Challenging and Defending Local Authority Child Care Decisions: A Practical Guide

CELEBRATING
150 YEARS

JORDANS

Challenging and Defending Local Authority Child Care Decisions: A Practical Guide

Elizabeth Isaacs QC
St Ives Chambers, Birmingham

Jeremy Weston QC
St Ives Chambers, Birmingham

Lorna Meyer QC
No5 Chambers, Birmingham, London, Bristol

Carmel Shepherd
Children's Guardian
Local Authority panels chair
Trainer and consultant

Family Law

Published by Family Law
A publishing imprint of Jordan Publishing Limited
21 St Thomas Street
Bristol BS1 6JS

British Library Cataloguing-in-Publication Data

A catalogue record for this book is available from the British Library.

ISBN 978 1 84661 317 3

Typeset by Letterpart Ltd, Reigate, Surrey

Printed in Great Britain by CPI Antony Rowe, Chippenham and Eastbourne

ACKNOWLEDGMENTS

Grateful thanks to all those who helped in the painful transition of this book from idea to reality. You all know who you are.

To Áine, Diane and Donna the true stars of the No5 library for their unfailing good humour and unerring ability to track down the impossible.

To Denise who performed similar miracles at St Ives.

FOREWORD

The arrival of this new work on *Challenging and Defending Local Authority Child Care Decisions* comes at a time when its contents will be much-needed by all those in local authorities who make important child care decisions, and all those who experience the impact of those decisions. The book rightly highlights the enhanced responsibility that will be placed upon local authorities to reach prompt and soundly-based conclusions, as a result of the changes being introduced following the Family Justice Review, and the programme to modernise family justice which has been driven by the judiciary. Although 'D-Day' for the final and full implementation of these changes is likely to be in the Spring of 2014, many of the new practices are already being developed and are now a feature of the decision-making process, both in and outside the court arena.

This book delivers what it sets out to do. It is balanced and provides advice to those who have to make decisions for children who are the subject of proceedings under Part IV of the Children Act 1989, and advice to those who seek to challenge them. Although written by lawyers (one of whom has a social work background), and based upon a comprehensive and up-to-date understanding of the law and practice, the text throughout remains true to the stated aim of providing a 'practical guide'. The chapters on 'Litigation without a lawyer' and the 'Uses and misuses of CA 1989, section 20' will be of particular value to family members who are seeking to navigate these complicated waters without legal assistance.

Inevitably, the authors have had to put the book to bed and press the 'print' button at a time when much of the detail of the new law and procedure has still to be clarified. Whilst this indicates the near certainty of a second edition in 2014, the first edition, which is needed now, is able to look forward to many of the likely changes by including detail throughout the text based upon what is already known from the Family Justice Review and government statements.

Two principal aims of the Family Justice Review's recommendations are to reduce delay and to reduce the court's reliance on professional input from outside local authority social services. It was certainly not an aim of the Family Justice Review that the quality of decisions made for, and about, children in public care should be eroded in any way. In this brave new world, where local authority decisions will need to be taken more promptly and with greater reliance upon 'in-house' social work expertise, the need for the sage advice contained within these pages is all too clear, in order that both the process of decision-making and each decision made can be, so far as possible, the best for each child and every child.

Andrew McFarlane
Royal Courts of Justice
11 March 2013

PREFACE

In a climate of financial constraint and increasing public scrutiny the pressures on local authorities to deliver high quality services and good outcomes for children have never been higher.

The Family Justice Review Final Report[1] acknowledged the effects of such pressures on the quality of social work practice with children and families:

> 'Local authorities are critical to proceedings. We acknowledged in the interim report the pressures on them and we have challenged the ready assumption that they are incompetent in what they do. This is far from the case and we have seen ample evidence of good practice. But we have also seen that poor practice happens.'

The Family Justice Review also reiterated the concerns about the effect on children of delay in decisions about their welfare that have been consistently expressed for at least the last twenty years. In particular, the Family Justice Review highlighted the harmful effects to children of delay caused by court proceedings:

> 'Delay really matters. All our understanding of child development shows the critical importance of a stable environment to allow development of firm attachments to caring adults. Yet our court processes lead to children living with uncertainty for months and years with foster parents, in care homes, or with one parent in unresolved conflict with the other. A baby can spend their first year or much longer living with foster parents, being shipped around town for contact with their birth parents, while courts resolve their future. The longer the case the greater the stress, both for children and adults ... Professionals working within the family justice system need to be aware of the urgency of children's developmental timeframes. Very young children are more likely to develop secure attachments to permanent carers before the age of one. If they are left too long in abusive or neglectful families whilst the decision-making process runs its course, they may suffer a double jeopardy. Their long-term wellbeing may be compromised by the far-reaching consequences of maltreatment and they may suffer from the rupturing and loss of secure attachments made with temporary carers. They will also become more difficult to place in permanent placements as they grow older. Early and decisive action is needed and acceptable timescales need to be agreed and widely disseminated.'[2]

---

[1] Family Justice Review Final Report (November 2011), para 3.97.
[2] Ibid, para 1.2.9.

The Family Justice Review concluded that it is unacceptable for courts to take on average more than a year to deal with public child care cases, correctly reminding us that the harm caused to a child in such a period of uncertainty is unjustifiable in anything other than the most exceptional circumstances.

The financial implications of such delay was also expressed in the clearest possible terms:[3]

> 'This all comes at a high financial cost both to the taxpayer and the individual. The estimate of the overall system cost to the public purse in 2009/10 is now put at £1.6 billion ... We are not convinced these resources are spent in the most efficient and effective way. And with no more money to be had it is all the more important to use resources to best effect.'

The government accepted almost all of the Family Justice Review's proposals in full and identified the impact of the proposed series of reforms as follows:

- For parents – a simpler, more straightforward system that they understand and have confidence in, and that will give them the support they need quickly and effectively.

- For social workers – a streamlined system which supports and inspires them to use their professional expertise to achieve the best outcomes for children.

- For local authorities – a less resource-intensive system which allows them the flexibility to determine how best to meet a child's needs, without unnecessary additional scrutiny.

- For courts and the judiciary – a process which is easier to manage, less bureaucratic and more focused on the needs of the child.

- For the wider family – a clear sense of roles and responsibilities, the ability to input and be listened to, and understanding of the process.

- For children – a faster system which recognises, listens and responds to their needs and concerns; protects their welfare and secures their safety; and one that helps them enjoy their childhood in the most stable environment possible.

In November 2011 the Lord Chief Justice appointed Mr Justice Ryder to prepare a judicial response setting out solutions to the problems identified in the Family Justice Review.

---

[3]   Ibid, para 2.12.

The judiciary's proposals for the reform of the family justice system were published in July 2012 and acknowledged the cross party consensus for change in support of the Family Justice Review's conclusions.[4] There are two key elements to the proposals:

- strong judicial leadership and management; and

- robust case management of proceedings by the requirement to have a welfare timetable for each child based on evidence and research.

It is proposed that courts will use evidence-based good practice to control the material which it receives, in particular that of expert witnesses. The government has agreed with the Family Justice Review's analysis that in too many cases experts are commissioned to provide assessments which add little value to proceedings and introduce unnecessary delay. It is therefore proposed that the court should seek material from an expert witness only when that information is not available and cannot properly be made available from parties already involved; independent social workers should be used only exceptionally. The new Part 25 of the Family Procedure Rules 2010[5] now confirms that expert evidence will be restricted to that which in the opinion of the court is necessary to assist the court to resolve the proceedings.[6]

Such context has obvious and fundamental implications for the development of social work practice with children and families in the future; for example:

(a) decisions by local authorities are increasingly being made within a context of avoiding unnecessary delay, in-house assessments and other related cost;

(b) there should be limited and reduced scrutiny of local authority practice by children's guardians (not least because of the resource constraints on CAFCASS);

(c) there should be limited and reduced court scrutiny of local authority care plans; and

(d) local authorities should assume responsibility for making decisions about whether adoption is in a child's best interests (rather than adoption panels).

Plainly the impact on social work practice with children and families of such proposals has yet to be evaluated. However, just as social workers will be required to make decisions more quickly, so the opportunities for families to

---

[4] *Judicial proposals for the modernisation of family justice* – The Judiciary of England and Wales, July 2012 http://www.judiciary.gov.uk/Resources/JCO/Documents/ Reports/ryderj_recommendations_final.pdf.

[5] In force from 31 January 2013.

[6] Rule 25.1 of the Family Procedure Rules 2010.

navigate and challenge local authority concerns are likely to become more limited and complex. It is therefore more essential than ever for professionals (and, increasingly, self-representing litigants) to be vigilant in evaluating the quality and transparency of local authority decision-making in order to challenge or defend such decisions as appropriate.

This book takes a practical approach in exploring the roles and powers of local authorities with an emphasis on understanding the usefulness and accessibility of the various available remedies. All major forms of challenge to local authority decision-making are considered.

The law is stated as at 17 February 2013.

CONTENTS

TABLE OF CASES

References are to paragraph numbers.

TABLE OF STATUTES

References are to paragraph numbers.

TABLE OF STATUTORY INSTRUMENTS

References are to paragraph numbers.

INTRODUCTION

The companion volume to this book, *Social Work Decision-Making: A Guide for Child Care Lawyers*[1] describes comprehensively the wide scope of local authority practice and decisions in relation to child care law that can be challenged. However, recent policy and legal developments culminating in the Children and Families Bill (put before Parliament in January 2013) make it clear that the scope of challenge is only likely to increase in the near future.

The publication of the Family Justice Review in November 2011 reflected a consensus for the need to change among the judiciary and professionals of all disciplines. In particular the Family Justice Review proposed a number of changes to the structure of the family justice system including the introduction of a unified Family Court, strengthened judicial continuity, and increased judicial case management and training.

Following consultation and consideration of the Family Justice Review's recommendations, the judiciary's proposals for the modernisation of family justice were published in July 2012 envisaging full implementation by 2014. The core principle underpinning the proposals is the need to prevent delay and reduce costs in decision-making for children in care proceedings.

At the time of writing (January 2013) it remains unclear to what extent the new proposals will affect local authority practice. However, there are a number of areas which suggest increased scope for challenge in the future, especially when taking into account the renewed pressures on the local authority to act early, speedily and with reduced costs. Four key areas may be open to renewed challenge and scrutiny, although these are by no means exhaustive.

The decision about whether a child should be placed for adoption

In cases where the local authority is acting as an adoption agency, it must have access to an adoption panel (or an adoption and permanency panel) to assist it in meeting its requirements under the Adoption Agencies Regulations 2005.[2] The Adoption Panel has a central role within the adoption agency in terms of contributing to an effective adoption service. One of the key areas of responsibility of the Adoption Panel was previously to recommend whether a specific child should be placed for adoption.

---

[1]   Jordan Publishing, 2nd edn, 2012.
[2]   SI 2005/389.

However, this requirement has been removed to reduce duplication of work that is done by the court with the intention of reducing delay in planning for looked after children.

The Adoption Agencies Regulations 2005 have been amended to reflect this change.[3] The new requirement provides that in cases where the local authority is considering whether a child (who is not subject to a placement order) ought to be placed for adoption, the local authority *cannot* refer the case to the adoption panel. It is the local authority that must now deal with such matters itself by taking into account the child's permanence report, the child's health report, and the information relating to the health of each of the child's natural parents, and any other relevant information in coming to a decision about whether the child ought to be placed for adoption.[4]

Local authorities therefore now have new duties in decision-making about whether a child ought to be placed for adoption. Amended statutory guidance about such decision-making was issued in June 2012 and sets out the implications for local authorities. The principal changes for local authorities include:[5]

(a)   The child's social worker will still be required to prepare the Child Permanence Report (CPR) but it is now the agency decision-maker (ADM) alone who will make the decision about whether a child ought to be placed for adoption.

(b)   An ADM may not delegate their authority to another person. Local authorities can appoint more than one ADM, but care needs to be taken to ensure consistency of approach. The ADM should be a senior person within the adoption agency.[6]

(c)   The CPR, the guardian's views and all relevant expert reports from care proceedings must be considered by the ADM as part of their decision making.

(d)   The relevant papers must be referred to the ADM by the agency adviser. The agency advisor to the Panel alone will be responsible for monitoring the quality of the CPR and deciding whether the report is adequate for submission to the ADM.

---

[3]   Regulation 17(2) of the Adoption Agencies Regulations 2005 (as amended by reg 5 of the Adoption Agencies (Panels and Consequential Amendments) Regulations 2012 – in force from 1 September 2012).

[4]   Regulation 19(1A) of the Adoption Agencies Regulations 2005 (as amended by reg 6 of the Adoption Agencies (Panel and Consequential Amendments) Regulations 2012 – in force from 1 September 2012).

[5]   BAAF Briefing for Agency Decision Makers and Agency Advisers on the Implications of implementing the Adoption Agencies (Panel and Consequential Amendments) Regulations 2012 (9 August 2012).

[6]   The qualifications, knowledge and experience required by an ADM are set out in the Adoption National Minimum Standards (March 2011) paragraph 23.17 (can be downloaded at https://www.education.gov.uk/publications/standard/Adoptionandforstering/Page1/DFE-00028-2011).

(e)   The ADM can discuss the case with the medical adviser, legal adviser and agency adviser, but not have a joint meeting with them. The guidance does not preclude the ADM from consulting the advisers and seeking additional information from the social worker. However, there is no provision for referring a case to the Adoption Panel for advice. The Guidance is clear that in cases where the court is involved, a referral to the Panel for any reason is prohibited and would constitute a breach of the Regulations and of data protection principles.

(f)   The ADM must consider the welfare checklist in s 1(4) Adoption and Children Act 2002 (ACA 2002) as well as all of the information provided in the CPR and the other relevant reports.

(g)   The ADM must make a decision within 7 working days of receipt of the reports. There is no provision for adjourning the ADM's decision to allow time for taking advice (although they may adjourn the case if they consider the reports to be insufficient). Local authorities therefore need to ensure that the relevant advisers are available to the ADM within the set timeframe.

(h)   When recording their decision the ADM must list all the material that they have taken into account in reaching their decision (including any discussions that they have with the agency or medical advisers), identify the key arguments in the case and set out their reasons for making the decision.

(i)   The outcome of any discussion, as well as the decision itself and its reasons must be recorded on the child's and/or prospective adopters' case record as applicable. It should be made available to the adoption panel when it makes its recommendations in respect of matching the child (after a placement order being granted) with specific adopters.

(j)   Local authorities will need to introduce a new timetable for papers being submitted to the ADM, and medical and legal advisers will need to be available to the ADM during the 7 day period of decision-making.

(k)   The child's parents and the prospective adopters should be informed orally of the local authority's decision within 2 working days, and written confirmation should be sent to them within 5 working days.

The amended Adoption Guidance takes account of the new obligations on local authorities and reinforces the earlier guidance set out by the Court of Appeal about the way in which the decision-maker should approach a case. In *Hofstetter v LB Barnet and IRM*[7] the Administrative Court said that it would be good discipline and appropriate for the decision-maker to list the material taken into account in reaching the decision, identify key arguments and state the reasons for their decision. Before making a considered and professional decision, the decision-maker will need to consider (among other things) the exercise of powers under s 1 ACA 2002 and all the information surrounding the case including the relevant reports.

---

[7]   [2009] EWHC 3282 (Admin).

Local authorities should therefore expect the decision-making by ADMs to be subject to the same levels of scrutiny as previously given to decision-making by panels.[8] Just as adoption panels are required to give full reasons for their recommendation, so should ADMs explain their decisions.[9] Failure to show that the ADM has read and fully considered all the appropriate information and arguments may present a fruitful ground of challenge by legal representatives for parents and children.

Similarly, it is clear that where the decision that a child should be placed for adoption has been made without reference to the panel, any panel advice on contact arrangements, placement with siblings or adoption support will now be *limited* to the consideration at the matching panel. Therefore the quality assurance functions of panels in considering and reporting on CPRs presented to them will be restricted. The task now facing local authorities will be to ensure that the quality assurance function previously held by the adoption panel is maintained while the scope for challenge by those representing parents and children is greatly increased.

Scrutiny of the care plan

At present s 31(3A) CA 1989 provides that no care order may be made with respect to a child until the court has considered a s 31A care plan. However, the Act does not specify how complete the plan needs to be. In *Re S (Minors) (Care Order: Implementation of Care Plan); Re W (Care Orders: Adequacy of Care Plan)*[10] the House of Lords held that the care plan should be 'sufficiently firm and particularised for all concerned to have a reasonably clear picture of the likely way ahead for the child for the foreseeable future'.

However, the Family Justice Review Final Report expressed concern about what it called the progressive extension of court interest in proposed care plans and relied on 'call for evidence' submissions from Lord Phillips and Lady Hale, in the Supreme Court, as follows:

'If parental rights and responsibilities are to be changed or rearranged, article 6(1) of the ECHR requires that the decision be made by a court after a fair hearing. A fair process is also required by article 8 where the state interferes with the right to respect for family life. But the court's current close involvement with the formulation of the care plan in care proceedings goes beyond what was originally envisaged when the Children Act was passed and probably beyond what is required by the ECHR. Article 8 requires that the courts have some control over the contact between parents and children in care and also over the decision to sever contact with the birth family. But it does not require that the courts have control

---

[8]   See *Re B (Placement Order)* [2008] EWCA Civ 835, [2008] 2 FLR 1404.
[9]   See *Hofstetter v London Borough of Barnet and IRM* [2009] EWHC 3282 (Admin) at para 133.
[10]   [2002] UKHL 10.

over how the child is looked after in care. Courts cannot look after children or conjure up the resources with which to do so.'

The Family Justice Review concluded that at present court scrutiny of the plan can go beyond what is needed to be satisfied that a care order is required:

'... [The court] ... can try to determine how the child should be parented and not just by whom. The motivation is honourable but the result is to cause delay for that child and others, and to waste time and money, particularly bearing in mind that a court can only consider a child's needs at one point in time. The needs and circumstances are highly likely to change, potentially negating the value of the detailed scrutiny. To take responsibility away from the local authority contributes to a lack of confidence and decisiveness on their part, undermining their parental authority.'

The proposals by the Family Justice Review provoked a strong and mixed response. Some respondents argued that as a point of principle scrutiny of the detail of care plans is a right and proper function of the court, that court scrutiny can improve the care plan, and that other safeguards are not adequate, including particularly independent reviewing officers (IROs) who are overburdened and not truly independent of local authorities.[11] The Family Justice Review considered that the thrust of such arguments was fuelled by an undercurrent of deep scepticism about the ability of local authorities to deliver adequate care for children. However, the Family Justice Review could not point to any research on whether changes to the detail of local authority care plans ordered or induced by the court process lead to better outcomes for children:

'Care planning is bound to be difficult and uncertain. Many plans change after the care order – inevitable if children are in care for many years ... Court involvement is certainly not a guarantee of success and courts are not well equipped to carry out the care planning role. We also need to set alongside the possible benefit the cost and time taken by court scrutiny and the effect of that both on that child and other children not yet before the court ... The courts have a legitimate interest in the quality of social work practice ... However, to try to improve the quality of social work from the bench on an individual case-by-case basis is likely to be ineffective and costly.'[12]

The Family Justice Review made it clear that it did not advocate wholesale departure from the principles in *Re S (Minors) (Care Order: Implementation of*

---

[11] For example, the consultation response by the Association of Lawyers for Children argued that the proposals were '... misconceived and wholly contrary to the interests of children' – Family Justice Review Final Report (November 2011), para 3.20.

[12] Family Justice Review Final Report (November 2011), paras 3.30–3.31.

Care Plan); Re W (Care Orders: Adequacy of Care Plan)[13] and that the requirement for the care plan to be 'sufficiently certain' should remain.

The Family Justice Review Final Report therefore reiterated that while courts must continue to play a central role in public law in England and Wales, they should refocus on the core issues of whether the child is to live with parents, other family or friends, be removed to the care of the local authority or be adopted. The report went on to recommend that when determining whether a care order is in a child's best interests the court will not normally need to scrutinise the full detail of a local authority care plan for a child. Instead the court should consider only the core or essential components of a child's plan.

Such components were specifically identified as follows:

- Planned return of the child to their family.
- A plan to place (or explore placing) a child with family or friends.
- Alternative care arrangements, including adoption.
- Contact with birth family to the extent of deciding whether that should be regular, limited or none.[14]

The Judicial Proposals for the Modernisation of Family Justice ('the Judicial Proposals') (July 2012) confirmed that Phase 2 of the modernisation programme[15] will describe a more focused scrutiny of the final care plan. However, although the scope of the expected scrutiny of placement proposals and care plans is to be set out in due course within a Family Court Guide which will signpost good practice, the precise nature of the permitted scrutiny remains to be seen.[16]

Plainly, any restriction or limitation on the degree of scrutiny of the care plan by the court will need to be balanced against the extent of the factors that the court must consider in the welfare checklist in s 1(3) CA 1989 in care cases and in the welfare checklist in s 1(4) ACA 2002 in adoption cases. We suggest that potentially there is a difficult tension between the need to resolve cases quickly

---

[13]   [2002] UKHL 10.

[14]   The Family Justice Review Final Report also recommended that the government should consult on whether s 34 of the CA 1989 should be amended to promote reasonable contact with siblings, and to allow siblings to apply for contact orders without leave of the court. Such consultation has been undertaken and results are awaited at the time of writing.

[15]   Due to be completed in the summer of 2014 with the anticipated implementation of the Children and Families Bill.

[16]   At the time of writing (February 2013) the collection of 'expectation documents' developed by the Family Justice Board in collaboration with the judiciary is open to a consultation process. The documents set out the key contributions and good practice which the family courts can expect of CAFCASS, local authorities, the Legal Aid Agency and HMCTS. The documents do not introduce new requirements for agencies nor do they provide an exhaustive list of agencies' legal responsibilities. Rather, the aim is to provide a clear, concise and accessible summary of the main contributions and good practice which the courts can look to agencies to provide and which all agree are central to the just and efficient progression of cases and more timely decision-making for children – see http://www.justice.gov.uk/about/moj/advisory-groups/family-justice-board/good-practice-consultation.

by limiting court scrutiny of the local authority's care plan, and the requirement for the court to consider such factors as the child's physical, emotional and educational needs,[17] the likely effect on the child (throughout his life) of having ceased to be a member of the original family and become an adopted person,[18] or the risk of harm to the child.[19] Such tension is only likely to increase, rather than diminish, the likelihood of challenge to local authority decision making in the near future.

The limited role of the guardian

The reduction in scrutiny of care plans by the court may not be the only reason for the likelihood of increased challenge to local authority decision-making in the near future. There is also likely to be a reduction in independent scrutiny of the local authority's work by the children's guardian.

The Family Justice Review considered the role of the guardian in its final report and recommended that children should continue to be parties to proceedings. Respondents to the Family Justice Review consultation indicated a high degree of consensus around the need for guardians to:

- Meet the child and work with them to ensure their wishes and feelings are listened to and heard.
- Represent those wishes and feelings to the court.
- Focus proceedings at all times on the child's best interests.
- Provide the court with their independent view of the child's welfare.
- Meet the parents and read all local authority files.

Respondents generally considered that the current statutory duties and responsibilities of guardians were appropriate. However, the continuing role of the guardian in the detailed scrutiny of the court plan was more contentious.

The Family Justice Review Final Report concluded that the guardian's scrutiny of the care plan should be limited in line with the limitations to be imposed on the courts, although no change to the statutory framework is proposed. It was reiterated that in public law cases it is important that the guardian:

- Ensures the child is aware of what is happening and understands the decisions to be made.
- Gives age-appropriate support to ensure that the voice of the child is heard.
- Gains and maintains the necessary skills to be able to understand and interpret the child's views.
- Ensures the child is given the chance to decide how they wish to hear the outcome of the case and from whom.

---

[17] Section 1(3)(b) CA 1989 and s 1(4)(b) ACA 2002.
[18] Section 1(4)(c) ACA 2002.
[19] Section 1(3)(e) CA 1989 and s 1 (4)(e) ACA 2002.

However, the Review went on to emphasise that court social work services must be managed efficiently and that the input of the guardian has to be proportionate and appropriate to the needs of the case, reflecting the complexity of cases and the stage they are at:

> 'We understand concerns about any reduction of guardian involvement. No public law case is unimportant. But the system has to be able to put resource where it is most needed. It cannot do everything so choices have to be made.'

In light of this approach, the Family Justice Review made various recommendations about the future scope of the guardian's role, stressing that none of these is incompatible with the independence of the guardian in an individual case:

- The guardian should carry out an initial assessment of how much support is needed from themselves and the solicitor when the case is received.
- The guardian should carry out an assessment of the quality and sufficiency of the authority's work at the outset of the case.
- There should be dialogue between the judge, guardian and solicitor throughout a case to agree what the guardian should focus on, without compromise to the guardian's independence.
- Guardian and solicitor should both attend court only if necessary.

However, in submissions to the Family Justice Review's consultation, CAFCASS itself has expressed concern about the possible effects of limitations on the role of the guardian in scrutinising the local authority's work and care plans, although it does accept that a lighter touch is sufficient in well managed local authority cases:[20]

> 'In relation to the future role of CAFCASS, it is vital that poor or incomplete local authority assessments, and poor or incomplete care plans, have independent social work oversight, and are effectively challenged and improved when necessary. It would be negligent to remove this essential safeguard for children in inadequately prepared cases ... IROs also potentially have a powerful role to play in constructively challenging poor pre-proceedings practice in their local authorities.'

The changing role of the guardian remains to be seen, but it seems inevitable that, in the current context of limited resources and emphasis on avoiding delay, the extent of scrutiny of the local authority's decisions and plans is likely to be less rather than more. As already discussed, the reduction in independent oversight is likely to lead to greater scope for challenge of local authority decision-making.

---

[20] CAFCASS Response to Family Justice Review Interim Report (June 2011).

The reduction in use of independent experts

The Family Justice Review Final Report made it plain that in some cases there can be no substitute for expert evidence in child care cases. For example, medical testimony may be critical to determining whether a child was harmed by accident or not. However, the report identified a trend towards an increasing and unjustified use of expert witness reports, with consequent delay for children.

The Family Justice Review therefore made a number of proposals in relation to experts which have implications for the way in which local authorities may approach their work. In particular, the Review recommended that judges should be given clearer legislative powers to enable them to refuse expert assessments and that independent social workers should only be employed to provide new information to the court, not as a way of replacing the assessments that should have been submitted by the social worker or the guardian. In summary, it concluded that the child's timescales must exert a greater influence over the decision to commission reports and judges must order only those reports they truly need.

The inevitable outcome of this approach is that the burden and reliance on local authority social workers is likely to increase. It will increasingly fall to social workers, rather than experts or independent social workers to base their decision-making on good quality, thorough assessments of children and families. This change of focus lies at the heart of the Family Justice Review recommendations, was central to the recommendations of the Munro Review of Child Protection[21] and is endorsed within the Judicial Proposals. The recent amendments introduced by the new Part 25 of the Family Procedure Rules 2010 also enshrine the duty on the courts to restrict expert evidence. Rule 25.1 confirms that expert evidence will be restricted to that which in the opinion of the court is necessary to assist the court to resolve the proceedings.

The new approach is also likely to be reinforced in the forthcoming Children and Families Act due to be implemented in 2014:[22]

> 'Local authorities are critical to proceedings. We acknowledged in the interim report the pressures on them and we have challenged the ready assumption that they are incompetent in what they do. This is far from the case and we have seen ample evidence of good practice. But we have also seen that poor practice happens ... A major change programme is now beginning in both England and Wales to reduce bureaucracy and refocus social work practice onto direct work with families. There will be fresh emphasis on increasing the amount of time social workers spend working directly with children and families and providing them with early help. There should be less

---

[21] The Munro Review of Child Protection: Final Report (May 2011, Cm 8062, TSO).
[22] Family Justice Review Final Report (November 2011), paras 3.97–3.101.

bureaucratic process. Social workers, as with all professionals across the family justice system, will need to develop a stronger understanding of child development and the impact of delay when making decisions about children.'

However, despite the well-intentioned sentiments of such an approach, the lack of a consistent and sufficiently stocked pool of well-qualified, skilled social work practitioners working under increased pressures within local authorities means that the intended improvements in the quality of local authority decision-making may be more difficult and complex to achieve. This, together with the reduced availability for independent assessment by experts and the more limited oversight envisaged for guardians will inevitably widen rather than narrow the scope for challenge to local authority decision-making. The importance of careful analysis of the decision-making carried out by local authorities at the pre-proceedings stages, as well as during proceedings, cannot be overestimated. This includes, but is by no means limited to:

- Were local authority decisions transparent and understandable?
- Were local authority decisions carried out in accordance with the relevant internal and/or LSCB policies and procedures?
- Were local authority decisions made in accordance with the relevant government guidance?
- Were families and young people properly consulted, informed and involved in key decision-making?
- Were key local authority assessments carried out in a timely and appropriate fashion?
- Were the assessments completed by suitably qualified social work professionals?
- Were decisions about removal of children from their families made on the basis of proper assessment, planning and review?
- Were decisions about placing children in foster care rather than friend or family placements made appropriately and on the basis of informed assessment and review?
- Were decisions about delay in completing kinship assessments of potential friends or family placements justified?
- Were decisions about whether or not to place siblings together in foster care made appropriately and on the basis of informed assessment?
- Were decisions about whether or not children were placed in close proximity to home made appropriately and on the basis of informed assessment and consultation?
- Did the local authority seek external assessments (for example, by psychologists or specialist learning disability or mental health professionals) where appropriate?
- Were decisions about contact made on the basis of informed social work assessment and consideration?
- Were statutory reviews conducted regularly and appropriately?

- Did the IRO (if involved) act appropriately and promptly in scrutinising the actions and decision-making of the local authority?
- Were decisions leading to key changes in care planning (for example, changes from rehabilitation to adoption) made on the basis of informed assessment, planning and consideration?
- Was any decision by the local authority that a child ought to be placed for adoption made on the basis of informed assessment, planning and review?

The future?

Only time will tell whether the proposed changes identified above will lead to an improvement in the decision making for children by those responsible for ensuring their safety and safeguarding their welfare. It remains to be seen whether the pressures on the systems identified above will operate instead in a negative fashion and further reduce confidence of children and parents in the systems designed to help them.

The aim of this book is to bring together for lawyers, professionals, self-representing litigants and families the tools to ensure that whatever the future holds:

- important decisions in planning for a child are made on sound foundations;
- alternative routes of scrutiny of decisions are identified;
- disagreements are resolved if possible without litigation;
- the right course of action is chosen in the event that legal challenge is necessary; and
- the initial steps, procedures and sources of support are readily available.

Part 1

CONTEXT

Chapter 1

THE ROLE OF THE LOCAL AUTHORITY

SECTION 1 – IMPLICATIONS FOR CHILD CARE LAW

1.1   It is unlawful for a public authority to act in a way which is incompatible with an ECHR Convention right.[1] In most cases involving children in the public law context it may seem obvious and beyond question that the subject of challenge to a decision or omission should be the local authority.

1.2   However, extensive functions delegated to local authorities in relation to children and families are increasingly delegated from local authorities to and commissioned from external, non-statutory providers; for example:

- chairing statutory reviews;

- chairing child protection conferences;

- carrying out assessments of friends and family carers;

- commissioning parenting assessments from independent social workers pre-proceedings;

- placing children in residential assessment units or placements managed by voluntary organisations or private companies;

- arranging placements for looked after children with private fostering or adoption agencies;

- referring children for treatment or direct work to therapeutic care facilities managed by voluntary organisations or private companies;

- commissioning external independent visitors or personal advisors for young people.

1.3   It is therefore essential for those seeking to challenge (or indeed defend) a decision in such a case to be able to determine whether it is a *local authority* that should be challenged or whether *a commissioned service provider* is the most appropriate subject of challenge. Not only is it vital to understand the

---

[1]   Human Rights Act 1998, s 6(1).

distinction for the purposes of service, but also to ensure that any applications are issued in a timely fashion given the tight timescales that apply in judicial review and human rights proceedings.

SECTION 2 – DEFINING A PUBLIC AUTHORITY

1.4   The term 'public authority' is not exhaustively defined in statute or caselaw.

1.5   Some assistance is provided by s 6(3)(b) Human Rights Act 1998 (HRA 1998) which defines 'public authority' as:[2]

> Any person certain of whose functions are functions of a public nature.

However, s 6(5) provides that:

> In relation to a particular act, a person is not a public authority by virtue only of subsection (3)(b) if the nature of the act is private.

1.6   It is the distinction between public and private acts that lies at the heart of much legal debate in relation to whether and when it may be appropriate to challenge local authorities.

The functions-based test

1.7   Traditionally it was the source of a body's powers that was held to be fundamental in defining what was or was not a public authority. However, in the last twenty five years the emphasis has shifted away from this test. The current position is that it is an examination of both the source and nature of the functions performed by the body that will determine whether it should be regarded as a public body or not. This is known as the functions-based test. This has inevitably resulted in some non-statutory bodies which have been set up to carry out public functions being deemed public bodies for the purposes of challenge by judicial review.

The decision in Datafin

1.8   The turning point in clarifying the definition of a public authority came with the Court of Appeal's consideration of the test in *R v Panel on Takeovers and Mergers ex p Datafin*.[3] In *Datafin* the Court of Appeal considered the jurisdictional issue of whether the decisions of the relevant body, namely, the Panel on Takeovers and Mergers (the Panel) were susceptible to judicial review. The function of the Panel was to promulgate the City Code on Takeovers and Mergers which necessarily gave it a very wide ambit; among the companies to

---

2   'Public authority' is also defined as a court or tribunal (s 6(3)(a) HRA 1998), but challenges to court or tribunal decisions fall outside the scope of this book.

3   [1987] QB 815, CA.

which the Code applied were all listed public companies considered by the Panel to be resident in the United Kingdom.

1.9 The Court of Appeal defined the Panel's role as follows:[4]

'... indistinguishable in its effect from a delegation by the council of the Stock Exchange to the Panel, a group of people which includes its representative, of its public law task of spelling out standards and practices in the field of take-overs which listed companies must observe if they are to enjoy the advantages of a Stock Exchange listing and of determining whether there have been breaches of those standards and practices.'

1.10 The following factors in relation to the Panel's nature and function were held to be particularly relevant:[5]

• it operated wholly in the public domain;

• its jurisdiction extended throughout the United Kingdom;

• it operated as an integral part of a system which has a public law character;

• it was supported by public law in that public law sanctions are applied if its edicts are ignored;

• without doubt it was performing a public duty and an important one;

• its duties included the duty to act judicially at times;

• it could not conveniently be controlled by established forms of private law;

• the fact that the Panel was self-regulating made it not less but more appropriate that it should be subject to judicial review by the courts because it was not subject to regulation by others.

1.11 In particular it was held, per Lloyd LJ:[6]

'So long as there is a possibility, however remote, of the Panel abusing its great powers, then it would be wrong for the courts to abdicate responsibility. The courts must remain ready, willing and able to hear a legitimate complaint in this as in any other field of our national life ... And if the courts are to remain in the field, then it is clearly better, as a matter of policy, that legal proceedings should be in the realm of public law rather than private law, not only because they are quicker, but also because the requirement of leave ... will exclude claims which are clearly unmeritorious.'

---

4   Per Nicholls LJ at p 58D.
5   Summarised at p 26B.
6   At p 46G.

1.12 It was therefore confirmed that the source of power and functions performed by a body were *both* relevant factors which should be given different weight according to the circumstances:[7]

> 'I do not agree that the source of the power is the sole test whether a body is subject to judicial review ... Of course the source of the power will often, perhaps usually, be decisive. If the source of power is a statute, or subordinate legislation under a statute, then clearly the body in question will be subject to judicial review. If, at the other end of the scale, the source of the power is contractual, as in the case of private arbitration, then clearly the arbitrator is not subject to judicial review ... But in between these extremes there is an area in which it is helpful to look not just at the source of the power but at the nature of the power. If the body in question is exercising public law functions, or if the exercise of its functions have public law consequences, then that may ... be sufficient to bring the body within the reach of judicial review.'

1.13 The position was summarised concisely by Lloyd LJ[8] thus:

> '... it is not just the source of the power that matters, but also the nature of the duty.'

Developments since Datafin

1.14 In determining whether a body is a public body, the fact that the decisions of that body have or may have serious implications for those who are subject to such decisions is not a relevant factor. Similarly, nor is it important that the body might play an important role in public life.[9]

1.15 However, it is clear that in subsequent case law since *Datafin* there has been a focus on the nature of the function of the body, rather than the body itself. Two key cases in which the issue was considered in detail are *Poplar HARCA v Donoghue*[10] and *R (Heather) v Leonard Cheshire Foundation*.[11]

The Poplar case

1.16 The issue of whether a body performing functions which a public body would otherwise be obliged to perform necessarily renders the function a public function was considered by the Court of Appeal in *Poplar HARCA v Donoghue*.[12] In *Poplar* it was held that public bodies can use private bodies to perform their functions without the nature of the function thereby inevitably being considered public so as to turn the private body into a public body for the purposes of s 6 HRA 1998.

---

[7]   At p 48F.
[8]   At p 52B.
[9]   See *R v Football Association Ltd ex p Football League Ltd* [1993] 2 All ER 833.
[10]   [2001] EWCA Civ 595.
[11]   [2002] EWCA Civ 366.
[12]   [2001] EWCA Civ 595.

1.17 In the *Poplar* case the issue related to whether a housing association was a public authority.

The facts

1.18 D was a tenant at a local authority property that was later transferred to Poplar Housing Association (Poplar). Poplar had been created as a housing association by the local authority in order to transfer to it a substantial proportion of the council's housing stock. The local authority issued proceedings for possession against D but, upon discovering that it was not the landlord, withdrew the proceedings. Poplar subsequently commenced possession proceedings against D pursuant to s 21(4) Housing Act 1988 (HA 1988). There is no ambiguity in the terms of s 21(4) HA 1988 and the court was required to make the possession order if D had a tenancy which was subject to s 21(4) and the proper notice had been served. It was agreed in the case that but for the HRA 1998 arguments, there would be no possible basis for interfering with the court's decision.

The arguments

1.19 D argued that Poplar was a public authority within the meaning of Art 6 and had breached her Art 8 rights in seeking a possession order. D argued that Poplar fell within the definition of public authority under s 6(1) as it was performing public functions. In particular, D argued that the obligation to provide interim accommodation (under Part 7 (homelessness) of the Housing Act 1996) pending inquiries owed to a homeless applicant was clearly a public function, and that a housing association which provides that accommodation is thus fulfilling a public function. In particular, D argued that where the duty was originally owed by the local authority but subsequently transferred to the housing association *whilst the duty was ongoing*, then the public nature of a function was made all the clearer.

1.20 In reply, Poplar disputed that it was a public authority and argued that it had not breached D's Art 8(2) rights because a housing association was not a public body or performing a public function. In particular, Poplar (supported by the government intervening) drew attention to various features of housing associations in support of this proposition:

(a) housing associations vary vastly in size;

(b) their structure is that of an ordinary private law entity;

(c) each housing association is given freedom to decide how it achieves what is expected of it;

(d) members of the housing association are not appointed by, or answerable to, the government but are private individuals who volunteer their services;

(e)   although a housing association is funded in part out of public funds, the major source of its income is its rental income.

The issues

1.21   The key issue before the court (aside from procedural issues, Art 8 and remedy issues) was therefore whether Poplar was a public body or whether it was performing functions of a public nature.

1.22   The obvious importance of this issue was that the HRA 1998 would only apply to Poplar if it was deemed to be a public body or performing public functions.

The decision

1.23   The Court of Appeal agreed that the definition of who is a public authority, and what is a public function, for the purposes of s 6 of the HRA 1998, should be given a generous interpretation. It was confirmed that housing associations as a class are not standard public authorities. It was also agreed that if housing associations are to be a public authority, this must be because a particular function performed by an individual housing association is a *public* as opposed to a *private* act. In such circumstances, the housing association would then be a functional, or hybrid, public authority.

1.24   It was held that the fact that a body performs an activity which otherwise a public body would be under a duty to perform, cannot mean that such performance is necessarily a public function. It was held that a public body, in order to perform its public duties, can use the services of a private body. Section 6 should not be applied so that if a private body provides such services, the nature of the functions are inevitably public. The Court of Appeal gave as examples a small hotel providing bed and breakfast accommodation as a temporary measure at the request of a housing authority or a hospital requesting a private company to carry out specialist services such as analysing blood samples, and held that this was not what the HRA 1998 intended.

1.25   Section 6(3) means that hybrid bodies – who have functions of a public and private nature – are public authorities, but *not* in relation to acts which are of a private nature:[13]

> 'The purpose of section 6(3)(b) is to deal with hybrid bodies which have both public and private functions. It is not to make a body, which does not have responsibilities to the public, a public body merely because it performs acts on behalf of a public body which would constitute public functions were such acts to be performed by the public body itself. An act can remain of a private nature even though it is performed because another body is under a public duty to ensure that that act is performed.'

---

[13]   At para [59].

1.26 The Court of Appeal held that Poplar *was* a public authority by taking account of the following:

(a) While s 6 requires a generous interpretation of who is a public authority, it is clearly inspired by the approach developed by the courts in identifying the bodies and activities subject to judicial review. The emphasis on public functions reflects the approach adopted in judicial review by the courts and text books since the decision of the Court of Appeal (judgment of Lloyd LJ) in *Datafin*.

(b) The local authority, in transferring its housing stock to Poplar, does *not* transfer its primary public duties to Poplar. Poplar is no more than a means by which the local authority seeks to perform those duties.

(c) The act itself of providing accommodation to rent is not, without more, a public function for the purposes of s 6.

(d) The fact that a body is a charity or is conducted not for profit does not point to the body being a public authority. In addition, even if such a body performs functions that would be considered to be of a public nature if performed by a private body, nevertheless such acts may remain of a private nature for the purpose of s 6(3)(b) and (5).

(e) What can make an act which would otherwise by private, public, is a feature or combination of features which impose a public character or stamp on the act. Statutory authority for what is done can help to mark the act as being public, so can the extent of control over the function exercised by a public authority. The more closely the acts that could be of a private nature are enmeshed in the activities of a public body, the more likely they are to be public. However, the fact that the acts are supervised by a public regulatory body does not necessarily indicate that they are of a public nature.

(f) The closeness of the relationship between the local authority and Poplar – Poplar was created to take a transfer of local authority housing stock, several of its board members were also members of the local authority, and Poplar was subject to the local authority's guidance as to the manner in which it acted towards D.

(g) D was, at the time of transfer, a sitting tenant of Poplar and it was intended that she would be treated no better and no worse than if she remained a tenant of the local authority. While she remained a tenant, Poplar therefore stood in relation to her in very much the position previously occupied by the local authority.

1.27 However, the Court of Appeal made it plain that whilst these were the most important factors, it was desirable to step back and look at the situation as a whole:[14]

> '... As is the position on applications for judicial review, there is no clear demarcation line which can be drawn between public and private bodies and functions. In a borderline case, such as this, the decision is very much one of fact and degree.'

1.28 It was therefore held that the role of Poplar was so closely assimilated to that of the local authority that it was performing public and not private functions. Poplar was therefore determined to be a functional public authority, although it was emphasised that this did not mean that all Poplar's functions were public.

The Leonard Cheshire case

1.29 A comparable position arose in the case of *R (Heather) v Leonard Cheshire Foundation*[15] where the Court of Appeal considered that a residential home was manifestly *not* performing public functions and refused a challenge brought by two residents in relation to the local authority's decision to close the home. The *Leonard Cheshire* case was considered in the light of the earlier guidance in *Poplar*.

The facts

1.30 The claimants were long stay patients in a residential home which was owned and run by the Leonard Cheshire Foundation (*Leonard Cheshire*). They appealed against the dismissal of their application for judicial review of *Leonard Cheshire's* decision to close the home. Their application was dismissed after a preliminary hearing at which it was held that *Leonard Cheshire* was not a public authority within the meaning of the term in s 6 HRA 1998. The correctness of that conclusion formed the subject of their appeal. At the time the home, based in Hampshire, was *Leonard Cheshire's* first and largest home with 42 long stay residents including the residents who had both lived there for periods of more than 17 years. *Leonard Cheshire* is the UK's leading voluntary sector provider of care and support services for the disabled. The majority of the residents at the home, including the appellants, had been placed there by the social services departments of their local authority or by their health authority. A smaller group of residents were privately funded. In making the placements and providing the funding which the placements required, the authorities were exercising statutory powers. *Leonard Cheshire* decided to redevelop the home as three or four smaller community based homes to be located in surrounding towns and the residents were to be relocated in the community based units.

---

[14]   At para [66].
[15]   [2002] EWCA Civ 366.

The arguments

1.31 The local authority was obliged to provide accommodation for the claimants by virtue of s 21(1) National Assistance Act 1948 (NAA 1948) which provides:

21 Duty of local authorities to provide accommodation

(1) Subject to and in accordance with the provisions of this Part of this Act, a local authority may with the approval of the Secretary of State, and to such extent as he may direct shall, make arrangements for providing –

(a) residential accommodation for persons aged eighteen or over who by reason of age, illness, disability or any other circumstances are in need of care and attention which is not otherwise available to them; and

(b) residential accommodation for expectant and nursing mothers who are in need of care and attention which is not otherwise available to them.

1.32 The accommodation, which the authorities arrange, may be provided by the authority *or by another authority* by virtue of s 21(4) and (5) of the NAA 1948 (as amended). Under the NAA 1948 the authority may also make arrangements for the accommodation to be provided by third parties under s 26(1) which deals particularly with the provision of accommodation in premises maintained by voluntary organisations:

26 Provision of accommodation in premises maintained by voluntary organisations

(1) Subject to subsections (1A) and (1B) below, arrangements under section 21 of this act may include arrangements made with a voluntary organisation or with any other person who is not a local authority where –

(a) that organisation or person manages premises which provide for reward accommodation ... and

(b) the arrangements are for the provision of such accommodation in those premises.

This is how the claimants in the case came to be living at the *Leonard Cheshire* home in Hampshire.

1.33 Arrangements for the payment for the accommodation are made by virtue of the powers in s 26(2) NAA 1948 (as amended):

(2) Any arrangements made by virtue of ... this section shall provide for the making by the local authority to the other party thereto of payments in respect of the accommodation provided at such rates as may be determined by or under the arrangements ...

1.34 The claimants were opposed to such a move and argued that in making this decision *Leonard Cheshire* was exercising functions of a public nature within the meaning of s 6(3)(b) HRA 1998 and so, as a public authority, was required not to act in a way which was incompatible with Art 8 ECHR. It was argued that *Leonard Cheshire* had contravened Art 8 by not respecting the claimants' right to a home and failing to take into account, inter alia, promises made to them that the home would be their 'home for life'.

1.35 The issue in *Leonard Cheshire* was therefore very simple – in providing accommodation for the claimants was *Leonard Cheshire* performing a public function?

The decision

1.36 The Court of Appeal confirmed in *Leonard Cheshire* that if the authority itself provides accommodation, it is performing a public function. It is also performing a public function if it makes arrangements for the accommodation to be provided by *Leonard Cheshire*.

1.37 However, the Court of Appeal went on to find that if a body which is a charity (like *Leonard Cheshire*) provides accommodation to those to whom the authority owes a duty under s 21 (in accordance with an arrangement under s 26), it *does not follow* that the charity is performing a public function.

1.38 Again it was confirmed that a public authority can be a hybrid body – namely, a public authority in relation to some of its functions and a private body in relation to others. This is the combined consequence of s 6(3) and (5) HRA 1998.

1.39 Section 6(5) provides that:

> (5) In relation to a particular act, a person is not a public authority by virtue only of subsection (3)(b) if the nature of the act is private.

1.40 The Court of Appeal distinguished the position in *Leonard Cheshire* from that in *Poplar* by finding that in *Poplar* the Housing Association could be considered to be performing a public function by looking at the situation *as a whole*. In *Poplar* the Court of Appeal came to that conclusion because the role of the Housing Association was 'so closely assimilated' to that of the Housing Authority. When the same analysis was applied to the facts in *Leonard Cheshire*, the Court of Appeal found that there was little support for the argument that in providing accommodation for the claimants, *Leonard Cheshire* was performing a public function. All the factors in *Leonard Cheshire* could point to was that the activity of *Leonard Cheshire* was regulated which could be an indicator that a function is public.

1.41 The Court of Appeal concluded that it was not the situation in this case where the local authority could divest itself of its Art 8 obligations by contracting out to a voluntary sector provider its obligations under s 21 NAA 1948. It was held that the local authority remains under an obligation by virtue of s 21 NAA 1948 and therefore retains an obligation under Art 8 to the appellants even though it has used its powers under s 26 to use *Leonard Cheshire* as a service provider. It was held that the role *Leonard Cheshire* was performing manifestly did not involve the performance of public functions. The fact that *Leonard Cheshire* was a large and flourishing organisation did not change the nature of its activities from private to public. It was not in issue that it is possible for *Leonard Cheshire* to perform some public functions and some private functions. In *Leonard Cheshire* it was contended that this hybrid function was exactly what had happened because some residents were privately funded and some residents were publicly funded.

1.42 However, the Court of Appeal dismissed this argument and found that there was no material distinction between the nature of the services *Leonard Cheshire* had provided for those residents funded by a local authority and those provided to residents who were funded privately. It was held that while the degree of public funding of the activities of an otherwise private body is certainly relevant as to the nature of the functions performed, by itself it is not determinative of whether the functions are public or private.

1.43 In *Leonard Cheshire* it was held that there was no other evidence of there being a public flavour to the function of *Leonard Cheshire* or the organisation itself:[16]

> '... *Leonard Cheshire* is not standing in the shoes of the local authorities. Section 26 of the NAA provides statutory authority for the actions of the local authorities but it provides *Leonard Cheshire* with no powers. *Leonard Cheshire* is not exercising statutory powers in performing functions for the appellants.'

1.44 It was therefore confirmed that, on the approach adopted in *Poplar*, it could be said quite clearly that *Leonard Cheshire* was *not* performing any public function.

SECTION 3 – HYBRID BODIES

1.45 The cases of *Poplar* and *Heather* demonstrate the functional nature of the test that needs to be applied in relation to hybrid bodies (ie, those bodies exercising some public and some private functions).

1.46 The fact that the decisions of the body have serious implications for those who are subject to them or the fact that the body might play an important role in public life are not relevant factors to whether a body is a public body.[17]

1.47 However, in *Parochial Church Council of the Parish of Aston Cantlow v Wallbank*[18] the House of Lords confirmed that there could be no universal test of what is a public function, given the diverse nature of governmental functions and the variety of means by which these functions may be discharged. The House of Lords offered guidance in terms of the various factors that can be

---

[16]   At para 35(ii).
[17]   *R v Football Association Ltd ex p Football League Ltd* [1993] 2 All ER 833.
[18]   [2003] UKHL 3 WLR 283.

taken into account when determining whether a particular action or activity should be defined as a public function include the extent to which, in carrying out the relevant function, the body is:

- publicly funded;

- exercising statutory powers;

- taking the place of central government;

- taking the place of local authorities;

- providing a public service.

1.48   While it is clear that it is the *source* of the powers that is regarded as a critical part of the functional test when considering whether the body is a public authority in relation to a particular action or activity, the issue in relation to child care law decisions remains far from straightforward.

Chapter 2

LOCAL AUTHORITY DUTIES AND RESPONSIBILITIES

SECTION 1 – THE LEGAL FRAMEWORK

2.1 Local authority duties when dealing with children and families are numerous and complex.[1] The key duty on local authorities is the duty to safeguard and promote children's welfare and includes:

(a) The duty to work together with other agencies.

(b) The duty to carry out an investigation.

(c) The duty to work with children.

2.2 The statutory legislation most relevant to local authority work with children and families is provided within the Children Act 1989.

2.3 The Children Act 1989 created a single coherent framework to deal with the private and public law relating to children. It aims to strike a balance between the rights of children to express their wishes on decisions made about their lives, the rights of parents to exercise their responsibilities towards their children, and the duty of the state to intervene where the child's welfare requires it.[2]

2.4 The Children Act 1989 is based on the belief that children are generally best looked after within the family with their parents playing a full part in their lives and with least recourse to legal proceedings. The principles underpinning social work practice with children and families are informed by the Children Act 1989 (reinforced in the Children Act 2004), and can be summarised as follows:

- safeguarding children and promoting their welfare;

---

[1] For a comprehensive overview and analysis of local authority duties in working with children and families see *Social Work Decision-Making: A Guide for Childcare Lawyers* (Jordan Publishing, 2nd edn, 2012).
[2] Department for Children, Schools and Families *The Children Act 1989 Guidance and Regulations*, Volume: Court Orders (2nd edn, 2008).

- recognising parental responsibility (and the ability of unmarried fathers to share that responsibility by agreement with the mother, by joint registration at birth, or by court order);

- providing family support and services to children in need, including services for disabled children, to enable children to remain in their own homes as far as possible;

- taking account of race, culture, language, religion and disability;

- working in partnership with children and their families;

- the local authority's duty (unless not reasonably practicable or consistent with the child's welfare) to promote contact between a looked after child and his or her parents (or relevant others);

- the local authority's duty to return a child looked after by them to his or her family unless it is not in the child's interests;

- giving due weight to children's wishes and feelings.

The statutory legislation

2.5   The statutory legislation most relevant to work to safeguard and promote the welfare of children is as follows:

- Children Act 1989 (Pts I, III and IV);

- Children Act 2004;

- Children (Leaving Care) Act 2000;

- Adoption and Children Act 2002;

- Children and Young Persons Act 2008;

- Human Rights Act 1998;

- European Convention on Human Rights (the European Convention for the Protection of Human Rights and Fundamental Freedoms) 1950 (ECHR);

- United Nations Convention on the Rights of the Child 1989 (UNCRC);

- United Nations Convention on the Rights of Persons with Disabilities 2006.

The duty to promote and safeguard children's welfare

2.6   The Children Act 1989 (CA 1989) places a duty on local authorities to promote and safeguard the welfare of children in need in their area. The primary focus of legislation about children in need is on how well they are progressing and whether their development would be impaired without the provision of services.

2.7   Section 17 of the CA 1989 deals with the general duties of local authorities to safeguard and promote children's welfare. Local authorities carry the lead responsibility for establishing whether a child is in need and for ensuring that services are provided to that child as appropriate.

2.8   This does not necessarily require local authorities themselves to be the provider of such services. Section 17(5) of the CA 1989 enables the local authority to make arrangements with others to provide services on their behalf.

> **CA 1989, s 17(1) and (10)**
>
> (1)   It shall be the general duty of every local authority ...
>
> (a)   to safeguard and promote the welfare of children within their area who are in need; and
>
> (b)   so far as is consistent with that duty, to promote the upbringing of such children by their families,
>
> by providing a range and level of services appropriate to those children's needs.
>
> (10)   ... a child shall be taken to be in need if –
>
> (a)   he is unlikely to achieve or maintain, or to have the opportunity of achieving or maintaining, a reasonable standard of health or development without the provision for him of services by a local authority under this Part;
>
> (b)   his heath or development is likely to be significantly impaired, or further impaired, without the provision for him of such services, or
>
> (c)   he is disabled ...

2.9   The thrust of the government guidance remains that only in exceptional cases should there be compulsory intervention in family life, for example where necessary to safeguard a child from significant harm. Such intervention should, as long as it is consistent with the child's safety and welfare, support families in making their own plans for the welfare and protection of their children. As well as being responsive to children's direct requests for help and advice, professionals also need to engage with parents at the earliest opportunity when doing so may prevent problems or difficulties becoming worse.

2.10   Where it appears to a local authority that there is a child in need within its area, Sch 2, para 3 of the CA 1989 enables the local authority to assess that child's needs. At the same time as carrying out an assessment under this part of the Children Act 1989, account should be taken of assessment requirements contained in any other legislative framework. This could include an assessment of the needs of a disabled person under the Chronically Sick and Disabled Persons Act 1970, the Disabled Persons (Services, Consultation and Representation) Act 1986, or an assessment of the child's special educational needs under the Education Act 1996, Part IV.

2.11 Section 17(4A) of the CA 1989[3] requires local authorities, where practicable, to take account of children's wishes and feelings before determining what services to provide or what action to take.

CA 1989, s 17(4A) (as amended)

(4A)   Before determining what (if any) services to provide for a particular child in need in the exercise of functions conferred on them by this section, a local authority shall, so far as is reasonably practicable and consistent with the child's welfare –

(a)   ascertain the child's wishes and feelings regarding the provision of those services; and

(b)   give due consideration (having regard to his age and understanding) to such wishes and feelings of the child as they have been able to ascertain.

2.12 Local authorities are obliged to comply with statutory guidance issued under s 7(1) of the Local Authority Social Services Act 1970 (LASSA 1970) when carrying out their duties relating to children and families, unless there are exceptional circumstances which justify a variation.

LASSA 1970, s 7(1)

(1)   Local authorities shall, in the exercise of their social services functions, including the exercise of any discretion conferred by any relevant enactment, act under the general guidance of the Secretary of State.

2.13 If the local authority fails to follow statutory guidance (issued under the LASSA 1970, s 7(1)), in relation to any function under the CA 1989, the Secretary of State has the power to declare them in default.

2.14 *Working Together*,[4] the key statutory guidance,[5] requires local authorities, in common with all organisations that provide services or work with children and young people, to:

---

[3]   As amended by s 53(1) of the Children Act 2004.

[4]   *Working Together to Safeguard Children: A guide to inter-agency working to safeguard and promote the welfare of children* (DCSF, 4th edn, 2010). It should be noted that Wales now operates under a different system through the Welsh Assembly. The Welsh version of Working Together is entitled *Safeguarding Children: Working together under the Children Act 2004* which is currently under review (February 2013); individual chapters have been separately updated (available to download at wales.gov.uk). See also chapter 10 for further discussion of the Welsh Guidance.

[5]   At the time of writing (February 2013) the guidance in *Working Together* is subject to wholesale revision although the timetable for implementation remains unknown – see http://www.education.gov.uk/childrenandyoungpeople/safeguardingchildren/protection.

- have senior managers who are committed to children's and young people's welfare and safety;

- be clear about people's responsibilities to safeguard and promote children's and young people's welfare;

- check that there are no known reasons or information available that would prevent staff and volunteers from working with children and young people;

- have procedures for dealing with allegations of abuse against members of staff and volunteers;

- make sure staff get training that helps them do their job well;

- have procedures about how to safeguard and promote the welfare of young people; and have agreements about working with other organisations.

2.15 The guidance in *Working Together* makes it quite clear that safeguarding and promoting the welfare of children is the responsibility of the local authority, working in partnership with other public organisations, the voluntary sector, children and young people, parents and carers, and the wider community. A key objective for local authorities is to ensure that children are protected from harm. Other functions of local authorities that make an important contribution to safeguarding are housing, sport, culture and leisure services, and youth services.

The duty to work together with other agencies

2.16 Section 27 of the CA 1989 also places a specific duty on local authority services and health bodies to co-operate in the interests of children in need. An underlying principle of the CA 1989 is to encourage such collaboration between agencies in order to achieve a holistic view of a child's needs. It is not sufficient for the local authority simply to identify and consider specific problems; rather, the local authority must take account of other services provided by other agencies, including voluntary organisations, and should facilitate the provision of services by others which the local authority may provide.

CA 1989, s 27

(1) Where it appears to a local authority that any authority or other person mentioned in subsection (3) could, by taking any specified action, help in the exercise of any of their functions under this Part, they may request the help of that other authority or person, specifying the action in question.

(2) An authority whose help is so requested shall comply with the request if it is compatible with their own statutory or other duties and obligations and does not unduly prejudice the discharge of any of their functions.

(3)   The persons are –

    (a)   any local authority;

    (b)   any local education authority;

    (c)   any local housing authority;

    (d)   any health authority; and

    (e)   any person authorised by the Secretary of State for the purposes of this section.

2.17   The legislation therefore envisages a shared responsibility and the need for effective joint working between agencies and professionals with different roles and expertise in order to protect children and promote their welfare; it is envisaged that this approach will be continued and reinforced in the forthcoming legislation. Effective joint working is reliant on constructive relationships between individual practitioners, promoted and supported by the commitment of senior managers to safeguard and promote the welfare of children, and reliant on the establishment of clear lines of accountability.

2.18   Achieving good outcomes for children requires all those with responsibility for assessment and the provision of services to work together according to an agreed plan of action.

2.19   *Working Together to Safeguard Children* is the key piece of statutory guidance issued under the LASSA 1970, s 7(1),[6] which provides a clear framework of guidance about how individuals and organisations should work together to safeguard and promote the welfare of children. *Working Together* is intended to provide a national framework within which agencies and professionals at local level – individually and jointly – draw up and agree on their own ways of working together to safeguard and promote the welfare of children. It applies to England. Part 1 is statutory guidance. Part 2 is non-statutory practice guidance. Non-statutory guidance is not underpinned by any legal duty and does not give rise to any binding obligations on the part of the local authority. However, any non statutory guidance is recognised as standards of good practice and any variation from non statutory guidance need to be explained and justified.

2.20   All parts of *Working Together* are suggested as required reading for lawyers working in the field of public law child care.

2.21   The guidance in *Working Together* is addressed to:

* all practitioners and front-line managers who have particular responsibilities for safeguarding and promoting the welfare of children;

---

[6]   The Department of Health, the Home Office and the Department for Education and Skills *Working Together to Safeguard Children* (TSO, 4th edn, 2010) (can be downloaded from www.everychildmatters.gov.uk).

- senior and operational managers in organisations that are responsible for commissioning or providing services to children, young people, parents and carers;

- senior and operational managers in organisations that have a particular responsibility for safeguarding and promoting the welfare of children.

2.22 An essential tenet of the CA 1989 and *Working Together* is that promoting and safeguarding the welfare of children is not just the responsibility of the local authority; an integrated approach by all relevant agencies working together is a fundamental element of good practice.

2.23 Section 11 of the Children Act 2004 places a duty on key persons and bodies to make arrangements to ensure that in discharging their functions, they have regard to the need to safeguard and promote the welfare of children.

2.24 The thrust of government guidance and thinking around interagency working is therefore clear – all organisations working with children and families share a commitment to safeguard and promote children's welfare. For many agencies this is underpinned by a statutory duty or duties.

2.25 The guidance in *Working Together* reinforces this duty by linking the safeguarding and promotion of children's welfare – and in particular the protection of children from significant harm – to the need for effective joint working between agencies and professionals that have different roles and expertise. Individual children, especially some of the most vulnerable children and those at greatest risk of suffering harm and social exclusion, will need co-ordinated help from health, education, early years, children's social care, the voluntary sector and other agencies, including youth justice services.

2.26 For those children who are suffering, or likely to suffer, significant harm, joint working is essential to safeguard and promote their welfare.

The duty to carry out an investigation

2.27 Section 47 of the CA 1989 places the local authority under a duty to make enquiries in certain circumstances to decide whether they should take any action to safeguard or promote the welfare of a child.

CA 1989, s 47

(1) Where a local authority –

    (a)   are informed that a child who lives, or is found, in their area –
        (i)   is the subject of an emergency protection order; or
        (ii) is in police protection; or
    (b)   have reasonable cause to suspect that a child who lives, or is found, in their area is suffering, or is likely to suffer, significant harm,

the authority shall make, or cause to be made, such enquiries as they consider necessary to enable them to decide whether they should take any action to safeguard or promote the child's welfare.

2.28   Section 47(9), (10) and (11) of the CA 1989 place a statutory duty on any local authority, any local education authority, any local housing authority, and any health authority, to help the local authority in carrying out its social services functions in undertaking s 47 enquiries (unless it would be unreasonable in all the circumstances of the case).

The duty to work with children

2.29   Section 47(5A) of the CA 1989[7] requires local authorities, where practicable, to take account of children's wishes and feelings before determining what action to take during investigations.

2.30   The guidance in *Working Together* (2010) confirms the approach to be taken by social workers in situations when it is not possible to ascertain the child's wishes and feelings. In those circumstances professionals should record in writing why it was not reasonably practicable or consistent with the child's welfare to elicit his or her wishes or feelings.[8]

> **CA 1989, s 47**
>
> (5A)   For the purposes of making a determination under this section as to the action to be taken with respect to a child, a local authority shall, so far as is reasonably practicable and consistent with the child's welfare –
>
> (a)   ascertain the child's wishes and feelings regarding the action to be taken with respect to him; and
>
> (b)   give due consideration (having regard to his age and understanding) to such wishes and feelings of the child as they have been able to ascertain.

2.31   The guidance in the *Framework for the Assessment of Children in Need and their Families* (2000) provides the structure for helping to collect and analyse information obtained in the course of s 47 enquiries.

2.32   The 2008 Laming Review of the progress across England to implement effective arrangements for safeguarding children[9] reiterated the importance of frontline professionals getting to know children as individual people and, as a matter of routine, considering how their situation feels to them.

2.33   The Children and Young Persons Act 2008 came into force in November 2008 and fulfils the commitments made in the White Paper, *Care Matters: Time for Change*. The new legislation extended the statutory framework for children in care in England and Wales and was intended to ensure that children in care are able to share the same aspirations as those in supportive family homes by

---

[7]   As amended by Children Act 2004, s 53(3).
[8]   *Working Together to Safeguard Children* (4th edn, 2010), para 1.17.
[9]   *The Protection of Children in England: A Progress Report* (TSO, March 2009).

receiving high quality care and services which are focused on and tailored to their needs. The new legislation was intended to improved the stability of children's placements and improve the educational experience and attainment of young people in local authority care or about to leave care. Most of the changes have been incorporated into the statutory framework by additions or substitutions in the Children Act 1989 and the Care Standards Act 2000.

2.34 Key elements of the Children and Young Persons Act 2008 include:

* enabling local authorities to operate a different model of organising social care by discharging (although not delegating) social work functions to other bodies (any such arrangements must be exercised in favour of qualified social workers);

* strengthening the role of the independent reviewing officer (IRO);

* obliging local authorities to visit young people in their care;

* ensuring that there will be a designated member of staff at maintained schools whose specific responsibility it will be to promote the educational achievement of children in care who attend that school;

* ensuring that looked-after children (up to 18) are not moved out of an existing placement before they are ready;

* requiring the local authority to provide assistance to young people in care or who have recently left care to pursue education and training;

* improving the stability of placements for children in care, limiting 'out of authority' placements, and securing higher placement standards;

* improving the support for family and friend carers, including allowing local authorities to make longer-term financial payments to family carers in circumstances where otherwise the child would be accommodated by the local authority, where this would be appropriate.

2.35 The most important provisions of the recent legislation in relation to local authority duties and responsibilities are:

* the duty for local authorities to make arrangements to promote co-operation between the local authority, each of the local authority's relevant partners and such other bodies (or people) working with children in the area as the local authority considers appropriate (CA 2004, s 10);

* the setting up of Local Safeguarding Children Boards (CA 2004, ss 13–16).

SECTION 2 – THE CHILDREN'S COMMISSIONER

2.36 The statutory inquiry into the death of Victoria Climbié (2003)[10] and the first joint Chief Inspectors' report on safeguarding children (2002)[11] highlighted the lack of priority status given by local authorities (as well as other agencies) to safeguarding children. The government's preliminary response to these findings was set out in the Green Paper *Every Child Matters*, and was enacted in the Children Act 2004[12] which includes the provision for a Children's Commissioner.[13]

2.37 The role of the Children's Commissioner is focused on promoting and protecting the rights of children, in line with the Articles of the UN Convention on the Rights of the Child (UNCRC) to which the government is a committed signatory.

2.38 The argument for having a Children's Commissioner is that children are generally more vulnerable than adults and are therefore more likely to have their rights abused.

2.39 The role of the Children's Commissioner is currently defined in s 2 Children Act 2004 as:

- having the function of promoting awareness of the views and interests of children in England;

- encouraging people exercising functions or engaged in activities affecting children to take account of their views and interests;

- advising the Secretary of State on the views and interests of children;

- considering or researching the operation of complaints procedures so far as relating to children;

- considering or researching any other matter relating to the interests of children;

- publishing reports on any matters considered or researched by him or her;

- ensuring that children are made aware of his/her function and how they may communicate with him or her; and

- consulting children, and organisations working with children, on the matters he or she proposes to consider or research.

---

[10] *The Victoria Climbié Inquiry Report* (TSO, 2003).
[11] The Department of Health *Safeguarding Children: a Joint Chief Inspectors Report on Arrangements to Safeguard Children* (TSO, 2002).
[12] In force since 15 November 2004.
[13] Children Act 2004, s 2.

2.40   The mission statement of the Children's Commissioner states that:[14]

'We will use our powers and independence to ensure that the views of children and young people are routinely asked for, listened to and that outcomes for children improve over time. We will do this in partnership with others, by bringing children and young people into the heart of the decision-making process to increase understanding of their best interests.'

2.41   In July 2010 the government commissioned an independent review of the office, role and functions of the Children's Commissioner by Dr John Dunford. Although it was acknowledged that the Commissioner had had a significant impact on the lives of some children and young people, the overall impact of the role was felt to have been disappointing partly due to the limited remit set out in the 2004 legislation and partly due to a failure to establish credibility with government and other policy makers. The Dunford Review therefore particularly aimed to look at the Commissioner's powers, remit and functions, value for money and the relationship with other government funded organisations carrying out related functions.

2.42   The Dunford Review was published in November 2010 and recommended that the remit, powers and independence of the Commissioner should be strengthened to set the Commissioner apart from the many children's organisations and provide him or her with a unique role.

2.43   In July 2012 the government confirmed that it had accepted in principle all of the Dunford Review's recommendations and that legislative changes were needed to ensure that the Commissioner would, in future, have greater impact on children and young people's lives, stating:[15]

'The Government aim to make the UK the most child-friendly country in Europe. Children are generally more vulnerable than adults and do not have the same opportunities to make their views known or to raise concerns about the impact of new policies or legislation. It is therefore important that they have a strong advocate to represent their interests, particularly when they are in vulnerable situations.'

2.44   The proposed reforms to the Commissioner's role are set out within the draft legislation that will in due course be contained within the forthcoming Children and Families Bill.[16] In particular, the Commissioner will have powers to:

- carry out investigations;

- carry out assessments of the impact of new policies and legislation on children's rights;

---

[14]   Mission statement of the Children's Commissioner – see www.childrenscommissioner.gov.uk.

[15]   Children's Minister Written Ministerial Statement to Parliament 11 July 2012.

[16]   Due to be introduced to Parliament in January 2013.

- undertake research;

- monitor the effectiveness of complaints and advocacy services for children and young people;

- access places where children are cared for or accommodated away from home, so that their concerns can be heard;

- request the information needed to carry out full and robust investigations; and

- require those to whom recommendations are made to set out how they intend to respond.

2.45 The draft legislation is intended to make the Commissioner more independent from government and more directly accountable to Parliament, in particular through an annual report to Parliament that will allow for stronger scrutiny of the Commissioner's performance. Future Commissioners are to be granted a single six-year term of office. It is proposed that the Children's Commissioner for England would retain responsibility for non-devolved matters, but would be able to delegate his or her powers of investigation to the Children's Commissioners in the devolved Administrations. The Children's Commissioner for England would also be required to consult the Children's Commissioners in the devolved Administrations before conducting an investigation in a non-devolved matter within their jurisdictions or across the UK.[17]

SECTION 3 – LOCAL SAFEGUARDING CHILDREN'S BOARDS (LSCBS)

2.46 The current accountability structure for child protection in local areas was prescribed in the Children Act 2004 with the statutory positions of Director of Children's Services (DCS) and Lead Member for Children's Services being designated as the respective key points of professional and political accountability within the local authority. Around these key positions other services, such as the police and health, play key roles through local partnership structures, ie the Children's Trust Board and the Local Safeguarding Children Board (LSCB).[18]

2.47 Guidance about the LSCB role and functions is set out in detail in chapter 3 of the current edition of *Working Together*.[19] However, LSCBs are

---

[17] See http://www.publications.parliament.uk/pa/jt201213/jtselect/jtrights/83/8304.htm for greater detail about the government's proposals in relation to the expanded role of the Children's Commissioner.

[18] See chapter 10 for discussion of the Welsh LSCBs and the Welsh LSCB regulations.

[19] The government's plans for maintaining the roles of LSCBs and the Children's Trust Boards remain unknown at the time of writing (January 2013); however, the draft revised guidance in

primarily scrutiny bodies which monitor whether local partners, through the Children's Trust Board, are effectively safeguarding and promoting the welfare of children and young people in their local area. Like the Children's Trust Board, the LSCB is a statutory body. As part of their scrutiny function each LSCB produces and publishes an annual report about safeguarding and promoting the welfare of children in its local area, and submits a copy of this report to the Children's Trust Board. The majority of LSCBs are independently chaired, meaning that they are in a better position to provide scrutiny and challenge to the local authority and its Children's Trust Board partners.

2.48 Although the LSCB coordinates the effectiveness of arrangements to safeguard and promote the welfare of children in that locality, the LSCB is not accountable for the operational work of the Board's partners. Each Board partner retains their own existing lines of accountability.[20]

2.49 The LSCB is the key statutory mechanism for agreeing how the relevant organisations in each local area will co-operate to safeguard and promote the welfare of children, and for ensuring the effectiveness of what they do.

2.50 In an overall analysis of the social work relating to a child and/or family, it is plainly important to consider whether the local authority's work has complied with the LSCB policies and procedures for that area.

Working Together does not envisage any significant changes – see http://www. workingtogetheronline.co.uk/chapter_three.html#lscb.

[20] The government's plans for maintaining the roles of LSCBs and the Children's Trust Boards remain unknown at the time of writing (January 2013).

Chapter 3

LITIGATION WITHOUT A LAWYER

SECTION 1 – SELF-REPRESENTING LITIGANTS

Why?

3.1 A party is at liberty to choose to represent him/herself at any stage throughout court proceedings.[1]

3.2 There are many reasons why a party should find themselves in this position:

- Through choice as they believe they are in the best position to understand and present their own case.

- Through choice as they have found it hard to accept the legal advice they have been given as to prospects of achieving their desired outcome.

- Due to limitations of availability of public funding or availability of lawyers conducting public funded work.

- Due to a financial situation excluding them from public funding but insufficient to fund their own representation.

3.3 There are now greater and greater pressures on the provision of public funding for litigants caught up in the family justice system.

3.4 In July 2009 the Centre for Social Justice published a report entitled *Breakthrough Britain: Every Family Matters*.[2] In this report the following was noted:

> 'all those who we met in consultation in the preparation of this report and who had any experience of the legal aid system were unanimous: family legal aid is in its final throes of meltdown. It has barely sustained a discernible public service over several years, and has done so only through incredible commitment and financial sacrifice of many family lawyers. It is doubted whether there is any long term future for family legal aid in that there will be very few practitioners sufficiently experienced to undertake the necessary work. The present fee

---

[1] Brief consideration will be given to the power of the court to control vexatious litigants later see **3.88** et seq.

[2] http://www.centreforsocialjustice.org.uk.

structures and arrangements for legal aid are driving even more solicitors away from providing family legal aid services, restricting future access to justice for low income members of the public.

Morever, even as our report was being prepared, there were new proposals from the Legal Services Commission to reduce even further the level of fees paid to lawyers undertaking family work.[3] The real anxiety and concern is twofold. First, will there be solicitors and barristers experienced in family work spread across the country willing to undertake legal aid work? Secondly, will their expertise be sufficient for the complex cases in which representation is required? If, as we were told, there are genuine fears that one or both of the above will not continue to exist then many deserving parties will simply have no access to representation. This will in return result in dramatically increased numbers of parties acting in person, many more cases of injustice as one party is unable to properly represent their position and additional delays and costs in running the family justice system.'[4]

3.5   Since the publication of the report quoted above further cuts to legal aid funding have come into effect in the family sphere.

3.6   Very little research data is available as to the impact upon the court system, outcome of cases and litigants of the unrepresented litigant within family proceedings. In 2005 the Department of Constitutional Affairs published *Litigants in Person: Unrepresented Litigants in First Instance Proceedings*.[5] The Report acknowledged that there was no longitudinal data on family cases but indicated that the interview data supported the anecdotal evidence that there had been an increase in non-represented parties.

3.7   The report raised the following issues of concern:

- The available information pointed to unrepresented litigants increasing the workload of family courts.[6]

- Data suggested that unrepresented litigants achieved poorer outcomes.[7]

- Non-representation tended to slow down the progress of the case.[8]

---

3   The CSJ report cites the LSC press release 12 February 2009; see http://www.legalservices.gov. uk/ aboutus/press_releases_9297.asp.
4   *Breakthrough Britain: Every Family Matters*, para 4.3.1.
5   DCA Research Series 2/05 March 2005 authors Professor Richard Moorhead and Mark Sefton, Cardiff University. The underlying data for the report was collected from spring 2002 to summer 2003.
6   Ibid, p 173.
7   Ibid, p 221. It was suggested that this was essentially for two reasons. Firstly lack of representation frequently meant they were unable to present their cases in the best light, secondly a proportion brought cases which were inherently weak either because they did not have the benefit of lawyers discouraging them from bringing cases in the first place or because they were motivated to bring poor cases because of other grievances against their opponents or a broader disregard for the relevance of law to their dispute.
8   Ibid, pp 242 and 257.

3.8 For those working within the family justice system there has been growing concern that the numbers of litigants in person (the most commonly used name until recently when the Civil Justice Council Report of November 2011 replaced this with the term self represented litigants) in private law children's cases but also in care cases has been on the increase. It is anticipated that numbers of litigants in person will continue to rise.[9]

3.9 These concerns were reflected in the Family Justice Review final report in November 2011:

'The legal aid cuts may lead to a reduction in numbers of family solicitors and barristers and closure of some firms. There is also a risk that lower funding may dissuade future entrants to this area of the profession. The effects will be felt directly in private law but may also reduce the availability of family lawyers for public law particularly outside the largest cities ... we are particularly concerned that a consequence of the proposed changes in legal aid will inevitably see a rise in the number of litigants in person.'

3.10 In June 2011 the Ministry of Justice carried out a literature review of research on litigants in person and concluded that:

- They tend to be younger, and have lower income and educational levels, than those who obtain representation.

- They face problems in court, of understanding evidential requirements, identifying legally relevant facts and dealing with forms. One study found these problems also existed for those engaging in mediation without legal representation.

- They create an extra burden for court staff and judges.

- Help given to them could breach requirements for impartiality.

- The weight of the evidence indicated that lack of representation negatively affected case outcomes.

- Users and court staff appreciate court based support services, though there is little evidence about their impact.[10]

3.11 Obviously the types of claims and applications to court identified in this book are equally ones where parties may either choose, or find themselves forced into, self-representation.

---

[9] See for example Sir Nicholas Wall, President of the Family Division's Resolution Address 2012 July [2012] Fam Law 817 and the particular problems he envisaged such an increase will cause.
[10] Quoted from Family Justice Review Final Report Nov 11 para 4.178/4.180 including extract from K Williams *Litigants in person: A literature review* (Ministry of Justice, 2011).

3.12   The problems faced by self-representing parties, and those that they pose to the court and the other party, are also acknowledged in the Judicial Studies Board Equal Treatment Bench Book Chapter 1.3.

3.13   This identifies the perhaps obvious issues that most unrepresented parties are stressed and worried, operating in an alien environment with effectively a foreign language, that the outcome of the case may well have profound and long term consequences upon their life. However, it also identifies that they may have agonised over whether the case was worth the risk to their health and finances, and therefore they may feel passionately about their situation.

3.14   Practical guidance for the judiciary includes:

• Judges should be aware of the feelings and difficulties experienced by unrepresented parties.

• The importance of maintaining patience and an even-handed approach.

• The importance of maintaining a balance between assisting and understanding what the unrepresented party requires, while protecting their opponent against the problems that can be caused by the unrepresented party's lack of legal and procedural knowledge is the key.

• The aim is to ensure that unrepresented parties understand what is going on and what is expected of them at all stages of the proceedings – before during and after any attendances at a hearing.

3.15   In order to achieve the above, guidance for the judiciary recommends that unrepresented parties should have access to appropriate information (rules, practice directions and guidelines – whether from publications or websites), should be informed about what is expected of them in good time to comply and be given, wherever possible, sufficient time according to their needs.

3.16   Court staff cannot give legal advice under any circumstances though may be able to assist with information on the practical steps of how a case may be pursued.

3.17   The family justice system, however, cannot ignore the requirements of Art 6(1) of the European Convention on Human Rights (ECHR) when considering the correct manner in which to approach such litigants and the peculiar problems they face and indeed the peculiar problems they pose both to the courts and opposing parties:

'In the determination of his civil rights and obligations or of any criminal charge against him, everyone is entitled to a fair and public hearing within a reasonable time by an independent and impartial tribunal established by law. Judgment shall be pronounced publicly but the press and public may be excluded from all or part of a trial in the interest of morals, public order or national security in a democratic society, where the interests of juveniles or the protection of the private life of the parties so require, or to the extent strictly necessary in the opinion of the court in special circumstances where publicity would prejudice the interests of justice ...'

3.18   The right to a fair trial has been interpreted as including the following implied rights:

• practical and effective access to a court;

• a real opportunity to present a case (including presence at an adversarial hearing and ability to cross-examine);

• equality of arms;

• fair presentation of the evidence;

• a reasoned judgment;

• implementation of judicial decisions.

3.19   The principles of access to a court and equality of arms however are not strictly transferrable to confirm a right to the provision of legal aid and therefore legal representation in civil cases. A refusal of legal aid will not automatically equate to denial of rights of access. Access to a court can be achieved through other routes including simplification of court procedures, provision of pro bono services or other forms of non public-funded assistance.

3.20   However there may be cases where the absence of a lawyer to represent a party may render the proceedings unfair.[11] Public law proceedings which involve the state (usually legally represented) seeking to interfere with family life by the imposed removal of a child or children are more likely to require true equality of arms with the provision of legal representation for the parent than private law proceedings where parents are at odds between themselves as to the arrangements for their children.

3.21   The current proposals for modernisation of family justice have given consideration to the needs of self representing litigants indicating that '... the immediate challenge is to develop effective methods of assisting self-representing litigants in private law cases, while maintaining fairness to all parties'.[12]

---

[11]   See for example *P, C and S v UK* [2002] 2 FLR 631, ECtHR.
[12]   Mr Justice Ryder *Judicial Proposals for the Modernisation of Family Justice* (July 2012).

3.22   The draft proposals include:

- materials to be contained in a virtual Family Court Guide – designed to signpost good practice and the content of the rules and practice directions to the court, including:

  — Local authority work to prepare for proceedings.
  — The content of social work evidence.
  — How to make the decision which is the timetable for the child.
  — What is key issue identification?
  — What is the threshold?
  — How and when to use experts.
  — How to represent an incapacitated adult party and how to identify and ask for special measures to assist vulnerable parties and witnesses.
  — How to obtain third party disclosure and manage concurrent proceedings.
  — What scrutiny is to be expected of placement proposals and care plans
  — How to use published and peer-reviewed research in court.

In addition:

  — A statement of evidential principles for use in children proceedings will be published.

The draft proposals also suggest:

- that new materials by way of practice notes and explanatory guidance will be provided for self-representing litigants and McKenzie friends

- a consistent but firm approach will be developed to litigants, whether represented or not, to ensure that issues remain in focus and that they are addressed within the timetable set by the court. That will require a new culture of compliance.

The draft proposals further explain:[13]

- that in private law cases the pathway likely to describe information for self represented litigants would set out what the court can and cannot do and how it does it, a procedure that helps to identify safeguarding issues ie risk and urgent cases and an inquisitorial environment within which most decisions will be made. In a conventional case that may involve restrictions on the right of one party to cross-examine another, relying instead on each party having their say, the judge identifying the issues

---

[13]   Mr Justice Ryder *The Family Justice Modernisation Programme* (6th Update).

upon which he or she needs further assistance and then the judge asking questions of each party himself or herself.

SECTION 2 – MCKENZIE FRIENDS

3.23 The combination of the above features will go some way to explain the increasing use by unrepresented litigants of McKenzie friends and the need for the court to give guidance both in 2008 and 2010 as to the circumstances in which they should be permitted to act and the limitations of their roles.

Who and what are McKenzie friends?

3.24 The best place to start is the 12 July 2010 Practice Note issued by Lord Neuberger of Abbotsbury MR and Sir Nicholas Wall P reported at [2010] 1 WLR 1881.[14]

3.25 The Practice Note guidance applies to civil and family proceedings in the Court of Appeal (Civil Division), the High Court of Justice, county courts and family proceedings courts.

3.26 The Practice Note is stated to supersede the earlier guidance in *Practice Note (Family Courts: McKenzie Friends) (No 2)*[15] which is now withdrawn. It is intended to remind courts, litigants and representatives of the principles set out in the case authorities.

3.27 When referring to the principles drawn from the current Practice Note the language used will reflect that of the [2010] note rather than update it to refer to 'self representing parties'.

3.28 The principles:

- Litigants have the right to reasonable assistance from a lay person (sometimes known as a McKenzie friend).

- Litigants assisted by McKenzie friends remain litigants in person.

- McKenzie friends have no independent right to provide assistance.

- McKenzie friends have no right to act as advocates or to carry out the conduct of litigation.

---

[14] The Practice Note (which is expressly not issued as a practice direction) supersedes the guidance contained in the earlier practice note of 2008. It is said to be issued as a result of the increase in litigants in person in all levels of civil and family courts.
[15] [2008] 1 WLR 2757.

3.29   McKenzie friends **may**:

- provide moral support;

- take notes;

- help with case papers;

- quietly give advice on any aspect of the conduct of the case.

3.30   McKenzie friends **may not**:

- act as the litigant's agent in relation to the proceedings;

- manage litigant's cases outside court for example by signing court documents;

- address the court;

- make oral submissions;

- examine witnesses.

McKenzie friends **do not** have a right of audience or a right to conduct litigation.

3.31   It is a criminal offence to exercise rights of audience or to conduct litigation unless properly qualified and authorised to do so by an appropriate regulatory body.[16] In the case of an otherwise unqualified or unauthorised individual, such as a lay individual including a McKenzie friend, the court may grant rights of audience on a case by case basis.[17]

3.32   Earlier cases have identified the benefits of the McKenzie friend being someone who can advise and assist the litigant throughout the process providing an essential element of continuity.

When can McKenzie friends be used?

3.33   The court retains the power to refuse to permit a litigant the assistance of a McKenzie friend but may only do so where it is satisfied that in the case in question the interests of justice and fairness do not require the litigant to receive such assistance.

3.34   If the court considers that there are grounds for preventing the use of a McKenzie friend or if one of the other parties objects to the use of the

---

[16]   See for example ss 12–19 and Sch 3 of the Legal Services Act 2007.
[17]   See below for further detail on rights of audience and McKenzie friends.

McKenzie friend it is not for the litigant seeking to rely on their assistance to justify why they should be able to do so; it is for the objecting party or court to provide sufficient reasons why the litigant should not receive such assistance.

3.35 However where the proceedings are in closed court[18] the litigant is required to justify the McKenzie friend's presence in court. It is stated that the presumption in permitting a McKenzie friend to attend such hearings and to enable litigants to exercise the right to assistance, is a strong one.

3.36 The right to a fair trial is engaged when the use of a McKenzie friend is disputed. The matter therefore will need very careful consideration.

3.37 The decision to refuse such assistance may be made at the start of the hearing or during the course of a hearing.

3.38 The ground for refusing such assistance would appear to be that the McKenzie friend may give, has given or is giving, assistance which impedes the efficient administration of justice.

3.39 If it appears during the course of the hearing that a McKenzie friend is acting in such a way that may result in the court reaching such a conclusion the court should, before determining that the McKenzie friend is likely to impede the efficient administration of justice, consider whether a firm and unequivocal warning to the litigant and/or the McKenzie friend might suffice in the first instance.

3.40 A decision by the court not to curtail assistance from a McKenzie friend should be regarded as final. However subsequent misconduct by the McKenzie friend or where the court reaches the view that the McKenzie friend's continuing presence will impede the efficient administration of justice the decision can be revisited. If the court takes this route then a short judgment should be given setting out why the court has decided to curtail the right to assistance.

3.41 Litigants may appeal such decision but McKenzie friends have no right to do so.

3.42 If the McKenzie friend is assisting in care proceedings the court should consider the McKenzie friend's assistance at any advocates' meetings directed by the court. Those responsible for organizing such meetings should note the provisions of FPR 2010, PD12A, para 14.2 which provides:

> '… where there is a litigant in person the court will consider the most effective way in which that person can be involved in the advocates' discussions and give directions as appropriate including directions relating to the part to be played by an McKenzie Friend.'

---

[18] The practice note explains this as meaning where the hearing is in chambers, is in private, or where the proceedings relate to a child.

3.43 The High Court can, under its inherent jurisdiction, impose a civil restraint order on McKenzie friends who repeatedly act in ways that undermine the efficient administration of justice.

How do McKenzie friends become involved?

3.44 A litigant who wishes to exercise the right to receive reasonable assistance from a McKenzie friend should:

- inform the judge of that wish as soon as possible; and

- indicate who the proposed McKenzie friend will be.

3.45 The proposed McKenzie friend should:

- produce a short curriculum vitae or other statement setting out relevant experience;

- confirm that he or she has no interest in the case; and

- confirm that he or she understands the McKenzie friend's role and the duty of confidentiality.

3.46 Where the ability to use a McKenzie friend is in dispute the litigant seeking to receive assistance should be given a reasonable opportunity to argue the point and the proposed McKenzie friend should normally be allowed to help the litigant at the hearing determining whether his/her assistance will be permitted or circumscribed. The McKenzie friend therefore should not be excluded from the hearing of this preliminary issue.

3.47 Litigants are permitted to communicate any information, including filed evidence, relating to proceedings to McKenzie friends for the purpose of obtaining advice or assistance in relation to the proceedings.

3.48 Legal representatives should ensure that documents are served on litigants in good time to enable them to seek assistance regarding their content from McKenzie friends in advance of any hearing or advocates' meeting.

3.49 If the litigant is seeking for the McKenzie friend or other lay-person to be granted a right of audience the application must be made at the start of the hearing. If a right to conduct litigation is sought the application must be made at the earliest possible time and in any event must be made before the lay-person does anything which would amount to the conduct of litigation.[19]

---

[19] 'Rights of audience' effectively means the right to appear before and address the court , including the right to call and cross-examine witnesses. 'Conduct of litigation' means the issuing of proceedings before any court in England and Wales, the commencement, prosecution and defence of such proceedings and the performance of any ancillary functions in relation to such proceedings.

3.50 The right of audience and the right to conduct litigation are two distinct rights if both rights are sought their grant must be applied for individually and each application must be separately justified.

Factors to be considered

3.51 The following factors should **not** be taken to justify the court refusing to permit a litigant receiving the assistance of a McKenzie friend; however, they will be issues considered by the court:

- The case or application is simple or straightforward.

- The hearing is only a directions or case management hearing.

- The litigant appears capable of conducting the case without assistance.

- The litigant is unrepresented through choice.

- The other party is not represented.

- The proposed McKenzie friend belongs to an organisation that promotes a particular cause.

- The proceedings are confidential and the court papers contain sensitive information relating to a family's affairs.

A litigant may be denied the assistance of a McKenzie friend because its provision might undermine or has undermined the efficient administration of justice.

3.52 Examples of circumstances where this might arise include:

- The assistance is being provided for an improper purpose.

- The assistance is unreasonable in nature or degree.

- The McKenzie friend is subject to a civil proceedings order or a civil restraint order.

- The McKenzie friend is using the litigant as a puppet.

- The McKenzie friend is directly or indirectly conducting the litigation.

- The court is not satisfied that the McKenzie friend fully understands the duty of confidentiality.

SECTION 3 – RIGHTS OF AUDIENCE/CONDUCT OF LITIGATION

3.53 As set out above the court does have the power on a case by case basis to grant rights of audience/conduct of litigation to otherwise unqualified or unauthorised individuals including McKenzie friends.

3.54 The practice note urges caution however setting out that the courts should be slow to grant any application from a litigant for a right of audience or right to conduct litigation to any lay person including a McKenzie friend.

3.55 The practice note warns that this caution is because persons exercising such rights should normally be properly trained, be under professional discipline (which will include the obligation to insure against liability for negligence) and be subject to an overriding duty to the court. These requirements are deemed to be necessary for the protection of all parties to litigation and are essential to the proper administration of justice.

3.56 Any such application will need to be considered very carefully and the court should only be prepared to grant the application where there is good reason to do so taking in to account all the circumstances of the case.

3.57 Such rights should not be granted to lay persons automatically, or without due consideration. They should not be granted for mere convenience.

3.58 It is for the litigant to persuade the court that the circumstances of the case are such that it is in the interests of justice for the court to grant a lay person a right of audience or a right to conduct litigation.

3.59 Once the court has granted either a right of audience or a right to conduct litigation (or having granted each right), the court retains the power to remove either right. The granting of such rights in one set of proceedings cannot be relied upon as a precedent supporting their grant in future proceedings.

3.60 Examples of circumstances which have been found to justify the grant of a right of audience to a lay person include the following:[20]

- The person is a close relative of the litigant.

- Health problems prevent the litigant addressing the court or conducting the litigation and the litigant cannot afford to pay for a qualified legal representative.

---

[20] It must be remembered however that even seemingly similar cases can have different factual backgrounds, as these facts can vary tremendously and since the issue must be decided on a case-by-case basis these examples should not be regarded as establishing a precedent.

- The litigant is relatively inarticulate and prompting by that person may unnecessarily prolong the proceedings.

3.61 The fundamental principle in relation to lay people seeking to exercise rights of audience is that they should be properly trained and under a professional discipline as protection for all parties. The approach of the court to the use of lay persons who hold themselves out as professional advocates or professional McKenzie friends or lay people who seek to exercise such rights on a regular basis (whether for reward or not) will be that the grant of a right of audience or right to conduct litigation to such a person will only be granted in exceptional circumstances. It is considered that to apply any lesser test would be likely to subvert the will or intention of parliament.

3.62 It would not appear that the test of 'exceptional circumstances' applies as a general principle when considering whether to grant rights of audience or to conduct litigation to the truly 'lay' McKenzie friend.

3.63 Rights of audience and the right to conduct litigation are two separate and distinct rights. The grant of one right to a lay person does not mean that that the grant of the other right has automatically or implicitly also been made.

Recent examples in practice

3.64 Attention is drawn to the, as yet, unreported case of *Re H (Children)*.[21] Both the first instance and Court of Appeal decision came after the bringing into operation of the 2010 Practice Note. The Court of Appeal comprised of Sir Nicholas Wall P, Arden LJ and Sullivan LJ.

3.65 The father had sought the assistance of a particular individual as a McKenzie friend and also applied for the McKenzie friend to be granted rights of audience. The judge at first instance rejected both applications on the basis that the McKenzie friend was intimidating towards the mother. The judge however did not oppose the father using a different McKenzie friend.

3.66 The first instance judge had heard evidence from both the father and the proposed McKenzie friend and from the children's representative and was anxious to achieve equality of arms.

3.67 Although the determination of the judge was seen as a swift, rough and ready case management decision the Court of Appeal declined to interfere. The reasons given by the judge were said to be perfunctory but it was acknowledged that reasons given did not have to be elaborate. The judge had referred to the Practice Guidance. In the circumstances of the case the judge had been entitled to decide as she did.

---

[21] Unreported, 20 June 2012, Court of Appeal (Civil Division) – analysis obtained through assistance of Westlaw.co.uk.

3.68 Whilst decided in the Administrative rather than family court another, as yet unreported, case of *R (Koli) v Maidstone Crown Court*[22] is a useful illustration of the approach of the court to the use of 'professionals' in the role of McKenzie friends for whom rights of audience are sought.

3.69 The litigant applied for permission for the grant of a right of audience to an individual who was an unqualified paralegal on the basis that his case was a complex one that raised a constitutional issue.

3.70 In response to a court request that a statement be filed by the individual setting out what his qualifications were, whether he had ever been convicted, whether he had ever been declared a vexatious litigant and how he came to be instructed by the litigant, the individual informed the court at the start of the hearing that he was an unqualified self-employed paralegal who had provided assistance in various Scottish cases, that he was not a vexatious litigant and that he had convictions for counterfeiting and unlawfully providing immigration advice (although he stated that the latter conviction was the subject of judicial review) and maintained that he and the litigant had come across each other through a friend of a friend.

3.71 The court rejected the application for rights of audience on the basis that the individual was an unqualified individual seeking to supply an advocacy service and that it was as such that he had come into contact with the litigant. It was clear that if granted rights of audience in the case he would rely upon such grant in future cases and it would simply serve to bolster his paralegal status and subvert the statutory provisions as to who could be granted rights of audience. Rights of audience to such individuals should be granted in exceptional circumstances only.

3.72 The court further determined that it could not be said that the judicial review claim which the litigant sought to bring was so complex in fact or law that it would be appropriate to allow the individual to act as an unqualified advocate rather than as a McKenzie friend. Therefore it was appropriate to refuse him rights of audience but instead to allow him to assist as a McKenzie friend.

3.73 The following case pre-dates the 2010 practice note but remains a helpful illustration of the manner in which a McKenzie friend can overstep the boundaries of legitimate conduct and emphasises the need for the McKenzie friend to understand and comply with the duties of confidentiality whatever their role in the outside world.

3.74 *HBCC v LC (by her Litigation Friend the Official Solicitor), JG and SG*[23] involved a McKenzie friend who was also an elected local councillor. The court advised that:

---

[22] Unreported, 10 May 2011, Queens Bench Division (Admin) – analysis obtained through assistance of Westlaw.co.uk.

[23] [2010] EWHC 1527 (Fam), [2011] 1 FLR 463.

'any elected representative who took up an issue on behalf of a constituent must be cautious not to find himself or herself in conflict with any role as a McKenzie Friend; if such conflict emerged then it was incumbent upon the person to withdraw from one of the roles forthwith.'

3.75 The McKenzie friend in the case had taken up arms against the local authority on behalf of the litigant resulting in two areas of potential if not actual conflict. These were breach of the duty of confidentiality as a McKenzie friend and of s 12(1) of the Administration of Justice Act 1960 (which would amount to contempt of court within the Court of Protection proceedings) and the actions would also amount to a breach of the guidance that a McKenzie friend should not act as an agent of the litigant.

3.76 It appears to be the case that the approach of the family courts has been more relaxed in the use of McKenzie Friends than has been the case in other civil proceedings.

Payment for McKenzie friends

3.77 Litigants can enter into lawful agreements to pay fees to McKenzie friends for the provision of reasonable assistance in or out of court. Such assistance could include photocopying documents, preparing bundles, delivering documents to the court and other parties or provision of advice in connection with court proceedings. Such fees cannot be lawfully recovered from the opposing party.

3.78 Fees incurred by McKenzie friends for carrying out the conduct of litigation, in the absence of the court granting such a right to the McKenzie friend cannot be lawfully recovered either from the litigant for whom they carry out such work or from the opposing party.

3.79 If the court has granted a right to conduct litigation to a McKenzie friend then in principle such fees incurred in such work are recoverable from the litigant for whom such work is done. They cannot be lawfully recovered from the opposing party.

3.80 If the court has granted a right of audience to a McKenzie friend the fees incurred in exercising such a right are in principle recoverable from the litigant on whose behalf the right is exercised. In addition they are in principle recoverable from the opposing party as a recoverable disbursement.[24]

3.81 Parties and legal representatives are at risk of adverse costs orders particularly in relation to wasted costs arising from misconduct. Section 51(6) of the Senior Courts Act 1981 indicates that the court may disallow or (as the case may be) order the legal or other representative concerned to meet the whole of any wasted costs or such part of them as may be determined in accordance with rules of court. Section 51(13) defines 'legal or other

---

[24] CPR 1998, rr 48.6(2), (3)(a)(ii).

representative' in relation to a party to proceedings as including any person exercising a right of audience or right to conduct litigation on his behalf. This provision appears therefore to place at risk of wasted costs orders anyone to whom the court has granted such rights.

SECTION 4 – OTHER SOURCES OF SUPPORT

3.82 In addition to proposals to streamline court procedures and to make greater materials and guidance available to self representing litigants there has been an increase in other independent forms of support being made available for people involved in the court process.

3.83 Litigants can access support and assistance from local Personal Support Units (PSU)[25] and the Citizen's Advice Bureau.[26] Offices of both organisations can be found at the Royal Courts of Justice in London.

3.84 The PSU is an independent charity which describes itself as supporting litigants in person, witnesses, victims, their family members and other supporters attending court in the following locations:[27]

- Royal Courts of Justice.

- Principal Registry of the Family Division.

- Wandsworth County Court.

- Manchester Civil Justice Centre.

- Cardiff Civil Justice Centre.

- Birmingham Civil Justice Centre.

- Liverpool Civil and Family Court.

Contact can be made with the PSU either in advance of a hearing or by contacting them on the day of a hearing.

3.85 The PSU staff and volunteers can offer non-legal and practical help in the following ways:

- attending court with litigants;

---

[25] The personal support unit at the Royal Courts of Justice can be contacted on 020 7947 7701 or by email at cbps@bello.co.uk or rcj@thepsu.org.uk at the inquiry desk.

[26] The Citizen's Advice Bureau at the Royal Courts of Justice can be contacted on 020 7947 6564 or at the inquiry desk.

[27] The personal support unit's website can be accessed on http://thepsu.org and gives the precise locations for the units at the identified courts.

- helping litigants find out how to obtain the right forms, find relevant information on the internet, complete forms if the litigant knows what they want to say, and take paperwork to the appropriate customer service desk or court office;

- speaking to court staff if necessary;

- helping the litigant to think clearly before, during and after the hearing;

- sorting through the litigant's paperwork;

- helping to find the way round the court buildings;

- referring litigants to other agencies.

3.86 As with the situation for court staff the PSU cannot offer legal advice, cannot offer an advocacy service or represent the litigant at hearings.

3.87 PSU is a charity which describes its service as free, confidential[28] and independent.

SECTION 5 – PROTECTION FROM VEXATIOUS LITIGANTS

3.88 The Civil Procedure Rules 1998 enable the court to make civil restraint orders, which can inhibit and control the issuing of applications by vexatious litigants.

3.89 Civil restraint orders (CRO) are orders refraining a party from:

(a) making any further applications in current proceedings – *a limited civil restraint order*;

(b) from issuing certain claims or making certain claims or applications in specified courts – *an extended civil restraint order* (ECRO);

(c) from issuing any claim or making any application in specified courts – *a general civil restraint order* (GCRO).[29]

3.90 In addition to the Rules and Practice Direction, the Practice Note should also be considered – see *R (Kumar) v Secretary State for Constitutional Affairs*.[30]

---

[28] This should not be misinterpreted as providing any legal professional privilege.
[29] CPR 1998, r 2.3 (interpretation provisions). Please note this is a different creature from an order pursuant to s 91(14) of the Children Act 1989.
[30] [2006] EWCA Civ 990, [2007] 1 WLR 536.

3.91 CPR 1998, r 3.11 provides for a practice direction to set out the circumstances in which the court has the power to make a civil restraint order against a party to the proceedings, the procedure where a party applies for a CRO against another party and the consequences of making a CRO.[31]

3.92 Practice Direction PD3C indicates that the use of CROs are for situations where a party has issued claims or made applications that are totally without merit.

3.93 Limited civil restraint orders can be made by a judge of any court where a party has made two or more applications which are totally without merit.

3.94 If made, the order will restrain the party from making any further applications in the proceedings in which the order is made without first obtaining the permission of a judge identified in the order. The order will, unless otherwise specified, remain in effect for the duration of the proceedings and is limited to those particular proceedings.

3.95 If the party restrained makes an application without first obtaining leave then the application will be dismissed without the need for any further order of the judge and without the need for the other party to respond.

3.96 Extended civil restraint orders may be made by judges of the Appeal Court, High Court or by a designated civil judge of the county court or his appointed deputy, where a party has persistently issued claims or made applications which are totally without merit. This will restrict the party from issuing claims or making applications concerning any matter involving, relating to, touching upon or leading to the proceedings in which the order was first made in any court (if made by the Court of Appeal) in the High Court or county court (if made by a High Court judge) or in any county court identified in the order where made by the designated civil judge or his appointed deputy without first obtaining the permission of a judge identified in the order. Again any application/claim made without permission will automatically be struck out/dismissed.

3.97 A general civil restraint order may be made by any of the judges able to make an ECRO where the party against whom the order is made persists in issuing claims or making applications which are totally without merit in circumstances where an extended civil restraint would not be sufficient or appropriate. This restrains the party from applying for any claim or making any application in any court (if made by Court of Appeal Judge) in the High Court and county court (if made by a High Court judge) or any county court identified in the order (if made by a designated civil judge or his appointed deputy) without first obtaining the permission of a judge identified in the order.

---

[31] What follows is a very brief summary of the provisions. If proposing to make an application for such an order, or seeking to discharge one, due regard must be had for the detailed provisions in the practice direction.

3.98 ECROs and GCROs will last for the period specified in the order which may not exceed 2 years. CPR 1998, PD3A, Part 3, para 7 contains the provisions relating to vexatious litigants.

SECTION 6 – ADDITIONAL TIPS[32]

3.99 Although this guide may not necessarily apply to all the proceedings envisaged in this book, certain elements of the advice given there to self-representing litigants are likely to be of universal application.

3.100 The following should be noted:

- A litigant who is acting in person faces a heavier burden in terms of time and effort than does a litigant who is legally represented, but all litigation calls for a high level of commitment from the parties. No intending litigant should underestimate this.

- If the rules or court orders require documents to be prepared in a certain manner a document which does not comply with those requirements may be struck out as may documents which are garbled or abusive.

- Applications for adjournment of hearings will not readily be granted where opposed by other parties. Good reason will need to be shown and if the reason is illness an original medical certificate signed and dated by a medical practitioner setting out the reasons why attendance at court is not possible is likely to be required.

- Parties are reminded that they are expected to act with courtesy and respect for the other parties present and for the proceedings of the court.

- Punctuality is particularly important, as being late for hearings is unfair to other parties and other court users as well as being discourteous to them and the court.

---

[32] The Queen's Bench Guide has been prepared by the Senior Master and provides a general explanation of the work and practice of the Queen's Bench Division and is designed to make it easier for parties to use and proceed in the QBD.

Chapter 4

SPECIAL FORMS OF REPRESENTATION

SECTION 1 – LITIGATION FRIENDS

4.1   There are some special forms of representation that are available (and in some cases necessary) within court proceedings. The aim of this chapter is to provide a basic working understanding of circumstances in which special forms of representation may be used and the procedure for appointing them or the terms under which they will operate.

4.2   Many of the legal remedies referred to within this book include applications which may be made by a child. Where those applications are governed by the Civil Procedure Rules 1998 (CPR 1998) (so for example freestanding human rights applications not made within existing care proceedings, civil claims for damages, judicial review applications) there are provisions that require that the child should be represented by a 'litigation friend'.[1]

4.3   For example, the independent reviewing officer has a role to play in referring matters to CAFCASS Legal where a child may wish to complain, or where it may be appropriate for the child (or an appropriate adult on the child's behalf) to initiate court proceedings.[2]

4.4   Various different terms have historically been used for this role, some of which will continue to be in use and some of which now have other completely different meanings. The term 'litigation friend' now replaces the earlier roles in civil proceedings of 'next friend' and 'guardian ad litem'.

Civil proceedings

4.5   Any application proposed by or on behalf of a child, which is governed by the civil procedure rules as opposed to the family procedure rules, must take into account CPR 1998, Part 21 and associated Practice Direction PD21 which will not be replicated here.

---

[1]   For use of litigation friends within family proceedings, see FPR 2010, Part 15 (protected parties) and Part 16 (children).

[2]   See chapter 7.

4.6   The need for a litigation friend arises not only with respect to children but also in relation to any party who lacks capacity within the meaning of the Mental Capacity Act 2005 to conduct the proceedings. The latter category is referred to as a protected party.

4.7   In summary CPR 1998, r 21.2 directs that:

(a)   a protected party must have a litigation friend to conduct proceedings on his behalf;

(b)   a child must have a litigation friend to conduct proceedings on his behalf unless the court makes an order permitting a child to conduct proceedings without one.[3]

4.8   A child, or a litigation friend already acting for the child, can make the application for permission for the child to act without a litigation friend. If the child making the application for permission already has a litigation friend then notice of the application must be given to the existing litigation friend.

4.9   If a child is acting without a litigation friend under the rules and it subsequently appears to the court to be desirable for a litigation friend to conduct the proceedings on the child's behalf the court can appoint one.[4]

4.10   Unless the child has been given permission to act without a litigation friend a person may not (unless with the permission of the court) make an application against a child before proceedings have started or take any step in proceedings, except issuing and serving a claim form or applying for the appointment of a litigation friend until the child has a litigation friend.[5]

4.11   Appointment of a litigation friend can take place without a court order under CPR 1998, r 21.4.

4.12   A person may act as a litigation friend if he or she:

(a)   can fairly and competently conduct proceedings on behalf of the child;

(b)   has no interest adverse to the child; and

(c)   where the child is a claimant, undertakes to pay any costs which the child may be ordered to pay in relation to the proceedings, subject to any right he or she may have to be repaid from the assets of the child.

4.13   Each of the above criteria must be met before a person can be appointed as a litigation friend.

---

[3]   See CPR 1998, r 21.2(2) and (3).
[4]   See CPR 1998, r 21.2(4) and (5).
[5]   CPR 1998, r 21.3.

4.14 In order to be appointed as the litigation friend without the need for a court order the procedure in r 21.5 must be followed. This involves filing a certificate of suitability stating that the above conditions are met and that the litigation friend consents to act and confirms that he or she knows or believes the person is a child. The certificate must be served on everyone upon whom r 6.13 requires a claim form to be served. A certificate of service will need to be filed with the certificate of suitability. The certificate of suitability should be completed in the CPR Form N235.[6]

4.15 An alternative procedure for appointment exists and that is set out in r 21.6. This route is appointment by court order. This application may be made by a person wishing to become a litigation friend or by a party. Effectively this route will be used where someone who is not entitled to act as a litigation friend has filed a defence or where no litigation friend has been appointed and a claimant wishes to take some step within the proceedings. The application will need to be made in accordance with CPR 1998, Part 23.

4.16 The same qualification criteria must be met. In appropriate circumstances the Official Solicitor may be appointed to act. The appointment of the Official Solicitor is regarded as a last resort. Any order appointing the Official Solicitor will be expressed as being subject to his consent. Provision will need to be made for the payment of the Official Solicitor's costs.

4.17 The rules give power for the court to direct that a person may not act as a litigation friend, to terminate the appointment of a litigation friend and to appoint a new litigation friend in substitution for an existing one. An application for this to happen will need to be supported by evidence.[7]

4.18 It is important to note that where a claim is made by or on behalf of a child or against a child no settlement compromise or payment or acceptance of money paid into court will be valid without the approval of the court.[8]

4.19 Rule 21.12 contains the provisions which enable a litigation friend to recover expenses to the extent that they have been reasonably incurred and are of a reasonable amount. It is necessary to make an application to the court and there are caps on the level that may be claimed. If they are expenses which could be recoverable on an assessment of costs but have been disallowed in whole or in part they cannot be recovered by an application under these provisions. It will be necessary to file a witness statement setting out the nature and amount of the expenses and the reason why the expense was incurred.

Family proceedings

4.20 Where the applications are governed by the Family Procedure Rules 2010 the provisions of FPR 2010, Part 15 and PD15A (relating to representation of

---

[6] See Form N235 in Part 4 (resources section).

[7] CPR 1998, r 21.7.

[8] CPR 1998, r 21.10.

protected parties) and FPR 2010, Part 16 and PD16A (relating to representation of children) will need to be consulted.

4.21   Within family proceedings where the child is a party to the proceedings but not the subject of those proceedings, he or she must have a litigation friend to conduct proceedings on his behalf. This applies[9] unless the child has ether obtained the court's permission to act without a litigation friend or a solicitor considers that the child is able (having regard to the child's understanding) to give instructions in relation to the proceedings and has accepted instructions from that child to act for that child in the proceedings and, if the proceedings have already begun, the solicitor is already acting.[10]

4.22   The provisions relating to the appointment of a litigation friend without court order and by court order together with the provisions for terminating or preventing the appointment of a particular litigation friend very closely mirror the CPR provisions already considered above. The main differences relate to the ability to compromise proceedings and to accept money on the child's behalf.

4.23   Where the child is the subject of the proceedings and those proceedings are 'specified' under s 41(6) Children Act 1989[11] then particular provisions will apply for the appointment of a 'children's guardian' for the child. This chapter is not intended to deal with these types of children in proceedings in any greater depth and consideration will need to be given to s 41 Children Act 1989 and FPR 2010, r 16.3.

SECTION 2 – THE OFFICIAL SOLICITOR

4.24   Brief reference has been made in the section on litigation friends as to the role that the Official Solicitor may play as a last resort litigation friend in civil proceedings governed by the CPR 1998. Similar provision is made within the Family Procedure Rules 2010 for the appointment of the Official Solicitor within family proceedings both for protected parties and for children.[12]

4.25   The Official Solicitor to the Senior Courts can be contacted at 81 Chancery Lane, London, WC2A 1DD. Telephone 020 7911 7127.

4.26   For further guidance on the use of the Official Solicitor see Practice Note dated 2 April 2001.[13]

---

[9]   In proceedings under the Children Act 1989, in proceedings under Part 4A of the Family Law Act 1996, adoption, placement or related proceedings or proceedings under the court's inherent jurisdiction with respect to children.

[10]   See FPR 2010, rr 16.5 and 16.6.

[11]   Mainly proceedings regarded as public law proceedings for example applications for care/supervision orders or their discharge, applications for orders for contact with a child in care, making or revocation of placement orders etc.

[12]   FPR 2010, Parts 15 and 16.

[13]   [2001] 2 FLR 155.

4.27 Where the issue within the family proceedings is to determine matters relating to the child's welfare then CAFCASS will represent the child. In care proceedings where the child is the subject of the proceedings this will be by way of the appointment of a children's guardian.

4.28 Where the child is a party to family proceedings but not the subject of them the child must have a litigation friend unless FPR 2010, r 16.6 applies which allows the child to conduct their own proceedings if given permission by the court, or if a solicitor considers, having regard to the child's understanding, that the child is able to give instructions in relation to the proceedings and has accepted instructions to act.

4.29 FPR 2010, r 16.11 replicates the provision in the CPR 1998 for the court to appoint by order a litigation friend. The Official Solicitor is specifically identified as someone who may be appointed but they will not necessarily be appointed in every case.

4.30 The existing practice guidance, which does not appear to have been updated since the introduction of the Family Procedure Rules 2010, indicates that the Official Solicitor will act for a non subject child in the absence of any other willing and suitable person. They may also act for a child who is likely to lack capacity on reaching the age of 18 as CAFCASS cannot act beyond a child's 18th birthday.

4.31 The Practice Note indicates that it can be helpful for any question of the proposed instruction of the Official Solicitor to be discussed in advance by telephone on the number given above.

4.32 Where the court is considering making an order for the involvement of the Official Solicitor any order appointing him should be subject to his consent. The order, the court file and any bundle containing a summary, statement of issues and chronology should also be sent.

4.33 It should be noted in all cases that where the Official Solicitor is invited to act and consents to do so his investigations are likely to result in delays whilst their investigations are conducted.

SECTION 3 – ADVOCATES TO THE COURT

4.34 Sometimes the court will require assistance from advocates who do not represent the views of any specific party. This usually arises where there is a danger of an important or difficult point of law being decided without the court hearing all relevant arguments on the point. Previously this role was referred to as being an 'amicus curiae'.

4.35 The function of the advocate to the court is to give the court assistance on the relevant law and its application to the particular facts of the case. The advocate will not normally call evidence, cross-examine witnesses or investigate disputed facts.

4.36 CAFCASS Legal and the Official Solicitor may in appropriate cases be invited to act as advocate to the court.

4.37 Helpful guidance on the procedure to be adopted and the cases in which it may be appropriate can be found in the Attorney-General's memorandum of 19 December 2001.[14]

4.38 The current contact details for the Attorney General's Office are 20 Victoria Street, London, SW1H 0NF. Telephone 020 7271 2492. Email correspondence@attorneygeneral.gsi.gov.uk.

4.39 In situations where the experience of CAFCASS or the Official Solicitor in representing children and adults under a disability is likely to be of assistance, then they should be approached.

4.40 The requests should normally be made in writing and be accompanied by the relevant papers. It should be made clear whether the request is for written submissions or for attendance for oral submissions.

4.41 In urgent cases contact should be made by telephone.

SECTION 4 – SPECIAL ADVOCATES

4.42 In exceptional and very rare cases there may be the need to consider the appointment of a 'special advocate'. This will only be likely to arise where there are significant issues of risk of harm arising from the disclosure of material to one party in the proceedings and public interest immunity claims. Reported cases have included where the child and or parents are in protective police custody.

4.43 It is very rare indeed for this to be applicable in cases concerning decision making for children. The concept is more usually applied to cases involving detention of terrorist suspects.

4.44 Occasionally however, and in particular where the positive duty pursuant to Art 2 ECHR (right to life) falls upon the court and authorities, it may be a relevant consideration.

4.45 Use of a special advocate places great restrictions on the involvement of the party for whom the advocate acts. Material relied upon in the case will

---

[14] [2002] Fam Law 229.

become 'closed' to that party. That party will be prevented from knowing details and information upon which the court may base its decisions. They will be prevented from having a full lawyer client relationship with the 'special advocate' although they rely on that advocate to advance their case. The special advocate will have access to the closed material and will not be able to discuss it or its impact on the proceedings with them. Special advocates have been described as representing the interests of the party rather than representing that party.

4.46 If the facts and issues in the case indicate that this exceptional course may be necessary, then it is essential that a referral is made to the Attorney-General at an early stage.

4.47 There will be close scrutiny of the need to use such advocates due to the obvious risks of breaching Art 6 rights to a fair trial and Art 8 rights which themselves require procedural safeguards.

4.48 Helpful guidance can be obtained from the following recent cases: *BCC v FZ, AZ, HZ, and TVP*,[15] and *Re T (Wardship: Impact of Police Intelligence)*.[16]

---

[15] [2012] EWHC 1154 (Fam).
[16] [2009] EWHC 2440 (Fam), [2010] 1 FLR 1048.

Part 2

SCRUTINISING AND CHALLENGING DECISIONS

Chapter 5

METHODS OF CHALLENGING LOCAL AUTHORITIES

SECTION 1 – METHODS OF CHALLENGING LOCAL AUTHORITIES

5.1   There are various ways a person can use to challenge a decision, or omission, of the local authority:

- request that the decision or omission made by a social worker or a senior social worker be reviewed by a more senior officer within the local authority;

- make a complaint or representation to the local authority under the local authority's general complaints procedure established under s 26(3) of the Children Act 1989;

- make a complaint or representation to the local authority under s 7B of the Local Authority Social Services Act 1970 about any matter not within the scope of s 26(3) of the Children Act 1989;

- make a complaint about a child protection conference in accordance with the procedure in Working Together (2010) para 5.107;

- refer the decision or omission to the independent reviewing officer (IRO);

- refer the decision or omission to the relevant Children's Commissioner;

- refer the decision or omission to the Local Government Ombudsman;

- seek judicial review of the decision or omission;

- make an application for a contact order under s 34 of the Children Act 1989 (but only in relation to a child who is looked after by the local authority);

- make an application to discharge a care order under s 39(1) of the Children Act 1989, make an application to vary/discharge a supervision order under s 39(2) or to substitute a care order with a supervision order under s 39(4) of the Children Act 1989;

- make a freestanding application for a claim under ss 6 and 7 of the Human Rights Act 1998.

Chapter 6

INVOLVING CHILDREN AND FAMILIES IN DECISION-MAKING

SECTION 1 – INDEPENDENT VISITORS

6.1 The legal framework in relation to independent visitors is contained within s 23ZB(6)(a) of the Children Act 1989 (CA 1989) and Volume 2 CA Guidance.[1]

6.2 A responsible authority looking after a child has a duty to appoint a person to be a child's independent visitor where it appears to them to be in the child's interest to do so.[2] The appointment should be considered as part of the development of the care plan for the child or as part of a review of the child's case.

6.3 Being 'independent' means that an independent visitor must not be connected with the local authority in any way.

6.4 In identifying when an independent visitor should be appointed for a looked after child, the local authority should assess whether either of the following criteria is satisfied:

- it appears that communication between the child and a parent (or any person with parental responsibility) has been infrequent; or

- the child has not been visited (or has not lived with) a parent (or any person who has parental responsibility) during the preceding 12 months.

6.5 Decisions about whether to consider appointing an independent visitor should be determined according to the needs of the child. In deciding what factors should be taken into account when making such a decision, the local authority should consider the following:

- whether the child is placed at a distance from home, particularly where the placement is out-of-authority, which makes it difficult to maintain sufficient contact with friends;

---

[1] Children Act 1989 Guidance and Regulations Volume 2: Care Planning, Placement and Case Review (March 2010, DCSF).
[2] CA 1989, s 23ZB(6)(a).

- whether the child is unable to go out independently or whether he or she experiences difficulties in communicating or building positive relationships;

- whether the child is likely to engage in behaviour which will put him or her at risk as a result of peer pressure or forming inappropriate relationships with people who are significantly older;

- whether a child placed in a residential setting would benefit from a more individualised relationship; and

- whether it would make a positive contribution to promoting the child's education and health.

Who can act as an independent visitor?

6.6   In general the independent visitor role is envisaged as being undertaken by volunteers from a lay background, although in some circumstances they may have professional skills or experience which in other settings entitles them to work in a professional capacity with children.

6.7   In matching a child to an independent visitor the local authority should take account of the child's wishes and feelings. This means that the child must be part of the process of deciding whether an independent visitor should be appointed.

6.8   The child's social worker should be involved in the process of identifying whether the child would benefit from an independent visitor.

What is the purpose of the independent visitor?

6.9   The purpose of the independent visitor is to contribute to the welfare of the child. Therefore he or she should:

- promote the child's developmental, social, emotional, educational, religious and cultural needs;

- encourage the child to exercise his or her rights and to participate in decisions which will affect him or her;

- support the care plan for the child and his or her carers; and

- aim, as far as possible, to complement the activities of the carers.

6.10   The independent visitor's functions are primarily to visit, advise and befriend. However, the way in which these functions are carried out will vary according to the needs and wishes of the individual child.

6.11 The guidance expressly deals with what the independent visitor is *not* intended to do. Thus, the independent visitor should:

- not be anything other than child-focused (however sympathetic to other points of view);

- not be a substitute parent or carer;

- not allow personal prejudices to determine actions;

- not engage the child in intensive counselling involving complex situations; and

- not take on the role of a skilled advocate in complex situations.

The role of the independent visitor at meetings or in consultation processes

6.12 Where the local authority intends to make an application to court to keep the child in secure accommodation, the local authority must, if practicable, inform the child's independent visitor (if one has been appointed) of that intention as soon as possible.[3]

6.13 The independent visitor may also provide contributions to the review of a child's case either in writing or at review meetings to which he or she has been invited or at which the child has requested his or her attendance. The independent visitor can put views to the meeting as a friend of the child.

What should the independent visitor do if a skilled advocate is needed?

6.14 The guidance specifies the kind of situations where the child may have an urgent need for skilled advocacy:

- because he or she is dissatisfied with the current arrangements for his or her care;

- because of an absence of progress in achieving a plan for the future;

- because he or she feels that his or her views are being ignored; or

- because he or she is being abused.

6.15 The guidance makes it absolutely clear that the independent visitor is *not* expected to fulfil this role. Instead the independent visitor must be able to recognise the needs of the child in such serious situations and with the child's

---

3   Children (Secure Accommodation) Regulations 1991 (SI 1991/1505), reg 14(c).

agreement draw the concerns to the attention of his or her social worker (or, if necessary, a more senior officer in the local authority). In certain situations it may be appropriate to refer the matter to one of the voluntary organisations which specialises in advocacy.[4]

What should the independent visitor do if there are concerns?

6.16 If there are concerns about aspects of the child's case these should be discussed with the child's social worker. If having done so, the independent visitor is still not satisfied, then he or she should refer the case to the child's independent reviewing officer (IRO).

SECTION 2 – INDEPENDENT ADVOCATES

Relevance to child care lawyers

6.17 The requirement for children and young people to be able to participate meaningfully in decision-making concerning their care is a recurrent theme that has been emphasised in local authorities' policies and procedures for looked after children.[5] Notwithstanding this requirement, history demonstrates that meaningful participation of children and young people can sometimes be overlooked by professionals. To ignore participation is to marginalise the children and young people whose welfare the court and professionals are seeking to protect and does not serve to assist the local authority in making best interests decisions in respect of those individuals.

6.18 *Keeping Children Safe: the Government's Response to The Victoria Climbie Inquiry Report and Joint Chief Inspectors' Report Safeguarding Children* (2003) identified that an effective system to safeguard children should include:[6]

'Children and family members involved in making decisions about what services they receive.'

6.19 The views and interests of children and young people and the need for the same to be at the heart of decision-making was thereafter identified to be key in *Every Child Matters: Next Steps 2004* (Dfes 2004).

6.20 The need to establish a 'listening culture' was also identified in guidance issued by the Department for Education and Skills in 2004 entitled *Get it Sorted: Guidance on Providing Effective Advocacy Services for Children and Young People Making a Complaint under the Children Act 1989*:[7]

---

[4]   For example, the National Youth Advocacy Scheme (NYAS) www.nyas.net and The Children's Society www.childrensociety.org.uk.

[5]   For example, the Government's Objectives for Children's Social Services (issued in September 1999), the findings of the Waterhouse Inquiry and the Utting Report.

[6]   Paragraph 11.

[7]   At para 1.7.

'The Government wants advocacy and children's rights services to be linked to other activities which help professionals to listen to children, thereby creating a culture of openness where listening and responding to children and young people's concerns become an integral part of everyday practice.'

6.21   The provision of advocacy services is not limited to those children and young people wishing to make complaints, but also extends to their being able to make representations regarding their wishes and feelings in respect of a wide range of issues that impact on them as looked after children and young people (for which see s 26A of the CA 1989 below). It is recognised that whilst there are children who are adequately able to express their views, there will be a significant proportion who need support (in the form of an independent advocate) in order to be able to be listened to and have proper respect and regard shown to their wishes and feelings.

The legal framework

6.22   The legal framework in relation to independent advocates is contained within:

- The United Nations Convention on the Rights of the Child.

- The Children Act 1989.

- The Children Act 1989 Guidance and Regulations Volume 2: Care Planning, Placement and Case Review.

- National Standards for the Provision of Children's Advocacy Services 2002.

- The IRO Handbook.

- The statutory guidance – The Roles and Responsibilities of the Lead Member for Children's Services and the Director of Children's Services.

- The Children Act 1989 Guidance and Regulations Volume 3: Planning Transition to Adulthood for Care Leavers Including The Care Leavers (England) Regulations 2010.

- The Advocacy Services and Representations Procedure (Children) (Amendment) Regulations 2004 (SI 2004/719).

6.23   Article 12 of the United Nations Convention on the Rights of the Child provides:

> 1. States Parties shall assure to the child who is capable of forming his or her own views the right to express those views freely in all matters affecting the child, the views of the child being given due weight in accordance with the age and maturity of the child.

2. For this purpose, the child shall in particular be provided the opportunity to be heard in any judicial and administrative proceedings affecting the child, either directly, or through a representative or an appropriate body, in a manner consistent with the procedural rules of national law.

6.24   The Children Act 1989[8] provides:

Before making any decision with respect to a child who the local authority is looking after or proposing to look after, the authority must ascertain the wishes and feelings of the child and the local authority should give due consideration to those wishes and feelings.

6.25   Section 22(4) and (5) of the Children Act 1989 provides:

(4) Before making any decision with respect to a child whom they are looking after, or proposing to look after, a local authority shall, so far as is reasonably practicable, ascertain the wishes and feelings of –

(a)   the child;
(b)   his parents;
(c)   any person who is not a parent of his but who has parental responsibility for him; and
(d)   any other person whose wishes and feelings the authority consider to be relevant,

regarding the matter to be decided.

(5) In making any such decision a local authority shall give due consideration –

(a)   having regard to his age and understanding, to such wishes and feelings of the child as they have been able to ascertain;
(b)   to such wishes and feelings of any person mentioned in subsection (4)(b) to (d) as they have been able to ascertain; and
(c)   to the child's religious persuasion, racial origin and cultural and linguistic background.

6.26   The local authority is required, pursuant to s 26A of the 1989 Act,[9] to make arrangements for the provision of assistance to:

(a) persons who make or intend to make representations under section 24D of the 1989 Act.[10] Those persons are defined in section 24D(1) as being –

(i)   a relevant child for the purposes of section 23A[11] or a young person falling within section 23C;[12]
(ii)   a person qualifying for advice and assistance; or
(iii) a person falling within section 24B(2); and

(b) children who make or intend to make representations under section 26.

---

[8]   As amended by the Children Leaving Care Act 2000 and Children Act 2004, s 53.
[9]   Incorporating the amendments provided by Adoption and Children Act 2002, s 119 and the Children and Young Persons Act 2008, s 39, Sch 3, para 18.
[10] Representations include but are not limited to complaints.
[11] Section 23A(2) defining 'relevant child'.
[12] Section 23C(1) defining the continuing duties owed by the local authority in respect of former relevant children.

6.27   The assistance provided under the arrangements shall include assistance by way of representation[13] and every local authority shall give such publicity to their arrangements for the provision of assistance under this section as they consider appropriate.[14] The basic legal provision of each part is summarised below.

The Children Act 1989 Guidance and Regulations Volume 2: Care Planning, Placement and Case Review

6.28   Where a child has difficulty in expressing his/her wishes and feelings about any decisions being made about him/her, consideration must be given to securing the support of an advocate.[15]

6.29   The need for children to feel that they are 'active participants and engaged in the process' and for ascertaining a child's wishes and feelings during the care planning, placement and review process can be summarised as follows:

- when plans are being made for the child's future, s/he is likely to feel less fearful if s/he understands what is happening and has been listened to from the beginning;

- close involvement will make it more likely that s/he feels some ownership of what is happening and it may help him/her understand the purpose of services or other support being provided to him/her, his/her family and carer;

- many children have an understanding of what is causing their problems;

- what underlies their needs;

- they may have insight into what might or might not work in the context of their current circumstances and environment;

- they often know what sort of support they would most value and be able to access;

- engaging children helps to recognise their difficulties, develop their strengths; and

- promote their resilience.[16]

6.30   Ascertaining the wishes and feelings of children and young people is not a one off event, but needs to be a continuous process. Children's expressed views should always be discussed, recorded and given due consideration before

---

[13]   Section 26A(2).
[14]   Section 26A(5).
[15]   Paragraph 1.10.
[16]   Paragraph 1.10 and 1.11.

a placement decision is made, at every review meeting and at case conferences. The possibilities and options identified should be explained, discussed and, if necessary, reassessed in the light of the child's views. The social worker should be aware of and acknowledge that there may be good reasons why the child's views are different from those of his/her parents or the local authority.[17] This is a potentially ripe area for challenge in the context of care proceedings and the extent to which the views of the child have been ascertained, expressed, discussed, given due consideration and recorded will be a key area for scrutiny, whether a party is seeking to challenge or defend the actions of the local authority.

National Standards for the Provision of Children's Advocacy Services 2002

6.31 The Government recognised in the foreword provided by the Minister of State at the Department of Health:

'Too often in the past, we have seen situations where children and young people have tried to speak out but have not had their voices heard. This is not acceptable.'

6.32 There are ten standards identified as follows:

Standard 1:   Advocacy is led by the views and wishes of children and young people.

Standard 2:   Advocacy champions the rights and needs of children and young people.

Standard 3:   All advocacy services have clear policies to promote equalities issues and monitor services to ensure that no young person is discriminated against due to age, gender, race, culture, religion, language, disability or sexual orientation.

Standard 4:   Advocacy is well-publicised, accessible and easy to use.

Standard 5:   Advocacy gives help and advice quickly when they are requested.

Standard 6:   Advocacy works exclusively for children and young people.

Standard 7:   The Advocacy Service operates to a high level of confidentiality and ensures that children, young people and other agencies are aware of its confidentiality policies.

Standard 8:   Advocacy listens to the views and ideas of children and young people in order to improve the service provided.

Standard 9:   The Advocacy Service has an effective and easy to use complaints procedure.

Standard 10:   Advocacy is well managed and gives value for money.

---

[17]   Paragraph 1.12.

The IRO Handbook[18]

6.33 The role of the independent reviewing officer (dealt with in detail at chapter 7) includes the responsibility for considering the issue of an advocate.[19]

'When meeting with the child before every review, the IRO is responsible for making sure that the child understands how an advocate could help and his/her entitlement to one. Advocacy is an option available to children whenever they want such support and not just when they want to make a formal complaint. Some children will feel sufficiently confident or articulate to contribute or participate in the review process without additional help. Others may prefer the support of an advocate. This could be a formal appointment from a specialist organisation or might be an adult already in the child's social network.

Every child has the right to be supported by an advocate. The local authority must have a system in place to provide written, age appropriate information to each looked after child about the function and availability of an advocate and how to request one.'

The statutory guidance – the roles and responsibilities of the lead member for Children's Services and the Director of Children's Services

6.34 The responsibility on the local authority (as against the lead member for Children's Services and the Director of Children's Services) regarding the establishment of an effective system of contact as between looked after children and the local authority is contained at para 2.23:

'The Lead Member should also be satisfied that there is a system in place by which all children looked after by the local authority can contact the authority at an appropriate level. This should require the LM to pursue either an individual child's concerns or more general policy issues in response. The LM will wish to be kept aware of the needs and circumstances of particular groups of looked after children who may be especially vulnerable. These might include children living in placements at a distance from the local authority; children with disabilities; and looked after children in custody. The LM should also be satisfied that systems are in place to enable the voices of these young people to be heard, and to help inform the Council's strategy for corporate parenting.'

---

[18] IRO Handbook: Statutory guidance for independent reviewing officers and local authorities on their functions in relation to case management and review for looked after children (DCSF 2010).

[19] See the IRO Handbook at paras 3.14–3.15.

The Children Act 1989 Guidance and Regulations Volume 3: Planning Transition to Adulthood for Care Leavers Including the Care Leavers (England) Regulations 2010

6.35 Further guidance as to the need for the local authority to make all looked after children aware of the their entitlement to independent advocacy support is set out in paras 2.14 and 2.15 of the above Guidance:

> '2.14 Section 26A of the 1989 Act imposes duties on local authorities in respect of the provision of advocacy services.[20] All looked after children must be made aware of their entitlement to independent advocacy support and how they can access it. This entitlement is not just for when a looked after child or care leaver wishes to complain, it includes situations where young people need to make representations about the quality of the care and support provided by their responsible authority.
>
> 2.15 Access to advocacy will be particularly important where the local authority's decision-making processes concern the child's readiness to move from their care placement. Young people may frequently require independent support to enable them to put their view across and express their wishes and feelings about the help they feel they will need for the future, so that they are enabled to reach their potential.'

The Advocacy Services and Representations Procedure (Children) (Amendment) Regulations 2004 (SI 2004/719)

6.36 Persons who may not provide assistance with regard to advocacy services (provided pursuant to s 26A) are identified in reg 3 and are as follows:

(a) he is or may be the subject of the representations;

(b) he is responsible for the management of a person who is or may be the subject of the representations;

(c) he manages the service which is or may be the subject of the representations;

(d) he has control over the resources allocated to the service which is or may be the subject of the representations; or

(e) he is or may become involved in the consideration of the representations on behalf of the local authority.

6.37 Pursuant to reg 4, the local authority must, where they receive representations or become aware of an intention on the part of a person to make representations:

---

[20] *Get It Sorted: Guidance on Providing Effective Advocacy Services for Children and Young People Making a Complaint under the Children Act 1989* (DfES, 2004).

(a)   provide him with information about advocacy services; and

(b)   offer him help in obtaining an advocate.

6.38 The concept of independent advocates is not limited to family proceedings or looked after children. Such roles are also provided for under the Mental Capacity Act 2005,[21] Mental Health Act 2007[22] and Health and Social Care Act 2001.[23]

Provision of advocacy services

6.39 There are many different people that are able to advocate for children both informally and formally. Examples of such people include social workers, foster carers, teachers, nurses, health visitors, friends and relatives. Independent advocates are also provided by a number of voluntary organisations (eg the Children's Society, NSPCC etc). Many of those voluntary organisations themselves provide guidance and best practice for the provision of advocacy services. See for example, *Speaking Out A Guide for Advocates for Children and Young People with Learning Disabilities*.[24]

6.40 Despite the clear legislative framework providing for the provision of independent advocates to children and young people who are in the care of the local authority, the provision of such services has been patchy. The research by the Children's Society concludes:[25]

> 'We found that there is currently an inconsistency in access to advocacy for children in the looked after system driven by variation in spending between local authorities and variation in the skills available to effectively advocate for more vulnerable groups, such as children with communication difficulties and very young children.'

6.41 In cases both within and outside of proceedings, practitioners will have to pay close attention to the legislative framework underpinning the provision of advocacy services and consider whether, having regard to that framework, the child or young person can be said to have been able to properly express his views and engage in an effective and meaningful fashion in the decision making process concerning his future care/contact. This becomes a more significant role within the context of reduced services and availability of children's guardians.

---

[21]   Mental Capacity Act 2005, ss 35 and 36.
[22]   Mental Health Act 2007, s 30.
[23]   Health and Social Care Act 2001, s 12.
[24]   Produced by the NSPCC in association with Voice UK in 2005.
[25]   Entitled *The Value of Independent Advocacy for Looked After Children and Young People* (Children's Society, September 2012, Pona and Hounsell).

SECTION 3 – CHILD PROTECTION CONFERENCES

6.42 Child protection conferences (CPCs) have been in general use since the 1970s with the emergence of the child protection register. Their operation has been prescribed by a series of departmental circulars since 1974. Guidance about the procedure relating to CPCs is contained in *Working Together*.[26]

6.43 A child protection conference is a multi-agency meeting to discuss the case of a particular child that is convened at the request of either the local authority or any other agency involved, but chaired by a local authority officer.

6.44 The decision of the child protection conference is not binding upon the local authority, but is a recommendation to the local authority or to a particular agency for action.

6.45 There are three types of CPCs:

• Initial child protection conference;

• Review child protection conference;

• Pre-birth child protection conference.

6.46 The local authority has the lead role in convening and arranging CPCs although they are *multi-agency* meetings. The aim of a child protection conference is to:

• Enable professionals most involved with the child and family to assess all relevant information in making decisions about whether the child is at continuing risk of significant harm.

• Enable professionals to make an interagency plan about how to safeguard the child and promote welfare if the child is at continuing risk of significant harm.

• Involve the child's family in assessing and planning how to protect the child.

6.47 The local authority is responsible for arranging the CPC, but there will be an independent chair with special skill and experience in child protection social work.[27]

6.48 Until the early 1990s it was highly unusual for parents (or children where appropriate) to be invited to attend CPCs. Social workers and other

---

[26] The Department of Health, the Home Office and the Department for Education and Skills *Working Together to Safeguard Children* (TSO, 4th edn, 2010).

[27] Historically an NSPCC worker, but currently most local authorities will provide or utilise a specialist independent reviewing and chairing service.

professionals attended CPCs in private to discuss their concerns about the child and to formulate a child protection plan without the involvement of the family. The plan would then be explained to the family by the social worker after the meeting.

6.49 The emphasis on working in partnership embodied in the Children Act 1989 and the accompanying guidance, combined with research findings and the campaigning by organisations such as the Family Rights Group and the NSPCC, has now ended the universal practice of parents being excluded from CPCs as a matter of course – 'exclusion should be kept to a minimum and needs to be especially justified'.[28]

6.50 Local Safeguarding Children Board (LSCB) procedures should set out criteria for excluding a parent or care-giver, including the evidence required. A strong risk of violence or intimidation by a family member at or subsequent to the conference, towards a child or anybody else, might be one reason for exclusion. The possibility that a parent or care-giver may be prosecuted for an offence against a child is not in itself a reason for exclusion although in these circumstances the chair should take advice from the police about any implications arising from an alleged perpetrator's attendance. If criminal proceedings have been instigated, the view of the Crown Prosecution Service should be taken into account. The decision to exclude a parent or care-giver from the child protection conference rests with the chair of the conference, acting within LSCB procedures. If the parents are excluded, or are unable or unwilling to attend a child protection conference, they should be enabled to communicate their views to the conference by another means.

6.51 Including parents and other relevant family members (and children if appropriate) in the discussions, planning and decision-making at CPCs requires particular sensitivity, thought and preparation by the allocated social worker, the chair of the Conference, and by the other professionals attending. With strong leadership from the chair and the commitment of all professionals to be open and honest, parents can participate in CPCs and assist in effective decision-making.[29] Inclusion of parents enables both professionals and families:

- To be clear about the allegation of abuse.

- To be directly informed about the findings of the professionals.

- To join in decision-making about further work (including the nature and extent of future partnership).

---

[28] The Department of Health, the Home Office and the Department for Education and Skills *Working Together to Safeguard Children* (TSO, 4th edn, 2010), para 6.15.

[29] See The Department of Health *The Challenge of Partnership in Child Protection: A Practice Guide* (HMSO, 1995).

6.52   Preparation for attendance at CPCs is essential and requires work by the social worker and the chair, as well as work to prepare the family. It may not be possible for all family participants to remain in the meeting throughout the discussions. There may be conflicts of interest between participants and these may necessitate partial withdrawal of some people at some stages. For example, some young people will decline to be in the room with an alleged abuser or will be unable to speak in front of a parent or relative, but might necessarily want the opportunity to speak with professionals without the presence of those adults. Many adults and children will find it helpful to have a supporter at the CPC, but the nature and extent of the supporter's role should always be examined and clarified. It will certainly help adults (and children) to contribute more effectively to CPCs if they are assisted beforehand to think through their own interpretations of the events which are causing concern.[30]

6.53   Before a conference is held, the purpose of a conference, who will attend, and the way in which it will operate, should always be explained to a child of sufficient age and understanding, and to the parents and involved family members. Where the child or family members do not speak English well enough to understand the discussions and express their views, an interpreter should be used. The parents (including absent parents) should normally be invited to attend the conference and helped to participate fully. Social workers should give parents information about local advice and advocacy agencies, and explain that they may bring an advocate, friend or supporter. The child, subject to consideration about age and understanding, should be invited to attend, and to bring an advocate, friend or supporter if he or she wishes. Where the child's attendance is neither desired by him or her nor appropriate, the social worker (or other professional) who is working most closely with the child should ascertain what his or her wishes and feelings are, and make these known to the conference.

6.54   The local authority should provide a written report summarising and analysing the information from the assessment. The local authority will also usually request written reports from other professionals.

6.55   The written report should summarise and analyse the information obtained by the local authority during the initial assessment. Reports should include as much information as possible to enable the CPC to devise an effective child protection plan for the child. Information in the social worker's report should include:

- a chronology of significant events;

- information about the child's health and development in all domains;[31]

---

[30]   See *Social Work Decision-Making: A Guide for Childcare Lawyers* (Jordan Publishing, 2nd edn, 2012) for more detailed information about how to analyse the local authority's approach to child protection conferences.

[31]   See chapter 5.

- information about the capacity of the parents and other family members to protect the child from harm and to promote the child's development;

- the wishes and feelings of the child, parents and other family members about the protection plan;

- analysis of the implications of the information obtained for the child's future safety;

- a clear recommendation about future planning for the child.

6.56 It is good practice for parents to be provided with a copy of the social worker's report in advance and for them to have been given an opportunity to discuss the contents and recommendations of the report with the social worker.

6.57 A policy of refusing to allow a solicitor for the parents to attend a CPC is unlawful. A policy of refusing to provide parents with the minutes of a CPC is also unlawful.[32] It is good practice to invite solicitors or representatives from the firm representing parents and the child to attend the CPC.[33]

6.58 Other professionals or people who may have a relevant contribution to make may include:

- the child, or the child's representative;

- family members (including the wider family);

- local authority staff who have led and been involved in an assessment of the child and family;

- foster carers (current or former);

- residential care staff;

- professionals involved with the child (for example, health visitors, midwife, school nurse, children's guardian, paediatrician, school or nursery staff, GP);

- professionals involved with the parents or other family members (for example, family support services, adult mental health services, probation, GP);

- professionals with expertise in the particular type of harm suffered by the child or in the child's particular condition, for example, a disability or long-term illness;

---

[32] *R v Cornwall County Council, ex p LH* [2000] 1 FLR 236.
[33] Guidance document produced by the Law Society's Family Law Committee (in consultation with the Professional Ethics Division) (1997).

- professionals involved in investigations (for example, the police);

- local authority legal services (child care);

- NSPCC or other involved voluntary organisations;

- a representative of the armed services, in cases where there is a Service connection.

6.59 The relevant Local Safeguarding Children Board (LSCB) protocol should specify a required quorum for attendance, and list those who should be invited to attend, provided that they have a relevant contribution to make. As a minimum, at every CPC there should be attendance by the local authority and at least two other professional groups or agencies that have had direct contact with the child who is the subject of the CPC. In addition, attendees may also include those whose contribution relates to their professional expertise or responsibility for relevant services. In exceptional cases, where a child has not had relevant contact with three agencies (that is, the local authority and two others), this minimum quorum may be breached.

6.60 Professionals and agencies who are invited but are unable to attend should submit a written report.

Initial child protection conferences

6.61 The timing of an initial child protection conference will depend on the urgency of the case and on the time needed to obtain relevant information about the child and family. If the CPC is to reach well-informed decisions based on evidence, it should take place following adequate preparation and assessment. Cases where children are at risk of significant harm should not be allowed to drift. Initial child protection conferences should take place within 15 working days of the strategy discussion.

6.62 The purpose of the initial child protection conference is to formulate a multi-agency outline child protection plan in as much detail as possible. The CPC should decide whether the child's name needs to be placed on the child protection register and under which category.

6.63 The tasks of the initial child protection conference will be to:

- appoint a key worker (usually the social worker);

- identify members of the core group of professionals and family members who will develop and implement the child protection plan;

- establish how parents, children and the family should be involved in the planning process;

- establish timescales for meetings of the core group, production of the child protection plan and for child protection review meetings;

- identify in outline what further core and specialist assessments are required;

- outline the child protection plan, including specific details of what needs to change;

- consider the need for a contingency plan; and

- clarify the purpose of the initial child protection conference, the core group and the review child protection conference.

6.64 The outline child protection plan should:

- identify the risks of significant harm to the child and ways in which the child can be protected through an inter-agency plan based on assessment findings;

- establish short-term and longer-term aims and objectives that are clearly linked to reducing the risk of harm to the child and promoting the child's welfare;

- be clear about who will have responsibility for what actions (including actions by family members) within what specified timescales; and

- outline ways of monitoring and evaluating progress against the plan.

6.65 The initial child protection conference should also agree a date for the first review child protection conference, and under what circumstances it might be necessary to convene the review child protection conference before that date.

6.66 When determining whether the child should be the subject of a child protection plan the CPC should consider whether the child is at continuing risk of significant harm.

6.67 The test in considering this question is two-fold:

- Can the child be shown to have suffered ill-treatment or impairment of health or development as a result of physical, emotional, or sexual abuse or neglect, and is it the judgment of the professionals that further ill treatment or impairment is likely? Or

- Is it the judgment of the professionals (substantiated by the findings of enquiries in this individual case or by research evidence), that the child is likely to suffer ill treatment or the impairment of health or development as a result of physical, emotional, or sexual abuse or neglect?

6.68 If the CPC decides that the child is at continuing risk of significant harm, it will automatically be the case that safeguarding the child requires inter-agency help. In these circumstances intervention with the family will need to be delivered through a formal child protection plan.

6.69 Conference participants should base their judgments on:

- all the available evidence obtained through existing records;

- the initial assessment;

- the in-depth core assessment undertaken following the initiation of s 47 enquiries.

6.70 The method of reaching a decision within the CPC on whether the child should be the subject of a child protection plan should be set out in the relevant LSCB protocol. The decision-making process should be based on the views of all agencies represented at the conference, and also take into account any written contributions that have been made.

6.71 The decision of the conference and, where appropriate, details of the category of abuse or neglect, the name of the key worker, the lead professional and the core group membership should be recorded in a manner that is consistent with the initial child protection conference report and circulated to all those invited to the conference within one working day.

6.72 The record of the CPC is a crucial working document for all relevant professionals and the family. It should include:

- the essential facts of the case;

- a summary of discussion at the conference, which accurately reflects contributions made;

- all decisions reached, with information outlining the reasons for decisions;

- a translation of decisions into an outline or revised child protection plan enabling everyone to be clear about their tasks.

6.73 In *Re X (Emergency Protection Orders)*[34] McFarlane J (as he then was) reiterated the guidance in Working Together and set out some basic requirements in respect of the recording of confidential information shared during CPCs:

---

[34]   [2006] 2 FLR 701 at [29].

- if the circumstances are sufficient to justify the exclusion of the parents from part of a CPC (or the parents are otherwise absent), a full minute should nevertheless be taken of everything that is said during the CPC;

- if it is considered necessary to treat part of what is minuted as confidential from the parents, that part of the minutes should be disclosed for approval to the professionals who attended the CPC, but that part of the approved minutes should be maintained separately from the body of the minutes, which are sent to the parents;

- the non-confidential section of the minutes should expressly record at the appropriate stage that confidential information was disclosed or discussed;

- the need for continued confidentiality with respect to confidential sections of the minutes should be kept under review by the CPC chair, with confidentiality only being maintained if it continues to be necessary.

6.74   After the initial child protection conference the following actions should be implemented:

- a key worker will be appointed (this will normally be the social worker acting as the lead professional);

- members of a core group will be appointed and meetings of the core group arranged and coordinated by the key worker or the lead professional;

- a child protection plan will be formulated and implemented.

The review child protection conference

6.75   The first review child protection conference should take place within three months of the initial child protection conference and further reviews should be held at intervals of no more than six months for as long as the child remains subject of a child protection plan. This is to ensure that momentum is maintained in the process of safeguarding the registered child.

6.76   The purpose of the review child protection conference is to:

- review the safety, health and development of the child against intended outcomes set out in the child protection plan;

- ensure that the child continues adequately to be safeguarded; and

- consider whether the child protection plan should continue in place or should be changed.

6.77 Every review child protection conference should consider explicitly whether the child continues to be at risk of significant harm, and therefore whether the child's welfare should continue to be safeguarded through the provision and implementation of a child protection plan.[35] If not, then the child will no longer need to remain subject of a child protection plan.

6.78 The child protection plan should be based on the findings from the assessment and follow the dimensions relating to the child's developmental needs, parenting capacity and family and environmental factors, drawing on knowledge about effective interventions.

6.79 The aim of the child protection plan is:

- To ensure the child is safe and to prevent the child from suffering further harm.

- To promote the child's welfare, health and development.

- To support the family and wider family members to safeguard and promote the welfare of their child (provided it is in the best interests of the child).

6.80 The child protection plan should set out what work needs to be done, why, when and by whom.

6.81 The child protection plan should contain:

- A description of the identified developmental needs of the child, and what therapeutic services are required.

- Specific, achievable, child-focused outcomes intended to safeguard and promote the welfare of the child.

- Realistic strategies and specific actions to achieve the planned outcomes.

- A contingency plan to be followed if circumstances change significantly and require prompt action.

- Clearly defined roles and responsibilities of professionals and family members, including the nature and frequency of contact by professionals with children and family members.

- Clearly defined points at which progress will be reviewed, and the means by which progress will be judged.

---

[35] For more detailed information about analysing child protection plans, see *Social Work Decision-Making: A Guide for Childcare Lawyers* (Jordan Publishing, 2nd edn, 2012).

- Clearly defined roles and responsibilities of professionals who will have routine contact with the child and professionals who will provide specialist or targeted support to the child and family.

6.82   The child protection plan should take into consideration the wishes and feelings of the child, and the views of the parents, insofar as they are consistent with the child's welfare. The key worker should make every effort to ensure that the children and parents have a clear understanding of the planned outcomes, that they accept the child protection plan and are willing to work to it.

6.83   Parents should be clear about the evidence of significant harm that resulted in the child becoming the subject of a child protection plan, about what needs to change, and what is expected of them as part of the plan for safeguarding and promoting the child's welfare. All parties should be clear about the respective roles and responsibilities of family members and different agencies in implementing the plan. The parents should receive a written copy of the plan so that they are clear about who is doing what, when and the planned outcomes for the child.

Chapter 7

INDEPENDENT REVIEWING OFFICER (IRO)

7.1　Detailed guidance about the role of the independent reviewing officer (IRO) is found in the Care Planning, Placement and Case Review (England) Regulations 2010[1] and in the guidance within the IRO Handbook: Statutory guidance for independent reviewing officers and local authorities on their functions in relation to case management and review for looked after children.[2]

SECTION 1 – THE INTRODUCTION OF IROS

7.2　IROs were introduced on a statutory basis in 2004. The scheme was brought in by the Review of Children's Cases (Amendment) (England) Regulations 2004[3] and the *Independent reviewing officers' Guidance 2004*. At the same time the Children and Family Court Advisory and Support Service (Reviewed Case Referral) Regulations 2004[4] extended the functions of CAFCASS so that on a referral from an IRO they could consider bringing proceedings for breaches of the child's human rights, judicial review and other proceedings.

SECTION 2 – INITIAL FAILINGS OF THE SCHEME

7.3　The IRO initiative was not regarded as successful and a Green Paper consultation[5] found that:

- IROs were not sufficiently robust in challenging decisions made by local authorities even where professional practice was obviously poor.

- Not every statutory review was being conducted in a way that encouraged a challenging analysis of the proposals for meeting the child's needs.

---

[1]　SI 2010/959.
[2]　DCSF, 2010. Issued under s 25B(2)(b) of the CA 1989 (as amended by the Children and Young Persons Act 2008 which created a new power for the Secretary of State to issue statutory guidance to IROs) and s 7 of the Local Authority Social Services Act 1970.
[3]　SI 2004/1419.
[4]　SI 2004/2187.
[5]　*Care Matters* Cmd 6932 (2006).

- Insufficient weight was being given to the views of the child or to those of his or her parents, carers, or other professionals with a role in securing his or her welfare.

- Unless care plans are rigorously examined the review is no longer an opportunity for informed reflection on the child's progress and planning for the child's future; instead it becomes merely a sterile 'box ticking' exercise.

7.4   Professional criticism of the performance of the IRO system was also recorded in *S (A Child Acting by the Official Solicitor) v Rochdale Metropolitan Borough Council and the Independent Reviewing Officer*.[6]

7.5   In this case care proceedings were issued in relation to a teenage mother's baby, and the Official Solicitor was appointed to act on behalf of the teenage mother, who was not competent to give instructions. The Official Solicitor took the view that the local authority should have issued care proceedings in respect of the teenage mother (S), who was an extremely vulnerable young person, in respect of whom nobody had been exercising parental responsibility for some time, and who, in his view, was suffering significant harm. The local authority declined to do so.

7.6   The Official Solicitor applied for judicial review of the authority's decision and brought a claim for relief under the Human Rights Act 1998. Eventually, after S had been placed in secure accommodation to prevent further absconding, the authority did issue care proceedings, and the judicial review proceedings were withdrawn. S, acting by the Official Solicitor, persisted with the human rights claim against the local authority and the IRO. Eventually the court approved a compromise between the parties, but at the hearing one of the issues that remained was whether wider issues concerning the duties owed to looked-after children should be dealt with.

7.7   The court attached to the case report for public record the concerns expressed by the Official Solicitor about the IRO. In particular, the court endorsed the Official Solicitor's complaints about the local authority's failure to take the rudimentary step of assessing S's needs adequately. The court agreed that what it described as 'a largely impotent or supine IRO' played a significant contribution to the overall systemic failures in the case.

7.8   The court also made general comments about the overall failure of the IRO and CAFCASS initiative:[7]

> 'Not one single referral has been made by CAFCASS in respect of an 'accommodated' child since the office of the IRO was created. There has still not been any case where a child's circumstances have been referred to CAFCASS post

---

6   [2008] EWHC 3283 (Fam).

7   *S (A Child Acting by the Official Solicitor) v Rochdale Metropolitan Borough Council and the Independent Reviewing Officer* [2008] EWHC 3283 (Fam) at [96].

care order, and that despite the fact that the office was created in response to a consistent concern by the courts as to the appropriate remedies to be taken when a local authority failed to implement a care plan which had been approved by the court and on the basis of which the court had ceded its control to the local authority.'

7.9   The court made particular reference to the inadequacy of the statutory reviews for S, and concluded that:

- the statutory review process appeared to have been largely a 'tick box' exercise;

- the basic review pro-formas were incomplete with records of at least two reviews missing entirely;

- there was no evidence of any contribution to S's care planning by any other professional other than an unqualified social worker;

- there was no action taken in respect of a delay in referring S to the appropriate mental health team (CAMHS);

- although the statutory requirement to provide a personal education plan for S was acknowledged in the course of review its absence was never remedied;

- there was never any suggestion that S be referred to a clinical or educational psychologist notwithstanding the fact that she had attended for education on only 14 days in her 2 years as an accommodated child and her behaviour frequently involved excessive alcohol consumption, self harm, illicit drugs and sexual activity with much older men and frequent absconding from her accommodation.

7.10   The court found that all these factors ought to have been obvious to the IRO and attached as an appendix to the judgment a summary of the Official Solicitor's analysis about the key concerns and broader lessons to be learned in the case. The particular recommendations about the role, and deficits, of the IRO (within a wider context of overall concerns and systemic failures) included:

- Statutory reviews of 'looked after' children must be rigorously conducted. Where an action or assessment is recommended, time limits should be set to ensure compliance with a named individual identified to put the plan into action.

- Thought should be given, in the case of every looked after child, as to whether reviews of the child's circumstances should be held more frequently particularly at times of crises for the child.

- Any assessments or important information should be made available to the IRO sufficiently in advance of statutory reviews to provide him or her with the opportunity to consider them fully. The fact that it is not contemplated that a court or a guardian will review the case files should not mean that any lesser standard is acceptable. Case management and recordings should be regarded as requiring a universal standard of competence either in or outside proceedings.

- Where a recommendation is made, or has been made earlier and there has been a failure to comply, the IRO should be proactive in ensuring compliance with timetables, bearing in mind his or her obligation to make a referral to CAFCASS if he or she feels a child is not being sufficiently protected.

- The IRO should at all times bear in mind that to discharge his or her function effectively he or she must have access to all relevant documentation. In particular he or she should review the social workers' files and read the records to ensure that they are up to date.

- Greater participation in the process of care planning would enhance the IRO's credibility and confidence in challenging the decision-making processes of the local authority from a platform of improved knowledge about the child's individual circumstances.

- In line with the recommendations in *Care Matters: Transforming the Lives of Children and Young People in Care*,[8] every child should be allocated a named IRO. The name of the officer should be communicated to the child who, in an age appropriate manner, should be told of the IRO's function.

- Where parents have consistently failed to attend statutory reviews the IRO should ensure that a planned program to support their renewed involvement is devised with identified markers to evaluate its success.

SECTION 3 – THE REVISED REGIME

7.11   Following the concerns raised in the Green Paper consultation in 2006[9] (and echoed in *S (A Child Acting by the Official Solicitor) v Rochdale Metropolitan Borough Council and the Independent Reviewing Officer*[10]), the CYPA 2008 included widespread reforms to the IRO service.

7.12   Since April 2011 IROs have been subject to a revised regime as provided for by the CYPA 2008 amendments to the CA 1989. The government's

---

[8]   *Care Matters: Transforming the Lives of Children and Young People in Care* CM 6932 (TSO, October 2006).
[9]   *Care Matters* Cmd 6932 (2006).
[10]   [2008] EWHC 3283 (Fam).

commitment to IROs as a key element in improving care planning and securing better outcomes for looked after children is clearly stated within the most recent guidance.

7.13   As such, the role of the IRO is to provide a quality assurance role within the care planning and review process. The IRO's responsibilities have now been extended from monitoring the performance by the local authority of their functions in relation to a child's review, to monitoring the performance by the local authority of their functions in relation to a child's case in accordance with s 25A(1) of the CA 1989.[11]

7.14   The intention of such changes is stated in the guidance as being to enable the IRO to have an effective independent oversight of the child's case and to ensure that the child's interests are protected throughout the care planning process:[12]

> 'These are detailed responsibilities. To carry them out properly needs time and care.'

7.15   The functions of the IRO are set out in s 25B(1) of the CA 1989 and reg 45 of the Care Planning, Placement and Case Review (England) Regulations 2010. Where there is a need for significant changes to the care plan, then the date of the child's review should be brought forward. The social worker must inform the IRO in the event of a significant change or event in the child's life. No significant change to the care plan can be made unless it has been considered first at a review, unless this is not reasonably practicable.

7.16   The IRO should chair all review meetings of looked after children. Part of the IRO's duties is to ensure that any poor practice and/or failure to review the case in accordance with regulations is brought to the attention of persons at an appropriate level of seniority within the responsible authority.

7.17   Under the Care Planning, Placement and Case Review (England) Regulations 2010, the IRO now has the power to adjourn reviews if he or she is not satisfied that sufficient information has been provided by the responsible authority to review the child's care plan in accordance with Sch 7.[13] For example:

- the IRO is not satisfied that the local authority has complied adequately with all the requirements relating to reviews (eg the duty to consult the child, the child's parents and others before taking decisions with respect to the child, or appropriate planning and paperwork being available) and considers that such omissions will adversely affect the efficacy of the review; or

---

[11]   Inserted by s 10 Children and Young Persons Act 2008.
[12]   *Re A and S (Children)* [2012] EWHC 1689 (Fam) at para 195.
[13]   The Care Planning, Placement and Case Review (England) Regulations 2010, reg 36(2).

- the IRO is not satisfied that the child has been properly prepared for the meeting.

7.18 However, the guidance recommends that careful consideration should be given before taking such action and the wishes and feelings of the child, the carer and, where appropriate, the parents should be sought before any decision is made. The IRO should consider the effects on the child of delaying a meeting for which he or she has been prepared and will need to weigh up the benefits between proceeding with the meeting on limited information and the delay in decision-making as a result of adjournment. However, responsibility for deciding whether or not a review should be adjourned rests solely with the nominated IRO for the child concerned. In such circumstances the review may be adjourned once but should be completed within 20 working days of the original scheduled date.

7.19 Where disagreements or differences in opinion arise in the course of the review process between those present, every effort should be made to resolve the matter on an informal basis. Where agreement cannot be reached, the responsible local authority should ensure that the child, parents, carers and others involved with the child are aware of the representations procedure they are required to have in place.

7.20 The IRO is under a duty to advise the child of his or her right to make a complaint and of the availability of an advocate to assist the child in making a complaint.

7.21 Where the IRO is of the view that the responsible local authority:

- has failed to address the needs of the child set out in the revised plan; and/or

- has failed to review the case in accordance with the regulations; and/or

- has failed to implement effectively any decision made at a review; or

- is otherwise in breach of its duties to the child in any significant way,

the IRO must advise staff at an appropriate level of seniority of this failure. It will be important that senior managers then work to resolve the failure within a timescale that meets the needs of the individual child.

7.22 The IRO has the statutory power to refer a case to CAFCASS (or a Welsh family proceedings officer) if the IRO considers it appropriate to do so.[14] The IRO will encounter a wide range of situations in which there are concerns about the plan for the child or the service that is being provided. In most cases it will be possible to address these through:

---

[14]   CA 1989, s 25B(3).

- discussion with the local authority, including access to the dispute resolution procedure;

- use of the complaints procedure, either by the child directly or by an adult who is authorised to act on the child's behalf; or

- application to the court for an order under the CA 1989, either by the child or by an appropriate adult who is able and willing to act.

7.23 When considering whether to make a referral to CAFCASS, the IRO should consider the impact that a referral would have for the child. In some cases, there will be time available first to pursue the full dispute resolution procedure within the local authority. In other situations, the matter will be of sufficient urgency that the dispute resolution process needs to be curtailed. It is the responsibility of the IRO to make the decision about whether and when a referral is necessary, based on the timetable for the child.

7.24 The Family Justice Review final report (November 2011) considered the role of the IRO in detail and recommended that there need to be effective links between the two roles and that the working relationship between the guardian and the IRO needs to be stronger.

7.25 The Family Justice Review noted the widespread distrust – often ill-founded – of local authority ability and willingness to implement a care plan in the best interests of the child. In particular, it concluded that such distrust was often associated with discussion of the role of the IRO and concern about workloads and independence from their employer, the local authority:[15]

> 'For as long as the IRO is employed by the local authority there is the possibility that their independence will be compromised and this will be detrimental to the welfare of the child ... The role of the IRO is pivotal to ensuring that appropriate care plans are agreed and delivered, their independence is essential and can only be guaranteed if the role is moved outside of the local authority.'

7.26 However, the Family Justice Review concluded that to remove the role from day-to-day local authority management would simply leave a gap that the local authority would have to fill under another name. It therefore recommended that the role should remain within the management of the local authority but with overall review of the efficiency of the service to be carried out. Section 11 of the CYPA 2008 was intended to develop the IRO service beyond the scope of the local authority by enabling the government to establish a new corporate body to discharge the IRO functions and/or to confer such functions on CAFCASS. Those functions included the provision of training, accreditation, appointment and management of IROs. However, this part of the 2008 Act remains to be enforced at the time of writing (January 2013).

---

[15] Consultation response by National Youth Advocacy Service, cited in Family Justice Review Final Report (November 2011) at para 3.113.

Consequently, the training, appointment and management of IROs currently remains within the remit of local authorities.

7.27 One concern raised within the final Family Justice Review report was that the lack of referrals to CAFCASS, and via them to the courts, indicated a lack of effectiveness by IROs in scrutinising the local authority's management of the case. Just eight formal referrals were noted as having been made to CAFCASS since the process was introduced in 2007. It was however observed that informal advice is sought more frequently. The Family Justice Review rejected this as a criticism of the IRO role, instead seeing it as an indication of the effectiveness of the increased use of dispute resolution being used within local authorities:[16]

> 'The formal referral mechanism is one to be used by exception and the threat is often effective without the use. The figures suggest to us that the informal route is used and helping to resolve issues without court action.'

7.28 This issue was considered at length in *Re A and S (Children)*,[17] a case which echoes the shortcomings previously identified in *S (A Child Acting by the Official Solicitor) v Rochdale Metropolitan Borough Council and the Independent Reviewing Officer*.[18]

7.29 In *Re A and S*, two boys, now teenagers, came into local authority care as infants and were in due course freed for adoption. After a time the search for adopters was abandoned but the freeing orders were never discharged and all links with the boys' family were cut. They remained under the freeing orders for 11 years, moving from foster placement to foster placement and becoming increasingly unsettled and disturbed. They were found to have suffered irreparable harm and the court made declarations that the local authority had acted incompatibly with the children's rights under Arts 8, 6 and 3 of the ECHR.

7.30 The court also made declarations in relation to the independent reviewing officer as follows:

(a) the IRO failed to identify that the children's human rights had been and were being infringed (breach of Art 8);

(b) the IRO failed to take effective action to ensure that the local authority acted upon the recommendations of looked after child (LAC) reviews (breach of Art 8); and

(c) the IRO failed to refer the children's circumstances to CAFCASS Legal (breach of Art 8).

---

[16] Family Justice Review Final Report (Nov 2011) at para 3.115.
[17] [2012] EWHC 1689 (Fam).
[18] [2008] EWHC 3283 (Fam).

7.31 The primary failings in the case were front line social work failings, compounded by abusive behaviour in two foster homes (as reflected in the greater balance of the HRA 1998 declarations in respect of the local authority's actions). However, the inadequacy of the IRO system was held to be an important secondary contributor, in that it did not pick up on and remedy the primary problem.

7.32 The IRO apologised unreservedly to the children and accepted the following specific shortcomings on his part in both a detailed statement and in frank oral evidence:

(a) not monitoring the social work response to and the compliance with his recommendations and advice from the LAC reviews (for example, recommendations about contact, revoking the freeing order, applying to the Criminal Injuries Compensation Authority);

(b) not identifying who would implement the LAC review recommendations or the timescale within which they would be implemented;

(c) not checking that the key social worker had recourse to his own manager and if appropriate, the Legal Department, in order to implement review recommendations;

(d) not verifying information provided by social workers;

(e) not addressing and resolving the repeated failures by the social workers to implement the recommendations;

(f) not referring the cases to CAFCASS Legal;

(g) allowing the children to be in adoptive limbo and thereby deprived of the legal rights that care orders would have provided to them and to their family members on their behalf;

(h) not promoting the rights of the children to independent legal advice and advocacy by identifying an appropriate individual or resource to give them legal advice and support;

(i) not promoting the rights of the children to have the best chance of a settled and secure home throughout their childhood.

7.33 It was held that the local authority defaulted on its duties towards two children and its independent reviewing system did not call it to account. The matter was never returned to court as it should have been and as a result the local authority's actions did not come under independent scrutiny. It was also held that the IRO reviewing system within the local authority had been utterly ineffective and that there was a pressing need for the independent reviewing system to work more effectively than it did for the boys in this case.

Chapter 8

COMPLAINTS

SECTION 1 – COMPLAINTS PROCEDURES

What is a complaint?

8.1   Making a complaint is the first *formal* step available for children and their families or their advocates to voice dissatisfaction with the services they receive (or do not receive). Solving problems should be at the forefront of the local authority's approach and making a complaint is the first formal step for challenging social work decision-making. However, children and/or their families must take few steps before making a complaint to give the local authority the opportunity to try to resolve any dissatisfaction they may experience informally.

8.2   In the first instance the child/young person (or any person acting on their behalf) needs to tell someone (eg their social worker/residential worker/foster carer/independent reviewing office) what it is they are unhappy about. The local authority should first attempt to resolve the problem/issue raised by the child immediately and without recourse to the formal complaints procedure.

8.3   The child should then be informed what should happen next if they continue to be unhappy with the solution offered to them and give them a complaints leaflet; go through it with them and/or give them the contact details of whom to contact next. This should be the complaints manager.[1] The complaints manager (for details see below in **8.37–8.39**) is responsible for dealing and processing complaints effectively and within timescales. The complaint procedure must be well advertised, easily understood and available to all children and their families known to the local authority.

8.4   It is not always easy for a child/young person to make a request/voice unhappiness about the solution offered and then for the local authority to recognise what the child has said as a matter that should be dealt with under the complaint procedure. A simple example: A child is in a permanent placement with foster carers under a care order. The girl wants to join the football team of a professional club who saw her play football in school. Her foster carer is able to transport the girl to the club after school but not collect her at the end of the session two hours later. The foster family were unable to identify a reliable alternative and the local authority refused to meet the

---

[1]   Also known as compliments and complaints managers. They are usually located in Policy and/or Performance section of Children's Services.

additional costs of a transport service and told the girl that there was nothing they could do. This could be the end of a future football career for a girl in care whose potential was thwarted before it even started. To allow the girl to reach her full potential, the local authority's decision must be challenged.

8.5   In the first instance, the girl and/or her foster family must first voice the need for help in transport. It requires confidence, resilience, advocacy and good working relationships between child/foster family/social worker. In the absence of any of these ingredients or a combination of them, the child may remain silent and/or the foster family may feel too powerless.

8.6   Having succeeded in making the request, the child/foster family/advocate needs to voice their dissatisfaction (to either the social worker or the IRO) about the failure of the local authority to recognise the girl's wish to play and train with a professional football team as an 'unmet need' and/or that an alternative solution offered (for example the offer that the girl should join the more local, walking distance football club which is ill equipped) is not good enough. The child and/or family must voice their dissatisfaction to the resolution offered and decide to MAKE A COMPLAINT.

8.7   This difficult process is recognised in the statutory guidance and it is recommended that families approach people and agencies in the community who provide independent advice (eg advocacy services, Family Rights Group or lawyers) who may assist in problem solving (and may prevent dissatisfaction developing into complaints).

8.8   The guidance specifies that local authority staff should ensure that attempts at problem solving are not used to divert an eligible person from making a complaint under the statutory procedure. Nevertheless, the guidance also specifies that the local authority should continue to make efforts to resolve the dissatisfaction of children and young people so that the matter complained about can be resolved, including during consideration of a formal complaint.

8.9   Attempts at resolution should not end once a complaint has been made. Rather, local authorities should consider introducing alternative ways of resolving the complaint while any given stage in complaint investigation is ongoing. In any case, resolution should be in the best interests of the child concerned.

8.10   There are a number of methods of resolution that do not require a full investigation that can be applied, including:

- the provision of an apology or explanation;

- conciliation and mediation;

- a re-assessment of the children or young person's needs;

- practical action specific to the particular complainant;

- a review of practice; and

- an assurance that the local authority will monitor the effectiveness of its remedy.

Alternative dispute resolution

8.11 Alternative dispute resolution (ADR) may be offered as an alternative to the complaints procedure if this is agreed by both complainant and complaints manager. A complainant can opt back into the complaints process at any time. Conciliation meetings are used to resolve complaints without the need for protracted investigations. The aim is to provide better outcomes for complainants with a focus on resolution over process. However, the complainant may decide to terminate ADR at any time and refer back to the complaints procedure

Independent reviewing officers (in cases of complaints from or on behalf of children in care)

8.12 Independent reviewing officers (IROs) do not have a role in instigating the complaints procedure themselves, and should not stand in the way of complaints being made. They will have a role when they meet children to inform them that they have a right to make complaints to the local authority, and of the local authority's responsibility to provide them with an independent advocate should the child so wish.

8.13 The IRO may be part of the solution to the problem, and the complaints manager may consult with the IRO to determine what options are available. An outstanding formal complaint using the local authority's complaints procedure should not prevent the IRO from fulfilling their role in resolving problems by negotiation. The IRO may have a role in communicating both with the child and with the complaints manager. The IRO should not prejudice the complaints procedure but their work may help to speed up the process or even hold a key to its resolution. The IRO should become involved in serious complaints concerning children's care plans. They should not usually need to get involved in more minor complaints about a child's day-to-day care.

8.14 In all cases the welfare of the child is the primary concern. IROs will need to make a judgment about whether a problem raised via a complaint is serious enough to constitute a breach of the child's human rights such as to justify making a referral to CAFCASS, or whether it would be reasonable to await a resolution through the complaints procedure, with or without additional support of the IROs own negotiation.[2]

---

[2] For more information on the role of the independent reviewing officer see the Care Planning, Placement and Case Review (England) Regulations 2010 and accompanying IRO handbook.

The legal framework

8.15 The key legislative framework for complaints is underpinned by the Children Act 1989, s 26(3) (support for families and children). It was amended by the Children Act 1989 Representations Procedure (England) Regulations 2006.[3]

8.16 The Guidance *Getting the Best from Complaints, Social Care Complaints and Representations for Children, Young People and Others* (Department for Education and Skills) accompanies the Children Act 1989 Representations Procedure (England) Regulations 2006.

8.17 This guidance applies to England only and sets out the changes arising from the Adoption and Children Act 2002 which amended and extended the scope of Representations Procedure (England) Regulations in the Children Act 1989. In the main it inserted a new section (s 26A) into the Children Act 1989, which requires local authorities to arrange for the provision of advocacy services to children and young people making or intending to make representations, including complaints.

8.18 The Welsh version of this guidance is *Listening and Learning: A Guide to handling complaints and representations in local authority social services in Wales*.[4]

Other relevant regulations

8.19 The Advocacy Services and Representations Procedure (Children) (Amendment) Regulations 2004[5] came into force on 1 April 2004. These Regulations require local authorities to provide advocacy services for children and young people making or intending to make a complaint under s 24D or s 26 of the Children Act 1989.

8.20 All children must be given a copy of the current relevant complaint leaflet by their social worker when they become looked after but a child may choose someone else as an advocate if s/he wishes to do so.

8.21 Local authorities have a statutory duty, arising from the Children Act 1989, to have a system for receiving representations by, or on behalf of, children who use the social care services they provide or commission and to produce an annual report about the operation of the complaints procedure relation to an individual child about the local authority's exercise of its

---

[3]   The Local Authority Social Services and National Health Service Complaints Regulations 2009 (England) apply to adults social care and is outside the scope of this book.

[4]   (2005) Available to download at Listening and learning: A guide to handling complaints and representations in local authority social services in Wales
http://wales.gov.uk/topics/health/publications/socialcare/guidance1/listening/
?lang=en See also Your Rights to Complain – Children and Young Persons www.cymru.gov.uk
http://wales.gov.uk/docs/dhss/publications/110426childcomplaintsen.pdf.

[5]   SI 2004/719.

functions under Part III and para 4 of Sch 7 of the Children Act 1989 and matters in relation to children and young people accommodated by voluntary organisations and registered children's homes.

8.22 The Data Protection Act 1998 gives the general right to any person to read personal information held about themselves in social work records. Certain information can be withheld but as a general rule it is advisable to seek access to the records held before or when making a formal complaint.

Definitions

8.23 A complaint is defined in the guidance of *Getting the Best from Complaints* as an expression of dissatisfaction or disquiet (verbally or written) in relation to an individual child or young person, which requires a response. Complaints of a general nature which are not concerned with an individual case would therefore fall outside the statutory definition, as do anonymous complaints.[6]

8.24 Section 26(3) of the Children Act 1989 provides that all functions of the local authority under Part 3 of the Act may form the subject of a complaint. This would include complaints about:

- an unwelcome or disputed decision;

- concern about the quality or appropriateness of a service;

- delay in decision making or provision of services;

- delivery or non-delivery of services including complaints procedures;

- quantity, frequency, change or cost of a service;

- attitude or behaviour of staff;

- application of eligibility and assessment criteria;

- the impact on a child or young person of the application of a local authority policy; and

- assessment, care management and review.

8.25 The Regulations provide that the following may also be the subject of a complaint:

---

[6]   Anonymous complaints however, should be recorded. The fact that the complaint is from an anonymous source should not in itself justify a decision not to pursue the matter. Nor should it rule out referral to other procedures as relevant.

- the decision by the local authority to initiate care and supervision orders (s 31);

- the effect of the care order and the local authority's actions and decisions where a care order is made (s 33);

- control of parental contact with children in care (s 34);

- how supervisors perform their duties where a supervision order is in force (s 35);

- matters that do not relate to the court and which are specifically actions of the local authority can be considered, regarding applications for and duties in relation to child assessment orders (s 43); and

- matters relating to applications for emergency protection orders and decisions relating to the return of children who have been removed (s 44).

Where social work information or a social work report has gone to court, the child or young person can make a complaint about the report, for example its quality or accuracy, distinct and separate to the subsequent actions of the court. If this complaint is upheld, the local authority should advise the child or young person what action it proposes to take with regard to the court action.

8.26 The Regulations also provide that the following adoption-related functions may also be the subject of a complaint:

- provision of adoption support services (as prescribed in reg 3 of the Adoption Support Services Regulations 2005[7]) insofar as these enable adoptive children to discuss matters relating to adoption;

- assessments and related decisions for adoption support services as prescribed in reg 3 of the Adoption Support Services Regulations 2005 (Parts 4 and 5 of the Adoption Support Services Regulations 2005);

- placing children for adoption, including parental responsibility and contact issues (ss 18–29 of the 2002 Act);

- removal of children who are or may be placed by adoption agencies (ss 30–35 of the 2002 Act);

- removal of children in non-agency cases (ss 36–40 of the 2002 Act);

- duties on receipt of a notice of intention to adopt (s 44 of the 2002 Act);

- duties set out in regulations in respect of:

---

[7]   SI 2005/691.

-   a local authority considering adoption for a child (Part 3 of Adoption Agency Regulations 2005[8]);
-   a proposed placement of a child with prospective adopters (Part 5 of Adoption Agency Regulations 2005);
-   placement and reviews (Part 6 of Adoption Agency Regulations 2005);
-   records (Part 7 of Adoption Agency Regulations 2005);
-   contact (Part 8 of Adoption Agency Regulations 2005); and

-   parental responsibility prior to adoption abroad (Part 3 of Adoptions with a Foreign Element Regulations 2005).

8.27 The Regulations also provide that the following special guardianship related functions may also be the subject of a complaint:

-   financial support for special guardians;

-   support groups for children and young people to enable them to discuss matters relating to special guardianship;

-   assistance in relation to contact;

-   therapeutic services for children and young people; and

-   assistance to ensure the continuation of the relationship between the child or young person and their special guardian or prospective special guardian.

Exemptions from the complaints procedure

8.28 The complaints procedure does not apply when:

-   the person wishing to complain does not meet the requirements of 'who may complain' and is not acting on behalf of such an individual;

-   the complaint is not in regard of the actions or decisions of the local authority complained to, or of anybody acting on its behalf; or

-   the same complaint has already been dealt with at all stages of the procedure.

8.29 Regulation 8 provides the local authority with discretion in deciding whether to consider complaints where to do so would prejudice any of the following concurrent investigations:

-   court proceedings;

---

[8] SI 2005/389.

- tribunals;

- disciplinary proceedings; or

- criminal proceedings.

If the local authority decides not to consider or further consider complaints subject to these concurrent investigations, they must write to the complainant explaining the reason for their decision and specifying the relevant concurrent investigation (reg 8(3)).

8.30 Once the concurrent investigation has been concluded the complainant may resubmit their complaint to the local authority as long as it is within one year of the conclusion of the concurrent investigation.

Who may complain

8.31 Sections 26(3) and 24D of the CA 1989 and s 3(1) of the Adoption and Children Act 2002 require the responsible authority to consider representations including complaints made to it by:

- any child or young person (or a parent of his or someone who has parental responsibility for him) who is being looked after by the local authority or is not looked after by them but is in need;

- any local authority foster carer (including those caring for children placed through independent fostering agencies);

- children leaving care;

- special guardians;

- a child or young person (or parent of his) to whom a special guardian order is in force;

- any person who has applied for an assessment under s 14F(3) or (4);

- any child or young person who may be adopted, their parents and guardians;

- persons wishing to adopt a child;

- any other person whom arrangements for the provision of adoption services extend;

- adopted persons, their parents, natural parents and former guardians; and

- such other person as the local authority consider has sufficient interest in the child or young person's welfare to warrant his representations being considered by them.

Complaints made on behalf of a child

8.32 Where a complaint is received from a representative acting on behalf of a child or young person, the local authority should normally confirm where possible that the child or young person is happy for this to happen and that the complaint submitted reflects his or her views.

8.33 The local authority has the discretion to decide whether or not the representative is suitable to act in this capacity or has sufficient interest in the child's welfare. If the local authority considers that the representative does not have sufficient interest, s/he should notify the representative in writing, explaining that no further action should be taken.

8.34 The local authority is also likely to receive complaints by adults that relate to a child or young person but are not made on the child's behalf. The Children Act 1989 gives discretion to local authorities to decide in cases where eligibility is not automatic whether or not an individual has sufficient interest in the child's welfare to justify his own complaint being considered by them. In reaching a decision, where possible the local authority may wish to check with the child or young person that it is happy with the person making a complaint.

Complaints relating to more than one local authority

8.35 Where a complaint relates to two or more local authorities, the complaint should be considered by the authority which is looking after the child or in any other case by the authority within whose area the child is ordinarily resident. Under s 27 of the Children Act 1989, there is a duty to cooperate. Good practice would suggest the local authority responding to the complaint should ensure good communication with the other local authority/authorities.

Key principles for complaint procedures

8.36 Local authorities have the duty to formulate a complaint procedure according to the key principles identified in the guidance within *Getting the Best from Complaints*:

- Clear and easy to use complaints procedure.

- The people who use the service should be treated with dignity and respect, are not afraid to make a complaint, and have their concerns taken seriously.

- It should ensure, as far as is possible, even-handedness in the handling of complaints.

- Any concerns about the protection of children should be referred immediately to the relevant social services team or to the police.

- Complaints should be resolved swiftly and satisfactorily at the local level.

- Be a fair process with adequate support for everyone involved in the complaint.

- The child or young person should receive a full response without delay.

- Any local authority purchasing services in the independent sector, should be able to exercise its continuing duty of care.

- Safeguard the child or young person's rights of access to other means of redress, such as the Local Government Ombudsman.

- Local authorities should monitor their performance in handling complaints, deliver what they have promised, learn from complaints and use this learning to improve services for everyone who uses them.

The complaints manager

8.37 The Regulations require local authorities to designate an officer, known as a complaints manager. The local authority should ensure that the complaints manager has sufficient clarity of purpose and authority to enable complaints to be dealt with swiftly and effectively. The complaints manager should be independent of operational line management and of direct service providers.

8.38 The complaints manager should also take an active role in facilitating resolution of complaints by identifying appropriate colleagues and external people (including investigating officers and advocates) to contribute to complaints work. The complaints manager should foster good working relationships with key bodies and partner agencies.

The role of the complaints manager

8.39 The role of the complaints manager includes:

- managing, developing, resourcing and administering the complaints procedure;

- overseeing the receipt and investigation of complaints that arise from problems that could not be resolved initially;

- liaising with the independent reviewing officer where appropriate to identify options for resolution;

- appointing investigating officers, review panellists and independent persons;

- ensuring that there are no conflicts of interest at any stage between parties involved in delivering the procedure;

- co-operating with such other persons or bodies as may be necessary in order to investigate or resolve complaints;

- promoting local resolution;

- monitoring the progress of the investigation and ensuring its smooth running;

- making recommendations to the local authority on any other action to take following an investigation;

- working closely with the panel chair on the organisation of stage 3 review panels;

- monitoring and reporting on time scales;

- maintaining a written record of complaints made, the procedure followed and the outcome;

- compiling the annual report.

- providing help and advice to children and young people and others who may wish to make a complaint so that they understand the options available for resolution both within the complaints procedure or alternatives routes of remedy and redress;

- ensuring that advocacy services are explained, offered and provided when required;

- ensuring the complainant is kept informed at all stages;

- offering advice on the response of the authority; and providing practical support to complainants; and

- supporting staff involved in all stages of the complaints procedure.

The procedure for complaints investigations and resolutions

8.40 There are three stages to any complaints procedure:

- Stage 1 – local resolution;

- Stage 2 – investigation; and

- Stage 3 – review panel.

Time Scales

8.41 There are also time scales for the investigation process. These are as follows:

- 10 days at stage 1 (with a further 10 days for more complex complaints or additional time if an advocate is required);

- 25 days at stage 2 (with maximum extension to 65 days);

- 20 days for the complainant to request a review panel;

- 30 days to convene and hold the review panel at stage 3;

- 5 days for the panel to issue its findings; and

- 15 days for the local authority to respond to the findings.

8.42 The intention of the regulations is that in most circumstances complaints should be considered at stage 1 in the first instance. This is the local resolution stage which requires the local authority to resolve a complaint as close to the point of contact with the child or young person as possible (ie through front line management of the service). In doing so the local authority should consider the wishes of the complainant about how the complaint should be dealt with.

Receiving a complaint

8.43 Local authorities are required to put in place systems for complaints to be made verbally to a member of staff or in writing (including electronically) (reg 6). Complaints handling by local authorities must be child and young person friendly and appropriate to the age and understanding of the child. The concerns of children and young people should be listened to. If a child or young person wishes to make a complaint, local authorities are required to provide him with information about advocacy services and offer help to obtain an advocate (see below about advocacy).

8.44 If a complaint is made to a member of staff, the complaints manager should be informed as soon as possible so that he or she can record the complaint and monitor progress. It should be remembered that there may be no need to engage the complaints procedure if the matter is resolved immediately.

8.45 As soon as it becomes apparent that someone wishes to make a complaint, the complainant should be given information about the authority's complaints procedure including how to contact the complaints manager.

8.46 The complainant retains the right to approach the Local Government Ombudsman at any time and the local authority should make this clear in its publicity. However, the Ombudsman would ordinarily expect the local authority to consider the complaint initially and may refer the complaint back to the relevant complaints manager if this has not been done.

Time limit for making a complaint

8.47 Local authorities do not need to consider complaints made more than one year after the grounds to make the representation arose (reg 9). In the event of late complaints, the complaints manager should write to advise the complainant that their complaint cannot be considered and explaining the reasons why he or she has adopted this position. This response should also advise the complainant of his or her right to approach the Local Government Ombudsman. However, as with deferred/freezing decisions (see below), decisions need to be made on a case-by-case basis and there should generally be a presumption in favour of accepting the complaint unless there is good reason against it.

8.48 The time limit can be extended at the local authority's discretion if it is still possible to consider the representations effectively and efficiently. Local authorities may also wish to consider such complaints if it would be unreasonable to expect the complainant to have made the complaint earlier. For example, where the child was not able to make the complaint or did not feel confident in bringing it forward in the year time limit.

8.49 Though not exclusive, possible grounds for accepting a complaint made after one year are:

- genuine issues of vulnerability;

- the local authority believes that there is still benefit to the complainant in proceeding;

- there is likely to be sufficient access to information or individuals involved at the time, to enable an effective and fair investigation to be carried out; and

- action should be taken in light of human rights-based legislation.

Advocacy services

8.50 During the course of making a complaint, the local authority should support the child or young person by actively providing information and advice. The child or young person is entitled to advocacy support that is independent and confidential.[9]

8.51 The complaints manager should ensure that a suitable person meets the child or young person to discuss the complaints process and ensure that any questions or concerns that the complainant may have are fully addressed. Where an advocate is being used, the local authority needs to ensure that the advocate is acting with the informed consent of the young person. The local authority should not rely on the advocate to ensure the child or young person understands the procedure.

8.52 The local authority should also consider how to meet the varying needs of complainants. This should be particularly important in relation to complainants whose first language is not English and those with communication difficulties. The authority may wish to consider publicising any facilities available to complainants from voluntary organisations and local community or self-help groups.

Advocates in the complaints procedure

8.53 The role of the advocate was established under the Advocacy Services Representations Procedure (Children) (Amendment) Regulations 2004. The advocate should provide independent and confidential information, advice, representation and support to the child or young person making the complaint.[10] The role of the advocate in the complaints procedure is:

- to empower the child or young person by enabling him to express his views wishes or feelings, or by speaking on his behalf;

- to seek the resolution of any problems or concerns identified by the child or young person by working in partnership with child or young person and only with his agreement;

- to support the child or young person pursuing a complaint through every stage of the complaints procedure and to provide him with information about his rights and options, helping him or her clarify the complaint and the outcomes he or she is seeking; and

---

[9]   See *Get It Sorted: Providing Effective Advocacy Services for Children and Young People making a Complaint under the Children Act 1989* (DfES, 2004).

[10] For detailed discussion about the advocacy services in Wales – see the Children's Commissioner's March 2012 report *Missing Voices* (pp 13–15 set out the history of the advocacy legislation for Wales including the most recent 2009 and 2011 reviews).

- to speak for or represent the child or young person at any stage of the complaints process, including at the informal stage or at any formal hearing or interviews.

Stage 1 – local resolution

8.54 A complaint is made on the date on which it is first received by the local authority.

8.55 The expectation is that the majority of complaints should be considered (and resolved) at stage 1. However, if the local authority or the complainant believes that it would not be appropriate to consider the complaint at stage 1, they should discuss this together. Where both parties agree, the complaint can move directly to stage 2.

8.56 At stage 1, staff at the point of service delivery – including the independent reviewing officer where appropriate – and the child or young person should discuss and attempt to address the complaint as quickly as possible. They should discuss the issue and exchange information and thinking behind decisions and try to agree a way forward.

8.57 Regulation 14(1) places a 10 working day time limit for this part of the process. Most stage 1 complaints should ideally be concluded within this time limit.

8.58 Where the local authority cannot provide a complete response it can implement a further 10 days' extension (reg 14(5)). If necessary, the local authority may also suspend stage 1 until an advocate has been appointed (reg 14(3)). The maximum amount of time that stage 1 should take is 20 working days. After this deadline the complainant can request consideration at stage 2 if he or she so wishes. The complaints manager should inform the complainant that he or she has the right to move on to stage 2 if the time scale has elapsed for Stage 1 and the complainant has not received an outcome. It may be that the complainant is happy to put this off for the time being (for example, if the reason that resolution is delayed due to a key person being off sick or on leave), so this period can be extended with the complainant's agreement or request.

8.59 If the matter is resolved, the local authority must write to the complainant confirming the agreed resolution and the complaints manager should be informed of the outcome as soon as possible. Otherwise, a letter should be sent by the local authority to the complainant (or a meeting offered, if this is more appropriate) responding to the complaint.

8.60 Where the matter is not resolved locally, the complainant has the right to request consideration of the complaint at stage 2. There is no time-limit within which s/he must request this, but local authorities may wish to recommend that the complainant does this within 20 working days so that momentum in resolving the complaint is not lost. The local authority is under a duty to operate expeditiously throughout the complaints handling process (reg 10).

Stage 2 – investigation

8.61 Consideration of complaints at stage 2 is normally achieved through an investigation conducted by an investigating officer and an independent person. Stage 2 commences either when the complainant requests it or where the complainant and the local authority have agreed that stage 1 is not appropriate (reg 17(1)).

8.62 If the complaint has been submitted orally, the complaints manager must ensure that the details of the complaint and the complainant's desired outcome are recorded in writing and agreed with the complainant. This may be achieved either by correspondence or by meeting the complainant to discuss, followed by a written record of what was agreed. He or she may wish to do this in conjunction with the investigating officer and independent person appointed to conduct stage 2 (see below). Should the complainant amend the written record of his complaint, the stage 2 timescale will start from the date that the complaint is finalised.

8.63 The complaints manager should arrange for a full and considered investigation of the complaint to take place without delay. He or she may also request (in writing) any person or body to produce information or documents to facilitate the investigation.[11] Consideration of the complaint at stage 2 should be fair, thorough and transparent with clear and logical outcomes.

8.64 The complaints manager should ensure that the authority appoints an investigating officer (IO) to lead the investigation of the complaint and prepare a written report for adjudication by a senior manager.

8.65 A copy of the complaint should be sent to any person who is involved in the complaint, unless doing so would prejudice the consideration of the complaint. Where this may be the case, the complaints manager should advise senior management, who should inform staff of the details of the complaint through normal line management.

8.66 The investigation should be completed and the response sent to the child or young person within 25 working days (reg 17(3)). However, this may be impractical in some cases, eg where the complaint involves several agencies, all or some of the matters are the subject of a concurrent investigation (such as a disciplinary process), if the complaint is particularly complicated or if a key witness is unavailable for part of the time.

8.67 Where it is not possible to complete the investigation within 25 working days, stage 2 may be extended to a maximum of 65 working days (reg 17(6)).

---

[11] Consideration should be given to matters of disclosure and confidentiality.

All extensions should be agreed by the complaints manager. The important thing is to maintain dialogue with the complainant and where possible reach a mutual agreement as to what is reasonable where a response in 25 working days is not feasible.

8.68 The local authority must inform the child or young person as soon as possible in writing of:

- the reason for the delay; and

- the date by which he or she should receive a response (reg 17(6)).

8.69 Where one or more agencies are involved in considering the complaint, it would be good practice for these bodies to aim for whichever is the shorter of the timescales to produce their final responses.

The investigating officer (IO)

8.70 The IO may be employed by the local authority or be brought in from outside the authority, appointed specifically for this piece of work. The IO should not, however, be in direct line management of the service or person about whom the complaint is being made.

8.71 The IO should have access to all relevant records and staff. These should be released within the bounds of normal confidentiality and with regard to relevant legislation in the Freedom of Information Act 2000 and the Data Protection Act 1998.

8.72 The investigating officer's undertakings may include:

- providing a comprehensive, open, transparent and fair consideration of the complaint through:

    – sensitive and thorough interviewing of the complainant;
    – consideration of social work records and other relevant information;
    – interviewing with staff and other people relevant to the complaint; and
    – analysing information;

- preparation of the report of the investigation in a clear, plain language;

- effectively liaising with the complainant and/or his/her advocate, the independent person and the complaints manager as appropriate; and

- identifying solutions and recommending courses of action to resolve problems.

The investigating officer must have due regard to the regulated timescales for investigation.

The independent person (IP)

8.73 An independent person (IP) must be appointed to the investigation (reg 17(2)). This person should be in addition to the IO and must be involved in all aspects of consideration of the complaint including any discussions in the authority about the action to be taken in relation to the child. The person appointed should be neither an elected member nor an employee of the local authority, nor a spouse of an employee or member of the authority. Former local authority staff are eligible, but good practice would suggest at least three years have elapsed since they were employed by the local authority.

8.74 The independent person may not undertake any other roles in the consideration of the same complaint (such as an advocate or review panellist).

8.75 The independent person should:

- ensure that the process of investigation is open, transparent and fair;

- work alongside the investigating officer to provide an independent and objective view to the investigation of complaints;

- see the same relevant files and documents as the investigating officer;

- participate in all interviews and discussions relevant to the investigation;

- read the investigating officer's report and produce his own report on the investigation;

- comment on each of the complaints and state whether he or she agrees with the investigating officer's findings on them; and

- explain, where necessary, his or her reasons for considering an investigation to be unfair or incomplete and to advise the complainant of these in his or her report.

The investigation process

8.76 The process is identified in Annexe 2 of the guidance. This requires the IO to:

- be aware of the timescale and the importance of providing a thorough investigation;

- work closely with the complaints manager, independent person and advocate where appropriate on all aspects of the investigation and report writing including keeping the complainant informed of progress;

- if the media is involved (eg local/national press, television or radio) notify the complaints manager and maintain strict confidentiality;

- consider the environment the investigations are conducted in – some places may be intimidating or distressing for children and young people in particular;

- question whether an unannounced visit to the establishment complained of to check normal practice would be helpful; and

- adhere to relevant conventions and legislation such as Data Protection Act 1998, Health and Safety Act 1974 and the Human Rights Act 1998 and the United Nations Convention on the Rights of the Child.

Steps to be undertaken by the IO

8.77

(1) Contact the complainant, ideally by phone, to offer a meeting in person. This meeting should explain the investigation procedure and:

    (a) allow the complainant to explain how s/he feels and express any strong emotions – s/he should feel as if the complaint has been accepted;

    (b) clarify the complaint and all its individual parts and produce a written record;

    (c) ask what the complainant wants in terms of solution or outcome;

    (d) check whether the complainant needs support of any kind, in order to understand the discussion properly; and

    (e) determine whether s/he needs support during the process eg an advocate.

(2) Read background on the complaint and the relevant legal and administrative policies and procedures.

(3) Consider whether the complaint could be resolved without further investigation.

(4) Assess whether the complaints procedure is the most appropriate way of handling this complaint. Consider alternative possible procedures, for example alternative dispute resolution (such as mediation), appeals to tribunals, legal action and police involvement. If the complaints procedure is not appropriate, discuss the alternatives with the complaints manager.

(4) Obtain all documentation needed including original versions of documents such as files, log books and timesheets.

(6) Produce a chronology of the sequence of events from the files and identify the names of the individuals most directly involved in the content of the complaint.

(7)   Analyse and categorise the complaint into its different elements.

(8)   Identify a list of interviewees and notify them that you wish to hold interviews with as much notice as possible. Supply them with relevant information on the complaint in advance of the interview.

(9)   Arrange the order of interviews in a logical sequence as relevant to the particular complaint.

(10) Inform all those to be interviewed that they may be accompanied by a friend or trades union representative, provided that this person is not within normal line management arrangements with the interviewee and that there are no issues of confidentiality.

(11) Consider whether a witness of a particularly difficult interview is needed.

(12) Prepare the line of questioning for each interviewee.

(13) Explain the complaint and your role clearly to the interviewee and confirm that they understand the complaints procedure and their role in it.

(14) Conduct the interviews in an informal and relaxed a manner, while ensuring that due process is adhered to:

   (a)   use open not leading questions;
   (b)   do not express opinions in words or attitude; and
   (c)   ask single not multiple questions, ie one question at a time.

(15) Try to separate hearsay evidence from fact by asking interviewees how they know a particular fact.

(16) Persist with questions if necessary. Do not be afraid to ask the same question twice. Make notes of each answer given.

(17) Deal with conflicting evidence by seeking corroborative evidence. If this is not available, discuss with the complaints manager the option of a meeting between the conflicting witnesses.

(18) Make a formal record of the interview from the written notes as soon as possible while the memory is fresh. Show the interviewee the formal record, ask if he or she has anything to add, and to sign the record as accurate.

Stage 2 investigation report

8.78

(1) On completion of consideration of the complaint, the IO should write a report on his/her investigations including:

    (a) details of findings, conclusions and outcomes against each point of complaint (ie 'upheld' or 'not upheld'); and

    (b) recommendations on how to remedy any injustice to the complainant as appropriate.

(2) The report should be written in plain language, avoiding jargon, so that everyone can understand it. It should distinguish between fact, feelings and opinion.

(3) Good practice suggests that the IP should also provide a report to the local authority once s/he has read the IO's final report. S/he may wish to comment on:

    (a) whether s/he thinks the investigation has been conducted entirely in an impartial, comprehensive and effective manner;

    (b) whether all those concerned have been able to express their views fully and fairly;

    (c) whether the IO's report provides an accurate and complete picture of the investigation; and

    (d) the nature of the recommendations or make his own recommendations as necessary.

(4) Annex 2 of the guidance recommends that the investigation report should include:

    (a) chronology;

    (b) list of interviewees;

    (c) the complaints set out in a numbered list;

    (d) your analysis and findings for each point of complaint;

    (e) a record of relevant policy, practice and legislation;

    (f) your recommendations and response to the complainant's desired outcomes;

    (g) any other relevant information;

    (h) a separate addendum for any other issues for the local authority; and

    (i) consider comments from relevant persons such as the complaints manager, independent person and amend the report as necessary.

The adjudication process

8.79 Once the IO has finished the report, a senior manager should act as adjudicating officer and consider the complaints, the IO's findings, conclusions, and recommendations, any report from the IP and the complainant's desired outcomes.

8.80 The purpose of adjudication is for the local authority to consider the reports and identify:

- its response;

- its decision on each point of complaint; and

- any action to be taken (with timescales for implementation).

8.81 The adjudicating officer should normally be a senior manager, reporting to the Director responsible for Children's Services. The adjudicating officer will prepare a response to the reports, with her/his decision on the complaint, actions s/he will be taking with timescales for implementation.

8.82 The adjudicating officer may wish to meet the complaints manager, IO and IP, to clarify any aspects of the reports. The adjudicating officer should also consider liaising with the complaints manager in drafting the adjudication.

8.83 The adjudicating officer may wish to meet the child or young person as part of the adjudication process or afterwards to explain the details of the adjudication ie the outcome of the complaint and any actions that he or she proposes.

8.84 The adjudicator for the local authority should then write to the complainant with their response containing:

- a complete copy of the investigation report;

- any report from the IP; and

- the adjudication, which would include:

    – confirmation of the local authority's response to the investigation report;
    – a view on whether the investigation has been thorough and complete;
    – the local authority's position on the investigating officer's and independent person's findings against each point of complaint;
    – any actions that s/he will be taking and their timescale for implementation;
    – confirmation of the complainant's right to request stage 3 within 20 working days (reg 17(8)); and

  –   reminding the complainant of his/her right to approach the Local
      Government Ombudsman at any time.

8.85 The adjudicating officer should ensure that any recommendations
contained in the response are implemented. The complaints manager should
monitor implementation and report to the Director on what action has been
taken on a regular basis.

Stage 3 – review panels

8.86 Where stage 2 of the complaints procedure has been concluded and the
complainant is still dissatisfied, s/he will be eligible to request further
consideration of the complaint by a review panel (reg 18).

8.87 The complaints manager should assess requests for the review panel as
they are presented on a case-by-case basis. The complaints manager should also
confer with the chair, following the chair's appointment, regarding
arrangements for the panel.

Purpose of review panels

8.88 Review panels are designed to:

•   listen to all parties;

•   consider the adequacy of the stage 2 investigation;

•   obtain any further information and advice that may help resolve the
    complaint to all parties' satisfaction;

•   focus on achieving resolution for the complainant by addressing his
    clearly defined complaints and desired outcomes;

•   reach findings on each of the complaints being reviewed;

•   make recommendations that provide practical remedies and creative
    solutions to complex situations;

•   support local solutions where the opportunity for resolution between the
    complainant and the local authority exists;

•   identify any consequent injustice to the complainant where complaints are
    upheld, and to recommend appropriate redress; and

•   recommend any service improvements for action by the authority.

8.89 As a general rule, the review panel should not reinvestigate the
complaints, nor should it be able to consider any substantively new complaints
that have not been first considered at stage 2.

8.90   The guidance specifies that, ideally, no party should feel the need to be represented by lawyers at the review panel. The purpose of the panel is to consider the complaint and, wherever possible, work towards a resolution. It is *not* a quasi-judicial process and the presence of lawyers can work against the spirit of openness and problem-solving. However, the complainant has the right to bring a representative to speak on his behalf and there is nothing in the regulations and guidance that specifies this cannot be a lawyer.

Local authority representative at the review panel

8.91   The local authority should ordinarily be represented at the stage 3 review panel by the same senior manager who acted as adjudicating officer. Where the adjudicating officer delegates this role, he or she should do so to a member of staff with sufficient status in the local authority to represent it.

8.92   The local authority representative should:

- provide further information to support the local authority's position;

- consider whether any other member of staff should attend to address specific issues and request their attendance through the chair;

- prepare a presentation to give to the panel on the day;

- keep all staff involved in the complaint, but who are not attending the panel, informed of the proceedings; and

- act on any recommendations from the panel (as required by the Director).

Review panellists

8.93   The panel consists of a chair and two other people appointed by the local authority. All panel members must be independent – this means people who are neither members nor officers of the local authority to which the representations have been made, nor the spouse or civil partner of such people. In appointing the panel chair, former members or officers of the local authority may be considered on a case-by-case basis, but good practice suggests that three years should have elapsed.

8.94   The panellists should:

- read panel papers in advance of the meeting;

- attend for the entirety of the panel and contribute to the consideration of the complaint through the chair;

- support the chair by taking an active part in the decision-making process;

- contribute to deliberations and the wording of the panel's findings; and

- provide relevant opinion based on any specialist skills, knowledge and awareness that they have in respect of the presenting complaint.

Independent chair of the review panel

8.95 The role of the chair is to:

- confer with the complaints manager about the specific needs of the complainant;

- agree who will attend as the local authority representative and request the attendance of any other persons who may assist in understanding the complaint and its context;

- chair the panel meeting by ensuring that the complaint is heard in full;

- operate flexibly in response to the individual needs of each panel member;

- ensure that the panel runs smoothly and that each participant is given an opportunity to contribute appropriately;

- ensure that all participants are treated with respect throughout the process;

- in consultation with the other panellists, ensure that the pre-meeting, presentations and deliberations are of proportionate length to ensure appropriate consideration of the complaint and to enable the panel to reach its conclusions;

- manage the panel's deliberations to produce a timely and full response to the complainant and local authority within five working days of the panel meeting;

- ensure that any disagreements of position among the panellists are recorded and seek to reach a majority decision where necessary; and

- be available to meet local authority staff, if needed, after the panel meeting to discuss any recommendations arising.

Clerk to the panel

8.96 It is the duty of the local authority to provide administrative support for the operation of the panel which may be in the form of a clerk. It may be sensible for this role to be filled by a separate officer to that of the complaints manager. The clerk should assist in the appointment of the panel through to the production of its final recommendations to the local authority.

8.97   Tasks the clerk might undertake include:

- organising the venue, facilities and refreshments;

- distributing written submissions from the complainant and the authority;

- supporting the complaints manager and chair as required;

- ensuring that procedure on the day is adhered to;

- taking notes to facilitate the panellists' decisions;

- confirming with the complainant whether he or she will be bringing any representatives or witnesses with him and assist as necessary; and

- providing administrative support to the chair and panel to produce and issue the final recommendations to the local authority complainant and other attendees within five working days.

General principles for the review panel

8.98   The review panel should be alert to the importance of providing a demonstrably fair and accessible process for all participants. Many complainants, particularly children and young people, may find this stage to be a stressful experience. It is important that the panel is customer-focused in its approach to considering the complaint and child or young person-friendly. This may include limiting the total number of local authority representatives attending to a workable minimum to avoid the possibility of overwhelming the complainant.

8.99   In particular, the following principles should be observed for the conduct of the panel:

- The local authority should recognise the independence of the review panel and in particular, the authority of the chair.

- Panels should be conducted in the presence of all the relevant parties with equity of access and representation for the complainant and local authority.

- Panels should uphold a commitment to objectivity, impartiality and fairness, and ensure that the rights of complainants and all other attendees are respected at all times.

- The local authority should consider what provisions to make for complainants, including any special communication or mobility needs or other assistance.

- Panels should observe the requirements of the Human Rights Act 1998, the Data Protection Act 1998, and other relevant rights-based legislation and conventions in the discharge of their duties and responsibilities;

- The standard of proof applied by panels should be the civil standard of 'balance of probabilities' and not the criminal standard of 'beyond all reasonable doubt.' This standard will be based on evidence and facts.

- It will be at the chair's discretion to suspend or defer proceedings in exceptional circumstances where required, including the health and safety of all present.

8.100 The local authority should be mindful of the specific needs of children and young people either using the complaints procedure or who are affected by complaints. Local authorities should ensure that:

- the review panel acts in accordance with the United Nations Convention on the Rights of the Child;

- the review panel safeguards and promotes the rights and welfare of the child or young person concerned;

- the wishes and feelings of such children and young people are ascertained, recorded and taken into account;

- the best interests of such child or young person are prioritised at all times; and

- where the complaint is made by a person deemed to have a sufficient interest in the child's welfare, they should where appropriate, seek the child or young person's views with regard to the complaint.

Local authority representative at the review panel

8.101 The local authority should ordinarily be represented at the stage 3 review panel by the same senior manager who acted as adjudicating officer. Where the adjudicating officer delegates this role, he or she should do so to a member of staff with sufficient status in the local authority to represent it.

8.102 The adjudicating officer should represent the local authority. However, where he or she has rejected any of the investigating officer's findings at stage 2 or where the panel chair requests his attendance, the local authority representative should:

- provide further information to support the local authority's position;

- consider whether any other member of staff should attend to address specific issues and request their attendance through the chair;

- prepare a presentation to give to the panel on the day;

- keep all staff involved in the complaint, but who are not attending the panel, informed of the proceedings; and

- act on any recommendations from the panel (as required by the Director).

Summary of Stage 3 timescales

8.103

Action	Time
Complainant requests review panel	Up to 20 working days after receipt of the Stage 2 adjudication
Complaints manager acknowledges request	Within 2 working days
Complaints manager appoints chair and confirms attendees and content of panel papers with chair	Within 10 working days of the complainant's request for review panel
Local authority agrees the other panellists and date for review panel	Within 30 working days of the complainant's request for review panel
Local authority circulates panel papers	Within 10 working days of the date for the review panel
Review panel produces its written report (including any recommendations)	Within 5 working days of the review panel
Relevant Director issues his response	Within 15 working days of receiving the review panel's report

Withdrawing a complaint

8.104 The complaint may be withdrawn verbally or in writing at any time by the complainant (reg 7). The local authority must write to the complainant to confirm the withdrawal of the complaint. In these circumstances, it would also be good practice for the local authority to decide on whether or not it wishes to continue considering the issues that gave rise to the complaint through an internal management review. The local authority should then use this work to consider the need for any subsequent actions in the services it delivers.

8.105 Should the complainant then seek to reinstate the complaint, the local authority could use the review to produce a response as necessary.

SECTION 2 – MONITORING COMPLAINTS ARRANGEMENTS BY LOCAL AUTHORITIES

Recording

8.106 Local authorities must monitor the complaints arrangements that they have in place to ensure that they comply with the regulations (reg 13). They must keep a record of:

- each representation/complaint received;

- the outcome of each, ie the decisions made in response to the representation/complaint and any action to be taken; and

- whether there was compliance with the time limits.

8.107 The overall purpose of recording is to enable:

- children and young people to see that their concerns and suggestions are being dealt with and that a thorough and fair consideration has taken place;

- the organisation to demonstrate that complaints are taken seriously and how they are resolved; and

- feedback from representations and complaints to lead to improvement in service planning and delivery.

Record management and data protection

8.108 All functions of the complaints procedure must adhere to the requirements of the Data Protection Act 1998 and the Freedom of Information Act 2000. Particular attention is drawn to the need to ensure that any personal information obtained in relation to a complaint is only used for that purpose.

8.109 Records of complaints, any investigation reports, panel reports and letters of response from the local authority should be placed on the relevant service user's file, unless there are specific reasons not to do so (for example, if the reports would cause distress to the child). Those involved in the investigation should have access to notes of their own interview in order to confirm the accuracy of the content. The investigation report and all other relevant papers should be held by the complaints manager in a separate complaints file.

Confidential complaints

8.110 A frequent worry of children and young people is that details of the complaint might be given to other people who do not need to know about it.

Children see privacy and confidentiality as vital, and must be able to make 'confidential complaints' – sometimes to avoid 'come-backs' on themselves. Therefore details of a child's personal complaint should not be put into a complaints book that others can read.

8.111 Particular attention is drawn to the need to ensure that personal information obtained in relation to a complaint is used only for that purpose.

Making complaints information accessible

8.112 For children and young people with difficulty reading, writing or speaking English, the local authority should identify a suitable method of communication so that these children can express and follow progress on their complaint in full; this might involve the provision of information (including responses to complaints) in large print, translation or in other formats. In the case of complainants with special needs or within specific community groups, the local authority should meet the complainant to explain any reports in person.

8.113 For people with special needs, such as learning disabilities, sensory or physical impairment or with mental health problems, the complaints manager should liaise closely with the authority's specialist teams and relevant voluntary bodies to ensure that the complainant is able to express their complaint in full (using advocacy and support services if appropriate). The child or young person should have confidence that the authority can provide as thorough consideration as for any other service user.

Diversity monitoring

8.114 Local authorities should, where possible and appropriate, ensure that they ask the complainant to define their own ethnic origin, gender, any disability and age. It is important that authorities seek to identify for the complaints procedure:

- an accurate picture of use by ethnic origin, age, gender, sexual orientation and disability;

- where take-up or use could be improved or reviewed;

- a base-line for planning, target-setting and measuring change;

- equal accessibility to all sections of the community;

- whether any distinct needs exist amongst members of minority groups, for which special provision may be necessary; and

- that it does not inadvertently discriminate against any particular group.

Annual report

8.115 Local authorities must publish an annual report (reg 13(3)) each financial year. This should draw upon the information already gathered for recording purposes. However, this annual report is a separate requirement and should not contain personal information that is identifiable about any individual complainant.

8.116 The annual report should be arranged by the complaints manager and should provide a mechanism by which the local authority can be kept informed about the operation of its complaints procedure. The report should be presented to staff, the relevant local authority committee and should be made available to the regulator and the general public. It should provide information about:

- representations made to the local authority;

- the number of complaints at each stage and any that were considered by the Local Government Ombudsman;

- which customer groups made the complaints;

- the types of complaints made;

- the outcome of complaints;

- details about advocacy services provided under these arrangements;

- compliance with timescales, and complaints resolved within extended timescale as agreed;

- learning and service improvement, including changes to services that have been implemented and details of any that have not been implemented;

- a summary of statistical data about the age, gender, disability, sexual orientation and ethnicity of complainants; and

- a review of the effectiveness of the complaints procedure.

8.117 In order to demonstrate learning from complaints, analysis of trends and closer working with relevant bodies (such as the NHS), individual local authorities may wish to agree a common format for their reports and reporting cycles with relevant key agencies.

Monitoring and quality assurance

8.118 Local authorities should monitor the operation and effectiveness of their complaints procedure as well as how information about complaints is being used to improve services and delivery. Local authorities should ensure that their quality assurance systems include a cycle of planning with outcomes fed back into operational delivery. All local authorities should provide a system for:

- the dissemination of learning from complaints to line managers;

- the use of the complaints procedure as a measure of performance and means of quality control; and

- information derived from complaints to contribute to practice development, commissioning and service planning.

8.119 Monitoring should also highlight how effective communication is within the authority and to the children and young people receiving their services, where staff training is required and whether resources are targeted appropriately. This should be fed back into the system in order to facilitate and improve policy and practice.

General principles of redress

8.120 Under s 92 of the Local Government Act 2000, local authorities are empowered to remedy injustice arising from maladministration. Remedies will include, but are not restricted to, financial redress.

8.121 Each case should be considered on its own merits, and local authorities should develop their own policies to assure consistency across similar injustices. These should ensure that any remedies are implemented reasonably quickly or to take action within a defined framework.

8.122 Any application of remedies should:

- be appropriate and proportionate to the injustice;

- put the complainant in the position he or she would have been in except for the fault;

- consider financial compensation, where the above is not possible;

- take into account the complainant's views and desired outcomes; and

- take into account the effect of the complainant's own actions (such as delay on his part).

Financial redress

8.123 There are different reasons why financial redress may arise. These include:

- compensation;

- quantifiable loss;

- loss of a non-monetary benefit;

- loss of value;

- lost opportunity;

- distress; and

- time and trouble.

8.124 When considering financial redress, the local authority should also consider the following issues:

- whether it is appropriate to offset compensation in instances where the complainant owes money to the authority. This would apply for any costs owed to the authority as a whole, rather than to a single service;

- where the complainant has incurred expenses or suffered financial loss, the authority should also consider whether it is appropriate to pay for loss of interest as well. The Local Government Ombudsman recommends the standard rate set by the county court; and

- it may also be appropriate to calculate a financial remedy as a formula which takes into account all known factors.

Deferring (freezing) decisions

8.125 If the complaint is about a proposed change to a care plan, a placement or a service, the decision may need to be deferred (frozen) until the complaint is considered. However, care should be taken if deferring a decision is likely to have a significant effect upon the mental or physical wellbeing of an individual.

8.126 The decision to defer should normally be made through detailed discussion and risk assessment between the complaints manager and the manager responsible for the service, within the context of the work being undertaken with the child or young person. Decisions need to be made on a case-by-case basis, but there should generally be a presumption in favour of freezing, unless there is a good reason against it (for example, if leaving a child or young person where they are would put them at risk). In cases where decisions are met with opposing views, advice should be sought from the appropriate director in the local authority.

SECTION 3 – THE RELATIONSHIP WITH OTHER PROCEDURES

Working with other procedures

8.127 Every local authority is likely to have other procedures that have a significant bearing on the complaints procedures. These might include:

- child protection procedures;

- court proceedings;

- grievance procedures; or

- disciplinary procedures.

8.128 It is important that relationships between different procedures are clear and that the content is consistent. Procedures may also need to link with those within the NHS and other agencies contributing to services (eg the Local Authority Social Services and National Health Service Complaints Regulations 2009 or when NHS staff may become involved in family support and child protection work). Other agencies who may be involved in services to children include education establishments, housing authorities, voluntary and private child care organisations, the Probation Service and the police.

8.129 It is essential that local authorities separate out complaints appropriate to other procedures and cases where joint action is required. The complaints manager should provide advice to staff, including consideration of whether to freeze social work decisions until any concurrent investigations are resolved. There should be effective coordination between the agencies involved and complainants should be provided with clear information as to how inter-agency matters will be dealt with.

8.130 In considering a complaint which is subject to concurrent investigation under one of the above procedures, local authorities should be careful not to do anything that may compromise or prejudice the other investigation. In such circumstances, the complaints manager should be mindful of developments and liaise closely with other staff.

Grievance and disciplinary procedures

8.131 Complaints procedures should be kept separate from grievance procedures, (which concern staff issues such as conditions of service) and disciplinary procedures (which apply to the actions of staff in relation to failures to comply with job descriptions).

8.132 Where complaints contain an element of grievance or discipline, the local authority should keep the child or young person and its staff informed about progress in handling both the complaints and the disciplinary or grievance elements as appropriate having regard to normal staff confidentiality.

8.133 Staff can feel confused and intimidated by systems which reinforce an implication of culpability if a member of staff is named in a complaint. Staff should be reassured that they should not be held personally liable for carrying out resource decisions or allocations of service, according to the authority's criteria. In most cases they will have been named because they are the person best known to the user or carer.

Concurrent investigations

8.134 The handling of a complaint may coincide with action under the disciplinary procedures or on occasion, police investigation.

8.135 The local authority should ensure that alternative procedures can run concurrently with the complaints procedure. For example, a complaint about a deficiency in service may also bring to light issues of a disciplinary nature. If there are still substantive issues around the deficiency in service to be resolved, the fact that disciplinary procedures commence is not a reason to stop the complaints process carrying on in respect of the service issue (unless to do so would compromise or prejudice the concurrent investigation).

8.136 Decisions on how to proceed should be based on individual cases. Local guidance may be necessary on how priorities are identified and decisions made in relation to them. Local guidance should draw clear distinctions between a complaint, a grievance, legal proceedings and the reporting of a matter that is a criminal offence. The local authority will need to consider how best to inform children and young people which procedure is being applied in their case and why.

8.137 The local authority should also make clear to staff (and trades unions and professional associations) that consideration of the complaint is separate to any necessary action under the grievance or disciplinary procedures. Staff should be kept informed of progress of the complaint, but not given any details that would breach confidentiality or work against the child or young person's best interest.

8.138 The local authority has discretion not to commence the complaints investigation where to proceed with it would compromise a concurrent investigation under another statutory or internal procedure (reg 8). If the local authority decides not to commence the complaints process, it must write to the complainant explaining the reasons for its decision and specifying the relevant concurrent investigation. The local authority should also inform the complainant of his right to resubmit his complaint once the concurrent investigation is concluded and that he or she must do this within 1 year of the conclusion of the concurrent investigation (reg 8(5)). The local authority should also keep the complainant up to date with progress on the concurrent investigation.

Cross-boundary issues

8.139 A potential area of confusion can arise around boundaries between the local authority's responsibilities and those of other bodies delivering services on behalf of the authority. This can happen, for example, where the local authority provides domiciliary care to the household of a child with disabilities through a private agency, and the child wishes to complain about aspects of this service.

8.140 Cross boundary issues can occur among:

- children's homes;

- children's day care providers;

- domiciliary care services;

- contracted agencies and multi-agency services;

- multi–agency health service packages; and

- single or joint assessments.

8.141 It is important that the local authority is alert to cross-boundary issues and that the complaints manager has protocols in place for the successful handling of these complaints. Partner agencies should have appropriate procedures of their own in place for responding to complaints in the first instance.

Complaints made to a local authority about an NHS body

8.142 Sometimes a complaint crosses over boundaries between a local authority and the NHS. Where this happens, children and young people should not have to worry about who they should approach with complaints about different aspects of the service they receive. Instead, the complaint can be made in its entirety to any one of the bodies involved.

8.143 The local authority has a responsibility to work with other bodies to establish which agency should lead on handling the complaint and to ensure that the complainant is kept informed and receives as comprehensive a reply as possible. Both bodies should aim to address the complaints as fully as possible by answering questions, providing information and attending meetings in connection with the consideration of the complaints where appropriate. Both the local authority and the NHS staff should consider meeting the child or young person together if this will facilitate a more effective outcome.

8.144 Ideally, both investigations should be completed simultaneously and reports delivered to the child or young person together. In order to facilitate this, the two bodies should aim to work to the shorter of their respective complaints procedure timescales.

8.145 The arrangements set out above for identifying a lead body apply only where the matters raised concern both bodies. However, sometimes, one body receives a complaint about the actions of another. This can happen where the child or young person does not understand which organisation is responsible for which service, but can also happen where there is an important issue of trust – a child or young person might, for example speak to a social worker he or she trusts about concerns over his treatment by the NHS or approach a district nurse about a carer employed by the local authority.

8.146 The complaints manager of the body receiving the complaint should record the outline of the complaint and, with the consent of the complainant, refer it formally to the other. It should then be for the complaints manager of the body complained against to make sure the complaint is dealt with properly.

Complaints involving regulated services

8.147 With regard to those services that are regulated (including local authority functions) specific complaints procedures are required under separate regulations and national minimum standards under the Care Standards Act 2000. They are therefore distinct from the complaints procedures for local authorities that are outlined in this guidance. Understandably, confusion may sometimes exist about which complaints procedure is appropriate for specific sets of circumstances.

8.148 Complaints are likely to arise from the following issues:

- commissioning;

- placement arrangements;

- placement monitoring;

- personal needs reassessments;

- funding;

- contractual arrangements;

- service agreements;

- service quality; and

- care regime matters not covered by regulations and national minimum standards.

8.149 If the complaints manager receives such a complaint, he or she will need to consider whether it is most appropriately dealt with by any complaints process that is operated within the relevant regulated service or setting or whether it is a matter that relates more directly to the exercise of the local authority's Children Act 1989 functions, covered by this procedure. Where the local authority is responsible for the original assessment of need that led to a placement and associated funding, then the complainant will (in most instances) have recourse to this procedure. However, access to this complaints procedure does not apply to people with private self-funding arrangements.

8.150 The complainant should be able to make a single complaint to the provider or the local authority and have this considered by the relevant parties as necessary. The complaints manager should therefore ensure good communication with all other parties, and organisations should discuss the details of the complaint to ensure a seamless response.

8.151 It is possible for someone to have two complaints ongoing at the same time. One to a residential placement, for example, about how it meets the regulations and/or standards, and one to the local authority about how it has fulfilled its function in relation to the provision of services to meet the needs of the child or young person.

8.152 The local authority has responsibilities in terms of fulfilling its children's social services functions, and the regulator has the responsibility for ensuring that regulated providers (eg care homes) meet the appropriate Regulations and national minimum standards.

8.153 When local authorities receive a complaint that is about services provided under the Children's Homes Regulations 2001[12] they should refer the relevant parts of the complaint to the registered provider within 5 working days. The local authority should also inform the child or young person of this. Details of the relevant parts of the complaint should also be sent to the local authority's care management team and the contract monitoring team. Any issues of safeguarding and potential vulnerability of the child should be confirmed by the complaints manager with the child or young person before releasing the complaint to the relevant care service provider.

8.154 Where the complaint consists of elements relating to both social services functions and services provided under the Children's Homes Regulations 2001 the local authority should co-operate with the provider to ensure that the complainant receives one response dealing with all aspects of

---

[12]   SI 2001/3967.

the complaint. The local authority should, within 10 working days, send details of the complaint to the registered provider and determine which parts of the complaint relate to local authority social services and which to services provided by the care provider. It should also advise the complainant which parts of the complaint the local authority is considering.

8.155 If the child or young person considers that he or she has suffered an injustice as a result of any significant delay or failure by the authority to refer his complaint to the registered person he or she is entitled to raise concerns to the local authority. The local authority should then deal with this matter under the appropriate procedure.

Building a seamless service with the local authority's other complaints procedures

8.156 Where a complainant has other related complaints that do not fall within this statutory procedure, the local authority may wish to consider whether there are advantages in accepting these into a single investigation. Local authorities are encouraged to offer a complete single response where possible, for example where a child or young person has complaints relating to both a local authority's housing service and its children's services. If the local authority does not feel that would be beneficial it should apply the following guidance.

8.157 The complaints manager responsible for children's services should liaise with other staff as relevant. These members of staff should agree who will take the lead, to make sure that the complainant is kept informed and, wherever possible, gets a single, clear reply that covers all aspects.

8.158 The local authority should also respond as promptly by meeting the shorter of whichever timescales apply and should ensure that this process is not confusing for the child or young person.

Child protection and child protection conferences

8.159 Where consideration of a complaint leads to concerns about the welfare of children, these should be referred immediately to local authority children's social care or the police. The handling of any associated complaint can be suspended if necessary.

8.160 The welfare of children is a corporate responsibility of the entire local authority. The local authority should work in partnership with other public agencies, the voluntary sector, and service users and carers. Local authorities have the lead responsibility for the establishment and effective functioning of Local Safeguarding Children Boards (LSCBs), which co-ordinate the way local agencies including the police, education services and housing services work together to safeguard and promote the welfare of children.

8.161 Where enquiries have been conducted under s 47 of the Children Act 1989, a child protection conference may be held. This brings together family members, the child (where appropriate), and those professionals most involved with the child and family to consider information about the child's developmental needs (ie health and development) and decide what future action is required to safeguard and promote the welfare of the child.

Complaints about a child protection conference[13]

8.162 Parents/caregivers and, on occasion children, may have concerns about which they may wish to make representations or complain, in respect of one or more of the following aspects of the functioning of child protection conferences:

• the process of the conference;

• the outcome, in terms of the fact of and/or the category of primary concern at the time the child became the subject of a child protection plan; and/or

• a decision for the child to become, or not to become, the subject of a child protection plan or not to cease the child being the subject of a child protection plan.

8.163 Complaints about individual agencies, their performance and provision (or non provision) of services should be responded to in accordance with the relevant agency's complaints handling process (eg s 26 of the Children Act 1989).

8.164 However, complaints about aspects of the functioning of conferences described in this section should be addressed to the conference chair. Such complaints should be passed on to local authority children's social care. In considering and responding to complaints, the local authority should form an inter-agency panel made up of senior representatives from LSCB member agencies. The panel should consider whether the relevant inter-agency protocols and procedures have been observed correctly and whether the decision that is being complained about follows reasonably from the proper observation of the protocol(s).

8.165 The panel may make one or more of the following decisions based on a majority decision:

• to conclude that the child protection conference procedures were followed correctly and support the original child protection conference decision;

---

[13]   *Working Together* (2010).

- to recommend that the child protection conference be reconvened with the same or a different conference chairperson to reconsider the previous decision regarding the child protection plan and/or reconsider the categories of abuse or neglect;

- to decide that they have insufficient information to make a decision and set out a timescale for completing the task and set a date for a further hearing.

8.166 If there are subsequent complaints about the work of individual agencies, or their performance or the provision or non-provision of services, these should be handled in line with the particular agency's complaints process.

Court orders

8.167 The procedure outlined in this chapter is not an appeals procedure. People wishing to appeal against court orders should approach the court.[14] However, dissatisfaction about a local authority's management or handling of a child's case, even where related to a court order, may be appropriately considered by the complaints procedure, for example, conduct of social work staff involved in court procedures. It is for the complaints manager to identify whether these circumstances might be considered under this procedure. The child or young person should also be informed that the complaints procedure cannot overturn a court decision.

8.168 The local authority should also consider whether any possible complaint relating to records used in court may also constitute a challenge to accuracy of the records it holds under the Data Protection Act 1998.

SECTION 4 – THE LOCAL GOVERNMENT OMBUDSMAN

8.169 Where the presenting facts indicate that reasonable, appropriate consideration of the complaint has been undertaken at stage 2 and that further consideration by the review panel would not produce a demonstrably different outcome, the complaints manager should discuss with the complainant the possibility of referring the complaint to the Local Government Ombudsman.

8.170 The authority can only consider this option once stage 2 has been concluded and the complainant has received the authority's final position on the complaints.

8.171 There are a number of important safeguards that must be in place before proceeding with this option. Stage 2 must have delivered:

- a very robust report;

---

[14] See chapter 15.

- a complete adjudication;

- an outcome where all complaints have been upheld (or all significant complaints relating to service delivery in respect of the qualifying individual); and

- the local authority is providing a clear action plan for delivery; and

- the local authority agrees to meet the majority or all of the desired outcomes presented by the complainant regarding social services functions.

8.172 Where this is the case, and the complainant agrees, the complaints manager can then approach the Local Government Ombudsman and ask him to consider the complaint directly, without first going through a review panel.

8.173 It is important to note that the Ombudsman has the power to investigate complaints made by members of the public in writing. Therefore the local authority and the complainant will need to agree a written statement of the complaint for release, by the authority, to the Ombudsman.

8.174 The Ombudsman will then apply a test of reasonableness to this decision. If the Ombudsman concludes that early referral was incorrect, he or she may select from a range of responses. This may include proposing that the complaint is considered by the local authority at a stage 3 review panel in the normal manner.

8.175 Early referral of the complaint will not restrict the Ombudsman from later consideration of the complaint if he or she so chooses.

SECTION 5 – GUIDANCE ON UNREASONABLY PERSISTENT COMPLAINANTS

8.176 When local authorities are committed to dealing with all complaints fairly and impartially and to providing a high quality service to those who complain, they will not normally limit the contact complainants have with their offices. However, there are a small number of complainants who, because of the frequency of their contact with the local authority, hinder consideration of their own complaints.

8.177 Where a local authority encounters irresolvable and persistent complaints, it should consider all aspects of why this situation may be developing. It is also important to distinguish between people who make a number of complaints because they really think things have gone wrong, and people who make unreasonably persistent complaints.

8.178 If the complainant is persisting because his complaints have not been considered in full then the local authority must address this (normally by invoking the next stage). However, if the authority has already done so and has demonstrated this to the complainant, then the complaints manager should consider whether the complainant is now inappropriately persistent. The following guidance should only be pursued where absolutely necessary.

Persistent complainants

8.179 Features of a 'persistent complainant' may include:

- a person who makes the same complaint repeatedly (with minor differences), but never accepts the outcomes;

- a person who seeks an unrealistic outcome and persists until it is reached; or

- a person with a history of making other unreasonably persistent complaints.

Unreasonably persistent complaints

8.180 An unreasonably persistent complaint is likely to include some or all of the following:

- an historic and irreversible decision or incident;

- frequent, lengthy, complicated and stressful contact with the local authority staff;

- the complainant behaving in an aggressive manner to staff or being verbally abusive or threatening;

- the complainant changing aspects of the complaint partway through the investigation or review panel;

- the complainant making and breaking contact with the local authority on an ongoing basis; and

- the complainant persistently approaching the local authority through different routes about the same issue in the hope of getting different responses.

8.181 There are a number of principles that the authority can apply. The most important being that the complainant receives the same standard of response as any other service user, and that the authority can show that it has not discriminated against the persistent complainant.

8.182   If the situation is challenging but it is possible to proceed, staff should avoid giving unrealistic expectations on the outcome of the complaint.

Action in response

8.183   Where the relationship becomes unworkable, the complaints manager should ensure that he or she demonstrates that he or she has considered the complaints as fully as is appropriate. This should normally be through advising the complaint that:

- he does not constitute a person who may complain and/or that his complaints do not fall within the relevant criteria for what may be complained about;

- the local authority has either offered or provided consideration of the issues through another procedure (eg the corporate complaints procedure);

- the local authority will consider the substantive issues at all stages of the complaints procedure; or

- the matters raised are not sufficiently different to justify being considered as a new complaint.

8.184   Where the local authority has attempted to move the complaint on to the next stage but the complainant has either refused or delayed such progression through excessive objection to the process rather than addressing the substantive issues of the complaint themselves, the local authority should advise the complainant that this is causing delay and is unreasonable use of the complaints procedure.

8.185   In some instances, abusive, threatening or other unreasonable behaviour may be a feature of the complainant's disease or mental illness (eg chronic anxiety). In such cases, if possible, the local authority should consider securing a whole case review from all professionals involved.[15]

8.186   In all cases where the complaints manager decides to treat someone as an unreasonably persistent complainant, he or she should write to tell the complainant why he or she believes his behaviour falls into that category, what action he or she is taking and the duration of that action. He or she should also inform the complainant how he or she can challenge the decision if he or she disagrees with it (this should normally include information regarding the Local Government Ombudsman).

---

[15]   The local authority should refer to the Mental Capacity Act 2005 if appropriate.

8.187 Where a complainant's complaint is closed and he or she persists in communicating about it, the complaints manager may decide to terminate contact with that complainant.

Restricting access

8.188 The decision to restrict access to the complaints procedure should be taken by the complaints manager and should follow a prior warning to the complainant. Any restrictions imposed should be appropriate and proportionate. The options that the complaints manager is most likely to consider are:

- requesting contact in a particular form (for example, letters only);

- requiring contact to take place with a named officer;

- restricting telephone calls to specified days and times;

- asking the complainant to enter into an agreement about his future contact with the local authority; and

- informing the complainant that if he or she still does not cooperate with the advice given, any further correspondence that does not present significant new matters or new information will not necessarily be acknowledged, but will be kept on file.

8.189 Any new complaints from people who come under this policy should be treated on their individual merits.

8.190 In extreme cases, the local authority may consider the following actions:

- referring the complaint to the Local Government Ombudsman before the complaints procedure has been exhausted (see Annex 3); or

- advising the complainant that it cannot assist further and informing them of their right to approach the Local Government Ombudsman.

8.191 The distinction between the two options above is that early referral to the Local Government Ombudsman is a positive action that can only be undertaken in agreement between the local authority and the complainant. This is therefore the less likely option with persistent complainants.

8.192 Option 2 may arise where the local authority does not agree with the complainant that the complaints are substantively valid and the two parties disagree on the way forward. This is more likely with a persistent complainant. Should the local authority take this option, it should not contact the Local Government Ombudsman directly, but should indicate to the complainant that he or she may make this approach. The local authority should confirm to the complainant that it is not responding to the complaint further.

8.193 The Local Government Ombudsman is likely to apply the test of reasonableness over the local authority's response in a similar manner to an early referral and will have a range of options open to him.

Terminating contact

8.194 Where a complainant continues to behave in a way which is unacceptable, the local authority may decide to terminate contact with the complainant and discontinue any investigation into the complaint.

8.195 Where the behaviour is so extreme that it threatens the immediate safety and welfare of staff, the authority should consider other options, for example reporting the matter to the Police or taking legal action. In such cases, the authority may not give the complainant prior warning of that action.[16]

---

[16] In following this guidance, the complaints manager should refer to the Mental Capacity Act 2005 and all relevant human rights based legislation.

The procedure for Children Act 1989 complaints

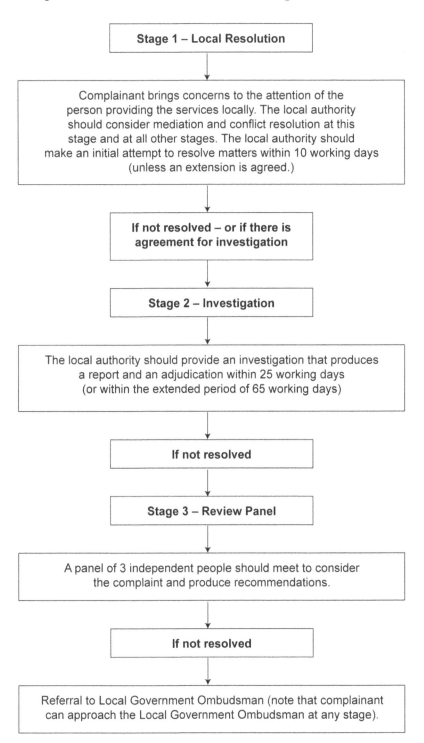

Stage 1 – Local Resolution

Complainant brings concerns to the attention of the
person providing the services locally. The local authority
should consider mediation and conflict resolution at this
stage and at all other stages. The local authority should
make an initial attempt to resolve matters within 10 working days
(unless an extension is agreed.)

**If not resolved – or if there is
agreement for investigation**

Stage 2 – Investigation

The local authority should provide an investigation that produces
a report and an adjudication within 25 working days
(or within the extended period of 65 working days)

If not resolved

Stage 3 – Review Panel

A panel of 3 independent people should meet to consider
the complaint and produce recommendations.

If not resolved

Referral to Local Government Ombudsman (note that complainant
can approach the Local Government Ombudsman at any stage).

Chapter 9

USE AND MISUSE OF SECTION 20

SECTION 1 – INTRODUCTION

9.1 The idea of a system of 'voluntary accommodation' alongside the more formal and confrontational route of obtaining emergency protection orders or interim care orders through the court process, persists although the phrase is not found anywhere in the Children Act 1989.

9.2 In reality s 20 of the CA 1989 sets out a mixture of duties imposed upon the local authority to provide accommodation alongside discretionary powers to do so, depending on circumstances, age of child and the position of those who hold parental responsibility for the child.

9.3 Parents approaching the local authority for help either in crisis situations, or where there is a more settled desire to relinquish care of their child, can take advantage of this consensual route of providing alternative care. The parents retain all their legal rights and at the end of an agreed period or even at an earlier stage they can demand the return of the child. The local authority in these circumstances has no legal right to prevent the return of the child.

9.4 Problems in the use of, or with the limits to, the powers in this section however can be perceived to arise, or actually arise where:

- the consent/agreement is arrived at where the crisis situation impacts on the ability of the parent to give a valid or fully informed consent;

- some other reason is in operation to call the capacity of the parent to consent into question;

- the option of consensual accommodation is presented as a last chance as a way of avoiding court proceedings where the granting of an order would be in doubt;

- it is used to secure removal at birth;

- accommodation under the section is used over extensive periods before formal proceedings are taken;

- parents and local authority do not agree on day to day care issues including issues of contact with the child;

- local authorities feel the need to exercise a degree of parental responsibility for the child in their care;

- parents do not seek the return of the child but wish to exercise a degree of control over placement and manner in which their child should be brought up;

- an older child's views and those of his/her parents do not coincide;

- the child's parents views on aspects of their upbringing do not coincide.

9.5   The use of s 20 can epitomise both the best and worst in the Children Act 1989. It can be a way to ensure the true working in partnership or it can be used as a potential threat or an improper exercise of control. It can show the State and parents working together to achieve the best for the child in the spirit of the 'no order' principle but can also place them at loggerheads with no readily apparent mechanism for achieving a resolution.

9.6   The complaints procedure and role of the independent reviewing officer are highly relevant to the child accommodated under s 20 arrangements. Reference should be made to the specific chapters dealing with them as, whilst mentioned here, they will not be dealt with in detail.

9.7   Getting the approach wrong when making decisions for a child who is looked after under the s 20 regime can lead to breaches of both Art 6 and Art 8 of the ECHR and open the local authority to challenge through various of the routes discussed in this book.

SECTION 2 – THE LEGAL FRAMEWORK

9.8   Section 20 provides:[1]

20 Provision of accommodation for children: general

(1) Every local authority **shall** provide accommodation for any **child in need** within their area who appears to them to require accommodation as a result of –

   (a)   there being no person who has parental responsibility for them;
   (b)   his being lost or having been abandoned; or
   (c)   the person who has been caring for him being prevented (whether or not permanently, and for whatever reason) from providing him with suitable accommodation or care

(2) [*not directly relevant for the purposes of this chapter*]

---

[1]   Key words in the subsection have been highlighted for ease of reference.

(3) Every local authority **shall** provide accommodation for any **child in need** within their area who has reached the **age of sixteen** and whose welfare the authority consider is likely to be seriously prejudiced if they do not provide him with accommodation.

(4) A local authority **may** provide accommodation for **any child** within their area (even though a person who has parental responsibility for him is able to provide him with accommodation) if they consider that to do so would safeguard or promote the child's welfare.

(5) A local authority **may** provide accommodation for any person who has reached the **age of sixteen but is under twenty-one** in any community home which takes children who have reached the age of sixteen if they consider that to do so would safeguard and promote his welfare.

(6) Before providing accommodation under this section, a local authority shall, so far as is reasonably practicable and consistent with the child's welfare –

(a)   ascertain the child's wishes and feelings regarding the provision of accommodation; and
(b)   give due consideration (having regard to his age and understanding) to such wishes and feelings of the child as they have been able to ascertain.

(7) A local authority **may not provide accommodation** under this section for any child if any person who –

(a)   has parental responsibility for him; and
(b)   is willing and able to –
(i)   provide accommodation for him; or
(ii)   arrange for accommodation to be provided for him

objects.

(8) Any person who has parental responsibility for a child may at any time remove the child from accommodation provided by or on behalf of the local authority under this section.

(9) Subsections (7) and (8) do not apply while any person –

(a)   in whose favour a residence order is in force with respect to a child;
(aa) who is a special guardian of the child; or
(b)   who has care of the child by virtue of an order made in the exercise of the High Court's inherent jurisdiction with respect to children,
agrees to the child being looked after in accommodation provided on or behalf of the local authority.

(10) Where there is more than one such person as is mentioned in subsection (9) all of them must agree.

(11) Subsections (7) and (8) do not apply where a child who has reached the age of sixteen agrees to being provided with accommodation under this section.

9.9   Other key provisions in the Children Act 1989:[2]

---

[2]   This should not be regarded as an exhaustive rehearsal of all provisions of the Act applying to children accommodated pursuant to s 20 but the most relevant to the issues discussed in this chapter. Careful attention should be applied to all provisions contained in ss 20 to 23, 25, 26 and chapters 6, 7, and 8 of this book.

Section 2: Parental Responsibility for Children

(9) A person who has parental responsibility for a child may not surrender or transfer any part of that responsibility to another but may arrange for some or all of it to be met by one or more persons acting on his behalf.

Section 3: Meaning of "parental responsibility"

(1) In this Act "Parental Responsibility" means all the rights, duties, powers, responsibilities and authority which by law a parent of a child has in relation to the child and his property.

(5) A person who –

    (a)   does not have parental responsibility for a particular child; but
    (b)   has the care of the child

may (subject to the provisions of this Act) do what is reasonable in all the circumstances of the case for the purpose of safeguarding or promoting the child's welfare.

Section 22: General duty of local authority in relation to children looked after by them[3]

(3) It shall be the duty of any local authority looking after any child –

    (a)   to safeguard and promote his welfare; and
    (b)   [*not replicated here*]

(3A) The duty of a local authority under subsection (3)(a) to safeguard and promote the welfare of a child looked after by them includes in particular a duty to promote the child's education.

(4) Before making any decision with respect to a child whom they are looking after, or proposing to look after, a local authority shall, so far as is reasonably practicable, ascertain the wishes and feelings of –

    (a)   the child;
    (b)   his parents;
    (c)   any person who is not a parent of his but has parental responsibility for him
    (d)   any other person whose wishes and feelings the authority consider to be relevant,

regarding the matter to be decided.

(5) In making any such decision a local authority shall give due consideration –

    (a)   having regard to his age and understanding, to such wishes and feelings of the child as they have been able to ascertain
    (b)   to such wishes and feelings of any person mentioned in subsection 4(b) to (d) as they have been able to ascertain; and
    (c)   to the child's religious persuasion, racial origin and cultural and linguistic background.

---

[3]   Please note that the full text is not repeated here but only those provisions most relevant to the issues in this chapter.

The Children Act 1989 Guidance and Regulations

9.10 Very little additional assistance on the specific problems relating to s 20 highlighted above is provided in the guidance issued alongside the Children Act but attention is drawn to the following important references:

Volume 1 – Court Orders

9.11 Paragraph 2.16 provides:[4]

> 'The position of the temporary carer is clarified by section 3(5) which provides that a person who has the care of the child but does not have parental responsibility may do "what is reasonable in all the circumstances of the case for the purpose of safeguarding or promoting the child's welfare" (section 3(5)). This covers actions taken by people looking after a child who is being accommodated by a local authority under section 20, provided that these are reasonable in the circumstances. What is reasonable will depend on the urgency and gravity of what is required and the extent to which it is practicable to consult with a person with parental responsibility.'

Volume 2 – Care Planning, Placement and Case Review[5]

9.12 This volume applies to Part 3 of the Children Act 1989, which includes s 20 and sets out the functions and responsibilities of local authorities and partner agencies under Part 3. It states that the guidance describes how local authorities should carry out their responsibilities in relation to care planning, placement and case reviews for looked after children[6] and notes that these responsibilities are designed to support the local authority in its primary duty set out in s 22(3A) of the 1989 Act to safeguard and promote the welfare of the looked after child and to act as good corporate parents to enable each looked after child to achieve his or her full potential in life.[7]

9.13 Some of the key principles which are identified include:[8]

- Parents should be expected and enabled to retain their responsibilities and to remain as closely involved as is consistent with their child's welfare, even if that child cannot live at home either temporarily or permanently.

---

[4] This wording is taken from the 2008 version of Volume 1, which, on this element, remained the applicable guidance at the time of writing (the 2008 version was updated with Annexes to cover the Public Law Outline). It is likely that this volume will be updated shortly (at the time of writing in February 2013) and care should be taken to ensure any subsequent version is consulted.

[5] These are taken from the March 2010 version which was the most recent at the time of writing.

[6] The term 'looked after children' encompasses those accommodated by virtue of s 20.

[7] This guidance accompanies the Care Planning, Placement and Case Review (England) Regulations 2010.

[8] See Volume 2, paras 1.5 and 1.6.

- If children have to live apart from their family, both they and their parents should be given adequate information and helped to consider alternatives and contribute to the making of an informed choice about the most appropriate form of care.

- Parents should be encouraged to exercise their responsibility for their child's welfare in a constructive way and where compulsory intervention in the family is necessary it should, where possible, support rather than undermine the parental role. The 1989 Act places a strong emphasis on the local authority working in partnership with parents when undertaking their statutory functions.

9.14 In considering *the care plan for the voluntarily accommodated child*[9] the guidance states that most children who start to be looked after have been known to children's services for some time. It advises that where a child is to be voluntarily accommodated it should therefore be possible to begin the care planning process in advance of the care episode. Where this is not possible a care plan must be prepared within 10 working days of the start of the first placement. Where the young person who is to be accommodated is over the age of 16 and agrees to be provided with accommodation under s 20 the care plan should be agreed with the young person.[10]

9.15 On contact issues the guidance offers this advice for *contact arrangements for an accommodated child*.[11] Arrangements for contact with an accommodated child are a matter of negotiation and agreement between the responsible local authority, the child, parents and others seeking contact. The responsible authority should ensure that parents and others wishing to have contact with the child know where to seek advice about contact matters. In the event of a dispute about contact the guide advises that if such dispute cannot be resolved and the complaints procedure has not provided a solution, a s 8 order may be made on the application of the child, a parent or other person.

9.16 This approach does not appear adequately to reflect the absence of any parental responsibility vesting in the local authority. Where local authorities and parents cannot agree on the correct contact arrangements it must be debatable whether the effect of s 3(5) is, in fact, sufficient to put the onus on to the parents to seek orders. There does not appear to be any clear decision on this point. However it is correct that the restriction imposed by s 9 CA 1989 on the making of a s 8 order with respect to a child in the care of a local authority does not extend to a child who is merely accommodated. The phrase 'in care' is interpreted as a child who is the subject of a care order.

---

[9] See specifically Volume 2, paras 2.36 and 2.37.
[10] For detailed consideration of what should be included in the care plan see Care Planning, Placement and Case Review (England) Regulations, reg 5 and Sch 1 and para 2.44 onwards of The Children Act Guidance and Regulations Volume 2.
[11] See Volume 2, paras 2.91 and 2.92.

SECTION 3 – AREAS OF POTENTIAL CONFLICT

Removal at birth

9.17 Removal of a child from its parents at or shortly after the moment of birth is likely to be regarded as the most draconian interference possible with the rights of both child and parents to respect for their private and family life.

9.18 Great care therefore is needed to ensure that the planning and decision-making is properly conducted and that the removal, if it is to occur, is a proportionate response to the perceived risk to the child.

9.19 Great care is also required to ensure that the parent is both able to participate in the planning process and understands exactly what is being proposed.

9.20 Understanding of the local authority proposals and plans is not the same as consenting to those plans.

9.21 If there is no valid consent given then s 20 cannot be used to facilitate the removal of the child and other legal authority must be obtained.

9.22 Pre-birth consent may not still be in operation even immediately after birth and, if not, other legal authority must be obtained before a removal can be considered lawful.

9.23 The above statement of principle can be illustrated by *R (G) v Nottingham City Council*[12] and *R (G) v Nottingham City Council and Nottingham University Hospital.*[13] The background to the above cases involved an 18 year old who had herself been in the care of the local authority and who, during the course of judicial review proceedings challenging a deficient and inadequate pathway plan for herself, gave birth to a baby boy who within a matter of hours of birth had been removed from her care and placed in a separate room in the hospital.

9.24 The original judicial review proceedings came on for hearing the day after the birth. At that hearing lawyers for the mother sought an order from the court for the immediate re-unification of mother and child alleging the removal had been without any lawful authority. There was a pre-birth plan, as recorded in the child protection conference recommendations, for an interim care order (ICO) to be sought upon birth, for the baby to remain in hospital until taken into foster care, for the baby not to be removed by the mother from hospital and identifying that an EPO would need to be obtained if an ICO was not in place. Neither order had been obtained at the time of the separation of mother and child.

---

[12] [2008] EWHC 152 (Admin), [2008] 1 FLR 1660 (the February judgment).
[13] [2008] EWHC 400 (Admin), [2008] 1 FLR 1668 (the March judgment).

9.25   Munby J[14] explained:

'... the law is perfectly clear but perhaps requires re-emphasis. Whatever the impression a casual reader might gain from reading some newspaper reports, no local authority and no social worker has any power to remove a child from its parents or, without the agreement of the parent, to take a child into care, unless they have first obtained an order from a family court authorising that step: either an emergency protection order in accordance with section 44 of the Children Act 1989 or an interim care order in accordance with section 38 of the Act or perhaps, in an exceptional case (and subject to s 100 of the Act) a wardship order made by a judge of the Family Division of the High Court.'[15]

9.26   He further underlined that:[16]

'...section 46 of the Children Act 1989 permits a police constable to remove a child where he has reasonable cause to believe that the child would otherwise be likely to suffer significant harm, and that power can be exercised without prior judicial authority. But the powers conferred on the police by section 46 are not given to either local authorities or social workers.'

9.27   He took care to identify that this approach was subject to two qualifications:

- A social worker or nurse is entitled to intervene if that is necessary to protect a baby from immediate violence at the hands of a parent.

    Not because they have any special power or privilege entitling them to intervene but by application of a wider principle that anyone who happens to be present is entitled whether by restraining the assailant or by removing the defenceless victim from the assailant's reach, to intervene to prevent an actual or threatened criminal assault taking place in front of their very eyes.

- Where circumstances might properly justify action taken pursuant to s 3(5) of the Children Act 1989 where a person who has care of a child may do what is reasonable in the circumstances of the case for the purpose of safeguarding or promoting the child's welfare.

    The illustration given in *R (G) v Nottingham CC* was of a hospital being entitled to separate mother and child where a premature baby desperately needed placing in a special unit or on a ventilator, where medical necessity dictated even if the mother objected.

---

[14]   As he then was.
[15]   See para 15 of the February 2008 judgment.
[16]   See para 16 of the February 2008 judgment. For further consideration of the ability of police to remove children in an emergency see *Langley and Others v Liverpool City Council* [2006] 1 FLR 342 in chapter 18.

9.28 The post-script to the February 2008 judgment noted that care proceedings were started with respect to the baby the day before his judgment was completed and upon the conclusion of the separate care proceedings an interim care order was made.

9.29 In the March 2008 judgment the following guidance was set out:

- A mother could not be said to have given consent to the removal of her baby merely because, knowing of a local authority plan to remove the child, she did not object to it, and because at the moment of separation she did not actively resist.

- Absence of objection could not be conflated with actual consent and equating helpless acquiescence with consent was unprincipled and fraught with potential danger.

    'Mr Justice Munby reminded local authorities that the law of England and Wales had long recognised that women in the aftermath of birth may not be as able to act wisely as at other times and that compassionate regard for those realities underlay statutory provisions as disparate as section 1 of the Infanticide Act 1938 and section 52(3) of the Adoption and Children Act 2002.'

- Although consent to the accommodation of a child in accordance with s 20 of the 1989 Act did not have to be in writing, a prudent local authority would always wish to ensure that an alleged parental consent in such a case was properly recorded in writing and evidenced by the parent's signature.

- That there can be cases where a woman is able to give a valid consent to the accommodation of her newly born baby by the local authority immediately after birth for example where she had entered the labour ward with a settled intention to hand over the baby for adoption immediately after birth and followed up that intention by leaving the hospital within a short time of the birth, requesting that she be adopted and not wishing to see the child.[17]

- That it was the responsibility of the NHS Trust to ensure that it was acting with lawful authority not simply to rely on the 'mere say so' of a social worker that the separation of mother and child was lawful.

9.30 Declarations regarding the separation of mother and child were granted in the case in the following terms:

---

[17] Reference was made by way of example to *Re L, X County Council v C* [2008] 1 FLR 1079.

- The separation of G's new born baby from his mother on the 30 January 2008 at the NHS Trust was a breach of G's rights under Art 8 ECHR in that the local authority had neither lawful authority nor any consent from G for the said action.

9.31 The issue as to whether the mother was entitled to financial compensation for the unlawful separation or whether the declaration amounted to just satisfaction within the meaning of Art 41 of the Convention were, in the absence of agreement, left by the court to be dealt with on another day.[18]

9.32 A number of local authorities through their safeguarding boards now have guidance or protocols for pre-birth plans and hospital birth plans to avoid the problems experienced in the *Nottingham* case and many of these can be accessed online.[19]

9.33 Nothing highlighted below removes the need for the correct process of assessment and planning in advance where a family is already known to a local authority or are referred to children's services early in a mother's pregnancy. The advice given below relates to emergency or urgent scenarios where a temptation might exist to regard the use of s 20 accommodation as the most expeditious way forward and hopefully operates as a checklist to ensure that if s 20 is used it is only used in circumstances where it is appropriate and lawful to do so.

9.34 Where the pre-birth child protection conference decides, or where the imminent birth of a child only becomes known to a local authority at the last minute in circumstances that indicate that the risks to an unborn child are so great that a child protection plan and EPO are likely to be required upon birth the following key points are stressed:

9.35 The baby may only be separated from his or her mother with valid parental consent or by obtaining a court order or in valid circumstances through police protection procedures. It is not possible to obtain an order until the child is born.[20]

9.36 Whilst a father who does not hold parental responsibility does not have the ability to veto a mother's consent to s 20, a father with parental responsibility does have such ability. A father with parental responsibility may remove a child from accommodation provided by the local authority.

---

[18] On the issue of human rights damages and the idea of just satisfaction see chapter 18 herein.

[19] For example Nottingham Safeguarding Children Board *Safeguarding babies at birth where the risks are too great to leave them in care of their parents: Practice Guidance and Toolkit.*

[20] But see *Re D (Unborn Baby)* [2009] 2 FLR 313 where in exceptional circumstances Munby J granted an anticipatory declaration, in advance of the birth, that it would be lawful for the local authority to remove the child at birth without forewarning the parents of its intention to do so. Note: The declaration dealt only with the lawfulness of the non-involvement of the mother and her partner in the birth planning for the future child and did not alter the power to remove through the usual process of s 46 CA 1989 upon birth, if appropriate and the need for a subsequent application for an EPO.

9.37 Further where a person with parental responsibility objects to the local authority accommodating the child under s 20 the local authority may not accommodate that child. This is subject to the condition, however, that the person objecting is both willing and able to either provide accommodation, or to arrange for accommodation to be provided, for the child.

9.38 It is therefore desirable to have both parents' consent. It should be remembered that married parents both automatically acquire parental responsibility for the child on birth.

9.39 Where there is a conflict between the parents on the issue of consent legal advice should be sought by the local authority as it may be necessary to secure an order if any separation is to be lawful.

9.40 The child protection plan needs to be explicit about actions to be undertaken and by whom immediately following the birth of the child.

9.41 If the plan includes the need to separate a baby from its parents there should be recognition that this can be traumatic for the family, the planning needs to be clear for all professionals involved and the steps necessary to achieve such aim need to be carried out sensitively and fairly.

9.42 The specific safeguarding risks and steps required to manage those risks need to be assessed and clearly spelt out.

9.43 The steps required must be proportionate to the risks identified. There would need to be good reasons for deciding that the baby would be at risk of significant harm if left in the mother's care whilst on the same ward post birth such as a reason for believing an imminent risk of physical harm, significant neglect through inappropriate handling, feeding or supervision likely to result in harm to the baby, attempts to leave the hospital with the baby placing the baby at risk of significant harm. The risk identified would also need to be supported by a professional judgment based on proper assessment that it is not possible to manage these risks in any other fashion.

9.44 The assessment should include consideration of the nature of any support that maternal and paternal families may be in a position to give.

9.45 The precise legal basis for separation needs to be properly considered and it is advisable for the workers to obtain legal advice at an early stage.

9.46 If consent to accommodation is given in advance of admission to hospital for the birth (or in advance of the birth) the issue of consent should be discussed and reviewed with the parents throughout the process on a regular basis.

9.47   The closer to birth that the consent is obtained the greater the risk that the consent will not be regarded as informed consent due to the impact of emotions and the vulnerability of the mother close to birth.

9.48   The parents should be advised to seek independent legal advice to assist them in making any decision to consent to the baby's accommodation. Any consent or disagreement to accommodation should be recorded.

9.49   Acknowledgment that a mother understands a birth protection plan that involves removal at birth is not the same as consent by the mother to that plan and cannot be relied upon to legalise any removal in the absence of valid consent.

9.50   Following the birth of the child the issue of consent to accommodation must be revisited with the parent.

9.51   It must be remembered and acknowledged that although a mother may have consented to an advance birth protection plan and have signed consents pre-birth she is entitled to change her mind at any point and in particular can do so after the birth. In these circumstances pre-birth consent cannot render lawful a post-birth removal. The voluntary nature of s 20 accommodation should not be overlooked.

9.52   The local authority will need to ensure that:

- consent is explicitly given;

- the parent giving consent is fully informed of their options;

- the parent fully understands the implications of consent;

- the parent has the capacity to consent (eg that the mother's ability to consent is not affected by her mental state after childbirth).

9.53   Contingency plans should be considered and recorded to enable swift recourse to these plans if parental consent is withdrawn or if a professional dealing with the parent is no longer satisfied that there is valid consent.

9.54   The issue of when to revisit the question of parental consent is a sensitive one and will need to be decided on a case-by-case basis. Proper assistance should be sought from professionals working with the mother (such as midwives, nursing staff etc) as to what is a reasonable period to leave after the birth before raising the topic with the mother again.

9.55   Wherever possible any consent should be evidenced in writing signed by the parent. It is advisable to make a record of any reason why it may not have been possible for the consent to be evidenced in writing.

9.56 It should be clear whether the separation is regarded as being temporary or more permanent in nature as issues for consent are likely to differ in each circumstance.

9.57 It should clear whether there is to be a lapse of time before separation and if so whether there can be contact during this period.

9.58 It is advisable for local authority legal teams to be notified when the mother has gone into labour to enable them to run through a checklist with the workers on the ground.

9.59 Ideally parents should have access to their own legal advice before consenting. Attempts should be made to contact any solicitor instructed by the mother and to enable the solicitor and mother to have time to discuss matters post-birth but prior to any removal.

Where there are issues relating to capacity

9.60 The use of s 20 accommodation at birth again came to the attention of the courts in *Coventry City Council v C, B, CA and CH*.[21]

9.61 Hedley J used this opportunity to give guidance to social workers in respect of obtaining parental consent under s 20 for the removal of a child immediately or soon after birth to the care of the local authority. In this case particular attention was paid to the provisions of the Mental Capacity Act 2005 and the impact issues of capacity would have for the s 20 voluntary regime.

9.62 This guidance is also likely to be of assistance in other s 20 situations not involving new-born babies.

9.63 The views expressed by Hedley J in Part V, para 46 of the judgment regarding the ambit of s 20 agreements were seen in advance by the then President of the Family Division and specifically approved.

9.64 The court recognised that the emphasis of Part III of the Children Act 1989 is on partnership. It acknowledged that any attempt to restrict the use of s 20 ran the risk both of undermining that partnership element and of encroaching upon a parent's right to exercise parental responsibility in any way they saw fit in order to promote the welfare of their child. However the judge gave clear warning that the use of s 20 was not unrestricted and must not be compulsion in disguise.

9.65 In order for any s 20 agreement to be lawful the parent must have the requisite capacity to make the agreement.

---

21   [2012] EWHC 2190 (Fam).

9.66   All consents given under s 20 must be considered in the light of ss 1–3 of the Mental Capacity Act 2005.

9.67   Even where there is capacity the court underlined that it is essential that any consent so obtained is properly informed and, at least where it results in detriment to the giver's personal interest, is fairly obtained. Such requirements are implicit in a due regard for the giver's rights under Arts 6 and 8 of the European Convention on Human Rights.

9.68   Lawful separation of mother and baby at the time of birth (assuming there were reasonable grounds for believing that such a separation should take place) could be obtained in one of four ways:

- by agreement under s 20;

- by emergency protection under s 44;

- by the police under s 46;

- or under an interim care order under s 38.

9.69   Even where removal is justified there remains a need for minimum intervention and to work in partnership with parents.[22]

9.70   The judgment stresses that it can never be permissible to seek agreement to do that which would not be authorised by order solely because it is known, believed or even suspected that no such authorisation would be given and in order to circumvent that position. Such an approach would breach all requirements of good faith and of fairness.

9.71   There will be cases where it is perfectly proper to seek agreement to immediate post-birth accommodation. Three obvious examples cited in the judgment being:

- where the mother's intention always has been and remains to have the child placed for adoption;

- where a parent has always accepted that the child must be removed and has consistently expressed a willingness to consent (rather than just acquiescence);

- where a parent by reason of supervening physical health or personal circumstance positively seeks accommodation of the child by social services.

---

[22]   See for example *A v East Sussex CC and Another* [2010] 2 FLR 1596.

9.72 These examples were not to be regarded as an exhaustive list of the appropriate use of s 20 for new-born children. The court acknowledged that there would be other circumstances and that the right to exercise parental responsibility by requesting accommodation under s 20 and the local authority's power of response under s 20(4) must be respected.

9.73 Every parent has the right, if they have the capacity to do so, to exercise their parental responsibility to consent under s 20 to have their child accommodated by the local authority and every local authority has power under s 20 so to accommodate provided that it is consistent with the welfare of the child.

9.74 Every social worker obtaining such consent is under a personal duty (the outcome of which may not be dictated to them by others) to be satisfied that the person giving consent does not lack the capacity to do so.

9.75 In taking any such consent the social worker must actively address the issue of capacity and take into account all the circumstances prevailing at the time and consider the questions raised by s 3 of Mental Capacity Act 2005 and in particular the mother's capacity at that time to use and weigh all relevant information.

9.76 If the social worker has doubts about capacity no further attempt should be made to obtain consent on the occasion that the doubt arose and advice should be sought from the social work team leader or management.

9.77 If the social worker is satisfied that the person whose consent is sought does not lack capacity the social worker must be satisfied that the consent is fully informed.[23] The following questions should be considered:

- Does the parent fully understand the consequences of giving such consent?

- Does the parent fully appreciate the range of choices available and the consequences of refusal as well as giving consent?

- Is the parent in full possession of all the facts and issues material to the giving of consent?

9.78 If not satisfied that the answers to these questions are 'yes' no further attempt should be made to obtain consent on that occasion and advice should

---

[23] On the specific facts of the case Hedley J identified two matters which may have resulted in the mother's consent not being properly informed: (i) she was not told that her refusal to agree to s 20 accommodation would have resulted in the child staying in the hospital for another day or so whilst an urgent hearing was sought; (ii) she was told this was only a temporary arrangement and was not told that the local authority would oppose a return of the child to her care.

be sought as above. The social work team should further consider taking legal advice if there is any doubt or if considered necessary.

9.79 If the social worker is satisfied that the consent is fully informed, then it is necessary to be further satisfied that the giving of such consent and the subsequent removal is both fair and proportionate. In considering this issue it may be necessary to ask:

- What is the current physical and psychological state of the parent?

- If they have a solicitor, have they been encouraged to seek legal advice and/or advice from family and friends?

- Is it necessary for the safety of the child for her to be removed at this time?

- Would it be fairer in this case for this matter to be the subject of a court order rather than an agreement?

9.80 If having done all this and, if necessary, having taken further management and legal advice, the social worker then considers that a fully informed consent has been received from a capacitous mother in circumstances where removal is necessary and proportionate, consent may be acted upon.

9.81 Having outlined the above steps the court warned that, in the light of that guidance, local authorities may want to approach with great care the obtaining of s 20 agreements from mothers in the aftermath of birth, especially where there is no immediate danger to the child and where probably no order would be made. Where it is perceived that care proceedings are likely to be necessary the matters set out above will have particular relevance.

SECTION 4 – LIMITS OF SECTION 20

9.82 Where a child is in the care of a local authority through the making of a care order (whether interim or final) specific provisions enabling the local authority to limit the parents' exercise of parental responsibility are provided under s 33(3)(b) CA 1989 where it is necessary to do so in order to safeguard and promote the child's welfare. This power is not replicated where the child is accommodated under s 20.

9.83 *R v Tameside Metropolitan Borough Council Ex p J*[24] illustrates the approach taken by the court in cases where a child is looked after by a local authority under s 20 and is therefore in the physical care of the authority but where the authority does not hold parental responsibility.

---

[24]   [2000] 1 FLR 942.

9.84 This case involved the accommodation of a disabled child. After 3 years the local authority suggested moving the child from a residential home for disabled children to a foster placement. The child's parents opposed the move but the local authority decided to move the child anyway and set about organising contact with the foster family. The parents sought judicial review of the local authority's decision. Granting the judicial review and declaring that the authority had no power to place the child with foster parents without her parent's consent the court held that, where a child was accommodated under a voluntary arrangement, parents retained parental responsibility which included the right to decide where a child lived.

9.85 A local authority providing a child with accommodation under a voluntary arrangement rather than a care order had what the court described as 'mundane' day-to-day powers of management but they were not entitled to make the kind of decisions ultimately exercised by those with parental responsibility for a child.

9.86 The court explained that accommodation under a voluntary arrangement was a matter for co-operation between the parents and the local authority. Where such co-operation had broken down, the local authority had no power to move the child against the express wishes of the parents, notwithstanding their duties to children in need in within their area and equally the parents had no right to dictate where the authority must accommodate their child.

9.87 If the local authority took the view that there was a risk of significant harm to the child if their own view of the child's accommodation needs did not prevail, they should apply to the court for a care order. If there was no such risk, the local authority was ultimately entitled to offer the parents the choice between caring for the child themselves or agreeing to a solution acceptable to the authority.[25]

9.88 A commonly encountered problem when a child is accommodated is the arrangements for contact between the accommodated child and parents or other people (siblings, relatives, godparents) where the local authority and parental responsibility holders do not agree. Therefore where negotiation and agreement cannot achieve what in the eyes of the local authority is a safe regime of contact, consideration should be given to whether the risks of the contact sought or proposed by the parents are such as to amount to significant harm warranting the issuing of care proceedings. The guidance suggests that a s 8 order can be applied for where parents are faced with what they regard as intransigence by the local authority in setting up a contact regime that meets their requirements. This raises the question as to whether the s 8 order can direct the local authority to make the child available for contact as the wording of the Act provides that a contact order is an order requiring the person with

---

[25] The judge appeared to conclude that the provisions of s 105 and s 3(5) refer to a child who was the subject of a care order. A question must arise as to whether this in fact is the correct meaning of s 3(5) but this does not impact upon the decision.

whom the child lives to allow the child to visit or stay with the person named.[26] Is this then to be made against the foster carer if the child is in foster care? Who would be the appropriate person if the child is in residential care? Certainly it is appropriate in these circumstances for the matter to be brought before the court.

9.89 The Court of Appeal recently removed any doubt on the issue as to whether wardship and s 20 accommodation can run side-by-side in the case of *E (A Child)*.[27]

9.90 The Court of Appeal determined that there was nothing either explicitly or implicitly stated within s 100 Children Act 1989[28] which prevented a wardship order being made where a child was not required to be accommodated but was, in fact, voluntarily accommodated.

9.91 Where agreement existed between the local authority as to the fact that a child should be cared for by the local authority, where the placement in which a child should reside is agreed as between parents and local authority but there are disagreements as to levels of contact, religious activities, education etc then it would appear that the wardship regime may allow the appropriate forum for determination of such issues between local authority and parents.

9.92 In *E (A Child)* the judge at first instance made a care order but stated that the use of wardship would meet the welfare of the child more appropriately than the making of a care order for the following reasons:[29]

- it would be an appropriate means of rendering both the local authority and parents accountable to the court;

- it would enable the court to oblige the local authority to keep the parents informed about progress in arranging therapy;

- it would ensure that the parents received information as proposed in the child's care plan; and

- it would provide a route by which contact could be regulated .

9.93 The Court of Appeal stated that if the accommodation agreement is terminated by either or both of the parties to the agreement, then obviously the court is not in a position to require the local authority to accommodate or

---

[26] As distinct from the wording of the s 34 orders for contact with a child in care which specifically directs that the 'local authority' shall allow contact. Section 34 orders can be enforced as against a local authority by the use of committal orders *Re P-B (Contact: Committal)* [2009] 2 FLR 66.

[27] [2012] EWCA Civ 1753. For further consideration of wardship see chapter 14.

[28] For additional guidance see FPR 2010, PD12D in Part 4 (resources section).

[29] Permission to appeal to the court of appeal was granted by the first instance judge.

supervise but, so long as the s 20 placement remains the judge was not prevented from making the wardship order.[30]

9.94 Problems may also arise (particularly where the accommodated child is an older child) where there is a desire to limit the information about placement and progress that is provided to those holding parental responsibility even though there may not be any disagreement over placement.

9.95 The general duties imposed on a local authority by s 22 apply to children who are accommodated under s 20 as do the Care Planning, Placement and Review (England) Regulations 2010.

9.96 A child who has reached the age of 16 can agree to the provision of accommodation and such agreement will override any parental objection and render any removal of the child by the parent unlawful. However where an accommodated child is under 16 years of age the expressed views of that child, which may include a desire to limit their parents' role in their lives and to restrict the passage of information to their parents about their location, schooling, and social activities, are unlikely, by themselves, to be sufficient to absolve the local authority from complying with their statutory duties.

9.97 The court cannot make any of the s 8 of the Children Act 1989 orders (save for a residence order) where a child is in the care of the local authority by virtue of a care order. This restriction[31] will not apply if the child is accommodated by virtue of s 20. A local authority cannot apply for a residence order or a contact order.[32] The court cannot exercise its powers to make a specific issue order or prohibited steps order with a view to achieving a result which could be achieved by making a residence or contact order or in any way denied to the High Court as a result of s 100(2).[33] Section 100(2) would prevent for example any order requiring a child to be placed in the care or under the supervision of the local authority, so as to require the accommodation of the child or for the purpose of giving the local authority power to determine any question which has arisen or may arise relating to the exercise of parental responsibility.

9.98 There is nothing to prevent a specific issue order or prohibited steps order being made with respect to a child who is accommodated rather than 'in care'. These orders may be used to:

- limit or prevent a particular course of action by a parent;

- determine a specific dispute over the manner in which a particular aspect of parental responsibility should be exercised.

---

[30] See also the case of *Re K (Children with Disabilities: Wardship)* [2012] 2 FLR 745.
[31] Section 9(1) Children Act 1989 read with section 105(1).
[32] Section 9(2) CA 1989.
[33] Section 9(5) CA 1989.

9.99   These orders cannot be used however to:

- give the local authority the decision making power on those issues;

- determine where the child should live; or

- place the child in care/accommodation or under supervision.

9.100   If a local authority intends to use a prohibited steps order or specific issue order to determine any issue arising between itself and the parents of an accommodated child it will need to obtain the permission of the court.[34]

9.101   This s 8 route would also be available to the accommodated child where they sought to limit the role played by their parents in their day-to-day lives. The child would also need to seek the permission of the court to commence any such application. The court would need to be satisfied that the child had sufficient understanding to make the proposed application before it could grant permission to issue the application.

9.102   In appropriate circumstances it may be necessary for declaratory relief to be sought from the court to enable such limits to be imposed.

9.103   This was the approach adopted in *Re C (Care: Consultation with Parents Not in Child's Best Interests)*.[35] Although that case involved a child in the care of the local authority through a care order there is nothing to suggest that it would be an inappropriate procedure to adopt where the same issues arise in the voluntary accommodation setting.

9.104   The child in *Re C* was 13 years of age, had been raped and indecently assaulted by the father and now clearly stated that she did not want any form of contact with him or for him to be consulted about major decisions or to be given information about her progress.

9.105   The court indicated that it is only a very exceptional case that would attract this kind of relief. A parent is entitled to be fully involved, normally, in the decision-making process relating to his or her child and if not involved, then at least informed about it. In so far as this engaged the father's rights to a family life, then by the same token it engaged the child's right to privacy and a family life. In reaching the decision that the child's rights overwhelmed all others in the case the court noted that the local authority was not making any very significant decision about the child such as adoption or a move abroad, but was merely working out the details of the child's care.[36]

9.106   As can be seen from the cases referred to during the course of this chapter remedies detailed in this book including complaints, judicial review,

---

[34]   Section 10(2) and (3).
[35]   [2006] 2 FLR 787.
[36]   See also *Re P (Children Act 1989 ss 22 and 26: Local Authority Compliance)* [2000] 2 FLR 910.

declaratory relief and human rights challenges should also be considered by local authorities, parents and children where a child is accommodated and the limits of exercise of parental responsibility cannot be agreed.

Chapter 10

DEATH AND SERIOUS HARM TO CHILDREN

SECTION 1 – SERIOUS CASE REVIEWS, CHILD PRACTICE REVIEWS AND CHILD DEATH REVIEWS

Introduction

10.1 Elsewhere in the book we have considered the way in which decisions or outcomes in individual cases can be challenged, for example by applications for judicial review or damages claims arising out of negligence or breach of human rights. However, very often a real consideration for families faced with the consequences of mistakes made by the State is not merely a need for explanations as to how this has happened to them and their child, but also a desire to prevent it happening to others.

10.2 These combined questions of how did it happen and how can we prevent it happening again lead to a brief consideration of the role that local authorities and families can play in the processes which follow the death or serious injury of a child. These processes are not limited to children already known to or in the care of the local authority.

10.3 Child-care lawyers are probably familiar with the idea of a serious case review but less so with the operation of inquests. What follows below is an introduction to the statutory provisions and primary factors affecting the operation of both processes. Families may wish to know what voice they can have in attempting to understand what went wrong.

10.4 At the time of writing (February 2013) the serious case review systems, both English[1] and Welsh[2] (which have notable differences), are undergoing review. The inquest system also faces the prospect of changes if outstanding

---

[1] On the 12 June 2012 Tim Loughton MP Parliamentary Under Secretary of State for Children and Families launched the English consultation process on revised child protection statutory guidance. The consultation document covering serious case reviews is entitled *Learning and Improvement Guidance*. The consultation process closed on 4 September 2012.

[2] The Welsh Government consultation process opened on 9 January 2012 and closed on 2 April 2012. The proposals for the new system were contained in a document entitled *'Welsh Government: Protecting Children in Wales Arrangements for Multi Agency Child Practice Reviews'*. The draft guidance consultation document was issued under Number WG-14087 and the consultation response dated June 2012 under Number WG-15962. The new framework and regulations took effect on 1 January 2013. See footnote 7.

provisions in existing legislation are brought into force.[3] People referring to these parts of this work should therefore be aware of the need to check whether or not the prospective changes highlighted below have come into effect by the time of reading.

Local Safeguarding Children Board functions

10.5 The Children Act 2004 established Local Safeguarding Children Boards (LSCB) for each local authority area.[4] The board was to have such functions as the Secretary of State prescribed by regulation; in particular reference was made to the functions of review or investigation.[5]

10.6 For local authorities in England, s 16 requires the local authority and each of their board partners to have regard to any guidance given by the secretary of state concerning the exercise of their functions relating to LSCBs. Section 34 makes similar provision for Wales with the requirement that the authority must have regard to guidance issued by the Welsh Assembly.

10.7 Separate regulations exist for both England and for Wales.

English LSCB Regulations[6]

10.8 In the English version, reg 5(1)(e) makes provision for the LSCB to undertake reviews of serious cases and to advise the authority and their Board partners on lessons to be learned. Regulation 5(2) defines a 'serious case' for this purpose as a case where abuse or neglect of a child is known or suspected and either the child has died; or the child has been seriously harmed and there is cause for concern as to the way in which the authority, their Board partners or other relevant persons have worked together to safeguard the child. This responsibility arises where the child concerned is a child in the area of the authority by which the Board was established.

10.9 In addition to serious case reviews the Boards are invested with additional functions relating to child deaths by reg 6.[7] These include not only the collection and analysing of information about each death of a child normally resident in the area of the authority, but also the putting into place of procedures for ensuring that there is a co-ordinated response by the authority, their Board partners and other relevant persons to an unexpected death. The child death review functions are compulsory.

---

3   See Coroner's and Justice Act 2009.
4   See s 13 for England and s 31 for Wales.
5   See s 14 for England and s 32 for Wales.
6   Local Safeguarding Children Boards Regulations 2006 (SI 2006/90).
7   There is not currently a separate child death review process in Wales. Pilot projects were set up and in 2012 an evaluation was published. The resulting report *Evalution of the Child Death Review Pilot Project in Wales* Government Social Research Number 10/2012: Cordis Bright Ltd recommended continuation of funding to allow the continuation of the system.

Welsh LSCB regulations[8]

10.10 In the 2006 Welsh version, pre-amendment, reg 3(1)(e) made provision for the Board to undertake serious case reviews in accordance with reg 4. Regulation 4 contained detailed provisions that were not replicated in the English statutory instrument but were instead, in the main, dealt with within the English guidance. In Wales, the Board was required to undertake a review (a 'serious case review') where within the area of the Board, abuse of a child is known or suspected, and a child had died, or had sustained a potentially life-threatening injury, or had sustained serious and permanent impairment of health or development. The Board was also empowered to undertake such a review where a child within its area suffered harm which did not fall within the preceding definitions.

10.11 The regulations set out the purpose of the serious case review as identifying steps that might be taken to prevent a similar death or harm occurring.

10.12 In the 2006 Welsh regulation, pre-amendment, reg 4(4)–(6) made provision as to the production of an overview report and of an anonymised summary. The regulations also provided the framework as to the circulation and publication of the reports.

10.13 The 2012 amendments to the 2006 regulations, which came into effect on the 1 January 2013,[9] replace serious case reviews with *'child practice reviews'* which include *'concise child practice reviews'* and *'extended child practice reviews'*.[10] Regulation 4 is revoked and replaced with new regs 4A and 4B.

The concise child practice review

10.14 The concise child practice review is to be undertaken where there is a death, potentially life threatening injury or serious and permanent impairment of health or development where the child was neither on the child protection register nor a looked after child on any date during the 6 months preceding the death or injury (for cases involving death or injury), or on any date during the 6 months preceding the date upon which the local authority identifies that a child has sustained serious and permanent impairment of health or development.

The extended child practice review

10.15 The duty to conduct an extended child practice review arises where the child was on the child protection register and/or was a looked after child on any date during the 6 months preceding the death or injury or date upon which the

---

[8] The Local Safeguarding Children Boards (Wales) Regulations 2006 as amended by the Local Safeguarding Children Boards (Wales) (Amendment) Regulations 2012 which came into force on 1 January 2013.

[9] The Local Safeguarding Children Boards (Wales) (Amendment) Regulations 2012 (W 222) (SI 2012/1712).

[10] For assistance on the associated guidance see **10.62** et seq below.

authority identifies that a child has sustained serious and permanent impairment of health and development.

10.16   The purpose of the child practice review is to identify any steps that can be taken by Board partners or other bodies to achieve improvements in multi-agency child protection practice.

10.17   In undertaking a child practice review the Board is required to ensure that the perspective of the child who is the subject of the review is obtained and that the child's perspective contributes to the process so far as is practicable and appropriate to the circumstances of the case. In addition the Board must ensure that the perspectives of members of family of the child who is the subject of the review are obtained and that these perspectives contribute to the process so far as is practicable and appropriate to the case.

10.18   The production and distribution of written reports differs under the new reg 4 to that under the previous system. The reports will feed into a new multi-agency learning event.

10.19   The new system places emphasis on the use of multi-agency professional forums as the foundation for learning and improving the quality of work with families. The forums have two key purposes (i) case learning and (ii) dissemination of new knowledge and findings.

10.20   As with the separate statutory instruments for England and Wales there is separate guidance for the two countries. The source materials, key elements and impending changes are set out in the following paragraphs.

Guidance – English

Chapters 7 and 8: working together to safeguard children (2010)

10.21   Chapter 7 deals with guidance on child death review processes whilst Chapter 8 deals with serious case reviews.

10.22   Both Chapters are contained within Part 1 of the guide and as such are issued in the form of statutory guidance under s 7 of the Local Authority Social Services Act 1970. The guidance should therefore be complied with by local authorities carrying out their social services functions, unless local circumstances indicate exceptional reasons that justify a variation.

10.23   In addition Chapters 7 and 8 are issued under s 16 of the Children Act 2004 requiring children's service authorities and their statutory partners to have regard to any guidance given to them, in exercising their functions relating to LSCB, by the Secretary of State. They must, therefore, take the guidance into account and if they decide to depart from it they must have clear reasons for doing so.

Child death review processes

10.24   There are two main processes under this heading:

- The broader overview of all child deaths up to the age of 18 years.

- The rapid response by a group of key professionals who come together for the purpose of enquiring into and evaluating each unexpected death of a child.

It is the latter category that will be considered in the greatest detail.

Involvement of parents and family

10.25   Local Safeguarding Children Boards are reminded within the guidance at para 7.7 that it is vitally important to establish mechanisms for appropriately informing and involving parents and other family members in both processes.

10.26   In appropriate circumstances reference to 'parents' should be taken to include carers and 'family members' to include siblings.

10.27   It is acknowledged that in addition to the need to inform parents and family members that the child's death is to be reviewed these individuals often have significant information and questions to contribute to the review process. Paragraph 7.36 includes within the functions of the child death overview panel the seeking of relevant information not only from professionals but also from family members. Further the panel must provide relevant information to those professionals involved with the child's family so that they in turn can convey that information in a sensitive and timely manner to the family.

10.28   It is important however to recognise that there are limits to the review process. Family members should understand that the key to the process is the learning of lessons in order to improve the health, safety and well-being of children generally and to assist in preventing further such deaths. The process is not undertaken with the aim of establishing culpability or apportioning blame.

10.29   Arrangements should be made by the responsible panel[11] to ensure that wherever necessary arrangements are made for the family to meet with relevant professionals to help answer their questions.

10.30   A further function of the panel identified in para 7.36 is monitoring the support and assessment services offered to families of children who have died.

---

[11]   The LSCB sub-committee responsible for the reviewing information on child deaths is the child death overview panel.

10.31 The extent of the provision of information to family members may be affected by the existence of parallel enquiries such as those by the police and the coroner. It is suggested that any limitations however are kept under regular review by all agencies involved.

Definition of unexpected death[12]

10.32 This is the death of an infant or child (less than 18 years old) which:

- was not anticipated as a significant possibility, for example 24 hours before the death; or

- where there was a similarly unexpected collapse or incident leading to or precipitating the events which led to the death.

Specific responsibilities relating to unexpected death[13]

10.33 The guidance intends that those professionals involved with a child (both before and/or after the death) should come together to respond to that death. The examples cited in the guidance include the following: paediatrician, GP, nurse, health visitor, midwife, mental health professional, substance misuse worker, social worker, youth offending team worker, probation or police officer and other workers specific to that child's circumstances. Not mentioned in the guidance but one area of professional contact, which perhaps ought to be considered, is a member from the teaching profession involved with any child.

10.34 The joint responsibilities of these professionals as identified in the guidance include:

- Responding quickly to the unexpected death of a child.

- Making immediate enquiries into and evaluating the reasons for and circumstances of the death, in agreement with the coroner (the guidance also indicates that a protocol should be agreed with the local coronial service).

- Undertaking the types of enquiries/investigations that relate to the current responsibilities of their respective organisations when a child dies unexpectedly including liaising with those who have ongoing responsibilities for other family members.

- Collecting information in a standard nationally agreed manner.

- Providing support to the bereaved family, and where appropriate referring on to specialist bereavement services.

---

[12] See para 7.21 of the guidance.
[13] See paras 7.48–7.50 of the guidance.

- Following the death through and maintaining contact at regular intervals with family members and other professionals who have ongoing responsibilities for other family members, to ensure they are kept informed and are kept up to date with information about the child's death.

Reporting to the coroner[14]

10.35 When a child dies unexpectedly and no doctor is able to issue a medical certificate of the cause of death, the child's death must be reported to the coroner. Information relating to the death arising from the rapid response process should also be passed to the coroner. Where the coroner is involved a review of all relevant medical, social and educational records should be included in a report to the coroner prepared jointly by the lead professionals in each agency.[15] This report should be delivered to the coroner within 28 days of the death unless some of the crucial information is not yet available.

Serious case reviews

10.36 The guidance stresses that the purpose of a serious case review (SCR) is for agencies and individuals to learn lessons to improve the way in which they work.

In particular they are to:[16]

- establish what lessons are to be learned from the case about the way in which local professionals and organisations work individually and together to safeguard and promote the welfare of children;

- identify clearly what those lessons are both within and between agencies, how and within what timescales they will be acted on, and what is expected to change as a result; and

- improve intra and inter agency working and better safeguard and promote the welfare of children.

10.37 The guidance specifically states they are **not to**:

- inquire into how a child died or was seriously harmed

- inquire into who is culpable

It indicates that these are issues for the coroner and criminal courts to determine as appropriate.

---

[14] More detailed consideration is given to the role of the coroner under the separate heading of inquests at **10.78** et seq below.
[15] See for example para 7.84 of the guidance.
[16] See paras 8.5–8.7 of the guidance.

10.38 Further the guidance specifies that serious case reviews are **not** part of any disciplinary inquiry or process relating to individual practitioners. Whilst they may be conducted at the same time as any disciplinary procedures they should be conducted separately from disciplinary action.

10.39 Clearly when a child dies or is seriously harmed, and abuse or neglect is known or suspected to be a factor, the first priority of local organisations should be to consider immediately whether there are other children who are suffering or likely to suffer, significant harm and who require safeguarding. Where concerns exist about the welfare of an individual child or, for example, siblings of a child who has died, been neglected or injured the usual child protection procedures should be followed. Then organisations should consider whether there are any lessons to be learned about the ways in which they work individually and together to safeguard and promote welfare of children within their area generally.

When should a serious case review be undertaken

10.40 A SCR must always be undertaken when:[17]

- A child dies (including death by suspected suicide) and abuse or neglect is known or suspected to be a factor in the death. This is irrespective of whether children's social care has been, or is, involved with the child or the family. This category would include the need to hold a review into the death of a child killed by a parent or close relative with mental illness, known to substance abuse or to perpetrate domestic violence.

- A child dies in custody (whether in police custody, on remand or following sentencing, in a young offenders institution (YOI) or a secure training centre (STC)).[18]

- A child dies in a secure children's home.

- A child dies whilst detained under the Mental Capacity Act 2005.

10.41 In addition the LSCB should consider undertaking a SCR whenever a child has been seriously harmed in the following circumstances:[19]

- a child sustains a potentially life threatening injury or serious and permanent impairment of physical and/or mental health and development through abuse and neglect; or

- a child has been seriously harmed as a result of being subjected to sexual abuse; or

---

[17] See paras 8.9–8.10.
[18] Deaths in custody or during transport to and from custody are also likely to involve the Prisons and Probation Ombudsman.
[19] See para 8.11–8.12.

- a parent has been murdered and a domestic homicide review is being initiated under the Domestic Violence Act 2004; or

- a child has been seriously harmed following a violent assault perpetrated by another child or an adult,

and the case gives rise to concerns about the way in which local professionals and services worked together to safeguard and promote the welfare of children.

10.42 The guidance also suggests that it would be appropriate in other circumstances to conduct a serious case review where it is likely that the review could result in useful lessons; these include:

- Where there was clear evidence of a child having suffered or been likely to suffer significant harm which was not recognised by organisations in contact with the child, or which was not shared with other organisations or which was not acted upon appropriately.

- Where the abuse occurred in an institutional setting (which might include schools, nurseries, children's or family centres, YOI, STC, immigration removal centres etc).

- Where the child was looked after by the local authority including when the child had run away from a care setting.

- Where the child was a member of a family only recently moved to the UK such as asylum seekers or temporary workers.

- Where the child was the subject of or had previously been the subject of a child protection plan or been on the child protection register.

Who may start the SCR process?

10.43 Any professional or agency may refer a case to the LSCB if they believe that there are important lessons for intra- and/or inter-agency working to be learned from the case. Likely sources of referrals will be local authorities, children's guardians, independent reviewing officers as well as health professionals.

Responsibility for determining whether to hold a SCR

10.44 Ultimately it is the responsibility of the chair of the LSCB to determine whether or not a SCR should take place in any particular case. The LSCB chair is likely to receive advice and recommendations on this aspect, and on the terms of reference, from a SCR sub-committee. Once the decision is taken to conduct a SCR a SCR panel should be convened to manage the process. The chair of the SCR panel should not be a member of any LSCB involved in the SCR, an employee of any of the agencies involved in the SCR or the overview report author.[20]

10.45 If the criteria are not met for a full SCR then it may be valuable to complete 'individual management reviews' within agencies concerned where there are lessons to be learned about the way in which staff worked within one agency rather than how the agencies worked together. In any event if there is to be a SCR each relevant service should undertake an individual management review of its involvement with the child and family. An important element of these individual reviews will be the drawing up of chronologies. Further assistance as to the scope and format of the individual management reviews is given in the guidance.[21] Those conducting the management reviews should not have been directly concerned with the child or family nor should they have been the immediate line managers of any practitioners involved with the child or family.

10.46 The guidance again, when considering the scope of the review, stresses that consideration should be given to how the child (in cases not involving a death), surviving siblings, parents and other family members should contribute to the SCR and who should be responsible for facilitating their involvement.[22] Thought should also be given to how they are informed of the findings of the SCR.

The overview report and executive summary

10.47 The purpose of the overview report is to bring together and draw overall conclusions from the information available through the individual management reports, child death review process and reports commissioned from any other relevant interests. Where appropriate the overview report may include findings from other relevant processes such as care or criminal proceedings, an inquest or inquiry. The outline format for the overview reports is again set out in the guidance.[23]

10.48 The author of the overview report should be a person who is independent of all the local agencies and professionals involved and of the LSCB. The author should not be the chair of the LSCB, the SCR sub-committee or the SCR panel.

10.49 An executive summary should be prepared in accordance with the outline format set out in the guidance and should be made public. The guidance stipulates that the content of the executive summary will need to be suitably anonymised in order to protect the identity of children, relevant family members and others and to comply with the Data Protection Act 1998.

---

[20] For fuller detail on composition of SCR sub-committee and panel see paras 8.14–8.16.
[21] See for example paras 8.34–8.39.
[22] See para 8.20.
[23] See para 8.40.

Changes to the original 2010 scheme were identified in a letter from Tim Loughton (Parliamentary Under Secretary of State for Children and Families) dated 10 June 2010. This required the publication of the overview reports (rather than just the executive summaries) for all new SCRs initiated on or after 10 June 2010.[24] It identified the need for the overview report and executive summary to be anonymised and not to contain identifying details. The overview reports should therefore be published with the executive summaries unless there are compelling reasons relating to the welfare of any children directly concerned in the case for this not to happen.

10.50 The revised guidance set out in this letter retained the principle that the individual management reviews should not be made publicly available.

10.51 The identities of those to whom the overview report or executive summary should be circulated are specified in the guidance.[25] The guidance recognises that the child who was seriously harmed and members of the child's family have an interest in the completed SCR (as well as professionals, the public and the media). It also acknowledges that the competing interests involved are difficult to balance as they involve principles of confidentiality with respect to personal information, accountability of public services and the maintenance of public confidence in the process of internal review.

10.52 Not surprisingly the publication of serious case reviews and executive summaries can lead to strong feelings from parents, family members and on behalf of children (as well as professionals whose actions or inactions may come under public scrutiny) particularly in cases where a family member or member of the child's household is ultimately, through other court processes, identified as being responsible for the death of a child.

10.53 The issue of publication has recently proven amenable to challenge and determination through the court process as a result of the need to obtain the correct balancing of competing Art 8 and Art 10 rights. This is illustrated in *Re X and Y*,[26] a case heard in the Court of Appeal which arose under the Welsh system of serious case reviews.

10.54 The first instance judge, exercising the inherent jurisdiction, ruled on a local authority's application to vary a reporting restriction order to allow them to publish the anonymised executive summary. The relaxation of the order was supported by various media organisations but opposed by the parents and the children. There was no argument that the High Court judge had correctly directed himself as to the law to be applied but the appellant (the children) asserted that he had failed to apply the proper approach and was plainly wrong when reaching a decision that (subject to further redaction) the order should be relaxed so as to permit the publication of the executive summary. In particular

---

[24]   The government published two SCR overview reports relating to Peter Connelly on the 26 October 2010.
[25]   See paras 8.43–8.46
[26]   [2012] EWCA Civ 1500.

the appellant asserted that the judge had failed to provide the intense focus on the children's interests as demanded by Lord Steyn in *Re S*.[27]

10.55   The Court of Appeal accepted that a more drastic form of redaction than that approved by the judge was required if the balance between the public interest in the publication of the executive summary and the private interests of the children was to be struck properly and appropriately. This was against the background noted by Lord Justice Munby in para 55 of the judgment that:

> 'here were children in a fragile situation about whose welfare the judge had "very real concerns". If the executive summary is published in the form authorised by the judge, the children will suffer from the inevitable media reporting which is likely to be extremely upsetting to them. The children, Y in particular, will have to live with the realisation that a painful part of their intensely private family history has now been exposed to the world and his wife. And this public knowledge of what has hitherto been private may well expose Y in particular to unkind treatment or worse at the hands of other children at school or others in the local community. None of the proposed redactions will render these consequences either less likely or less damaging.'

10.56   However it is important to note that the Court of Appeal expressed the view that the statutory scheme contemplates, and compliance with the convention, requires that what is published must be anonymised to such extent as is necessary (in the Strasbourg sense) to protect Art 8 interests of the relevant children, family members and others. The Court of Appeal also considered that, whilst there could be circumstances where the Art 8 claims are so dominant as to preclude publication altogether, these would be very rare. The court also accepted that if all that could be published were recommendations about disembodied events that, whilst unsatisfactory, must be better than publishing nothing.

Impending changes: Working together to safeguard children – 2012 draft statutory guidance on learning and improvement

10.57   Tim Loughton's letter of the 10 June also announced the appointment of Professor Eileen Munroe to conduct an independent review to improve child protection. Her review resulted in the consultation process on three documents to replace the 2010 *Working Together* guidance. The detailed guidance for serious case reviews and child death reviews is to be replaced by the document *Statutory Guidance on Learning and Improvement*. The consultation opened in June 2012 and closed in September 2012.

10.58   As at the 14 January 2013 the government's response to enquiry as to when the guidance might be reissued was as follows:

---

[27]   *In Re S (A Child) (Identification: Restrictions on Publication)* [2004] UKHL, [2005] 1 AC 593.

'The Government is currently considering the consultation responses received on the revised guidance. We are now working with Directors of Children's Services, The Royal Colleges and others to get this right. We will be publishing the revised guidance in due course.'

10.59 The emphasis in the revised guidance is on the principle that learning reviews (including child death reviews, serious case reviews and management reviews of a child protection incident falling below the threshold for an SCR) are not ends in themselves but their purpose is to identify improvements that are needed. The findings should be translated into programmes of action which lead to sustainable improvements and the prevention of death, serious injury or harm to children. Transparency and accountability are stressed.

10.60 The notable changes proposed relating to serious case reviews and child death reviews include:

- Reports from cases meeting the SCR criteria must be published in full, including the LSCBs response to the review findings. The reports therefore must be written with publication in mind and should not contain personal information relating to surviving children, family members or others. This would include detailed chronologies, family histories and genograms.

- LSCBs should also make other information available to the public about the issues identified in the reviews and the audits and actions taken in response.

- The requirement that the SCRs and management reviews are conducted using systems methodology as recommended by Professor Munro so that information is gathered not only about what professionals did in the case but why they took that action and what this reveals about the way in which local services operate.

- More specific requirements as to the qualifications of those to conduct the reviews are set out.

- The principle of proportionality of approach to the scale and level of complexity of the issues being examined is introduced.

- The responsibilities of the child death overview panel will include determining whether the death was deemed preventable.[28]

The guidance is significantly shorter than the 2010 version.

---

[28] The proposed definition of 'preventable death' is set out Appendix 1 as 'those in which modifiable factors may have contributed to the death. These factors are defined as those which, by means of nationally or local achievable interventions, could be modified to reduce the risk of future child deaths. In reviewing the death of each child, the CDOP should consider modifiable factors, for example in family provision, and consider what action could be taken locally and what action could be taken at a regional or national level'.

10.61 The guidance reiterates the need for clarity about how families including surviving children will be involved in the reviews and how their expectations are to be met. Similarly the guidance reiterates the importance of the need to keep families up to date with information about the children's death. (Note both the 2010 and 2012 proposed guidance include flow charts for child deaths and unexpected deaths.)

Guidance: Welsh

10.62 The new guidance to be applied from the 1 January 2013 is entitled *Protecting Children in Wales: Guidance for Arrangements for Multi-Agency Child Practice Reviews*. The guidance is available on the Welsh Government Website at www.cymru.gov.uk. The guidance replaces chapter 10, *Serious Case Reviews in Safeguarding Children: Working Together Under the Children Act 2004*. The other existing chapters remain in force, although they are due to be revised to reflect the new legislative framework currently contained in the Social Services and Well-being (Wales) Bill.

10.63 Published at the same time is the associated guidance *Protecting Children in Wales: Child Practice Reviews: Guide for Facilitating Learning Events*. Only key points in the guidance or differences from the previous guidance will be highlighted in this section.

10.64 The guidance identifies that there are important features in the new framework which marked it out from the existing case review system. The following statements should perhaps be highlighted:

- It involves agencies, staff and families in a collective endeavour to reflect and learn from what has happened in order to improve practice in the future, with a focus on accountability and not on culpability.

- It recognises the impact of the tragic circumstances of non-accidental child deaths or serious harm on families and on staff and provides opportunities for serious incidents to be reviewed in a culture that is experienced as fair and just by all concerned.

- It focuses on key learning identified through the review process to result in relevant recommendations and action to improve future practice recorded in anonymised reports which are published by LSCBs.

10.65 As with the proposed changes to the English system it is stated to provide a more streamlined and proportionate approach with more constructive use of resources than the previous system. The focus is on key learning identified through the review and on action to improve future practice.

10.66 Key principles are identified which include taking account of the wishes and views of children and families in individual cases. The new framework is stated to be in accord with the Convention on the Rights of the Child.

10.67 A referral of a case will in the first place be made to the LSCB business manager child practice review who will ensure the LSCB chair is informed and will arrange for the referral to be sent on to the LSCB standing child practice review sub-group or sub-committee.

The concise review

10.68 Once the decision is taken to hold a concise review a multi-agency review panel will be established. A time-line of a maximum of 12 months preceding the incident should be prepared (this should only be exceeded in exceptional circumstances).[29] Agencies that have been involved with the child and family will be requested to provide information of contact with the family, a timeline of significant events and a brief analysis of the situation and recommendations if appropriate. These will replace the existing independent management reviews. The panel may ask for further clarification from the agencies involved and the terms of reference for the review may be amended or extended.

The reviewer

10.69 The panel will identify and commission a reviewer who must be independent of the case management. The quality and experience of the reviewer is crucial and the skills needed include a thorough knowledge of child protection systems, issues, responsibilities and practice, an understanding of multi-disciplinary working, an ability to enquire and communicate about practice with professionals and with children and family members.

Involvement of family in concise review[30]

10.70 In order to incorporate the perspective and experience of family members (such as the child, siblings, parents, carers, grandparents or other appropriate significant family members) into the review process, the review panel will need to consider how this may be most effectively achieved. Suggestions in the guidance include contacting and talking to family members about the purpose of the review and identifying messages or questions they would want to contribute. The form of this contact is not prescribed but may include the appointed reviewer meeting the child and family members. Appropriate arrangements will also need to be made for reporting back at the conclusion of the review.

Child practice review report and outline action plan

10.71 In the annex to the guidance a template is provided for this anonymised report which is to be prepared and submitted to the review panel at the end of

---

[29] In addition the timeline may be extended to include decisions and actions following the incident.
[30] See for example paras 5.30–5.35.

the process. The report is to be published on the LSCB website for a minimum of 12 weeks as well as being provided to the Safeguarding team of the Welsh Government. The publication of the report will be the same with the extended review. An outline action plan should also be prepared and discussed. The plan should reflect the learning identified in the review report, should focus on outcomes and should indicate how the actions are intended to make a difference to local systems and child protection practice. It is intended that the finalised action plan will be reviewed and progress monitored by the review sub group and reported on to the board. Once the action has been completed the plan will be signed off by the board and a report made to the safeguarding team of the Welsh Government and to the Inspectorates.

10.72 The Welsh Government should be informed of every case that meets the criteria for a concise review that has been considered by the review sub-group. If the final decision of discussions between the chair of the LSCB and the Board has been to decline to hold a review, this will also need to be notified to the Welsh Government in writing with reasons and highlighting any conflicting views.

Extended child practice reviews

10.73 The additional issues to be addressed by the extended review will include:

- whether previous relevant information or history about the child and/or family members was known and taken into account in the assessment, planning and decision making for the child and family;

- whether the child protection, looked after child or pathway plans were robust and appropriate;

- whether the plan was effectively implemented, monitored and reviewed;

- whether agencies challenged each other regarding the effectiveness of the plan;

- whether respective statutory duties of agencies working with the child and family were fulfilled and whether there were obstacles or difficulties preventing agencies from fulfilling their duties.

10.74 The 12-month timeline for the concise review may be extended in the extended review when necessary to reflect the time the child was on the child protection register or within the care system. The guidance suggests that it can be extended up to two years where circumstances warrant but the focus of the analysis should remain on current practice.

10.75 The extended review should be conducted by two reviewers, rather than one. One reviewer should provide an external perspective and one reviewer should deal with the local context. Both will be responsible for writing the child practice review report.

10.76 The draft guidance includes as an Annex a separate reviewer's guide. This guide also includes reference to the involvement of family members in the process and in 'debriefing' or feedback whether through a further visit, letter or phone call.

Further thoughts

10.77 It remains to be seen just how the increased involvement of family members will be received both by professionals and by families. Will this greater role lead to reassurance that all information has been traced and lessons have been learned from the circumstances of their child's death or injury? Will this greater role simply lead to frustration at the lack of the review system providing a direct way of ascribing blame and redress and so feed into the challenges identified elsewhere in this book? Will the review processes themselves now in fact add extra fertile ground for challenge such as judicial review of decisions not to hold a SCR or CPR where the mandatory criteria are not met, or disputes over publication of details in reports?

SECTION 2 – INQUESTS

10.78 As referred to above, it is the inquest system that is designed to answer the question as to how a death occurred. The relevance of inquests to this work relates to the need to consider whether the inquest system can in any way be used to hold a local authority to account where they have, no doubt by omission, been responsible in part for failing to prevent the death of a child known to them. It is after all the duty of the coroner to conduct a full, fair and fearless investigation into the circumstances of the deceased's death.[31]

10.79 Article 2 of the European Convention of Human Rights (ECHR) is not one which child-care practitioners need to refer to on a regular basis. The right to life however is of significant importance to the issues that fall to be considered by the coroner during the course of an inquest.

10.80 It is important to have a basic understanding of the roles and responsibilities of the coroner and the real purpose of the inquest in order not to raise expectations of bereaved family members or indeed to lose sight of the proper role for local authorities within this process.

---

[31] See for example *R (Takoushis) v Inner North London Coroner and another* [2006] 1 WLR 461.

10.81 For very basic assistance on these issues a helpful starting point is the Ministry of Justice *Guide to Coroners and Inquests* (March 2012). This can be found online at www.justice.gov.uk.

The statutory framework and questions for the inquest

10.82 The Coroner's Act 1988 and the Coroner's Rules 1984 still govern the inquest process.

10.83 Section 8 of the Act provides that it shall be the duty of the coroner to hold an inquest where he is informed that the body of a person is lying within his district and there is reasonable cause to suspect that the deceased died a violent or unnatural death, a sudden death where the cause is unknown or has died in prison.

10.84 The inquest may be held either with or without a jury however s 8(3) prescribes the circumstances in which the coroner must summon a jury. These include deaths in prison, in police custody or as a result of an injury caused by a police officer in the purported execution of his duty and further where the death occurred in circumstances the continuance or possible recurrence of which is prejudicial to the health or safety of the public or any section of the public.

10.85 The coroner may exercise his discretion to summon a jury in other cases as provided for by s 8(4).

10.86 Section 11(5) sets out the matters that the coroner shall at the end of the process certify. These are:

* who the deceased was;

* how, when and where the deceased came by his death.[32]

10.87 Rule 36(1) of the Rules clarifies that neither the coroner nor the jury shall express any opinion on any other matters.

10.88 Section 11(5) provides that where the deceased came by his death by murder, manslaughter or infanticide the purpose of the proceedings shall not include the finding of any person guilty of the murder, manslaughter or infanticide.

---

[32] The 'how' may be interpreted in its narrow sense or in a broader sense meaning 'how and in what circumstances'. The narrow interpretation will lead to what has become known as a *Jamieson* inquest (after *R v North Humberside Coroner ex p Jamieson* [1995] QB 1); the broader will lead to what has become known as a *Middleton* inquest after *R (Middleton) v West Somerset Coroner* [2004] 2 AC 182 (HL). For assistance on when the broader inquest will be permitted see the paragraphs on the relevance of Art 2 right to life obligations at **10.94** et seq below.

10.89 Rule 42 of the rules clarifies that no verdict shall be framed in such a way as to appear to determine any question of criminal liability on the part of a named person or of civil liability.

10.90 Rule 22 also provides that no witness at an inquest shall be obliged to answer any question tending to incriminate himself.

10.91 Rule 43 however states the following:

> A coroner who believes that action should be taken to prevent the recurrence of fatalities similar to that in respect of which the inquest is being held may announce at the inquest that he is reporting the matter in writing to the person or authority who may have power to take such action and he may report the matter accordingly.

10.92 In *R (Middleton) v West Somerset Coroner*,[33] Lord Bingham of Cornhill indicated that the prohibitions set out above in rr 36 and 42 should continue to be respected even though *Middleton* itself changed the interpretation to be given to the question 'how' a deceased came by his death in certain types of cases. In considering these provisions he stated:

> 'The prohibition in rule 36(2) of the expression of opinion on matters not comprised within sub-rule (1) must continue to be respected. But it must be read with reference to the broader interpretation of "how" in section 11(5)(b)(ii) and rule 36(1) and does not preclude conclusions of fact as opposed to expressions of opinion. However the jury's factual conclusion is conveyed, rule 42 should not be infringed. Thus there must be no finding of criminal liability on the part of a named person. Nor must the verdict appear to determine any question of civil liability. Acts or omissions may be recorded, but expressions suggestive of civil liability, in particular "neglect" or "carelessness" and related expressions should be avoided.'

10.93 Rule 20 sets out the entitlement to examine witnesses. Rule 20(2) identifies the people who shall have the right to examine a witness at an inquest either in person or by an authorised advocate. These include a parent, child, spouse, civil partner, partner and any personal representative of the deceased. A further category of person entitled to examine witnesses is any person whose act or omission or that of his agent or servant may in the opinion of the coroner have caused, or contributed to the death of the deceased. The coroner can also determine that someone is a properly interested person and this will confer the right to examine witnesses.

10.94 The coroner has a duty to notify a spouse, near relative or personal representative of the deceased (if their name and address are known to him) of the date hour and place of the inquest. This duty also extends to any other person who in the opinion of the coroner falls within r 20(2), or anyone who has asked the coroner to notify him of the date of the inquest and has provided him with a telephone number or address for the purpose.

---

[33] [2004] UKHL 10, [2004] 2 AC 182, [2004] 2 All ER 465, [2004] 2 WLR 800.

10.95 *Interested persons referred to above in rule 20(2)*: relatives who do not fall within the precise definition specified in r 20(2)(a) may be able to bring themselves within the definition of a 'properly interested person'. In order to qualify as a properly interested person the interest must be more than merely trivial and contrived.

10.96 Section 5(2) of the Coroner's and Justice Act 2009 (when brought into force) will add the additional wording which is discussed in the case law that:

> '... where necessary to avoid a breach of any convention rights (within the meaning of the Human Rights Act 1998) the purpose mentioned in subsection (1)(b) is to be read as including the purpose of ascertaining in what circumstances the deceased came by his or her death.'

The relevance of Article 2

10.97 European and domestic law recognises three possible duties or obligations on the state arising from Art 2:[34]

(i)   **The general duty**. In brief the duty not to take life without justification and to establish a framework of laws, precautions, procedures and means of enforcement which will, to the greatest extent reasonably practicable, protect life.[35] This positive duty to protect life is in place at all times.

(ii) **The procedural duty**. In brief the duty upon the state to investigate. This is only triggered where there is evidence of an arguable or prima facie breach of the duty to protect life. This will require an effective public investigation by an independent official body.[36] This could be discharged by full criminal proceedings or if there are none by an inquest or other suitable and sufficient enquiry. Where the inquest is relied upon to discharge this duty it will need to take the form of the enhanced enquiry known as a '*Middleton*' inquest in the sense that the question to be answered must be how, in the full sense of by what means and in what circumstances, the deceased came by his death.[37]

(iii) **The operational duty**. In brief this adds an additional duty on the state to protect life where an individual is in its care. To establish that the authorities have violated their positive general duty to protect life it must be shown that they knew or ought to have known at the time of the existence of a real and immediate risk to the life of an identified

---

[34]   The categories as set out here are taken from the summary at paras 35–41 of the judgment of Mr Justice Foskett and HHJ Peter Thornton QC in *R (Kent County Council) v HM Coroner for the County of Kent* [2012] EWHC 2768 (Admin).

[35]   *R(Middleton) v West Somerset Coroner* [2004] 2 AC 182 (HL), para [2], Lord Bingham of Cornhill.

[36]   *Middleton* para [3].

[37]   See also the attempts of the Court of Appeal to explain/simply the test for engagement of Art 2 in *LSC v R(on the Application of Humberstone)* [2010] EWCA Civ 1479.

individual and that they failed to take measures within the scope of their power which, judged reasonably, might have been expected to avoid that risk.[38]

10.98 It is important to note that whatever mode of inquiry is adopted an effective investigation requires sufficient public scrutiny to secure accountability and an appropriate level of participation by the next of kin to safeguard their legitimate interests.[39] This has further been interpreted as leading to a duty to provide representation where it is likely to be necessary to enable the next of kin to play an effective part in the proceedings.[40]

10.99 Consideration of the position of family members was also commented upon in *Middleton* where Lord Bingham stated at para [18]:

> '... the deceased's family or next of kin ... like the deceased may be victims. They have been held to have legitimate interests in the conduct of the investigation which is why they must be accorded an appropriate level of participation. An uninformative jury verdict will be unlikely to meet what the House in *Amin* held to be one of the purposes of an article 2 investigation "that those who have lost their relative may at least have the satisfaction of knowing that lessons learned from his death may save the lives of others."'

10.100 Certainly in the European context there is clear authority for the view that a family member of a 'disappeared person' can be a victim of treatment contrary to Art 3 where there are special factors which give the suffering of the family member a dimension and character distinct from the emotional distress which may be regarded as inevitably caused to relatives of a victim of a serious human rights violation so as to amount to inhuman and degrading treatment. It has been suggested that the essence of the violation lies not so much in the disappearance but rather concerns the authorities reactions and attitudes to the situation when it is brought to their attention.[41] Proximity of the family tie will be relevant with weight attaching to the parent-child bond.

10.101 It may be useful to note that whilst not every act which adversely affects moral or physical integrity will interfere with the right to respect for private and family life under Art 8, European case law does not exclude the possibility that treatment which does not reach the severity required for a breach of Art 3 may still be sufficient to breach Art 8.

The relevance to local authority children's services

10.102 The use of the coroner's system has brought intense scrutiny to deaths occurring as a result of police actions, whilst in custody or in situations where negligence has arisen in hospital or mental health settings. It seems so far,

---

[38] *Osman v United Kingdom* (2000) 29 EHRR 245.
[39] *R (Amin) v SSHD* [2003] UKHL 51, [2004] 1 AC 653.
[40] See for example *LSC v R(on the application of Humbestone)* [2010] EWCA Civ 1479.
[41] See for example *Kurt v Turkey* (1998) 27 EHRR 373 and *Timurtas v Turkey* (2001) 33 EHRR 6.

certainly in the sense of reported case law, that the same focus has not yet highlighted deaths within the care system through the prism of the coroner's court. This may be as a result of the approach taken to serious case reviews or it may simply be that with the increasing use and understanding of the Art 2 arguments this will prove to be an area which finds itself increasingly under the spotlight in the future.

10.103 The following are two examples of reported cases where the consideration of a death of a child known to children's services has come under scrutiny.

R (Kent County Council) v HM Coroner for the County of Kent[42]

10.104 The case considers the application by Kent County Council for judicial review of the decisions of HM Coroner for Kent that:

(i)   Article 2 of the European Convention of Human Rights applied to the inquest of a child aged 14 years at the time of his death (Edward Barry); and

(ii) the inquest should be held with a jury.

Brief facts

10.105 Edward was found dead in the flat of a friend of an apparent self-administered overdose of methadone. The social services department had been involved with Edward and his family some nine months prior to his death when his parents sought support due to problems Edward was experiencing including absences from home, the use of drink and drugs, sleeping rough, being brought home by the police drunk or drugged and associating with street drinkers and drug takers. Both his parents and his school expressed concerns to the local authority. His parents sought, through social services, alternative accommodation for him. A consultant psychiatrist, at the time of a local authority core assessment, indicated to the local authority that Edward was at risk, the local authority closed the file, it is said, indicating that the responsibility for him lay with his parents. A request by the parents for a multi-agency intervention was not actioned by the local authority. Approximately 4 months after the core assessment the psychiatrist recommended a secure placement for Edward. The local authority assessed him as being a child in need within s 17 of the Children Act 1989. In accordance with the parents' wishes attempts were made to find a 7 day respite foster placement for him but none was available. A subsequent request by the family for the provision of accommodation was refused. Both the Coroner's Court and the Administrative Court were provided with the serious case review executive summary which suggested there were 'many missed opportunities' and a large number of shortcomings on the part of the local authority.

---

[42] [2012] EWHC 2768 (Admin).

Acknowledged failings

10.106　For the purposes of the judicial review hearing the council did not challenge the findings of the SCR that the local authority:

- should have given greater consideration to providing respite foster care;

- took an overly optimistic view of his parent's ability to assume sufficient responsibility for his welfare;

- failed to refer him to a drug and alcohol counsellor with a local authority resource supporting adolescents or to the independent substance misuse agency;

- failed to put in place a child protection plan.

The coroner's decisions

10.107　The inquest, once opened, was adjourned until the SCR report was concluded. At a pre-inquest hearing the family raised the argument that Art 2 was engaged. The coroner ruled that Art 2 applied to the inquest and ordered that it should take place with a jury.

The arguments for the local authority on judicial review

10.108

- There was no breach of the substantive obligation under Art 2 because the statutory systems for children in need of care were in place and wholly adequate. There was no systemic failure which could lead to an arguable breach.

- There was no breach of the operational obligation because Edward was not sufficiently under the state's control. Nor was there any real or immediate risk to life.

- Even if Art 2 was potentially engaged it did not apply because the claimant had done all that it could by way of prompt and effective process to remedy its mistakes.

The findings on judicial review

10.109

- The case involving as it did a vulnerable child with the factual background as set out above entered into the potential territory of operational duty; therefore the question to be determined is whether there was a real and immediate risk to the child in the period before his death.

- The answer to that question as determined by the administrative court was that although the child in question was undoubtedly vulnerable and at risk that risk, viewed objectively, was not a risk to life and certainly not a real and immediate risk to life. It was a risk of harm but that should not (based on hindsight) be equated with a risk to life.

- Although the child told the local authority that he had previously attempted suicide that was 9 months prior to his death and there was no evidence that he took his life in the end and none of the incidents in the few months before his death could be described as obviously life-threatening.

- There was no evidence to justify the coroner's averred view that the local authority had actual or constructive knowledge of a real and immediate risk to Edward's life.

- There was they held, despite the tragic circumstances, no operational duty in place at the time of the death and therefore no scope for the Art 2 extended inquest. The local authority did not have parental responsibility for him. He was not 'in care' in the sense that no proceedings had been commenced under s 31 of the Children Act 1989, he was not therefore living within the control or under the direct responsibility of the local authority. As there was no operational duty in place there could be no breach of it and therefore there could not have been any breach of the general duty to protect life.

- If there was no breach of the general duty to protect life no procedural duty to investigate arises; therefore a '*Middleton*' type enhanced inquest was not required.

- Whilst the child had been a child in need under s 17 of the Children Act 1989 the court found that it would not be proportionate to require that the local authority exercise sufficient control over all the children served through s 17 so as to lead to an operational duty being exercised in every case.

- The operational duty should be interpreted in a way that does not impose an impossible or disproportionate burden on the authorities particularly in terms of priorities and resources.[43]

- On the question of the use of the jury the court held that the coroner was entitled to conclude, even for the non enhanced '*Jamieson*' (as opposed to enhanced '*Middleton*') inquest that it was his public duty to investigate the death so as to avoid the recurrence of the tragic and troubling death of a

---

[43]   The court cited both *Osman v UK* (1998) 29 EHRR 245 and *Rabone v Pennine Care NHS Foundation Trust* [2012] UKSC 2 on this point.

vulnerable 14-year old who was away from home and they could not fault the decision therefore for the use of a jury.

Comment

10.110 Counsel for the local authority accepted, though in the light of their decision on the issue of operational duty it was not necessary for the court to determine the issue, that although there had been a SCR as the report had not been made public there had been little public scrutiny of the role of the local authority. It would appear therefore that if an operational duty had been found to exist the argument that the SCR itself provided an alternative and sufficient enquiry rendering a *Middleton* inquest unnecessary would have failed. It is yet to be seen whether the revised SCRs and CPRs considered above will be sufficiently public and involve the family members to sufficient degree to avoid Middleton type inquests in the future for children who die whether through suicide or at the hands of a known violent parent/carer. See also the doubts expressed by Collins J in *R (Smith) v Oxfordshire Asst Deputy Coroner*[44] as to whether the existence of other procedures means that the narrow form of inquest is all that would be needed.

R (Plymouth CC) v HM Coroner for the County of Devon and Secretary of State for Education and Skills[45]

10.111 This case considered an application by Plymouth City Council for judicial review of the coroner's decision:

(i)   That the scope of the inquest should not be limited to the two days preceding the death of the child (Perrin) but should extend to the role played by the child protection agencies including the local authority during the child's life and specifically to whether, by act or omission, they had contributed to his death.

Brief facts

10.112 Perrin died at the age of 9 months. At the time of his death he was (with his two sisters) in the care of his mother and her new partner. Prior to his birth the local authority had substantial concerns about the parenting capacity of his mother. Throughout his life the authority provided substantial professional support for the family and sought to closely monitor his well-being and that of his sisters. A month after his birth a child protection plan was drawn up providing for weekly visits to the family by a social worker, weekly visits by a family support worker and weekly visits by a health visitor. 5 months before his death further crisis intervention assessment was undertaken. 8 weeks prior to his death proceedings were initiated for a supervision order and 5 weeks prior to his death an interim supervision order was granted.

---

[44]   [2008] 3 WLR 1284 (QBD).
[45]   [2005] EWHC 1014 (Admin), [2005] 2 FLR 1279.

10.113 The medical evidence found that the cause of death was bronchopneumonia which, although in its early stages, proved fatal because he was in a debilitated and dehydrated state. The dehydration had developed over the two days prior to his death. Had his mother sought medical assistance even only 10 hours before his death it could have been averted. His mother and her partner pleaded guilty to an offence of acting with cruelty towards Perrin. Initially the Part 8 review (SCR), although initiated, was suspended pending resolution of all care, criminal and coroner's proceedings. A detailed guardian's report from the children's guardian in the continuing proceedings for the sisters, which was said to contain detailed criticisms of the local authority was not disclosed to the coroner in line with an order from the family court partially on the basis that the Part 8 review would adequately meet any investigative duty as might exist under Art 2. A subsequent application for disclosure by the coroner (the first application had been made by the guardian) met with more success but was suspended pending the outcome of the judicial review applications.[46]

The coroner's decisions

10.114 The coroner decided that the investigation should be broadened to extend to the role played by the statutory child protection agencies during his life on the basis that:

- The statutory child protection agencies, as public authorities, had or might have, failed to protect Perrin's life under Art 2.

- A duty was therefore cast upon the state by Art 2 to conduct an investigation into whether any such agency has indeed infringed his right to life (the investigative duty).

- The investigative duty was not discharged by any other investigation which was being conducted, into the role played by the child protection agencies in relation to Perrin and therefore it fell to the coroner's court to discharge it.

The findings on judicial review

10.115

- Article 2 imposed three distinct duties on the state:

    - A negative duty – a duty not, by its agents, to intentionally take a life save in the circumstances specified in the article itself.
    - A positive duty – a duty to take all reasonable steps to protect a person's right to life. The state is required to take all reasonable care to protect the life of a person involuntarily in its custody.

---

[46] Note Andrew McFarlane QC (as he then was) acted as counsel to the inquest. The local authority, CAFCASS and the solicitor for the child in the supervision proceedings were all (amongst others) represented at the inquest.

- A second positive duty collateral to the above being an investigative duty – a duty to furnish an appropriate investigation into the cause of a death which has been or may have been caused or contributed to by a breach of the state's protective duty. The procedural obligation introduced by Art 2 was said to have three interlocking aims; to minimise the risk of future deaths; to give the beginnings of justice to the bereaved; and to assuage the anxieties of the public.

- The coroner impeccably stated the law that it was his duty to consider whether there was or might have been a breach by the state of its protective duty under Art 2 and that a breach will be found if it is established that the authorities did not do all that could be reasonably expected of them to avoid a real and immediate risk to life of which they have or ought to have knowledge.

- The central question therefore was not whether the local authority should at some stage have applied for an interim care order with a plan to take him into foster care (and plainly if this had been done he would not had died) but whether his very life was, or should have been, known to be at real and immediate risk.

- On the evidence before the coroner there was no justification for such a conclusion and therefore the investigative duty under Art 2 was not triggered.

Comment

10.116 The Court expressed views (albeit once again it did not fall to be determined) whether the other investigations aside from the coroner's might meet the Art 2 investigative duty had it been triggered. Doubt was cast on the criminal proceedings being sufficient if there were guilty pleas, comment was made that some care proceedings relating to siblings of a deceased child where the local authority had arguably breached its protective duty might (if the conclusion were made public) be sufficient. Wilson J suggested that it may be worthwhile for care judges to consider whether in fact theirs would be a convenient forum for the discharge of such duty. Even where there are deaths which could have been avoided, however, care judges can be loath to delve deeply into the failings of local authorities if there are concessions by parent/carers as to the direct causation of death or where there is no argument over care plans.

10.117 Time constraints may mean this more in depth investigation is unlikely to find favour in future care fact-findings. When considering the Part 8 enquiry whilst commenting that they would be likely to be rigorous with contributions from many fields and were also likely to be sufficiently independent Wilson J commented that there was no hearing at which oral evidence was given and no facility for assertions to be directly tested by or on behalf of next of kin. The major problem he foresaw was that the system concentrated on inter-agency failings rather than establishment of breach of Art 2 duty to take all reasonable steps to protect the child's life. Under the new systems it is felt this is likely to remain the same.

10.118 Local authorities in public law care cases are dealing with exceptionally vulnerable children and many of those are either accommodated, placed in the care of the local authority or come to their attention either living at home or in the community. As a result the duties set out above and highlighted in cases such as *Rabone v Pennine Care NHS Foundation Trust*[47] in the context of risk of suicide are readily understandable. Local authorities will also need to have regard to similar duties where there are issues arising of serious domestic violence or past physical abuse of the child or other children by a person who is likely to be a carer for or visitor to the child with whom they are concerned.

---

[47]   [2012] UKSC 2.

Part 3
REMEDIES

Chapter 11

APPLICATIONS WITHIN PROCEEDINGS

SECTION 1 – INTRODUCTION

11.1 There are likely to be a large range of decisions made by the local authority within proceedings that may well give rise to a need for justification by a local authority and to be the subject of challenge by a party affected by such decisions.

11.2 Some of those decisions will be capable of justification or resolution without the need for the issue of an application to court but there will remain those that require an application to be issued within proceedings.

11.3 This chapter is not intended to be an exhaustive list of every application that might be issued within proceedings but instead will explore applications and principles that are most likely to be needed by a local authority seeking to defend its decisions and to those seeking to challenge such decisions.

SECTION 2 – THE LEGAL FRAMEWORK

11.4 Section 34 of the Children Act 1989 provides:

34 Parental contact etc with children in care

(1) Where a child is in the care of a local authority, the authority shall (subject to the provisions of this section) allow the child reasonable contact with –

    (a)   his parents;

    (b)   any guardian or special guardian of his;

    (ba) any person who by virtue of section 4A has parental responsibility for him;

    (c)   where there was a residence order in force with respect to the child immediately before the care order was made, the person in whose favour the order was made; and

    (d)   where, immediately before the care order was made a person had care of the child by virtue of an order made in the exercise of the High Court's inherent jurisdiction with respect to children, that person.

(2) On an application made by the authority or the child, the court may make such order as it considers appropriate with respect to the contact which is to be allowed between the child and any named person.

(3) On an application made by –

    (a)   any person mentioned in paragraphs (a) to (d) of subsection (1); or

(b)   any person who has obtained the leave of the court to make the application,

the court may make such order as it considers appropriate with respect to the contact which is to be allowed between the child and that person.

(4) On an application made by the authority or the child, the court may make an order authorising the authority to refuse to allow contact between the child and any person who is mentioned in paragraphs (a) to (d) of subsection (1) and named in the order.

(5) When making a care order with respect to a child, or in any family proceedings in connection with a child who is in the care of a local authority, the court may make an order under this section, even though no application for such an order has been made with respect to the child, if it considers that the order should be made.

(6) An authority may refuse to allow the contact that would otherwise be required by virtue of subsection (1) or an order under this section if –

(a)   they are satisfied that it is necessary to do so in order to safeguard or promote the child's welfare; and
(b)   the refusal –
(i)   is decided upon as a matter of urgency; and
(ii)   does not last for more than seven days.

(7) An order under this section may impose such conditions as the court considers appropriate.

(8) The Secretary of State may by regulations make provision as to –

(a)   the steps to be taken by a local authority who have exercised their powers under subsection (6);
(b)   the circumstances in which, and conditions subject to which, the terms of any order under this section may be departed from by agreement between the local authority and the person in relation to whom the order is made;
(c)   notification by a local authority of any variation or suspension of arrangements made (otherwise than under an order under this section) with a view to affording any person contact with a child to whom this section applies.

(9) The court may vary or discharge any order made under this section on the application of the authority, the child concerned or the person named in the order.

(10) An order under this section may be made either at the same time as the care order itself or later.

(11) Before making a care order with respect to any child the court shall –

(a)   consider the arrangements which the authority have made, or propose to make, for affording any person contact with a child to whom this section applies; and
(b)   invite the parties to the proceedings to comment on those arrangements.

11.5   Section 39 of the Children Act 1989 provides:

39 Discharge and variation etc of care orders and supervision orders

(1) A care order may be discharged by the court on the application of –

    (a)   any person who has parental responsibility for the child;

    (b)   the child himself; or

    (c)   the local authority designated by the order.

(2) A supervision order may be varied or discharged by the court on the application of –

    (a)   any person who has parental responsibility for the child;

    (b)   the child himself; or

    (c)   the supervisor.

(3) On the application of a person who is not entitled to apply for the order to be discharged, but who is a person with whom the child is living, a supervision order may be varied by the court in so far as it imposes a requirement which affects that person.

(3A) On the application of a person who is not entitled to apply for the order to be discharged, but who is a person to whom an exclusion requirement contained in the order applies, an interim care order may be varied or discharged by the court in so far as it imposes the exclusion requirement.

(3B) Where a power of arrest has been attached to an exclusion requirement of an interim care order, the court may, on the application of any person entitled to apply for the discharge of the order so far as it imposes the exclusion requirement, vary or discharge the order in so far as it confers a power of arrest (whether or not any application has been made to vary or discharge any other provision of the order).

(4) Where a care order is in force with respect to a child the court may, on the application of any person entitled to apply for the order to be discharged, substitute a supervision order for the care order.

(5) When a court is considering whether to substitute one order for another under subsection (4) any provision of this Act which would otherwise require section 31(2) to be satisfied at the time when the proposed order is substituted or made shall be disregarded.

SECTION 3 – CONTACT TO CHILD IN CARE

11.6   The issue of contact to a child in care is governed by s 34 of the Children Act 1989.

11.7   Where a child is in the care of the local authority the authority is required to allow that child 'reasonable contact' with those identified below:[1]

•   his parents;

•   any guardian or special guardian of his;

---

[1]   CA 1989, s 34(1).

- a step-parent;

- where there was a residence order in force with respect to the child immediately before the care order was made, the person in whose favour the order was made; and

- where, immediately before the care order was made, a person who had care of the child by virtue of an order made in the exercise of the High Court's inherent jurisdiction with respect to children, that person.

11.8 It is of note that the list of persons above to whom the local authority must allow reasonable contact does not include a vast array of friends, relatives and connected persons that in many cases may represent important links for the looked after child who is placed away from his family in local authority care. Indeed, s 34 is specifically entitled 'Parental contact etc with children in care.'

11.9 However, the issue of the promotion and maintenance of contact between a looked after child and his family is instead encompassed in the duty owed by the local authority pursuant to Sch 2, para 15 of the Children Act 1989 which provides:

> (1) Where a child is being looked after by a local authority, the authority shall, unless it is not reasonably practicable or consistent with his welfare, endeavour to promote contact between the child and –
>
> (a)   his parents;
> (b)   any person who is not a parent of his but who has parental responsibility for him; and
> (c)   any relative, friend or other person connected with him.

11.10 Before making a decision regarding contact, the local authority is required, so far as is reasonably practicable, to ascertain the wishes and feelings of the child, his parents, any person who is not a parent of his but who has parental responsibility and any other person whose wishes and feelings the local authority consider to be relevant.[2]

What is 'reasonable contact'?

11.11 'Reasonable contact' in one case may be indirect contact but in another case direct unsupervised contact. Therefore, 'reasonable contact' is entirely fact specific to the case in question and there is no case authority or statutory definition of this issue.

New born babies

11.12 Arguments often arise with regard to the issue of contact as between parents and new-born babies who have been accommodated by the local

---

[2]   CA 1989, s 22(4) and (5).

authority. Heavy reliance (and at times misinterpretation) was in the past placed on the 'concluding thoughts' of Munby J (now President) in the case of *In the Matter of Unborn Baby M R (X and Another) v Gloucestershire County Council*[3] where at para 44 he stated:

> '(iv) If a baby is to be removed from his mother one would normally expect arrangements to be made by the local authority to facilitate contact on a regular and generous basis. It is a dreadful thing to take a baby away from his mother: dreadful for mother, dreadful for father and dreadful for the baby. If the state, in the guise of a local authority, seeks to intervene so drastically in a family's life – and at a time when, ex hypothesi, its case against the parents has not yet even been established – then the very least the State can do is to make generous arrangements for contact. And those arrangements must be driven by the needs of the family, not stunted by lack of resources. Typically, if this is what the parents want, one will be looking to contact most days of the week and for lengthy periods. And local authorities must be sensitive to the wishes of a mother who wants to breast-feed and must make suitable arrangements to enable her to do so – and when I say breast-feed I mean just that, I do not mean merely bottle-feeding expressed breast milk. Nothing less will meet the imperative demands of the Convention. Contact two or three times a week for a couple of hours a time is simply not enough if parents reasonably want more.'

11.13   However, the reliance to be placed upon those 'concluding thoughts' was fully considered by Bodey J in *Kirklees MBC v S (Contact to Newborn Babies)*[4] where he found as follows:

> '[28] It is important to note that *Re M* was an application for leave to apply for judicial review of a decision by a local authority to commence care or other protective proceedings under the Children Act 1989. The aim of such intended judicial review was to secure an injunction restraining the local authority from going ahead with its intended Children Act proceedings. Munby J, who of course has very great experience of sitting both in the Administrative Court and in the Family Division, unsurprisingly rejected that application for leave to bring such judicial review proceedings. It was in those circumstances that he added his "Concluding thoughts". In my judgment, therefore, Mr Hayes was correct in characterising such thoughts as "obiter".

> [29] I would not, however, wish to dissent from Munby J's observations in *Re M (Care Proceedings: Judicial Review)* [2003] EWHC 850 (Admin) [2003] 2 FLR 171, provided they are not elevated into principles and provided it is not understood from them that the words "most days of the week" imply daily contact including at weekends. The judge was clearly comparing the sort of level of contact which he thought appropriate for babies removed from their mothers where supervision by or on behalf of the local authority is required (viz "most days of the week and for lengthy periods") with contact "two or three times a week for a couple of hours at a time", which he said would clearly not constitute reasonable contact.

---

3   [2003] EWHC 850 (Admin).
4   [2006] 1 FLR 333.

[30] Nor do I consider that Munby J's comment that such contact arrangements "must be driven by the needs of the family, not stunted by lack of resources" was intended to mean that resources are a wholly irrelevant consideration. It is clear that the practicalities of arranging contact by a mother to a baby have to be borne in mind as part of deciding what quantum of contact would constitute "reasonable" or "appropriate" contact under s 34, within which decision-making process at least some regard must generally be had to the extent to which the quantum of contact would be likely to impose unreasonable burdens either on the foster carer's abilities to sustain it, and/or on the resources of the local authority to facilitate it.

[31] An order for daily contact to a child in foster care, where supervision by or on behalf of the local authority is required, is, on any view, (to put it at its lowest) exceptionally unusual, a fact which was inferentially recognised in the submissions made to me on behalf of the mother and the children's guardian.

[32] Had the existing order been expressed to run for a medium or long-term period of time, then, in my judgment, it would not have constituted "reasonable" or "appropriate" contact, and could not have been sustained at this appeal hearing. There was no evidence to support the proposition relied on by the family proceedings court that it is "vital that contact between a parent and a child of L's age should be daily to establish maternal bonds", a proposition which is not, in my experience, borne out by the way in which this type of case is generally dealt with by the courts, and which goes far wider in its ambit ("a child of L's age") than was necessary to determine this particular case.

[33] I do not regard Munby J's observations in *Re M* as supporting any such proposition, still less as laying down any "principles", to use the word of the family proceedings court; nor do I consider that he would have expected his observations to be so understood.

[34] ...

[35] At the risk of repeating myself (and I realise I am doing so), Munby J did not refer to "daily" contact, but to "contact most days of the week". Nor was anything which he said, in my judgment, intended to detract from the fact that each such case has to be looked at on its own particular merits, with welfare of the child paramount, so as to determine what quantum of contact would be "reasonable" or "appropriate" under the relevant subsections of s 34.'

11.14 In summary, therefore, whilst the above cases will inevitably be relevant in any argument concerning the issue of contact with a new born baby, each case will be considered on its own facts and by reference to the welfare checklist and the welfare of the child being the court's paramount consideration. There cannot be any general principle as to the quantum of such contact and the court will consider the particular circumstances of each case when assessing 'reasonable contact.'

Orders for contact

11.15 Upon the application by the local authority or the child, the court may make such order as it considers appropriate with respect to the contact which is to be allowed between the child and any named person.[5]

11.16 Upon an application being made, any person set out in s 34(1) or any person who has obtained the leave of the court, may make an application for a contact order, the court may make such order as it considers appropriate with respect to the contact which is to be allowed between the child and that person.[6]

11.17 Individuals required to apply for leave of the court to make such an application will need to adopt the procedure as set out in the Family Procedure Rules 2010, Part 18. When deciding the application for leave (permission), the court will consider the matters set out in s 10(9) of the Children Act 1989 and will apply the principles identified by Sumner J in *Re W (Care Proceedings: Leave to Apply)*.[7]

11.18 Any substantive application for contact under s 34 (as opposed to the application for leave to apply) is a question with respect to the upbringing of a child; hence the child's welfare must be the court's paramount consideration.[8]

11.19 In the event that a person applies for an order under s 34 and the application is refused, that person will have to obtain the leave of the court to make any further application in respect of that child if a period of less than six months has elapsed since the refusal.[9]

The local authority refusing to allow contact

11.20 The local authority may refuse to allow contact that would otherwise be required by virtue of its duty to allow reasonable contact or by virtue of an order under s 34(2), without recourse to court if:

    (a)   they are satisfied that it is necessary to do so in order to safeguard or promote the child's welfare; and

    (b)   the refusal –

        (i)   is decided upon as a matter of urgency; and

        (ii) does not last for more than seven days.[10]

11.21 In the event of a local authority requiring authority to refuse to allow contact for a period any longer than the seven days provided for in s 34(6) then this would have to be the subject of an application pursuant to s 34(4).

---

5   CA 1989, s 34(2).
6   CA 1989, s 34(3).
7   [2004] EWHC 3342 (Fam), [2005] 2 FLR 468.
8   CA 1989, s 1(1).
9   CA 1989, s 91(17).
10   CA 1989, s 34(6).

11.22   An area of likely challenge in the course of ongoing proceedings is a case in which the local authority seeks an order pursuant to s 34(4) of the Children Act 1989 to authorise its refusal to allow contact. The grant of such an order represents a significant interference in family life and will require a local authority to identify cogent and compelling evidence in support of the order. Per Munby J in *Re K (Contact)*:[11]

> '[25] It is a very drastic thing indeed to interfere with a young mother's contact with her newborn baby, and his contact with her, particularly at a time when "threshold" (see s 31(2) of the Act) is yet to be established. It is an even more drastic thing to deny contact altogether, and something which lies at the very extremities of the court's powers. Extraordinarily compelling reasons must be shown to justify an order under s 34(4) at this early stage in the proceedings.'

11.23   In *Re T (Termination of Contact: Discharge of Order)*,[12] the Court of Appeal indicated that a s 34(4) order should not be made:

(a)   whilst there remains a realistic possibility of rehabilitation of the child with the person in question; or

(b)   merely against the possibility that circumstances may change in such a way as to make termination of contact desirable. For an order to be justified, a probable need to terminate contact must be foreseeable and not too remote.

11.24   It is important to note that a refusal to allow contact (pursuant to s 34(6)) or the grant of an order under s 34(4) is *permissive*. It is therefore incumbent on the local authority to review the need for the continuation of the order and it is open to them to allow contact to resume should that be assessed to be in the child's best interests.[13]

11.25   In the event that the court does grant an interim s 34(4) order, it will be necessary for those acting for the parents to scrutinise very closely the actions of the local authority while that order is in force (and for the local authority itself to be ready to meet any such scrutiny). This is particularly important in relation to the extent of local authority assessment and work with the parents and child to explore whether there remains a need to refuse contact or whether with appropriate safeguards contact could safely take place.

11.26   Orders can be made under s 34 either at the same time as the care order itself or later.[14] Before making a care order the court shall consider the arrangements which the authority have made, or propose to make, for affording

---

[11]   [2008] 2 FLR 581.
[12]   [1997] 1 FLR 517.
[13]   Care Planning, Placement and Case Review (England) Regulations 2010 (SI 2010/959), reg 8.
[14]   CA 1989, s 34(10).

any person contact with a child to whom this section applies and invite the parties to the proceedings to comment on those arrangements.[15]

11.27   The arrangements for contact proposed by the local authority represent an issue that the local authority will require to demonstrate have been well thought out, are justified given the facts of the case and are in the best interests of the child. The court is entitled in an appropriate case, whilst approving the care plan and making a care order, to decline to approve the arrangements for contact and to make an order under s 34. In deciding whether to make a s 34 order the court is likely to undertake the balancing act clarified by Hale J (now Baroness Hale) in *Berkshire County Council v B*.[16] In that case, the Justices disapproved of the local authority care plan insofar as the arrangements for contact were concerned (the plan being only for two meetings a year between the child and his mother and indirect letter box contact) and instead made an order under s 34 for contact to take place twice weekly as between the mother and the child. The local authority appeal against that decision was dismissed.

11.28   When making a care order or in any family proceedings in respect of a child who is in the care of the local authority, the court may make an order under s 34, even though no application for such an order has been made, if it considers that the order should be made.[17] An order made under s 34 may impose such conditions as the court considers appropriate.[18]

Interim hearings

11.29   The making of an order at an interim hearing, terminating contact between the child and a parent pending a final hearing (and thereby effectively determining the case by ruling out rehabilitation) is likely in the vast majority of cases to be considered to be premature in the absence of exceptional and severe risk to the child being proven.[19]

11.30   The procedure adopted at an interim hearing in respect of applications under s 34 is an area, which like many others, will require to be justified by the local authority and the tribunal (whether justices or professional judge) and is likely to be an area for challenge by those affected by such orders. Guidance was provided by Cazalet J (with the approval of the President) in *Hampshire County Council v S*[20] in the following terms:

(1)   Justices should bear in mind that they are not, at an interim hearing, required to make a final conclusion; indeed it is because they are unable to reach a final conclusion that they are empowered to make an interim order. An interim order or decision will usually be required so as to

---

[15]   CA 1989, s 34(11).
[16]   [1997] 1 FLR 171.
[17]   CA 1989, s 34(5).
[18]   CA 1989, s 34(7).
[19]   See *A v M and Walsall MBC* [1993] 2 FLR 244.
[20]   [1993] 1 FLR 559.

establish a holding position, after weighing all the relevant risks, pending the final hearing. Nevertheless, justices must always ensure that the substantial issue is tried and determined at the earliest possible date. Any delay in determining the question before the court is likely to prejudice the welfare of the child (see s 1(2) of the Act).

(2) If justices find that they are unable to provide the appropriate hearing time, be it through pressures of work or for some other reason, they must, when an urgent interim order may have to be made, consider taking steps pursuant to r 14(2)(h) by transferring the proceedings laterally to an adjacent family proceedings court.

(3) At the start of a hearing which is concerned with interim relief, justices will usually be called upon to exercise their discretion under r 21(2) as to the order of speeches and evidence. Circumstances prevailing will almost certainly not permit full evidence to be heard. Accordingly, in such proceedings, justices should rarely make findings as to disputed facts. These will have to be left over for the final hearing.

(4) Justices must bear in mind that the greater the extent to which an interim order deviates from a previous order or the status quo, the more acute the need is likely to be for an early final hearing date. any disruption in a child's life almost invariably requires early resolution. Justices should be cautious about changing a child's residence under an interim order. The preferred course should be to leave the child where it is, with a direction for safeguards and the earliest possible hearing date.

(5) When an interim order may be made which will lead to a substantial change in a child's position, justices should consider permitting limited oral evidence to be led and challenged by way of cross-examination. However, it will necessarily follow that, in cross-examination, the evidence will have to be restricted to the issues which are essential at the interim stage. To this end the court may well have to intervene to ensure that this course is followed and that there is not a 'dress rehearsal' of the full hearing.

(6) Justices should, if possible, ensure that they have before them the written advice from the guardian ad litem. When there are substantial issues between the parties the guardian should, if possible, be at court to give oral advice. A party who is opposed to a recommendation made by the guardian should normally be given an opportunity to put questions to him or her in regard to advice given to the court.

(7) Justices must always comply with the mandatory requirements of the rules. These include compliance with: (a) r 21(1), which requires the justices to read, before the hearing, any documents which have been filed under r 17; (b) r 21(5), which requires the justices' clerk to make an appropriate written record of the hearing and in consultation with the

justices to record the reasons for the court's decision on any findings of fact; and (c) r 21(6), which requires the court, when making its order or giving its decision, to state the findings of fact and reasons for the court decision.

(8) If shortage of time or some other circumstance delays the court in the preparation of its written finding of fact and reasons, justices should adjourn the making of their order or the giving of their decision until the following court day or the earliest possible date. At that further hearing it is permissible for one of their number to return to court and state the decision, findings of fact and reasons (see r 21(6)). When the length of a hearing lasts beyond normal hours, it will often be sensible for the court to take this course so that it is not formulating its reasons and making perhaps a difficult decision under the sort of pressure which can arise when a sitting runs late into the day.

(9) When justices grant interim relief, they should state their findings and reasons concisely. Although it will not normally be open to them to make findings on disputed facts (because the court will not have heard the full evidence), it may assist if the justices summarise briefly the essential factual issues between the parties.

11.31 The case of *Hampshire County Council v S* and the guidance regarding procedure was approved and applied (albeit in the context of the grant of an interim care order as opposed to an interim s 34 order) in the case of *Re W (A Minor) (Interim Care Order)*.[21] The case of *Re W* was an appeal against the decision of a county court judge and whilst the guidance from *Hampshire County Council v S* derived from the decision of the justices in the family proceedings court, the guidance has equal application in respect of applications under s 34 in whatever tier of court an application is being considered.

Discharge of section 34 order

11.32 The court may vary or discharge any order made under this section on the application of the local authority, the child concerned or the person named in the order.[22]

11.33 In the event of an application to discharge the making of a s 34(4) order the court will treat the child's welfare as its paramount consideration and, additionally, will require to be satisfied that there has been a material change in circumstances between the making of the s 34(4) order and the application to discharge.[23]

---

[21] [1994] 2 FLR 892.
[22] CA 1989, s 34(9).
[23] *Re T (Termination of Contact: Discharge of Order)* [1997] 1 FLR 517.

SECTION 4 – APPLICATION TO DISCHARGE CARE ORDER

11.34   A care order may be discharged by the court on the application of:

(a)   any person who has parental responsibility for the child;

(b)   the child himself; or

(c)   the local authority designated by the order.[24]

11.35   Where a previous application has been made for the discharge of the care order (or the discharge of a supervision order or substitution of a supervision order for a care order – for which see below), no further application for discharge of the order can be made without leave of the court, unless the period between the disposal of the previous application and the making of the further application exceeds six months.[25]

Test to be applied

11.36   An application to discharge a care order is a question regarding the upbringing of a child and, accordingly, the welfare of the child shall be the court's paramount consideration.[26] Further, the court is required when considering whether to discharge the care order to have regard to the welfare checklist as identified in s 1(3) of the Children Act 1989.[27]

11.37   The case of *Re S (Discharge of Care Order)*[28] identifies the following principles:

- The jurisdiction to discharge a care order is discretionary.

- The issue has to be determined in accordance with the welfare of the child being paramount and applying the welfare checklist.

- When considering the welfare checklist the court must specifically consider (s 1(3)(e)):

  'any harm which he has suffered or is at risk of suffering ...'

- The risk to be considered is the risk current at the date of the discharge hearing.

---

[24]   CA 1989, s 39(1).
[25]   CA 1989, s 91(15).
[26]   CA 1989, s 1(1).
[27]   CA 1989, s 1(4)(b) and *Re S (Discharge of Care Order)* [1995] 2 FLR 639.
[28]   [1995] 2 FLR 639.

- In the great majority of discharge applications the court is likely to be concerned with evidence of recent harm and appraisal of current risk, in which conclusions reached by an earlier tribunal as to past harm or past risk would be of marginal relevance and historical interest only.

- However, there may be instances (likely to be extremely rare) in which the interest which every child has in seeing that justice is done to the claims of a natural parent will require the court hearing a discharge application to question, in the light of the evidence before it, not merely the relevance but also the soundness of antecedent findings reached by an earlier tribunal.

- In the general run of cases the family courts (including the Court of Appeal when it is dealing with applications in the family jurisdiction) will be every bit as alert as courts in other jurisdictions to see to it that no one is allowed to litigate afresh issues that have already been determined.

11.38 The case of *Re C (Care: Discharge of Care Order)*[29] also identifies the following principles applicable to an application for discharge of a care order:

- The burden is on the applicant to 'make out his case' for discharge of the care order and this is not limited to the listing of potential benefits.

- The judge is entitled to take into account the continuing effect, or lack of effect, of the care order.

- There might sometimes be cases where a care order ought to be preserved having regard to the potential advantages under the leaving care provisions to the child concerned.

11.39 Where a care order is in force with respect to a child the court may, on the application of any person entitled to apply for the order to be discharged, substitute a supervision order for the care order.[30]

SECTION 5 – APPLICATION TO VARY/DISCHARGE A SUPERVISION ORDER

11.40 A supervision order may be varied or discharged by the court on the application of:

(a) any person who has parental responsibility for the child;

(b) the child himself; or

---

[29] [2010] 1 FLR 774, applying the case of *Re S (Discharge of Care Order)* [1995] 2 FLR 639.
[30] CA 1989, s 39(4).

(c)   the supervisor.[31]

11.41   Ordinarily a supervision order lasts for a maximum period of one year in the first instance.[32] The making of a supervision order for a period less than one year is permissible.[33]

11.42   A supervisor can apply for a supervision order to be extended or further extended but the supervision order may not be extended so as to run beyond the end of the period of three years beginning on the date on which it was made.[34]

11.43   It is impermissible and the court has no jurisdiction to make a supervision order for a period of three years at the first application.[35] The capacity to extend the supervision order up to a period of three years remains available but the court cannot simply obviate the need for application(s) for further extension by making a three year supervision order at the outset. As to the timing of any application for extension, in *Wakefield District Council v T*,[36] Thorpe LJ doubted the need in most cases for any application to extend a supervision order of 12 months duration to be made before the last quarter of its first life.

11.44   The court does not have jurisdiction when considering an application to extend a supervision order to instead grant a care order. However, in cases where there is a justification for the grant of a care order as opposed to an extension of the supervision order, it is still open to the local authority to make a fresh application for a care order (pursuant to s 31 Children Act 1989), albeit that the local authority would have to satisfy the court afresh that the threshold criteria was established.[37]

SECTION 6 – OTHER APPLICATIONS WITHIN PROCEEDINGS

11.45   A potent application to be considered within proceedings is an application pursuant to the Human Rights Act 1998. Such applications are considered at chapter 12.

11.46   Additionally, claims for injunctive relief as against the local authority, particularly under the Human Rights Act 1998 also fall to be considered within proceedings and are considered at chapter 13.

---

[31]   CA 1989, s 39(2).
[32]   CA 1989, Sch 3, para 6(1).
[33]   *M v Warwickshire County Council* [1994] 2 FLR 593.
[34]   CA 1989, Sch 3, para 6(4).
[35]   *Wakefield District Council v T* [2008] 1 FLR 1569.
[36]   [2008] 1 FLR 1569.
[37]   *Re A (Supervision Order: Extension)* [1995] 1 FLR 335.

11.47 Finally, the exercise of the inherent jurisdiction of the High Court (including the wardship jurisdiction) also falls to be considered within proceedings and this issue is considered at chapter 14.

Chapter 12

HUMAN RIGHTS ACT APPLICATIONS

SECTION 1 – INTRODUCTION

12.1 The Human Rights Act 1998 came into force in the United Kingdom on 2 October 2000. An important development was the capacity of an individual to rely upon rights enshrined in the European Convention on Human Rights 1950 (ECHR) in domestic proceedings.

12.2 A substantial body of case law has emanated from the European Court of Human Rights and within the High Court. The topic is a large one and it is impossible to do it justice within the scope of this. The matters considered below are not intended to be an exhaustive discussion of the topic of Human Rights Act claims but instead focus on the aspects of such claims that are likely to be of direct relevance to the child care practitioner dealing with such issues.

SECTION 2 – THE LEGAL FRAMEWORK

12.3 Relevant legislation is as follows:

- The European Convention on Human Rights (ECHR).

- Human Rights Act 1998 (HRA 1998).

- Family Procedure Rules 2010, r 29.5.

- FPR 2010, Practice Direction 29A – Human Rights, Joining the Crown.

- FPR 2010, Practice Direction 29B – Human Rights Act 1998.

SECTION 3 – THE EUROPEAN CONVENTION ON HUMAN RIGHTS

12.4 In the context of child care law the following ECHR rights are likely to be applicable.

Article 3
Prohibition of torture

No one shall be subjected to torture or to inhuman or degrading treatment or punishment.

12.5 It will be unusual for allegations regarding breaches of Art 3 to be made against the local authority but in a suitable case the actions of the local authority might amount to inhuman or degrading treatment, for which see *A and S (Children) v Lancashire County Council (aka Re A and S (Children: Failed Freeing Orders)* set out below.[1]

12.6

Article 5
Right to liberty and security

1 Everyone has the right to liberty and security of person. No one shall be deprived of his liberty save in the following cases and in accordance with a procedure prescribed by law:

    (a)   the lawful detention of a person after conviction by a competent court;

    (b)   the lawful arrest or detention of a person for non-compliance with the lawful order of a court or in order to secure the fulfilment of any obligation prescribed by law;

    (c)   the lawful arrest or detention of a person effected for the purpose of bringing him before the competent legal authority on reasonable suspicion of having committed an offence or when it is reasonably considered necessary to prevent his committing an offence or fleeing after having done so;

    (d)   the detention of a minor by lawful order for the purpose of educational supervision or his lawful detention for the purpose of bringing him before the competent legal authority;

    (e)   the lawful detention of persons for the prevention of the spreading of infectious diseases, of persons of unsound mind, alcoholics or drug addicts or vagrants;

    (f)   the lawful arrest or detention of a person to prevent his effecting an unauthorised entry into the country or of a person against whom action is being taken with a view to deportation or extradition.

The rights under Art 5 have been found to be compatible with the making of a secure accommodation order[2] as long as the detention is for the purpose of educational supervision.

12.7 The rights under Art 5 are also likely to be engaged in cases where the court has exercised its inherent jurisdiction to detain a child for the purposes of medical treatment.[3]

---

[1]   [2012] EWHC 1689 (Fam), [2012] All ER (D) 173.

[2]   *Re K (Secure Accommodation Order, Right to Liberty)* [2001] 1 FLR 526; see also *DG v Ireland* (2002) EHRR 33.

[3]   *Re C (Detention: Medical Treatment)* [1997] 2 FLR 180.

12.8

Article 6
Right to a fair trial

1 In the determination of his civil rights and obligations or of any criminal charge against him, everyone is entitled to a fair and public hearing within a reasonable time by an independent and impartial tribunal established by law. Judgment shall be pronounced publicly but the press and public may be excluded from all or part of the trial in the interest of morals, public order or national security in a democratic society, where the interests of juveniles or the protection of the private life of the parties so require, or to the extent strictly necessary in the opinion of the court in special circumstances where publicity would prejudice the interests of justice.

2 Everyone charged with a criminal offence shall be presumed innocent until proved guilty according to law.

3 Everyone charged with a criminal offence has the following minimum rights:

(a)   to be informed promptly, in a language which he understands and in detail, of the nature and cause of the accusation against him;
(b)   to have adequate time and facilities for the preparation of his defence;
(c)   to defend himself in person or through legal assistance of his own choosing or, if he has not sufficient means to pay for legal assistance, to be given it free when the interests of justice so require;
(d)   to examine or have examined witnesses against him and to obtain the attendance and examination of witnesses on his behalf under the same conditions as witnesses against him;
(e)   to have the free assistance of an interpreter if he cannot understand or speak the language used in court.

An area that has been identified as highly contentious and likely to be the subject of challenge is the failure by local authorities to ensure that in care proceedings the parties have been provided with all relevant documents in advance of the hearing preventing them from engaging effectively in the proceedings as a whole, so as to respect their Art 6 rights.

12.9   In *Re L (Care: Assessment: Fair Trial)*, Munby J stated the following:[4]

'[150] The fairness which Arts 6 and 8 guarantee to every parent – and also, of course, to every child – in public law proceedings imposes, as Charles J recognised, a heavy burden on local authorities. But it must never be forgotten that, with the state's abandonment of the right to impose capital sentences, orders of the kind which judges of this Division are typically invited to make in public law proceedings are amongst the most drastic that any judge in any jurisdiction is ever empowered to make. It is a terrible thing to say to any parent – particularly, perhaps, to a mother – that he or she is to lose their child for ever.

[151] The state, in the form of the local authority, assumes a heavy burden when it seeks to take a child into care. Part of that burden is the need, in the interests not

---

4   [2002] 2 FLR 730.

merely of the parent but also of the child, for a transparent and transparently fair procedure at all stages of the process – by which I mean the process both in and out of court. If the watchword of the Family Division is indeed *openness* – and it is and must be – then documents must be made openly available and crucial meetings at which a family's future is being decided must be conducted openly and with the parents, if they wish, either present or represented. Otherwise there is unacceptable scope for unfairness and injustice, not just to the parents but also to the children. For as I pointed out in *Re B,* at para [68], referring to what Lord Mustill had said in *Re D (Minors) (Adoption Reports: Confidentiality)* [1996] AC 593, at 615F about "the interest of the child in having the material properly tested":

> "It is not only the individual litigant's right to a fair trial which may point in the direction of disclosure of the documents to him. The interests of the other litigants may well point in the same direction, for the children and other parties also have a right to a fair trial and, as part of their right to a fair trial, the right to have the forensic materials properly tested. It may well be that only if there is disclosure to *all* concerned can the children and other parties to the proceedings be confident that the materials have been properly tested. So it may often be that disclosure of the documents to the individual litigant is not merely for his benefit but also for the benefit of the others and the children in particular."

[154] If those involved in cases such as this are in future to avoid the criticisms which, understandably and, as it seems to me with no little justification, have been levelled against some of those involved in the present case they would be well advised to bear the following precepts in mind:

(i)　Social workers should, as soon as ever practicable:
　　(a)　notify parents of material criticisms of and deficits in their parenting or behaviour and of the expectations of them; and
　　(b)　advise them how they may remedy or improve their parenting or behaviour.

(ii)　All the professionals involved (social workers, social work assistants, children's guardians, expert witnesses and others) should at all times keep clear, accurate, full and balanced notes of all relevant conversations and meetings between themselves and/or with parents, other family members and others involved with the family.

(iii)　The local authority should at an early stage of the proceedings make full and frank disclosure to the other parties of all key documents in its possession or available to it, including in particular contact recordings, attendance notes of meetings and conversations and minutes of case conferences, core group meetings and similar meetings. Early provision should then be afforded for inspection of any of these documents. Any objection to the disclosure or inspection of any document should be notified to the parties at the earliest possible stage in the proceedings and raised with the court by the local authority without delay.

(iv)　Social workers and guardians should routinely exhibit to their reports and statements notes of relevant meetings, conversations and incidents.

(v)　Where it is proposed that the social workers and/or guardian should meet with a jointly appointed or other sole expert witness instructed in the case (what I will refer to as a 'professionals' meeting', as opposed to a meeting of experts chaired by one of the legal representatives in the case – usually the children's guardian's solicitor):

(a) there should be a written agenda circulated in advance to all concerned;

(b) clear written notice of the meeting should be given in advance to the parents and/or their legal representative, accompanied by copies of the agenda and of all documents to be given or shown to the expert and notice of all issues relating to or criticisms of a parent, or a non-attending party, which it is intended to raise with the expert;

(c) the parent, or non-attending party, should have a clear opportunity to make representations to the expert prior to and/or at the meeting on the documents, issues and/or criticisms of which he or she has been given notice;

(d) a parent or other party who wishes to should have the right to attend and/or be represented at the professionals' meeting;

(e) clear, accurate, full and balanced minutes of the professionals' meeting (identifying in particular what information has been given to the expert and by whom) should be taken by someone nominated for that task before the meeting begins;

(f) as soon as possible after the professionals' meeting the minutes should be agreed by those present as being an accurate record of the meeting and then be immediately disclosed to all parties.'

12.10 These principles as identified by Munby J were subsequently considered by the Court of Appeal[5] and were not rejected. However a caveat was given that trial judges should be extremely cautious in reading too much into the judgment in *Re L (Care: Assessment: Fair Trial)*,[6] which was merely intended to draw attention to certain principles of practice that deserved emphasis.

12.11 Accordingly, whilst the Court of Appeal has sounded a note of caution regarding the emphasis to be placed upon *Re L* it appears to remain good law and a key authority regarding the unqualified right to a fair hearing under Art 6.[7]

12.12 In any event, there are a number of further cases in which the need for the parents to be properly involved in the decision-making process, both before, during and after care proceedings has been confirmed.[8] A failure by a local authority to observe these basic principles is likely to be asserted to be a breach of the parents' Art 6 and Art 8 rights and is liable to leave the local authority vulnerable to challenge.

---

5 Per Thorpe LJ in *Re V (Care: Pre-Birth Actions)* [2005] 1 FLR 627 at para [24] and [30].

6 [2002] EWHC 1379 (Fam), para [154].

7 For a recent example of reliance being placed on *Re L* see the case of *RCW v A Local Authority* [2013] EWHC 235 (Fam) per Cobb J at para 19.

8 *Re G (Care: Challenge to Local Authority's Decision)* [2003] 2 FLR 42; *X Council v B (Emergency Protection Orders)* [2005] 1 FLR 341.

12.13

Article 8
Right to respect for private and family life

1 Everyone has the right to respect for his private and family life, his home and his correspondence.

2 There shall be no interference by a public authority with the exercise of this right except such as is in accordance with the law and is necessary in a democratic society in the interests of national security, public safety or the economic well-being of the country, for the prevention of disorder or crime, for the protection of health or morals, or for the protection of the rights and freedoms of others.

In the context of decisions concerning children (whether by the local authority or another party to proceedings) it is inevitable that arguments will centre on the Art 8 rights of the parties (both child and adult). These issues will potentially arise with regard to decisions made at interim stages of the case and at final hearing.

12.14   Article 8 is a qualified right and hence a breach of Art 8 will not be established if the justification in Art 8(2) can be established.

12.15   In family proceedings concerning the upbringing of a child, s 1 Children Act 1989 requires the court to treat the child's welfare as its paramount consideration. The Art 8 right to respect for private and family life is engaged insofar as the rights of the child are concerned but also with regard to the child's parents. The key question relates to the balance to be struck in the event that there is tension as between the Art 8 rights of the child and his parents.

12.16   The answer to this question is provided by the European Court of Human Rights decision in *Yousef v The Netherlands* where it is stated:[9]

'[73] The court reiterates that in judicial decisions where the rights under Art 8 of parents and those of a child are at stake, the child's rights must be the paramount consideration. If any balancing of interests is necessary, the interests of the child must prevail (see *Elsholz v Germany* (2002) 34 EHRR 58, [2000] 2 FLR 486, para 52 and *TP and KM v United Kingdom* (2002) 34 EHRR 2, [2001] 2 FLR 549, para 72).'

12.17   In the context of a child not exercising contact with a parent and/or being removed from the care of a parent, those acting for parents are likely to rely on the positive obligation that exists on the local authority to have *respect* (to use the word in Art 8 itself) for those rights.[10] Additionally, in the context of a failure on the part of the Finnish state authorities to take reasonable steps to

---

[9]   (Application No 33711/96) [2003] 1 FLR 210.
[10]   *Botta v Italy* (1998) 26 EHRR 241.

reunite a father and son and enforce contact orders, the European Court of Human Rights found that this constituted a breach of the Father's Art 8 rights in the case of *Hokkanen v Finland*.[11]

12.18 In *Hansen v Turkey*,[12] the issue of 'positive obligation' was further considered when the European Court of Human Rights found:

> [97] That being so, it must be determined whether there has been a failure to respect the applicant's family life. The court reiterates that the essential object of Art 8 is to protect the individual against arbitrary action by the public authorities. There are in addition positive obligations inherent in an effective "respect" for family life (see *Keegan v Ireland* (1994) 18 EHRR 342, para 49). In this context, the court has repeatedly held that Art 8 includes a right for parents to have measures taken that will permit them to be reunited with their children and an obligation on the national authorities to take such action (see *Eriksson v Sweden* (1989) 11 EHRR 183, para 71; *Margareta and Roger Andersson v Sweden* (1992) 14 EHRR 615, para 91; *Olsson v Sweden (No 2)* (1994) 17 EHRR 134, para 90; *Hokkanen v Finland* (1995) 19 EHRR 139, [1996] 1 FLR 289, para 55; *Nuutinen v Finland* (2002) 34 EHRR 15, para 127; *Ignaccolo-Zenide v Romania* (2001) 31 EHRR 7, para 94 and *Sylvester v Austria* (2003) 37 EHRR 17, [2003] 2 FLR 210, para 58).

> [98] However, the national authorities' obligation to take measures to facilitate reunion is not absolute, since the reunion of a parent with children who have lived for some time with the other parent may not be able to take place immediately and may require preparatory measures to be taken. The nature and extent of such preparation will depend on the circumstances of each case, but the understanding and co-operation of all concerned are always an important ingredient. Whilst national authorities must do their utmost to facilitate such co-operation, any obligation to apply coercion in this area must be limited since the interests as well as the rights and freedoms of all concerned must be taken into account, and more particularly the best interests of the child and his or her rights under Art 8 of the European Convention. Where contact with the parent might appear to threaten those interests or interfere with those rights, it is for the national authorities to strike a fair balance between them (see *Hokkanen v Finland* (1995) 19 EHRR 139, [1996] 1 FLR 289, para 58; *Ignaccolo-Zenide v Romania* (2001) 31 EHRR 7, para 94).

12.19 The message from this decision is that whilst the State has a positive obligation to facilitate rehabilitation of a child to a parent's care this is not absolute. The Art 8 rights of the child also fall to be considered in addition to an assessment as to what is in the best interests of that particular child.

12.20 An interesting and recent case with regard to a claim based upon a breach of Art 8 is that of *Coventry City Council v C and Others*.[13] In this case the court (Hedley J) gave important guidance regarding the proper approach to be taken by a local authority when seeking s 20 Children Act 1989 agreement to

---

[11] (1994) 19 EHRR 139.
[12] [2004] 1 FLR 142.
[13] [2012] EWHC 2190 (Fam).

accommodation.[14] The relevant aspect in that case is that the mother had also issued proceedings pursuant to s 7 of the Human Rights Act 1998 regarding the manner in which the local authority had obtained her s 20 agreement. Per Hedley J:

> '23. Substantial discussions took place on the first day of the hearing (and had of course been in train for some time) which resulted in the local authority conceding the mother's claim under Section 7 of the 1998 Act. The substance is recorded in the recitals to the order but in effect acknowledge two matters: first, that a Section 20 consent should not have been sought on 1st February 2012; and secondly, that such a removal was not a proportionate response to the risks that then existed. In the event the local authority accepts breaches of the Article 8 rights of both mother and child. The Order with its recitals is annexed to and should be read in conjunction with this judgment.

> 24. The mother, in discussion about damages, asked that they be applied to the costs of her receiving the therapeutic input that has long been advised. The parties have agreed the payment of damages and other provisions which all accept amount to 'just satisfaction' of both these claims.'

12.21   A further important case regarding the actions or inactions of the local authority and the human rights applications that flowed from such behaviour is that of *A and S (Children) v Lancashire County Council (aka Re A and S (Children: Failed Freeing Orders)*.[15] In this case the subject children sought declarations from the court that the local authority had acted incompatibly with their rights as guaranteed by Arts 3, 6 and 8 of the ECHR and the independent reviewing officer (IRO) had acted incompatibly with their rights as guaranteed by Arts 6 and 8 of the ECHR. The case concerned two brothers, *A* (aged 16) and *S* (aged 14) who were placed in the care of the local authority (Lancashire County Council) when they were aged 2 ¾ years and 6 months old. Both boys were made the subject of freeing orders in 2001 but neither was found a suitable home. The boys had numerous foster placements (*A* moving between foster placements 77 times and *S* moving 96 times) and had suffered 'irreparable harm'. In at least one of those foster placements the boys were the subject of an assault leading to the foster care pleading guilty to assault. No adoptive placement was identified for the boys and in 2004 the local authority formally abandoned the plan for adoption and the care plan changed to long term fostering. Notwithstanding this change in care plan the local authority did not apply to revoke the freeing orders. On being placed in care the boys had lost all links with their birth family but had not gained a substitute adoptive family. The boys had no direct contact with their birth family after 2002 despite their requests for contact to be arranged.

12.22   In the 12 years from 1999–2011 each of the boys was subject to 35 looked after children (LAC) reviews. The IRO named in the action chaired 16 of those reviews. In 2011 the local authority decided to move *A* from his foster

---

[14]   See chapter 9 of this book with regard to the use and misuse of s 20 agreement.
[15]   [2012] EWHC 1689 (Fam), [2012] All ER (D) 173. See chapter 7 where this case is also discussed in detail in relation to the role of IROs.

placement in which he had been for almost 3 years to live instead at a children's home. *A* went to see solicitors in an attempt to prevent his removal from his foster placement and his solicitor secured the agreement of the local authority that he would not be unilaterally moved and it was proposed that the local authority would apply to revoke the freeing order. Even at that stage the local authority did not apply for a revocation of the freeing order and the child *A* himself applied to the High Court for revocation of the freeing order.

12.23 When the application made by *A* came before the court the judge was highly concerned at the history of the case and granted leave to *A* to apply to invoke the inherent jurisdiction of the High Court. An order was made preventing the local authority from removing a child from the care of his foster carers without the permission of the court.

12.24 The IRO accepted that he had failed adequately to carry out his role in respect of the boys and accepted a number of specific shortcomings including that he had not addressed or monitored the repeated failures of social workers or promoted the rights of *A* and *S*. The IRO highlighted a number of difficulties which he faced which included a caseload of three times the good practice guidance at times, lack of training and absence of access to legal advice. In due course the court made declarations that the independent reviewing officer for *A* and *S* had acted incompatibly with the rights of those children as guaranteed by Arts 6 and 8 of the ECHR in that he:

(a)   failed to identify that *A* and *S's* human rights had been and were being infringed;

(b)   failed to take effective action to ensure that the local authority acted upon the recommendations of the Looked After Child Reviews; and

(c)   failed to refer the circumstances of *A* and *S* to CAFCASS legal.

12.25 The courts made similar declarations with regard to the conduct of the local authority in this case. Specifically, it was declared that the local authority had acted incompatibly with the rights of *A* and *S* as guaranteed by Arts 3, 6 and 8 of the ECHR in that it:

(a)   Failed to provide *A* and *S* with a proper opportunity of securing a permanent adoptive placement and a settled and secure home life.

(b)   Failed to seek revocation of the orders freeing *A* and *S* for adoption causing a number of identified consequences for them.

(c)   Permitted *A* and *S* to be subjected to degrading treatment and physical assault and failed adequately to protect their physical and sexual safety and their psychological health.

(d) Failed to provide accurate information concerning *A* and *S's* legal status to the independent reviewing officers.

(e) Failed to ensure that there were sufficient procedures in place to give effect to the recommendations of the looked after child reviews.

(f) Failed to promote the rights of *A* and *S* to independent legal advice.

(g) Specifically, failed to act as the 'responsible body' to enable *A* and *S* to pursue any potential claims for criminal injuries compensation, tortious liability and/or breach of human rights arising from their treatment by their mother, or by the H's or by Mrs B.

It is fair to point out that both the local authority and the independent reviewing officer readily accepted that they had breached the boys' rights under the ECHR.

12.26 The court, having made the declarations under the Human Rights Act 1998, ordered that the claim to damages (under the HRA 1998) should be transferred to the Queen's Bench Division to be heard with their claim for breach of statutory duty and negligence against the local authority.

12.27 This case is obviously an extreme example of the actions/inactions of the local authority resulting in proceedings under the Human Rights Act 1998 and the court exercising its inherent jurisdiction (to prevent the removal by the local authority of *A* from his foster placement). However, its principles have direct application in all cases where the decision-making of the local authority falls to be considered.

SECTION 4 – PROCEEDINGS UNDER THE HUMAN RIGHTS ACT 1998

12.28 The local authority is a 'public authority' having regard to the definition provided at s 6(3) of the 1998 Act.[16]

12.29 It is unlawful for a public authority to act in a way which is incompatible with a Convention right.[17]

12.30 Section 7 of the HRA 1998 provides that a person who claims that a public authority has acted (or proposes to act) in a way which is made unlawful by s 6(1) may:

(a) bring proceedings against the authority under this Act in the appropriate court or tribunal, or

(b) rely on the Convention right or rights concerned in any legal proceedings,

---

[16] See chapter 1 for detailed consideration of the definition of a public authority.
[17] HRA 1998, s 6(1).

but only if he is (or would be) a victim of the unlawful act.

12.31   The issue of proceedings under s 7 of the HRA 1998 is well recognised in the arena of public law children cases and the decisions/actions of local authorities.

12.32   In *Re M (Care: Challenging Decisions by Local Authority)*,[18] in the context of care proceedings, the local authority held a permanency planning meeting to which, by reason of a breakdown in communication, the parents were not invited. The meeting concluded that rehabilitation of the child to the parents was ruled out and that in the event that an extended family placement was not viable then adoption would be the plan. Both parents commenced actions under s 7 of the Human Rights Act 1998 claiming:

(1)   that the manner in which the local authority had reached its conclusion at the meeting was incompatible with their right to respect for their family life under Art 8(1) of the European Convention for the Protection of Human Rights and Fundamental Freedoms 1950, and that the decision was accordingly made unlawful by virtue of s 6(1) of the 1998 Act; and

(2)   that the combined effects of ss 6, 7 and 8 of the Act required that the current plans of the local authority should be reviewed and sanctioned by the court.

12.32   Both parents also applied under s 39 Children Act 1989 for discharge of the care order.

12.33   The court found that the manner in which the local authority had reached its decision was in breach of Art 8 of the ECHR having regard to the circumstances of the case and the serious nature of the decisions to be taken, the parents had not been involved in the decision-making process to a degree sufficient to provide them with the proper protection of their interests. Therefore, the court found that the local authority had acted unlawfully and that the decision made at the meeting to pursue permanence by way of adoption was quashed. The court did not direct the manner in which the local authority would now be required to reconsider that decision.

12.35   The case of Re *S (Minors) (Care Order: Implementation of Care Plan); Re W (Minors) (Care Order: Adequacy of Care Plan)*[19] confirms the capacity for claims under the HRA 1998 to be pursued in appropriate cases. The following principles emerge from the case:

•   While a care order is in force the court's powers under its inherent jurisdiction are expressly excluded (s 100(2)(c) and (d), (para [23]).

---

[18]   [2001] 2 FLR 1300.
[19]   [2002] 1 FLR 815 (HL). See also Wall LJ at para 93 and 94 in *Re S and W (Care Proceedings)* [2007] 2 FLR 275.

- Where a care order is made the responsibility for the child's care is with the authority rather than the court. The court retains no supervisory role in monitoring the authority's discharge of its responsibilities (para [25]).

- The court has no power to impose conditions in a care order (para [26]).

- Section 6 of the Human Rights Act 1998 makes it unlawful for a public authority to act in a way which is incompatible with a convention right. Section 7 enables victims of conduct made unlawful by s 6 to bring court proceedings against the public authority in question. Section 8 spells out, in wide terms, the relief a court may grant in those proceedings. The court may grant such relief or remedy, or make such order, within its powers as it considers just and appropriate. Thus if a local authority conducts itself in a manner which infringes the Art 8 rights of a parent or a child, the court may grant appropriate relief on the application of a victim of the unlawful act (para [45]).

- The question whether the authority has acted unlawfully, or is proposing to do so, is a matter to be decided in the proceedings. Relief can be given against the authority only in respect of an act, or proposed act, of the authority which the court finds is or would be unlawful (para [49]).

- Clearly if matters go seriously awry, the manner in which a local authority discharges its parental responsibility to a child in its care may violate the rights of the child ... under Art 8. The local authority's intervention in the life of the child, justified at the outset when the care order was made, may cease to be justifiable under Art 8(2). Sedley LJ pointed out that a care order from which no good is coming cannot be sensibly be said to be pursuing a legitimate aim (para [54]).

- Thus if a local authority fails to discharge its parental responsibilities properly, and in consequence the rights of the parents under Art 8 are violated, the parents may, as a long stop bring proceedings against the authority under s 7 (para[62]).

- In discharging its responsibility the local authority has the duty of respecting the convention rights of the child ... if a dispute arises whether this duty has been breached in any particular case the person aggrieved can now invoke the court's jurisdiction to determine it under s 7 of the Human Rights Act 1998 if no other route is available (para [109]).

12.36 In the event that a freestanding application under s 7(1)(a) is pursued the proceedings must be brought before the end of the period of one year beginning with the date on which the act complained of took place or such longer period as the court or tribunal considers equitable having regard to all the circumstances.[20] A freestanding application must be brought under Part 8 of the Civil Procedure Rules 1998.

12.37 In the event that there is a challenge/complaint regarding the care plan of the local authority then such issues should be heard in the Family Division of the High Court and preferably before a judge with experience of sitting in the Administrative Court: *CF v The Secretary of State for the Home Department*[21] and *Re S and W (Care Proceedings)*.[22]

12.38 In the event that issues under the ECHR and Human Rights Act 1998 are raised within care proceedings they are almost always more appropriately considered within those proceedings as opposed to the issue of separate HRA 1998 proceedings. The making of an application under the HRA 1998 within existing proceedings must be brought under Part 18 of the Civil Procedure Rules 1998.

12.39 Confirmation of the appropriateness of issues under the HRA 1998 being litigated within ongoing care proceedings without the need for a freestanding application to be made was confirmed in *Re L (Care Proceedings Human Rights Claims)* per Munby J:[23]

> 'There was an important distinction to be drawn between cases where care proceedings had come to an end, where a freestanding application under section 7(1)(a) of the Human Rights Act 1998 was the appropriate remedy, and cases where care proceedings were still on foot, where section 7(1)(b) provided and appropriate remedy within the care proceedings themselves. Human Rights Act complaints which arose before the making of a final care order should normally be dealt with in the context of the care proceedings and by the court dealing with the care proceedings.'[24]

12.40 In the event that a party seeks to rely on breaches of the ECHR, and in particular, alleged breaches of Arts 6 and 8, it is imperative that they act without delay and seek interim relief immediately.

12.41 *Re P (Adoption: Breach of Care Plan)*[25] concerned an application by a father for leave to appeal against freeing for adoption orders made in respect of his two children. The children were aged 10 and 5. There was divided opinion between the professionals as to whether adoption was the correct path. In recognising those issues the care plan provided for a plan to pursue long term fostering concurrently with adoption. Based on that care plan the parents consented to a care order and were reassured by the local authority who made it clear that they would be considered and kept informed throughout the

---

[20] HRA 1998, s 7(5).
[21] [2004] 2 FLR 517.
[22] [2007] 2 FLR 275.
[23] [2003] 2 FLR 160.
[24] See also Wall LJ at para 91 in *Re S and W (Care Proceedings)* [2007] 2 FLR 275.
[25] [2004] 2 FLR 1109.

placement process. Subsequently, and unbeknown to the parents, the local authority reneged on the plan and identified prospective adopters. The children were placed with the adopters and the local authority made arrangements for the parents to have a final goodbye contact session with the children. There were ongoing disputes between the father and the local authority and the father issued applications for the discharge of the care orders. The parents' applications were heard at the same time as the applications by the local authority for freeing for adoption orders.

12.42   The judge granted the freeing orders. The father appealed and argued that his rights under Arts 6 and 8 of the ECHR had been breached due to the manner in which the local authority had behaved. Permission to appeal was refused, Thorpe LJ stating:

> '[20] When the father sensed, as he inevitably must have done, that the denial of contact was both a breach of the care plan and a breach of his rights, then it was to the judge that he should have gone immediately. This failure to apply for interim relief is as significant, in my judgment, as the failure to apply under s 7 of the Human Rights Act 1998. Indeed, in my judgment, it is more significant because, although there may be some professional unfamiliarity with the s 7 route, and there may be difficulties in obtaining public funding for a s 7 application, all with any experience of public law litigation know that the judge is available at short notice to restore any rights that are being arbitrarily denied or withheld by local authorities in possession of care orders. The local authority's duty to ensure and promote contact was plain. The application for a termination order under s 34 of the Children Act 1989 had been withdrawn. This was, therefore, the plainest case for an urgent application to the judge to intervene. In all these submissions in relation to the dismissal of the contact application and in relation to human rights breaches, I attach great significance to the father's failure to protest those breaches prior to the trial in mid-December.'

12.43   If a party proposes to raise HRA 1998 applications in the context of interim care applications useful guidance is provided by the Court of Appeal (Wall LJ) in *Re S (Care Proceedings: Human Rights)*:[26]

> '[9] The reason I prefer this approach is that it immediately focuses the mind of the tribunal on Art 8 of the European Convention. If (and it is not a practice which I wish to encourage) parties are to make HRA applications in care proceedings, it would, I think, be helpful if those hearing such cases were to focus on the European Convention when making or refusing to make interim orders. Thus if – as here – a judge plainly takes the view that the conduct of the local authority represents a breach or breaches of a party's Arts 6 and 8 European Convention rights he or she will:
>
> (a)   be able to invite argument on the point then and there; and
> (b)   will be able to make appropriate findings in the context of the application before the court. Much time and expense could thereby be saved.'

---

26   [2010] EWCA Civ 1383, [2012] 2 FLR 209.

12.44 The grant of injunctive relief under the HRA 1998 is considered in more detail in chapter 13 where the case of *Re H (Care Plan: Human Rights)*[27] is also discussed. This case confirms that there was jurisdiction pursuant to s 8(1) to injunct a local authority from separating a mother and child and that this jurisdiction flowed from the cases of *Re W and B; Re W (Care Plan)*[28] and *Coventry City Council v O (Adoption)*.[29]

12.45 The very recent case of *RCW v A Local Authority*[30] is also an example of the grant of injunctive relief pursuant to the HRA 1998 against a local authority to prevent the removal of a child from a prospective adopter. This case is also considered more fully in chapter 13.

---

[27] [2012] 1 FLR 191.
[28] [2001] EWCA Civ 757.
[29] [2011] EWCA Civ 729.
[30] [2013] EWHC 235 (Fam).

Chapter 13

INJUNCTIVE RELIEF

SECTION 1 – INTRODUCTION

13.1 This chapter explores the capacity for the court to grant injunctive relief in the context of public law proceedings in respect of children. In particular, the chapter will focus on the injunctive powers available both to the local authority but also those that are permitted to be used against a local authority.

13.2 The chapter will very briefly focus on the court's powers under the Family Law Act 1996 and the Protection from Harassment Act 1997 insofar as injunctive provisions are concerned, particularly with regard to injunctions intended to protect children, and provide an overview of the same. It is not intended that this chapter should be an exhaustive and fully detailed description of those topics, as to do so would be to stray from the context of this book regarding decisions of the local authority and would represent in any event a topic too wide to consider properly.

13.3 The chapter will also consider the legislative basis for the grant of injunctive relief provided by the County Courts Act 1984 and by the Senior Courts Act 1981.

13.4 Additionally, and very much a 'hot topic' at the time of writing (February 2013), is the capacity for a party to seek injunctive relief pursuant to the Human Rights Act 1998. Chapter 12 deals with the wider topic of Human Rights Act claims but this chapter will specifically consider the grant of injunctive relief pursuant to the 1998 Act. Chapter 16 deals with the grant of injunctions within judicial review proceedings.

SECTION 2 – THE LEGAL FRAMEWORK

13.5 Relevant legislation is as follows:

- Children Act 1989.

- Family Law Act 1996.

- Protection from Harassment Act 1997.

- County Courts Act 1984, s 38.

- Senior Courts Act 1981, s 37.

- Human Rights Act 1998, s 8.

SECTION 3 – JURISDICTION OF THE COUNTY COURT

13.6   The availability of remedies (which include the grant of injunctive relief) in the county court is also provided by s 38 of the County Courts Act 1984:

> (1) Subject to what follows, in any proceedings in a county court the court may make any order which could be made by the High Court if the proceedings were in the High Court.
>
> (2) Any order made by a county court may be –
>
>> (a)   absolute or conditional;
>> (b)   final or interlocutory.

13.7   Jurisdiction to grant injunctive relief, particularly in the context of the protection of children may also derive from the following statutory provisions:

- Family Law Act 1996;[1]

- Protection from Harassment Act 1997.

13.8   The Family Law Act 1996 provides jurisdiction, amongst other matters, regarding the grant of non-molestation orders and/or occupation orders (regulating occupation of a dwelling house) in order to protect associated persons and/or children. Those powers are likely to be the first port of call in any case in which the need for injunctive relief arises. In the event that those provisions are not applicable to the situation and/or do not extend to the situation in question it is then that the court will consider its other powers (eg under s 38 County Courts Act 1984).

13.9   The Protection from Harassment Act 1997 is also available but there is likely to be a substantial overlap with the provisions of the Family Law Act 1996. The remedies under the 1997 Act are only available to 'a person' and the local authority as an entity does not come within that definition. Therefore the local authority is not able to apply for an order under this Act. Indeed, the capacity for individual social workers (as affected persons) to apply for such orders may also be limited and inappropriate.[2]

13.10   The jurisdiction of the county court is a creature of statute. Unlike the High Court the county court does not possess any inherent jurisdiction to grant injunctions. Accordingly, the grant of injunctive relief in the county court must

---

[1]   As amended by the Domestic Violence Crime and Victims Act 2004.
[2]   *Tameside MBC v M (Injunctive Relief: County Courts: Jurisdiction)* [2001] Fam Law 873 considered below **13.16**.

be based on the available statutory powers as opposed to the wider inherent jurisdiction exercisable by the High Court.

13.11 In *D v D (County Court: Jurisdiction: Injunctions)*[3] a father alleged physical abuse by the mother against their children in the context of private law proceedings. The father had made a complaint to the police who in turn had alerted social services and the children were the subject of a medical examination. At a directions hearing the judge was highly critical of the father's actions and the actions of the police and social services. The judge made a number of interim orders regulating the residence and contact issues but also made a direction that neither the police nor social services should take any further steps regarding the children without further referral of the matter to the court. At a further hearing, at which the local authority was represented, the local authority indicated that it intended to pursue a s 47 of the Children Act 1989 investigation. Nevertheless, the order against the police and social services was confirmed with minor modifications. The father, local authority and the police appealed against that order arguing that the court lacked jurisdiction to so order.

13.12 The appeal was allowed. The Court of Appeal found that the county court had no inherent jurisdiction to grant injunctions to restrain a local authority from exercising its statutory powers in relation to children, or the police from exercising their statutory or common law powers, and had no statutory jurisdiction to do so under the Children Act 1989. The Court of Appeal did, however, find that the making of a prohibited steps order (pursuant to s 8 of the Children Act 1989) to restrain a party holding parental responsibility from involving those other agencies if it was satisfied that in so doing that party was acting in a way detrimental to the welfare of the children was permissible.

13.13 The jurisdiction of the county court to grant injunctive relief to supplement public law orders was also considered in the case of *Devon County Council v B*.[4] In that case the local authority sought an order freeing the child for adoption and an order under s 34(4) of the Children Act 1989. The local authority also pursued an application for an injunction under the inherent jurisdiction restraining the mother from entering or attempting to enter the town where the child was living with his father and stepmother because the local authority was investigating the possibility of placing him with them. The judge (sitting in the county court) ordered, amongst other things, adjournment of the freeing application for 'review' and granted an injunction in terms similar to those sought. The mother appealed against the judge's decision.

13.14 The appeal was allowed and the Court of Appeal reiterated that the county court did not have jurisdiction to grant the injunction sought. Applying s 100(3) of the Children Act 1989, no application for any exercise of the court's

---

3   [1993] 2 FLR 802.
4   [1997] 1 FLR 591.

inherent jurisdiction with respect to children could be made by a local authority without the leave of the court, namely the High Court. The county court did not have an inherent jurisdiction to grant injunctions in relation to the exercise by local authorities of their statutory powers in public law applications under the 1989 Act.

13.15   However, case authority[5] does exist for the proposition that the county court has jurisdiction to grant injunctions to protect the staff of a local authority and to allow for its functions under the care order to be properly discharged and that such orders are properly made under s 38 of the County Courts Act 1984.

13.16   In *Tameside MBC v M (Injunctive Relief: County Courts: Jurisdiction)*[6] four children were made the subject of care orders based on permanence by way of long term fostering or adoptive placements. The parents had made regular threats of violence against social workers, had threatened to 'firebomb' houses, caused criminal damage to social workers cars, obtained home telephone numbers and addresses of professionals and followed social workers home. Undertakings given by the parents as to their behaviour had been breached and the social work staff were described as being very frightened. The local authority sought injunctive relief under the Protection from Harassment Act 1997 and, in the alternative, relief within the care proceedings, either through the exercise of the court's inherent jurisdiction, or in the exercise of its statutory jurisdiction under s 38 of the County Courts Act 1984. These proceedings were heard on the day the care orders were made.

13.17   The court declined to grant injunctive relief under the Protection from Harassment Act 1997 or by reason of any inherent jurisdiction but instead granted injunctive relief in the exercise of its statutory jurisdiction under s 38 of the County Courts Act 1984. The court confirmed the principle that the county court did not have any inherent jurisdiction to grant an injunction, but held that a statutory jurisdiction existed to do so when, as in this case, the local authority had established a statutory right, by virtue of the care order granted by the court. The grant of injunctive relief was found to be just and convenient and was required to enable the local authority to implement its care plan and in accordance with its parental responsibility for each of the children.

SECTION 4 – JURISDICTION OF THE HIGH COURT

13.18   The power of the High Court to grant injunctive relief is provided by s 37 of the Senior Courts Act 1981:

> (1) The High Court may by order (whether interlocutory or final) grant an injunction or appoint a receiver in all cases in which it appears to the court to be just and convenient to do so.

---

5   This case is a first instance decision of a county court judge and has not been the subject of consideration by the Court of Appeal.

6   [2001] Fam Law 873.

(2) Any such order may be made either unconditionally or on such terms and conditions as the court thinks just.

13.19 In common with the county court, the High Court retains jurisdiction to grant injunctive relief for the purpose of the protection of children and others and this is derived from the following statutory provisions:

•   Family Law Act 1996;[7]

•   Protection from Harassment Act 1997.

13.20 In addition, and unlike the county court, the High Court does have the power to make injunctions pursuant to the inherent jurisdiction in cases where the interests of the child require the making of such orders.

Section 37

13.21 The case of *C v K (Inherent Powers: Exclusion Order)*[8] is an often cited case authority with regard to the jurisdiction of the High Court insofar as the grant of injunctive relief is concerned. Wall J was considering the issue of whether the court had jurisdiction to exclude a joint tenant from a property. The circumstances of the case were that the applicant (C) was looking after her grandson and she had previously been in a relationship with K. They had ceased living as husband and wife but K sporadically returned to the property and was abusive towards both the applicant and her grandson. C and K were joint tenants of the property. At an interim hearing, C had been granted a residence order in respect of her grandson and an injunction had been granted excluding K from the property pending the final hearing. The issue at the final hearing was whether the court had jurisdiction to grant injunctive relief.

13.22 The court made clear that this case did not concern the '*parens patriae*'[9] jurisdiction of the High Court over children who had been made wards of court. The following principles emerge from this case:

•   Jurisdiction exists in both the High Court and the county court to protect children from harm which is exercisable irrespective of the proceedings in which the issue of the need to protect the children arises.

•   There is a co-existing jurisdiction given in the High Court by s 37 of the Senior Courts Act 1981 and in the county court by s 38 of the County Courts Act 1984 to grant injunctive relief in support of legal and equitable rights.

---

[7]   As amended by the Domestic Violence Crime and Victims Act 2004.

[8]   [1996] 2 FLR 506.

[9]   Per Lord Denning in *Re L (An Infant)* [1968] 1 All ER 20 and deriving from the right and duty of the Crown as parens patriae to take care of those who are not able to take care of themselves.

- The powers exercisable under ss 37 and 38 of the respective statutes may be invoked in support of the rights and duties conferred on a person by a residence order and the powers of the court in this context extend to orders against molestation and to ouster injunctions.

- The powers exercisable by the court under ss 37 and 38 extend to the grant of injunctions against third parties. Thus, a person who is not a parent of the child may be restrained from interfering with the exercise of parental responsibility by a person who has a residence order in relation to the child. The powers of the court to grant injunctive relief include the power to exclude the stranger from property in which he or she has a beneficial interest.

- The powers of the court to exclude a person from property in which he or she has a proprietary interest should be exercised with extreme caution. By analogy with s 100(4) of the Children Act, the jurisdiction is likely only to be exercised where the court is satisfied that if the jurisdiction is not exercised the child is likely to suffer significant harm. In reaching any conclusion the court must look at all the circumstances of the case, including of course the circumstances of each of the parties and the conduct of the parties towards each other and the child. The court must make findings of fact upon which the assessment of likely future harm can be made.

- Whilst the jurisdiction exists to make a final order excluding a person from occupation of property in which he or she has a proprietary interest, without limitation of time, the court cannot by these means vary proprietary interests and must in every such case consider whether an indefinite order is required in order to protect the child from the likelihood of significant harm, and to achieve a result which is just.

13.23 The case of *C v K* was also applied in *Re P (Care Orders: Injunctive Relief)*[10] in which the power of the High Court to grant injunctive relief was further considered. There had been serious concerns regarding the sporadic attendance of the child (who was described as highly intelligent) at school which had led to the child being removed from the parents care and placed in foster care. The local authority subsequently sought a final care order with placement of the child at home with her parents on the condition that the parents supported the child's attendance at college. The local authority sought injunctions ancillary to the care order requiring the parents to allow the child to attend the college without interference and permitting the local authority to monitor the family. An issue arose as to whether such injunctions should be granted pursuant to the inherent jurisdiction (pursuant to s 100 of the Children Act 1989) or whether s 37 of the Senior Courts Act 1981 (described then as the Supreme Court Act 1981) could be invoked in support of the local authority's statutory duties towards children in its care.

---

[10] [2000] 2 FLR 385.

13.24   In granting the injunctions sought, it was held that (per Charles J):

- The powers conferred on the court by the Supreme Court Act 1981 (now known as the Senior Courts Act 1981), s 37 were available to support the rights conferred by the Children Act 1989, s 33, and in particular s 33(3) after a care order had been made.

- The Children Act 1989, s 100 did not apply to the general statutory power to make injunctions, therefore it was not necessary for the local authority to have leave to apply for the injunctive relief sought.

SECTION 5 – INHERENT JURISDICTION

13.25   The case of *Re S (Minors) (Inherent Jurisdiction: Ouster)*[11] supports the proposition that in circumstances where no other means exists to achieve the result, the court retains an inherent jurisdiction to remove a person from a home in order to protect the welfare of those children living in that home. However, as was observed by Wall J in *C v K* above, no issue was taken by the father against whom the ouster order was sought, as to the court having inherent jurisdiction (as opposed to jurisdiction founded upon s 37 of the Senior Courts Act 1981) to oust a person from a home. Indeed, the father expressly conceded that the High Court had jurisdiction to oust an individual under the inherent jurisdiction but that the circumstances of the case were such that this jurisdiction should not be exercised. For those reasons, it is a case authority that should be approached with some caution and in any event is superseded by the conclusions of *C v K*.

See chapter 14 for more detailed consideration of the inherent jurisdiction and wardship.

SECTION 6 – WITHOUT NOTICE ORDERS

13.26   There will be situations where the circumstances of the case justify the grant of a without notice order. However, it is imperative that practitioners consider the following principles with regard to such without notice applications. Failure to have proper regard for these principles will expose practitioners to a real risk of adverse consequences including the making of a costs order.

13.27   In *Re S (Ex Parte Orders)* it was held (per Munby J) that:[12]

- Those applying for ex parte relief were under a duty to make the fullest disclosure of all the relevant circumstances known to them, including all relevant matters, whether of fact or law.

---

[11]   [1994] 1 FLR 623.
[12]   [2001] 1 FLR 308.

- Those who obtained ex parte injunctive relief were also under an obligation to bring to the attention of the respondent, at the earliest practicable opportunity, the evidential and other persuasive materials on the basis of which the injunction had been granted.

- Generally, when granting ex parte injunctive relief in the Family Division the court would require the applicant and, where appropriate, the applicant's solicitors, to give the following undertakings:

  (a) where proceedings had not yet been issued, to issue and serve proceedings on the respondent, either by some specified time or as soon as practicable, in the form of the draft produced to the court or otherwise as might be appropriate;

  (b) where the application had been made otherwise than on sworn evidence, to cause to be sworn, filed and served on the respondent as soon as practicable an affidavit or affidavits substantially in the terms of the draft affidavit(s) produced to the court or, as the case might be, confirming the substance of what was said to the court by the applicant's counsel or solicitors; and

  (c) subject to (a) and (b) above, to serve on the respondent as soon as practicable:

      (i)   the proceedings,
      (ii) a sealed copy of the order,
      (iii) copies of the affidavit(s) and exhibit(s) containing the evidence relied on by the applicant, and
      (iv) notice of the return date including details of the application to be made on the return date.

- A person who had given an undertaking to the court was under an unqualified obligation to comply to the letter with that undertaking, and when the undertaking was to do something by a specified time then time was of the essence. A person who found himself unable to comply timeously with his undertaking should either:

  (i)   apply for an extension of time before the time for compliance had expired; or
  (ii) pass the task to someone who had available the time in which to do it.

- Whether or not express undertakings were given, an applicant who obtained ex parte injunctive relief was under an obligation to carry out the steps set out above, as was the solicitor.

- Any ex parte order containing injunctions should set out on its face, either by way of recital or in a schedule, a list of all affidavits, witness statements and other evidential materials read by the judge. The applicant's legal representatives should whenever possible liaise with the associate to ensure that the order as drawn contained this information, and if the order did not, should take urgent steps to have it amended under the slip rule.

- Because persons injuncted were entitled to be given proper information about without notice hearings it would be prudent for those acting for the applicant in such a case to keep a proper note of proceedings, lest they found themselves embarrassed by a reasonable request for information which they were unable to provide.

13.28 A further example of the court providing guidance as to best practice regarding without notice applications is that of *B Borough Council v S (by the Official Solicitor)*[13] in which the exceptional nature of a without notice application was confirmed. The court was critical of the number of unnecessary and inappropriate without notice applications being made which were not supported by appropriate evidence. Charles J[14] found that good practice, fairness and common sense demanded that on a without notice application the applicant should provide the court with:

(a) a balanced, fair and particularised account of the events leading up to the application and thus of the matters upon which it is based. In many cases this should include a brief account of what the applicant thinks the respondent's case is, or is likely to be;

(b) where available and appropriate, independent evidence;

(c) a clear and particularised explanation of the reasons why the application is made without notice and the reasons why the permission to apply to vary or discharge the injunction granted should be on notice (rather than immediately or forthwith as in the standard collection and location orders) and why the return date should not be within a short period of time; and

(d) (in many cases) an account of the steps the applicant proposes concerning service, the giving of an explanation of the order and the implementation of an order. This is likely to be of particular importance in cases such as this where emotional issues are involved and family members of a person who lacks capacity are the subject of the injunctions and orders. In such cases, as here, information as to those intentions is likely to inform issues as to the need for, and the proportionality of, the relief sought and granted.

---

[13]   [2007] 1 FLR 1600.
[14]   Endorsing the guidance given by Munby J in *Re S (Ex Parte Orders)* [2001] 1 FLR 308.

SECTION 7 – EXCLUSION ORDERS

13.29 In the event that the court finds there are reasonable grounds to believe that the circumstances with respect to a child, as set out in s 31(2)(a) and (b)(i) Children Act 1989 (ie the threshold criteria), are satisfied and the court makes an interim care order, then in an appropriate case it may make an order pursuant to s 38A of the Children Act 1989 to exclude a person from a dwelling house in which a child lives.

13.30 The conditions for making such an order are, pursuant to s 38A(2):

(a) that there is reasonable cause to believe that, if a person ("the relevant person") is excluded from a dwelling-house in which the child lives, the child will cease to suffer, or cease to be likely to suffer, significant harm, and

(b) that another person living in the dwelling-house (whether a parent of the child or some other person) –

(i) is able and willing to give to the child the care which it would be reasonable to expect a parent to give him, and
(ii) consents to the inclusion of the exclusion requirement.

13.31 The court may attach a power of arrest to a s 38A exclusion order and in that event a constable may arrest without warrant any person whom he or she has reasonable cause to believe to be in breach of that requirement.[15]

13.32 Similar provisions with regard to the inclusion of an exclusion requirement are also applicable on the court granting an emergency protection order.[16]

SECTION 8 – THE HUMAN RIGHTS ACT 1998

13.33 See chapter 12 for a more detailed analysis of claims under the Human Rights Act 1998.

13.34 In respect of an act (or proposed act) of a local authority (as a public authority) which the court finds is (or would be) unlawful, the court may grant such relief or remedy, or make such order, within its powers as it considers just and appropriate.[17] Further to the case authorities set out below, such relief can include injunctive relief as against a party, including the local authority.

13.35 The case of *Re H (Care Plan: Human Rights)*[18] provides an example of a fairly typical issue arising in a care case regarding the suitability or otherwise of the local authority care plan and guidance from the Court of Appeal as to how that situation should have been managed having regard to the Human Rights Act 1998.

---

[15]   Section 38A(5) and (8).
[16]   CA 1989, s 44A.
[17]   Human Rights Act 1998, s 8(1).
[18]   [2012] 1 FLR 191.

13.36   In that case the local authority's care plan was for the mother and child to be placed together in a safe environment under the auspices of an interim care order. However, at a subsequent hearing the local authority changed its interim care plan and sought to remove the child from the care of the mother and place the child in foster care. The judge indicated her disapproval of the care plan insofar as it provided for the child to be placed in foster care. The judge expressed the view that the removal of the child from the care of the mother was not necessary and was a disproportionate response and amounted to a breach of both the mother's and child's rights pursuant to Art 8 of the European Convention for the Protection of Human Rights and Fundamental Freedoms 1950. Therefore, the judge invited the local authority to reconsider and amend its interim care plan. The local authority declined to amend its care plan and sought an interim care order based on a care plan of removal of the child to foster care. Despite her strong disapproval of the care plan the judge felt constrained to grant the interim care order endorsing a care plan for removal. The mother's representatives made submissions that included reliance on s 8 of the Human Rights Act 1998. The judge indicated a willingness to hear an application for injunctive relief under the Human Rights Act 1998. Therefore, two days later the mother applied for an injunction under s 8(1). That application was subsequently dismissed when the judge found that she had no jurisdiction to grant an injunction under s 8(1) Human Rights Act 1998 once an interim care order had been made.

13.37   The mother appealed against that decision and the appeal was allowed. The Court of Appeal granted interim relief and concluded that there was jurisdiction pursuant to s 8(1) Human Rights Act 1998 to injunct a local authority from separating a mother and child and that this jurisdiction flowed from the cases of *Re W and B; Re W (Care Plan)*[19] and *Coventry City Council v O (Adoption)*.[20] The Court of Appeal also found that the application for an injunction under s 8(1) Human Rights Act 1998 and the application for an interim care order should have properly been considered by the judge at the same time.

13.38   However, it is of note that the two judgments of the Court of Appeal from Thorpe LJ and Black LJ indicate that this outcome was intended only to be a pragmatic solution in a case requiring urgent consideration. The issues raised by the skeleton arguments in this case were recognised to be important and manifestly demanded a suitable three judge constitution (which had not been possible given the time constraints). Accordingly, whilst this is good authority for the proposition that there is power to injunct a local authority pursuant to the Human Rights Act 1998 it is inevitable that there will be further Court of Appeal guidance on this issue when the full arguments in a suitable case reach a suitably constituted three judge Court of Appeal.

---

[19]   [2001] EWCA Civ 757.
[20]   [2011] EWCA Civ 729.

13.39 The very recent case of *RCW v A Local Authority*[21] is a further example, at first instance, of a court granting an urgent application for injunctive relief pursuant to the Human Rights Act 1998. The injunctive relief granted was to prevent a local authority from removing a child from the care of a prospective adopter who had lost her sight after surgical intervention to remove a tumour on the brain. The prospective adopter asserted that the removal of the child from her care would infringe both her and the child's Art 8 rights under the ECHR, that the decision making of the local authority was flawed and that she had been excluded from any involvement in that decision making. The court held (per Cobb J):

> 'On the information before me I am satisfied that LBX failed to give RCW a full and informed opportunity to address its concerns about the future care arrangements for SB. In this respect, LBX had acted in breach of the procedural rights guaranteed by Article 8 and Article 6 and of the common law principle of fairness.'

---

[21] [2013] EWHC 235 (Fam) per Cobb J at para 32.

Chapter 14

INHERENT JURISDICTION AND WARDSHIP

SECTION 1 – INTRODUCTION

14.1 As identified in chapter 13 the inherent jurisdiction is a creature of the High Court. The county court and the family proceedings court do not have any corresponding inherent jurisdiction. Therefore, reference to the inherent jurisdiction within this chapter refers exclusively to the exercise of the inherent jurisdiction of the High Court.

14.2 This chapter explores the extent to which invoking the inherent jurisdiction is available to both the local authority and to other parties and the limitations that exist in the exercise of that jurisdiction.

14.3 The inherent jurisdiction of the High Court includes, but is not limited to, wardship. This chapter considers the wardship jurisdiction and procedure and identifies occasions when the protection of the child will justify an application to make the child a ward of court.

SECTION 2 – THE LEGAL FRAMEWORK

14.4 Relevant legislation is as follows:

- Children Act 1989, s 100.

- Family Procedure Rules, Part 12, Chapter 5.

- Family Procedure Rules 2010, Practice Direction 12D.

SECTION 3 – INHERENT JURISDICTION

14.5 The origins of the exercise of the inherent jurisdiction of the High Court are well established and are variously described in a number of cases; the dicta of Lord Denning MR in *Re L (An Infant)* is most apposite and reads as follows:[1]

---

[1] [1968] 1 All ER 20.

'I think that counsel takes altogether too limited a view of the jurisdiction of the Court of Chancery. It derives from the right and duty of the Crown as *parens patriae* to take care of those who are not able to take care of themselves. The Crown delegated this power to the Lord Chancellor, who exercised it in his Court of Chancery. In the ordinary way he only exercised it when there was property to be applied for the infant (see *Wellesley v Duke of Beaufort* (1827) 2 Russ 1 at pp 20, 21). The child was usually made a ward of court, and thereafter no important step in the child's life could be taken without the court's consent; but that was only machinery. Even if there was no property and the child was not a ward of court, nevertheless the Court of Chancery had power to interfere for the protection of the infant by making whatever order might be appropriate. That was made clear by Lord Cottenham LC in *Re Spence*, where the infants were not wards and there was no property. Lord Cottenham LC said ((1847) 2 Ph at p 251):

> "I have no doubt about the jurisdiction. The cases in which this court interferes on behalf of infants are not confined to those in which there is property ... This court interferes for the protection of infants, qua infants, by virtue of the prerogative which belongs to the Crown as parens patriae, and the exercise of which is delegated to the Great Seal."

This wide jurisdiction of the old Court of Chancery is now vested in the High Court of Justice and can be exercised by any judge of the High Court.'

14.6   The nature of inherent jurisdiction proceedings is described in Practice Direction 12D[2] as follows:

'1.1 It is the duty of the court under its inherent jurisdiction to ensure that a child who is the subject of proceedings is protected and properly taken care of. The court may in exercising its inherent jurisdiction make any order or determine any issue in respect of a child unless limited by case law or statute. Such proceedings should not be commenced unless it is clear that the issues concerning the child cannot be resolved under the Children Act 1989.

1.2 The court may under its inherent jurisdiction, in addition to all of the orders which can be made in family proceedings, make a wide range of injunctions for the child's protection of which the following are the most common –

(a)   orders to restrain publicity;
(b)   orders to prevent an undesirable association;
(c)   orders relating to medical treatment;
(d)   orders to protect abducted children, or children where the case has another substantial foreign element; and
(e)   orders for the return of children to and from another state.

1.3 The court's wardship jurisdiction is part of and not separate from the court's inherent jurisdiction. The distinguishing characteristics of wardship are that –

(a)   custody of a child who is a ward is vested in the court; and

---

2   Supplementing the FPR 2010, Part 12, Chapter 5.

(b) although day to day care and control of the ward is given to an individual or to a local authority, no important step can be taken in the child's life without the court's consent.'

14.7 More recent confirmation of the exercise of the inherent jurisdiction and the interplay with wardship is provided by Parker J in *MA v DB (Inherent Jurisdiction)* from which the following principles emerge:[3]

*   proceedings pursuant to the inherent jurisdiction of the court in relation to children are 'family proceedings' as defined by s 8(3) of the Children Act 1989 and hence the court may make any s 8 order of its own motion;[4]

*   it is not necessary for a child to be made a ward of court in order for the inherent jurisdiction of the High Court to be invoked;

*   the court has the power to dispense with all formalities in order to bring proceedings to a mutually agreed conclusion.

The local authority as applicant

14.8 The use of the inherent jurisdiction (particularly with regard to wardship) by the local authority needs to be seen in the light of the restrictions imposed by s 100(2) of the Children Act 1989:

(2) No court shall exercise the High Court's inherent jurisdiction with respect to children –

(a) so as to require a child to be placed in the care, or put under the supervision, of a local authority;

(b) so as to require a child to be accommodated by or on behalf of a local authority;

(c) so as to make a child who is the subject of a care order a ward of court; or

(d) for the purpose of conferring on any local authority power to determine any question which has arisen, or which may arise, in connection with any aspect of parental responsibility for a child.

14.9 The local authority requires leave to make an application for any exercise of the court's inherent jurisdiction with respect to children.[5]

---

[3] [2011] 1 FLR 724.
[4] CA 1989, s 10(1)(b).
[5] CA 1989, s 100(3).

14.10   Leave may only be granted if the court is satisfied that:

(a)   the result which the authority wish to achieve could not be achieved through the making of any order of a kind to which subsection (5) applies[6]; and

(b)   there is reasonable cause to believe that if the court's inherent jurisdiction is not exercised with respect to the child he or she is likely to suffer significant harm.[7]

14.11   A court considering whether to grant leave to a local authority to make an application to invoke the inherent jurisdiction should not adopt a restrictive construction of s 100.[8]

14.12   *Re P (Care Orders: Injunctive Relief)*[9] establishes that in a case involving application for injunctive relief pursuant to s 37 of the Senior Courts Act 1981, s 100 of the Children Act 1989 does not apply and, therefore, it is not necessary for the local authority to have leave to apply for the injunctive relief sought.

14.13   In cases where the court is considering whether to grant leave, the court will plainly have a focus on whether the result that the local authority wishes to achieve could be secured by the making of orders other than under the inherent jurisdiction.[10]

14.14   An example of a case in which such issues arose is *Islington London Borough Council v E*[11] which involved care proceedings where the agreed care interim care plan was for the child to be placed with his father in Turkey. The issue was whether this could be achieved by invoking the inherent jurisdiction or by the child being placed under an interim care order. The judge ultimately found that the course proposed by the local authority contravened s 100(4)(a) of the Children Act 1989 because the local authority's proposed plan could be secured by the making of an interim care order and permission to place the child abroad by virtue of Sch 2, para 19 of the Children Act 1989.

14.15   Where a child is in the care of the local authority and issues arise that require the determination of the court the options are more limited for a local authority. In these circumstances an application under the inherent jurisdiction may be the only avenue available. A child in the care of the local authority

---

6   This subsection applies to any order –
     (a) made otherwise than in the exercise of the court's inherent jurisdiction; and
     (b) which the local authority is entitled to apply for (assuming, in the case of any application which may only be made with leave, that leave is granted).
7   CA 1989, s 100(4).
8   Per Thorpe LJ in *Devon County Council v S and Another* [1994] 1 FLR 355.
9   [2000] 2 FLR 385.
10   CA 1989, s 100(5).
11   [2011] 1 FLR 1681.

cannot be made a ward of court.[12] The local authority will also be bound by the provisions of s 9 of the Children Act:

(1) No court shall make any section 8 order, other than a residence order, with respect to a child who is in the care of a local authority.

(2) No application may be made by a local authority for a residence order or contact order and no court shall make such an order in favour of a local authority.

14.16 In the event that a child is not in care then a local authority will need to consider whether the result it seeks to achieve might be secured by seeking leave to make an application for a specific issue order or a prohibited steps order.[13] An example of such a course is *Re C (HIV Test)*[14] where the local authority successfully applied for and was granted a specific issue order directing that a baby should be tested for the presence of the HIV virus where the mother was herself HIV positive and both she and the father opposed the baby being subjected to such testing. Any application made by a local authority for a specific issue order or a prohibited steps order will have to ensure that it does not contravene s 9(5) of the Children Act 1989, namely:

'No court shall exercise its powers to make a specific issue order or prohibited steps order –

(a) with a view to achieving a result which could be achieved by making a residence or contact order; or

(b) in any way which is denied to the High Court (by section 100(2)) in the exercise of its inherent jurisdiction with respect to children.[15]

14.17 The local authority is entitled to seek to make application to the court under the inherent jurisdiction in cases where there are difficult or disputed issues as to what is in the best interests of a child and the court is required to resolve those issues or questions. Inevitably the cases involving the invoking of the inherent jurisdiction will represent the more unusual or novel issues or those that cannot be resolved by recourse to the relevant statutory provisions, in particular, the Children Act 1989.

14.18 *Re M (Care: Leave to Interview Child)*[16] is an example of a case in which the inherent jurisdiction was invoked. In this case the father was charged with rape of his daughters and his criminal solicitor sought permission to interview the father's two sons for the purpose of preparing the father's defence. The two boys were the subject of interim care orders and an issue arose between the local authority and a father as to the extent and manner in which those interviews should take place. The court determined that issue and identified that its jurisdiction so to do emanated from the inherent jurisdiction.

---

[12] CA 1989, s 100(2)(c) and Senior Courts Act 1981, s 41(2A).
[13] CA 1989, ss 9(5) and 10(2)(b), (9).
[14] [1999] 2 FLR 1004.
[15] See also *Nottinghamshire County Council v P* [1993] 2 FLR 134.
[16] [1995] 1 FLR 825.

14.19 In *London Borough of Brent v S*,[17] the local authority were concerned with the welfare of a 17-year-old Afghan national (S) who had been accommodated by the local authority on his arrival to the UK as an unaccompanied minor having previously left Afghanistan and travelled via Pakistan and then onto the UK for his own safety. He was unaware as to the whereabouts of family members and local authority efforts to trace them had proved unsuccessful. S wanted to travel to Pakistan to trace his family who he believed were refugees living there. The local authority opposed the trip on the grounds of safety and sought and obtained interim orders to prevent S from going on such a trip. The judge ultimately discharged the injunctions preventing S from travelling. However, with regard to the intervention of the local authority and the application to court, Sumner J stated:

> '[32] I would add a few words about the position of the local authority. They have been sympathetic to S, though the delay in reaching the decision and the manner in which it had to be carried out may not have been helpful. However I fully support them in deciding that, in such a difficult and anxious matter as this, they should seek a decision of the court. It would not have been an easy request to accept, even if the immigration position was not fully known. I hope nothing I have said discourages local authorities, in appropriate cases such as this, seeking the assistance of the court for which they are not to be criticised.'

Applicants other than local authority

14.20 Any individual can apply to invoke the inherent jurisdiction of the court.

14.21 The case of *A and S (Children) v Lancashire County Council (aka Re A and S (Children: Failed Freeing Orders)*[18] is more fully considered in chapter 12 in respect of human rights applications in the context of a party seeking declarations that the local authority and the independent reviewing officer had acted incompatibly with their Arts 3, 6 and 8 rights under the European Convention for the Protection of Human Rights and Fundamental Freedoms 1950 (ECHR). However, this case is also an example of the High court at an interim stage granting leave to A (a 16-year-old child) to apply to invoke the inherent jurisdiction of the High Court. Subsequently, an order was made under the inherent jurisdiction preventing the local authority from removing A from the care of his foster carers (that being the intended care plan of the local authority) without the permission of the court.

Procedure

14.22 Procedure for applications under the inherent jurisdiction is governed by FPR 2010, Part 12, Chapter 5, rr 12.36–12.42. Any party applying under the inherent jurisdiction must also have regard to FPR 2010, PD2D.

---

[17]   [2009] EWHC 1593 (Fam).
[18]   [2012] EWHC 1689 (Fam), [2012] All ER (D) 173.

14.23 Applications under the inherent jurisdiction must be issued in the High Court.[19]

SECTION 4 – THE EXERCISE OF THE INHERENT JURISDICTION

14.24 It is not possible to provide an exhaustive list of issues that are likely to require the court to be invited to exercise its inherent jurisdiction. In any event the scope of this book concerns the challenging and defending of decisions of the local authority and it is in this context that the inherent jurisdiction must be considered as opposed to the far wider issues that the inherent jurisdiction is available to address. Instead, what follows are headline topics of areas in which the inherent jurisdiction may be appropriately exercised and are matters that might also concern decision-making on the part of the local authority.

Orders to restrain publicity

14.25 A difficult and sometimes complex issue that appears to often be raised in proceedings (whether public law or private law) is the extent to which orders to restrain publicity are required.

14.26 The confidentiality of proceedings concerning children is well established and there exist a number of statutory provisions (considered briefly below) that regulate such confidentiality:

- Section 97(2) Children Act 1989 provides that no person shall publish to the public at large or any section of the public any material which is intended, or likely, to identify any child as being involved in any proceedings under the Children Act 1989 or the Adoption and Children Act 2002 or an address or school as being that of a child involved in any such proceedings.

- FPR 2010, Part 12, Chapter 7, rr 12.72–12.75 regulate the communication of information (including the disclosure of documents) in specified circumstances without the leave of the court requiring to be obtained.

- The Administration of Justice Act 1960,[20] s 12(1) prohibits the publication (whether in its widest sense (ie to the media) or more limited (ie to an individual)) of information relating to proceedings under the inherent jurisdiction, Children Act 1989, the Adoption and Children Act 2002 or proceedings that otherwise relate wholly or mainly to the maintenance or upbringing of a minor.

---

[19] FPR 2010, r 12.36(1).
[20] See *Re B (A Child) (Disclosure)* [2004] 2 FLR 142 per Munby J for a guide to the application of AJA 1960, s 12.

- The Contempt of Court Act 1981, s 11, provides the court with power to allow a name or other matter to be withheld from the public in proceedings before the court and to give directions prohibiting the publication of that name or matter in connection with the proceedings as appear to the court to be necessary for the purpose for which it was so withheld.

- The Children and Young Persons Act 1933, s 39 allows the court to direct that no newspaper report shall reveal the name, address or school, or include any particulars calculated to lead to the identification, of any child or young person concerned in the proceedings. This includes the power to prohibit a picture being published in any newspaper as being or including a picture of any child or young person involved in the proceedings.

14.27 Notwithstanding the existence of the statutory framework identified above, there are often issues raised as to whether those powers are sufficient or whether they require to be supplemented by orders under the inherent jurisdiction. The case of *A v M (Family Proceedings: Publicity)*[21] is just one example of that situation. This case involved protracted proceedings in which the aggrieved mother made allegations to the media. The father applied to the court for injunctive relief to prevent further disclosure to the media by the mother and her partner. Charles J considered the statutory provisions applicable (including the AJA 1960 and Family Procedure Rules) but concluded that relief over and above that which was provided was required in the circumstances of this case.

14.28 Often when public law proceedings are ongoing there are concurrent criminal proceedings and issues of disclosure/identification of individuals is an issue that the court requires to regulate given the public nature of criminal proceedings. See *Re S (Identification: Restriction on Publication)*[22] where the House of Lords held:

- Since the coming into force of the Human Rights Act 1998, the preceding case-law about the existence and scope of inherent jurisdiction of the High Court to restrain publicity need not be considered in this or similar cases. In a case such as the present the foundation of the jurisdiction to restrain publicity now derived from rights under the European Convention for the Protection of Human Rights and Fundamental Freedoms 1950 (ECHR). The case-law on the inherent jurisdiction was, however, not wholly irrelevant as it might remain of some interest in regard to the ultimate balancing exercise to be carried out under the European Convention provisions.

---

[21]   [2000] 1 FLR 562.
[22]   [2005] 1 FLR 591.

- The Art 8 rights of the child were engaged but the competing rights of freedom of the press under Art 10 were also engaged and were not, in these circumstances, outweighed by the rights of the child under Art 8.

- Full contemporaneous reporting of criminal trials in progress promoted public confidence in the administration of justice and promoted the values of the rule of law.[23]

- Given the weight traditionally given to the importance of open reporting of criminal proceedings, it had been important for the judge, in carrying out the exercise required by the ECHR, to begin by acknowledging the force of the argument under Art 10 before considering whether the right of the child under Art 8 was sufficient to outweigh it.

Orders to protect abducted children or where the case has a substantial foreign element

14.29   In *Re S (Wardship: Peremptory Return)*,[24] the local authority sought an emergency protection order in respect of a 7-year-old child that was alleged to be being seriously neglected. The justices refused to grant an emergency protection order and the mother promptly removed the child from England and went to Spain where the father was living. The local authority initiated care proceedings and also applied for leave to invoke the wardship jurisdiction under s 100(4)(a) of the Children Act 1989 with a view to ensuring that the child returned to the jurisdiction. The court accepted that the local authority could not achieve the result sought by any means other than wardship, made the child a ward of court and required the parents to return her to the jurisdiction. The parents appealed, arguing that the child had lost her habitual residence in England and was now habitually resident in Spain and that, therefore, there had been no jurisdiction to ward the child. The parents argued that the child's removal from the jurisdiction had been entirely lawful, in that the mother had merely exercised her parental responsibility in choosing to take the child abroad, and that they were, as parents, entitled to retain the child in Spain. The Court of Appeal held:

- The order for wardship was properly made but set aside the order for peremptory return.

- That it was permissible for a court to conclude that if there had been a lawful removal and a lawful retention abroad, and if the Hague Convention did not apply, then the only basis upon which the child could be returned to the jurisdiction was by wardship, and to conclude that s 100(4)(a) of the Children Act 1989, therefore, applied.

---

[23]   See also s 12 HRA 1998 which applies if a court is considering whether to grant any relief which, if granted, might affect the exercise of the Convention right to freedom of expression.
[24]   [2010] 2 FLR 1960.

- On the information provided by the local authority in this case it had been open to the judge, on an emergency basis, to say that there was a likelihood that if the inherent jurisdiction were not exercised the child was likely to suffer significant harm and to ward the child.

Orders for the return of children to and from another state

14.30   Albeit in the context of private law proceedings, see *B v D (Abduction: Inherent Jurisdiction)*[25] which is authority for the making of orders under the inherent jurisdiction as a mechanism for achieving the return of children removed to another country notwithstanding the initiation of proceedings under the Hague Convention of International Child Abduction 1980.

SECTION 5 – WARDSHIP

14.31   The use of wardship is still available to the court pursuant to the inherent jurisdiction but its use has been substantially reduced since the implementation of the Children Act 1989.

Jurisdiction

14.32   Wardship is part of the inherent jurisdiction of the High Court with regard to the protection of minors. Accordingly, the wardship jurisdiction only applies to persons under the age of 18 years.

14.33   An unborn child cannot be made a ward of court[26] but the capacity does exist to seek anticipatory declaratory relief in respect of an unborn child.[27]

14.34   The court does not have jurisdiction to make orders in wardship in respect of a child who was not and never had been habitually resident or present in the England.[28]

Effect of wardship

14.35   On the making of a wardship order the custody of a child who is a ward is vested in the court and no important step can be taken in the child's life without the consent of the court.[29]

---

[25]   [2009] 1 FLR 1015.
[26]   *Re F (In Utero) (Wardship)* [1988] 2 FLR 307.
[27]   *Re D (Unborn Baby)* [2009] 2 FLR 313.
[28]   *H v H (Jurisdiction to Grant Wardship)* [2011] EWCA Civ 796, [2012] 1 FLR 23.
[29]   Practice Direction 12D, para 1.3; *Re E (SA) (A Minor) (Wardship)* [1984] 1 All ER 289.

14.36 A plain advantage in utilising the wardship jurisdiction is that the child automatically becomes a ward of court, and is thereby protected, on the making of a wardship application.[30]

14.37 It is not possible to identify every scenario in which an application for a wardship order will be appropriate. Wardship is not a jurisdiction that is derived from statute and hence its development must be considered in the light of the case law.

Challenging the local authority

14.38 In the event that an individual seeks to challenge the decision of a local authority and complains that the local authority has acted improperly, unfairly or unlawfully the case authorities would not support wardship (or otherwise invoking the inherent jurisdiction) as being an appropriate course.

14.39 In *A v Liverpool City Council*,[31] attempts to challenge the actions of the local authority by way of wardship proceedings were robustly rejected.

Per Lord Wilberforce:

> 'Parliament has by statute entrusted to the local authority the power and duty to make decisions as to the welfare of children without any reservation of a reviewing power to the court.'

14.40 Per Lord Roskill:

> 'I am of the clear opinion that while prerogative jurisdiction of the court in wardship cases remains, the exercise of that jurisdiction has been and must continue to be treated as circumscribed by the existence of the far-ranging statutory code which entrusts the care and control of deprived children to local authorities. It follows that the undoubted wardship jurisdiction must not be exercised so as to interfere with the day to day administration by local authorities of that statutory control.'

14.41 Those principles were confirmed in *Re W (A Minor) (Care Proceedings: Wardship)*[32] per Lord Scarman:

> 'The High Court cannot exercise its powers, however wide they may be, so as to intervene on the merits in an area of concern entrusted by Parliament to another public authority.'[33]

14.42 Instead, an individual aggrieved by the actions of the local authority will need to challenge that decision by means other than wardship, including

---

[30] Senior Courts Act 1981, s 41(2).
[31] (1981) 2 FLR 222.
[32] [1985] FLR 879, applying *A v Liverpool City Council* (1981) 2 FLR 222.
[33] See also *Re S (Minors) (Care Order: Implementation of Care Plan); Re W (Minors) (Care Order: Adequacy of Care Plan)* [2002] 1 FLR 815.

consideration of an application for judicial review (for which see chapters 16 and 17) and/or a claim under the Human Rights Act 1998 (for which see chapter 12).

Invoking wardship jurisdiction

14.43 The case of *Re W and X (Wardship: Relatives Rejected as Foster Carers),*[34] a decision of Hedley J is an example of wardship being invoked to protect the interests of the children. In the context of care proceedings it was not in issue that the four children could not return to the care of their parents. The care plan for the youngest child was permanence by way of adoption. The care plan of the local authority in respect of the three older children was that they should remain in the care of the maternal grandparents. However, the local authority had previously rejected the maternal grandparents as foster carers. In the event that a care order was made, the impact of the Children Act 1989 and the Fostering Services Regulations 2002[35] was that the local authority would be required to remove the children from the care of the maternal grandparents. The court invoked the court's inherent jurisdiction in wardship and made the three older children wards of court. The reasoning for such an approach was that the circumstances of the case warranted continuing external control of the placement to ensure the children's welfare and that the invoking of the inherent jurisdiction filled a significant lacuna in the applicable statutory provisions.

14.44 In the case of *Re F (Mental Health Act: Guardianship),*[36] the Court of Appeal approved the invoking of the wardship jurisdiction as opposed to the grant to the local authority of a guardianship order under the Mental Health Act 1983 in respect of a 17-year-old child (assessed to be mentally operating in the 5–8 year range) who wished to return home to her parents in circumstances where the local authority considered that she would be exposed to risk. The Court of Appeal identified an immediately advantageous consequence of making the child a ward of court would be the appointment of the Official Solicitor as guardian ad litem thereby granting the advantage of separate representation, and in practical terms would have enabled one judge to consider the needs of all eight children in consolidated proceedings.

14.45 *Re K (Children with Disabilities Wardship)*[37] is a further example of a case where the court considered that the needs of the children demanded that they be made wards of court. The case concerned care proceedings in respect of five children between 17 and 3, three of whom suffered from severe and complex neuro-disabilities including cerebral palsy and epilepsy. Both parents suffered from mental and physical ill-health as a result of the demands of caring for the children. The local authority was granted permission to withdraw proceedings under Part IV of the Children Act 1989 and the three children with

---

[34]   [2003] EWHC 2206 (Fam), [2004] 1 FLR 415.
[35]   SI 2002/57.
[36]   [2000] 1 FLR 192.
[37]   [2012] 2 FLR 745.

disabilities were made wards of court. The judge's reasoning for the making of wardship orders included the conflicted history of the case, the desirability that a legal structure was in place and served as a reminder that all parties remained accountable to the court regarding the arrangements for the children and confirmed the court's powers over the control and delegation of parental responsibility.

14.46 In the context of a private law dispute, the case of *T v S (Wardship)*[38] is a reminder that in cases involving high levels of parental conflict the invoking of the wardship jurisdiction is, in a suitable case, an appropriate course.

14.47 In *Re E (A Child)*[39] the Court of Appeal concluded that the court was not precluded by virtue of s 100 of the Children Act 1989 from making a child a ward of court where that child had been accommodated pursuant to s 20 of the Children Act 1989.

---

[38] [2012] 1 FLR 230.
[39] *Re E (A Child) (Wardship Order: Child in Voluntary Accommodation)* [2012] EWCA Civ 1753, [2012] All ER (D) 262 (Nov).

Chapter 15

APPEALS

SECTION 1 – INTRODUCTION

15.1 This chapter will not attempt to be a full technical explanation of all the provisions and procedures for appeal but aims to provide the reader with a quick fingertip reference to the most essential elements.

15.2 It will focus on the immediate steps you will need to take where a court dealing with public law children's cases makes a decision with which you take issue.

15.3 We will also set out below important information that will assist in emergency situations where time is at its most limited and pressure at its highest.

15.4 Finally we hope to identify, and give you the knowledge to avoid, the most common 'elephant traps' likely to catch the unwary.

15.5 For more in depth consideration of the procedural steps reference should be made to the helpful tables and commentary on the statutes as contained in works such as the *Family Court Practice*[1] and the *White Book*.[2]

SECTION 2 – APPLICABLE RULES

Civil Procedure Rules 1998, Part 52 and PD52A and 52C[3]

15.6 These Rules govern appeals to the Court of Appeal and will apply to civil appeals[4] and most appeals likely to be made to the Court of Appeal with respect to child-care proceedings.[5]

---

[1]   Jordan Publishing, 2013.
[2]   Sweet and Maxwell, 2012.
[3]   Note that as from 1 October 2012 the old PD52 has been replaced by PD52A–PD52E.
[4]   For appeals against refusal of permission to apply for judicial review specific regard must be had to CPR 1998, r 52.15 and the exceptionally short timescale for appealing set out therein.
[5]   However please see below for those anomalies where appeals cannot be made under the heading 'Can I appeal? (**15.114–15.122**).

Civil Procedure Rules 1998, Part 52 and PD52A and 52B

15.7 These Rules govern appeals (in non-family proceedings) to the High Court and county court with the aim of providing a uniform procedure for appeals

Family Procedure Rules 2010, Part 30 and PD30A

15.8 These Rules govern appeals in family proceedings to the High Court and to a county court. They effectively codify for the lower courts the rules and practice that have grown up over the years with respect to appeals to the Court of Appeal. They therefore reflect the rules of that court but they do not apply to appeals to the Court of Appeal.

Appeals to High Court and county court

Children Act 1989, section 94

15.9 The effect of this section is that appeals from:

- orders made by a magistrates' court under the Children Act 1989 and the Adoption and Children Act 2002; and

- the refusal of a magistrates' court to make any order under those Acts,

are to be made to the county court and are no longer to be heard by the High Court.

Access to Justice Act 1999 (Destination of Appeals) (Family Proceedings) Order 2011[6]

15.10 The effect of this statutory instrument is that appeals from:

- a district judge of the High Court; and

- a district judge of the Principal Registry of the Family Division,

are to be made to the High Court irrespective of whether the decision appealed was made in the High Court or by the Principal Registry when it was treated as a care centre, adoption centre or as a county court (for the purposes of appeals from decisions of a magistrates' court under s 94 of the Children Act 1989).[7]

---

[6] SI 2011/1044.
[7] See art 2(1) and (2) of the Order.

15.11 Additionally appeals from a district judge or deputy district judge of the county court are to be made to a judge of the county court (obviously for this purpose the term 'judge of the county court' does not include a district judge or deputy district judge).[8]

Appeals to the Supreme Court

15.12 These are not considered in this work as such appeals are unlikely to be one of the 'immediate steps' that this chapter is designed to cover. They require careful attention to the formulation of the questions for the appeal and strict adherence to procedural rules.

15.13 Appeals to the Supreme Court are governed by the Supreme Court Rules 2009[9] and the associated practice directions. The statutory instruments and court forms can be accessed through the court website on www.supremecourt.gov.uk.

15.14 In specific circumstances a 'leapfrog appeal' may be made direct from the High Court to the Supreme Court. This will be governed by ss 12–16 of the Administration of Justice Act 1969. This route can only be considered if the case is one where the judge of the High Court certifies that a point of general public importance is involved and that it either:

- relates wholly or mainly to the construction of an enactment or statutory instrument, and has been fully argued in the proceedings and fully considered in the judgment of the judge in the proceedings,

- is one in respect of which the judge is bound by a decision of the Court of Appeal or of the Supreme Court in previous proceedings and was fully considered in the judgments given by the Court of Appeal or the Supreme Court (as the case may be) in those previous proceedings.

Do not assume that the same procedural steps and time limits apply as with appeals to the lower courts.

---

8   See art 3.
9   SI 2009/1603.

SECTION 3 – BARE ESSENTIALS

Permission

Appeal to Court of Appeal

15.15   Permission to appeal is required against all decisions made by the judge in the county court or High Court **except** committal orders, a refusal to grant habeas corpus or secure accommodations orders under s 25 of the Children Act 1989.[10]

15.16   Application for permission may be made to the court that made the decision that is to be appealed (unless that decision was itself a decision made on an appeal[11]) or to the Court of Appeal in an appeal notice.

15.17   If the application for permission is made to the court below and is refused an application for permission can still be made (within the time limits) to the Court of Appeal.

15.18   Usually the permission application will be dealt with as a paper application although if permission is refused then the appellant is entitled to request that the matter of permission be reconsidered at an oral hearing[12] (unless the Court of Appeal has determined that the appeal is totally without merit and has, pursuant to r 52.3(4A), barred any such application).

Appeal to High Court or county court

15.19   Permission to appeal is required against all decisions made by the district judge **except** committal orders or secure accommodation orders under s 25 of the Children Act 1989.

15.20   Permission to appeal is not required where the decision appealed is made by the magistrates' court.[13]

15.21   Application for permission may be made to the court which made the decision which is to be appealed or to the court which will hear the appeal in an appeal notice.[14]

15.22   Once again in civil proceedings the permission application will usually be dealt with as a paper application with the ability to seek an oral hearing if permission is refused on paper unless the High Court or Circuit Judge directs that the application is totally without merit and makes an order preventing the appellant from requesting reconsideration at an oral hearing.[15] It does not

---

[10]   See CPR 1998, r 52.3 and PD52A, para 4.1 et seq.
[11]   See CPR 1998, r 52.13 and **15.22** in the text above under 'second appeals'.
[12]   See CPR 1998, r 52.3(4).
[13]   See FPR 2010, r 30.3 and PD30A, para 4.1 or CPR 1998, r 52.3.
[14]   See FPR 2010, r 30.3(3) or CPR 1998, r 52.3(2).
[15]   See CPR 1998, r 52.3(4) and (4A).

appear that the FPR have yet been amended to include this power to bar an oral hearing for reconsideration of permission to appeal.[16]

Second appeals

15.23 If the order that you wish to appeal is an order made by the High Court or county court which was itself an order on an appeal (for example from a magistrates court or district judge) then the application for permission to appeal must be made to the Court of Appeal.

Permission – additional tips

15.24 Whilst the rules allow for the permission application to be made to the appeal court the expectation is, and good practice dictates, that the application should be made orally in the court below at the conclusion of the judgment.

15.25 In some courts there is a growing practice of judgments being reserved and even of reserved judgments being handed down in written form in the absence of the trial advocates. Careful consideration will need to be given to the possible impact of appeal time limits in these circumstances. As soon as it is known that the judgment is to be reserved thought should be given to the need to raise with the judge the issue of when the time for appeal will start to run.[17]

15.26 With increasing acceptance of the use of electronic forms of communication between the court and parties to a case it may be that advanced agreement can be reached with the court that any application for permission to appeal may be made by email. If this is acceptable then it is essential that the application is copied to *all* parties in the case. There should not be any single-party electronic communication with the court or judge. Hard copies of the full email chain must be kept. Any such communication should be appropriately formal.

Time limits

Appeal to Court of Appeal

15.27 Unless another time limit has been set by the court below the appellant must file the appellant's notice no later than **21 days** after the date of the decision of the lower court that the appellant wishes to appeal.[18]

15.28 The court below can at the time of the decision set a time limit which is either longer or shorter than the 21 days set out above.

---

[16]   See FPR 2010, r 30.3(5).
[17]   There may also be a need to consider in advance of receipt of judgment the setting up a directions hearing after receipt of judgment, so any issues arising from lack of reasons can be properly dealt with; see the warnings in 'Amplification of first instance judgments' (at **15.48** et seq).
[18]   CPR 1998, r 52.4(2).

15.29   However, if the lower court grants permission to appeal once the time limit for appealing has expired, in the absence of any such extension of time, the permission will be ineffective.

15.30   If an extension of time therefore is needed once the period specified by the lower court has expired or after 21 days, if the lower court did not specify a different timescale, any application for an extension of time will need to be made to the Court of Appeal in the appeal notice.

15.31   Where an application for extension of time is needed the reasons for the delay in appealing will need to be set out together with all steps taken after the decision appealed and the making of the application.

Appeal from refusal of permission to apply for judicial review[19]

15.32   Where permission to apply for judicial review has been refused at a hearing in the High Court the person seeking that permission may apply to the Court of Appeal for permission to appeal. The application must be made within **7 days** of the decision of the High Court to refuse to give permission to apply for judicial review. On this application the Court of Appeal may instead of giving permission to appeal, give permission to apply for judicial review.[20]

Appeal to High Court or county court

15.33   Unless another time limit has been set by the court below the appellant must file the appellant's notice no later than **21 days** after the decision of the lower court that the appellant wishes to appeal.[21]

Appeal against interim care order

15.34   Note the much more restrictive time limit for appealing an order under s 38(1) of the Children Act 1989 (interim care or supervision order) when made by the magistrates court, a district judge of the High Court, or district judge or deputy district judge in the county court. In these circumstances the limit is **7 days**.[22]

15.35   There does not appear to be a similar restriction of time where you are appealing to the Court of Appeal. However, it must be noted that applications for permission to appeal should be brought on expeditiously. Just because 21 days are allowed by statute this does not make it an appropriate timescale in such children's cases.

---

[19]   For more detailed consideration of judicial review appeals see chapter 17.
[20]   CPR 1998, r 52.15(1), (2) and (3).
[21]   FPR 2010, r 30.4(4) or CPR 1998, r 52.4(2).
[22]   FPR 2010, r 30.4(3).

Request for oral hearing where permission to appeal is refused by Court of Appeal

15.36 The request must be filed within 7 days after service of the notice that permission to appeal has been refused.[23]

15.37 Where an appellant who seeks a request for reconsideration of refusal of permission to appeal at an oral hearing is in receipt of services funded by the LSC the appellant must also send a copy of the court's reasons for refusing permission to the LSC as soon as it has been received. The Court will require confirmation that this has been done.[24]

Time limits – additional tips

15.38 Time will start to run from the date of the decision, not the date when the order is drawn up.

15.39 If you can foresee, in advance, circumstances that will impact upon the ability to file an appellant's notice within the statutory time frame, then it is open to you to ask the court below at the time of judgment, or reserving of judgment, to extend the timescale beyond the set period. Bearing in mind the need for children's cases to be dealt with swiftly there will need to be very good grounds for making such an application and the period of additional time should be kept to a minimum.

15.40 Exceptional circumstances which might justify seeking an extension in advance may include situations where it is anticipated that one of the lay parties will face substantial difficulties in being able to consider the terms of the judgment and give instructions (such as where they are in prison, about to give birth, have fluctuating or limited understanding or require any handed down judgment to be interpreted) or where a period of national public holiday is about to begin.

15.41 To understand how time is calculated see CPR 1998, Part 2, r 2.8. For example, unless the time limit is 5 days or less, weekends and public holidays will count. The day on which the time period begins is not included.

---

[23] CPR 1998, r 52.3(5).
[24] CPR 1998, PD52C, para 17.

SECTION 4 – STANDARD TESTS

For permission

Appeal to Court of Appeal

15.42   Permission to appeal can only be given if the court considers that the appeal would have a real prospect of success or there is some other compelling reason why the appeal should be heard.[25]

Appeal to High Court or county court

15.43   Permission to appeal can only be give if the court considers that the appeal would have a real prospect of success or there is some other compelling reason why the appeal should be heard.[26]

15.44   The Court of Appeal in 2007 helpfully explained, in order to assist self representing litigants (known at the time as litigants in person) that the only matter for the Court of Appeal at the permission stage was 'whether or not the appellant had an arguable case fit to present to the full court on appeal that the order of the judge below was plainly wrong'.[27]

15.45   That question was then broken down further into the following four questions:[28]

(a)   Did the judge arguably make any error of law in reaching his conclusion?

(b)   Was there, arguably, insufficient material on which the judge could properly make findings of fact and the assessments of the witnesses he did make?

(c)   Is it arguable that the order made was not properly open to him in the exercise of his judicial discretion?

(d)   Is there, arguably, an error in the exercise of that discretion which enables the appeal court to say that his order was, arguably, plainly wrong?

It is only if the answer to any one of these is 'yes' that the appeal court can give permission to appeal.[29]

---

[25]   CPR 1998, r 52.3(6).

[26]   FPR 2010, r 30.3(7).

[27]   *Re W (Permission to Appeal)* [2007] EWCA Civ 786, [2008] 1 FLR 406, para [16].

[28]   *Re W (Permission to Appeal)*, para [20].

[29]   As the Family Procedure Rules 2010 relating to appeals mirror the CPR 1998 on the permission issue it is suggested that this approach is equally applicable to appeals to the High Court and county court.

For permission for second appeal

15.46   Permission will only be granted where:

- The appeal would raise an important point of principle or practice (in the sense of one which has not already been established in the higher court).

- There is some other compelling reason for the Court of Appeal to hear it (it is likely that this would need the existence of facts indicating that the previous appeal process was somehow tainted by some procedural irregularity which rendered it unfair although other grounds may be available to provide sufficient compelling reason).

For full appeal

15.47

- Clearly the grounds set out above in the test for the permission stage are relevant.

- Was there an error of law (for example a failure to apply the correct legal test) or is the appeal against the manner in which the judge exercised his discretion (for example a failure by the judge to give sufficient weight to, or the excessive reliance on, certain factors)?

- *Re W* restated the approach of the House of Lords in the following leading case on children's appeals where the appeal is based an erroneous exercise of judicial discretion.

- *G v G (Minors Custody Appeal)*:[30]

  'Appeals in custody cases, or in other cases concerning the welfare of the children were not subject to special rules. Even if the appellate court would itself have preferred a different conclusion it must leave the decision of first instance undisturbed unless it could say that decision was wrong. The limited role of the appellate court in custody cases was not that such appeals were subject to any special rules but that there were often two or more possible decisions any one of which the court of first instance might reach without being held to be wrong. The appellate court should only interfere when it was satisfied that the court of first instance had not merely reached a decision with which the appellate court might disagree but had exceeded the generous ambit within which a reasonable disagreement was possible and had reached a decision which was so plainly wrong that it must have erred in the exercise of its discretion. Where the decision of the court of first instance, not being dependent on an assessment of witnesses, was vitiated by an error in the balancing exercise, being an erroneous weighing of the relevant factors, the appellate court could interfere.'

---

[30]   [1985] FLR 894, HL.

- There is a need to beware of taking hopeless appeals. The Court of Appeal will not simply excuse such a course of action because the subject matter of the appeal involves the welfare of vulnerable children. See the warning in *Re N (Residence: Hopeless Appeals)*:[31]

  'Per curiam: the more difficult the decision and finely balanced the conclusion the less prospect there is of that conclusion being successfully appealed. Those mounting such an appeal, likely to involve the waste of public funds ... ought to consider very carefully the wisdom of doing so.'

- Lack of reasons: it is a well established principle that a judgment should sufficiently explain what the judge had found and what he had concluded as well as the process of reasoning by which he arrived at his findings and conclusions. Within this heading also sits the need for the judge to explain the reasons for any departure from the recommendations of the guardian.[32] Please note however that this potential ground for appeal comes with a serious health warning. See 'Amplification of first instance judgments' at **15.48** et seq.

For extension of time

15.48 It is likely that the criteria set out in CPR 1998, r 3.9 will be applied to any application to the Court of Appeal for permission to appeal out of time. These include (but are not limited to):

- the interests of the administration of justice;

- whether the application has been made promptly;

- whether the failure to comply was intentional;

- whether there is a good explanation for the failure;

- whether the failure to comply was caused by the party or his legal representatives;

- the effect the failure to comply had on each party; and

- the effect that the granting of relief would have on each party.

Amplification of first instance judgments

15.49 It must be noted that there is a responsibility on a party to seek amplification and/or clarification of a judgment prior to considering any issue of an appeal.

---

[31] [1995] 2 FLR 230.
[32] See by way of example para 37 of *Re D (Grant of Care Order: Refusal of Freeing Order)* [2001] 1 FLR 862.

15.50   *Re A and L (Appeal: Fact-finding)*[33] leaves no doubt that:

> 'it was the responsibility of the advocate, whether or not invited to do so by the judge, to raise with the judge and draw to his attention any material omission in the judgment, any genuine query or ambiguity which arose on the judgment, and any perceived lack of reasons or other perceived deficiency in the judges reasoning process.'

Further it was noted that:

> 'whether or not the advocates had raised the point with the judge, where permission was sought from the trial judge to appeal on the grounds of lack of reasons, the judge should consider whether the judgment was defective for lack of reasons and if he concluded that it was, he should set out to remedy the defect by the provision of additional reasons.'

15.51   If neither of the above steps are taken the appeal court may well simply remit the case to the trial judge with an invitation for him to provide additional reasons for the decision or clarification of an ambiguity. If the case is remitted for this purpose the appeal court may define the distinct areas upon which the judge's assistance is required.

15.52   The Court of Appeal in *Re B (Appeal: Lack of Reasons)*[34] made it crystal clear that the practice as set out in *English Emery Reimbold and Strick Ltd*[35] applied with equal force to family cases.

15.53   Commenting on the appeal in *Re B* Thorpe LJ indicated that:

> '... In a perfect world counsel for the parents would have set up a hearing in reaction to the receipt of His Honour Judge Barber's written judgment, and canvassed with him the many points that have been canvassed in pursuit of the application for permission to appeal.'

15.54   The duty arises whether it is an extempore oral judgment given immediately upon conclusion of the evidence and submissions, or whether the judge has adjourned to prepare a written judgment, or indeed adjourned to prepare a judgment that is then read out by the judge in court.

15.55   See for example *Re A and L (Fact-Finding Hearing: Extempore Judgment)*.[36] Per Curiam:

> 'A common dilemma familiar to any family judge was whether to adjourn to prepare a written judgment, with all the further delays that might cause, or to

---

[33]   [2012] EWCA Civ 1205, [2012] 1 FLR 134. Also reported as *In Re A (Children) (Judgment: Adequacy of Reasoning) (Practice Note)* [2012] 1 WLR 595.

[34]   [2003] EWCA Civ 881, [2003] 2 FLR 1035.

[35]   *English v Emery Reimbold and Strick Ltd: DJ and C Withers (Farms Ltd) v Ambic Equipment Ltd, Verrechia (Trading as Freightmaster Commercials) v Commissioner of Police of the Metropolis* [2002] EWCA Civ 605, [2002] 1 WLR 2409, [2002] 3 All ER 385, CA.

[36]   [2011] EWCA Civ 1611, [2012] 1 FLR 1243.

deliver an immediate extempore judgment so that plans for the children could be moved forward with minimal delay. Extempore judgments were not to be discouraged. The safeguard was the duty of the parties to seek further elaboration or explanation from the judge if they felt something was missing.'

15.56 Care must be taken that this approach is restricted to the seeking of further explanation or correcting obvious factual mistakes (as opposed to challenging findings made on disputed facts) and is not misused as an attempt to introduce new arguments or to re-argue points already determined by the judge in the judgment.

15.57 It is not only the advocates who must ensure that this procedure is used in the correct manner. Judges must also take care that they do not inappropriately attempt to use this process in order to reverse a previously stated conclusion. The following paragraphs illustrate the risks inherent in this approach.

15.58 On the 20 February 2013 the Supreme Court handed down the judgment *In the matter of L and B*.[37] The issue for the Supreme Court was whether and in what circumstances a judge who has announced her decision is entitled to change her mind and whether the prinicples were any different in the context of care proceedings.

15.59 The initial fact finding hearing had resulted in a judgment recording that the father was responsible for the non-accidental injuries to his daughter. Counsel for the father in line with *Re A* requested that the judge address a number of issues in an addendum judgment. A court order was drawn up recording that the father was seen to have caused the injuries and directing further steps in the case. Unknown to the parties the order was not immediately sealed by the court. A further directions hearing was held and the judge indicated that a perfected judgment would be made available.

15.60 The perfected judgment when delivered expanded upon the earlier judgment in some respects but also reached a different conclusion. This time the court noted that 'given the uncertain nature of the evidence after the passage of so much time I am unable to find to the requisite standard which of the parents it was who succumbed to the stress to which the family was subject. It could have been either of them who injured [the child] and that is my finding'. At the final hearing a few days after the perfected judgment was delivered counsel for the mother asked the judge to explain why she had changed her mind and why she had not given the parties an opportunity to make further submissions before doing so. Unknown to the parties the original court order was only sealed by the court a week after this further hearing.

15.61 The mother (who was represented through the Official Solicitor due to incapacity) appealed to the Court of Appeal. *Re L-B (Reversal of Judgment)*[38]

---

[37]   [2013] UKSC 8 on appeal from [2012] EWCA Civ 984.
[38]   [2012] EWCA Civ 984 (Rimer LJ dissenting).

sets out the judgment of the majority of the Court of Appeal which appeared to reach the conclusion that the power to expand or supplement the terms of the judgment allowed the judge only to expand reasons in further support of the already stated conclusions not to reverse a previously stated conclusion.[39]

15.62 The father appealed to the Supreme Court. Allowing the appeal the Supreme Court stated as follows:

- It has long been the law that a judge is entitled to reverse his decision at any time before his order is drawn up and perfected (see para 16).

- The judge therefore has jurisdiction to change his mind up until the order is drawn up and perfected. Under the Civil Procedure Rules an order is now perfected by being sealed by the court. In considering whether to exercise this jurisdiction the overriding objective must be to deal with the case justly. A relevant factor must be whether any party has acted upon the decision to his detriment. A carefully considered change of mind can be sufficient. Every case is going to depend upon its particular circumstances (see paras 19 and 27).

- The Court of Appeal applied an exceptionality test which was not the correct approach. The majority of the Court of Appeal were right, however, to stress the importance of finality and Rimer LJ was right to express the view that 'no judge should be required to decide the future placement of a child upon what he or she believes to be a false basis' (para 29).

- On the suggestion that the judge should have given the parties notice of her intention and a further opportunity to address the court it was noted that in the circumstances of the particular case it was difficult to see what any further submissions could have done, other than to re-iterate what had already been said (see para 30).

- The judge has no jurisdiction to change his mind after the order is sealed unless the court has an express power to vary its own previous order (see para 19).

- A judge in care proceedings is entitled to revisit an earlier identification of the perpetrator if fresh evidence warrants it. There are two legal issues in care proceedings (i) has the threshold been crossed? (ii) what does the paramount consideration of the child's welfare require to be done about it? In such a composite enquiry, the judge must be able to keep an open mind until the final decision is made, at least if fresh evidence or further developments indicate an earlier decision is wrong (see paras 33–35).

---

[39] Whether this was in fact the conclusion was a matter of debate in the Supreme Court. Baroness Hale finally concluding that what the Court of Appeal must have meant was that the judge did have jurisdiction to change her mind but should not have exercised it on the facts of the case (see para [15] of the Supreme Court judgment).

- Both the Civil Procedure Rules and Family Procedure Rules make it clear that the court's wide case management powers include power to vary or revoke their previous case management orders. Where there is power to vary or revoke there is no magic in the sealing of the order. The question becomes whether or not it is proper to vary the order (see para 37).

- The power does not enable a free-for-all in which previous orders may be revisited at will. It must be exercised 'judicially and not capriciously'. It must be exercised in accordance with the overriding objective. In family proceedings the overriding objective is 'enabling the court to deal with cases justly, having regard to any welfare issues involved' (see para 38).

- If the later development is simply a judicial change of mind this is a difficult issue upon which arguments are finely balanced. It would be difficult for any judge to get his final decision right for the child, if, after careful reflection, he was no longer satisfied that his earlier findings of fact were correct. However if a judge in care proceedings is entitled simply to change his mind, it would destabilize the platform of established facts which it was the very purpose of the split hearing to construct, it would throw the hearing at the second stage into disarray and would probably result in delay. If a judge were entitled to change his mind a party would presumably be entitled to invite him to do so, in effect the judge would be invited to hear an appeal against himself (see paras 39–45).

- As the court order had not in fact been sealed at the time of the judge's change of mind the point did not arise for determination. The arguments relating to this point were so finely balanced that the Supreme Court refrained from expressing even a provisional view upon it. The preferable solution was to avoid the situation from arising in the first place. A properly reasoned judgment in the case would have addressed the matters raised by counsel with the judge. If the judge had not changed her mind the father would have had the opportunity of appealing against her findings to the Court of Appeal (see paras 45 and 46).

15.63 If you fail to take the appropriate steps to invite amplification of the judgment and seek instead to move straight to an appeal then you must be prepared for robust criticism from the appeal court in the following manner. Per Ward J:[40]

> 'it was high time that the Family Bar woke up to the fact that *English v Emery Reimbold* ... applied to family cases including both private and public law children cases, as much to any other case. After judgment was given counsel had a positive duty to raise with the judge not only any alleged deficiency in the judge's reasoning process but also any genuine ambiguity that arose on the judgment: judges should welcome this process and any who resented it were likely to find themselves the subject of criticism in the Court of Appeal. In this case, following receipt of the judgment counsel should have raised with the judge any queries that arose, inviting

---

[40]   *Re M (Fact-Finding Hearing: Burden of Proof)* [2008] EWCA Civ 1261, [2009] 1 FLR 1177.

the judge to deal with them; had this happened it was most unlikely that the perpetrator aspect of this case would have reached the Court of Appeal. Henceforth advocates who failed to follow *Re B* ... and *Re T*[41] were likely to find themselves in some difficulty; it was to be hoped that in the future the Court of Appeal would not be faced with matters that were plainly within the province of the judge, and were properly capable of being resolved at first instance, immediately after the relevant hearing.'

15.64 If all of the above does not make it clear enough then the relevant practice direction for an appeal to the county court and High Court should leave no doubt.

FPR 2010, Part 30 PD30A: Material omission from a judgment of the lower court.

'4.6 Where a party's advocate considers that there is a material omission from a judgment of the lower court or, in a magistrates' court, the written reasons for the decision of the lower court (including inadequate reasons for the lower court's decision), the advocate should before the drawing of the order give the lower court which made the decision the opportunity of considering whether there is an omission and should not immediately use the omission as grounds for an application to appeal.[42]

SECTION 5 – TIPS FOR URGENT MATTERS

Stays

15.65 It must be noted that applying for permission to appeal and/or the lodging of an appellant's notice does not act as a stay. If therefore it is essential that the order which is to be appealed is not put into effect (for example because it would have the effect of moving the place where the children are to live or because it would discharge the care order) the first step must be to ask the judge making the order to also order a stay

15.66 If the judge below refuses a stay then the next step should be to invite the judge to delay implementation or enforcement of the order for a sufficient period of time to allow the appellant to approach the Court of Appeal.

15.67 If the judge refuses to delay implementation immediate contact can be made by representatives with the Court of Appeal (following the urgent steps set out below) to request an urgent stay until an on-notice hearing can take place.[43]

---

[41] *Re T (Contact: Alienation: Permission to Appeal)* [2002] EWCA Civ 1736, [2003] 1 FLR 531.

[42] See also para 4.8 for the duty on the court where an application for permission to appeal based on a material omission in the judgment is made. The duty is to consider whether there is a material omission and if there is to provide additions to the judgment. This paragraph does not apply to a magistrates' court.

[43] See *Re S* below, also *Re A (Residence Order)* [2007] EWCA Civ 899 para 27 'when a judge considers that a significant change in the arrangements for a child needs to be made in effect

15.68   If such an application, due to its urgent nature, cannot be covered by public funding, the Court of Appeal will be likely to accept an undertaking from the party's legal adviser to file the appellant's notice once funding is granted.

15.69   An immediate application will need to be made for the public funding certificate to be extended which will need to be treated by the LSC as a matter of the greatest urgency.

15.70   In *NB v Haringey LBC*[44] Mostyn J drew attention to the following matters applying to applications for a stay pending appeal:

> 'The existence of an arguable appeal with reasonable prospects of success was the minimum requirement before a court could even consider granting a stay.'

15.71   Where the prospective appeal had a strong likelihood of success that by itself may be sufficient to underpin a stay.

15.72   Where the prospective appeal is simply arguable then further grounds are likely to be needed before a stay will be granted for example if the appeal is likely to be rendered nugatory if a stay is not granted then this will be a highly persuasive factor.

15.73   The following principles have been identified:

- The court must take into account all the circumstances of the case.

- A stay is the exception rather than the general rule.

- The party seeking a stay should provide cogent evidence that the appeal will be stifled unless a stay is granted.

- The court should apply the balance of harm test in which the likely prejudice to the successful party must be carefully considered.

- The court should take into account the prospects of the appeal succeeding and only where strong grounds of appeal or a strong likelihood of success are shown should a stay be considered.

15.74   Mostyn J noted that whilst their were numerous authorities dealing with the issue of the granting of a stay pending appeal there were none on

---

forthwith and learns that there is an aspiration to appeal to this court, he should in my view always give serious consideration to making an order which affords the aspiring appellant a narrow opportunity to approach this court for further, temporary relief before his order takes effect. No doubt the welfare of the child remains paramount; but, subject thereto, the judge needs to consider whether a refusal to afford a narrow opportunity for such an approach unfairly erodes the facility for effective appeal'.

[44]   [2012] 2 FLR 125.

whether the test was modified in a case involving children. He commented that the test he set out had to be seen through the welfare prism that overarches all family proceedings.

15.75 It should be noted that there is authority to indicate that the magistrates' court does not have the power to stay the implementation of its own orders[45] although it was suggested that under s 11 of the Children Act 1989 the court could give directions as to when an order made by them was to come into force.

Urgent and out of hours appeals

15.76 *Re S (Child Proceedings: Urgent Appeal)*,[46] *Re A (A Child)*[47] reminded practitioners of the following:

- Emergency facilities were always available to deal with urgent child cases and could be speedily accessed by the profession by telephone where necessary.

- The practice of the Court of Appeal in relation to urgent applications concerning children was that:

  - *in office hours*: the potential appellant who wished to apply for an immediate stay should contact the Court of Appeal office at the Royal Courts of Justice on the conventional telephone number.
  - *out of office hours*: the potential appellant should contact the security offices of the Royal Courts of Justice and request to speak to the Duty Judge.

- In either event the appellant would be able to speak to a Deputy Master, who, in turn would speak to a Lord Justice.

- The Lord Justice, if satisfied that the matter was appropriately urgent and that a short stay was called for would either grant a stay, or arrange for the matter to be listed at short notice for an oral hearing, on notice to the other parties, within the time frame permitted by the judge at first instance.

- These facilities are designed to cater for urgent cases and must not be abused.

- For the contact details see **15.78–15.80** below.

---

[45] *Re O (A Minor) (Care Order: Education: Procedure)* [1992] 2 FLR 7, *Re J (A Minor) (Residence)* [1993] 2 FCR 636.
[46] [2007] 2 FLR 1044.
[47] [2007] EWCA Civ 899.

15.77 Further, the potential appellant should ensure that they are in a position as soon as possible to provide the Court of Appeal with documents such as a note of the judgment, the terms of the order and draft grounds of appeal which may be faxed or emailed to the court.

Expedited appeals

15.78

- Requests may be made for the hearing of the appeal to be expedited.

- Any such request should be made by letter, or in an email if time is short, setting out the grounds why an early hearing is thought to be needed.

- The request must be marked for the immediate attention of the court and copied to the other parties.

15.79 Assistance with contacting the Court of Appeal can be found on the relevant website at www.justice.gov.uk under Court of Appeal Civil Division.

15.80 At the time of printing the telephone number for the Civil Appeals Office for the issue of new appeals in office hours is 020 7947 7121/6533.

15.81 For out of hours contact the number for the security office at the Royal Courts of Justice is 020 7947 6000 or 020 7947 6260.

15.82 For contact regarding an appeal which has already been issued then contact during office hours should be made with the relevant case progression group. In family cases this is likely to be case progression group B. The relevant number is 020 7947 6910.

15.83 For guidance on the use of online filing in urgent matters, see below.

15.84 Specific reference is now contained in CPR 1998, PD52C at para 26 to the procedure for expedited appeals. It is made clear that any expedited hearing will be listed at the convenience of the court and not according to availability of counsel.

Adoption appeals

15.85 See *Re PJ (Adoption: Practice on Appeal)*. Per Curiam:[48]

> 'if an adoption were to be challenged by appeal the respondent below should immediately apply for a stay to prevent the meeting between the judge and the children. That application should be coupled with an application to the Court of Appeal for an expedited hearing.'

---

[48]   [1998] 2 FLR 252.

Orders pending appeal

15.86 There is surprisingly little by way of decided authority on the question of the powers of the Court of Appeal to make orders preventing the removal of children from accommodation provided by the local authority (such as a foster home/children's centre) when there is no longer parental consent and where there is not at the time of the application for permission to appeal an interim care order in existence.

15.87 Section 40 of the Children Act 1989 (orders pending appeal in cases about care or supervision orders) provides as follows:

> (1) where –
>
> (a) the court dismisses an application for a care order; and
> (b) at the time when the court dismisses the application, the child concerned is the subject of an interim care order.
>
> the court may make a care order with respect to the child ...
>
> (5) where –
>
> (a) an appeal is made against any decision of a court under this section; or
> (b) any application is made to the appellate court in connection with a proposed appeal against that decision,
>
> the appellate court may extend the period for which the order in question is to have effect but not so as to extend it beyond the end of the appeal period.

15.88 The issue fell to be briefly considered in *Croydon London Borough Council v A (No 2 (Note))*[49] on an appeal against the refusal of the justices to make care orders to the High Court. The children were not the subject of interim care orders, the only order placing the children in particular local authority premises was an undertaking from the parents not to remove the children from those premises. Hollings J decided that there was no power in the High Court in the circumstances to make an interim care order pursuant to s 40 of the Children Act 1989. At p 349, para E in considering the impact of s 100(2) he went on to explain:

> 'I had considered that an appellate court under its inherent jurisdiction always has, I should have thought, a right to make holding orders such as stays of execution. An interim care order could be of the nature of a stay of execution but section 100, it could be said, relates to the inherent jurisdiction in respect of children, not the inherent jurisdiction in respect of the management of appeals – if such exists. It is a nice point but I do not propose to take advantage of that nice point. I leave that for further consideration at another time. In the circumstances, I think the only safe course is to make an interim order under section 38 of the 1989 Act for 28 days.'

15.89 The Court of Appeal itself has given consideration (in the field of immigration) as to whether the Court of Appeal has an inherent jurisdiction.

---

[49] [1992] 2 FLR 348.

In *YD(Turkey) v Secretary of State for the Home Department*,[50] it held that it possessed an inherent jurisdiction to order the Home Secretary to refrain from removing the applicant between the filing of an out of time application for an extension of time and the determination of the application and indicated that such an order would not be a stay in the ordinary sense of staying further actions within the proceedings but an order preserving the status quo. In reaching such a decision Lord Justice Brooke reviewed the existence, use and continued development of the inherent jurisdiction (see paras 15–24). It appears therefore that an inherent jurisdiction in respect of management of appeals does in fact exist.

15.90   The issue raised its head in the context of a care case in *Re MA (Care: Threshold)*.[51] The High Court judge declined to find that the threshold had been met, the children had not been the subject of interim care orders but were accommodated with parental consent pursuant to s 20 CA 1989. On dismissing the application for care orders the High Court judge felt compelled, due to his finding on threshold, not to make interim care orders pending appeal. He also declined permission to appeal. The single Lord Justice on the urgent application for permission to appeal granted an injunction to prevent the removal of the children from foster care prior to the matter coming before the appeal court. The parents raised objections to this course of action with the Court of Appeal including the argument that it breached the provisions of s 100 CA 1989. However by the time of the conclusion of the oral hearing of the appeal the parents had been persuaded to observe the injunction without pressing their request for an opportunity to challenge its lawfulness. In the words of Wilson LJ 'in the event this conundrum must await this court's resolution on another day'.

15.91   Consideration should be given in appropriate cases to s 38(3) which makes provision that, if on an application for a care or supervision order, the court makes a residence order with respect to the child concerned it should also make an interim supervision order with respect to that child unless it is satisfied that the child's welfare will be satisfactorily safeguarded without an interim order being made.

SECTION 6 – REPRESENTATION ON APPEAL

15.92   Although each party in the case should be treated as a respondent to the appeal this does not necessarily mean that it is appropriate that each party appears and is separately represented within the appeal hearings.

15.93   Particularly where the parties are dependent on public funding (and whether that is through the LSC and legal aid, or the fact that the local authority funding is itself a drain on the public purse) care should be taken that it is only where it is really necessary that separate appearance and

---

50   [2006] EWCA Civ 52, [2006] 1 WLR 1646.
51   [2010] 1 FLR 431.

representation are undertaken. Over-representation is likely to lead to the costs of such representation being disallowed.

15.94 See the advice and warning in *Oxfordshire County Council v X, Y and J*[52] per curiam:

> 'it is only where it was clear that there was an unavoidable conflict of interest between two parties, as a matter of law, should they have separate legal representation, especially where public money was involved. This should also be borne in mind by judges when awarding costs.'

15.95 In paras [45]–[48] Lord Neuberger on behalf of the court emphasised this point in the strongest possible terms and added:

> 'The fact that parties may have different factual points, or that one party's case may be seen as stronger than the other's, or that parties legal advisers may see the legal arguments or prospects somewhat differently, are not good reasons for their incurring the expense and court time of separate representation.
>
> When it appears that a hearing may involve more than one set of legal representation to support the same outcome, very careful consideration should be given by legal advisers as to whether there really is a need for more than one legal representation …
>
> We accept, of course, that in some circumstances, it is unavoidable that two parties who support the same outcome have to be separately represented, because the conflict between them, is as a matter of law, such that they cannot be jointly represented. However even in such cases, very careful consideration should be given to the question of whether both parties should be represented at the hearing by separate advocates. In many such cases, it should be possible for one of the parties to limit himself or herself to written representations …'

SECTION 7 – NOTICES, FORMS AND SKELETONS

Court of Appeal

15.96 Forms and guidance can be found on the Court Service Form Finder website (address www.hmctsformfinder.justice.gov.uk).

15.97 Appellant's notice – Form **N161**, Guidance **N161A:**[53]

- The form provides a checklist of documents which are to be filed with the appeal notice but regard should also be had to the relevant practice directions which give directions on the documents to be filed, time limits, preparation of bundles etc.

---

[52]   [2010] EWCA Civ 581, [2011] 1 FLR 272.
[53]   See the forms in Part 4 (resources section).

- It is necessary to state the grounds of appeal in the notice. The detailed argument should not be contained in the grounds but in the skeleton argument which should be filed with the notice of appeal.[54]

- The grounds of appeal should identify as concisely as possible the respects in which the judgment of the court below is either (a) wrong or (b) unjust because of a serious procedural or other irregularity.

15.98   Respondent's notice – Form **N162**:[55]

- Must be issued where a respondent to an appeal wishes to seek any variation in the order of the court below.

- Must be issued where a respondent is happy with the outcome of the case below but wishes to ask the appeal court to uphold the order of the court below on different, or additional, grounds to those relied upon by the lower court.

- If seeking to vary the order then permission to appeal will be required and must be requested in the respondent's notice.

- Time limits apply to the filing of the respondent's notice. These are set out in the revised Practice Direction PD52C Section V – Timetable.[56]

- A skeleton argument should be filed by a respondent who wishes to be heard on the appeal (whether or not there is a respondent's notice) as if there is not either a respondent's notice or respondent's skeleton argument the respondent will be limited to arguments made in the lower court and may not be heard on any additional arguments in the Court of Appeal.

15.99   Electronic filing of appellant's and respondent's notices:

- In some cases where the appellant/respondent is represented by a solicitor it is possible to file the appellants notice by email.

---

[54]   The CPR rules and revised Practice Directions themselves do not make any reference to the ability to file the skeleton within 14 days of the appeal notice although this still seems to appear on the guidance N161A for completing the appellant's notice.

[55]   These provisions are consistent with r 52.5 regarding the use of a respondent's notice; however the revised Practice Direction PD52C, para 8(1) indicates that a respondent who seeks to appeal against any part of the order made by the court below must file an appeal notice and PD52C, para 8(2) indicates that a respondent who seeks a variation of the order of the lower court must file an appeal notice and must obtain permission to appeal. See Form N162 in Part 4 (resources section).

[56]   See the timetable in Part 4 (resources section). The time limit is 14 days from granting of permission by the court below (or if permission is not required) or of notification that permission has been granted by the Court of Appeal or of notification that the permission application will be listed with the appeal to follow.

- Email correspondence will not be given priority over postal or fax correspondence.

- At the time of writing the guidelines for this procedure can be found at www.justice.gov.uk under Court of Appeal Civil Division – Electronic Filing.

- Prior to October 2012 the relevant section of the practice direction was 52PD para 15.1A and 15.1B (the latter dealing with the procedure for completing and submitting online forms) but this does not appear to have been replicated in the revised practice directions now supplementing Part 52

- The current email address for filing is given as civilappeals. registry@hmcts.gsi.gov.uk.

- You must note that emails are only checked twice daily.

- Emails received before 10.00am will not be dealt with until the office opens for business that day.

- Emails received after 4.30pm will not be dealt with until the following day and will be treated as having been filed on the next working day.

- In order to be accepted the email must contain:

  (i)   the sender's name together with confirmation that the sender is authorised to give undertakings on behalf of the firm of solicitors concerned; and
  (ii) an undertaking by the firm of solicitors to pay the requisite fee as soon as practicable and in any event no later than 7 days from the date on which the email is sent.

- Any attachment must be in Microsoft Word or Adobe Acrobat (.pdf).

- The document must not exceed 20 pages in length, 2 megabytes in file size or contain colour content.

- Urgent Appeal via email.

- If the matter is urgent and you wish to utilise the email filing system you will need to ensure that the you follow the above steps, that you do so as early as possible during the course of the day and that you telephone the Registry of the Civil Appeals Office to inform them on either 020 7947 6533 or 7121.

15.100   Skeleton arguments:

- See CPR 1998, PD52A[57] and PD52C.[58]

- The skeleton arguments must:

    - be concise;
    - define and confine the areas of controversy;
    - have numbered paragraphs;
    - be cross referenced to the appeal bundle;
    - be self contained (therefore not refer to arguments contained in separate or earlier skeleton arguments);
    - be printed on A4 paper in not less than 12 point font and 1.5 line spacing.

- The skeleton must not:

    - include extensive quotations from documents or authorities;
    - normally exceed 25 pages.

- Where authorities are cited the skeleton argument must state the proposition of law that the authority demonstrates and identify the parts of the authority that support that proposition.

- The appellant's skeleton argument should accompany the appellant's notice.

- Where the appellant has filed a skeleton argument in support of an application for permission to appeal the same skeleton argument may be relied upon for the appeal hearing. However PD52C Section V – Timetable, at para 21 allows for the service of an appeal skeleton argument (without bundle cross-references) by the appellant 21 days after the letter from the Civil Appeals Office notifies the parties of the window within which the appeal is likely to be heard. The time appears to run from the date of the letter (rather than receipt).

- The respondent's skeleton argument if a respondent's notice has been filed is due within 14 days of the filing of the respondent's notice. If no respondent's notice has been filed the respondent's skeleton must be served 42 days after the letter from the Civil Appeals Office notifies the parties of the window within which the appeal is likely to be heard.

- Consideration should also be given as to whether it would be helpful to provide:

---

[57]   CPR 1998, PD52A, section V.
[58]   CPR 1998, PD52C, para 31.

- a list of people featuring in the case and their relationship (personal or professional) to the child who is the subject of the proceedings;
- a chronology of relevant events (most likely to be needed).

- CPR 1998, PD52C now makes additional provision for a 'replacement skeleton argument' which is one filed by both appellant and respondent and is described as a skeleton argument which has been amended in order to include cross references to the appeal bundle. According to the section V timetable such replacement argument is due from the appellant no later than 14 days before the appeal hearing and from the respondent no later than 7 days before the date of the hearing.[59] This is not the same as a supplemental skeleton which is only to be filed where strictly necessary and only with the permission of the court.[60]

Written statement for oral permission hearing

15.101 At least 4 days before the oral permission hearing the appellant's advocate must file a brief written statement setting out:[61]

(a) the points which are to be raised on the hearing

(b) the reasons why permission should be granted notwithstanding the reasons given for refusal of permission.

Position of respondent before permission granted[62]

15.102 A respondent who is content with the order of the court below is not expected to take any action on an appeal until:

(a) directed by the court to do so;

(b) notified that permission to appeal has been granted;

(c) notified that permission to appeal will be considered at the hearing of the appeal.

High Court and county court

15.103 The Appeal Notice Form N161[63] is also for use in civil appeals to the High Court and county court.[64]

---

[59] CPR 1998, PD52C, paras 1 and 21.
[60] CPR 1998, PD52C, para 32.
[61] CPR 1998, PD52C, para 16.
[62] See for example CPR 1998, PD52C, paras 16, 19 and 21 but see the responsibility to file an appeal notice in para 8.
[63] See the forms in Part 4 (resources section).
[64] CPR 1998, PD52B, para 4.1.

15.104   The Practice Direction suggests[65] that skeleton arguments should only be filed and served if:

(a)   there is a direction of the court to do so; or

(b)   the complexity of the issues of fact or law in the appeal justify them; or

(c)   the skeleton arguments would assist the court in respects not readily apparent from the papers in the appeal

SECTION 8 – HUMAN RIGHTS ISSUES

15.105   Where an appellant seeks to rely on any issue under the Human Rights Act 1998, or any remedy available under that Act for the first time on the appeal, the appeal notice will need to contain the details required by CPR 1998, PD16, paras 15.1 and 15.2.

15.106   In brief this means that the appellant must:

- state the fact that he relies on the provisions of or seeks a remedy under that Act;

- give precise details of the Convention right which, it is alleged, has been infringed;

- give details of the alleged infringement;

- state whether the relief sought includes a declaration of incompatibility in accordance with s 4 of the HRA 1998 in which case the appellant must also state:

   – the precise details of the legislative provision alleged to be incompatible; and
   – the details of the incompatibility;

- state whether the relief sought includes damages in respect of a judicial act to which s 9(3) of the HRA 1998 applies in which case the appellant must also state:

   – the judicial act complained of; and
   – the court or tribunal which is alleged to have made it.

15.107   CPR 1998, r 19.4A will apply and PD19A must be complied with. These provisions set out the details as to whom notice should be given and joinder of parties (eg giving notice to the Crown and/or the Lord Chancellor).

---

65   CPR 1998, PD52B, para 8.3.

SECTION 9 – PRACTICE DIRECTION RE CITATION OF AUTHORITIES

15.108 There is a tendency in care hearings to refer to specialist law reports when citing authorities to the court (such as FLR – family law reports) and for ease of search and printing to rely on copies of cases from resources such as Lawtel and Bailii. Neutral citations have made tracking cases down on-line much simpler.

15.109 It is important to note however that when it comes to citing case authority in skeleton arguments and preparing the authorities bundles for the Court of Appeal that there is a preferred hierarchy of report which should be complied with.

15.110 See the guidance and warnings in *TW v A City Council*,[66] per curiam:

'the attention of the Family Bar was drawn to Practice Direction 52PD 66 – Appeals, which supplemented the Civil Procedure Rules, Part 52 and also the note at 52.12.3 of the White Book 2010, which referred to s 8 of the Practice Statement (Supreme Court: Judgments) [1998] 1 WLR 825. In particular the profession should remember that the relevant authorities were to be copied from the official law reports and that it was only if a case did not appear in the official law reports that a case report from the All England Law Reports or a specialist law report series should be used. Bailiii reports (with neutral citation numbers) should be used only if no other recognised reports were available and the case really needed to be cited. The relevant passages in the authorities on which counsel would be seeking to rely must be marked.'[67]

15.111 The reference to the official law reports is a reference to those law reports that are cited by reference to the following abbreviations after the year 'AC' (appeals cases) 'QB' (Queens bench) 'Fam' (Family) 'Ch' (Chancery)

15.112 The hierarchy then is that it is only if an authority is not reported in the first on the following list that you can move onto the next in the list and only if it does not appear there that you can move onto the next and so on:

(a) Official law report series (AC, QB, Ch, Fam etc).

(b) Weekly Law Reports (WLR).

(c) All England Law Reports (All ER).

(d) Specialist (eg FLR).

(e) Bailii neutral citation numbers – only if no other recognised reports are not available and the case really needs to be cited.

---

[66] [2011] EWCA Civ 17, [2011] 1 FLR 1597.
[67] Please note the relevant practice direction is now PD52C, para 29.

Remember the authorities bundle should not contain more than 10 authorities unless the scale of the appeal really warrants more extensive citation.

15.113 CPR 1998, PD52C now indicates that in addition to the above the following should also be followed when providing bundles of authorities:

- any photocopies of authorities should not be in landscape format or have reduced size of type;

- the marking of the relevant passage should be by way of a vertical line in the margin.

15.114 The bundle of authorities must bear a certificate by the advocates responsible for arguing the case that all of the above requirements have been complied with for each and every authority included.[68]

SECTION 10 – CAN I APPEAL?

Against refusal of permission to appeal

15.115 If both the lower court and the appeal court refuse permission to appeal (save for the limited step of seeking an oral hearing if the Court of Appeal refusal was a 'paper refusal') there is no ability to appeal that refusal to a higher court. A refusal of permission to appeal to the Court of Appeal (even after a fully contested argument with all parties represented) by the Court of Appeal as opposed to the dismissal of the Appeal and a refusal of permission to appeal to the Supreme Court will prevent any appeal to the Supreme Court.[69]

Against case management decisions

15.116 Yes: but see CPR 1998, PD52A, para 4.6, where the application is for permission to appeal a case management decision, the court dealing with the application may take into account whether:

(a) the issue is of sufficient significance to justify the costs of the appeal;

(b) the procedural consequences of an appeal (eg loss of trial date) outweigh the significance of the case management decision;

(c) it would be more convenient to determine the issue at or after trial.

15.117 Any appeal against a case management decision must be made quickly – do not sit back thinking that you have the luxury of the 21 day time limit.

---

[68]   CPR 1998, PD52C, para 29.
[69]   Access to Justice Act 1999, s 54(4).

15.118 Remember that in most cases the case management decision is an exercise of judicial discretion and will be unlikely to involve an error of law. If the court below has taken into account all relevant matters and weighed all the pros and cons before reaching its decision and has given a clear explanation (which does not mean lengthy) as to why the particular application/direction sought was refused or granted then it is unlikely that the Court of Appeal will seek to interfere with that exercise of discretion.

15.119 The impact of the additional considerations for appeals involving case management decisions have resulted in the impression that a high threshold will need to be met before permission will be granted.

Against magistrate's refusal of jurisdiction

15.120 Section 94 Children Act 1989 makes provision which means that an appeal cannot be made against a decision of the magistrates' court to decline jurisdiction on the basis that it considers the case can more conveniently be dealt with by another court.

Against the making of an EPO

15.121 Section 45(10) Children Act 1989 makes provision which means that an appeal cannot be made against the making of or refusal to make an emergency protection order – the extension or refusal to extend the period of operation of an EPO – the discharge or refusal to discharge of an EPO and the giving or refusal to give directions connected with such an order.[70]

SECTION 11 – WARNINGS

15.122 It must be noted that compliance with the time limits and provisions of the practice directions is not meant to be aspirational. There are various sanctions for non-compliance.

By way of example:

- costs of preparing a skeleton argument which does not comply with the requirements or which was not filed in time will not be allowed on assessment except as directed by the court;[71]

- a respondent who unreasonably opposes an application for extension of time for filing an appellant's notice may be ordered to pay the costs of the application;[72]

---

[70] Section 45(8) makes provision however for applications for discharge of emergency protection orders.
[71] CPR 1998, PD52A, para 5.1(5).
[72] CPR 1998, PD52C, para 4(3)(b).

- if a respondent is legally represented and proposes to address the court the respondent must lodge a skeleton argument;[73]

- the court may refuse to hear argument on a point not included in a skeleton argument filed within the prescribed time;[74]

- a respondent who at the permission stage voluntarily makes submissions or attends a hearing will not normally receive an order of costs in their favour.[75]

15.123 It is also wise to note the duty of the appeal court (whether Court of Appeal, High Court or county court) set out in CPR 1998 r 52.10(5) when it refuses an application for permission to appeal, strikes out an appellant's notice or dismisses an appeal where it considers that the application or appellant's notice was totally without merit. In these circumstances, it must record the fact that it considers the application, notice or appeal to be totally without merit and must at the same time consider making a civil restraint order.[76]

---

[73] CPR 1998, PD52C, para 13.
[74] CPR 1998, PD52C, para 31(3).
[75] CPR 1998, PD52C, para 20.
[76] For brief consideration of civil restraint orders please see chapter 3.

Chapter 16

JUDICIAL REVIEW – THE LAW

SECTION 1 – DEFINITIONS

16.1 Judicial review is a common law supervisory process by which the High Court scrutinises decisions or actions of government, local authorities and other public bodies. The process is used to correct errors of law or decisions taken in a public law context to ensure that an individual is given fair treatment by the decision-making authority. Judicial review is defined in the *Pre-action Protocol for Judicial Review* (the Protocol) at para 1 as follows:

> 'Judicial review allows people with a sufficient interest in a decision or action by a public body to ask a judge to review the lawfulness of:
>
> - An enactment; or
> - A decision, action or failure to act in relation to the exercise of a public function.'

16.2 However, judicial review is not an appeals process and is not concerned with the merits of the original decision or action; it is simply concerned with the procedure followed or not followed and the decision-making process. The court will not substitute its own decision for that of the original body that made the decision:[1]

> 'Judicial review is concerned with reviewing not the merits of the decision in respect of which the application for judicial review is made, but the decision-making process itself. It is thus different from an appeal. The purpose of the remedy of judicial review is to ensure that the individual is given fair treatment by the authority to which he has been subjected: it is no part of that purpose to substitute the opinion of the judiciary or of individual judges for that of the authority constituted by law to decide the matters in question.'

16.3 In judicial review proceedings the court will only be concerned with whether the decision-making authority (for these purposes, the local authority):

(a) exceeded its powers; or

(b) committed an error of law; or

(c) reached a decision which no reasonable body could have reached; or

---

[1] *Chief Constable of the North Wales Police v Evans* [1982] 1 WLR 1155 at 1173, per Lord Brightman.

(d)   abused its powers.

16.4   The judicial review process is therefore designed effectively to prevent the abuse of power by public authorities. However, judicial review only extends to decisions of inferior courts. It therefore cannot be used as a method of reviewing decisions made by the High Court or the Court of Appeal.

16.5   The judicial review process can be used to seek:

- A mandatory order requiring the public body to do something (previously known as an order of mandamus).

- A prohibiting order preventing the public body from doing something (previously known as an order of prohibition).

- A quashing order quashing the public body's decision (previously known as an order of certiorari).

- A declaration.

- An injunction.

- Human Rights Act 1998 (HRA 1998) damages.

16.6   Claims for judicial review can either be heard by a single judge or a divisional court (comprising a court of two judges). The Administrative Court sits in London, Birmingham, Cardiff, Leeds and Manchester (although in appropriate cases arrangements may be made for sittings at alternative locations).

Note

16.7   The Woolf reforms to the civil justice procedure have affected the way in which judicial review cases are reported. Previously judicial review cases were reported as *R v Jeremy Weston QC ex p Elizabeth Isaacs*. They are now reported as *R (Jeremy Weston QC) v Elizabeth Isaacs*. Given the historical scope of cases referred to within this book, the reader will see cases referred to under both schemes.

SECTION 2 – THE LEGAL FRAMEWORK

16.8   The rules governing judicial review are contained within:

- Senior Courts Act 1981 (SCA 1981), s 31;

- CPR 1998, Part 54;

- CPR 1998, PD54;

- Administrative Court Guidance: Notes for Guidance on Applying for Judicial Review (the Guidance);

- Pre-action Protocol for Judicial Review (the Protocol).

16.9 A decision or other administrative act of a public authority is subject to the presumption of legality. This simply means that such decisions or actions are presumed to be lawful until the court grants an appropriate remedy to quash the decision or declare it void. The effect of such a remedy is that the decision or action is recognised as being ultra vires and void – in short, it is as if it had never existed.

16.10 The main grounds on which an individual may seek judicial review are:

(a) Illegality.

(b) Irrationality.

(c) Procedural impropriety.

(d) Lack of proportionality.

16.11 The judicial review process also interacts with the ECHR and the HRA 1998 in that an individual may also seek to challenge the action or omission of a public authority on the grounds that the action or omission is incompatible with the ECHR. Section 6(1) HRA 1998 provides that it is unlawful for a public authority to act in a way which is incompatible with ECHR rights which have effect for the purposes of the HRA 1998.[2]

SECTION 3 – IMPLICATIONS FOR CHILDCARE LAW

16.12 In the majority of cases the family courts will be able to investigate and evaluate the merits, or otherwise, of the local authority's case in detail. The role of the Administrative Court hearing an application for judicial review is much narrower.

16.13 In the Administrative Court the focus of the court's investigation will generally not be on the **merits** of the local authority's case, but rather on the much more limited question of the **legality** of the local authority's decision-making process, leading up to and embracing its decision to apply for an order. There are only fairly limited grounds on which the Administrative Court can intervene. Save in only wholly exceptional cases, it will simply not be appropriate to bring judicial review proceedings where the object of the proceedings is to prevent a local authority commencing emergency protection or care proceedings.[3]

---

[2] See chapter 1, section 1.
[3] Confirmed in *Re M (Care Proceedings: Judicial Review)* [2003] EWHC 850 (Admin).

16.14 Judicial review is a remedy of last resort and should not be used where there is available another equally effective and convenient remedy.[4] However, judicial review is also '... a singularly blunt and unsatisfactory tool when the matters in issue are as sensitive and difficult as they inevitably are in care and similar types of cases'.[5]

16.15 It is also important to remember that remedies in judicial review are always discretionary and may not be applied even if the court finds that a decision was unlawful.

16.16 Potential claimants should therefore ensure that all other possible remedies have been exhausted before making a claim because such action, or failure to act, will almost certainly affect the court's overall consideration of the matter and exercise of its discretion. This requires potential claimants, as well as local authorities, to have a clear understanding of the scope of local authority internal review and complaints procedures as well as potential legal routes to challenge local authority decision-making.[6]

16.17 It is also important to remember that judicial review may not necessarily lead to the substantive remedy that is sought, but could simply just lead to the matter being reconsidered by the decision-maker who may in turn simply make the same decision again on the merits as long as the decision is approached lawfully. All the court can do in judicial review is to scrutinise the decision to ensure that it was lawful. Potential claimants must be advised that the court will not substitute its own decision for the original decision.

16.18 The following is a suggested (but not exhaustive) list of factors that potential claimants should bear in mind when considering whether judicial review is the most appropriate form of challenge to a local authority decision:

- Are there other alternative remedies available?

- Is the application in time and has the claimant acted promptly?

- If necessary can an extension of time for a judicial review application be obtained?

- Is the court likely to deal favourably with any delay?

- Is the application being made at the right time?

---

[4]   See for example *R (T) v Royal Borough of Kingston-upon-Thames* [1994] 1 FLR 798, *R (W) v East Sussex County Council* [1998] 2 FLR 1082 and *Re M (Care Proceedings: Judicial Review)* [2003] EWHC 850 (Admin).

[5]   *Re M (Care Proceedings: Judicial Review)* [2003] EWHC 850 (Admin), *Re L (Care Proceedings: Human Rights Claims)* [2003] EWHC 665 (Fam).

[6]   See the companion volume to this book *Social Work Decision-Making: A Guide for Childcare Lawyers* (Jordan Publishing, 2nd edn, 2012) for more detail about local authority social work practice and procedure.

- Is the claim dealing with a decision or a continuing policy?

- Is the claim dealing with more than one decision?

- Is the application premature?

- Has there been full and frank disclosure?

- Are there appropriate grounds for a claim?

SECTION 4 – REMEDIES

16.19 When considering what, if any, remedy should be made available in dealing with a claim for judicial review, the court will exercise its discretion. It should be remembered that all remedies are only discretionary. In certain circumstances the court may find that the public authority acted unlawfully but then go on to decline to grant a remedy.

When can relief be refused?

16.20 There are some specific grounds available to the court when refusing relief as a matter of discretion.

- **The remedy is of no practical use**
  In some cases a remedy may have become of no practical use or the issues have now become academic. In circumstances where an issue of law arises where the court's authoritative guidance is required or where similar cases may arise in the future, the court may decide to hear the case and give a judgment to clarify the law but not grant any specific remedy.

- **There has been no prejudice suffered**
  In some cases although there may have been an error, no real prejudice to the claimant has been sustained. For example, the court may find that the local authority had failed to disclose relevant material at an early stage of the decision making process, but that the mistake had been rectified before the final decision was taken.

- **The decision was not influenced by error**
  In some limited cases the courts may refuse to quash a decision where it is confirmed that the decision-maker would have reached the same decision, even if it is also found that he or she erred in law or failed to act in accordance with procedure. However this approach will only be adopted in cases where the court can be absolutely clear that it is not substituting its own views for those of the decision-maker and where the decision-maker would have reached the same conclusion.

- **The claim raises hypothetical issues**

  In cases where the claim raises hypothetical issues the court may refuse to grant a remedy. For example, the claim may be being raised prematurely because the facts may not yet have arisen or because the decision may not yet have been made. This approach is most likely to be adopted in cases where a clear issue of law arises and where unnecessary costs or unfairness to an individual may be prevented by the court's early determination of the issues.

- **The claim has not been brought promptly**

  The court will normally decline to grant permission to apply for judicial review in cases where a claim has not been brought promptly and within three months of the date when the grounds of challenge first arose. However, even in cases where the time limit has been extended, the court may still refuse a remedy where it would be likely to cause substantial hardship or prejudice to any party.

- **There would be an adverse effect on third parties**

  The court will be reluctant to grant a remedy in cases where the defect is procedural and it is confirmed that in fact the same decision might be reached even if the proper procedure was followed. In such cases the court will take account the likely administrative inconvenience of quashing the decision.

- **There are adequate alternative remedies available**

  The court will not grant a judicial review remedy where alternative remedies were available, but not used by the claimant. This approach will be taken most commonly at the permission stage, but may also be applicable at the full hearing stage. In considering whether the claimant should have used alternative remedies, the court will consider the real nature of the complaint and whether the appeal process was in fact suitable to deal with the issues. This will be particularly relevant in cases where the real issues being challenged relate to issues of fact rather than issues of law. In challenging decisions of local authorities claimants should therefore always ensure that they utilise the internal complaints procedures first. However, there may be some situations where the case raises issues of law on which the court is required to provide an authoritative decision where the issue is also being dealt with by an alternative remedy. In some situations the case may be urgent and may require the particular speed of resolution or the interim relief allowed by a judicial review remedy. In other situations the alternative remedy may not be adequate or appropriate.

What remedies are available?

16.21 There are various remedies available on an application for judicial review as follows:

(a)   Quashing orders.

(b)   Prohibiting orders.

(c)   Mandatory orders.

(d)   Declarations.

(e)   Injunctions.[7]

(f)   Damages (in limited, defined circumstances).[8]

Quashing orders

16.22   A quashing order is a prerogative remedy which is appropriate when the court is considering past actions or decisions.

16.23   A quashing order (previously known as an order of certiorari) is an order of the High Court which quashes the decisions of an inferior court or tribunal or public authority (or any other body as discussed earlier). The primary purpose of a quashing order is to quash decisions which are ultra vires. The effect of a quashing order is to confirm that the decision is a nullity and should not be regarded as having any effect at all from the time it was made.

16.24   In addition to making a quashing order, the court may remit the matter back to the decision-maker and direct it to reconsider the matter and to reach a decision in accordance with the judgment of the court. Alternatively, if there would be no point in remitting the matter back to the original decision maker, the court may now, subject to any statutory provision to the contrary, take the decision itself.[9] However, it is unclear to what extent the court will use this power which effectively substitutes its own view for that of the primary decision maker.

Prohibiting orders

16.25   A prohibiting order (previously known as prohibition orders) is a prerogative remedy which will become appropriate once it is obvious that a decision has been made in circumstances when the court is then considering future actions or decisions, and it may sometimes be appropriate for the court to make a prohibiting order alongside a quashing or declaratory order. For example, a prohibiting order could be used to prevent the implementation of an unlawful decision which is the subject of a quashing order or a declaration of invalidity.

---

[7]   See chapter 13 for discussion about injunctive relief.
[8]   See chapter 18 for discussion about damages.
[9]   CPR 1998, r 54.19(3).

16.26   A prohibiting order is an order which forbids the relevant inferior court or tribunal, or public authority (or any other body as discussed earlier) to act in excess of or to abuse its statutory or other public law powers. Generally the claimant must apply for a prohibiting order as soon as the decision has been made or is about to be made.

16.27   The effect of a quashing order is to set aside a decision or other administrative action so that such decision or action is seen as if it was never capable of producing any effect as a matter of law.

Mandatory orders

16.28   A mandatory order (previously known as an order of mandamus) is a prerogative order which requires the directed person, public authority or inferior court or tribunal to do the particular thing or take the particular action specified in the order which has a statutory duty to perform. However, the court will generally prefer to declare that the public authority is under a duty to do the specified act and then rely on the public authority's compliance with the declaration.

Declarations

16.29   As already indicated, the court will often grant a declaration or an injunction as well as or instead of one of the prerogative orders. However, a declaration or an injunction is not limited to such circumstances and can be made as the sole order in the case if it is most appropriate. The test for the court in considering whether or not to make such an order will be whether it is just and convenient to do so.

16.30   The court will grant a declaration or injunction if it considers that it would be just and convenient having regard to:

(a)   the nature of the matters in relation to which relief may be granted by way of a quashing order, a prohibiting order or a mandatory order;

(b)   the nature of the bodies against whom relief may be granted by the making of such orders; and

(c)   all the circumstances of the case.

16.31   A declaration will declare the nature and scope of the current legal position or of the parties' legal rights. Declarations can be formulated in a flexible manner to identify the nature and consequences of the particular illegality of the action. However, declarations should do more than simply state the past position of the parties; they must relate to some particular required action at the time of the hearing or alternatively at some specified point in the future. The effect of a declaration that a decision or action is ultra vires or unlawful is that the decision is incapable of ever having produced a legal effect.

16.32 It is possible for courts to grant interim declarations which might, in some cases, be preferable to interim injunctions.

Injunctions

16.33 Injunctions are discretionary orders which can be prohibitory or mandatory. They can be imposed even in circumstances where compliance may cause difficulty for the subject public bodies or authorities.

16.34 A prohibitory injunction restrains the subject from carrying out the imminent threat, action or continuation of unlawful actions in the future.

16.35 A mandatory injunction requires and compels the subject to take particular action, to remedy past failings or to rectify past damage.

SECTION 5 – IDENTIFYING REVIEWABLE LOCAL AUTHORITY DECISIONS

16.36 In order to decide whether judicial review is the appropriate form of challenge to a local authority decision it must be established that the decision exists in public law. If the decision cannot be identified as falling within public law, then the claimant must bring an action in private law under Pt 7 CPR 1998. Remedies in private law may not be appropriate or adequate to rectify the injustice being challenged.

16.37 In most cases involving child law decisions, it will almost never be in dispute that the decision-maker is a public body, ie, the local authority.[10] However, it is still important to analyse the nature of the decision or the act so that it can clearly be identified as existing in public law. It is not necessarily fatal if an act or decision is misidentified and challenged under the wrong procedure because r 54.20 CPR 1998 gives the court a comprehensive power to transfer cases in or out of the Administrative Court. The rules are sufficiently flexible to manage justifiable errors of procedure without leading to a claim being struck out.

16.38 For the purposes of establishing a claim for judicial review, potential claimants must be able to identify correctly that the decision or action being challenged is founded in public law rather than private law. Correct classification of the action as falling within public law will determine whether any HRA 1998 claim is available.

16.39 In addition, any claim seeking damages for breach of a public law duty would otherwise fail because there is no right to damages for breach of a public law duty in English law. In the key case of *O'Reilly v Mackman*[11] the House of

---

[10] See chapter 1.
[11] [1983] 2 AC 237.

Lords held that as a general rule it was contrary to public policy and an abuse of the court's process to allow a dissatisfied applicant to proceed by way of an ordinary action (now brought under CPR 1998, Part 7) when the substance of the complaint was founded in public law. The reasons for this were to prevent the claimant evading the legal and procedural rules governing judicial review claims under CPR 1998, Part 54 which are designed to provide safeguards for local authorities against applications without grounds or merits. These safeguards include the requirement on claimants for permission to apply for judicial review within strict time limits, the need for a statement of facts giving full and frank disclosure of all relevant facts confirmed by a statement of truth, and the court's powers to control disclosure and cross-examination of witnesses.

16.40　In *O'Rourke v Camden LBC*[12] it was held that the question of whether any private law duty exists depends on whether, on a correct construction of the statute, such a duty has been intended by Parliament.[13] The principles in relation to whether a statutory duty is owed were dealt with comprehensively by the House of Lords in *X (Minors) v Bedfordshire CC*[14] and *Stovin v Wise*.[15]

16.41　In light of this test, in circumstances where the local authority is given a wide discretion and judgment about how to discharge any duty which does arise, it is highly likely that the courts will interpret such a duty as a *public law duty* rather than as a private law duty. This is because it is unlikely to be held that Parliament would have intended for errors of such discretion and judgment on the part of the local authority to give rise to a private law cause of action. Similarly, where the local authority's duty arises under a statutory scheme which sets out a detailed and specific procedure for enforcing its duties, it is most likely that the courts will interpret such duty as falling within the scope of public law.

16.42　In most child law cases it is therefore highly likely that the decisions being challenged will fall within the scope of public law, being predominantly derived from the Children Act 1989, the Children Act 2004, the Children and Young Persons Act 2008, the Adoption and Children Act 2002, the Children (Leaving Care) Act 2000 (and the associated statutory regulations and guidance).[16]

16.43　Judicial review in family cases is usually concerned with decisions arising out of duties requiring elements of discretion or judgment on the part

---

[12]　[1998] AC 188, HL.

[13]　See *R (Morris) v Newham London Borough Council* [2002] All ER (D) 402 (May); and also *Anufrijeva (As Personal Representative of the Estate of Kuzjeva) v Southwark London Borough Council* [2002] All ER (D) 37 (Dec); *X v Hounslow London Borough Council* [2008] EWHC 1168 (QB).

[14]　[1995] 2 AC 633, HL.

[15]　[1996] AC 923, HL.

[16]　See chapter 2, section 1.

of the local authority. Such discretion or judgment can be phrased within the statutory framework in a number of ways:

(a)   The duty only arises *if* certain subjective criteria are satisfied (such as – if it appears to the local authority that ... then the local authority shall ...):

- For example, s 47(5ZA)(a) Children Act 1989 provides that where, as a result of any such enquiries, it appears to the authority that there are matters connected with the child's education which should be investigated, they shall consult the local authority who maintain any school at which the child is a pupil.

(b)   The duty itself contains subjective elements (such as – the duty to provide *suitable* ...):

- For example, s 22A Children Act 1989 provides that when a child is in the care of a local authority, it is their duty to provide the child with accommodation.

16.44   Local authority powers, as well as duties, can also be subject to judicial review no matter how subjectively worded. However, the drafted basis of the power will affect the likely success of any judicial review claim.

SECTION 6 – UNREVIEWABLE DECISIONS

16.45   Not every local authority decision can be the subject of challenge by judicial review. There are some local authority powers and duties which, although clearly existing in public law, cannot be enforced by an individual's claim against the local authority.

- **Target duties**
  Some powers and duties are known as target duties because they identify a target for the local authority to aim at but failure to comply fully or at all will not necessarily mean that an individual is then automatically entitled to seek judicial review. Where these sorts of target duties are concerned, they are regarded as being owed to society as a whole or a specific section of it, rather than to individuals and it is assumed that Parliament did not intend to confer specific rights on individuals. For example, in *R (A) v Lambeth LBC*[17] the House of Lords held that the local authority's duty under s 17(1) CA 1989 to safeguard and promote the welfare of children within their area who are in need was a target duty only.

---

[17]   [2003] UKHL 57.

- **Alternative remedies were available**

  There will also be some other local authority decisions where, although suitable for challenge by judicial review, there is in fact another more appropriate alternative remedy which the court would require the claimant to have utilised.

- **Judicial review is inappropriate**

  Other decisions may be harder to distinguish as being excluded from judicial review but nonetheless will be inappropriate.

  – In *Re C (Adoption: Religious Observance)*[18] it was held that judicial review was normally a wholly inappropriate method of challenging a local authority's decisions concerning a child where care proceedings were already under way and could be resolved within those proceedings.

  – In *Re L (Care Proceedings: Human Rights Claims)*[19] it was held that where there are separate applications under ss 7 and 8 Human Rights Act 1998 the proper form forum for litigating these issues will almost always be the court (at whatever level) where the care proceedings are being held. Only in a wholly exceptional case would it ever be appropriate to make a separate or freestanding Human Rights Act application in such a case.

  – In *Re M (Care Proceedings: Judicial Review)*[20] the parents were refused an injunction to prevent the local authority from applying for an EPO in relation to their then unborn baby. It was held that, save in a wholly exceptional case, it was simply not appropriate to bring judicial review proceedings where the object of the proceedings is to prevent a local authority commencing emergency protection or care proceedings.

16.46 In *Re M (Care Proceedings: Judicial Review)*[21] it was suggested that the only sorts of situations where it might be proper to exercise the judicial review jurisdiction would be:

- where the court would have no jurisdiction to hear those other proceedings; or

- where the other proceedings would be vexatious or otherwise an abuse of process; or

- where a party to the existing proceedings would be severely prejudiced by the issue of further proceedings.

---

[18]   [2002] 1 FLR 1119.
[19]   [2003] EWHC 665 (Fam), [2003] 2 FLR 160.
[20]   [2003] EWHC 850 (Admin).
[21]   [2003] EWHC 850 (Admin).

SECTION 7 – ALTERNATIVE REMEDIES

16.47 As already discussed, judicial review is regarded as a remedy of last resort – see *R (G) Immigration Appeal Tribunal*.[22] This principle is clearly set out at the beginning of the Protocol (para 2):

> 'Judicial review may be used where there is no right of appeal or where all avenues of appeal have been exhausted.'

16.48 If the court finds that such a remedy was available but that the claimant failed to use it, permission for judicial review is highly unlikely to be granted.[23]

16.49 A claimant must therefore be able to demonstrate that he or she has exhausted any proper available alternative remedies. However, this is unlikely to include the existence of an alternative statutory procedure which is more appropriately viewed as one of the factors to be considered within the court's discretion as to whether relief should be granted.[24]

16.50 It is also unlikely that simply the mere existence of an alternative remedy will prevent the possibility of using judicial review. The important questions for the court will relate to the convenience of the alternative remedy and the common sense of the situation.[25]

16.51 The Protocol also requires both claimants and defendants to ensure that all alternative forms of dispute resolution (ADR) have been pursued:

> **3.1** The parties should consider whether some form of alternative dispute resolution procedure would be more suitable than litigation, and if so, endeavour to agree which form to adopt. Both the Claimant and Defendant may be required by the Court to provide evidence that alternative means of resolving their dispute were considered. The Courts take the view that litigation should be a last resort, and that claims should not be issued prematurely when a settlement is still actively being explored.

16.52 The issue of suitability or effectiveness of an alternative remedy is a matter for the court to decide.[26]

---

22 [2005] 1 WLR 1445.
23 See *R v Chief Constable of Merseyside Police ex p Calvely* [1986] QB 424; *R v Secretary of State for the Home Office ex p Swati* [1986] 1 WLR 477, CA; *R (Whitehead) v Chief Constable of Avon and Somerset* [2001] EWHC 433 (Admin); *Medical Council of Guyana v Dr Muhammed Mustapha Hafiz* (2010) 77 WIR 277.
24 See *Leech v Deputy Governor of Parkhurst Prison* [1988] AC 533 at 580C–580D.
25 See *R v Metropolitan Stipendiary Magistrate ex p London Waste Regulation Authority* [1993] 3 All ER 113 at 120B.
26 See *R ex p Waldron* [1986] QB 824 at 852F–853A and *Southern Hotel Sligo Ltd v Iarnrod Eireann* [2007] IEHC 254.

16.53 The Protocol[27] provides some guidance as to the types of ADR that might be considered suitable for these purposes, although such guidance is inevitably not exhaustive:

> '**3.2** It is not practicable in this protocol to address in detail how the parties might decide which method to adopt to resolve their particular dispute. However, summarised below are some of the options for resolving disputes without litigation:
>
> - Discussion and negotiation.
> - Ombudsmen – the Parliamentary and Health Service and the Local Government Ombudsmen have discretion to deal with complaints relating to maladministration …
> - Early neutral evaluation by an independent third party (for example, a lawyer experienced in the field of administrative law or an individual experienced in the subject matter of the claim).
> - Mediation – a form of facilitated negotiation assisted by an independent neutral party.'

16.54 However the Protocol also recognises the limitations of ADR and provides that:

> '**3.4** It is expressly recognised that no party can or should be forced to mediate or enter into any form of ADR.'

In those circumstances, the lack of participation in an ADR process will not prevent a claim for judicial review.[28]

16.55 An alternative remedy is also likely to be regarded as unhelpful or inadequate where the court's guidance about the issues in dispute is plainly required.[29]

16.56 Alternative forms of dispute resolution in child care cases could include:

(a)   Internal complaints procedures.

(b)   Family group conferences.

(c)   Requesting a meeting with the LA.

(d)   The pre-proceedings meeting.

(e)   Correspondence.

(f)   The independent review mechanism (IRM) in adoption.

---

[27]   At para 3.1.
[28]   See www.resolution.org.uk/alternatives_to_court.
[29]   See *R (A) v Kingsmead School Governors* [2003] ELR 104 at [45].

(g) Use of an independent social work mediator or social worker from another team or local authority.

(h) Review meetings.

16.57 The claimant should therefore specify within the claim form:

(a) whether or not there is any other adequate alternative remedy to judicial review; and if so,

(b) reasons for why that alternative remedy has not been used, including reasons for why the alternative remedy is generally not adequate or why it is unsuitable for the circumstances of this particular case.

SECTION 8 – REVIEWING CONTINUING POLICIES

16.58 In some cases the claimant may wish to challenge the public authority's continuing failure to act lawfully, rather than an actual decision. For example, this might include:

• a local authority's policy of refusing to place children at home with parents subject to care orders; or

• a policy of only conducting full connected persons assessments (lasting 16 weeks) rather than expedited assessments, except in absolutely exceptional circumstances.

16.59 In these sorts of cases the claim cannot be based on a failure to make any decision at all; rather it will be based on the public authority's continuing failure to make a lawful decision. The claimant may seek to argue that the decision arises from an unlawful policy which remains in place and which therefore continues to inform any new decision.

16.60 In these cases, it will be more difficult to identify or calculate when time starts to run because it is highly likely that the policies leading to such decisions will be older than three months prior to the proposed commencement of judicial review proceedings.

16.61 However, this situation does not mean that such decisions or polices are excluded from challenge by judicial review. Illegality of a policy is generally considered a good reason for extending time, where otherwise the unlawful policy continue in operation – see *R v Westminster CC ex p Hilditch*[30] where it was held:

---

[30] Unreported, 14 June 1990 but cited in *R v Rochdale BC ex p Schemet* [1994] ELR 89, QBD at 100–101.

'... if a policy is unlawful, prima facie it should be discontinued. The mere fact that the policy has been in place for nearly three years is not a sufficient reason for the court countenancing its continuing implementation for the indefinite future ...'

SECTION 9 – DEALING WITH MORE THAN ONE DECISION

16.62 As already discussed, the burden is on the claimant to act promptly once the final decision which is challenged has been made.

16.63 However, what is the position where, as often happens, a public authority makes more than one reviewable decision in relation to the same circumstances of the case? This is particularly relevant where having been asked to review a decision, the public authority then confirms the decision. In these cases it is generally *the later decision* that should be challenged via judicial review, particularly where it replaces, supersedes or confirms the original decision.

16.64 If the claimant's request for a review of the original decision was refused, then the refusal itself may be considered as a reviewable decision, although arguably it is likely to be less persuasive to the court than the substance of the original decision.

16.65 It is therefore important to specify on the claim form:

(a)   whether any other part of the decision-making process is being challenged as well as the original decision; and if so,

(b)   the nature of all parts of the decision-making being challenged.

(c)   the reasons why all parts of the decision-making (not just the original decision) are detrimental to the claimant.

16.66 It is equally important for defendants to explain in the acknowledgment of service the reasons for actions taken at each stage of the decision-making process, and particularly the impact on the defendant of any challenge to subsequent decision-making.

SECTION 10 – GROUNDS FOR JUDICIAL REVIEW

16.67 The claimant must state the legal basis for any claim for judicial review in the claim form.[31] The claim form must include a detailed statement of the claimant's grounds for bringing the claim for judicial review and a statement of the facts relied on.[32]

---

[31]   CPR 1998, r 8.2(b)(ii) (as applied by r 54.6(1)).
[32]   CPR 1998, PD54A and rr 5.6(1) and (2).

16.68 Failure to do so is likely to lead to the application for permission being refused, although claimants are allowed to provide reasons where such information may not be currently available.[33] However, it is essential that, where at all possible, claimants give a clear explanation as to how the claim fits within the scope of the legal grounds available for judicial review, the limits of the remedies available and the extent of the court's powers.

16.69 Grounds can generally be amended without much difficulty *before* the permission stage of the proceedings. However, this only applies where a proposed amendment develops or extends grounds; leave to amend is unlikely to be granted in cases where a completely new issue is being raised. The claimant should therefore provide a copy of the proposed amended grounds to the court and the parties as soon as possible before the permission hearing.

16.70 Grounds may be amended *after* the permission hearing with the leave of the court.[34] In such circumstances no written evidence may be relied upon unless the court gives permission.[35] Where the claimant intends to rely on additional grounds at the hearing of the claim for judicial review, he or she must give notice to the court and to any other person served with the claim form no later than 7 clear days before the hearing (or the warned date where appropriate).[36]

16.71 In such circumstances the claimant must therefore ensure that:

- any additional grounds satisfy the test for granting permission;

- they give notice to all parties; and

- they serve copies of the proposed amendments or additional written evidence within 7 clear days.

16.72 It is also critically important for defendants to understand the full scope of possible grounds for judicial review in order to detect possible legal errors. Defendants are required to set out within the acknowledgment of service a summary of the grounds for contesting a claim.[37] Defendants (and any other person served with the claim form) who wish to contest the claim or support it on additional grounds should file and serve detailed grounds for contesting the claim or supporting it on additional grounds and any written evidence within 35 days after service of the order giving permission.[38]

16.73 It is therefore important that defendants are able to identify whether the proposed claim does in fact fall within one of the recognised categories of

---

[33] CPR 1998, PD54A and r 5.8.
[34] CPR 1998, r 54.15.
[35] CPR 1998, r 54.16(2)(b).
[36] CPR 1998, PD54A, para 11.1.
[37] CPR 1998, r 54.8(4)(a)(i).
[38] CPR 1998, r 54.14 (1).

grounds for judicial review and in such circumstances, to state the reasons for such legal error within the acknowledgment of service and subsequent response. Speedy analysis of such legal error may mean that the court can be invited to dismiss the claim at an early stage in proceedings.

Categories of grounds

16.74   The three main categories of grounds for judicial review were confirmed in *Council of Civil Service Unions v Minister for the Civil Service* as follows:[39]

- Illegality.

- Irrationality.

- Procedural impropriety.

16.75   However, it has long been recognised that the different categories of grounds for judicial review are not necessarily easily distinguishable from each other – see the classic proposition by Lord Greene MR in *Associated Provincial Picture Houses Ltd v Wednesbury Corporation:*[40]

> 'Bad faith, dishonesty – those of course, stand by themselves – unreasonableness, attention given to extraneous circumstances, disregard of public policy and things like that have all been referred to, according to the facts of individual cases, as being matters which are relevant to the question. If they cannot all be confined under one head, they at any rate, I think, overlap to a very great extent.'

16.76   In *Council of Civil Service Unions v Minister for the Civil Service*[41] the House of Lords made it clear that the commonly understood list of three grounds for judicial review was not an exhaustive list:

> '... That is not to say that further development on a case by case basis may not in course of time add further developments. I have in mind particularly the possible adoption in the future of the principle of "proportionality".'

16.77   In practice, this is exactly what has happened. Proportionality is now recognised as both a separate ground for judicial review which can be relied upon in cases where human rights issues are engaged. Alternatively it is recognized as an important element of the ground of unreasonableness in cases where it is argued that a decision was so disproportionate that it was irrational or unreasonable.

16.78   Factual disputes are not generally regarded as falling within the scope of judicial review because it is the *route* to a decision that is at issue, rather than the factual basis of a decision. The court will therefore generally be very

---

[39]   [1985] AC 374 at 410D.
[40]   [1948] 1 KB 223.
[41]   [1985] AC 374, HL.

cautious about interfering with the decision-maker's own evaluation of the evidence and factual basis which underpinned or was the basis for its decision.

16.79 However, there are certain exceptions to this rule and if necessary judicial review can be adjusted so as to enable issues of fact to be resolved.[42] Judicial review can be used to deal with issues of fact in the following situations:

- **Fundamental mistakes of fact**
  Judicial review is available where a decision-maker has made a fundamental mistake of fact.[43] In such circumstances the court may be invited to find that the decision-maker's factual basis for the decision was irrational. The claimant must demonstrate four matters in such cases (although this list is not a precise code and is open to variation):

  (i)   There must have been a mistake as to an existing fact, including a mistake as to the availability of evidence on a particular matter.
  (ii) The fact or evidence must have been 'established' in the sense that it was uncontentious and objectively verifiable.
  (iii) The claimant, or his legal advisers, must not have been responsible for the mistake.
  (iv) The mistake must have played a material (although not necessarily decisive) part in the decision-making.

- **The asserted facts do not exist**
  In some cases it can be argued that the facts which triggered the decision-maker's power to act do not actually exist. In other words the decision-maker (public authority) acted outside its jurisdiction because the condition precedent to the exercise of its powers did not exist. In rare cases where a precedent fact is required before a decision is taken, then it is open to the court to decide whether that fact exists when considering an application for judicial review.[44]
  If the court finds that determination of this issue is essential in considering the overall application for judicial review, then it may permit additional evidence to be submitted..[45] If the relevant statutory provision is that the local authority has power or jurisdiction where it is 'satisfied' of particular matters or where certain matters 'appear' to the local authority, then the court will generally only intervene if the local authority's finding that the necessary facts existed was not one which a reasonable person,

---

42   See *Doherty v Birmingham City Council* [2009] 1 AC 367 at 416 and 443D and see *Manchester City Council v Pinnock* [2010] 3 WLR 1441 at 1461B.

43   See *R (Alconbury Developments Ltd) v Secretary of State for the Environment, Transport and the Regions* [2003] 2 AC 295; *Naz Foundation v Delhi* [2009] 4 LRC 838, *R (Animal Defenders International) v Secretary of State for Culture, Media and Sport* [2008] UKHL 15.

44   See *R v Oldham Metropolitan Borough Council ex p Garlick* [1993] AC 509; *R (A) v LB Croydon; R (M) v LB Lambeth* [2008] EWCA Civ 1445.

45   See *R v Secretary of State for the Home Department, ex p Rahman* [1998] QB 136.

properly instructed as to the question to be determined, could have come to, or if the body is not in fact satisfied as to the relevant matters.

However, in general terms the court is more likely to conclude that it is for the decision-maker, rather than the court itself, to determine the factual basis behind any decision taken.

16.80   Therefore disputed issues of fact or errors of fact only become relevant in judicial review cases where they relate directly to errors of law which are relied upon as the basis of challenge to a decision. In all other circumstances, the Administrative Court will not be concerned about issues of fact and it will be assumed that the factual basis of a claim for judicial review is correct, clear and agreed.

The ground of illegality

16.81   A public authority will not be acting lawfully if it acts outside the limits of its jurisdiction or powers. This is often described as 'ultra vires' and means that any act done or decision made by a public authority outside or in excess of its powers will generally be void. The presumption is that the acts of public bodies (including decisions) are lawful and valid unless and until declared otherwise by the court.[46]

16.82   The ground of illegality was defined in *Council of Civil Service Unions v Minister for the Civil Service* as follows:[47]

> '... By "illegality" as a ground for judicial review I mean that the decision-maker must understand correctly the law that regulates his decision-making power and must give effect to it. Whether he has or not is par excellence a justiciable question to be decided, in the event of dispute, by those persons, the judges, by whom the judicial power of the state is exercisable.'

16.83   The court can intervene to ensure that the powers of public authorities are exercised lawfully when making decisions. Illegality is therefore usually relied upon in circumstances where a decision-maker has failed to direct himself or herself properly about the law – see for example *Akbarali v Brent London Borough Council and Other Cases*[48] where a local authority was held to have failed to direct itself correctly re the meaning of a statutory provision providing for the payment of grants to students. Section 6(1) of the HRA 1998 may also be engaged in cases relying on illegality as a ground of judicial review in relation to alleged breaches of the ECHR by providing that:

> 6(1) It is unlawful for a public authority to act in a way which is incompatible with a Convention right.

---

[46]   See *Boddington v British Transport Police* [1999] 2 AC 143 at 155, HL, *R (Draga) v Secretary of State for the Home Department* [2011] EWHC 1825 (Admin), *R v SE Searby Ltd* [2003] EWCA Crim 1910.

[47]   [1985] AC 374 at 410D.

[48]   [1983] 2 AC 309 at 350D.

Other relevant examples for child care lawyers could involve alleged breaches of the Equality Act 2010 or the Disability Discrimination Act 1995.

16.84 It is for the court, not the public authority, to decide whether in the whole circumstances of the case, the words of the relevant statute apply to the facts which form the basis of the public authority's decision when given their ordinary usage. A decision based on a public authority's conclusion that the facts of the case fit the relevant statutory definition will not normally be regarded as an error of law, or an illegal decision, within the context of judicial review proceedings.

16.85 Where a public body errs in law in reaching a decision, the court may quash that decision. A public body will err in law in the following circumstances if it:

- acts in breach of fundamental human rights;

- misinterprets a statute or a rule of common law;

- misinterprets a legal document;

- takes a decision on the basis of secondary legislation, or any other act or order, which is itself ultra vires;

- takes legally irrelevant considerations into account;

- fails to take relevant considerations into account;

- fails to follow the proper procedure required by law;

- fails to fulfil an express or implied duty to give reasons for its decision;

- otherwise abuses its power.

16.86 However, even where it is shown that the decision-maker has applied the law wrongly to a particular set of facts, it will still remain open to the court to decide whether such illegality is relevant.[49],[50] Judicial review remains at all times a discretionary remedy and the court will need to be satisfied that the decision is founded on a relevant error of law, ie: an error in the actual making of the decision which affected the decision itself.[51] The court is highly unlikely to interfere in cases where an error of law was not directly relevant to the decision being challenged. Even in those circumstances where the error of law

---

[49] *R v Lord President of the Privy Council* [1993] AC 682.
[50] *Secretary of State for Education and Science v Tameside Metropolitan Borough Council* [1977] AC 1014, HL.
[51] See *R v Hull University Visitor ex p Page* [1993] AC 682 at 702C.

is relevant, the court may still exercise its discretion not to quash the decision where it would have been no different had the error not been committed.[52]

Unlawful delegation of powers or duties

16.87 It is a well-established, fundamental principle of administrative law that a decision must be made by the decision-maker to whom it has been entrusted – this is known as the doctrine of *delegates non potest delegare*. Public authorities therefore cannot evade their duties by delegating their decisions to others unless they have specific power to do so and have done so properly.[53]

Secret policies

16.88 It is unlawful for a public authority to keep a policy hidden from the person(s) to whom such policy applies. In *Salih and Rahmani v The Secretary of State for the Home Department*[54] the court considered the different categories of information about legal rights that should be made plain to individuals:

> 'It is a fundamental requisite of the rule of law that the law should be made known. The individual must be able to know of his legal rights and obligations.'

16.89 The court confirmed that the publication of statutes and statutory instruments plainly falls within this category. The court also identified a number of contexts, particularly where important rights of the individual are concerned, where Parliament has imposed a legal duty on public authorities to inform the individual affected of his rights or to give him legal advice. However, in *Salih and Rahmani v The Secretary of State for the Home Department*[55] the court also confirmed that there may be other circumstances in which extra-statutory policies relating to the exercise of a statutory discretion may be just as important:

> '... an extra-statutory policy relating to the exercise of a statutory discretion, moreover a policy that does not in terms require that support be provided, but only sets out the qualifications for eligibility for support (and describes what may be provided). However, the policies of public authorities may have a significance approaching or approximating to a law and may be equally important to the individual ... On principle a policy ... should be made known to those who may need to avail themselves of it ... it is inconsistent with that policy not to make available information about it: the restriction on information in practice excludes persons ignorant of it from the benefit of the policy in a manner that is not set out in or implicit the policy.'

16.90 There are obvious implications of such a principle when considering the ways in which local authorities formulate policies in relation to looked after children and child protection practice; for example, although social workers may refer in evidence to a local authority's policy of not placing children

---

[52] See *R v Bedwellty Justices, ex p Williams* [1997] AC 225, HL.
[53] See *Allingham v Minister of Agriculture and Fisheries* [1948] 1 All ER 780.
[54] [2003] EWHC 2273 (Admin) at [45].
[55] [2003] EWHC 2273 (Admin) at [48]–[53].

subject to care orders at home with their parents, such policies are often not explicitly confirmed in writing or made known to parents. When faced with declarations or statements by local authorities relating to 'policy decisions', practitioners may well find it useful to request disclosure of such policies, the date on which a policy was formulated, and the way in which it has been (or has not been) disseminated within and beyond the local authority.

The importance of reasons for a decision

16.91 In some cases it will be extremely difficult to argue that a public authority has misdirected itself about the law and that a decision has been made illegally if there are no documentary reasons given for a decision. The duty to give reasons for an administrative decision need not be express and can be implied. This is particularly relevant in child law cases where decisions are often made by social workers or their managers quickly and 'on the hoof'. In such cases it is particularly important to seek disclosure of all possible written material relating to the decision. It is also important to consider whether the *lack* of documentary evidence about the reasons for a decision might be relied upon to demonstrate that a public authority has failed to direct itself correctly about the law, particularly if the local authority's own procedures indicate the expectation of a requirement for reasons about important decisions to be documented.

16.92 It is important to remember that, in the absence of a statutory or policy requirement to provide documentary reasons for a decision, there is no general common law duty on a public authority to provide reasons. However, the implied requirement for local authorities to give reasons has been repeatedly confirmed. It is also well established in administrative law that fairness demands that reasons for decisions should be given. In *R (Wooder) v Feggetter and Another*[56] the Court of Appeal held that while there is no general duty to give reasons for a decision, there are classes of cases where there is such a duty and where the court may take account of fairness as follows:

(a) The subject matter is an interest so highly regarded by the law that fairness requires that reasons, at least for particular decisions, be given as of right. In child care cases it is suggested that decisions involving adoption or permanent separation of a child from his birth family could all reasonably be argued as falling within this category.

(b) The decision appears aberrant and fairness may require reasons so that the subject of the decision may know whether the aberration is lawful or open to challenge.[57] Decisions involving radical departures from previously agreed care plans could reasonably be argued as falling within this second category.

---

[56] [2003] QB 219.
[57] See also *R v Civil Service Appeal Board ex p Cunningham* [1991] 4 All ER 310 at 319B, *R v Higher Education Funding Council ex p Institute of Dental Surgery* [1994] 1 WLR 242.

16.93 In *R (Wooder) v Feggetter and Another*[58] the Court of Appeal confirmed:

> '... the common law implies a duty to give reasons ... where the subject-matter is an interest so highly regarded by the law ... that fairness requires that reasons ... be given as of right'.

16.94 It is also suggested that it is not just the fact of whether reasons have been given that will be important for child care lawyers. It is also the *transparency, quality* or *substance* of the reasons given that will be of critical importance.[59]

16.95 Given the obvious importance of examining the reasons for any decision that is to be challenged, the burden is on the claimant (or prospective claimant) to ask for reasons for a decision as soon as possible. Such a request should be put in writing (either directly by the claimant or on his behalf by legal representatives) whenever possible and should be set out in the clearest possible terms. It is likely to prove extremely difficult to argue later that reasons for a challenged decision were not provided or were defective in some way if the claimant did not actually seek or pursue a copy of the reasons.[60]

16.96 This is important regardless of whether the decision-maker had a statutory obligation or not to give reasons for a decision.[61] Failure or refusal by the decision-maker to provide reasons can itself form the basis of a claim for judicial review on the grounds that such failure or refusal was unfair or irrational.

16.97 The principles relating to the content of adequate reasons for a decision were confirmed by the House of Lords in *Save Britain's Heritage v Number 1 Poultry Ltd*:[62]

(a) Reasons must be proper.

(b) Reasons must be intelligible.

(c) Reasons must be adequate.

(d) Reasons must enable the reader to understand why the matter was decided as it was and what conclusions were reached on the 'principal important controversial issues', disclosing how any issue of law or fact was resolved.

---

[58] [2003] QB 219. Applied in *R (O) v West London Mental Health NHS Trust* [2005] EWHC 604 (Admin) where the common law duty to give reasons was reiterated.

[59] See *Re L-B (Children)* [2013] UKSC 8 (on appeal from [2012] EWCA Civ 984). Also see *R (Asha Foundation) v Millenium Commission* [2003] ACD 50, *Save Britain's Heritage v Number 1 Poultry Ltd* [1991] 1 WLR 153, *English v Emery Reimbold and Strick Ltd* [2002] 1 WLR 2409, *Norouzi v Sheffield City Council* [2011] IRLR 897.

[60] See *R v The Crown Court of Southwark ex p Samuel* [1995] COD 249.

[61] See *R v Secretary of State for the Home Department ex p Fayed* [1997] 1 All ER 228.

[62] [1991] 1 WLR 153.

(e) Reasons can be briefly stated as long as they set out the substance of the decision.[63] The degree of particularity required will depend entirely on the nature of the issues falling for decision.[64]

(f) The reasoning must not give rise to a substantial doubt as to whether the decision-maker erred in law (for example, by misunderstanding some relevant policy or some other important matter or by failing to reach a rational decision on relevant grounds) BUT such adverse inference will *not* readily be drawn and the reasons need refer only to the main issues in the dispute, not to every material consideration.[65]

16.98 In summary, if it is established that reasons satisfy the key principles outlined above, address the relevant issues between the parties and explain how the decision-maker reached a decision/conclusion about those issues, then it is highly unlikely that the court will find that the reasons were inadequate. Claims for judicial review based on a ground that inadequate reasons were given are unlikely to succeed without the relevant deficiencies being established.

Rectification of deficient or inadequate reasons

16.99 In some situations the local authority may become alive to the issue that its stated reasons for a decision are inadequate, perhaps after a pre-action letter has been received from a claimant, and may seek to rectify the error. In these sorts of situations, it is essential that the only additional reasons provided serve simply to amplify and explain the earlier decision and do not set out wholly new reasons.[66]

16.100 In most such cases the court is highly unlikely to allow such rectification to take place because it will be concerned to ensure that the amended reasons are the real reasons and not simply an attempt by the local authority to rectify or justify the earlier decision.[67] Consequently the court is highly unlikely (or at any rate, will be extremely circumspect) to allow the local authority to fill material gaps in evidence by providing additional evidence in affidavit. In other words, a decision-maker who gives one set of reasons cannot, when challenged, come up with another set of reasons.[68]

16.101 However, in *R (Bancoult) v Secretary of State for Foreign and Commonwealth Affairs*[69] the Divisional Court granted the applicant permission to re-amend his judicial review claim to add two new grounds to his existing challenge; the applicant was also granted permission to rely on further

---

63 *R v Civil Service Appeal Board, ex p Cunningham* [1991] 4 All ER 310, CA.
64 See *Stefan v General Medical Council* [1999] 1 WLR 1293 at 1340B. See also *R v Southwark Crown Court ex p Brooke* [1997] COD 81.
65 See *R (Duncan) v General Teaching Council for England* [2010] EWHC 429 (Admin) at [6].
66 See *R v Westminster City Council ex p Ermakov*, and *Re L-B (Children) (Injuries to Children: Identity of Perpetrator)* [2012] EWCA Civ 984.
67 See *S v Special Educational Needs Tribunal* [1995] 1 WLR 1627 at 1637B.
68 See *R v Westminster City Council ex p Ermakov* (1996) 28 HLR 819 at 829.
69 [2012] EWHC 3281 (Admin).

evidence. This was because the subject matter of the instant proceedings differed from previous proceedings, and the decision not to raise the grounds in earlier proceedings did not make it an abuse of process to raise it in the present context. In addition, in such a sensitive case where the applicant also complained of difficulties in obtaining disclosure of documents over several years, he or she should not be prevented from advancing an arguable case which he or she contended had become apparent only because of documents discovered within the preceding six months.

16.102 In *R (O) v West London Mental Health NHS Trust* it was held:[70]

> '... it may well be proper to explain or expand in certain circumstances. But where a key issue has not properly, or indeed at all, been dealt with in the original reasons, it becomes very difficult to accept that it should be possible to supplement those matters subsequently when a challenge is raised.'

16.103 In *Re L-B (Children) (Injuries to Children: Identity of Perpetrator)*[71] the Court of Appeal held that if a judgment appeared to be incomplete or deficient, counsel was obliged to invite the judge to expand or supplement it rather than to rely on the deficiency as ground for an application for permission to appeal. However, that practice allowed the judge to only expand reasons in further support of his stated conclusions, not to reverse a previously stated conclusion. However, the decision was very recently reversed by the Supreme Court in *Re LB (Children)*[72] where it was held that a judge in care proceedings is entitled to revisit an earlier identification of the perpetrator if fresh evidence warrants it. The Supreme Court confirmed that the judge must be able to keep an open mind until the final decision is made, at least if fresh evidence or further developments indicate an earlier decision was wrong.[73]

16.104 The Supreme Court confirmed that both the Civil Procedure Rules and Family Procedure Rules make it clear that the court's wide case management powers include power to vary or revoke their previous case management orders. However, the power does not enable a free-for-all in which previous orders may be revisited at will. The power must be exercised 'judicially and not capriciously' and must be exercised in accordance with the overriding objective.[74]

16.105 In *Re A and L (Children)*[75] the judge had given brief but sufficiently clear reasons for his judgment. It was held that neither ex tempore judgments, nor judicial brevity were to be discouraged, the safeguard being the duty of the parties to seek explanation or elaboration from the judge.

---

[70] [2005] EWHC 604 (Admin).
[71] [2012] EWCA Civ 984.
[72] [2013] UKSC 8 (on appeal from [2012] EWCA Civ 984).
[73] See chapter 15 for more detailed consideration of the Supreme Court decision in the context of appeals.
[74] In family proceedings the overriding objective is 'enabling the court to deal with cases justly, having regard to any welfare issues involved'.
[75] [2011] EWCA Civ 1611.

The ground of irrationality (Wednesbury unreasonableness)

16.106 Irrationality amounting to an error of law is often defined as *Wednesbury* unreasonableness, having been considered in *Associated Provincial Picture Houses Ltd v Wednesbury Corporation* as follows:[76]

> 'What, then, is the power of the courts? They can only interfere with an act of executive authority if it be shown that the authority has contravened the law ... When an executive discretion is entrusted by Parliament to a body such as the local authority ... what appears to be an exercise of that discretion can only be challenged in the courts in a strictly limited class of case ... The exercise of such a discretion must be a real exercise of the discretion ... Unreasonable really meant that it must be proved to be unreasonable in the sense that the court considers it to be a decision that no reasonable body could have come to. It is not what the court considers unreasonable, a different thing altogether. If it is what the court considers unreasonable, the court may very well have different views to that of a local authority on matters of high public policy ...'

16.107 Therefore a decision held to be so unreasonable that no reasonable body, properly directing itself as to the law to be applied, could have reached such a decision will be quashed.

16.108 Unreasonableness or irrationality was confirmed as one of the grounds for judicial review in *Council of Civil Service Unions v Minister for the Civil Service* where it was defined as:[77]

> '... so outrageous in its defiance of logic or of accepted moral standards that no sensible person who had applied his mind to the question to be decided could have arrived at it.'

16.109 The principles in relation to unreasonableness have been considered at length in subsequent decisions, but can be summarised as follows:

(a) The standard of reasonableness varies with the subject matter of the decision being challenged.

(b) The claimant or prospective claimant must demonstrate an error of reasoning which effectively does not add up, is illogical or oppressive.

(c) There is a heavy burden on the claimant or prospective claimant to show that the unreasonableness is overwhelming.

(d) The circumstances in which a decision will be quashed for being unreasonable will be extremely limited.

---

[76] [1948] 1 KB 223.
[77] [1985] AC 374, HL at 410D.

(e)   The claimant must be careful to focus on an objective analysis of the irrationality or unreasonableness of the decision itself, rather than a simple assertion that the decision was wrong.

(f)   A simple disagreement about the conclusion reached by the decision-maker will not usually be sufficient to show that the decision was irrational or unreasonable.

16.110   The heavy burden on the claimant or prospective claimant in relation to pleading irrationality or unreasonableness means that a claim for judicial review is unlikely to succeed if it is based solely or largely on this ground. Claims are more likely to succeed if this ground is pleaded alongside other matters such as proportionality or a failure to take account of relevant factors (or taking account of irrelevant factors).

Consideration of relevant factors

16.111   The public authority's consideration of relevant factors in making a decision is therefore likely to be of particular significance in child care cases where local authorities and social workers exercise extensive discretion in coming to decisions about children and families. The definition of whether a factor is a relevant consideration or not will usually depend on the statutory or legal context. In cases where policy guidance exists in relation to the exercise of a public authority's discretion, such guidance will be a relevant factor which should be taken into account by the decision-maker.[78] In *R v Lincolnshire CC and Wealden DC, ex p Atkinson*[79] it was held that government guidance would be of relevance in any case, regardless of whether there was a statutory obligation to consider it, on the basis that such guidance will indicate matters which are themselves relevant.

16.112   It is also clear that the decision-maker must reach its own decision on each individual case and must not approach a decision with a predetermined policy on how all cases falling within a particular class will be treated. This does not mean that for public authorities to have policies will be unlawful per se, rather that the decision-maker must demonstrably approach each case on its own merits.[80]

16.113   It is important to consider the following factors (not an exhaustive list) in determining the merits of any claim or proposed claim based on this issue:

(a)   Is there a statutory basis of the relevant decision-making power?

---

[78]   See *R v Secretary of State for the Home Department, ex p Khan* [1984] 1 WLR 1337, CA and *R (Bhatt Murphy) v Independent Assessor; R (Niazi) v Secretary of State for the Home Department* [2008] EWCA Civ 755.

[79]   (1995) 8 Admin LR 529, QBD.

[80]   See *R v Secretary of State for the Environment, ex p Brent LBC* [1982] QB 593.

(b)   If so, does the statute give any express indication of the relevant factors to be taken into account by the decision-maker?

(c)   If not, can it be implied that a range of factors ought to have been taken into account by the decision-maker?

(e)   Did the decision-maker take account of the relevant factors (whether express or implied)?

(f)   Did the decision-maker properly ignore irrelevant factors in making the decision?

16.114   However, it is important to remember that any decision based on the exercise of discretion by the public authority will *not* necessarily be irrational or unreasonable because of a failure to take into account a consideration which the decision-maker was not obliged (by law or facts) to take into account. In order to succeed in showing that a failure to take relevant factors into account renders a decision irrational or unreasonable, it is also necessary to show that that the mistake was *material.* In other words, the claimant must be able to show that the decision could have been different if the relevant factors had been taken into account or the irrelevant factors had been ignored.[81]

16.115   It is important to remember that public authorities are entitled to give whatever weight they regard as appropriate in all the circumstances when making decisions. The weight to be given to a relevant consideration is a matter for the decision-maker and it will only be in the most exceptional cases that the court will consider quashing a decision arising from the public authority's exercise of discretionary powers involving a large element of policy consideration.[82]

16.116   The court will only intervene if it can plainly be shown that the decision is irrational although in some, limited, circumstances a decision may be quashed because insufficient or excessive weight was given to a consideration by the decision-maker.[83]

Inconsistent decisions

16.117   Inconsistency within a public authority's decision-making may provide an effective basis of a claim for judicial review within the overall grounds of irrationality. It may be argued that an inconsistent decision was illogical and therefore falls within the irrational or unreasonable category. However, such an argument is unlikely to succeed if the point of comparison for inconsistency is between the current case and another case. This is because the court is likely to consider that no two cases will ever be exactly the same.

---

[81]   See *Wellcome Foundation Ltd v Secretary of State for Social Services* [1988] 1 WLR 635, HL.

[82]   See *Council of Civil Service Unions v Minister for the Civil Service* [1985] AC 374, HL.

[83]   See *Secretary of State for Education and Science v Tameside Metropolitan Borough Council* [1977] AC 1014, HL.

16.118   Therefore in cases where inconsistency between cases is to be argued, it may be easier and more prudent to characterise decisions as generally unfair rather than inconsistent.

The ground of proportionality

16.119   The legal doctrine of proportionality simply means that there must be a reasonable relationship between the objective being sought, and the means used to obtain such objective.

16.120   Proportionality can arise in two different ways in relation to claims for judicial review:

(a)   It will be a relevant consideration for the court when reviewing cases for compatibility with the ECHR or HRA 1998.

(b)   Lack of proportionality may indicate an element of *Wednesbury* unreasonableness.

16.121   Generally the weight to be given by the public authority to a relevant factor when making a decision is a matter for the decision-maker. The court cannot interfere with such decisions. However, when considering the doctrine of proportionality, it may be appropriate and necessary for the court to consider the relative weight attached by the decision-maker to the various relevant interests and considerations.

16.122   In *R (Daly) v Secretary of State for the Home Department*[84] the House of Lords set out the three-stage test to be applied by the court when considering the issue of proportionality:

> '... whether (i) the legislative object is sufficiently important to justify limiting a fundamental right; (ii) the measures designed to meet the legislative imperative are rationally connected to it; and (iii) the means used to impair the right or freedom are no more than is necessary to accomplish the objective.'

16.123   Much academic debate has taken place in recent years in relation to the relationship between the traditional grounds of judicial review and the doctrine of proportionality as applied in human rights cases. In particular, the differences between the two approaches have been highlighted. In *R v Ministry of Agriculture, Fisheries and Food, ex p First City Trading Ltd* the court held as follows:[85]

> '... The difference between *Wednesbury* and European review is that in the former case the legal limits lie further back ... there are two factors. First, the limits of domestic review are not, as the law presently stands, constrained by the doctrine of proportionality. Secondly, at least as regards a requirement such as that of

---

[84]   [2001] UKHL 26.
[85]   [1997] 1 CMLR 250, QBD.

objective justification in an equal treatment case, the European rule requires the decision-maker to provide a fully reasoned case. It is not enough merely to set out the problem ... Rather the court will test the solution arrived at, and pass it only if substantial factual considerations are put forward in its justification: considerations which are relevant, reasonable and proportionate to the aim in view. But ... the court is not concerned to agree or disagree with the decision: that would be to travel beyond the boundaries of proper judicial authority, and usurp the primary decision-maker's function. Thus *Wednesbury* and European review are different models – one looser, one tighter – of the same judicial concept, which is the imposition of compulsory standards on decision-makers so as to secure the repudiation of arbitrary power'.

16.124   Essentially the *Wednesbury* test is not a flexible test but one which allows the decision-maker a very wide margin of appreciation. Therefore any decision may validly be taken as long as it was not made in error and a reasonable decision-maker could have taken it. In contrast, when considering a decision which is alleged to have challenged an ECHR right, the doctrine of proportionality is applied in a narrower context (the 'heightened (or anxious) scrutiny' test); it will vary according to the rights being asserted, the decision made and the facts of the case.[86]

16.125   The standard of review of proportionality that should be carried out by the court was considered at length by the House of Lords in *R (Daly) v Secretary of State for the Home Department*[87] where it was confirmed that the intensity of review is somewhat greater under the proportionality approach; three concrete differences were highlighted as follows:

'First, the doctrine of proportionality may require the reviewing court to assess the balance which the decision-maker has struck, not merely whether it is within the range of rational or reasonable decisions. Secondly, the proportionality test may go further than the traditional grounds of review inasmuch as it may require attention to be directed to the relative weight accorded to interests and considerations. Thirdly, even the heightened scrutiny test developed in *R v Ministry of Defence ex p Smith* [1996] QB 517 is not necessarily appropriate to the protection of human rights.'

16.126   In *R (Begum) v Headteacher and Governors of Denbigh High School*[88] it was held that:

'... it is clear that the court's approach to an issue of proportionality under the Convention must go beyond that traditionally adopted to judicial review in a domestic setting ... There is no shift to a merits review, but the intensity of review is greater than was previously appropriate, and greater even than the heightened scrutiny test ... The domestic court must now make a value judgment, an evaluation, by reference to the circumstances prevailing at the relevant time ... Proportionality must be judged objectively, by the court'.

---

[86]   See *R v Ministry of Defence ex p Smith* [1996] QB 517.
[87]   [2001] 2 AC 532.
[88]   [2007] 1 AC 100 *sub nom R (SB) v Governors of Denbigh High School* [2007] 1 AC 100. Applied in *Belfast City Council v Miss Behavin' Ltd* [2007] UKHL 19.

16.127 In *R (Samaroo) v Secretary of State for the Home Department*[89] the Court of Appeal proposed a two-stage test should be considered by the court when considering the issue of proportionality:

> 'At the first stage, the question is: can the objective of the measure be achieved by means which are less interfering of an individual's rights? ... At the second stage, it is assumed that the means employed to achieve the legitimate aim are necessary in the sense that they are the least intrusive of Convention rights that can be devised in order to achieve the aim'.

16.128 However, in *R (Association of British Civilian Internees (Far East Region)) v Secretary of State for Defence*[90] the Court of Appeal went on to highlight the increasing connection between the two doctrines:

> '... trying to keep the *Wednesbury* principle and proportionality in separate compartments is unnecessary and confusing. The criteria of proportionality are more precise and sophisticated ... It is true that sometimes proportionality may require the reviewing court to assess for itself the balance that has been struck by the decision-maker, and that may produce a different result from one that would be arrived at on an application of the *Wednesbury* test. But the strictness of the *Wednesbury* test has been relaxed in recent years even in areas which have nothing to do with fundamental rights ... The *Wednesbury* test is moving closer to proportionality, and in some cases it is not possible to see any daylight between the two tests.'

The ground of procedural impropriety

16.129 Procedural impropriety was confirmed as a ground for judicial review in *Council of Civil Service Unions v Minister for the Civil Service.*[91]

16.130 Procedural fairness, or the duty to act fairly and within the parameters of natural justice, refers to the procedural standards to which public authorities must adhere when making decisions. The flexible requirements imposed on public authorities will vary between cases and situations depending on the particular circumstances.[92] Procedural fairness falls squarely within the overall doctrine of natural justice.

16.131 There are two fundamental elements of natural justice – the right to be heard and the rule against bias. The distinction between impartiality and fairness was explained with great clarity by Lord Denning in *Kanda v Government of the Federation of Malaya* as follows:[93]

> 'The rule against bias is one thing. The right to be heard is another. Those two rules are the essential characteristics of what is often called natural justice. They

---

[89] [2001] UKHRR 1150.
[90] [2003] EWCA Civ 473.
[91] [1985] AC 374, HL at 410D.
[92] See *R v Secretary of State for the Home Department, ex p Doody* [1994] 1 AC 531.
[93] [1962] AC 322.

are the twin pillars supporting it ... They have recently been put in the two words, Impartiality and Fairness. But they are separate concepts and are governed by separate considerations.'

16.132 The common law principles of natural justice are now supplemented by Art 6 of the ECHR. The principles of natural justice relate to the manner in which a decision is taken, rather than to the issue of whether or not the decision is correct.

16.133 The duty to observe the rules of natural justice apply not just to courts and tribunals, but also to any public body making an administrative decision. The presumption will always be that any administrative decision will be taken fairly. The exact procedure to be followed in a given situation will inevitably vary depending on the nature and subject matter of the decision and all the circumstances of the case. However, in almost all circumstances, the issue will be the content of the duty to act fairly, rather than whether or not it actually applies at all.

The right to be heard

16.134 The right to be heard is a well established principle that applies just as much to local authority internal procedures as it does to court hearings; in *Kanda v Government of the Federation of Malaya*[94] the key decision of Lord Denning confirmed:

> '... the right to be heard ... must carry with it a right in the accused man to know the case which is made against him. He must know what evidence has been given and what statements have been made affecting him: and then he must be given a fair opportunity to correct or contradict them. The court will not go into the likelihood of prejudice. The risk of it is enough.'

16.135 Essentially, if a person is likely to be directly affected by the decision of the public authority, he or she is entitled to have notice of the details of the time, date and venue of any relevant hearing and of the nature of the case against him or her so that s/he has a proper opportunity to meet such case. The public authority must ensure that a person is provided with all reasonable facilities to help exercise the right to be heard. This can include the help of a friend to take notes and give advice.[95]

16.136 Although it is well established that decision-makers are usually entitled to determine and manage their own procedures, it is also the general rule that the more important the rights at stake arising from the decision, the more likely it is that fairness will require an oral hearing. The rule generally applies with the greatest force to the public authority's actions that lead directly to a final act or decision, rather than to preliminary or intermediary actions. Similarly, the rule is unlikely to apply with significant force to an ongoing investigation

---

[94] [1962] AC 322. Applied and endorsed by the Privy Council in *Diedrichs-Shurland v Talanga-Stiftung* [2006] UKPC 58.

[95] See *R v Leicester City Justices ex p Barrow* [1991] 2 QB 260, CA.

designed to obtain information for the purpose of a report or a recommendation on which a subsequent decision may be based. However, this does not mean that a person cannot or should not expect an investigation or inquiry to be conducted in a fair manner if the outcome of the investigation or inquiry is likely to expose him or her to substantial prejudice.

The rule against bias

16.137   The rule against bias means that no person may be a judge in his own cause. In some situations, it will be obvious that bias has occurred and the court will automatically quash the decision.

16.138   In *Locabail (UK) Ltd v Bayfield Properties Ltd*[96] the Court of Appeal gave as examples of cases in which a real danger of bias might well be thought to arise, cases in which:

> 'Where the credibility of any individual were an issue to be decided by the judge, he had in a previous case rejected the evidence of that person in such outspoken terms as to throw doubt on his ability to approach such person's evidence with an open mind on any later occasion.'

16.139   In other, less obvious situations the issue of whether bias has occurred will be a matter for the court. The test for the court remains as approved by the House of Lords in *Porter v Magill*,[97] namely:

> 'The question is whether the fair-minded and informed observer, having considered the facts, would conclude that there was a real possibility that the tribunal was biased.'

Legitimate expectations

16.140   A person may have a legitimate expectation of being treated in a particular way by a public authority even if there is no other legal basis on which he or she could claim such treatment.[98] Such expectation may arise from a representation or promise made by the public authority (including an implied representation), or from the authority's consistent past practice.

16.141   In such cases, the expectation arises from the public authority's conduct in relation to its decision-making and the general principles of fairness, predictability and certainty should not be disregarded. However, in order to rely on the doctrine, the claimant or prospective claimant must be able to demonstrate that he or she knew about the public authority's publicised procedure and relied upon it. Where a promise has been made by a person who has no power to make it, another decision-maker will not be bound to take it into account, even if it could amount to a legitimate expectation.[99]

---

[96]   [2000] QB 451.
[97]   [2001] UKHL 67.
[98]   See *O'Reilly v Mackman* [1983] 2 AC 237, HL.
[99]   See *R (Bloggs) v Secretary of State for the Home Department* [2003] EWCA Civ 686. See also

16.142   In *Abdi v Secretary of State for the Home Department* the Court of Appeal confirmed:[100]

> 'The search for principle surely starts with a theme that is current through the legitimate expectation cases. It may well be expressed thus. Where a public authority has issued a promise or adopted a practice which represents how it proposes to act in a given area, the law will require the promise or practice to be honoured unless there is good reason not to do so.'

16.143   In *Nyambi v Secretary of State for the Home Department* it was confirmed that:[101]

> 'In order to give rise to a legitimate expectation, the body concerned must have made a clear and unambiguous representation that it would act in accordance with the particular policy.'

16.144   The principles in relation to legitimate expectation fall within the overall ground of procedural impropriety and may serve as the basis for a judicial review claim. It is not always necessary for the claimant to show that he or she relied on a legitimate expectation to his detriment. However, claimants must specify clearly exactly how and in which of the various categories their legitimate expectation arose.

16.145   There are three categories of legitimate expectation:[102]

(a)   Cases where the decision-maker is only obliged to bear in mind its promise, giving the promise whatever weight it considers, before deciding whether to depart from it.

(b)   Cases where the promise induces a legitimate expectation that a certain procedure will be followed before taking a decision, such as a promise of consultation (leading to a procedural expectation).[103]

Nyambi v Secretary of State for the Home Department [2010] EWHC 1871 (Admin) where it was confirmed that a promise or representation by one public body cannot found a legitimate expectation against a different public body.

[100]   [2005] EWCA Civ 1363.

[101]   [2010] EWHC 1871 (Admin).

[102]   *R v North and East Devon Health Authority ex p Coughlan* [2001] QB 213. See also *R (Nadarajah) v Secretary of State for the Home Department* [2005] EWCA Civ 1363 where the Court of Appeal describes the principle of legitimate expectation in detail (and approved by the Supreme Court in *R (Lumba) v SSHD* [2011] UKSC 12); see also *Corporation of the Hall of Arts and Sciences v Albert Court Residents Association; Albert Court Residents Association v Westminster City Council* [2011] EWCA Civ 430).

[103]   See for example *R (National Association of Guardians ad Litem and Reporting Officers (NAGALRO)) v Children and Family Court Advisory and Support Service (CAFCASS)* [2001] EWHC 693 (Admin) where it was held that the CAFCASS decision not to offer guardians ad litem self-employed contracts was unlawful because NAGALRO had a legitimate procedural expectation that it would be given reasonable notice before any decision was made.

(c) Cases where the promise has induced a legitimate expectation of a substantial benefit (leading to a substantive expectation).

However, these categories are not exhaustive and are open to variation.

16.146 The court will apply three questions in all legitimate expectation cases, regardless of type:[104]

(a) To what has the public authority committed itself, whether by practice or by promise?

(b) Has the public authority acted, or does it propose to act, unlawfully in relation to its commitment?

(c) What should the court do?

---

[104] *R (Bibi) v Newham LBC* [2001] EWCA Civ 607. Recently approved in *Paponette v A-G of Trinidad and Tobago* [2010] UKPC 32.

Chapter 17

JUDICIAL REVIEW – PROCEDURE

17.1 There are three stages to the procedure for making an application for judicial review:

(a) the claimant must comply with various pre-action requirements;

(b) the claimant must apply for permission to apply for judicial review; and

(c) if permission is granted (but only if), then the claimant must make a full or substantive application for judicial review.

SECTION 1 – COMMENCING THE APPLICATION AT THE RIGHT TIME

17.2 Rule 54.5(1)(b) CPR 1998 provides that:

(1) The claim form must be filed –

(a) promptly; and
(b) in any event not later than 3 months after the grounds to make the claim first arose.

17.3 The issue as to when the time for an application for judicial review starts to run was considered in detail and determined by the House of Lords in *R (Burkett) v Hammersmith and Fulham LBC*.[1] It was held that the natural and obvious meaning of the requirement of the rule in r 54(1)(b) CPR 1998 was that the grounds for an application first arose *when the decision was made*. It was held that the fact that the illegality in a decision might have been foreseeable at some point before the decision was actually made did not detract from this meaning.

17.4 Various policy considerations in favour of this interpretation were set out by the House of Lords:

(a) The context weighed heavily in favour of a clear and straightforward interpretation of the rule which would lead to a readily ascertainable start

---

[1] [2002] UKHL 23, [2002] 1 WLR 1593. See also *R (Richardson) v North Yorkshire CC* [2003] EWCA Civ 1860, *R (Elliot) v Electoral Commission* [2003] EWHC 395 (Admin); *R (Young) v Oxford City Council* [2002] All ER (D) 226 (June).

date. Allowing the courts to ascertain the start date retrospectively was antithetical to the context of a time limit barring proceedings.

(b) Legal policy favours simplicity and certainty rather than complexity and uncertainty. The citizen and the decision-maker (and any interested third party) must know where they stand, particularly where the effect of the rule to be interpreted may result in the loss of the right to challenge an unlawful exercise of power. Retrospective decisions about the appropriate date could lead to a 'recipe for sterile procedural disputes and unjust results'.

(c) It is unreasonable to require the citizen to challenge a decision that may never actually take effect in light of the heavy burden on claimants of bringing a claim (the duty of full and frank disclosure, the obligation to present a full statement, evidence, supporting documents including skeleton arguments, bundles of authorities and so on). It would be unfair to subject the citizen to a retrospective decision by the court as to the date when the time limit for commencing proceedings was triggered.

17.5 In most cases the claimant will be expected to wait until a final decision has been taken before lodging an application. In *R (Burkett) v Hammersmith and Fulham LBC*[2] it was held that it would be premature to challenge a decision that might still change.

17.6 However, in some circumstances it may be possible to issue an interim challenge if it can be shown that there is a particularly good reason for preventing any delay. An application for relief at an interim stage should be made in exactly the same way as an application for a full claim.

17.7 Rule 54.5 CPR 1998 provides that:

(2) The time limit in this rule may not be extended by agreement between the parties.

(3) This rule does not apply when any other enactment specifies a shorter time limit for making the claim for judicial review.

17.8 This means that a judicial review claim will *not* necessarily be in time just because it is made within 3 months – what is important is that any claim is made promptly.

17.9 Claimants must therefore demonstrate not only that the claim is made within 3 months of the decision being challenged, but also that the claim was made promptly within the 3 month period. It is particularly important for

---

[2] [2002] UKHL 23, [2002] 1 WLR 1593.

claimants to act promptly when it is clear that the judicial review claim may have implications for the interests of third parties.[3]

17.10 Claimants should also be aware that a failure to act promptly cannot easily be mitigated by arguing that the claimant was unaware that grounds for judicial review existed at the time. This is because the court will regard time as starting to run regardless of the claimant's state of knowledge. However, the court is likely to look more favourably on this argument as justification for an extension of time.

SECTION 2 – EXTENDING TIME FOR APPLICATIONS

17.11 Rule 3.1(2)(a) CPR 1998 provides that:

(2) Except where these Rules provide otherwise, the court may –

(a) extend or shorten the time for compliance with any rule, practice direction or court order (even if an application for extension is made after the time for compliance has expired).

17.12 The court therefore has the power to extend time in any circumstances in relation to any of the rules relating to judicial review and time limits.

17.13 The burden is on the claimant to prove that there is a good reason for extending time. Any application for an extension of time or any issue relating to delay in issuing the claim should be addressed by the claimant within the claim form. The claim should include:

(a) an explanation as to why the claimant considers that the claim is being brought in good time; or if not,

(b) an application for an extension of time, including reasons for the delay, supporting documentary evidence (where possible) and explanations to mitigate any detriment to the defendant or third parties.

17.14 Section 5 of the Guidance states that:

'NB – If you are seeking an extension of time for the lodging of your application, you must make the application in the claim form, setting out the grounds in support of that application to extend time (CPR Part 54.5).'

17.15 However it is important to remember that the court will approach such applications on a case-by-case basis and even an apparently good reason for extending time may not lead to such application succeeding; see para 5.2 of the Guidance which states:

---

[3] The requirement for promptness does not arise in judicial review challenges relying on points of ECHR law – in such cases it is simply the requirement for claims to be brought within the 3 month period that is important.

'5.2 The court has the power to extend the period for the lodging of an application for permission to apply for judicial review but will only do so where it is satisfied there are very good reasons for doing so.'

17.16 It should be noted that there is no guidance in case law about whether one particular factor indicates any greater chance of success in arguing delay than any other factor. The most important consideration for the court will be the overall reasonableness of the claimant's conduct in leading to any delay. Within this analysis, the court will obviously examine very carefully the reasons for delay, the length of delay and evidence of any detriment to the defendant caused by such delay. It is therefore important for claimants to acknowledge and answer the likely detrimental effects of delay on the defendants within the claim form. It is equally important for defendants to set out the actual or likely impact of delay within their acknowledgement of service form.

17.17 The following is a (non-exhaustive) list of possible reasons that could be advanced to support an application for extending the time for making a judicial review application.

(a) *The delay was caused by difficulties or delay in obtaining public funding –* This may provide a good reason to support an application to extend the time limit for applications. However it is the extent of the effort made to chase up such funding in an attempt to prevent drift that is likely to influence the court much more than the delay itself.[4]

- In such cases claimants should ensure that copies of all relevant correspondence with the LSC and a detailed and comprehensive chronology are put before the court.

(b) *The delay was caused by mistakes by legal advisers –* (although see *R v Secretary of State for the Home Department ex p Oyeleye*[5] and *R v Tavistock General Commissioners ex p Worth*[6] where it was held that reliance on a legal adviser who was not legally qualified was no good reason for delay).

(c) *The delay was caused by claimant seeking alternative legitimate remedies –* as before, each case will be considered on its own facts. The pursuit of an alternative remedy in itself will not necessarily or automatically be considered as a good reason to extend time.[7]

---

4   See *R v Metropolitan Borough of Sandwell ex p Cashmore* (1993) 25 HLR 544; *R v University of Portsmouth ex p Lakareber* [1999] ELR 135.

5   [1994] Imm AR 268.

6   [1985] STC 564.

7   See *R v University College London ex p Ursula Riniker* [1995] ELR 213 at 215, *R v Essex County Council ex p Jackson Projects Ltd* [1995] COD 155, *R v Chief Constable of North Wales Police ex p Evans* [1982] 1 WLR 1155, *R v Secretary of State for the Home Department ex p Oladehinde* [1991] 1 AC 254, *R (Javed) v Secretary of State for the Home Department* [2001] EWCA Civ 789, [2002] QB 129, *R (J) v Secretary of State for the Home Department* [2004] EWHC 2069 (Admin).

(d)   *The delay was caused by compliance with the pre-action protocol (writing a letter before applying for judicial review)* – the pre-action protocol makes it quite clear that delay caused by the claimant writing a pre-action letter or by the local authority's time to respond is unlikely to succeed as an argument to support an application to extend time:

> 'Compliance with the protocol alone is unlikely to be sufficient to persuade the court to allow a late claim.'[8]

(e)   *The delay was caused by general correspondence between the parties* – the issue here will be the purpose and focus of such correspondence. If the correspondence demonstrates a clear will to settle the litigation or to clarify the local authority's actions, then the court is inevitably likely to look more favourably on an application to extend time. However, again the burden will be on the claimant to provide a detailed, comprehensive chronology of the course of the pre-proceedings conduct between the parties.[9]

(f)   *The delay is mitigated by the importance and strength of the case itself* – if the grounds for judicial review are particularly strong, then the court may consider that the strength of the case in itself is a good enough reason to consider the application to extend time favourably.[10] However, even very serious matters will not automatically lead to an application for an extension of time succeeding and again the court will consider applications on a case-by-case basis.

17.18   It is important to note that the time for lodging an application for judicial review may *not* be extended by agreement between the parties; the issue is categorically a matter for the court – see Section 5 of the Guidance.

SECTION 3 – DELAY

17.19   Delay is not just an important issue at the permission hearing. It is also an important and relevant consideration at the substantive hearing where the question for the court will be whether relief should be granted even if the decision being challenged is found to have been unlawful.[11]

17.20   In *R (Lichfield Securities Ltd) v Lichfield DC*[12] the Court of Appeal confirmed that s 31(6) SCA 1981 requires consideration of delay at the substantive hearing as a critical issue, regardless of whether arguments about promptness that were rehearsed earlier at the permission stage are repeated.

---

8   Footnote 1 to Judicial Review Pre-action Protocol.
9   See *R v Harrow LBC ex p Carter* (1994) 26 HLR 32, QBD and *R v Greenwich LBC ex p Patterson* (1994) 26 HLR 159.
10   See *R v Warwickshire County Council ex p Collymore* [1995] ELR 217 per Judge J at 228G.
11   See *R v Dairy Produce Quota Tribunal ex p Caswell* [1990] 2 AC 738, HL.
12   (2001) 3 LGLR 35.

17.21 Therefore, even if the court finds that time should be extended at the permission stage despite any delay in the case, it will not necessarily mean that delay should not be considered as an important matter at the substantive hearing. Section 31(6) SCA 1981 provides that:

> 31(6) Where the High Court considers that there has been undue delay in making an application for judicial review, the court may refuse to grant –
>
> (a)   leave for the making of the application; or
> (b)   any relief sought on the application,
>
> if it considers that the granting of the relief sought would be likely to cause substantial hardship to, or substantially prejudice the rights of, any person or would be detrimental to good administration.

The important phrase in s 31(6) is *may refuse to grant*; it is important to remember that s 31(6) allows the court *discretion* to refuse relief.

17.22 The issue therefore remains essentially one of practical case management for the second judge.

17.23 If the argument about delay was explored fully at the permission hearing and it was found that a claim for judicial review was brought promptly, then a defendant can only go on to rely on arguments about detriment caused by delay in the following very limited circumstances at the substantive hearing:[13]

(a)   if the judge hearing the initial application has expressly indicated that the issue of delay can be argued; or

(b)   if new and relevant material is introduced at the substantive hearing; or

(c)   if the issues, as they have developed at the substantive hearing, raise a different view about the question of promptness; or

(d)   if the judge at the permission stage has plainly overlooked some relevant matter or otherwise reached a decision per incuriam.

SECTION 4 – DISCLOSURE

The duty on claimants

17.24 The nature and purpose of the permission hearing is to filter out applications that are groundless or without real merit. The burden is therefore on the claimant to establish the legal and factual merits of the case by including reference to all the material facts known to him or her *whether or not they support his or her case*. The claimant should also draw the court's attention to any body of authority which is adverse to his or her case and give reasons for

---

[13]   See *R (Lichfield Securities Ltd) v Lichfield DC* (2001) 3 LGLR.

why the particular claim should be distinguished. This is particularly important where the application for permission is to be considered on the papers rather than at an oral hearing.[14] The full extent of the duty on the claimant within a paper application is set out in *R v Jockey Club Licensing Committee ex p Wright (Barrie John)*.[15]

(a) The claimant must show utmost good faith and make full and frank disclosure of the material facts.

(b) The material facts are those that it is material for the judge to know.

(c) Materiality is an issue to be decided by the court and not by the claimant's legal advisers.

(d) The claimant must make proper enquiries before applying for leave.

(e) The duty of disclosure includes a duty to disclose such facts as would have been known to the applicant had he or she made such enquiries.

(f) The extent of 'proper enquiries' will depend on all the circumstances of the case, including the nature of the case and the relief sought, the degree of urgency and the amount of time available for such enquiries to be made.

17.25 The duty on the claimant to give full and frank disclosure extends to:

• issues relating to delay;[16]

• the existence or extent of available alternative remedies;[17] and

• the provision of any defence that may be relied upon by the defendant.[18]

17.26 The duty is also not limited to matters known to the claimant and his or her legal advisers. Claimants are also obliged to disclose facts that could have been discovered if they had carried out proper enquiries.[19] It is not sufficient for the claimant simply to say that any failure to disclose material facts was made 'in good faith'.

---

[14] See *R v Crown Prosecution Service ex p Hogg* [1994] COD 237, QBD; *R v Secretary of State for the Home Department ex p Li Bin Shi* [1995] COD 135.

[15] [1991] COD 306, QBD.

[16] See *R v Bromley LBC ex p Barker* [2001] Env LR 1, QBD.

[17] See *R v Horsham DC ex p Wenman* [1995] 1 WLR 680.

[18] See *Lloyds Bowmaker Ltd v Britannia Arrow Holdings* [1988] 1 WLR 1337.

[19] See *Brink's Mat Ltd v Elcombe* [1988] 1 WLR 1350 at 1356H as applied in *R v Jockey Club Licensing Committee ex p Wright (Barrie John)* [1991] COD 306, QBD and *R (Konodyba) v The Royal Borough of Kensington and Chelsea* [2011] EWHC 2653 (Admin) at [27].

17.27   Discovery at a later stage that a claimant has failed to give full and frank disclosure can lead to permission being set aside.[20] Breach of the duty to disclose may also affect the issue of costs; r 44.3(4)(a) CPR 1998 provides that when considering costs orders, the court must have regard to all the circumstances, including the conduct of all of the parties.

17.28   The scope of the duty to disclose does not necessarily have to be extensive; it is sufficient for the claimant simply to ensure that the matter is not hidden by highlighting it for the court's attention in the grounds of the application without necessarily going into any more extensive detail.[21] However, the court has the usual discretion in the matter and it cannot necessarily be assumed that material non-disclosure will automatically lead to permission being refused, or being subsequently discharged if it has already been granted. In determining such issues, the court will consider whether the failure to disclose was deliberate or mistaken (in which case the speed with which the claimant sought to rectify the mistake will also be considered as a relevant matter).

17.29   Once an application for permission to apply for judicial review has been made and granted, the duty of disclosure on the claimant does not end. The duty to maintain full and frank disclosure continues throughout all stages of the proceedings.[22]

17.30   This continuing duty stretches to the claimant's position developing to the extent that he or she no longer wishes to seek judicial review but wishes to pursue the case as a test claim.[23]

17.31   Where both claimant and defendant agree that a claim has become unnecessary or academic, or where it appears to the claimant that the grounds of a claim have changed, the court should be informed of such developments as soon as possible. The parties should not wait for continuing developments to become certain before informing the court.

The duty on defendants

17.32   Although defendants are not required to file lengthy, fully argued defences or detailed evidence in reply in the acknowledgment of service at the permission stage, they too have a duty to identify any body of authority that is relevant to the matters before the court. Defendants therefore also have a high duty to assist the court with a complete and accurate explanation of all the

---

20   See *R (Webb) v Bristol CC* [2001] EWHC 696 (Admin).

21   See *R v Warwickshire County Council ex p Collymore* [1995] ELR 217 at 229F.

22   See *R (Tshikangu) v Newham London Borough Council* [2001] EWHC 92 (Admin), [2001] NPC 33.

23   See *R (Tshikangu) v Newham London Borough Council* [2001] EWHC 92 (Admin), [2001] NPC 33, *R (Done Brothers (Cash Betting) Limited) v The Crown Court at Cardiff* [2003] EWHC 3516 (Admin), *R (Johns) v Derby City Council* [2011] EWHC 375 (Admin).

facts relevant to the issues that the court must decide – see *R (Quark Fishing Limited) v Secretary of State for Foreign and Commonwealth Affairs*[24] where it was held that:

> '... it is the obligation of the respondent public body in its evidence to make frank disclosure to the court of the decision-making process.'

17.33 The rationale behind this extensive duty on public authorities relates to the fairness of proceedings for citizens; the citizen seeking to challenge the public authority should not be disadvantaged by having to speculate about the process by which the relevant decision was made.[25]

17.34 In the context of childcare law this duty on local authorities has been consistently reinforced by the courts. The local authority, when seeking to take a child into care, is under a heavy obligation to ensure that the procedure at all stages is transparent and fair, both in and out of court. Article 8 ECHR requires the local authority to involve parents fully in the decision-making process, at all stages of the child protection procedure, whether before, during or after the making of a care order. It is essential that the local authority keeps the parents properly involved in the planning process when care proceedings are initiated and the care plan is being formulated.[26] Likewise, it is essential to ensure that children are given the appropriate opportunity to participate in the decisions being made.

17.35 In *Re G (Care: Challenge to Local Authority's Decision)*[27] the local authority planned to remove children who were subject to care orders from their parents and readmit them to care but failed to invite the parents to a planning meeting to discuss this; this failure was held to constitute a breach of Art 8. In *Haase v Germany*[28] the emergency removal of eight children (including a 7 day old baby) from the applicants was not proportionate to the circumstances, failed to allow the applicants to participate in the decision-making process and was held to be a breach of Art 8.

17.36 Public authorities are not simply obliged to disclose all relevant facts and documents. They are also not obliged only to disclose information that is relevant in some way to the decision itself that is the subject of challenge. Documentation about the decision itself should be disclosed as a matter of course as the primary, best evidence. However the duty of disclosure on a defendant also extends to disclosure of *any information* that is relevant to the decision-making process.[29]

---

24 [2002] EWCA Civ 1409 at [50].
25 See *Re Brenda Downes* [2006] NIQB 77 at [35].
26 See *Re S (Minors) (Care Order: Implementation of Care Plan); Re W (Minors) (Care Order: Adequacy of Care Plan)* [2002] 1 FLR 815.
27 [2003] 2 FLR 42.
28 [2004] 2 FLR 39.
29 See *Tweed v Parades Commission for Northern Ireland* [2007] 1 AC 650 at 655G.

SECTION 5 – THE PRE-ACTION STAGE

Compliance with the Protocol

17.37 The *Pre-Action Protocol for Judicial Review* (the Protocol) applies to proceedings within England and Wales and has the status of a code of good practice which parties should generally follow before making a claim for judicial review (rather than obligatory or statutory guidance). The Protocol itself[30] requires that all claimants will need to satisfy themselves whether they should follow the Protocol, depending upon the circumstances of his or her case. Where the use of the Protocol is appropriate, the court will normally expect all parties to have complied with it and will take into account compliance or non-compliance when giving directions for case management of proceedings or when making orders for costs. The guidance[31] makes it clear that any claim for judicial review must indicate whether or not the protocol has been complied with. If the protocol has not been complied with, the reasons for failing to do so should be set out in the claim form.

17.38 The Court of Appeal has recently confirmed the importance of the Protocol. In *R (Scott) v London Borough of Hackney*[32] Hallett LJ analysed the conduct of the parties and acknowledged that compliance with or breach of the pre-action protocol must be a relevant factor to be taken into account. In *R (Bahta) v Secretary of State for the Home Department*[33] the Court of Appeal reiterated the importance of the Protocol in judicial review cases (when dealing specifically with the issue of costs):

> ' . . . what needs to be underlined is the starting point in the CPR that a successful claimant is entitled to his costs and the now recognised importance of complying with Pre-Action Protocols. These are intended to prevent litigation and encourage parties to settle proceedings, including judicial review proceedings, if at all possible.'

17.39 Situations when it will *not* be suitable to use the Protocol are defined within the Protocol itself as follows:

(a) Where the defendant does not have the legal power to change the decision being challenged (for example, decisions issued by tribunals such as the Asylum and Immigration Tribunal).

(b) In urgent cases (for example, when directions have been set or are in force for the claimant's removal from the UK).

---

[30]   Paragraph 7.
[31]   Paragraph 3.4.
[32]   [2009] EWCA Civ 217.
[33]   [2011] EWCA Civ 895.

(c)   Where there is an urgent need for an interim order to compel a public body to act where it has unlawfully refused to do so (for example, the failure of a local housing authority to secure interim accommodation for a homeless claimant).

17.40   However, even in emergency or urgent cases, it is recommended as good practice to fax to the defendant the draft claim form which the claimant intends to issue. Similarly, a claimant is also normally required to notify a defendant when an interim mandatory order is being sought.

Alternative Dispute Resolution (ADR)

17.41   The Protocol makes it plain that the parties should consider whether some form of alternative dispute resolution (ADR) procedure would be more suitable than litigation, and if so, endeavour to agree which form to adopt. Both claimants and defendants may be required by the court to provide evidence that alternative means of resolving their dispute were considered. The courts take the view that litigation should be a last resort and that claims should not be issued prematurely when a settlement is still actively being explored. Parties are warned within the Protocol that if the Protocol is not followed,[34] then the court must have regard to such conduct when determining costs.

17.42   Claimants are also strongly advised within the Protocol to seek appropriate legal advice when considering judicial review proceedings, and in particular, before sending the letter before claim to other interested parties or making a claim.

17.43   Although the Protocol does not address in detail how the parties might decide which method to adopt to resolve their particular dispute, it does summarise some of the options for resolving disputes without litigation:

- Discussion and negotiation.

- Ombudsmen – both the Parliamentary and Health Service and the Local Government Ombudsman have discretion to deal with complaints relating to maladministration.

- Early neutral evaluation by an independent third party (for example, a lawyer experienced in the field of administrative law or an individual experienced in the subject matter of the claim).

- Mediation – a form of facilitated negotiation assisted by an independent neutral party.

---

[34]   Including the requirements to consider ADR in para 3.1.

However, the Protocol goes on to state clearly[35] that it is expressly recognised that no party can or should be forced to mediate or enter into any form of ADR.

The stages of pre-action work

17.44 There are two distinct parts to the work required by the parties at the pre-action stage – the letter before claim (by the proposed claimant) and the letter of response (by the proposed defendant).

17.45 As already discussed, claimants are strongly advised within the Protocol to seek appropriate legal advice when considering judicial review proceedings, and in particular, before sending the letter before claim to other interested parties or making a claim.

The letter before claim

17.46 Before making a claim the claimant should send a letter to the defendant. The purpose of the letter is to identify the issues in dispute and to establish whether litigation can be avoided. However, a letter before claim will not automatically stop the implementation of a disputed decision.

17.47 Claimants should normally use the suggested standard format for the letter outlined at Annex A of the Protocol.[36]

17.48 The letter should contain the following information:

(a) The date and details of the decision, action or omission that is being challenged.

(b) A clear summary of the facts on which the claim is based.

(c) Details of any relevant information that the claimant is seeking and an explanation of why this is considered relevant.

(d) Details of any interested parties known to the claimant.

17.49 A copy of the letter should be sent to any interested parties known to the claimant before the claim for information is made.

17.50 A claim should not normally be made until the proposed reply date given in the letter before claim has passed, unless the circumstances of the case require more immediate action to be taken.

---

[35] Paragraph 3.4.
[36] See Part 4 (resources section). Also available to download at www.justice.gov.uk/forms.

17.51 The letter should normally give the defendant 14 days to reply, although a shorter or longer period may be appropriate depending on the particular circumstances of the case.

The letter of response

17.52 Defendants should normally respond to a letter before claim within 14 days using the standard format set out at Annex B in the Protocol.[37] Failure to do so will be taken into account by the court and sanctions may be imposed unless there are good reasons.

17.53 Where it is not possible to reply within the proposed time-limit the defendant should send an interim reply and propose a reasonable extension. Where an extension is sought, reasons should be given and, where required, additional information requested. This will not affect the time-limit for making a claim for judicial review nor will it bind the claimant where he or she considers this to be unreasonable. However, where the court considers that a subsequent claim is made prematurely it may impose sanctions.

17.54 If the claim is being conceded in full, the defendant's reply should say so in clear and unambiguous terms.

17.55 If the claim is being conceded in part or is not being conceded, the defendant's reply should say so in clear and unambiguous terms, and:

(a) Where appropriate, contain a new decision, clearly identifying what aspects of the claim are being conceded and what are not, or, give a clear timescale within which the new decision will be issued.

(b) Provide a fuller explanation for the decision, if considered appropriate to do so.

(c) Address any points of dispute, or explain why they can't be addressed.

(d) Enclose any relevant documentation requested by the claimant, or explain why the documents are not being enclosed; and

(e) Where appropriate, confirm whether or not they will oppose any application for an interim remedy.

17.56 The response should be sent to all interested parties identified by the claimant and contain details of any other parties who the defendant considers also have an interest.

---

[37] See Part 4 (resources section). Also available to download at www.justice.gov.uk/forms.

SECTION 6 – THE PERMISSION STAGE

17.57 All claims for judicial review under CPR 1998, Part 54 are dealt with in the Administrative Court.

Which court?

17.58 The guidance provides clear information about where claims for judicial review should be commenced and heard.

17.59 Claims may be issued at the District Registry of the High Court at Birmingham, Cardiff, Leeds or Manchester as well as at the Royal Courts of Justice in London.[38]

17.60 The general expectation is that proceedings will be administered and determined in the region with which the claimant has the closest connection. Cases started in London will normally be determined at the Royal Courts of Justice. Cases started in Birmingham will normally be determined at a court in the Midland region. Cases started in Cardiff will normally be determined at a court in Wales. Cases started in Leeds will normally be determined at a court in the North-Eastern region. Cases started in Manchester will normally be determined at a court in the North-Western region.

17.61 However, in determining where a case should be heard, the following considerations will apply:

(a)   any reason expressed by any party for preferring a particular venue;

(b)   the region in which the defendant, or any relevant office or department of the defendant, is based;

(c)   the region in which the claimant's legal representatives are based;

(d)   the ease and cost of travel to a hearing;

(e)   the availability and suitability of alternative means of attending a hearing (for example, by videolink);

(f)   the extent and nature of media interest in the proceedings in any particular locality;

(g)   the time within which it is appropriate for the proceedings to be determined;

---

[38]   See Part 4 (resources section) for details of all Administrative Court addresses.

(h)   whether it is desirable to administer or determine the claim in another region in the light of the volume of claims issued at, and the capacity, resources and workload of, the court at which it is issued;

(i)   whether the claim raises issues sufficiently similar to those in another outstanding claim to make it desirable that it should be determined together with, or immediately following, that other claim; and

(j)   whether the claim raises devolution issues and for that reason whether it should more appropriately be determined in London or Cardiff.

17.62 An application for directions as to venue for administration and determination should be made in Form N464.[39]

Making the application for permission

17.63 The application for permission to apply for judicial review must be made on the correct claim form – Form N461.[40]

17.64 The claim form must include or be accompanied by:

- a detailed statement of the claimant's grounds for bringing the claim for judicial review;

- a statement of the facts relied on;

- any application to extend the time limit for filing the claim form; and

- any application for directions.

Issues relating to human rights

17.65 If the claimant is seeking to raise any issue under the HRA 1998 or a remedy available under that Act, the claim form must also include the information required by para 15 of the Practice Direction supplementing Part 16 of the CPR 1998. This information is as follows:

> A party who seeks to rely on any provision of or right arising under the Human Rights Act 1998 or seeks a remedy available under that Act –
>
> (1)   must state that fact in his statement of case; and
> (2)   must in his statement of case –
>   (a)   give precise details of the Convention right which it is alleged has been infringed and details of the alleged infringement;
>   (b)   specify the relief sought;
>   (c)   state if the relief sought includes –

---

[39]   See Part 4 (resources section). Also available at www.justice.gov.uk/forms.
[40]   See Part 4 (resources section). Also available at www.justice.gov.uk/forms.

        (i)   a declaration of incompatibility in accordance with section 4 of that Act, or

        (ii)   damages in respect of a judicial act to which section 9(3) of that Act applies;

(d)   where the relief sought includes a declaration of incompatibility in accordance with section 4 of that Act, give precise details of the legislative provision alleged to be incompatible and details of the alleged incompatibility;

(e)   where the claim is founded on a finding of unlawfulness by another court or tribunal, give details of the finding; and

(f)   where the claim is founded on a judicial act which is alleged to have infringed a Convention right of the party as provided by section 9 of the Human Rights Act 1998, the judicial act complained of and the court or tribunal which is alleged to have made it.

17.66 If the claimant wishes to raise a devolution issue, the claim form must:

(a)   specify that the claimant wishes to raise a devolution issue;

(b)   identify the relevant provisions of the Government of Wales Act 1998; and

(c)   contain a summary of the facts, circumstances and points of law on the basis of which it is alleged that a devolution issue arises.

17.67 The guidance makes it clear that where it is not possible for the claimant to file all the above documents, he or she must indicate which documents have not been filed and the reasons why they are not currently available. The defendant and/or the interested party may seek an extension of time for the lodging of its acknowledgment of service pending receipt of the missing documents.

17.68 A court fee is payable when the claimant lodges the application for permission to apply for judicial review. A further court fee is payable if the claimant wishes to pursue the claim if permission is granted (Civil Proceedings Fees (Amendment) Order 2011).[41]

17.69 Claimants who are in receipt of certain types of benefits may be entitled to remission of any fee due as part of judicial review proceedings. Claimants who believe they may be entitled to fee remission should apply to the relevant Adminstrative Court Office using Form EX160 (Application for a Fee Remission) (or Form EX160B in the case of an emergency application); such application(s) should be lodged by the claimant with the claim form.[42]

---

[41] SI 2011/586. Details of up-to-date court fees can be found in Leaflet EX50 Civil and Family Court Fees available at www.justice.gov.uk/forms.

[42] Available at www.justice.gov.uk/forms.

What documents should be lodged?

17.70   The claimant should lodge the following documents in respect of any claim for permission to apply for judicial review:

(a)   the original claim form;

(b)   the original witness statement – this will usually set out the factual matters already referred to in the claim form;

(c)   a set of paginated and indexed copy documents for the court's use including:[43]

    (i)   any written evidence in support of the claim or application to extend time;

    (ii)   a copy of any order that the claimant is seeking to have quashed;

    (iii)   copies of any documents upon which the claimant proposes to rely – in children cases these can include:

- relevant correspondence;
- written agreements;
- policy documents;
- expert reports;
- social work statements;
- judgments or extracts from judgments;

    (iv)   copies of any relevant statutory material – this could include legislation, statutory instruments and practice directions as well relevant extracts from statutory or non-statutory guidance;

    (v)   a list of essential reading by the court (with page references to the passages relied upon). Where only part of a page needs to be read, that part should be indicated, by side-lining or in some other way, but not by highlighting. The essential reading list should usually include:

- the claim form;
- the witness statement(s);
- the decision letter;
- any other key documents which will help the court to understand the nature of the claim.

17.71   The guidance makes it clear that the documents should be paginated in consecutive page number order throughout the bundle. Claimants should also ensure that each page has a page number on it and provide an index, which lists the description of documents contained in the bundle together with their page reference numbers.

---

[43]   As referred to in para 7.5 (CPR 1998, Part 54.6 and PD54).

17.72 Claimants must also lodge sufficient additional copies of the claim form for the court to seal them (ie stamp them with the court seal) so that the claimant can serve them on the defendant and any interested parties. The sealed copies will be returned to the claimant by the court so that the claimant can serve them on the defendant and any interested parties.

17.73 If the claimant is legally represented, his or her solicitors must also provide a paginated, indexed bundle of the relevant legislative provisions and statutory instruments required for the proper consideration of the application.

17.74 If the claimant is acting in person he or she should also comply with this requirement if possible. Applications that do not comply with these requirements of CPR 1998, Part 54 and PD54 will not be accepted, save in exceptional circumstances. In this context a matter will be regarded as exceptional where a decision is sought from the court within 14 days of the lodging of the application. In such circumstances an undertaking will be required to provide compliance with the requirements of the CPR within a specified period. If the only reason given in support of urgency is the imminent expiry of the three month time limit for lodging an application, the guidance makes it clear that the papers will nonetheless be returned for compliance with Part 54 and Practice Direction 54. In those circumstances the claimant must seek an extension of time and provide reasons for the delay in lodging the papers in proper form.

When should the application for permission be made?

17.75 The claim form must be filed promptly and in any event not later than three months after the grounds upon which the claim is based first arose.[44]

17.76 The court has the power to extend the period for the lodging of an application for permission to apply for judicial review but will only do so where it is satisfied that there are very good reasons for doing so.

17.77 The time for the lodging of the application may only be extended by the court and cannot be extended by agreement between the parties.

17.78 If the claimant is seeking an extension of time for lodging the application for permission, then the application must be made in the claim form itself, setting out the grounds in support of that application to extend time.[45]

Who should be served with the application?

17.79 The sealed copy claim form (and accompanying documents) must be served by the claimant on the defendant and any person that the claimant

---

[44] CPR 1998, r 54.5.
[45] CPR 1998, r 54.5.

considers to be an interested party (unless the court directs otherwise) within 7 days of the date of issue (ie the date shown on the court seal). The court will *not* serve the claim on the defendant or any interested party.

17.80 Where the claim for judicial review relates to proceedings in a court or tribunal, any other parties to those proceedings must be named in the claim form as interested parties and served with the claim form.[46]

17.81 The claimant should lodge a certificate of service in Form N215 in the relevant Administrative Court Office within 7 days of serving the defendant and other interested parties.[47]

17.82 The date of deemed service is calculated in accordance with CPR 1998, r 6.14.[48]

Urgent applications

17.83 In the case of urgent applications for permission to be heard, considered by a judge as a matter of urgency, and/or to seek an interim injunction, the claimant must complete Form N463 (Request for Urgent Consideration).[49] Within the form the claimant must set out the reasons for urgency and the timescales sought for the consideration of the permission application, and the date by which the substantive hearing should take place. In cases where the claimant is seeking an interim injunction, the form must also be accompanied by a draft order and the grounds for the injunction.

17.84 The claimant must serve the claim form, the draft order and the application for urgency on the defendant and interested parties (by FAX and by post) advising them of the application and informing them that they may make representations directly to the court in respect of the claimant's application.

17.85 In urgent cases a judge will consider the application within the time requested and may make such order as he or she considers appropriate. The judge may refuse the claimant's application for permission at this stage if he or she considers it appropriate in the circumstances to do so. The judge may direct that an oral hearing must take place within a specified time. In those circumstances the court office will liaise with the claimant, the defendant and the interested parties (preferably their legal representatives) to fix a permission hearing within the time period directed.

17.86 In situations where a manifestly inappropriate urgent application is made, the court may consider, in appropriate cases, making a wasted costs order.

---

[46]   CPR 1998, PD54A, para 5.
[47]   Available at www.justice.gov.uk/forms.
[48]   See methods of service set out in Appendix – para 7.12 of the Guidance.
[49]   Available at www.justice.gov.uk/forms.

Acknowledging service

17.87   Any person who has been served with the claim form and who wishes to take part in the judicial review should file an acknowledgment of service (Form N462)[50] in the Administrative Court Office, within 21 days of service. This includes interested parties who have been served, as well as defendants.

17.88   Whilst there is no requirement upon the claimant to serve the defendant and any interested party with a Form N462 for completion by them, the guidance makes it clear that it is considered good practice to do so. The acknowledgement of service form must be served on the claimant and any other party to the claim either at the time that it is filed, or at the latest within seven days after it is filed.[51] The acknowledgement of service must be served by the defendant upon the claimant and any interested parties no later than 7 days after it is filed with the court. Failure to file an acknowledgement of service will make it necessary for the party concerned to obtain the permission of the court to take part in any oral hearing of the application for permission.

17.89   Claimants may wish to seek abridgement of time for the service of the acknowledgement of service at the time the claim form is filed. The court may also proceed to consider the application before the 21 day period has expired. Claimants should therefore ensure that the claim form is filed and served promptly.

What should be included within the acknowledgement of service form?

17.90   In Section A of the acknowledgement of service form the defendant must confirm whether he or she intends to contest all or part of the claim or not.

17.91   In Section B of the form the defendant must provide the name and address of any person considered to be an interested party (who has not previously been identified and served as an interested party).

17.92   In Section C of the form the defendant must outline a summary of grounds for contesting the claim. If the defendant is contesting only part of the claim, then he or she must set out which part is to be contested before then giving the grounds for contesting. Although all that is technically required at this stage is that the defendant simply indicates whether or not he or she intends to resist all or part of the claim as detailed within the claim form, this is clearly a vital part of the form. Given that almost all applications for permission to apply for judicial review will be considered on paper in the first instance, the grounds relied on by the defendant to resist the application are likely to have a vital part to play in the court's consideration.

---

[50]   See Part 4 (resources section). Also available at www.justice.gov.uk/forms.
[51]   CPR 1998, r 54.8(2)(b).

17.93 The summary in Section C should therefore indicate clearly the key points of resistance, including any relevant jurisdictional points and factual disputes, so that the court can identify the central issues in the case and determine the arguable merits, or otherwise, of the application for permission.

17.94 The summary should also deal with any issues relating to delay as this must be considered by the court at the permission stage.

17.95 It may be helpful for the defendant to attach witness statements or key documents to support the arguments raised in the acknowledgement of service form. However, defendants should take a proportionate approach to the scope and quantity of additional material submitted; all the court will be concerned with at this stage is whether the claim has an arguable chance of success. If the case is an arguable one on paper, then is not necessarily wise for defendants to submit unnecessarily detailed or extensive evidence at this stage.

17.96 In Section D the defendant must give details of any directions he or she will be asking the court to make, or alternatively must attach a separate application notice. This should hopefully avoid the need to make any interim applications between the court granting permission and a full hearing of the application. The onus is very much on the parties to be proactive in considering whether any interim directions are required. Such directions might include the need to expedite a hearing or to extend time for filing of certain parts of the evidence. If interim directions are to be sought, the defendant should refer to, and preferably attach, any relevant supporting evidence in the usual way.

What if the defendant fails to file an acknowledgement of service?

17.97 Failure to file an acknowledgement of service means that the defendant will not be able to take part in the permission stage of the case without the court's consent.

17.98 There is nothing to prevent the defendant from participating in the full hearing. However, the defendant's failure to file an acknowledgement of service may be taken into account when determining any future issue of costs, particularly if this caused the claimant to pursue the claim in circumstances when it might otherwise have been discontinued or abandoned.

Consideration of the application for permission

17.99 The papers will be forwarded to the judge by the Administrative Court Office upon receipt of the acknowledgement of service or at the expiry of the time limit for lodging such acknowledgement – whichever is earlier. The judge's decision and the reasons for it will be served upon the claimant, the defendant and any other person served with the claim form.

17.100 Applications for permission to proceed with the claim for judicial review are considered by a single judge on the papers. The purpose of this procedure is to ensure that applications are dealt with speedily, without unnecessary expense and to prevent the court's time being wasted with trivial complaints that are hopeless and without merit.

17.101 Permission to apply for judicial review will only be granted when the court considers that there is an arguable case which merits consideration at a full hearing.

17.102 In considering whether or not to grant permission, which is within the court's discretion, the court must take account of any alternative remedies that are available, and consider whether in light of those alternatives, it remains appropriate for the claim to proceed to judicial review. The general rule is that if an alternative remedy exists permission should not be granted.

17.103 When considering the appropriateness of any alternative remedy, the court will take account of the following points:

(a) Will the alternative remedy resolve the issue before the court fully and directly?

(b) Will the alternative remedy be quicker or slower than proceeding to full judicial review?

(c) Is the issue raised in the judicial review proceedings relate to any specialist area of knowledge plainly within the expertise or scope of the alternative remedy?

(d) Would judicial review circumvent an established statutory appeal framework which may be better equipped to deal with the issues raised in the judicial review?

(e) Would granting permission for judicial review lead to an unnecessary duplication of proceedings?

17.104 However it is important to remember that the court will not just focus on the nature and scope of any alternative remedy, but will consider all the material circumstances, the interests of the claimant and the wider public interest.

What happens if permission is refused?

17.105 If permission is refused, or is granted subject to conditions or on certain grounds only, the claimant is automatically entitled to have the application reconsidered at an oral hearing.

17.106 If the application for permission is refused at the paper stage, the court will serve an order to that effect. The order will also set out in summary terms a statement of the reasons why the application for permission has been refused.

The oral hearing of a renewed application

17.107 Any renewed application for an oral hearing must include the grounds which are relied upon in light of the reasons given by the judge who refused the application on paper.

17.108 Any request for an oral hearing must be filed within 7 days after service of the notification of the judge's decision upon the claimant;[52] a copy will be sent to the claimant at the same time as the judge's decision.

17.109 Where the judge directs an oral hearing or the claimant renews their application after refusal following consideration on paper, the claimant may appear in person or be represented by an advocate (if he or she is legally represented). If the claimant is not legally represented they may seek the court's permission to have someone speak on their behalf at the hearing.

17.110 Any application for permission to have someone speak on the claimant's behalf should be made to the judge hearing the application who will make such decision as he or she considers appropriate in all of the circumstances.

17.111 The claimant, the defendant and any interested parties will be given notice of the hearing by the Administrative Court List Office. An oral hearing will be listed in open court before a single judge and allocated a total of 30 minutes of court time. If it is considered that 30 minutes of court time is insufficient, the claimant should provide a written, realistic estimate of the time required for the hearing and request a special fixture.

17.112 Neither the defendant nor any other interested party need attend a hearing on the question of permission unless the court directs otherwise. However, unless the issue of costs prohibits attendance, it is probably wise for defendants and interested parties to attend.

17.113 If permission is granted at a renewed application hearing, the court will go on to consider any directions that are required, case management issues and any applications for a stay or for interim relief.

17.114 If a renewed application for permission is refused, the claimant may then appeal to the Court of Appeal.

17.115 It should be noted that where permission has been granted at a renewed application hearing the defendant is not able in these circumstances to apply to have the permission set aside. Nor is it open to the defendant to appeal against a decision to grant permission.

---

[52] CPR 1998, rr 54.11 and 54.12.

What happens if permission is granted?

17.116   If the judge grants permission and the claimant wishes to pursue the claim, he or she must lodge a further court fee[53] (or a further application for remission of fee (Form EX160) with the relevant Administrative Court Office within 7 days of service of the judge's decision. In the event that the claimant does not lodge the additional fee, the file will be closed by the court.

17.117   On granting permission the court may make case management directions[54] for the progression of the case. Case management directions may include directions as to venue, service of the claim form and any evidence on other persons and as to expedition.

Joining the Crown as a party

17.118   Where a claim is made under the Human Rights Act 1998, a direction may be made for the giving of notice to the Crown or joining the Crown as a party.[55]

17.119   The court may not make a declaration of incompatibility in accordance with s 4 of the Human Rights Act 1998 unless 21 days' notice, or such other period of notice as the court directs, has been given to the Crown. Where notice has been given to the Crown a Minister, or other person permitted by that Act, shall be joined as a party on giving notice to the court.

17.120   Where a party has included in his or her statement of case either a claim for a declaration of incompatibility in accordance with s 4 HRA 1998, or an issue for the court to decide which may lead to the court considering making a declaration, then the court may at any time consider whether notice should be given to the Crown and give directions for the content and service of the notice. A period of 21 days will be allowed before the court will make the declaration but the court may vary this period of time.

17.121   The court will normally consider any issues in relation to joining the Crown and give the relevant directions at the case management conference.

17.122   In cases where a party amends his or her statement of case to include either a claim for a declaration of incompatibility or an issue for the court to decide which may lead to the court considering making a declaration, then the court will consider whether notice should be given to the Crown and give directions for the content and service of the notice.

17.123   The notice given under r 19.4A must be served on the person named in the list published under s 17 of the Crown Proceedings Act 1947. The list, made

---

[53]   See Leaflet EX50 Civil and Family Court Fees available at www.justice.gov.uk/forms.
[54]   CPR 1998, r 54.10(1).
[55]   In those circumstances the requirements of r 19.4A CPR 1998 and para 6 of the Practice Direction supplementing Section I of Part 19 will apply.

by the Minister for the Civil Service, is annexed to CPR PD66. The notice will be in the form directed by the court but will normally include the directions given by the court and all the statements of case in the claim. The notice will also be served on all the parties. The court may require the parties to assist in the preparation of the notice.

17.124 Section 5(3) HRA 1998 provides that the Crown may give notice that it intends to become a party at any stage in the proceedings once notice has been given. Unless the court orders otherwise, the Minister or other person permitted by HRA 1998 to be joined as a party must, if he or she wishes to be joined, give notice of his or her intention to be joined as a party to the court and every other party. Where the Minister has nominated a person to be joined as a party the notice must be accompanied by the written nomination. Section 5(2)(a) HRA 1998 permits a person nominated by a Minister of the Crown to be joined as a party. The nomination may be signed on behalf of the Minister.

17.125 This procedure will also apply where a claim is made under ss 7(1)(a) and 9(3) HRA 1998 for damages in respect of a judicial act. In those circumstances notice must be given to the Lord Chancellor and should be served on the Treasury Solicitor on his behalf, except where the judicial act is of a court-martial when the appropriate person is the Secretary of State for Defence and the notice must be served on the Treasury Solicitor on his behalf. The notice will also give details of the judicial act, which is the subject of the claim for damages, and of the court or tribunal that made it.

SECTION 7 – THE FULL CLAIM STAGE

17.126 In the event that permission to apply for judicial review has been granted, any party upon whom the claim form has been served and who wishes to contest the claim (or to support it on additional grounds) must, within 35 days of service of the order granting permission, file and serve on the court and all of the other parties the following documents:

(a) detailed grounds for contesting the claim or supporting it on additional grounds; and

(b) any written evidence relied upon.

17.127 Any party who has filed and served such documents may then be represented at the hearing. Where the party filing the detailed grounds intends to rely on documents not already filed, a paginated bundle of those documents must be filed at the court when the detailed grounds are filed.

What should the detailed grounds contain?

17.128 The detailed grounds should set out the basis on which the claim is opposed or supported. In particular, the detailed grounds should set out the relevant legal and factual arguments which will be relied on at the full hearing of the claim in a logical and chronological/sequential manner. Written evidence which will be relied upon at the full hearing of the claim should be cross-referenced appropriately.

What should the evidence contain?

17.129 The claimant should serve all relevant evidence at the outset with the claim form. The combination of the evidence and the claim form should provide a comprehensive picture of the claimant's case.

17.130 The written evidence will include witness statements exhibiting any relevant documents. Taken as a whole, the witness statements should set out and explain all the issues of fact relied upon for the purposes of the defence to the claim. The defendant's witness statements should identify the points of dispute and the defendant's position about each point.

17.131 It is not necessary for a claimant to respond to the defendant's evidence although it may be advisable or desirable. In those circumstances, the claimant should apply under r 54.16 to file and serve evidence in reply if it is necessary and in response to a material issue in the defendant's evidence. The court will generally use its discretion to permit either party to file evidence which deals with matters that have arisen during the proceedings in order to ensure that the court has the most up-to-date information about the factual position at the hearing.

17.132 The usual civil rules of evidence apply to the witness statements, namely all relevant evidence will generally be admissible. However, it is important to remember that the court dealing with judicial review claims will not be evaluating the original decision as an appeal, and therefore the court is unlikely to be willing to allow fresh evidence to be admitted which could only be relevant if the proceedings were an appeal. There are however a number of situations where fresh evidence may be considered admissible by the court:

(a) Where the court's determination of issues of fact may actually decide the scope of the jurisdiction of the decision-maker. In these circumstances fresh evidence may be relevant and therefore admissible because the court is exercising its own jurisdiction.

(b) Where the claimant may be challenging the failure to consider a relevant matter and so the court will need to consider all the material circumstances so that it can properly assess the significance of the alleged failure by the decision-maker.

(c) Where fresh evidence is necessary to demonstrate the nature of the material that was considered by or put before the original decision-maker.

17.133 In all cases the purpose of the evidence is to assist the court in determining whether the original decision should be reviewed. Parties should therefore ensure that all evidence submitted is relevant and goes to the issue or issues at hand. For example:

(a) Where there is genuine confusion (rather than just a difference of opinion) as to the basis on which the original decision was taken and evidence is necessary to clarify or supplement the original decision.

(b) Where a mandatory or quashing order is sought, evidence will be necessary to demonstrate the facts making up the grounds of the claim.

17.134 The court has power to extend or abridge the time for lodging evidence.

Listing the hearing

17.135 In some circumstances the court may decide a claim for judicial review without a hearing where all parties agree.[56]

17.136 In most cases, however, when the time for lodging of evidence by the parties has expired, the case will then enter the court's warned list and all parties will be informed of this by letter. In cases where a direction has been given that the matter should be expedited, then the case will take priority over other cases waiting to be fixed and will enter an expedited warned list.

17.137 The parties (whether in person or via their legal representatives) will be contacted by the relevant Administrative Court List Office in order to seek to agree a date for the hearing. Parties will be offered a range of dates and will have 48 hours to take up one of the dates offered.

17.138 If the parties fail to contact the List Office within 48 hours, the List Office will fix the hearing on one of the dates offered without further notice and the parties will be notified of that fixture by letter.

17.139 Usually the court will give a fixed date for a hearing. However, there may also be a need to short warn a number of cases to cover the large number of settlements that occur in the list. Parties in cases that are selected to be short warned will be notified that their case is likely to be listed from a specified date, and that they may be called into the list at less than a day's notice from that date. If the case does not get on during that period, a date as soon as possible after that period will be fixed in consultation with the parties.

---

[56]   CPR 1998, r 54.18.

Adjournments

17.140 Where a hearing is listed in this way it will only be vacated by the Administrative Court Office if both parties consent and good reason is provided for the need to vacate the fixture using the adjournment form available from Administrative Court Listing Offices.

17.141 There will be a fee payable for any application to adjourn *unless* the application is made with the consent of all parties and lodged with the court no later than 14 days before the date of the hearing. If a party is entitled to fee remission, they must lodge an application for a fee remission (Form EX160) with the adjournment form.[57]

17.142 Where agreement to an adjournment cannot be reached, a formal application for adjournment must be made to the court on notice to all parties using Form AC001 for the relevant court (each court has its own form).[58] There will be a court fee payable[59] for any application to adjourn made without the consent of all parties, notwithstanding when it is lodged, unless the applicant is entitled to fee remission (in which case they must lodge the Form EX160) with the application.

17.143 Where all parties consent to an adjournment within 14 days of the hearing, a further court fee will be payable.

Applications for directions or further orders

17.144 There is no formal case management stage in judicial review cases. The issue of appropriate directions will of course be considered at the permission stage, but from that point it is expected that the parties will take a proactive role in deciding if any further directions or orders are needed.

17.145 In cases where case management decisions or directions are sought after permission has been granted, an application should be made under CPR 1998, Part 23 using Form PF244.[60] The application form should set out the terms of the order or directions being sought and refer to any evidence being relied on in support. The application may be heard in person or by telephone or video link.[61]

17.146 The applicant will be required to pay a court fee for such application[62] if all parties provide their written consent to the order being made, unless they are entitled to remission (in which case they should complete and submit Form EX160 with the application).

---

[57] Available at www.justice.gov.uk/forms.
[58] Available at www.justice.gov.uk/forms.
[59] See Leaflet EX50 Civil and Family Court Fees available at www.justice.gov.uk/forms.
[60] See Part 4 (resources section). Also available at www.justice.gov.uk/forms.
[61] As permitted by the Practice Direction under Part 23 CPR 1998.
[62] See Leaflet EX50 Civil and Family Court Fees available at www.justice.gov.uk/forms.

Trial bundles and skeleton arguments

17.147   The claimant must file a paginated and indexed bundle of all relevant documents required for the hearing of the judicial review. The bundle must also include those documents required by the defendant and any other party who is to make representations at the hearing. The bundle should be filed with the court and served on the other parties not less than 21 working days before the hearing.

17.148   Two copies of the bundle will be required by the court when the application is to be heard by a Divisional Court.

17.149   Any skeleton argument must be filed with the court and served on the other parties not less than 21 working days before the date of the hearing of the judicial review or the short warned date (in circumstances where the case has been short warned).

17.150   The defendant and any other party wishing to make representations at the hearing of the judicial review must file and serve a skeleton argument not less than 14 working days before the date of the hearing of the judicial review (or the short warned date).

17.151   There is no requirement for a self-representing litigant to lodge a skeleton argument, but equally there is nothing to prevent the person from doing so if they wish and if they consider that it would assist the court.

17.152   Any skeleton argument must contain the following information:

- a time estimate for the complete hearing, including delivery of judgment;

- a list of issues;

- a list of the legal points to be taken (together with any relevant authorities with page references to the passages relied on);

- a chronology of events (with page references to the bundle of documents);

- a list of essential documents for the advance reading of the court (with page references to the passages relied on) (if different from that filed with the claim form) and a time estimate for that reading; and

- a list of persons referred to.

Settlement before hearing

17.153   The court may decide a claim for judicial review without a hearing in circumstances where the parties agree.

17.154   If the claimant reaches agreement with the other parties as to the terms of the final order to be made, they must file at the court two copies of a document signed by all the parties setting out the terms of the proposed agreed order. There will be a further court fee payable[63] on lodging the consent order, unless the claimant is entitled to fee remission (in which case they must complete and submit Form EX60 (Application for a Fee Remission) with the application).[64]

17.155   If the claimant agrees with the other parties that a mandatory order is required the draft order should be accompanied by a statement of reasons relied on as justifying the proposed agreed order with copies of any authorities or statutory provisions relied on. If settlement is reached before permission is considered, the draft consent order must include provision for permission to be granted. Such a statement is not required where the agreement as to disposal (usually by way of withdrawal of the application) requires an order for costs or a detailed assessment of the claimant's Legal Services Commission costs. In those circumstances, the parties should file a draft consent order setting out the terms of settlement signed by all the parties.

17.156   If the parties agree that the application should be dismissed, they may apply for such an order by consent. Where the agreed order relates only to costs, the only requirement is that the parties file a document signed by them all which sets out the terms of the proposed order.

17.157   The court will consider the documents submitted by the parties and will make the order if it is satisfied that the order should be made without requiring the parties to attend.

17.158   If the court is not satisfied that the order should be made, the court will give directions and may direct that a hearing date be set for the matter to be considered further.

Discontinuing proceedings

17.159   A claimant may discontinue his claim at any time in accordance with Part 38 CPR 1998 using Form N279.[65]

17.160   There are two circumstances in which proceedings may be discontinued.

(a)   *Before service of the claim form* – if the sealed claim form and accompanying documents have not yet been served on any of the parties, then the prospective claimant may discontinue proceedings by notifying

---

[63]   See Leaflet EX50 Civil and Family Court Fees available at www.justice.gov.uk/forms.
[64]   Available at www.justice.gov.uk/forms.
[65]   Available at www.justice.gov.uk/forms.

the court in writing of his or her intention to do so. The court will accept a letter of withdrawal provided that it is confirmed in writing that service has not been effected on the parties.

(b) *After service of the claim form* – Part 38 CPR 1998 deals with discontinuance of a claim. The claimant must file a notice of discontinuance in Form N279 at the relevant court office and serve a copy on every other party. There is a right to discontinue a claim at any time except where:

- an interim injunction has been granted or an undertaking has been given – in those circumstances the permission of the court is required to discontinue the proceedings;
- interim payment has been made by the defendant – in those circumstances the consent of the defendant or the permission of the court is required to discontinue the proceedings;
- there is more than one claimant – in those circumstances the consent of every other claimant or the permission of the court is required to discontinue the proceedings.

17.161 A defendant may apply to set aside the notice of discontinuance within 28 days of being served with it.[66]

The hearing

17.162 The hearing of a claim for judicial review is normally before a single judge in open court. The hearing will usually consist of legal argument based on the skeleton arguments and the written evidence (predominantly the witness statements).

17.163 The claimant may act in person, but if the parties are legally represented then the usual practice is to allow each party's legal representative the opportunity to address the court. The claimant's argument will be heard first, followed by the defendant and the interested parties. The claimant will then be given an opportunity to reply to the submissions of the defendant and the interested parties.

17.164 The burden is on the claimant to establish his or her case to the civil standard of proof, ie on the balance of probabilities.

17.165 It will not necessarily be the case that every person who was served with the claim form or with the order granting permission will appear at the hearing. The court will usually seek to discourage the attendance of unnecessary or duplicated parties in order to save costs.

---

[66]   CPR 1998, r 38.4.

Costs

17.166 Discontinuing proceedings renders the claimant liable for any costs incurred by the other parties until the date of discontinuance. If the parties require any order for costs, then a draft order setting out the terms of the order sought is required. A notice of discontinuance is *not* required in those circumstances.

17.167 The general rule is that the party losing a substantive claim for judicial review will be ordered to pay the costs of the other parties. However, the judge considering the matter has discretion as to how to deal with the issue of costs as he or she considers appropriate in all of the circumstances. Costs may be awarded in respect of an unsuccessful paper application. Any application by the defendant and/or interested party for costs will normally be made in the acknowledgement of service.

SECTION 8 – APPEALS

17.168 Appeals can be made at either of the two stages within judicial review proceedings – the permission stage or the full hearing stage.

Appeals at the permission stage

Appeals by the claimant against the refusal of permission

17.169 Any claimant who has been refused permission to apply for judicial review following a hearing has a right of appeal to the Court of Appeal. The procedure for such appeals is set out in CPR, r 52.15.

17.170 In these circumstances the claimant must apply to the Court of Appeal for permission to appeal from the decision of the Administrative Court refusing permission within 7 days of the decision.

17.171 The standard form appellant's notice in Form N161[67] should be used. However, the requirements for the documents to be filed with the appellant's notice differ slightly from the usual list of documents required to be filed for appeals to the Court of Appeal.

17.172 The documents that should be filed with the appellant's notice are as follows:

- One additional copy of the notice for use by the Court of Appeal, and a further copy for each of the respondents to be sealed and returned by the Court of Appeal.

---

[67] Available at www.justice.gov.uk/forms.

- The order of the Administrative Court refusing permission to apply for judicial review.

- The appellant's notice in Form N161.

- A copy of the original decision which was the subject of the application to the Administrative Court.

- A copy of the bundle of documents used in the Administrative Court.

- Any witness statements or affidavits in support of any application (other than the application for permission to appeal) relied on before the Administrative Court.

- A copy of any skeleton argument relied on before the Administrative Court.

- A transcript of the judgment refusing permission to apply for judicial review.

17.173 In situations where not all those documents are available, then the appellant must explain as such to the Court of Appeal and provide an indication as to when they will be available.

17.174 A copy of the appeal notice, plus any accompanying skeleton argument, must be served on each respondent within 7 days after it has been filed.

How will the Court of Appeal proceed?

17.175 If the Court of Appeal does decide that a claim for judicial review should proceed, it will usually grant permission to apply for judicial review, rather than permission to appeal to the Court of Appeal.[68]

17.176 Permission to appeal to the Court of Appeal may be granted only where the appeal has a real prospect of success or there is some other compelling reason why the appeal should be heard, for example the case raises some issue of particular public importance.

17.177 Regardless of the outcome, the Court of Appeal will consider the appeal against refusal to grant permission to apply for judicial review by applying the same criteria as were applied by the Administrative Court, including whether there is an arguable case.

17.178 If the Court of Appeal grants permission to apply for judicial review, the case will be remitted to the Administrative Court for hearing, unless the

---

[68]   CPR 1998, r 52.15(3).

Court of Appeal considers and orders that it should hear the claim itself. This might occur in cases where an appeal to the Court of Appeal appears inevitable or where the issues are of urgent and public importance.

What if the Court of Appeal refuses to grant permission?

17.179   If the Court of Appeal refuses to grant permission to appeal from an order of the Administrative Court refusing permission to apply for judicial review, there is then no further avenue of appeal and that will be the end of the matter.

Appeals by the defendant against the grant of permission

17.180   It is extremely unlikely that the Court of Appeal will look kindly on an appeal by a defendant against the grant of permission and there is no provision for such a process within the CPR 1998. Defendants, and any interested parties who seek to object to the grant of permission to apply for judicial review should therefore ensure that their objections are fully set out before the court at the substantive hearing.

Appeals at the full hearing stage

17.181   Permission to appeal must be obtained from the Administrative Court itself at the hearing at which the decision was made, or subsequently from the Court of Appeal.

17.182   Permission to appeal will only be granted in cases where the Court of Appeal considers that the appeal would have a real prospect of success or where there is some important reason why the appeal should be heard, for example in cases of significant public importance.

17.183   In circumstances where permission to appeal was not sought from the Administrative Court itself, or where permission to appeal was sought but refused, then an application must be made to the Court of Appeal within 14 days of the decision. The application must be made in the form of an appellant's notice in Form N161.[69]

17.184   Such notice must be served upon the respondents within 7 days of being filed. However, the time limit for filing the respondent's notice will not actually commence unless and until permission is granted (except in cases where the application for permission to appeal and the appeal itself are to be heard at the same hearing).

17.185   The documents that should be filed with the appellant's notice are as follows:

---

[69]   See Part 4 (resources section). Available at www.justice.gov.uk/forms.

- One additional copy of the notice for the Court of Appeal, and a further copy for each of the respondents (to be sealed and returned by the Court of Appeal).

- A copy of the appellant's skeleton argument.

- A copy of the order being appealed.

- A copy of the order (if any) refusing permission to appeal, with a copy of any reasons.

- Any witness statements or affidavits in support of any application (other than the application for permission to appeal) included within the appellant's notice.

- A bundle of documents to support the appellant's case which should include:

  - statements of case;
  - a transcript of the reasons of the judgment of the Administrative Court;
  - relevant written evidence;
  - a copy of the original decision which was the subject of the judicial review application.

How will the Court of Appeal proceed?

17.186 The application for permission to appeal will be considered on paper by a single Lord Justice of Appeal.

What happens if permission is refused?

17.187 If permission is refused without an oral hearing, the appellant has the right to request that the application will be reconsidered at an oral hearing within 7 days of being served with the notice stating that permission has been refused.[70]

What happens if permission is granted?

17.188 In cases where permission is granted either by the Administrative Court or by the Court of Appeal, the appellant's bundle of documents will be served on the respondent. The respondent may then file a respondent's notice in Form N162.[71]

---

[70] See PD52, paras 4.11–4.14.
[71] See Part 4 (resources section). Available at www.justice.gov.uk/forms.

The respondent's notice

17.189   The respondent's notice may serve different purposes:

(a)   The respondent may wish to appeal part of the decision of the Administrative Court.

(b)   The respondent may wish to uphold the decision on different or additional grounds.

17.190   In cases where the Administrative Court has given permission to appeal, the respondent's notice must be served within 14 days of being served with the appeal notice.

17.191   In cases where the Court of Appeal has granted permission to appeal, the respondent's notice must be served within 14 days of being notified.

Chapter 18

DAMAGES AND LOCAL AUTHORITIES

SECTION 1 – INTRODUCTION

18.1 Anyone involved in child protection and care proceedings cannot help but notice how local authorities, according to certain sections of the media, cannot get it right: they act too soon, act too late, rely on minor parental failings to separate families, or miss major injuries.

18.2 Sometimes, as a result of these actions or inactions children, parents and families suffer damage. Examples that readily come to mind include the following:

- A child is physically, sexually or emotionally abused whilst in care.

- A child is physically, sexually or emotionally abused whilst in the care of their family despite prior local authority knowledge or involvement.

- The separation of parent and child without just cause or without legal authority.

18.3 Perhaps less obvious, but also with damaging effects, can be:

- The inadequate provision of information about a child to its adopters.

- The adverse consequences of local authority action on reputation and employment.

18.4 Elsewhere in this book consideration is given to the challenges that can be launched to the flawed decision making processes and how to prevent, overturn or discharge such interferences with family life. Chapter 19 deals with criminal injuries compensation which aims to assist those considering whether a child involved with the care system is entitled to a criminal compensation payment.

18.5 The aim of this chapter is to identify whether as a result of actions or inactions of the local authority, an employee of the local authority or a person or body responsible for carrying out child care tasks, any application can be made for financial compensation for any damage suffered.

18.6   There will be aspects where the issues overlap but claims for damages are considered under two broad headings of 'Civil Claims' and 'Human Rights Claims'. Damages will, in certain circumstances, be available in judicial review proceedings; these are considered briefly at the end of the chapter.

18.7   Civil claims will encompass matters such as negligence with its associated issues of breach of duty of care, vicarious liability, breach of statutory duty and trespass to the person. Human rights claims will, in the main but not exclusively, focus on alleged breaches of Art 3, Art 6 and Art 8.[1]

SECTION 2 – CIVIL CLAIMS

18.8   Establishing a cause of action against a local authority acting pursuant to its statutory child protection functions has not always proven as straightforward as might be expected. As a result there are numerous case authorities including House of Lords (as it then was) and European Court of Human Rights. What follows cannot replace detailed study of the main authorities but aims to identify the main points and pitfalls.

18.9   In each potential case careful consideration must be given to:

- Who is the correct claimant (parent or child or both)?

- Who is the correct respondent (local authority, individual employee, foster parent, expert) ?

- Does a common law duty of care exist?

- Has there been a breach?

- Can damage be demonstrated?

- Can causation be established?

- Limitation periods.

- What is the appropriate quantum?

Civil claims – legal background

18.10   In 1995 three appeals jointly came before the House of Lords[2] relating to an application where the claim for damages against the local authority was for breach of statutory duty and breach of a common law duty of care based

---

[1]   For more detailed assistance with the making of civil claims see for example Gumbel, Levision, Johnson and Scorer *APIL Guide to Child Abuse Compensation Claims* (Jordan Publishing, 2nd edn).

[2]   *X (Minors) v Bedfordshire County Council* [1995] 2 AC 633, [1995] 2 FLR 276.

on a background of reports of abuse and neglect of five children which had been disregarded by the authority for five years. The stark decision of the House of Lords can be summarised as follows:

(a)   for the alleged breach of statutory duty no claim for compensation could be made as:

> 'the claim based on breach of statutory duty simpliciter had been rightly struck out. All the statutory provisions relied upon by the authority had been made dependent upon the authority's subjective judgment, and to treat such duties as being more than public law duties was impossible.'

(b)   for the alleged breach of common law duty of care, despite the view that the local authority owed a direct duty of care to the claimant children, that the damage sustained was foreseeable and the relationship between the local authority and the children was sufficiently proximate the House of Lords concluded that:

> '... it would not be just and reasonable to superimpose a common-law duty of care on the authority in relation to the performance of its statutory duty to protect children in circumstances where a common-law duty of care would cut across the whole system set up for the protection of children at risk, where the task involved was extraordinarily delicate and where the imposition of damages might cause the authorities to adopt a more cautious and defensive approach. The courts should proceed with great care before holding liable in negligence those who had been charged by parliament with the task of protecting society from the wrongdoing of others.'

18.11   In 1996 the Court of Appeal[3] considered whether permission should be granted to appeal against an order striking out a claim alleging negligence of a local authority with respect to a child who had been physically and sexually abused by his foster father with whom the local authority had placed him. Relying on the *Bedfordshire* case the judge had determined that for the five following public policy reasons the council owed no duty of care:

(i)   the interdisciplinary nature of the system for protection of children at risk and the difficulties that might arise in disentangling the liability of the various agents concerned;

(ii)   the very delicate nature of the task of the local authority in dealing with children at risk and their parents;

(iii)   the risk of a more defensive and cautious approach by the local authority if a common law duty were to exist;

(iv)   the potential conflict between social workers and parents;

---

[3]   *H v Norfolk County Council* [1997] 1 FLR 384. Note that May LJ in *S v Gloucestershire CC* [2001] Fam 313 did not consider that *H v Norfolk* could withstand the *Barrett* case.

(v) the existence of alternative remedies under s 76 of the Child Care Act 1980[4] and the powers of investigation of the local authority ombudsman.

18.12 The Court of Appeal refused permission to appeal accepting that, for all the public policy considerations set out by the judge, the appeal was doomed to failure. The position of the relationship between the child and foster parents was considered not to be sufficiently different to that as between child and natural parents as to override those policy considerations.

18.13 In 1999 the House of Lords gave judgment in *Barrett v London Borough of Enfield*.[5] The claimant in the case had been taken into care at 10 months of age and did not leave care until age 18. He later brought an application for damages for psychiatric injury against the local authority alleging breach of statutory duty and negligence in the local authority's failure to place him for adoption, place him in foster care or reintroduce him to his mother. The Court of Appeal had upheld the striking out of the claim on the grounds that there was no jurisdiction to find that the authority was liable for negligence in exercising statutory discretion and that even if there was jurisdiction it would not be just and reasonable to impose liability on the authority. The House of Lords reinstated the claim concluding that

> 'it was possible for certain acts done pursuant to the lawful exercise of a statutory discretion, such as the local authority treatment of children taken into care, to be subject to a duty of care. It was only if a decision involved the weighing of competing public interests or was dictated by considerations which the courts were not fitted to assess that the courts would hold that the issue was non justiciable on the ground that the decision was made in the exercise of a statutory discretion. The decision whether to take a child into care was such a non-justiciable decision … it was not necessarily unjust or unreasonable to impose a duty of care on a local authority in relation to the children taken into its care. While it would be inappropriate to permit a child to sue his parents, it was not necessarily wrong for a child to sue a local authority, whose duties were not the same as those of a parent. Both in deciding whether a duty of care existed and whether, if a duty of care was owed, it had been broken the court must have regard to the statutory context and to the nature of the tasks involved, being careful to keep in mind the delicate and difficult factors involved in much local authority work, particularly child welfare work. However unless the court exercised its jurisdiction to consider those questions, the interests of the child would not be sufficiently protected. Requiring that the conduct of the local authority be measured against the standards of the reasonable man was in the public interest, not opposed to it.'

18.14 In *Barrett* great emphasis was placed on the fact that unlike the children in the Bedfordshire case the local authority had already taken the decision to

---

[4]   The Child Care Act 1980 has now been repealed. Today's equivalent of the s 76 provisions can be found in ss 3 and 4 of the Children Act 2004 and relate to the ability of the Children's Commissioner to conduct inquiries initiated by the Commissioner herself or by the secretary of State. For more information with regard to the Children's Commissioner see chapter 2 at **2.36** et seq.

[5]   [1999] 2 FLR 426.

remove the claimant from home and receive him into care allowing consideration of what kinds of acts or omissions thereafter by the local authority could ground a claim in negligence. Reviewing decisions not to take children into care was not felt to be appropriate by way of a claim for damages in negligence but was more amenable to other remedies such as judicial review or the ombudsman.

18.15   In 2000 the House of Lords considered the case of *W and Others v Essex County Council and another*.[6] The parents and their four children sought damages for personal injury arising out of the local authority placing with the family (which was a specialist foster placement) a foster child who was a known sexual abuser without informing the family of his history. The family had explicitly stated to the local authority that they were not prepared to foster children who were known, or suspected, sexual abusers. The parents alleged that the foster child had subsequently sexually abused children in the family resulting in serious psychiatric injury both for the children as primary victims and for the parents who had discovered the abuse. The parents' claims were struck out on the basis that the local authority did not owe them a duty of care and that they did not qualify as primary or secondary victims. The House reinstated the parent's claim indicating that it could not be said that the claim, that there was a duty of care to the parents and a breach of that duty, was unarguable in the sense of it being clear and obvious that it could not succeed.[7] Further the court indicated that it was impossible to say that the psychiatric injury claimed was outside the range of psychiatric injury recognised by law.

18.16   In 2001 the House of Lords considered the correct legal test to establish vicarious liability in the context of the sexual abuse of children at a school for children with emotional and behavioural difficulties. The school had a boarding annex and the warden of the annex, employed to care for the children living there, was the perpetrator of the abuse. The Court overruled an earlier Court of Appeal case which had formulated the test as to whether it could be said the employee's conduct was wrongful conduct outside the scope of the employment and instead altered the question to whether the torts were so closely connected with his employment that it would be fair and just to hold the employers vicariously liable for them.[8]

18.17   In 2001 two of the cases in *X v Bedfordshire* were considered by the European Court of Human Rights. The '*Bedfordshire*' element is reported under the title *Z and Others v United Kingdom*.[9] The court held that there had been violations of Arts 3 and 13 of the European Convention for Protection of

---

6   [2000] 1 FLR 657.
7   Hale LJ in the Court of Appeal commented on the different and more restrictive approach they were able to take to an issue of whether a common law duty of care was owed to prospective adopters in *A v Essex County Council* [2003] EWCA Civ 1848, [2004] 1 FLR 749 at para [44].
8   *Lister and others v Hesley Hall Ltd* [2001] UKHL 22, [2001] 2 FLR 307 overturning *Trotman v North Yorkshire County Council* [1999] LGR 584. For further consideration of the issue of vicarious liability and the current state of the law see **18.41–18.80**.
9   (Case 29392/95) [2001] 2 FLR 612.

Human Rights and Fundamental Freedoms. The decisions were based on the findings that the welfare system had failed to protect the children from serious, long term neglect and abuse in violation of Art 3, which prohibited torture, or inhuman or degrading treatment or punishment and which required the state to prevent the ill treatment of the which authorities had, or ought to have had, knowledge.

18.18   The court found a breach of Art 13, the right to an effective remedy before a national authority, due to the fact that the specific children, and others with the same complaint, could not sue the local authority in negligence for compensation no matter how foreseeable and severe the harm suffered, nor how unreasonable the conduct of the local authority in failing to take steps to prevent that harm.

18.19   The '*Newham*' element is reported under *TP and KM v United Kingdom*.[10] The Court held that there had been a breach of Arts 8 and 13. The Art 8 breach related to non-disclosure by the local authority to the mother of the video of the interview of the child, which when viewed demonstrated that there had been a mistake as to the person it was said the child had identified as her abuser.[11] The Art 13 breach again related to the absence of a means of claiming that the local authority's handling of the procedures was responsible for the damage they suffered and obtaining compensation for that damage. The court rejected the possibility of applying to the ombudsman and Secretary of State for redress as it did not provide the applicants with any enforceable right to compensation. The case provoked the following explanation of Art 13:

> '[107] As the Court has stated on many occasions, Art 13 of the Convention guarantees the availability at the national level of a remedy to enforce the substance of the Convention rights and freedoms in whatever form they might happen to be secured in the domestic legal order. Article 13 thus requires the provision of a domestic remedy to deal with the substance of an "arguable complaint" under the Convention and to grant appropriate relief ... the remedy required by Art 13 must be "effective" in practice as well as in law.

> The Court considers that, where an arguable breach of one or more of the rights under the Convention is in issue, there should be available to the victim a mechanism for establishing any liability of state official or bodies for that breach. Furthermore, in appropriate cases, compensation of the pecuniary and non-pecuniary damage flowing from the breach should in principle be available as part of the range of redress.'

18.20   The introduction of the Human Rights Act 1998 significantly altered the approach of the courts to the issue of whether a local authority owed children and parents a duty of care when exercising their child protection functions. As a result the reasoning in the *Bedfordshire* case must now be regarded with significant caution when considering claims by children.

---

[10]   (Case 28945/95) [2001] 2 FLR 549.

[11]   For further explanation of this particular element of breach please see **18.182** et seq.

18.21   Particular attention is drawn to *D v East Berkshire Community NHS Trust; MAK v Dewsbury Healthcare NHS Trust; RK v Oldham NHS Trust*[12] which held that the decision in Bedfordshire could not survive the Human Rights Act 1998. Lord Phillips MR explained the position with respect to the child in the following way:

> '[83] Insofar as the position of the child is concerned, we have reached the firm conclusion that the decisions in Bedfordshire cannot survive the Human Rights Act 1998. Where child abuse is suspected the interests of the child are paramount – see section 1 of the Children Act 1989. Given the obligation of the local authority to respect a child's European Convention Rights, the recognition of a duty of care to the child on the part of those involved should not have a significantly adverse effect on the manner in which they perform their duties. In the context of suspected child abuse, breach of a duty of care in negligence will frequently also amount to a violation of Art 3 or Art 8. The difference, of course, is that those asserting that wrongful acts or omissions occurred before October 2000 will have no claim under the Human Rights Act 1998. This cannot, however, constitute a valid reason of policy for preserving a limitation of the common law duty of care which is not otherwise justified. On the contrary, the absence of an alternative remedy for children who were the victims of abuse before October 2000 militates in favour of the recognition of a common law duty of care once the public policy reasons against this have lost their force.
>
> [84] It follows that it will no longer be legitimate to rule that, as a matter of law, no common law duty of care is owed to a child in relation to the investigation of suspected child abuse and the initiation and pursuit of care proceedings. It is possible that there will be factual situations where it is not fair, just or reasonable to impose a duty of care, but each case will fall to be determined on its individual facts.
>
> [85] In reaching this decision we do not suggest that the common law duty of care will replicate the duty not to violate Arts 3 and 8. Liability for breach of the latter duty and entitlement can arise in circumstances where the tort of negligence is not made out. The area of factual inquiry where breaches of the two duties are alleged is however likely to be the same.'

18.22   Since the decision of the Court of Appeal in *D v East Berkshire* it has been well established that a local authority that carries out investigations into suspected child abuse owes a duty of care to a child who is potentially at risk.[13] The position of parents however remains different to that of the child.

18.23   In *D v East Berkshire Community Health NHS Trust; MAK v Dewsbury Healthcare NHS Trust; RK v Oldham NHS Trust*.[14] The House of Lords considered the position of parents in three cases where each of their cases alleged that medical professionals had negligently misdiagnosed child abuse rather than the actual cause of the child's health problems. Their claims for damages for negligence which had disrupted family life and caused the parents

---

[12]   [2003] EWCA Civ 1151, [2003] 2 FLR 1166.
[13]   See the words of Swift J in *NXS v Camden LBC* [2010] 1 FLR 100 at 103.
[14]   [2005] UKHL 23, [2005] 2 FLR 284.

psychiatric injury had been struck out on the ground that public policy considerations militated strongly against the existence of a duty of care. Their appeal against the striking out was dismissed by the Court of Appeal.

18.24 Their Lordships noted that no-one sought to argue that the breadth of the decision by the House in the *Bedfordshire* case should be maintained in relation to claims by children. The Court of Appeal decision in the 2003 *East Berkshire* case, that the approach in *Bedfordshire* could not survive the Human Rights Act 1998 therefore went unchallenged.

18.25 As with the Court of Appeal the House of Lords in the 2005 *East Berkshire* case (Lord Bingham dissenting) dismissed the parent's appeal explaining that:

> 'Healthcare and other childcare professionals did not owe a common law duty of care to parents not to make negligent allegations of child abuse. Such duty would result in a conflict of interest; the doctor was under an obligation to act in the best interests of his patient, the child, rather than in the interests of the parent and if the doctor's suspicions were aroused he had to be able to act single-mindedly in the child's interests without regard to the possibility of a claim by the parent. The seriousness of child abuse as a social problem demanded that healthcare and other childcare professionals should not be subjected to conflicting duties when deciding whether a child might have been abused and what further steps to take.'

18.26 Subsequent claims founded on an assertion that the local authority owed a duty of care to a parent of a child when investigating and/or taking steps to protect children considered to be at risk of parental abuse resulted in the following statements:[15]

> 'The public interest in effective and fair investigation and prevention of criminal behaviour had fashioned the common law to protect those suspected of it from malice or bad faith but not from well-intentioned but negligent mistake. The basis for that distinction was the need to provide protection to those who had a duty to enforce the law in good faith from the imposition of a duty in negligence that could or might tend to inhibit them in the effective fulfilment of that duty; commonly this was labelled "conflict of interest".
>
> The development proposed would fundamentally distort the law of negligence in this area, putting at risk the protection of children which it provided in its present form ... the provision of a discrete Convention remedy through the Human Rights Act 1998 did not necessitate a change of the common law in the manner proposed.'

18.27 An earlier Court of Appeal decision[16] following a claim by mother and child for damages arising out of alleged negligence of the local authority in

---

[15]   *Lawrence v Pembrokeshire CC* [2007] EWCA Civ 446, [2007] 2 FLR 705.
[16]   *D v Bury Metropolitan Borough Council* [2006] EWCA Civ 1, [2006] 2 FLR 147.

failing to ensure that a residential risk assessment had been properly carried out, and in enforcing the separation of mother and child for four months, noted:

'Care professionals charged with questions of child protection and investigation of child abuse had to be free to exercise their professional functions without the burden of knowing that in the event that doubts about the injury or sexual abuse proved unfounded they might be exposed to damages claims. This freedom lasted throughout the investigatory process, which itself lasted until such time as a final care order was made. A local authority investigating the possibility of child abuse did not owe a duty of care to the parents of the child while the child was subject of an interim order, or while investigation continued under the aegis of that order.'

18.28 The Court of Appeal considered the application of *D v Bury Metropolitan BC* in *B v Reading BC and another*[17] in circumstances where the social worker and police formed the view that the father was responsible for sexual abuse of the child. After a fact finding hearing the father was found not to have sexually abused his daughter and she eventually went to live with him. It held that while it might be that in certain circumstances a direct duty could be owed to a person suspected of child abuse it was not correct to do so in the case before it.

18.29 More recent consideration of this issue by the European Court of Human Rights has appeared to support the approach of the domestic courts on this emphasis given to child protection as it acknowledged that:[18]

'Mistaken judgments or assessments by professionals did not per se render childcare measures incompatible with the requirements of Art 8. The authorities had duties to protect children and could not be held liable every time genuine and reasonably held concerns about the safety of children vis-à-vis members of their family were proved, retrospectively, to have been misguided ...'

18.30 However the lack of a remedy for parents prior to the 2 October 2000, when ss 7 and 8 of the Human Rights Act 1998 introduced a route by which parents could bring their grievances before the Court, led to a determination that the United Kingdom had violated the parents' rights pursuant to Art 13 of the European Convention in failing to make available to parents a means of claiming that the local authority's handling of the procedures was responsible for any damage which they had suffered and obtaining compensation for that damage.[19] This aspect is considered in greater detail below in the section on human rights claims.

18.31 It has been necessary to consider the recent history of the legal background to ensure an understanding of the type of claims that can in fact

---

[17] [2008] 1 FLR 797.
[18] *AD and OD v UK* (Application No 28680/06), [2010] 2 FLR 1, ECtHR.
[19] See for example *RK and AK v UK* (Application No 38000/05), (2009) EHRR 29 707, [2009] 1 FLR 274, ECtHR; see also *MAK and RK v UK* (Application Nos 45901/5 and 40146/06), [2010] 2 FLR 451, ECtHR.

be litigated. What follows is a more practical look at the essential elements of those claims and the information needed to be able to initiate such claims.

Negligence

18.32 The essential elements for establishing a claim founded on negligence are:

- The existence of a duty of care.

- A breach of that duty of care.

- Damage which can be demonstrated to flow from the breach.

18.33 From the way in which the claims have been formulated in reported cases the duty of care to the child can be seen to include, but not be limited to, the following:

- A duty to take reasonable steps to avoid or prevent the child from suffering personal injury.[20]

- A duty to investigate the history of the family.[21]

- A duty carry out proper assessment or investigation of the family before returning a child to their care.[22]

18.34 Elements amounting (individually or collectively) to breach can include the following:

- Failure to undertake an investigation in to the frequency and cause of more minor incidents of physical assault.

- Failure to assess the level of a parent or carer's motivation and ability to adequately care for the child.

- Infrequent and superficial observations of parent/child together.

---

[20]   See by way of illustration *NXS v Camden LBC* [2009] EWHC 1786 (QB), [2010] 1 FLR 100 – a claimant seeking damages 32 years after leaving local authority care having been accommodated at age 14. The claim was founded upon personal injury alleged to have been suffered as a result of the local authority's negligent failure to protect her from abuse (by her mother and maternal uncle) by her earlier removal into care.

[21]   See for example *ABB, BBB, CBB and DBB v Milton Keynes Council* [2011] EWHC 2745, [2012] 1 FLR 1157.

[22]   See for example the High Court decision *Pierce v Doncaster MBC* [2007] EWHC 2968 (QB), [2008] 1 FLR 922. The Court of Appeal considered this case in *Pierce v Doncaster MBC* [2008] EWCA Civ 1416, [2009] 1 FLR 1189 allowing an appeal only on the issue of constructive knowledge under s 14(3) Limitation Act 1980 but otherwise upholding the decision of the court below.

- Failure to undertake adequate risk assessment.

- Failure to consider the whole picture and cumulative effect of knowledge about the family members and their actions.

- Lack of proper supervision of social workers undertaking the direct work with the family.

- Lack of systematic monitoring of the family.

What is the standard of care required?

18.35   The standard to be applied when assessing whether in fact there has been a breach of the duty of care is the practice of a reasonably competent social services department or social worker, judged by the professional standards prevailing at the material time.[23]

18.36   It is interesting to note, however, the obiter comments of Lord Hutton in *Barrett v Enfield LBC*[24] as follows:

' ... when the decisions taken by a local authority in respect of a child in its care are alleged to constitute negligence at common law, the trial judge, bearing in mind the room for differences of opinion as to the best course to adopt in a difficult field and that the discretion is to be exercised by the authority and its social workers and not by the court, must be satisfied that the conduct complained of went beyond mere errors of judgment in the exercise of a discretion and constituted conduct which can be regarded as negligent.'

Trespass to the person

18.37   Where the act complained of as giving rise to a claim for damages is in the nature of physical or sexual abuse it may be simpler to consider phrasing the claim in the manner of trespass to the person, in reality an assault.

18.38   In order to qualify as an assault it will not always be necessary to demonstrate an element of 'physical battery' but as will be shown below it can incorporate for example inappropriate touching in sexual abuse cases that fall short of rape or buggery.

18.39   The law on vicarious liability has itself undergone changes which now mean that it is easier to hold local authorities responsible for the misconduct of their employees in cases of sexual abuse and it is no longer necessary to strain to be inventive and imaginative in bringing such acts under heads of breach of duty of care.

---

[23]   See for example *NXS v Camden LBC* [2010] 1 FLR 100 citing *Bolam v Friern Hospital Management Committee* [1957] 1 WLR 582.
[24]   [1999] 2 FLR 426 at 465.

18.40 It will also be seen below that pursuing a claim under the heading of trespass to the person rather than negligence may have the result of allowing a more flexible interpretation of the harm suffered as a result of the wrongdoing.

Vicarious liability

18.41 In brief, vicarious liability is the legal responsibility imposed on a defendant to compensate the victim for damage suffered by the victim caused by the negligent or other tortious act of the person committing the act even though the defendant is not personally at fault at all.

18.42 In its simplest form it is the legal responsibility imposed on an employer, although he himself is free from blame, for the assault/abuse committed by his employee in the course of his employment.

18.43 This approach led to the need to consider two stages before imposing liability on the employer:

(a) whether there was an employer/employee relationship between the defendant and the person committing the act; and

(b) whether the person committing the act was acting within the scope of his or her employment or whether he or she was on a frolic of his or her own.

18.44 In certain circumstances it was held that even though there was not a strict employer/employee relationship in existence the legal responsibility may fall on the blameless party. This approach resulted in the need to consider whether there existed:

• a relationship akin to employment;

• which is established by a connection between the defendant and the person committing the act which is sufficiently close so that;

• it is fair and just to impose liability on the defendant.

18.45 It has been stated that 'vicarious liability' is a fluid concept which has adjusted over the centuries to provide just solutions to the challenge of changing times and that the courts in their interpretation of the concept need to adapt to current demands.[25]

18.46 This is a topic that has recently been reviewed by both Court of Appeal and the Supreme Court. It may help to understand the issues and arguments involved in this difficult area by referring to older decisions before highlighting the central conclusions in the cases decided in the middle and end of 2012.

---

[25] See for example Lord Justice Ward in *JGE v The Trustees of the Portsmouth Roman Catholic Diocesan Trust* [2012] EWCA Civ 938.

18.47 *Lister and Others v Hesley Hall Ltd*[26] was a case where the central question for the House of Lords was whether as a matter of legal principle employers of the warden of a school boarding house, who sexually abused boys in his care, may, depending on the particular circumstances, be vicariously liable for the torts of their employee. The House determined that the test should not be whether the warden's conduct was wrongful conduct outside the scope of employment but whether the warden's torts were so closely connected with his employment that it would be fair and just to hold the employers liable for them.

18.48 Prior to the House of Lords ruling in *Lister* the test routinely applied was that a wrongful act is deemed to be done by a servant in the course of his employment only if it is either:

(a)   a wrongful act authorised by the master; or

(b)   a wrongful and unauthorised mode of doing some act authorised by the master.

18.49 The Court of Appeal in *Trotman v North Yorkshire County Council*[27] had concluded that sexual assaults were far removed from an unauthorised mode of carrying out a teacher's duties on behalf of his employer and that it was impossible to hold that the commission of acts of indecent assault can be regarded as a mode – albeit an improper and unauthorised mode – of doing what the deputy headmaster in the case was employed by the council to do.

18.50 The lower courts in *Lister* felt themselves bound by the approach in *Trotman*. Lord Steyn's view was that the approach in *Trotman* was wrong as rather than the employment furnishing a mere opportunity to commit sexual abuse the reality was that the council were responsible for the care of vulnerable children and employed the deputy head master to carry out that duty on its behalf and that the sexual abuse took place while the employee was engaged in duties at the very time and place demanded by the employment.

18.51 Lord Steyn concluded that the correct test was whether the warden's torts were so closely connected with his employment that it would be fair and just to hold the employers vicariously liable. Lord Millett commented that the law was mature enough to hold an employer vicariously liable for deliberate criminal wrongdoing on the part of an employee without resorting to the artificial use of allegations of failure to perform a duty to take care of the boys or failure of the warden to report his own wrong doing.

18.52 Although concerning the position of the Church's liability for acts of sexual abuse rather than that of a local authority the case of *Maga*[28] is a useful

---

[26]   [2001] UKHL 22, [2001] 2 FLR 307.

[27]   [1999] LGR 584.

[28]   *Maga v Trustees of the Birmingham Archdiocese of the Roman Catholic Church* [2009] EWHC 780 (QB); [2010] EWCA Civ 256.

one to consider when trying to understand the issue of vicarious liability and how the opposing arguments may be put and indeed received by the Court.

18.53   At first instance the Court approached the problem in the following way:

> 'questions as to vicarious liability of a church in respect of acts of sexual abuse of children by one of its priests may be both particularly difficult and sensitive. That arises from the wide duties of priests and the respect which the priesthood may be accorded. It is clear that ... "youth work" was a major part of Father Clonan's contribution to the parish. He did it in his capacity as a priest. It is submitted that his association with the claimant was carried out under that guise, that there was no other justification for it, and that association was accepted by the claimants parents because [he] was a priest. I accept it was [his] position as a priest which gave him the opportunity to abuse the claimant but ... that is not by itself sufficient. [His] association with the claimant was founded on the use of the claimant for money to wash his car, to do cleaning in the presbytery and in other houses, and to iron his clothes. That employment was not a priestly activity. [He] did not do anything to draw the claimant into the activities of the church. The association was not part of evangelization ... the assaults ... on the claimant were not so closely connected with Father Clonan's employment or quasi employment by the Church that it would be fair and just to hold the Church liable.'

18.54   On the wider claim that the Church were liable aside from the issue of vicarious liability under the separate head of negligence Mr Justice Jack made the following observations:

> '... suppose the managers of a care home appoint a person to work there without making any adequate checks on him, and he is in fact a paedophile, which should have been discovered: could managers say that they owed no duty to boys who were then in the home, or later came to it, and were abused by the employee? Plainly not. A close analogy can be drawn between the occupants of the home and boys within Father Clonan's congregation at the time of the claimants complaint and later. But the claimant was not within that congregation, and I have held that the circumstances of his association with the claimant were such that the Church is not vicariously liable for his assaults on the claimant ... If the assaults were carried out in circumstances where there is no vicarious liability because they were not sufficiently closely connected with the employment, then the victim should be outside any duty of care owed by the employer. That may be put in terms of a lack of proximity, or in terms of what is fair just and reasonable, or the two combined ...'

18.55   The Court of Appeal however, allowing the claimant's appeal against the dismissal of his claim, took the view that:

> 'there were a number of factors which, taken together showed that there was a sufficiently close connection between Father C's employment as a priest at the church and the abuse which he had inflicted on the claimant to render it fair and just to impose vicarious liability for the abuse on his employer.

- First Father C was normally dressed in clerical garb and was so dressed when he first met the claimant. At the very least that factor set the scene. A priest had a special role which involved trust and responsibility in a more general way even than a teacher, a doctor or a nurse. It was C's employment as a priest by the archdiocese which enabled him, indeed was intended to enable him, to hold himself out as having such a role and such authority.
- Second C's functions as a priest included a duty to evangelise or to bring the gospel to other people. Accordingly he was ostensibly performing his duty as a priest employed by the archdiocese by getting to know M.
- Third given that M was aged 12 or 13 when his association with C started, it was significant that C was given special responsibility for youth work at the church. It underlined the point that when getting to know and effectively grooming M C was ostensibly carrying out one of his specially assigned functions in the Church.
- Fourth C was able to develop his relationship with M by inviting him to a disco which was on church premises and which he organised as a priest at the church.
- Fifth the relationship was further developed when C got M to clear up after discos. That work on church premises at the request of the a priest at the church led M to do other work for C. Thus C's role as a priest in the archdiocese gave him the status and opportunity to draw M further into his sexually abusive orbit by ostensibly respectable means connected with his employment as a priest at the church.
- Sixth the fact that M was working at the request of a priest on premises, namely the presbytery, owned by the priest's archdiocese, adjoining the church where the priest worked, and which were lived in by the priest, was relevant to the issue of vicarious liability for the first three reasons mentioned above, namely moral authority, evangelisation and youth work.
- Seventh the opportunity to spend time alone with M, especially in the presbytery, had arisen from C's role as a priest employed as such by the archdiocese.'

18.56 Lord Neuberger MR acknowledged that the court should not be too ready to impose vicarious liability on a defendant as it was a type of liability for tort which involves no fault on the part of the defendant and for that reason alone its application should be reasonably circumscribed. Also the deleterious effect on schools and charities and social clubs aimed at the young of too readily imposing such a liability on employers for sexual abuse of children by their employees was rightly identified.

18.57 The mere fact that the opportunity to commit abuse arises as a result of employment is not enough. Although not actually required to determine the issue Lord Neuberger also held that the judge at first instance was wrong to conclude that the archdiocese did not owe a duty of care to the claimant indicating that the duty on the church (through another employee) was to keep a look out for, and to protect, young boys with whom C was associating, after a complaint that he had sexually abused a boy (particularly in the light of visits to the presbytery where the other employee also lived).

18.58 The conclusion of the judge below that if there was no vicarious liability for the assaults there was no duty of care was wrong in principle. It was easy to envisage circumstances where an employer could owe, and be in breach of, a duty of care, without being vicariously liable, in respect of sexual abuse committed by an employee. Lord Neuberger gave the example that a school would not normally be vicariously liable for sexual abuse committed against a pupil by a gardener employed at the school, but if the school had received previous allegations against the gardener of sexual abuse of pupils, failure to deal appropriately with those complaints so that he committed the abuse complained of would, at least on the face of it, give rise to a claim in negligence against the school.

18.59   The Court of Appeal grappled with the issue in July 2012 in *JGE v Trustees of the Portsmouth Roman Catholic Diocesan Trust*.[29] Lord Justice Ward in his judgment reviewed the development of the law relating to vicarious liability and in that exercise considered case authority from other countries.

18.60   The facts of JGE involved a claimant aged 48 years who at age 6½ was placed in a children's home run by the nuns of a convent. The claims were against one of the nuns by whom she was beaten but also against the Trustees of the Portsmouth Diocesan Trust due to the abuse of the claimant by the parish priest who visited the home which was located in his parish and who was alleged to have sexually abused the claimant both there and in the parish church. The claim against the Trust was based on vicarious liability for the actions of the priest.

18.61   A divided Court of Appeal upheld the decision of the court below on a preliminary issue as to whether, in law, the Trust may be vicariously liable for the alleged torts of the priest (the priest had by the time of the claim died).

18.62   Lord Justice Davis concluded that:

> 'although this was most certainly not an employment relationship or even a contractual relationship, the relationship between the Bishop and Father Baldwin nevertheless was sufficiently akin to that of employment: and at all events was one whereby, given the degree of control and connection and given the objectives of the Bishop in the appointment of Father Baldwin which it was intended he should further and promote, vicarious liability in respect of his activities in the parish is capable of arising ...

> To me the important fact here is that JGE on the alleged facts was resident (at the home) as a parishioner; and Father Baldwin's responsibilities, as part and parcel of his appointment by the bishop as parish priest, were designed to extend to ministering to those parishioners resident in the home, as part of the parish.'

18.63   Lord Justice Ward, having considered tests under the following headings:[30]

---

[29]   [2012] EWCA Civ 938.
[30]   For detailed consideration of these tests and how they were applied see paras 72–81 of the judgment of Ward LJ.

- Control.

- Organisation.

- Integration.

- Entrepreneur.

stated that:

> 'The result of each of these tests leads me to the conclusion that Father Baldwin is more like an employee than an independent contractor. He is in a relationship with his bishop which is close enough and so akin to employer/employee as to make it just and fair to impose vicarious liability. Justice and fairness here is used as a salutary check on the conclusion. It is not a stand alone test for a conclusion. It is just because it strikes a proper balance between the unfairness to the employer of imposing strict liability and the unfairness to the victim of leaving her without a full remedy for the harm caused by the employer's managing his business in a way which gives rise to the harm even when the risk of harm is not reasonably foreseeable.'

18.64 On the 21 November 2012 the Supreme Court gave judgment in *The Catholic Welfare Society and Others v Various Claimants and The Institute of the Brother's of the Christian Schools and Others.*[31]

18.65 Lord Phillips, delivering the judgment of the Court, considered the judgment of Ward LJ in *JGE*. He also commented that the law of vicarious liability is on the move.

18.66 Lord Phillips set out a number of propositions which have developed over the years which he regarded as sound and logical incremental developments of the law. These can be stated briefly as follows:

- It is possible for an unincorporated association to be vicariously liable for the tortious acts of one or more of its members.

- A defendant (D2) may be vicariously liable for the acts of another (D1) even though the acts in question constitute a violation of the duty owed to D2 by D1 and even if the acts in question are criminal offences.

- Vicarious liability can even extend to liability for a criminal act of sexual assault.

- It is possible for two different defendants (D2 and D3) each to be vicariously liable for the single tortious act of D1.

---

[31]   [2012] UKSC 56.

18.67 He formulated the two stages of the test as being:

(i)   First Stage: consider the relationship between D1 (the person committing the acts) and D2.

(ii)   Second Stage: consider the connection that links the relationship between D1 and D2 and the act or omission of D1.

18.68 He identified a number of reasons that usually make it fair, just and reasonable to impose vicarious liability on an employer when the employee commits a tort in the course of his employment:

- The employer is more likely to have the means to compensate the victim than the employee and can be expected to have insured against that liability.

- The tort will have been committed as a result of an activity being taken by the employee on behalf of the employer.

- The employee's activity is likely to be part of the business activity of the employer.

- The employer by employing the employee to carry on the activity will have created the risk of the tort committed by the employee.

- The employee will, to a greater or lesser degree have been under the control of the employer.

The significance of control today is that the employer can direct what the employee does, not how he does it.

18.69 The issue before the Supreme Court centred on the dispute between two sets of defendants to claims brought by 170 men in respect of alleged sexual and physical abuse they suffered at a residential school. In the lower court the managers of the school were held to be vicariously liable for the acts of abuse by teachers. The teachers were lay brothers of the Catholic Church and members of the Institute known as the Brothers of the Christian Schools. The managers of the school sought to challenge the finding that the Institute was not also vicariously liable for the acts of abuse committed by the members of the Institute.

18.70 In his judgment Lord Phillips set out the elements of the relationship between the teaching brothers and the Institute which were in the nature of the elements of a relationship between employer and employees:

- The Institute was divided into a hierarchical structure and conducted its activities as if it was a corporate body.

- The teaching activity of the brothers was undertaken because the head of the relevant district of the Institute directed the brothers to undertake it. The contracts of employment between the brothers and the managers of the school were entered into because the head of the relevant district of the Institute required the brothers to enter into such contracts.

- The teaching activity undertaken by the brothers was in furtherance of the objective or mission of the Institute.

- The manner in which the brothers were obliged to conduct themselves as teachers was dictated by the Institute's rules.

18.71 He also highlighted where the relationship differed from that of employer and employee.

- The brothers were bound to the Institute not by contract, but by their vows.

- The brothers entered into deeds under which they were obliged to transfer all their earnings to the Institute from which the Institute catered for their needs.

18.72 He concluded that these latter elements were not material and in fact rendered the relationship between the brothers and the Institute closer than that of an employer and its employees. He considered the relationship between the teaching brothers and the Institute to be sufficiently akin to that of employer and employees to satisfy stage one of the test of vicarious liability. He further added that there was a simpler analysis which also satisfied the test indicating that provided that a brother was acting for the common purpose of the brothers as an unincorporated association, the relationship between them would be sufficient to satisfy stage 1.

18.73 When considering the connection between the brother's acts of abuse and the relationship between the brothers and the institute for stage 2 of the test (the issue therefore of vicarious liability for sexual abuse) he noted that the precise criteria for imposing vicarious liability for sexual abuse are still in the course of refinement by judicial decision. Allusion was made to the 'Jimmy Saville Investigation' but he limited the case to the issue of liability of bodies that have, in pursuance of their own interests, caused their employees or persons in a relationship similar to that of employees, to have access to children in circumstances where abuse has been facilitated.

18.74 He identified that vicarious liability is imposed where a defendant, whose relationship with the abuser puts it in the position to use the abuser to carry on its business or to further its own interests, has done so in a manner which has created or significantly enhanced the risk that the victim or victims would suffer the relevant abuse. The essential closeness in the relationship between the defendant and the abuser and the acts of abuse thus involves a strong causative link. These were the criteria which established the necessary 'close connection' between relationship and abuse.

18.75   On the facts of the case he determined that the relationship between the Institute and the brothers enabled the Institute to place the brothers in teaching positions in the school and in particular in the position of headmaster there. The standing that the brothers enjoyed as members of the Institute led managers of the school to comply with the decisions of the Institute as to who should fill that key position. The running of the school was largely carried out by the headmaster. The headmaster was almost always the director of the Institute's community, living on the school premises. There was thus a very close connection between the relationship of the brothers and the institute and the employment of the brothers as teachers in the school.

18.76   Living cloistered on the school premises were vulnerable boys (vulnerable by virtue of being children in a school, by being virtually prisoners there and because their personal histories made it even less likely they would be believed if they attempted to disclose events).

18.77   The brother teachers were placed in the school to care for the educational and religious needs of these pupils. The acts of abuse were diametrically opposed to those objectives but, as explained by Lord Phillips, paradoxically that very fact was one of the factors that provided the necessary close connection between the abuse and the relationship between the brothers and the Institute which gave rise to vicarious liability on the part of the Institute.

18.78   The brothers who were members of the Institute were bound together by lifelong vows of chastity, poverty and obedience and by detailed and very strict rules of conduct. One chapter dealing with chastity included the provision that "they shall not touch their pupils through playfulness or familiarity, and they shall never touch them on the face". The status of a brother was treated by the managers of the school as an assurance that children could be safely entrusted to his care.

18.79   The placement of brother teachers in a residential school in which they also resided greatly enhanced the risk of abuse by them if they had a propensity for such misconduct.

18.80   As a result the Supreme Court concluded that this case was one where it was fair just and reasonable for the Institute to share with the managers of the school vicarious liability for the abuse committed by the brothers.

Damages

Types of damages

18.81   In brief the types of damage for which an award may be made include:

- physical injury;

- pain and suffering;

- loss of amenity;

- cost of treatment;

- future loss (for example earnings, disadvantage in the labour market).

18.82   Where considering the issue of psychiatric damage arising out of sexual and/or physical abuse in breach of parental, family or other trust and which involves children and/or vulnerable victims the court is likely to consider that the level of award should fall at the higher end of the bracket.

18.83   Guides issued by the Judicial Studies Board suggest that the factors to be taken into account when attempting to value such claims should include the following:

- The victim's ability to cope with life and work.

- The effect on their relationships with family, friends and others they come into contact with.

- Whether treatment has been sought and/or could alleviate the difficulties.

- Future vulnerability.

- The nature of the abuse.

- The nature of the relationship between victim and abuser.

- The duration of the abuse.

- The symptoms caused by the abuse.

18.84   Notionally the award will be assessed by reference to the following brackets – minor, moderate, moderately severe, severe. Currently post-traumatic stress disorder falls within its own category of psychiatric damage where there is a specific recognised diagnosis of the condition.

18.85 Thought is being given as to whether within these guides 'child abuse' should in fact form a separate category of damage rather than being assessed simply by reference to psychiatric injury.

18.86 When considering claims for damages flowing from negligence normal human emotions of a transient nature (such as fright, shock and grief) cannot justify an award in damages. Damages can only be awarded for harm recognised by the law such as physical harm or a recognisable psychiatric condition.[32]

18.87 Whilst experiences of distress and humiliation cannot in themselves amount to a personal injury which can sustain a free standing action it has always been possible to include a claim for such experiences in a claim for personal injury so long as they are related to the physical or psychiatric injury on which the claim is based.

18.88 In a case of rape or buggery, there is a sufficient physical injury on which to found a claim, even where no actual psychiatric harm has been caused. It has always been possible to claim for the humiliation and distress inherent in rape or buggery.[33]

18.89 The Court of Appeal in *AB v Nugent and Another*[34] commented that the effect of *Lister* was to make it much easier to show vicarious liability once trespass to the person in the form of sexual abuse has been established. The Court of Appeal confirmed that unlike the situation in a case where the cause of action is based in negligence, a cause of action based in trespass to the person does not require proof of physical or psychiatric damage. The tort of assault allowed damages not only for the physical injury which resulted but also afforded protection for the indignity, disgrace, humiliation and mental suffering even if no physical injury flowed from the assault.

18.90 The later High Court decision in *AB, JA, JPM, RM v Nugent Care Society*[35] took such an approach in the case of JA where the sexual abuse took the form of grabbing of genitals, masturbation and attempted oral sex without any element of rape or buggery.

18.91 The experts instructed in the case agreed that JA did not meet the criteria for personality disorder or mental illness but probably had some personality difficulties that impacted on his functioning and interpersonal relationships. The judge summarised that their attribution of problems related

---

[32]   See Ward LJ in *D v Bury Metropolitan Borough Council* [2006] 2 FLR 147. Note at para [91] his observations that whilst on the facts it did not arise in the case before him he agreed that harm caused by a local authority to a child which could properly be described as significant may well be of a sufficient nature and severity to found an action in tort for damages.

[33]   See para 28 of the judgment of Lady Justice Smith in *Albonetti v Wirrall Metropolitan BC* [2008] EWCA Civ 783.

[34]   [2009] EWCA Civ 827, [2010] 1 FLR 707.

[35]   [2010] EWHC 1005 (QB).

to difficulties that had distressed and troubled JA but left him without psychological abnormality. He further commented upon the conflicting aspects of their evidence:

> 'there can be no doubt that these are extremely difficult waters. The debate as to the proper degree of emphasis to place upon genetic inheritance, the effect of early childhood and personality development in the childhood environment, the contribution of rather later adverse experiences of an extreme kind, undergone whilst yet in early life, are questions which can never be solved in a case such as this. In my judgment, one is on surer ground in concluding that all of these components may have a major effect; that effect may vary greatly from individual to individual and that it is difficult to draw any precise conclusions from the scientific literature.'

18.92 The judge concluded that:

> 'In reality JA suffers from the consequences of the mechanisms he adopted to suppress and cope with the accumulated trauma of his young life. His emotional remoteness, his anger, his lack of trust in relationships are as much a consequence of how he dealt with what happened to him as of those experiences themselves ... Although falling short of a formal psychiatric injury, the effects have been marked.'

18.93 In making an award for damages he commented that:

> 'it seems to me the proper approach is to permit the negative psychological effects of an assault to sound in the general award alongside such things as the nature of the event, the immediate impact on the assault victim, and so forth. By definition we are not dealing with the more serious cases in terms of the consequences of assault, an outcome which will depend on the facts of the assault, the psychological resilience of the victim, the other factors affecting the victim for better or worse, and so forth. Therefore the approach I adopt in a case where no discrete psychiatric disorder is demonstrated, is to consider the adverse psychiatric consequences as part of the picture to be borne in mind when considering the level of damages at large for the assault itself.'

18.94 HHJ Hampton in *ABB and Others v MK Council*[36] commented that the assessment of damages for sexual abuse always presented its own particular difficulties. In many cases those who suffer adverse effects as a result of sexual abuse will have other unconnected difficulties in their lives. She stressed that they are not to be denied compensation simply because they do not have any diagnosed psychiatric illness. They are entitled to compensation for the pain and suffering caused by the abuse itself, as well as its consequences. In assessing damages where the local authority was in breach of its duty under s 47 Children Act 1989 she took into account that the claimants would have been likely to suffer difficulties either from the separation of their parents or if they had been cared for outside the family.

---

[36] [2012] 1 FLR 1157.

18.95 For a discussion regarding the limitations in tort when considering compensation for distress falling short of psychiatric injury and the history of case law in attempts to develop this as a separate head of damage see Lord Hoffman in *Wainwright v Home Office*.[37]

Time limits

18.96 Due to the nature of the abuse suffered by children and the circumstances in which they find themselves within the care system it is highly likely that, as a result of secrecy, disinclination to report or disbelief once reported, lack of access to independent advice as well as the limitations that can be expected to naturally flow from the age of the child itself, significant periods of time will elapse between the act or omission leading to a cause of action against an individual or authority and the time at which a decision is made to seek redress.

18.97 Time limits however cannot simply be ignored and it is necessary therefore to have at least a rudimentary understanding of the impact of the Limitation Act 1980.

18.98 Sections 11, 14, 28 and 33 of the Limitation Act 1980 are those most likely to be relevant to claims for personal injury arising from physical, sexual or emotional abuse.

Limitation Act 1980
Section 11: Special Time Limit in Respect of Personal Injury

(1) This section applies to any action for damages for negligence, nuisance or breach of duty (whether the duty exists by virtue of a contract or of provision made by or under a statute or independently of any contract or any such provision) where the damages claimed by the plaintiff for the negligence, nuisance, or breach of duty consist of or include damages in respect of personal injuries to the plaintiff or other person.

(1A) ...

(2) ...

(3) An action to which this section applies shall not be brought after the expiration of the period applicable in accordance with subsection (4) or (5) below.

(4) Except where subsection (5) below applies. The period applicable is three years from –

    (a)   the date on which the cause of action accrued; or
    (b)   the date of knowledge (if later) of the person injured.

(5) If the person injured dies before the expiration of the period mentioned in subsection (4) above the period applicable as respects the cause of action surviving for the benefit of his estate by virtue of Section 1 of the Law Reform (Miscellaneous Provisions) Act 1934 shall be three years from –

---

[37] [2004] 2 AC 406 (HL) paras 36–52 and Lord Foscote at para 60–63.

  (a)   the date of death, or
  (b)   the date of the personal representative's knowledge,

whichever is the later

(6) ....

(7) ....

Section 14 Definition of date of knowledge for purposes of sections 11 and 12

(1) Subject to subsection (1A) below, in sections 11 and 12 of this Act references to a person's date of knowledge are references to the date on which he first had knowledge of the following facts –

  (a)   that the injury in question was significant; and
  (b)   that the injury was attributable in whole or in part to the act or omission which is alleged to constitute negligence, nuisance or breach of duty; and
  (c)   the identity of the defendant, and
  (d)   if it is alleged that the act or omission was that of a person other than the defendant, the identity of that person and the additional facts support the bringing of an action against the defendant

and knowledge that any acts or omissions did or did not, as a matter of law, involve negligence, nuisance or breach of duty is irrelevant.

(1A) ...

(2) For the purposes of this section an injury is significant if the person whose date of knowledge is in question would reasonably have considered it sufficiently serious to justify his instituting proceedings for damages against a defendant who did not dispute liability and was able to satisfy a judgment.

(3) For the purposes of this section a person's knowledge includes knowledge which he might reasonably have been expected to acquire –

  (a)   from facts observable or ascertainable by him, or
  (b)   from acts ascertainable by him with the help of medical or other appropriate expert advice which it is reasonable for him to seek;

but a person shall not be fixed under this subsection with knowledge of a fact ascertainable only with the help of expert advice so long as he has taken all reasonable steps to obtain (and where appropriate to act on) that advice.

18.99   For the purposes of the Limitation Act 'personal injuries' include any disease and any impairment of a person's physical or mental condition.

Section 28 Extension of Limitation Period in case of Disability

(1) Subject to the following provisions of this section, if on the date when any right of action accrued for which a period of limitation is prescribed by this Act, the person to whom it accrued was under a disability, the action may be brought at any time before the expiration of six years from the date when he ceased to be under a disability or died (whichever first occurred) not withstanding that the period of limitation has expired.

(6) If the action is one to which section 11 or 12(2) of this Act applies, subsection (1) above shall have effect as if for the words "six years" there were substituted the words "three years".

'Under a disability' in this context will include children during their minority as well as people lacking capacity (within the meaning of the Mental Capacity Act 2005) to conduct legal proceedings.[38] The time limit therefore for a child complaining of physical, sexual or emotional abuse will not expire until three years from the date that the child attains their majority. This will therefore be when the claimant reaches the age of 21 years.

18.100   For the purpose of the Mental Capacity Act 2005 a person lacks capacity in relation to the matter if at the material time he or she is unable to make a decision for himself in relation to the matter because of an impairment of, or a disturbance in the functioning of, the mind or brain.[39]

18.101   When dealing with this type of claim the Limitation Act, unlike the situation with actions to recover land, does not contain an automatic maximum period after the date of the event that gave rise to the claim, the passage of which would render the action time barred. However this provision should not be read as preventing the action from being brought whilst the child is still a minor or whilst the person still lacks capacity.

18.102   There may in fact be good evidential reasons why the action should be brought at a much earlier stage as the inability to trace documents or witnesses intimately concerned with relevant events may cause substantial prejudice to the defendant.

Section 33 Discretionary exclusion of time limit for actions in respect of personal injuries or death

(1) If it appears to the court that it would be equitable to allow an action to proceed having regard to the degree to which –

   (a)   the provisions of section 11 or 11A or 12 of this Act prejudice the plaintiff or any person whom he represents; and

   (b)   any decision of the court under this subsection would prejudice the defendant or any person whom he represents

the court may direct that those provisions shall not apply to the action, or shall not apply to any specified cause of action to which the action relates

(3) In acting under this section the court shall have regard to all the circumstances of the case and in particular to –

   (a)   the length of, and the reasons for, the delay on the part of the plaintiff

---

[38]   See s 38(2) Limitation Act 1980. Please beware that some publications have continued to print the section with reference to the previous pre MCA 2005 wording of 'of unsound mind' which was amended by s 67 and Sch 6 of the MCA 2005.

[39]   See s 2(1) MCA 2005.

(b)   the extent to which, having regard to the delay, the evidence adduced or likely to be adduced by the plaintiff or the defendant is or is likely to be less cogent than if the action had been brought within the time allowed by section 11 ...

(c)   the conduct of the defendant after the cause of action arose, including the extent (if any) to which he responded to requests reasonably made by the plaintiff for information or inspection for the purpose of ascertaining facts which were or might be relevant to the plaintiff's cause of action against the defendant;

(d)   the duration of any disability of the plaintiff arising after the date of the accrual of the action;

(e)   the extent to which the plaintiff acted promptly and reasonably once he knew whether or not the act or the omission of the defendant, to which the injury was attributable, might be capable at that time of giving rise to an action for damages;

(f)   the steps, if any, taken by the plaintiff to obtain medical or legal or other expert advice and the nature of any such advice he may have received.

18.103   The reference to 'all the circumstances in the case' has been interpreted to include the court being entitled to consider factors such as:

- the ultimate prospects of the claim succeeding;

- the ability to have a fair trial; and

- any lack of prejudice to the defendant,

when weighing all the factors in the balance in the discretionary exercise required before deciding whether to direct that the time limit should not apply.

18.104   The list of specific factors set out in the statute itself should not be taken as fettering the ability of the court to consider additional factors, it is not an exhaustive list.

18.105   The overriding consideration, having proper regard to all the circumstances and the specific factors set out in the section, is whether it would be equitable or inequitable to allow the action to continue.

18.106   The burden will fall upon the claimant to establish that it is equitable for the court to disapply the time limit. It has been referred to as a heavy burden or an exceptional indulgence to a claimant to be granted only where equity between the parties demands it.

18.107   The House of Lords considered the operation of the Limitation Act 1980 in six cases concerning sexual assaults and abuse taking place many years before the commencement of proceedings in *A v Hoare, C v Middlesbrough Council, X and Another v Wandsworth LBC, H v Suffolk County Council, Young v Catholic Care (Diocese of Leeds) and another.*[40]

---

[40]   [2008] 1 AC 844, [2008] 1 FLR 771.

18.108   The issues underlying the case can be drawn from the summary as reported in the family law reports as follows; the six appeals all raised the question whether claims concerning sexual assaults and abuse that had taken place many years before the commencement of proceedings were barred by the Limitation Act 1980. Under s 2 of the 1980 Act the basic limitation period in tort was 6 years from the date on which the cause of action accrued. Under ss 11–14, the limitation period for personal injuries actions was 3 years from either the date on which the cause of action accrued, or from the 'date of knowledge', whichever was later. As defined in s 14 the date of knowledge involved a number of factors, including knowledge that the injury was 'significant'. Under s 14(2) an injury was significant if a person 'would reasonably have considered it sufficiently serious to justify his instituting proceedings for damages' against a defendant who admitted liability and who had sufficient funds to pay. Under s 33 the court had a discretion to extend the limitation period applicable to personal injuries or death. The claimants argued that the earlier case of *Stubbings v Webb*[41] in which the House of Lords held that s 11 did not apply to cases of deliberate assault, including acts of indecent assault, and claims directly based on them were therefore subject to a non-extendable limitation period of 6 years, had been wrongly decided. A Law Commission Review *Limitation of Actions (2001)(Law Com No 270)* had criticised the Lords' decision.

18.109   The House of Lords overruled *Stubbings v Webb* and held that s 11 did apply to a case of deliberate assault, including acts of indecent assault. For personal injury claims for damages arising out of sexual assaults and sexual abuse the relevant limitation period was 3 years from the date of knowledge, with judicial discretion to extend that period when it appeared that it would be equitable to do so.

18.110   This approach would therefore eliminate the anomaly that had allowed late claims to be brought against employers of those committing sexual abuse on proof of systematic negligence in failing to prevent the abuse but not on the more obvious and direct ground of vicarious liability for the abuse itself.[42]

18.111   Interpreting the test in s 14(2) as to whether an injury was significant they held that this was an entirely impersonal standard. You ask what the claimant knew about the injury he or she had suffered, you add any knowledge about the injury which may be imputed to him under s 14(3) and you then ask whether a reasonable person with that knowledge would have considered the injury sufficiently serious to justify instituting proceedings for damages against a defendant who did not dispute liability and was able to satisfy a judgment.

---

[41]   [1993] AC 498, [1993] 1 FLR 714.

[42]   Also the type of anomaly identified by Lord Hoffman and illustrated in *S v W (Child Abuse) Damages* [1995] 1 FLR where a claim by a child against a father as an intentional perpetrator of sexual abuse 10 years after the last act of abuse was struck out but the claim against the mother for negligent failure to protect the child against him fell under s 11 and the discretion was operated to allow the claim against the mother to continue.

The intelligence of the individual claimant was not relevant nor was the effect of the injuries on what he or she could reasonably be expected to do.

18.112 The question whether the actual claimant, having regard to his psychological state, could reasonably have been expected to institute proceedings was, however, to be taken into account by the court when considering whether to exercise the discretion to extend the limitation period under s 33 of the Act, not when calculating the date of knowledge by reference to s 14(2).

18.113 The inhibiting effect of sexual abuse upon a victim's preparedness to bring proceedings would therefore fall to be considered under s 33 rather than s 14(2).

18.114 The House reiterated that the discretion under s 33 was unfettered. Lord Hoffman and Lord Brown, however, drew attention to the sort of considerations that ought to be clearly in mind in sexual abuse cases particularly as the combined effects of the *Lister* case and the departure from *Stubbings* were anticipated to result in a substantially greater number of allegations being made may years after the abuse complained of.

18.115 These included:

- whether the complainant was for practical purposes disabled from commencing proceedings by the psychological injuries which he or she had suffered;

- when the complaint was first made and with what effect;

- whether the complaint had been made and recorded or the accused had been convicted of the abuse complained;

- whether the complaint had come out of the blue with no apparent support for it (other than perhaps that the alleged abuser has been accused or even convicted of similar abuse in the past);

- that not everyone who brings a late claim for damages for sexual abuse, however genuine the complaint may in fact be, can reasonably expect the court to exercise the s 33 discretion in his favour.

18.116 They concluded that a fair trial (which must include a fair opportunity for the defendant to investigate the allegations) was in many cases likely to be found quite simply impossible after a long delay.

18.117 What follows is a summary of recent examples of the Court putting such principles into practice to give the reader a flavour of the problems they may face and principles they may need to apply.

Albonetti v Wirral Metropolitan Borough Council[43]

18.118   The claimant had suffered sexual abuse, including anal rape, at the age of 15 while living in a children's home operated by the local authority. Proceedings were issued when he was 46 years of age. The claim related to negligence not vicarious liability as the alleged abuser was a visitor to the home. Expert evidence indicated that the claimant was suffering from post traumatic stress disorder caused by the abuse and which substantially accounted for previous psychiatric symptoms. For the purposes of s 14 in this case the injury to be considered was the immediate effect of the abuse namely the pain distress and humiliation that he experienced at the time. The court concluded that a person who had been raped whether vaginally or anally must know that he or she had suffered not only a grave wrong but also a significant injury thus the time began to run from the date of the claimant's majority and ran out in 1976. The issue of whether the court should exercise its discretion under s 33 was remitted for determination by the judge.

Albonetti v Wirral Metropolitan Borough Council[44]

18.119   When the s 33 discretion came to be considered in this case the court determined that it would not be appropriate to exercise its discretion to disapply the limitation period. The very great delay of 40 years was decisive. The alleged abuser had died many years before, he had not been convicted of the abuse and had not had any similar claims made against him, the house mother who ran the home at the relevant time had also died, there had been no complaint made by the complainant at the time of the alleged abuse and the claim had come out of the blue. The fact that the claim was for negligence rather than vicarious liability was regarded as important. The court also relied upon the fact that it would be of significant difficulty for the parties to adduce reliable expert evidence regarding the standards of the day, particularly now that more was known about the potential for abuse. A fair trial was simply impossible after such a long delay even though the reasons for the delay were understandable.

TCD v Harrow Council[45]

18.120   The first local authority placed the claimant in the home of a known sex offender subsequently allowing him and his wife to adopt her. The adoptive father began assaulting the claimant on her 8th birthday and almost three years later pleaded guilty of indecent assault on her. Following probation he was allowed to return to the family home. The adoptive parents separated and the father established a new home where the claimant was allowed by the second authority to spend time on access visits. 12 months later she moved to live with him in the third local authority area. He was granted custody. He began abusing the claimant again immediately after the move raping her on a number

---

43   [2008] EWCA Civ 783.
44   [2009] EWHC 832 (QB).
45   Full title *TCD v Harrow Council, Worcestershire County Council and Birmingham City Council* [2008] EWHC 3048 (QB), [2009] 1 FLR 719.

of occasions. After 2½ years of the abuse the claimant reported the matter to the authorities. The adoptive father was convicted of rape. The claimant gave evidence at the trial and the court criticised social services regarding their shortcomings in discharging their responsibilities towards the child. A CICA award was made. No claim was issued against the local authorities until the claimant was 37. The local authorities argued that her claims for remedies against them in respect of the child abuse suffered when she was aged 8 to 14 years should be struck out for being time barred.

18.121 The High Court struck out all three claims refusing to exercise its discretion under s 33. The court held that the claimant had been fixed with knowledge of relevant facts for the purposes of s 14 from the time of attaining her majority (she had known that the local authorities were aware of the father's conviction for her indecent assault and therefore knew enough to make it reasonable for her to begin to investigate whether or not she had a claim against any of the authorities).

18.122 Although the s 33 discretion was unfettered and was to be addressed in the light of all the individual circumstances of the case, the court should never lose sight of the public policy considerations underlying the legislative regime governing limitation periods. Public authorities, as well as commercial entities and individuals, should not remain exposed indefinitely to the threat of litigation based upon historical allegations. Fairness required a balancing of all relevant factors and their interests had to be taken into account.

18.123 There was a public interest in certainty and finality, and such considerations must not be lightly discounted, especially not on the basis of sympathy for an individual litigant.

NXS v Camden LBC[46]

18.124 Primary limitation expired on 21st birthday in 1996. Letter of claim 2005, initial claim form 2007 (allowed to lapse), active claim issued 2008 11½ years after expiration of primary limitation period. Events complained of included failure to remove into care between birth in 1975 and 1989 resulting in failure to protect from physical and sexual abuse and emotional neglect. Some 32 years had passed from the beginning of the abuse. Psychiatric expert evidence concluded that the claimant suffers from an emotionally unstable. personality disorder and dependency on drugs to which the physical and emotional abuse contributed. At various stages the claimant requested her records from the local authority and their failure to respond to those requests was a relevant factor for consideration under s 33 of the Limitation Act 1980 as their conduct made a significant contribution to the delays. Damages were granted in the agreed sum of £60,000.00.

---

[46] [2010] 1 FLR 100.

AB v Nugent Care Society[47]

18.125 The House of Lords decision in *A v Hoare* was, critically, to transfer the relevance of the question whether the actual claimant could reasonably have been expected to institute proceedings, taking into account his psychological state in consequence of the injury, from the enquiry whether the claimant had sufficient knowledge for the purposes of s 14 of the Limitation Act to the question whether the court should exercise its discretion to extend time under s 33.

18.126 The approach to the exercise of s 33 discretion set out in the *Bryn Alyn*[48] case remained valid, subject to appropriate amendment in the light of *A v Hoare*. The most significant amendment required was that in exercising the discretion the judge was now to give due weight to evidence that the claimant had been, for practical purposes, disabled from commencing proceedings by the psychological injuries

18.127

(i)   In brief the general guidance given by the Court of Appeal in *Bryn Alyn* was to the effect that in considering the discretionary exercise under s 33 the burden of showing that it would be equitable to disapply the limitation period lies on the claimant and it is a heavy burden, an exceptional indulgence to a claimant, to be granted only where equity between the parties demands it. Commenting on this starting point in *AB v Nugent* Lord Clarke indicated that it was only exceptional for the reason that but for the exercise of the discretion the claim would be time barred.

(ii)   Depending on the issues and the nature of the evidence going to them, the longer the delay the more likely, and the greater, the prejudice to the defendant.

(iii) A judge should not reach a decision effectively concluding the matter on the strength of any one of the circumstances specified in s 33(3) or on one of any other circumstances relevant to his decision, or without regard to all the issues in the case. He should conduct the balancing exercise at the end of his analysis of all the relevant circumstances and with regard to all the issues taking them all into account.

(iv)   If the issues under s 33 and the substantive issues in the case are being determined at the same hearing the judge should take care not to determine the substantive issues before determining the issue of limitation and in particular the effect of delay on the cogency of the evidence. Lord Clarke in *AB v Nugent* entirely agreed that to do otherwise would be to put the cart before the horse.

---

[47]   *AB v Nugent Care Society; GR v Wirral MBC* [2009] EWCA Civ 827, [2010] 1 FLR 707.
[48]   *KR and Others v Bryn Alyn Community Holdings Ltd & Another* [2003] EWCA Civ 85, [2003] 1 FLR 1203.

(v) Where a judge has assessed the likely cogency of the available evidence he should keep in mind in balancing the respective prejudice to the parties that the more cogent the claimant's case the greater the prejudice to the defendant of depriving him of the benefit of the limitation period. What is of paramount importance was not the loss of the limitation defence however but the effect of the delay on the defendant's ability to defend.

AB, JA, JPM and RM v Nugent Care Society[49]

18.128 The claimants had allegedly suffered abuse in children's homes run by the defendants in the 1960s and 1970s. Claims for damages were issued over 20 years later. On the question of whether the s 33 discretion should be exercised to allow JA's claim to proceed out of time some case report summaries indicate that the court concluded that some real significance had to be attached to the specific factor arising in sexual abuse cases that the tort itself had the tendency to inhibit the victim from complaining, reporting or suing. The text of the transcript details the expert evidence from both sides agreeing that the claimant had been:

> 'very reluctant to make a claim although he had knowledge that he had been harmed from the time of the alleged abuse onwards. However we agree that survivors of sexual abuse often account for their reluctance to complain in terms of the inherent shame in being sexually abused. This is particularly true for men and for those who find it hard to trust. This dynamic is well described in research literature in this area.'

18.129 In considering the s 33 factors Mr Justice Irwin stated:

> 'in my view this is a classic case where the nature and impact of the abuse has itself contributed to the delay. To adapt slightly the language of Lord Hoffman in *A-v Hoare* and others ...this is a case where for practical purposes, the claimant was disabled from commencing proceedings by the psychological consequences of the abuse he suffered.'

18.130 It should be noted that a debate exists as to whether it is appropriate for issues of limitation to be determined as a preliminary issue or whether it should form part of the substantive hearing.[50]

Other family examples of nature of claims possible

18.131 Examples where a duty of care has been asserted and the court has accepted either that such a duty exists or that at least it is arguable on the particular facts of the case in question include the following:

---

[49] [2010] EWHC 1005 (QB).
[50] See for example the discussions in the *Bryn Alyn and Nugent* cases, *T v Archbishop and Others* [2008] EWHC 3531 (QB), *Raggett v Society of Jesus Trust and Preston Catholic College Governors* [2010] EWCA Civ 1002.

• Failure to provide adoptive parents with relevant information about the children they were proposing to adopt[51] but in the circumstances of this case the Court of Appeal decided not to overturn the first instance judge's determination on liability but upheld it on entirely different grounds, those being that they saw no difficulty in finding a duty of care existed to communicate to prospective adopters that information which the adoption agency has decided they should have and which had not in fact been communicated as a result of administrative failures of the sort that commonly and regularly ground liability in negligence. The Court of Appeal however determined that it is not fair, just and reasonable to impose upon the professionals involved in compiling reports or adoption agencies a duty of care towards prospective adopters. Although they would not rule out a duty of care to the child (an issue which did not arise in the case before them).[52]

• Breach of a duty of care to children known to the local authority as having suffered sexual abuse from their father by a failure to investigate the history of the family to a standard that would be regarded as reasonable by a responsible body of social work opinion and a failure to make appropriate enquiries into the mother's circumstances and her ability to protect her children from him.[53] The local authority had become aware of the abuse some two years after it started but the father was allowed to reunite with the family after a brief period of separation and counselling. The abuse continued in total for a further 13 years. One child was awarded a total of £92,500 (for general damages, disadvantage in the labour market, and the costs of future cognitive analytic therapy), a second child was awarded £155,487 (for general damages, disadvantage in the labour market, past loss of earnings, past travel costs, future loss of earnings, future psychiatric counselling and other medical costs plus travel for the medical treatment), a third child received at total of £12,000 and the fourth child £59,476 (for general damages and future psychodynamic therapy or cognitive behavioural therapy).

• From same case: in considering quantum of general and special damages the family circumstances of the children had to be taken into account. The doctors who had reported on quantum also took into account the factors that had the children been separated from their family they inevitably would have suffered emotional difficulties and had their father

---

[51] *A v Essex County Council* [2003] EWCA Civ 1848, [2004] 1 FLR 749.

[52] The case considered the then relevant Adoption Agency Regulations 1983, regs 6 and 12 which contained the provisions under which information could be disclosed to prospective adopters. These provisions have been replaced in effect by reg 31 of the Adoption Agency Regulations 2005 (SI 2005/389) which appear provide a greater degree of disclosure. It remains to be seen whether the rejection of the duty of care to prospective adopters will survive the subsequent human rights approaches to the lack of an effective remedy and whether ss 6 and 7 HRA 1998 remedies will be regarded as sufficient remedies rather than the need to expand the extent of the duty of care in negligence.

[53] *ABB, BBB, CBB and DBB v Milton Keynes Council* [2011] EWHC 2745 (QB).

been removed from the home they would have been in the care of a single mother who had difficulty in coping.

SECTION 3 – CIVIL CLAIMS – PROCEDURE

18.132 Claims for negligence and personal injury will be governed by the Civil Procedure Rules 1998.

18.133 They will therefore be subject to the 'overriding objective'[54] of enabling the court to deal with cases justly. This includes:

- ensuring that the parties are on an equal footing;

- saving expense;

- dealing with the case in ways which are proportionate:

  - to the amount of money involved;
  - to the importance of the case;
  - to the complexity of the issues; and
  - to the financial position of each party;

- ensuring that it is dealt with expeditiously and fairly; and

- allotting to the case an appropriate share of the court's resources whilst ensuring that the parties are on an equal footing.[55]

18.134 It is likely that most claims of the nature discussed above will fall under Part 7 and its companion Part 16. Care must be taken to ensure that the contents of the relevant Practice Directions are taken into account these include CPR 1998, PD7A and PD16. Close attention should be paid however to Pre-Action Protocols (such as the one governing personal injury claims).

18.135 Where the claim is likely to fall within the jurisdiction of the High Court attention should also be paid to the Queens Bench Guide.

18.136 Courts will be minded to treat the standards set out in pre-action protocols as the normal reasonable approach to pre-action conduct. Once proceedings are issued the court will consider whether any non compliance with a protocol should result in adverse consequences. Although the level of damages sought in the types of cases that we are considering may be higher than that envisaged for the personal injury protocol it should be noted that in such higher value claims the court still expects the spirit of the protocol to be

---

[54] CPR 1998, r 1.1.
[55] Family lawyers should be familiar with these phrases in any event as a result of their incorporation (with only slight differences) into the Family Procedure Rules 2010 (SI 2010/2955).

followed. Therefore matters covered by the protocol such as letters before action, exchanging of information and documents and agreeing experts should be followed.

18.137   As is the norm in many court proceedings parties are urged to consider whether some form of alternative dispute resolution procedure would be more suitable than litigation. This may include simple discussion and negotiation, early neutral evaluation or mediation.

18.138   The pre-action protocol, sample letter of claim[56] and standard disclosure lists for personal injury claims can be found on the court website at www.justice.gov.uk, as can the Queen's Bench Guide. The relevant claim form is N1. The relevant documents are therefore the claim form, particulars of claim and statements of case.

18.139   The claim form can contain the particulars of claim, can have the particulars of claim accompanying it or can be followed by the particulars of claim. If the particulars of claim are to follow they will need to be served within 14 days of the service of the claim form and the claim form must contain a statement to that effect.[57]

18.140   Amongst other requirements the claim form must:[58]

- Contain a concise statement of the nature of the claim (eg the tortious act, breach of duty or other civil wrong complained of).

- Specify the remedy sought.

- If including a claim for money contain a statement of value[59] (including whether the claimant expects to recover not more than £5,000; more than £5,000 but not more than £25,000; or more than £25,000 or that the claimant cannot say how much is likely to be recovered. In addition in person injury claims the amount expected to be recovered as general damages for pain, suffering and loss of amenity being either not more than £1,000 or more than £1,000.)

- Contain such other matters as may be set out in a practice direction.

- If the claimant is claiming in a representative capacity state what that capacity is.

- Be verified by a statement of truth.[60]

---

[56]   See Part 4 (resources section) for pre-action protocol, sample letter of claim.
[57]   CPR 1998, rr 7.4 and 16.2(2).
[58]   CPR 1998, r 16.2.
[59]   CPR 1998, r 16.3.
[60]   CPR 1998, Pt 22.

18.141 The particulars of claim, amongst other things, must include:[61]

- A concise statement of the facts on which the claimant relies.

- Whether interest is claimed.

- Whether aggravated or exemplary damages are claimed and the grounds for claiming them.

- Whether provisional damages are claimed and the grounds for claiming them.

- Such other matters as may be set out in a practice direction.

For personal injury claims the Practice Direction[62] sets out additional information that must be included in the particulars of claim. These include the claimant's date of birth and brief details of the claimant's personal injuries.

18.142 The claimant must attach to the particulars of claim a schedule of details of any past and future losses which he or she claims; and where the claimant is relying on the evidence of a medical practitioner a report from a medical practitioner about the personal injuries he or she alleges in his claim must be attached to or served with the particulars of claim.

18.143 Additionally the Practice Direction sets out in para 8 specific matters which must be included in the particulars of claim if relied upon which include matters such as the type of any conviction relied upon as evidence under s 11 of the Civil Evidence Act 1968 and the issue in the claim to which it relates

18.144 Defendants will need to be aware of the provisions of Part 9, 10, 14, 15 and 16 for the filing of defences, admissions and acknowledgments of service. Once again reference must also be made to the associated practice directions.

18.145 Acknowledgements of service will need to be filed 14 days after the service of the claim form unless the claim form states that the particulars of claim are to follow, in which case it will need to be served 14 days after the service of the particulars of claim.[63]

18.146 A defence will need to be filed if the defendant wishes to defend all or part of the claim.[64]

18.147 The general rule is that the period for filing the defence is 14 days after service of the particulars of claim unless the defendant has filed an

---

[61] CPR 1998, r 16.4.
[62] CPR 1998, PD16, para 7.
[63] CPR 1998, r 10.3.
[64] CPR 1998, r 15.2.

acknowledgment of service in which case the period for filing the defence is 28 days after service of the particulars of claim.[65]

18.148 In the defence the defendant must state:[66]

- which of the allegations in the particulars of claim he or she denies;

- which allegations he or she is unable to admit or deny but which he or she requires the claimant to prove; and

- which allegations he or she admits.

18.149 Where the defendant denies an allegation he or she must state his or her reasons for doing so and set out his or her version of events if different from that of the claimant.[67]

18.150 If a defendant is silent on any allegation but has set out in his defence the nature of his case in relation to which that allegation is relevant he or she will be taken as requiring the claimant to prove that allegation. Otherwise failure to deal with an allegation will result in the defendant being treated as admitting the allegation.[68]

18.151 If there is a dispute as to the claimant's statement of value of the claim he or she must state why he or she disputes it and if he is able give his or her own value of the claim.[69]

18.152 The additional requirements imposed by the practice direction[70] for personal injury claims where the claimant has attached a medical report relating to the alleged injuries include the need for the defendant to state in the defence whether he or she agrees, disputes, neither agrees nor disputes but has no knowledge of, the matters contained in the medical report. If he or she disputes any part in the medical report he or she should give his reasons for doing so and where he or she has obtained his own medical report upon which he or she intends to rely in his defence he or she must attach it to the defence.

18.153 If the claimant has attached a schedule of past and future expenses and losses in connection with a personal injury claim the defendant should include or attach a counter schedule stating which items he or she agrees, disputes or neither agrees nor disputes but has no knowledge of. If he or she disputes any items he or she should supply alternative figures where appropriate.

---

[65]   CPR 1998, r 15.4.
[66]   CPR 1998, r 16.5(1).
[67]   CPR 1998, r 16.5(2).
[68]   CPR 1998, r 16.5(3) and (5).
[69]   CPR 1998, r 16.5(6).
[70]   CPR 1998, PD16, para 12.

18.154 Paragraph 13.1 requires the defendant to give details of the expiry of any relevant limitation period he or she relies upon.

18.155 CPR 1998, PD16 also makes provision in para 13.3 for any party to refer in the statement of case to any point of law on which his claim or his defence is based; to give the name of any witness he or she proposes to call and to attach or serve with the statement of case a copy of any document which he or she considers necessary to his or her claim or defence.

18.156 Specific provisions apply where a party seeks to rely on any provision or right arising under the Human Rights Act 1998 or seeks a remedy available under that Act. This will be set out in detail in the section dealing with human rights claims.[71]

18.157 When considering issuing these sorts of claims for damages careful thought will need to be given to the type of evidence that may be available and necessary. Steps may be required outside of the civil proceedings to seek release of documents private to the care proceedings for use in the civil proceedings.

18.158 It may be necessary to gain access to:

- Social services files or documents or computer records such as:

    - Case conference minutes;
    - LAC reviews;
    - Child protection plans;
    - Section 47 enquiries;
    - Core assessments;
    - Individual social work contact recordings;
    - Referrals to social services from other organisations;

- Medical records.

- Criminal convictions.

- Records held by the police (eg logs regarding domestic violence attendances).

- Fact-finding judgments or other judgments from the care proceedings.

- Serious case reviews.

- Section 37 reports.

- Guardian's reports.

---

[71] See **18.160** et seq in section entitled 'Human Rights'.

18.159 Care must be taken to ensure that confidential documents from the family proceedings are not used improperly or in breach of the Administration of Justice Act 1960, s 12 and the FPR 2010.[72]

SECTION 4 – HUMAN RIGHTS CLAIMS

18.160 As can be seen from above, prior to the introduction of the Human Rights Act 1998 the lack of a remedy for parents and children to hold local authorities to account in damages brought the United Kingdom into conflict with the European Court of Human Rights (ECtHR).

18.161 In order to understand the changes flowing from the introduction of the 1998 Act it will be helpful to consider both the wording of the Act and the individual articles which are most likely to be relevant in the family context.

18.162 The Law Commission and The Scottish Law Commission in October 2000 presented a report entitled *Damages Under the Human Rights Act 1998*.[73] Unusually the purpose of the report was information rather than law reform. In effect the report was requested to carry out:

- a review of the case law of the European Court of Human Rights in relation to the award and level of compensation under Art 41 of the convention;

- in the light of that case law to consider the principles of the Strasbourg jurisprudence which the courts should take into account when determining whether to award damages and the amount of award under s 8 of the Human Rights Act 1998.

It remains a helpful place to start when considering how questions of damages pursuant to the act are likely to be treated.

18.163 As will be seen below the UK domestic courts will need to continue to pay regard to the approach and decisions of the ECtHR when dealing with damages claims. The fact that the European Convention is a living instrument which must be interpreted in the light of present day conditions brings a significant degree of flexibility but with it difficulties of uncertainty and in identifying any strict coherent principles.

---

[72] Particular attention should be paid to FPR 2010, Part 12, Chapter 7, r 12.75 and FPR 2010, PD12G.

[73] Cm4853.

The basic essential provisions

Human Rights Act 1998

18.164

Section 6: Acts of Public Authority

(1) It is unlawful for a pubic authority to act in a way which is incompatible with a Convention right.

(2) Subsection (1) does not apply to an act if –

(a)   as the result of one or more provisions of primary legislation, the authority could not have acted differently; or

(b)   in the case of one or more provisions of, or made under, primary legislation which cannot be read or given effect in a way which is compatible with the Convention rights, the authority was acting so as to give effect to or enforce those provisions.

(3) In this section "public authority' includes –

(a)   a court or tribunal, and

(b)   any person certain of whose functions are functions of a public nature,

but does not include either House of Parliament or a person exercising functions in connection with proceedings in Parliament.

(4) (*repealed*)

(5) "An Act" includes a failure to act but does not include a failure to –

(a)   introduce in, or lay before, Parliament a proposal for legislation; or

(b)   make any primary legislation or remedial order.

Section 7: Proceedings

(1) A person who claims that a local authority has acted (or proposes to act) in a way which is made unlawful by section 6(1) may –

(a)   bring proceedings against the authority under this act in the appropriate court or tribunal

(b)   rely on the Convention right or rights concerned in any legal proceedings,

but only if he is (or would be) a victim of the unlawful act.

(2) In subsection (1)(a) "appropriate court or tribunal" means any such court or tribunal as may be determined in accordance with rules; and proceedings against an authority include a counterclaim or similar proceeding.

(3) If the proceedings are brought on an application for judicial review, the applicant is to be taken to have sufficient interest in relation to the unlawful act only if he is or would be a victim of that act.

(4) If the proceedings are made by way of a petition for judicial review in Scotland, the applicant shall be taken to have title and interest to sue in relation to the unlawful act only if he is, or would be a victim of that act.

(5) Proceedings under subsection 1(a) must be brought before the end of –

(a)   the period of one year beginning with the date on which the act complained of took place; or

(b)   such longer period as the court or tribunal considers equitable having regard to all the circumstances

but that is subject to any rule imposing a stricter time limit in relation to the procedure in question.

(6) In subsection 1(b) "legal proceedings" includes –

(a)   proceedings brought by or at the instigation of a public authority

(b)   an appeal against the decision of a court or tribunal.

(7) For the purposes of this section, a person is a victim of an unlawful act only if he would be a victim for the purposes of Article 34 of the Convention if proceedings were brought in the European Court of Human Rights in respect of that act.

[*Note: subsections 8–13 are not reproduced here*]

Section 8: Judicial Remedies

(1) In relation to any act (or proposed act) of a public authority which the court finds is (or would be) unlawful, it may grant such relief or remedy, or make such order, within its powers as it considers just and appropriate.

(2) But damages may be awarded only by a court which has power to award damages, or to order the payment of compensation, in civil proceedings.

(3) No award of damages is to be made unless, taking account of all the circumstances of the case, including –

(a)   any other relief or remedy granted, or order made, in relation to the act in question (by that or any other court), and

(b)   the consequences of any decision (of that or any other court) in respect of that act,

the court is satisfied that the award is necessary to afford just satisfaction to the person in whose favour it is made.

(4) In determining –

(a)   whether to award damages, or

(b)   the amount of an award,

the court must take into account the principles applied by the European Court of Human Rights in relation to the award of compensation under Article 41 of the Convention.

[*Note: subsections 5 and 6 are not reproduced here*]

Section 9: Judicial Acts

(1) Proceedings under section 7(1)(a) in respect of a judicial act may be brought only –

(a)   by exercising a right of appeal;

(b)   on an application (in Scotland a petition) for judicial review; or

(c)   in such other forum as may be prescribed by rules.

(2) That does not affect any rule of law which prevents a court from being the subject of judicial review.

(3) In proceedings under this Act in respect of a judicial act done in good faith, damages may not be awarded otherwise than to compensate a person the extent required by Article 5(5) of the Convention.

(4) An award of damages permitted by subsection (3) is to be made against the Crown; but no award may be made unless the appropriate person, if not a party to the proceedings, is joined.

[Note: subsection 5 is not reproduced here]

Section 11: Other Rights

A person's reliance on a Convention right does not restrict –

    (a)   any other right or freedom conferred on him by or under any law having effect in any part of the United Kingdom; or

    (b)   his right to make any claim or bring any proceedings which he could make or bring apart from sections 7 to 9.

Schedule 1: The Articles

18.165 (For the purposes of this chapter only those Articles most often referred to in children's care cases are reproduced here, being Arts 3, 6, 8, but practitioners should also be aware of the contents of Art 2[74] – right to life, Art 5 – right to liberty and Art 10 – freedom of speech as a minimum.)

Article 3: Prohibition of Torture

No one shall be subjected to torture or to inhuman or degrading treatment or punishment.

Article 6: Right to Fair Trial

1 In the determination of his civil rights and obligations or of any criminal charge against him, everyone is entitled to a fair and public hearing within a reasonable time by an independent and impartial tribunal established by law. Judgment shall be pronounced publicly but the press and the public may be excluded from all or part of the trial in the interests of morals, public order or national security in a democratic society, where the interests of juveniles or the protection of the private life of the parties so require, or to the extent strictly necessary in the opinion of the court in special circumstances where publicity would prejudice the interests of justice.

[Note: the remaining provisions of this article which relate to criminal offences are not reproduced here]

Article 8 – Right to Respect for Private and Family Life

1 Everyone has the right to respect for his private and family life, his home and his correspondence.

---

[74]   Please note that Art 2 of the Convention is considered in chapter 10.

2 There shall be no interference by a public authority with the exercise of this right except such as is in accordance with the law and is necessary in a democratic society in the interests of national security, public safety or the economic well-being of the country, for the prevention of disorder or crime, for the protection of health or morals, or for the protection of the rights and freedoms of others.

In addition regard must be had to the following Convention Articles which do not form part of the HRA 1998 Schedules:

Article 13: Effective Remedy

Everyone whose rights and freedoms as set forth in this Convention are violated shall have an effective remedy before a national authority notwithstanding that the violation has been committed by persons acting in an official capacity.

Article 41: Just Satisfaction

If the Court finds that there has been a violation of the Convention or the protocols thereto, and if the law of the High Contracting Party allows only partial reparation to be made, the Court shall, if necessary afford just satisfaction to the injured party.

18.166 Note: although omitted from the HRA 1998, Art 13 is relevant in understanding the case law. The Law Commission suggested that it was omitted as the HRA 1998 was designed to give effect to Art 13 by establishing a scheme under which the convention rights can be raised and provides an exhaustive code of remedies for those whose convention rights have been violated. Article 41 is also an essential element in understanding the European Court decisions relating to awards of damages and for interpreting s 8 of the HRA 1998.

18.167 For most family law practitioners the concept of damages is fairly alien to their normal daily work-load. The Law Commission Report is a helpful place to start in grappling with the likely issues and approach, although clearly care must be taken to ensure that more recent decisions both in this country and in Europe over the past 12 years are considered.

18.168 Lord Justice Wilson in *Re C (Breach of Human Rights Damages)*[75] quoting Hedley J highlighted the change in approach that would be needed for family practitioners thus:

"'I do not think" said Hedley J "that the concept of damages sits easily with the welfare jurisdiction of family law". The instincts of most family lawyers will be likewise, but by his thorough and energetic submission, Mr Tolson has persuaded me that as a result of the Human Rights Act, such instincts are misplaced.'

---

[75] [2007] 1 FLR 1957.

Thumb-nail sketch as to minimum requirements to establish breach

Article 2

18.169 Article 2 imposes a negative obligation on the State not to refrain from the intentional and unlawful taking of life.

18.170 It also imposes a positive obligation to protect life which is unqualified and self-evidently fundamental. To establish a breach it will be necessary to show that:

> 'the authorities knew, or ought to have known, at the time of the existence of a real and immediate risk to the life of an identified individual or individuals from the criminal acts of a third party and that they had failed to take measures within the scope of their powers which, judged reasonably might have been expected to avoid that risk.'[76]

18.171 For greater detail as to the application and interpretation of these duties and examples of cases relating to the child care context rather than associated with criminal activities and the duty of the police please refer to **10.97** et seq.

Article 3

18.172 Article 3 (like Art 2 but unlike Art 8) is cast in absolute terms there is no reference to any exception or proviso.

18.173 It imposes the negative obligation on public bodies to refrain from inflicting serious harm on persons but also requires them to take reasonable measures designed to ensure that individuals are not subjected to torture or inhuman and degrading treatment or punishment, including where such treatment is administered by private individuals.

18.174 The ill-treatment must attain a minimum level of severity if it is to fall within the scope of Art 3.

18.175 The assessment of this minimum is relative; it depends on all the circumstances of the case and will include consideration of the nature and context of the treatment, its duration, its physical and mental effects and in some instances, the sex, age and state of health of the victim.[77] It is likely to need an element of actual bodily injury or intense physical or mental suffering.

---

[76] See the approach of the ECtHR in *Osman v the UK* 29 EHRR 245 and *Van Colle v Chief Constable of the Hertfordshire Police* Court of Appeal decision at [2007] 1 WLR 1821 and House of Lords decision at [2009] 1 AC 225.

[77] *R (Bernard) v London Borough of Enfield* [2002] EWHC 2282 and *A v UK* [1998] 27 EHRR 611.

18.176 In order to amount to degrading treatment the court will need to consider whether the object is to humiliate and debase the person concerned but the absence of such intent cannot rule out finding a violation of Art 3.

18.177 Where treatment humiliates or debases an individual showing lack of respect for human dignity or arouses feelings of fear, anguish or inferiority capable of breaking an individual's moral and physical resistance it may be characterised as degrading.[78]

18.178 Article 3 cannot be relied upon where the distress and anguish, however deep, inevitably results from measures which are otherwise compatible with the convention unless there is a special element which causes the suffering to go beyond that inherent in their implementation.

18.179 Child protection measures will generally cause parents distress and on occasion humiliation particularly where they are suspected in some way of harming their child or otherwise failing in their parental responsibilities. Given the responsibility of the authorities under Art 3 to protect children from serious abuse, whether mental or physical, it would be contradictory to hold that authorities were automatically liable to parents under this provision whenever they erred, reasonably or otherwise, in the execution of their duties.[79]

18.180 Again Art 3 contains the positive obligation on authorities (as well as the negative obligation):

- To provide protection against a risk of treatment falling within Art 3 of which it knew or ought to have known about.

- The level of protection which it was required to provide was that which was reasonably available.

- It need not afford a guarantee against the danger but had to be reasonable, as a matter of practicality, common sense and humanity, taking into account the relevant policy decisions.

- Measures to be taken are those which afford a real prospect of avoiding the danger.

- The extent of risk will inform the extent to which protection should be provided.[80]

---

[78] *Pretty v UK* [2002] 35 EHRR 1, para 52.
[79] *MAK & RK v UK* (Applications Nos 45901/05 and 40146/06) [2010] 2 FLR 451, EctHR (final judgment 23/06/10).
[80] See eg *R (Mehmet Gezer) v SSHD* [2003] EWHC 860 (Admin).

Article 6

18.181 In principle the European Court will award monetary compensation under Art 41:

- Only where it is satisfied that the loss or damage complained of was actually caused by the violation it has found.

- It has repeatedly stressed that it will not speculate on what the outcome of proceedings would have been but for the violation.

- It has, however, on occasion been willing in appropriate cases to make an award if of the opinion that the applicant has been deprived of a real chance of a better outcome.[81]

- In the absence of a clear causal connection the standard response has been to treat the finding of violation without more as just satisfaction.

- It will require a case by case judgment.

- The court can make an award for anxiety and frustration (however described) if attributable to the violation. For very many people involvement in legal proceedings is bound to cause anxiety irrespective of any Article 6 breach and no award will be made in such cases but an award may be made if a person suffered anxiety and frustration attributable to the specific Art 6 breach.

- Sums awarded by European Court in this respect have been modest.

Article 8[82]

18.182 The main thrust of this provision is to prevent arbitrary interference by public authorities with an individual's private and family life.

18.183 The Article may also require public authorities to take positive measures to secure respect for private or family life.

18.184 Private life can include a person's physical and psychological integrity. It can cover the development of the personality of each individual in his relationships with other human beings. Family life includes the right to live together so that family relations can develop naturally and members of a family can enjoy one another's company.

---

[81]   *R (Greenfield) v Home Secretary* [2005] 1 WLR 673, HL.
[82]   The explanatory passages here are taken from a mixture of, *Anufrijeva v Southwark LBC* [2004] QB 1124; *R (Bernard) v London Borough of Enfield* [2002] EWHC 2282; *Markcx v Belgium* [1979] 2 EHRR 330; *Botta v Italy* [1998] 26 EHRR 241; Clayton and Tomlinson's *Law of Human Rights*.

18.185   Article 8 can, in appropriate circumstances, include the provision of welfare support (particularly where the welfare of children is at stake) if necessary to enable family life to continue.

18.186   There will be both negative and positive elements to the obligations under the Article. It should be remembered that the rights under Art 8 are qualified. The provisions of Art 8(2) mean that an interference which is both lawful and necessary in the interests of the protection of health or morals or the protection of rights and freedoms of others will not amount to a breach.[83]

18.187   Care must be taken that even in these circumstances the interference is proportionate to the risk anticipated.

Guidance on the approach to the specific remedy of damages

18.188   Damages through the domestic court will only be available as a remedy in relation to acts or omissions after the HRA 1998 came into force in October 2000. In many applications for judicial review there are also applications based on breach of human rights and the award of damages within those proceedings is often for this element.

18.189   Depending on the particular breach alleged the heads of damages can include:

- Pecuniary loss.

- Non-Pecuniary loss – which may itself include compensation for:

    - Pain.
    - Suffering.
    - Psychological harm.
    - Distress.
    - Frustration.
    - Inconvenience.
    - Humiliation.
    - Anxiety.
    - Loss of reputation.
    - Loss of relationship, love and companionship.

- Costs and expenses.

However an important concept is that an award will only be made if it is *'necessary to afford just satisfaction'*.[84]

---

[83]   Article 8(2) also includes reference to other interests such as national security etc.
[84]   Section 8 (3), 8(4) HRA 1998 and Art 41 of the Convention.

18.190 If the granting of another remedy by the court (or any other court) in relation to the breach or if the consequences of the court's decision (or that of any other court) is sufficient to achieve just satisfaction then damages should not be awarded. This encompasses the approach that the mere finding that there has been a violation of rights under the convention may itself amount to a remedy offering just satisfaction for the claimant.

18.191 In the light of this aspect of human rights damages local authorities may be well advised to heed the views of Sullivan J:[85]

> 'In my experience in this court, dealing with a wide range of complaints against public authorities, most citizens who have suffered as a result of some bureaucratic error are not motivated, or at least not primarily motivated by a desire for monetary compensation . They institute proceedings because they feel outraged by what they see as an injustice and want "them", the faceless persons in an apparently insensitive, unresponsive and impenetrable bureaucratic labyrinth, to acknowledge that something has gone wrong, to provide them with an explanation, an apology, an assurance that steps have been taken (so far as possible in an imperfect world) that the same mistake will not happen again. This assurance will at least give them the satisfaction of knowing that they have not suffered in vain.
>
> If a public body takes all of those steps reasonably promptly, once the problem had been drawn to its attention, then it may well be the case that nothing more is required by way of monetary compensation in order to afford 'just satisfaction' in very many cases.'

Understanding general principles relating to the award of damages

18.192 For a helpful summary of general principles see *Anufrijeva v Southwark LBC*.[86] This case gave the Court of Appeal its first opportunity to consider in detail the power of the courts to award damages under the HRA 1998 but must be read in the light of *R (Greenfield) v Secretary of State for the Home Department*.[87]

18.193 The *Anufrijeva* case related to three appeals having common features:

- All involved a claimant or claimants who came to the UK to seek asylum.

- Each complained of a failure by a public body to comply with a public law duty imposed by statute under which they claimed they were entitled to receive benefits.

- Each complained that the failure was due to maladministration.

---

[85] *R (Bernard)* [2002] EWHC 2282 (Admin), paras 39 and 40.
[86] [2003] EWCA Civ 1406, [2004] QB 1124.
[87] [2005] 1 WLR 673; see also **18.205** onwards below for further discussion of the impact of *Greenfield*.

- The maladministration amounted to a breach of the claimants' Art 8 rights.

- The allegations related to a failure to take the positive action that was necessary to ensure that their Art 8 rights were respected.

18.194   Lord Woolf CJ identified the key issues for the appeal as follows:

- What is the nature of the Art 8 rights?

- When does a duty arise under Art 8 to take positive action?

- In what circumstances does maladministration constitute breach of Art 8?

- When should damages be awarded?

- On what basis should damages be assessed?

- What procedures should be followed to ensure that the costs of obtaining relief are proportionate to that relief?

18.195   Concentrating on the principles identified with respect to the ability to award, and how to assess, damages the following points should be noted:

- Whereas damages are recoverable as of right in a case of damage caused by a tort the same is not true in the case of a claim brought under HRA 1998 for breach of the convention.[88]

- Reference should also be made to two articles of the convention not included in the Sch 1 to the HRA 1998:[89]

    (i)   Article 13 – which requires everyone whose rights and freedoms are violated to 'have an effective remedy'.
    (ii)   Article 41 – which requires the ECtHR to afford 'just satisfaction' to an injured party if this is not provided by a domestic court.

- Sections 6–8 of the Act together with Arts 13 and 41 establish a code governing the award of damages which has to be applied with due regard to the Strasbourg jurisprudence.[90]

- The code recognises the different role played by damages in human rights litigation and has significant features which distinguish it from the approach to the award of damages in a private law contract or tort action:[91]

---

[88]   Paragraph 50 of the judgment.
[89]   Paragraph 50 of the judgment.
[90]   Paragraph 52 of the judgment.
[91]   Paragraph 55 of the judgment.

(i) the award of damages under the HRA 1998 is confined to the class of unlawful acts of public authorities identified by s 6(1): see s 8(1) and (6);

(ii) the court has a discretion as to whether to make an award (it must be just and appropriate to do so) by contrast to the position in relation to common law claims where there is a right to damages: see s 8(1);

(iii) the award must be necessary to achieve 'just satisfaction'; language that is distinct from the common law approach where a claimant is invariably entitled, so far as money can achieve this, to be restored to the position he or she would have been in if he or she had not suffered the injury of which complaint is made;

(iv) the court is required to take into account in determining whether damages are payable and the amount of damages payable the different principles applied by the ECtHR in awarding compensation;

(v) exemplary damages are not awarded.

- In considering whether to award compensation and if so how much there is a balance to be drawn between the interests of the victim and those of the public as a whole.[92]

18.196 It is possible to identify one of the basic principles that the Court of Human Rights applies as follows:[93]

'The fundamental principle underlying the award of compensation is that the court should achieve 'restituto in integrum' – that is that the applicant should be placed in so far as possible in same position as if his convention rights had not been infringed.'

18.197 However a problem arises in relation to the consequences of breach of a convention right which do not clearly cause significant financial loss and which are not, therefore, capable of being computed in financial terms.

18.198 In considering what principles might be gleaned for these breaches Lord Woolf CJ commented that infringements can involve a variety of treatment of an individual which is objectionable in itself. For example the treatment might give rise to

- distress;

- anxiety;

and in extreme cases;

- psychiatric trauma.

---

92 Paragraph 56 of the judgment.
93 Paragraph 59 of the judgment.

He noted that the primary object of the proceedings will often be to bring the adverse treatment to an end.

18.199   If this is achieved is this enough to constitute 'just satisfaction' or is it necessary to award damages to compensate for the adverse treatment that has occurred? Should damages be awarded for anxiety and distress that has been occasioned by the breach? He identified that it was on these questions that Strasbourg failed to give a consistent or coherent answer.[94]

18.200   Lord Woolf indicated that courts dealing with claims for damages for maladministration should adopt a broad-brush approach, especially at first instance.[95]

18.201   Where no pecuniary loss is involved the question whether the other remedies that have been granted to a successful complainant are sufficient to vindicate the right that has been infringed should be decided without a close examination of the authorities or an extensive and prolonged examination of the facts.

18.202   Where there is an absence of guidance then the principles laid down by the HRA 1998 give great assistance:[96]

(a)   the critical message is that the remedy has to be 'just and appropriate' and 'necessary' to afford 'just satisfaction';

(b)   the approach is an equitable one, both as the reason for awarding damages and as the basis upon which to calculate them;

(c)   in appropriate cases the seriousness or manner of the violation can therefore be taken into account and, as a matter of fairness, result in an element of 'moral damages';

(d)   even though a claimant has suffered some form of non-pecuniary loss it can be insufficient to render an award of damages necessary, for example if the breach results in a mere annoyance and a sense of frustration which is not of such an intensity as would justify an award. It would seem therefore that the frustration and distress must be significant before an award can be justified.

18.203   The Court in *Anufrijeva*, whilst stressing again that the discretionary exercise of deciding whether or not to make an award of compensation under the HRA 1998 is not to be compared to the approach adopted where damages are sought for a breach of an obligation under civil law gave the following

---

[94]   Paragraph 59 of the judgment.
[95]   Paragraph 65 of the judgment.
[96]   Paragraph 66 of the judgment.

guidance on how to assess damages in those HRA 1998 cases where the court has decided it is appropriate to make an award:[97]

- The levels of damages awarded in respect of torts as reflected in the guidelines issued by the Judicial Studies Board, the levels of awards made by the criminal injuries compensation board and by the Parliamentary Ombudsman and Local Government Ombudsman may all provide some rough guidance where the consequences of the infringement of human rights are similar to that being considered in the comparator selected.

- In cases of maladministration (where consequences are not of a type giving rise to compensation under our civil law) the awards of the ombudsman may be the only comparator.

- There are good reasons where breach arises from maladministration, in those cases where an award of damages is appropriate, that the scale of such damages should be modest.

18.204 In order to control and ensure that costs expended in obtaining relief were proportionate to that relief the court gave the following guidance:[98]

(i) The courts should look critically at any attempt to recover damages under HRA 1998 for maladministration by any procedure other than judicial review in the Administrative Court.

(ii) A claim for damages alone cannot be brought by judicial review but in this case the proceedings should still be brought in the Administrative Court by an ordinary claim.

(iii) Before giving permission to apply for judicial review the Administrative Court should require the claimant to explain why it is not more appropriate to use any available internal complaint procedure or proceed by making a complaint to the Parliamentary Commissioner for Administration or Local Government Ombudsman at least in the first instance.

(iv) If there is a legitimate claim for other relief, permission, if appropriate, should be limited to that relief and consideration given to deferring permission for the damages claim, adjourning or staying that claim until use has been made of ADR (eg mediator or ombudsman) or remitting to a district judge or a master if it cannot be dismissed summarily on grounds that in any event an award of damages is not required to achieve just satisfaction.

---

[97] Paragraph 74 of the judgment.
[98] Paragraph 81 of the judgment.

The Court concluded this part of the judgment by noting that there were no doubt other ways in which proportionate resolution of this type of claim for damages could achieved. The court encouraged their use and did not intend for the above suggestions to be prescriptive.[99]

18.205 The House of Lords in *R (Greenfield) v Secretary of State for the Home Department*[100] indicated that although judges in England and Wales were not inflexibly bound by awards of the European Court, they should not aim to be significantly more or less generous than that court might be expected to be if it was willing to make an award at all.

18.206 The House of Lords expressed reservations about the practice of calculating quantum of awards by reference to domestic tortious awards or other guidelines as suggested in *Anufrijeva*[101] indicating that it was not a case on a breach of Art 6 but also stating in wider terms that such an approach should not be followed as:

- The HRA 1998 was not a tortious statute and its objects were different and broader.

- Even where the finding of violation is not judged to afford the applicant just satisfaction that finding will itself be an important part of the applicant's remedy and an important vindication of the right asserted.

- The purpose of incorporating the Convention in domestic law through the 1998 Act was not to give victims better remedies at home than they could recover in Strasbourg but to give them the same remedies without the delay and expense of resort to Strasbourg.

- Section 8(4) requires the court to take into account the principles applied by the European Court under Art 41 not only in determining whether to award damages but also in determining the amount of the award.

- There could be no clearer indication that the courts in this country should look to Strasbourg and not to domestic precedents.

18.207 The House of Lords in *Greenfield* in considering the approach to a breach of Art 6 stated that in deciding whether an award of damages was necessary to afford just satisfaction and, if so how much, the British courts had to look to the jurisprudence of the European Court of Human Rights for guidance. They emphasised that the focus of the convention was the protection of human rights rather than compensation and stressed in relation to Art 6 breaches the approach of the European Court was:

---

[99] It should be noted that the specific suggestions set out when followed in other cases have led to difficulty and may not in fact represent the best or proper course of procedure for specific cases. Care will need to be taken and they should not be regarded as a route map for each case.

[100] [2005] 1 WLR 673.

[101] See Lord Bingham of Cornhill at paras 18 and 19 of the judgment.

- that it would only award monetary compensation where it was satisfied that the loss or damage complained of was actually caused by the violation *although on occasion it had been willing to make an award if of the opinion that the applicant had been deprived of a real chance of a better outcome*;

- that awards for anxiety or frustration attributable to the breach had been made very sparingly and for modest sums;

- that awards were not precisely calculated but were such as were judged to be fair and equitable in the particular case.

18.208   The difference with Art 6 breaches, to breaches of for example Art 3 or 8, is that it did not follow from a finding that the trial process had involved a breach of an Art 6 right that the outcome of the trial process was wrong or would have been otherwise had the breach not occurred.

18.209   They warned that there was a risk of error if Strasbourg decisions given in relation to one article of the convention were read across as applicable to another.

Limitation period

18.210   The limitation period applies to all potential claimants including children and those under a disability. Section 7(5)(a) HRA 1998 states that the proceedings under s 7(1)(a) must be brought before the end of the period of one year beginning with the date upon which the act complained of took place.

18.211   A discretion is given to the court to extend the period to such longer period as the court or tribunal considers equitable having regard to all the circumstances. The time limit and discretion however are subject to any rule imposing a shorter time limit.

18.212   Whilst the discretion to extend cannot be fettered by any strict application of relevant factors issues of proportionality, public interest in proceedings being dealt with expeditiously and those matters of relevance to extension of limitation periods in ordinary civil damages cases are likely to be considered.

Meaning of victim

18.213   It is important for the purposes of s 7 to understand the concept of 'victim' and in order to do so reference has to be had to Art 34 of the Convention.[102]

---

[102]   Art 34 provides 'the court may receive applications from any person, non-governmental organisation or any group of individuals claiming to be the victim of a violation by one of the

18.214 For the purposes of damages in the care context it is probably unnecessary to consider the position of non-governmental organisations, artificial persons such as companies and public bodies as victims.

18.215 We are obviously concerned with the position of individuals such as parents, children and siblings. It is necessary for the claimant to be able to show that he or she is directly affected by the act or omission alleged to breach the convention rights.

18.216 But this is wide enough to include individuals who run the risk of being directly affected and is not limited to those who can demonstrate that they have suffered a detriment as a result of the act or omission.

18.217 Those who run the risk of detriment will need to be able to demonstrate a reasonable likelihood of being directly affected rather than mere suspicion that that would be the outcome.

18.218 In some situations a claimant can establish that they are a victim of a breach of a right affecting another person (usually in close family relationships).

Court having power to award damages

18.219 For stand-alone applications for damages for breach of Human Rights this is unlikely to cause much in the way of difficulty[103] but for cases within, or with a close connection to the public law care system, there remains limited practical guidance as to how this should be interpreted.

18.220 As far back as 2001 Lady Justice Hale (as she then was) expressed the following views about venue in *Re W and B; Re W (Care Plan)*:[104]

> '[73] There is no definition of "the appropriate court or tribunal" for the purposes of s 7(1)(a). The amended practice direction to Part 16 of the Civil Procedures Rules 1998 requires any party who seeks to rely on the Human Rights Act to state that and give certain particulars in his statement of case. A claim against a local authority under section 7(1)(a) might therefore be brought as an ordinary civil claim in the county court or High Court, in those proceedings, the court would clearly have power to grant injunctions or award damages.

High Contracting Parties of the rights set forth in the Convention or the protocols thereto. The High Contracting Parties undertake not to hinder in any way the effective exercise of this right'.

[103] Many judicial review proceedings will include claims for damages based on human rights breaches. Section 31(4) of the Senior Courts Act specifically enables the High Court to award damages in judicial review cases providing certain conditions are met. See **18.246** et seq.

[104] [2001] EWCA Civ 757, [2001] 2 FLR 582.

[74] Alternatively, a parent or a child could invoke the existing procedures in the Children Act 1989 to get the matter back before the care court and then rely upon section 7(1)(b) … in those proceedings, however, the court can only regulate contact or discharge the care order …

[75] In practice, we need a combination of these two procedures. Where the decision as to what is, or is not, unlawful in terms of 6(1) depends crucially upon the facts and merits of the case, it is much more appropriate for the cases to be brought in a court which is used to deciding such cases and evaluating the evidence. Furthermore, whereas only certain judges can exercise the care jurisdiction, all judges sitting in the county courts or High Court can grant injunctions and award damages. We need a court which can grant all the available remedies. The proceedings should be 'specified proceedings' under section 41 of the 1989 Act so that the child can be represented by a guardian ad litem. Applications under section 7(1)(a) should therefore be made, in the first instance, to the court which made the original care order (unless it was a family proceedings court where no remedies other than those under the 1989 Act are available). For my part I would not require a separate claim to be made under the Civil Procedure Rules 1998 and then consolidated with the Children Act 1989 application. I see no need to read the words 'in the proceedings' after the words 'within its powers' in s 8(1) of the 1998 Act. County Courts must now be able to exercise their powers to grant injunctions to prevent a local authority acting unlawfully even in a care case.'

18.221 The above comments on the issue of which court applications should be made to was not reviewed when the matter came before the House of Lords[105] although it should be noted that at para [62] of the judgment Lord Nicholls commented that s 7 offered a longstop remedy. He referred to the availability of independent visitors, children's complaints officers, children's rights officers, applications for discharge of care orders and judicial review. He did not expect proceedings to be launched under s 7 of the HRA 1998 until any other appropriate remedial route had been first explored.

18.222 There is no clear authority indicating that the ideal procedure as expressed by Hale LJ has been routinely accepted as the appropriate way of dealing with issues of damages arising within care proceedings.

18.223 See also the approach of Charles J to the issue as to whether the Court of Protection is a court with the power to award damages in *YA(F) v A Local Authority; YA(M); A NHS Trust and A Primary Care Trust*:[106]

- It was asserted that the claim for damages pursuant to HRA 1998 was not one within the jurisdiction of the Court of Protection and therefore should be transferred to the Queen's Bench Division.

- There was acceptance that the Court of Protection had jurisdiction to deal with HRA claims for declaratory relief.

---

[105] See *Re S; Re W* [2002] 1 FLR 815.
[106] [2010] EWHC 2770 (CoP).

- Paragraph 32 of the judgment highlights that the crucial sections are s 8(1) and (2) HRA 1998. Section 8(1) limits the remedies and relief that can be granted to those *within the power of the relevant court*. Section 8(2) focuses on the relevant court and provides that damages may be awarded only by a court which *itself* has power to award damages or to order the payment of compensation in civil proceedings.

- Sections 7 and 8 of the HRA 1998 do not of themselves create powers in the relevant courts and the focus is on the powers of the court.

- Arguments relating to convenience and/or what seems to be more practical do not themselves, and cannot themselves, confer jurisdiction.

- The powers of the High Court and county court flow from the provisions of the Senior Courts Act 1981, the County Courts Act 1984 and for the high court the assimilation of earlier jurisdiction and the inherent jurisdiction. The power in those courts then derives from the subject matter of the cases the court has jurisdiction to deal with.

- When applying s 8(2) one is looking at the general ability of the court to award damages excluding the power to do so conferred by the HRA itself.

- The judge's consideration of the provisions of the Mental Capacity Act 2005, s 47(1) and the Senior Courts Act 1981 led to his conclusion that both linguistically and purposively, albeit possibly against the instinct of a number of lawyers dealing with a welfare jurisdiction, the Court of Protection does have jurisdiction and thus power to award damages under HRA 1998.

- The judge however then went on to direct that when the matter returned before him he would treat it as proceedings in the QBD in respect of the mother's entire HRA claim and the son's claim for damages, not because he had any concern as to his conclusion, but to ensure that if the decision on jurisdiction was successfully appealed, or in the future in another case his conclusion was found to be wrong, any award in the proceedings would have a jurisdictional base.

18.224 The tendency, so far as reported cases are concerned, has been for the issue of damages arising from facts which are related to ongoing or recently concluded care proceedings to be transferred to the Queen's Bench Division rather than dealt with within the forum dealing with the care proceedings, although the High Court Family Division has certainly felt able to approve orders where payments of damages for breach of human rights arising from actions within or preceding the issue of care proceedings have been agreed by consent and recorded in the recitals to the orders. It is likely that the true meaning of a court which has the power to award damages will be the subject of further exploration.

Examples of domestic family based damages cases

18.225   *Re V (Care Pre-birth Actions)*[107]

- First instance decision of judge in a case where mother had already had two children removed pursuant to EPOs and subsequently made subject of full care orders, birth of her third child led to care proceedings with a further full care order. Complaints related to her pregnancy with fourth child and subsequent initiation of care proceedings.

- Whilst granting care and freeing orders the first instance judge found breaches under Art 6 relating to pre birth management in that the social worker could have said more to the mother and father about expectations and how to remedy and improve their parenting.

- Overturning first instance decision to award damages of £100 to each parent Court of Appeal held there was no breach on the basis that the court has to ascertain whether the proceedings considered as a whole were plainly wrong. It was not permissible to isolate one alleged incident and use it as basis for a finding of breach of Art 6 rights when relating to a social worker acting as such in the role exclusively before the birth of the relevant child and before the initiation of proceedings.

- The Court of Appeal, determining that as there was no breach the award of damages could not stand, noted that in any event the grant of the remedy is discretionary and specifically in relation to damages no award may be made unless, taking account of all of the circumstances of the case, the court is satisfied that the award is necessary to afford just satisfaction. They cautioned that if any application is made within proceedings of this kind (care proceedings) very close attention should be paid to the express provisions of s 8 before any court begins to consider making any such award.

- Holman J expressed the view that occasions when it could be necessary and just and appropriate to make such an award will be very rare indeed.

18.226   *Re C; Re P*[108]

- The issue for the Appeal Court was whether Hedley J was entitled to refuse the mother's damages claim in addition to his declaration that the local authority had breached the mother's human rights by deciding to abandon the care plan for her rehabilitation with her only child without giving her an opportunity to participate in the decision-making process.

---

[107] [2005] 1 FLR 627.
[108] [2007] EWCA Civ 2, [2007] 1 FLR 1957.

- The failure by the local authority to consult in the shift from one track to the other in a concurrent planning case was essentially a breach of a parent's Art 8 right to respect for family life.

- It was clear that the European Court of Human Rights generally favoured an award of damages in cases in which local authorities had infringed the rights of parents under Art 8 by shortcomings in the procedures by which they had taken children into care or kept them in care (the judge below had failed adequately to explain his refusal to award damages).

- The breach in this case, however, was purely procedural lying not in the decision to proceed to adoption but in reaching that decision without consulting the mother.

- The procedural breach had not been significant but was instead at the low end of the spectrum.

- It was not therefore necessary to afford to the mother any just satisfaction other than that resulting from the declaration finding a violation of her rights.

18.227   *Langley and Others v Liverpool City Council and Others*[109]

Background facts:

- Emergency protection order in existence.

- But the removal of one of children (C) from parents to foster care was undertaken by police pursuant to s 46 Children Act 1989.[110]

- Removal of two children from school by social workers.

Findings at first instance that:

- LA acted unlawfully in removal of three children.

- LA liable for assault and false imprisonment as well as for breach of Art 8 rights of the three children and both parents.

- Chief constable acted unlawfully in removal of one child (C) and liable for assault and false imprisonment.

- Damages awarded at first instance.

---

[109]   [2005] EWCA Civ 1773, [2006] 1 FLR 342.
[110]   Section 46 relates to the removal and accommodation of children by police in case of emergency.

- The judge at first instance found that once an emergency protection order had been granted under s 44 the police cannot remove a child to suitable accommodation under s 46.

Court of Appeal:

- Nothing in the Children Act 1989 which compels the conclusion that s 46 cannot be used where an EPO is in force pursuant to s 44.

- Where EPO is in force it is almost always preferable for the removal of children to be undertaken by professional social workers executing the EPO rather than police officers under s 46. Social workers may need to obtain police assistance and that is why s 48(9) is important.

- The failure of the police to ask themselves whether there were any compelling reasons why they should invoke s 46 rather than leave it to the LA to execute the EPO was unlawful.

- As this removal by the police was not 'in accordance with the law' (even though the officer acted in good faith in circumstances which justified the removal of the child by social workers to foster care) the police were therefore in breach of Art 8 with respect to the removal of one child (C).

- The decision of the LA to seek an EPO was a reasonable and proportionate response.

- The LA played a major part in securing the removal by the police of the one child C rather than asking them to ensure that he remained in the house until they could attend and execute the EPO. This failure by the LA rendered the LA liable to C and each of his parents.

- The removal of the other two children by social workers executing the EPO where an explanation had been given to the mother as to why the EPO had been obtained did not amount to a breach.

- Although the issue of damages was not before the Court of Appeal it commented that since it considered that the EPO with respect to C was justified and that it was appropriate to remove C to foster care it was difficult to see on what basis an award of substantial damages could properly be made on the basis that the removal was by the police rather than the LA.

18.228 *R (G) v Nottingham CC and Nottingham University Hospital*[111]

- Declarations granted that the local authority had acted unlawfully:

---

[111] [2008] EWHC 400 (Admin), [2008] 1 FLR 1668; for further consideration of this case see **9.23** onwards in chapter 9.

- – by failing to conduct a lawful assessment of the mother (an eligible child under Sch 2 para 19B of the CA 1989); and
- – by failing to produce a lawful pathway plan; and
- – by separating mother and baby without lawful authority.

- The issue of whether any breach of Art 8 rights should lead to a formal remedy to be determined in further hearing between mother and LA alone.[112]

- The questions of whether she was entitled to any financial compensation and, if so, what amount for the unlawful separation ,or whether as argued by the local authority the declarations itself was 'just satisfaction' were described as questions of some difficulty and complexity.

- Permission was granted to the mother to extend her claim to include common law damages. The explanation given for this part of the order was that the claim as framed was confined to damages pursuant to Section 8 HRA with no claim for common law damages. The court made an order designed to enable her if so advised to extend her claim to include common law damages. The court noted that no doubt her advisers would consider the important decision in the Court of Appeal in *F v Wirral MBC*[113] before embarking on that course.

18.229 *S (A Child Acting by the Official Solicitor) v Rochdale Metropolitan Borough Council and the IRO*[114]

- The background circumstances with respect to the claim involved a child S (age 18 by the time of the hearing) who had been accommodated pursuant to s 20 for approximately 5 years in a children's home and numerous foster placements and eventually secure accommodation.

- Matters were compromised between the parties with the local authority being ordered to pay £50,000.00 in costs but no order for damages.

- The HRA claims included alleged breaches by the local authority of its positive duty to guarantee respect for private life by:

- – failure to take adequate child protection measures;
- – failure to protect S's physical integrity and health;
- – failure in specific social services actions;

- Additional breaches were alleged under Arts 3 and 6 including:

- – failure to protect S from persistent exposure to degrading treatment;
- – failure to instigate public law care proceedings.

---

[112] The resolution of this aspect of the claim does not appear to have been reported.
[113] [1991] Fam 69.
[114] [2008] EWHC 3283 (Fam), [2009] 1 FLR 1090.

- Separate allegations were made with respect to the failings of the IRO with respect to her statutory obligations to S in monitoring and ensuring actions were carried out.

- A compromise agreement means limited information is available as to any concessions on the allegations or other financial arrangements that may have been made.

18.230 *A and S v Lancashire County Council*[115]

Background facts:

- Two brothers came into care as infants and were freed for adoption.

- After a time the search for adopters was abandoned but the freeing orders were never discharged and all links with their family were cut.

- The LA was responsible for the boys for 14 years.

- During this time the children were placed with subsequent sets of abusive foster carers involving both sexual and physical abuse.

- The LA defaulted on their duties to the children and the independent reviewing system did not call the LA to account.

- Human rights applications were issued against both the LA and its employee the independent reviewing officer.

- The High Court family judge granted declarations that the LA and IRO had acted incompatibly with the boy's Arts 8, 6 and 3 rights. Including:

  - permitting the boys to be subjected to degrading treatment and physical assault;
  - failing to adequately protect their physical and sexual safety and psychological health;
  - failing to provide a proper opportunity to the boys to secure a permanent adoptive placement and settled and secure home life;
  - failing to seek revocation of the freeing orders;
  - failing to promote their rights to independent legal advice;
  - failing to act as the responsible body to enable them to pursue any potential claims for compensation;
  - As against the IRO failing to identify that their human rights were being infringed;
  - failure to take effective action to ensure that the authority acted upon the recommendations of the LAC reviews;
  - failing to refer the circumstances of the boys to CAFCASS Legal.

---

[115] [2012] EWHC 1689 (Fam).

- Having made the declarations the High Court directed that the claims for damages under the HRA 1998 be transferred to the Queen's Bench Division to be heard with their claims for breach of statutory duty and negligence.

18.231   *Coventry City Council v C, B, CA and CH*[116]

- The local authority conceded the mother's claim under s 7 of the 1998 Act for breach of Art 8 based on the factual background that:

    – section 20 consent should not have been sought from this particular Mother in the circumstances that she found herself in; and
    – that removal of the child at birth was not a proportionate response to the risks that then existed.

- The mother's three previous children had at various times been made the subject of placement orders and placed for adoption.

- Pre-birth plans for her fourth child were drawn up, the mother was aware of the plan for immediate removal of the baby after birth when the baby was ready for discharge but had indicated her opposition to such a plan.

- She was admitted to hospital as an emergency and required life sustaining surgery. After the baby was born but whilst she was recovering from surgery the mother refused the social worker's request for agreement to the baby being accommodated, hospital staff voiced concerns as to the validity of any consent as might be given by the mother due to the effects of her treatment, subsequently after the mother had accepted morphine and was more comfortable and calm she was again approached for her agreement which she gave and the baby was accommodated.

- Agreement was reached about the payment of damages which together with the recitals identifying the breaches were accepted to amount to just satisfaction of both of the claims.

- The Court approved the manner in which the human rights claim was resolved.

Examples of European Court cases involving the UK

18.232   *Z v UK*[117]

- Acts complained of pre introduction of HRA 1998.

---

[116]   [2012] EWHC 2190 (Fam).
[117]   [2001] 2 FLR 612; also see at **18.17** above.

- Violations of Art 3 and Art 13 but not Art 6 (also a finding that no separate issue arose under Art 8).

- Four children became known to the local authority in 1987 despite many referrals regarding their care over the next three years, including descriptions of neglect and bruising, the children remained with their parents until voluntarily accommodated in 1992 followed by the making of care orders. During the time in the care of their parents the children are described as having suffered horrific experiences and been subject to appalling neglect over an extended period.

- In 1993 the Official Solicitor commenced proceedings on behalf of the children against the local authority claiming damages for negligence and/or breach of statutory duty. It was alleged that the local authority failure to act had resulted in psychological damage.

- The claim was struck out by the UK courts as revealing no cause of action.

- In 1997 CICB awards were made to the four children based on assessment that they had some physical and psychological injury inflicted upon them.

- With respect to the Art 3 claim the commission considered that there was a positive obligation on the Government to protect children from treatment contrary to this provision. The authorities had been aware of the serious ill-treatment and neglect suffered by the four children over a period of years at the hands of their parents and failed, despite the means reasonably available to them, to take any effective steps to bring it to an end.

- The ECtHR re-iterated that Art 3 enshrines one of the most fundamental values of democratic society. It prohibits in absolute terms torture or inhuman or degrading treatment or punishment. States were required to take measures designed to ensure that individuals within their jurisdiction are not subjected to torture or inhuman or degrading treatment, including such ill-treatment administered by private individuals.

- The measures should provide effective protection, in particular of children and other vulnerable persons and include reasonable steps to prevent ill-treatment of which the authorities had or ought to have had knowledge.

- With respect to the Art 13 claim it was found that the applicants did not have available to them an appropriate means of obtaining a determination of their allegations that the local authority failed to protect them from inhuman and degrading treatment and the possibility of obtaining an award of compensation for the damage suffered thereby and were therefore not afforded an effective remedy.

- The award of damages was for £32,000.00 for each applicant. The ECtHR commented that the description of the conditions which the children endured and the traumatic effects which this had on the children (including ongoing psychiatric illness for two of the children) left the court with no doubt that a substantial award to reflect their pain and suffering was appropriate.

- The ECtHR commented that the rates applied in domestic cases, though relevant, are not decisive.

18.233   *TP and KM v UK*[118]

- Acts complained of pre-introduction of HRA 1998.

- Violation of Art 8 and Art 13 but not Art 6.

- Child removed under place of safety order following concerns which included sexual abuse. Mother only allowed restricted contact which was then reduced to indirect contact following fears that she was trying to induce her daughter to change her evidence regarding the perpetrator of sexual abuse. The mother was not allowed access to the copy of the video of the child's interview by a consultant child psychiatrist.

- For a period of approximately 1 year the authority acted on the basis that the child had identified her mother's boyfriend. This was later called into doubt when the contents of the video were seen by lawyers for the mother.

- Mother and child were separated between November 1987 and November 1988.

- Proceedings were commenced by mother and child against the local authority, health authority and child psychiatrist, for negligence and breach of statutory duty resulting in a psychiatric disorder flowing from the enforced separation.

- The proceedings were struck out in the UK courts as revealing no cause of action.

- With respect to the Art 8 claim the ECtHR found that the removal of the child was supported by relevant and sufficient reasons and the use of the emergency procedure was proportionate. However the question of whether critical material (the video of interview) should be disclosed should not have been decided by the local authority or health professional conducting the interview. The positive obligation to disclose was not dependent upon the mother requesting disclosure.

---

[118]   (2002) 34 EHRR 2 42, [2001] 2 FLR 549. Also see at **18.19** above.

- The local authority's failure to submit this issue to the court for determination deprived the mother of an adequate involvement in the decision-making process concerning the care of her daughter and thereby of the requisite protection of their interests.

- With respect to the Art 13 claim the ECtHR considered that the applicants should have had available to them a means of claiming that the local authority's handling of the procedures was responsible for the damage which they suffered and obtaining compensation for that damage. As they did not they were not afforded an effective remedy.

- The court found that although it could not be asserted that they would have been reunited earlier if the video had been available at the initial stages of the proceedings it could not be excluded that it might have reduced the duration of their separation. Mother and child therefore suffered a loss of opportunity. In addition they certainly suffered non-pecuniary damage through distress and anxiety and in the case of the mother through feelings of frustration and injustice.

- The damage suffered was not sufficiently compensated by the finding of a violation.

- Making an assessment on an equitable basis the sum of £10,000.00 was awarded to each.

- Note: the report sets out the approach of Arden LJ sitting as an ad hoc judge by which she reached a lower figure for what she would have regarded as an appropriate award. Her method of reaching the figure of £6,000.00 is of interest.

18.234   *RK and AK v UK*[119]

- Acts complained of pre-introduction of HRA 1998.

- Violation of Art 13 but not Art 8.

- 1998 Misdiagnoses of fracture as non-accidental in origin rather than genetic disease resulting in very fragile bones leading to ICO and placement of child with aunt, then FCO and only return to parents after further injury 6 months later leading to correct diagnosis.

- Mistaken assessment by professionals did not as such make child care measures incompatible with Art 8. Social and medical authorities were under duties to protect children and could not be held liable every time that genuine and reasonably held concerns as to the safety of children were shown, retrospectively, to have been unfounded.

---

[119]   (2009) 48 EHRR 29 707.

- No breach of Art 8 as there had been relevant and sufficient reasons for the authorities to take protective measures. Those measures had been proportionate to the aim of protecting the applicant's daughter, due account had been given to the interests of the applicants and there had been no lack of appropriate expedition.

- Breach of Art 13 because the applicants' complaints as to the interference with their family life had been arguable; therefore should have had a means by which to claim that the local authorities had been responsible for any damage that they had suffered and by which they could have claimed compensation for that damage

- Such redress had not been available at the relevant time (as noted under Civil Claims above, the Court of Appeal and House of Lords had held that no duty of care was owed to parents of children in cases of suspected mistreatment and the HRA provisions were not yet in force).

- The damages were awarded upon the court not doubting that the applicants did as a result of the breach of Art 13 suffer frustration, stress and uncertainty which would not be redressed by a finding of violation alone.

- Having regard to awards in similar cases, making its assessment on an equitable basis awarded the applicants £10,000 jointly.

18.235   *MAK and RK v UK*[120]

- Acts complained of pre-introduction of HRA 1998.

- Violation of Art 8 but no violation of father's Art 3 rights, no violation of child's Art 6 rights.

- 9-year-old child taken to hospital on a number of occasions with bruising between 1997 and 1998. On the fourth occasion the child was admitted to hospital. Blood samples and photographs were taken of the child without having obtained the consent of the parents and, in fact, having been told that they should await the arrival of mother before any further examination or tests were undertaken. The local authority were also notified due to the doctor's suspicion of abuse.

- That evening the parents were informed by hospital that her father was not allowed to see his daughter, others on the ward witnessed this exchange, news was passed through the community and reached acquaintances in India. Thereafter visiting was limited to supervised on the basis of suspicion of sexual abuse.

---

[120] (Applications Nos 45901/05 and 40146/06) [2010] 2 FLR 451, ECtHR (final judgment 23/06/2010).

- 10 days after admission child was examined by a dermatologist who diagnosed Schamberg's disease a rare condition of the capillaries which is manifested by the eruption of purple patches on skin. The child was then discharged from hospital.

- Father's domestic claim for damages was struck out as the court held that no duty of care was owed. The child's claim was allowed to continue but legal aid was withdrawn on the basis that the likely costs were disproportionate to the value of the claim.

- Breach found of applicant's Art 8 rights on the basis that there was no legal authority to prevent the father visiting his daughter on the night of admission.

- Breach found of applicant's Art 8 rights on basis that whilst there were relevant and sufficient reasons for the authorities to suspect abuse at the time of the admission the delay in consulting a dermatologist extended the interference with the right to respect to family life.

- Breach found of child's Art 8 rights on basis of the blood samples and photographs being taken without consent.

- Breach of father's Art 13 rights on basis that his complaint regarding interference with respect to family life was arguable and there was no domestic redress available for a claim that the local authority's handling was responsible for any damage or for obtaining compensation.

Damages as follows:

- For father's Art 8 breaches £2,000 taking in to account the fact that the violation lasted only a few days during which time for most of the period he continued to have contact albeit supervised, it also took account of the humiliation experienced after he was publicly barred.

- For daughter's Art 8 breaches £4,500 for non pecuniary damage taking into account her age, the intimate nature of the photographs taken whilst she was alone at the hospital, together with the associated interference with her right to respect for family life. A pecuniary claim based on future counselling was declined on the basis that this was speculative.

18.236   *AD and OD v UK*[121]

- Acts complained of pre-HRA.

- Violation of mother and child's Art 8 and mother's Art 13 rights.

---

[121]   (Application No 28680/06) [2010] 2 FLR 1.

- Misdiagnosis of fractures as abuse rather than type 4 OI leading to interim care orders starting in May 1997, placement at family assessment unit for 12 weeks then child's separation from family and placement in foster care and subsequent discharge of ICO in July 1998 following numerous medical reports and the sustaining of a fracture whilst in foster care.

- Mother's claim for damages for negligence and personal injury was struck out on basis that the local authority owed no duty of care to a parent in care proceedings.

- Claims by child for negligence and personal injury were rejected on basis that the child had not been shown to have suffered any recognisable psychiatric damage or that alternatively any injury was transient and not compensatable by damages.

- The European Court reiterated that mistaken judgments or assessments by professionals do not per se render childcare measures incompatible with Art 8 requirements. The authorities both medical and social, have duties to protect children and cannot be held liable every time genuine and reasonably held concerns about the safety of their children vis-à-vis members of their family, are retrospectively found to have been misguided.

- The European Court whilst satisfied that there were relevant and sufficient reasons for the authorities to take protective measures the subsequent failings of the local authority (in not conducting the correct risk assessments whilst the family were at the family assessment unit and not utilising less intrusive measures including placement with relatives) of the local authority both extended and exacerbated the interference with the applicants' right to respect for their family life.

- As with RK and AK Art 13 violation found for mother due to lack of means of claiming redress.

- Damages £15,000 jointly to the applicants for Art 8 breach, no separate award for Art 13.

18.237 *E v UK*[122]

- The European Court of Human Rights held (at a time when the application of *Bedfordshire* meant that any application seeking damages from the local authority would inevitably fail) that an award by the CICB to victims of child sexual abuse, whilst potentially relevant to any

---

[122]   (App No 33218/96) reported as *E and Others v UK* [2003] 1 FLR 348 (judgment 26/11/2002).

subsequent question of just satisfaction, could not be regarded as providing a mechanism for determining the liability of social services for any negligence towards the children.

- In addition while a complaint to the local authority ombudsman might have led to an investigation of social services' management of the case, it would not have provided a binding determination as the ombudsman (at the time) only had the power to make recommendations.

- As a result the Court found that the children did not have a means of obtaining a determination of their allegations that the local authority had failed to protect them from inhuman and degrading treatment and there was in that respect a breach of Art 13.

Whether the approach in *Bury Metropolitan Borough Council v D*[123] will provide a route by which local authorities may be able to protect themselves from potential claims for damages by seeking prospective declaratory relief from the court as to the lawfulness of a proposed action remains to be seen. The case is probably limited to its very unusual facts and the route taken there should not be used as a matter of routine.

SECTION 5 – HUMAN RIGHTS CLAIMS – PROCEDURE

Practice Direction 16

Paragraph 15.1

18.238 A party who seeks to rely on any provision of or right arising under the Human Rights Act 1998 or seeks a remedy available under that Act:

(1) Must state that fact in his statement of case.

(2) Must in his statement of case:

  (a) Give precise details of the Convention right which it is alleged has been infringed and details of the alleged infringement.
  (b) Specify the relief sought.
  (c) State if the relief sought includes:

   (i) a declaration of incompatibility in accordance with s 4 of that Act; or
   (ii) damages in respect of a judicial act to which s 9(3) of that Act applies.

---

[123] [2009] 2 FLR 313.

(d)   Where the relief sought includes a declaration of incompatibility in accordance with s 4 of that Act, give precise details of the legislative provision alleged to be incompatible and details of the alleged incompatibility.

(e)   Where the claim is founded on a finding of unlawfulness by another court or tribunal give details of the finding.

(f)   Where the claim is founded on a judicial act which is alleged to have infringed a Convention Right of the Party as provided by s 9 of the Human Rights Act 1998, the judicial act complained of and the court or tribunal which is alleged to have made it.

18.239   Attention must also be paid to CPR 1998, Part 19 (in particular r 19.4A) and PD19A and the provision for notice to be given and parties joined in any of the circumstances in (c), (d) and (f) above.

18.240   In brief the result of these provisions is that the court may not make a declaration of incompatibility in accordance with s 4 of the Human Rights Act 1998 unless 21 days notice has been given to the Crown. Where there is a claim for damages in respect of a judicial act in accordance with s 9 of the Act notice must be given to the Crown.

18.241   The Courts Service provides a form EX503 which provides information for court user on the Human Rights Act 1998 in particular where the claim is for damages under that Act.

18.242   It sets out that there are three types of case involving the HRA 1998 that can be brought in the county courts or High Court:

- A claim for damages based on a breach of one or more rights protected by the HRA 1998.

- A claim for damages following a decision by a court that does not have the power to award damages (such as the Crown Court) that human rights have been breached.

- A non-damages application for an injunction or judicial review of the decision or action of the public authority (but identifies that a specific procedure exists for judicial review applications).[124])

18.243   As with non-human rights civil damages claims, claims for damages for less than £15,000 should start in the county court; claims above that level can be commenced in either the county court or the High Court.

18.244   Human Rights Act claims for damages (as with non-human rights claims) should be commenced on an ordinary N1 claim form marking the claim form appropriately to indicate that it includes a Human Rights Act point.

---

[124]   See chapter 17.

SECTION 6 – DAMAGES AND JUDICIAL REVIEW[125]

18.245 The Senior Courts Act 1981, s 31 and CPR 1998, r 54.3(2) define the circumstances in which damages can be award on an application for judicial review.

Senior Courts Act 1981

18.246 Section 31 provides:

> (1) An application to the High Court for one or more of the following forms of relief, namely –
>
> (a) a mandatory, prohibiting or quashing order;
> (b) a declaration or injunction under subsection (2); or
> (c) an injunction under section 30 restraining a person not entitled to do so from acting in an office to which that section applies
>
> shall be made in accordance with rules of court by a procedure to be known as an application for judicial review.
>
> (4) On an application for judicial review the High Court may award to the Applicant damages, restitution or the recovery of a sum due if –
>
> (a) the application includes a claim for such an award arising from any matter to which the application relates; and
> (b) the court is satisfied that such an award would have been made if the claim had been made in an action begun by the applicant at the time of making the application.

18.247 The above provisions make clear that it is not possible to make a standalone application for damages with judicial review proceedings. The claim for damages must be sought alongside some other form of judicial review relief, such as a mandatory, prohibiting or quashing order of a declaration or injunction.

18.248 Further in order to satisfy the test at (b) there must be an element to the judicial review claim for which there is a power to award damages. Breach of a public law right by itself does not found an award of damages. The claim therefore would need to have an additional element for which, if the matter had been brought to court by an ordinary claim, rather than judicial review, damages would have been available.

For example:

- Breach of human rights (see earlier in the chapter).

- An element of a private law action which would found a claim for damages such as the tort of false imprisonment.[126] This has been stated to

---

[125] The law and procedure for judicial review applications are dealt with in detail in chapters 16 and 17.

[126] Recent examples of this type of award see by way of illustration only *R (Mustafa Moussaoui)*

be a trespass to the person actionable in itself without proof of loss or damage. Awards for false imprisonment are based on normal compensatory principles and therefore the concept of merely nominal damages can in appropriate circumstances be applied.

- An element of a private law action which would found a claim for damages such as negligence (see earlier in the chapter).

- The tort of misfeasance in a public office. This has been described as deliberate and dishonest abuse of power by a public officer or a public body. It requires more than simply acting ultra-vires; the act complained of will need an element of malice or intent or knowledge that the act was unlawful (or reckless indifference as to whether it was lawful or not) and likely to cause injury to the claimant.[127]

18.249 Attention should be paid to the guidance given in the case of *Anufrijeva v London Borough of Southwark* already considered in detail above.[128]

18.250 Applicants may find that the issue of damages is dealt with after, and separately from, the determination of the judicial review merits.

---

v *SSHD* [2012] EWHC 126 and *R (Lumba) v SSHD* [2011] UKSC 12, [2012] 1 AC 245, *R (Kambadzi) v SSHD* [2011] UKSC 23, [2011] 1 WLR 1299.

[127] See for example *Three Rivers District Council & others and the Bank of England* [2000] 2 WLR 1220 and later at [2001] UKHL 16. See also *W v Essex County Council* [1999] Fam 90, [1998] 2 FLR 278 later considered by the House of Lords [2000] 2 WLR 601, [2000] 1 FLR 657.

[128] [2003] EWCA Civ 1406. See **18.192–18.194** above.

Chapter 19

CRIMINAL INJURIES COMPENSATION

SECTION 1 – RELEVANCE FOR CHILD CARE PRACTITIONERS

19.1 Local authorities, social workers, adopters, special guardians and other carers for children, together with family lawyers and children's guardians, will between them have many repeated experiences of taking responsibility and acting for abused children. Proper consideration should be given to whether such children are entitled to any compensation for the injuries (whether physical or mental) sustained by them as a result of an incident of maltreatment or a history of prolonged abuse.

19.2 It is important that ignorance of the avenues open to claim such compensation or inaction resulting in missed time limits do not operate to put such children at further disadvantage in their future lives.[1]

19.3 For children removed from their parents pursuant to the Children Act 1989 more often than not allegations of significant harm arise from the physical treatment of them by an adult that would include assaults of varying natures, both physical and sexual, similarly for children suffering abuse within the looked after care system. Many of these types of abuse (even if no prosecution or conviction ensues) would be considered as criminal in nature giving rise to possible criminal compensation. Sometimes the intervention of the state is brought about by the death of one parent at the hands of the other, a cohabitee or ex-partner. If the death arises as a crime of violence, criminal compensation may again be available.

19.4 This chapter therefore aims to set out sufficient information, by reference to the provisions of the Schemes, the guidance issued and case law, to provide a basic understanding of the features which might enable a child (or adult abused as a child) to qualify for compensation, the initial steps which need to be taken to both initiate a claim and to prevent or minimise reduction of an award.[2]

---

[1] Please see FPR 2010, PD12D, paras 6.1 and 6.2 for specific guidance with respect to CICA claims for children who are wards of court. The Practice Direction appears in Part 4 (resources section) of this book.

[2] For a more detailed study see Padley and Begley *Criminal Injuries Compensation Claims*: (The Law Society, 2005) and Begley, Downey and Padley *Criminal Injuries Compensation Claims 2008* (The Law Society, 2010).

19.5   The Scheme stresses that it is intended to be one of last resort with an expectation that other routes for compensation will have been initiated first.

19.6   There are cautionary tales in case law for local authorities and IROs who miss the opportunities to seek such compensation for children for whom they are responsible.

Primary Legislation

Criminal Injuries Compensation Act 1995 (CICA 1995)

19.7   By s 1(1), the Secretary of State[3] must make arrangements for the payment of compensation to, or in respect of, persons who have sustained one or more criminal injuries.

19.8   By s 1(2), any such arrangements must include the making of a scheme, providing in particular for the circumstances in which awards may be made, and the categories of person to whom awards may be made.

19.9   The Act identifies that the scheme will make provision for:[4]

- The basis upon which compensation is to be calculated (including the use of tariffs and the setting of a maximum amount for an award).

- The basic framework to be adopted for claims and awards (including the circumstances in which awards may be withheld or reduced and the use of trusts).

- The circumstances under which a decision may be reviewed.

- Rights of appeal.

19.10   The resulting Scheme applies to England, Scotland and Wales. In Northern Ireland criminal injuries compensation is the responsibility of the Department of Justice's Compensation Agency.

SECTION 2 – BASIC STRUCTURE OF THE SCHEME

19.11   The scheme is administered by the Criminal Injuries Compensation Authority (CICA).

19.12   Claims officers are responsible for determining the claims for compensation in accordance with the relevant scheme.

---

[3]   Secretary of State for Justice.
[4]   See ss 2–5 CICA 1995.

19.13 Their decisions are open to review[5] within the scheme provisions themselves and appeal thereafter lies to the First-Tier Tribunal.[6]

19.14 Even if a decision is made that an award is appropriate the amount of award may be reduced by reference to the criminal record of the applicant or their behaviour during or after the incident including their lack of co-operation with the police or the authority and delay in informing the police of the incident resulting in injury.

19.15 A decision made by a claims officer may be reconsidered at any time before the payment of a final award. The making of an interim payment does not prevent further consideration of issues of eligibility. New evidence or changes in circumstances may prompt reconsideration.[7]

19.16 Where there has been such a material change in the victim's medical condition after a final decision that it would result in injustice for the original assessment of compensation to stand, or where a victim has since died as a result of the injury, a claims officer may re-open the case.[8]

19.17 If the application to re-open comes more than two years after the final decision the claims officer will need to be satisfied that the application can be considered without a need for extensive further investigations.

19.18 The level of award is determined by a 'tariff' where each type of injury is given a value. The minimum tariff payment is £1,000.00. If the injury is not serious enough to qualify for a £1,000.00 payment an award will not be made. The maximum tariff payment for a single injury is £250,000.00. Additional payments may be available for loss of earnings and special expenses. The maximum overall payment is capped at £500,000.00.[9]

19.19 The applicant can seek a review of a decision of the claims officer in circumstances such as his refusal to waive or extend time limits, refusal to make an award, making a reduced award and refusing to re-open a case.[10]

19.20 The procedure for appeals to the First-Tier Tribunal is governed by the Tribunal Procedure (First-Tier Tribunal) (Social Entitlement Chamber) Rules 2008[11] supplemented by practice guidance issued by the principal judge. Currently the time limit for an appeal is 90 days from the date of the review decision.[12]

---

[5] See for example paras 100–102 and 117–124 of the 2012 Scheme.
[6] See paras 125–134 of the 2012 Scheme.
[7] See paras 109–113 of the 2012 Scheme.
[8] See paras 114–116 of the 2012 Scheme.
[9] The tariffs appear as schedules to the scheme in Annex E and the maximum cap in para 31 of the 2012 Scheme.
[10] This is no more than a very brief overview of the grounds for review attention will need to be given to the detailed provisions which are contained within paras 117–124 of the 2012 Scheme.
[11] SI 2008/2865.
[12] Rule 22(2)(b) of the 2008 Rules.

SECTION 3 – WHICH SCHEME IS APPLICABLE?

19.21 The scheme itself is kept under regular review resulting in the need for any applicant to ensure that their claim is made applying the correct terms and procedure for the scheme in force at the relevant time. This is effectively governed by the date upon which the application is received by the authority:

- Applications received[13] on or after 1 April 1996 but before 1 April 2001 fall to be considered under the '1996 Scheme'.

- Applications received on or after the 1 April 2001 but before 1 April 2008 fall to be considered under the '2001 Scheme'.

- Applications received on or after the 1 April 2008 but before the 1 April 2012 fall to be considered under the '2008 Scheme'.

- Applications received on or after the 1 April 2012 fall to be considered under the '2012 Scheme'.[14]

19.22 The Schemes can be found at www.justice.gov.uk/victims-and-witnesses/ cica. There are links from the site to the Northern Ireland Compensation Agency website. Alternatively the Northern Ireland Scheme can be accessed through www.dojni.gov.uk.

19.23 The Guide to the 2012 Scheme is also available online and the Guides to earlier Schemes can be obtain from the CICA on request. The 2001 Guide made reference to an additional guide TS10 Child Abuse and the Criminal Injury Compensation Scheme. However for the 2008 Scheme the specific guidance relating to child abuse was contained within Appendix 2 – claiming after a period of abuse. For the 2012 Scheme there appears to be no further separate Appendix and the time limits for applications by victims who were children at the time of injury is simply incorporated within the scheme.

19.24 The main principles and provisions relevant to those dealing with abused children are set out below and take the '2012 scheme' as the relevant Scheme, highlighting where necessary differences between this and the earlier schemes.

SECTION 4 – MAKING THE APPLICATION

19.25 The application must be on a form from the CICA (as must any application for review).

---

[13] Irrespective of when the injury was sustained.
[14] Paragraphs 1 and 2 of the Criminal Injuries Compensation Scheme 2012 and section 1, para 4 of the 2012 Guide.

Forms can be submitted on-line or by telephone. It would appear that in updating the scheme in 2012 the ability to apply by post has fallen by the wayside. Victim Support may also be able to support the applicant in making the claim or dealing with the agency on the applicant's behalf. Advice may additionally be sought from Citizen's Advice.

- For sample forms see www.justice.gov.uk/victims-and-witnesses/cica/apply-online.

- For telephone applications the contact is the customer service centre on 0300 003 3601.

19.26 Previously the postal forms fell under the following headings and this is likely to remain a good guide:

- I was injured because of a single violent crime.

- I was injured following a period of abuse.

- A loved one was killed because of a violent crime.

19.27 Supplemental forms included:

- I am claiming for loss of earnings or special expenses.

- I am applying on behalf of someone under 18.

- I am applying on behalf of an adult who is legally defined as incapable of managing their own affairs.

- I am applying as a representative (eg solicitor).

19.28 Basic information required at the time of completing the application form will include:

- A note of contact details for any medical practitioner who has provided relevant treatment (such as accident and emergency departments, hospital, GP and/or dentist).

- GP details even if not consulted in relation to the incident.

- The unique police ref number (crime reference number).

- The date of any court case.

- The name of the offender if known and address or addresses where the incident took place.

- A contact telephone number for the person making the application.

- National insurance number.

- Any criminal convictions for the applicant.

- Where the claim is made on behalf of a child an original birth certificate will need to be enclosed with the application form.

- Where the claim is made on behalf of a child in local authority care or subject to a residence (and it is assumed special guardianship) order a copy of the relevant order.

19.29 The forms previously indicated that if the injured person is aged 12 years or older they must sign the form. This would appear to be in addition to the person completing the form on their behalf. The 2012 Guide however refers to the need for someone who is applying on behalf of a child to complete the form as if they were the injured person and to ensure that they provide their own details and proof of their relationship to the child.

19.30 Signing the application form is taken as the giving of consent for the release to the Authority of all the records, evidence and other information which will assist the Authority in reaching a decision on the application. This will include release of medical information and reports including that relating to pre-existing conditions, evidence given by the applicant to the police and a criminal records check.

19.31 Even with the new rules as to permitted disclosure of information and judgments from care proceedings it would not appear that it is permissible (without the permission of the court) to disclose documents from those proceedings to the CICA to support an application for compensation.[15]

19.32 The issue of disclosure of documents from care proceedings to the CICA was considered by Munby J in *In the Matter of X (Children)*[16] where he felt that:

> 'those assessing [the child's] claim must have access to the appropriate documentation from the care proceedings which demonstrates the full gravity of the crime against her, for this will have a direct bearing on the level of compensation she receives.'

19.33 The 2008 Guide was less informative than the earlier forms of guidance in a number of respects. The 2001 TS10 guidance includes that, in relation to children, usually the person to act will be one of the child's parents but where the child has been subjected to abuse within the immediate family this may be impossible. If the child is in care the Authority will expect the claim to be

---

[15] The relevant provisions are found in FPR 2010, rr 12.73–12.75 and PD12G.
[16] [2008] EWHC 242 (Fam), [2008] 2 FLR 944.

lodged by or on behalf of the authority to which parental responsibility has been granted with the claim being signed by the Director of Social Work/Services or other responsible officer. The 2012 Guide offers no assistance on this point.

19.34 Clearly where the claim arises from abuse within the care system it is unlikely that the local authority will be the appropriate body to make the application on the child's behalf. A litigation friend will need to be identified and if there is not suitable person with parental responsibility then the Official Solicitor may need to act on the child's behalf.[17]

19.35 If an applicant is legally represented the costs of representation will not be met by the authority.

19.36 There are examples of local authorities bearing the burden of the funding of representation for children in their care. In other cases the funding of legal representatives is achieved through agreement with the applicant that the costs will be met from any award received. Currently very limited public funding is available for this area by way of 'legal help' only. Even this provision however will be short-lived as from the 1 April 2013 Criminal Injuries Compensation Authority cases will be out of the scope of legal aid.

19.37 A challenge based on the fact that the Scheme did not make provision for the costs of representation (rendering the Scheme incompatible with the Art 6 and Art 14 ECHR) failed, partially by reference to the fact that the CICA had limited public resources with which to operate a scheme that was for the public benefit. Imposing on the CICA the costs of paying a claimant's costs of representation would have a detrimental effect upon the administration of the scheme and was undesirable.[18]

SECTION 5 – TIME LIMITS

19.38 The application should be made as soon as possible after the incident giving rise to the injury and must be received by the authority within two years of the date of the incident.

19.39 The two-year time limit may only be disregarded in exceptional circumstances.

---

[17] For children who are wards of court the application must be made by the child's guardian or if no guardian has been appointed the person with care and control. See FPR 2010, PD12D para 6.1 and 6.2. The Practice Direction appears in Part 4 (resources section) of this book.

[18] *C v Secretary of State for the Home Department* QBD 22/05/2003 and on appeal [2004] EWCA Civ 234.

19.40 Any application for review of a decision must be received by the authority within 56 days of the date the decision was issued (although a period of extension may be granted).[19]

Waiver or extension of time limits

19.41   Under the 2001 Scheme, para 18:

> 'An application for compensation under this Scheme ... should be made as soon as possible after the incident giving rise to the injury and must be received by the Authority within two years of the date of the incident. A claims officer may waive this time limit where he considers that, by reason of the particular circumstances of the case, it is reasonable and in the interests of justice to do so.'

19.42   A tightening up of the ability to waive the time limit appeared to have taken place by the time of the 2008 Scheme and is highlighted by underlining in the wording below

19.43   Under the 2008 Scheme, para 18:

> 'An application for compensation under this Scheme ... should be made as soon as possible and must be received by the Authority within two years of the date of the incident. A claims officer may waive this time limit only where he or she considers that
>
> (a)   it is practicable for the application to be considered; and
> (b)   in the particular circumstances of the case, it would not have been reasonable to expect the applicant to have made the application within the two-year period.'

19.44   Paragraph 1 of the 2008 Guide referred to the time limit being disregarded only in 'exceptional circumstances' not a phrase that appeared within the Scheme itself.

19.45   Appendix 2 of the 2008 Guide contained the following additional guidance:

> '... these special circumstances may apply to a person who was sexually abused as a child but who could not report the abuse until they became an adult. However we would expect that the person reports the abuse as soon as it is reasonable for them to do so.'

19.46   The 2001 Guide TS10 Child Abuse and the Criminal Injuries Compensation Scheme approached the issue of waiver in the following manner:

> '... we adopt a sympathetic attitude towards late claims made on behalf of children, or by children themselves when made within a reasonable time of reaching 18.'

---

[19]   See the review provisions in paras 117–124 of the 2012 Scheme.

19.47   The 2012 Scheme continues the general two year time limit for adult victims in the following way:

Paragraph 87

'Subject to paragraph 88, an application must be sent by the applicant so that it is received by the Authority as soon as reasonably practicable after the incident giving rise to the criminal injury to which it relates, and in any event within two years after the date of the incident.'

19.48   The ability to extend the time limit under the 2012 Scheme has altered with the introduction to the scheme itself rather than just the guide of 'exceptional circumstances' preventing earlier application rather than the use of the milder 'it would not have been reasonable to expect.'

19.49   The 2012 Guide offers the following assistance as to how 'exceptional' may be interpreted. The authority will consider a claim if:

• there is medical or psychiatric evidence available which shows that it was not possible for the applicant to have applied earlier; and

• there is clear evidence available that there was a crime of violence and that the applicant was a victim. Whilst the authority will make basic enquiries of the police they state that the applicant will need to be able to provide evidence that they were a victim of a crime of violence and suffered an injury as a result.

Lack of knowledge of the scheme is not likely to satisfy the 'exceptional reason' approach.

19.50   It was to be hoped that the 'sympathetic approach' to child victims would continue but the new wording of the 2012 Scheme where it relates to child victims demonstrates a marked further tightening of the time limits.

19.51   Significant importance will now attach to the date of any reporting to the incident of the police particularly whether it was done before or after the victim's 18th birthday. If further significant enquiries are likely to be needed to be undertaken by the claims officer before the application could be determined this may well prove fatal to the application.

2012 Scheme – time limits for child victims

19.52   The Scheme now specifically provides as follows:

'2012 Scheme Paragraph 88 – time limit for application

(1) Where the applicant was a child under the age of 18 on the date of the incident giving rise to the criminal injury, the application <u>must be sent </u>by the applicant so that it is received by the Authority:

(a)   In the case of an incident reported to the police before the applicant's 18th Birthday, within the period ending on their 20th Birthday

(b)   In the case of an incident reported to the police on or after the applicants 18th Birthday, within two years after the date of the first report to the police in respect of the incident

(2) An application will not be accepted under this paragraph unless a claims officer is satisfied that the evidence presented in support of the application means that it can be determined without further extensive enquiries by a claims officer.

2012 Scheme Paragraph 89 – extension of time limit

A claims officer may extend the period referred to in para 87 or 88 where the claims officer is satisfied that:

(a)   due to exceptional circumstances the applicant could not have applied earlier

(b)   the evidence presented in support of the application means that it can be determined without further extensive enquiries by the claims officer.'

Both elements of the test for waiver must be satisfied.

19.53   Extreme care should be taken that delay by those responsible for the care of a child, who has provided them with information of sexual abuse at an earlier stage, does not result in an application being refused.

19.54   The Guide stresses that where a victim is under 18 it is best that someone applies on their behalf as soon as possible as it may be harder to provide the evidence that the child was injured as the result of a crime of violence if the application is left until the child has reached their majority or even delayed for a lesser period of time.[20]

19.55   The 2012 Guide contains the following warning:

'Section 2, paragraph 11

If you were abused as a child, we appreciate that you may not have felt able to report the incident for some time after the abuse happened. No matter how long ago the abuse took place, you should report it to the police before you make a claim. We need to check with the police that the crime has been reported. If you have not reported the incident to the police we will refuse your claim.'

19.56   *VL (A Child Suing by her Litigation Friend the Official Solicitor) v Oxfordshire County Council*[21] deals with the position of a local authority faced with an action for negligence flowing from their failure to ensure that an application for criminal compensation was made at a time before the system changed to a less generous one. The facts of the case involved a child placed at home under the auspices of a care order who became the victim of a violent

---

20   Section 2, paras 31–33 of the 2012 Guide.
21   [2010] EWHC 2091 (QB).

shaking by her father, resulting in permanent brain damage. The application on her behalf could have been made before the 1st April 2006 but was not. By the time the application was made the changes to the system operated to the victim's disadvantage. MacKay J made the following observations in paras 44-50:

> 'I am in no doubt that this defendant had the power to make a CICB claim on the claimant's behalf if it thought it advisable. Even if the mother objected it could do so ... that power does not mean it was under a duty in tort to maximise the economic position of a child by allocating time and resources to a pursuit of all available financial claims in a situation where a parent retains a share of parental rights. The primary focus of the defendant was on the physical welfare and safety of the child and the rebuilding of the family unit ... In my view it would not be fair just or reasonable by imposing the duty alleged in this claim to promote the claimant's financial security over the unity of the family, or even run the risk of doing so. While therefore the categories of negligence are never closed and the law of tort is a living thing I consider that to impose a duty of care of the type and scope contended for in this case would be neither fair just or reasonable in the circumstances.'

19.57 However in 2012 the failure by the local authority to pursue any potential claims for criminal injuries compensation arising from the mistreatment of children (by their mother and separate sets of foster carers) who had been placed in their care (and subsequently made the subject of orders freeing them for adoption) was held to be a breach of the children's Art 6 rights and was included in a declaration by the High Court to that effect.

19.58 The case *A and S v Lancashire County Council*[22] (Peter Jackson J) included evidence from the independent reviewing officer that this was a task he should have ensured was complied with. It was a recommendation during the LAC reviews that an application should be made to the CICA and he acknowledged a failure to monitor the social work response to and compliance with the recommendations and advice from the LAC reviews. The court also found this failure by the IRO to be a breach of the children's Art 8 rights.[23]

19.59 The independent reviewing officer will therefore have a significant role to play in monitoring such matters in addition to the primary responsibility upon the social workers and local authority legal team.

19.60 In the *A and S v Lancashire County Council*[24] case the claims for damages under the Human Rights Act 1998 were transferred to the Queen's Bench Division to be heard with their claims for breach of statutory duty and negligence against the local authority.

---

[22] [2012] EWHC 1689 (Fam).
[23] See chapters 7 and 12 for detailed discussion of this case.
[24] [2012] EWHC 1689 (Fam).

SECTION 6 – BURDEN AND STANDARD OF PROOF

19.61   The burden is on the applicant to establish the essential elements of his case including where necessary waiver of the time limit and why an award should not be reconsidered, withheld or reduced under any provision of the scheme.[25] The standard of proof will be the balance of probabilities.[26]

SECTION 7 – ELIGIBILITY

2012 Scheme: Eligibility to apply for compensation

19.62   Paragraph 4 provides:

> 'A person may be eligible for an award under this scheme if they sustain a criminal injury which is directly attributable to their being a direct victim of a crime of violence committed in a relevant place.[27] The meaning of "crime of violence is explained in Annex B".'[28]

19.63   Paragraph 5 – includes eligibility where the criminal injury is *directly attributable to their taking an exceptional and justified risk for the purpose* of for example apprehending an offender or suspected offender, preventing a crime, containing or remedying the consequences of a crime or assisting a constable.

19.64   Paragraph 6 – includes eligibility where the criminal injury is directly attributable to being present and witnessing an incident, or the immediate aftermath of an incident, as a result of which a loved one sustained a criminal injury falling within para 4 or 5. For definitions of 'loved one' and 'immediate aftermath' see below at **19.86**.

19.65   Paragraph 17 provides:

> 'A person is eligible for an award under this scheme only in relation to a criminal injury sustained on or after 1st August 1964.'

19.66   Note also paragraph 22:

> 'An award under this scheme will be withheld unless the incident giving rise to the criminal injury has been reported to the police as soon as reasonably practicable …'[29]

---

[25]   Previously contained in para 19 of the 2008 Scheme now effectively contained within the provisions of para 92 of the Scheme and in the Guide at for example section 3, para 2.

[26]   Section 3(2) CICA 1995.

[27]   For the 2012 Scheme 'relevant place' in this context means Great Britain or any other place specified in Annex C. Annex C includes things like aircraft, ships, lighthouses but excludes Northern Ireland.

[28]   Also see below in **19.76**.

[29]   See below at **19.113** et seq for what is meant by as soon as reasonably practical and the factors to be taken into consideration

19.67 There are also qualifying conditions as to residence, citizenship, nationality or membership of the armed forces. These are contained within paras 10–12 of the 2012 Scheme. It is important to check these provisions to see whether a potential applicant qualifies.

19.68 Specific provisions now exist in the 2012 Scheme to cover eligibility of asylum seekers and victims of trafficking (these relate to the conditions of residence rather than adding to the definition of being a victim of a crime of violence).

19.69 These are contained within paras 13–16 of the Scheme. There is the potential that the presence of children involved within public law care proceedings could be as a result of either asylum seeking or as a result of being trafficked. It is important to be aware therefore that they will not be eligible for any award unless they have been 'conclusively identified by a competent authority as a victim of trafficking in human beings' or have been 'granted temporary protection, asylum or humanitarian protection'.

19.70 In order to qualify as having been conclusively identified by a competent authority as a victim of trafficking the child will need to have:

(a) Completed the identification process required by Art 10 of the Council of Europe Convention against Trafficking of Human Beings (CETS No197, 2005), and upon completion

(b) a competent authority (meaning a person who is a competent authority of the United Kingdom for the purposes of that convention) must conclude that the child is such a victim.

The definition of 'victim of trafficking of human beings' is the definition under the Convention.[30]

---

[30] Article 4 of the Convention sets out the definition of 'trafficking of human beings' as meaning the recruitment, transportation, transfer, harbouring or receipt of persons, by means of the threat or use of force or other forms of coercion, of abduction, of fraud, of deception, of the abuse of power or of a position of vulnerability, or the giving or receiving of payments or benefits to achieve the consent of a person having control over another person, for the purpose of exploitation. Exploitation shall include, at a minimum, the exploitation of the prostitution of others or other forms of sexual exploitation, forced labour or services, slavery or practices similar to slavery, servitude or the removal of organs. In addition the recruitment, transportation, transfer, harbouring or receipt of a child for the purpose of exploitation shall be considered 'trafficking in human beings' even if this does not involve any of the means previously set out. A child is defined as a person under 18 years of age. 'Victim' is defined as any natural person who is subject to trafficking in humans beings as defined.

Meaning of 'criminal injury'

19.71 The 2008 Scheme use of 'personal injury' and the definition of this within the scheme provisions is not replicated.[31] The definition now appears in the 2012 Scheme in the following way.

'Annex A – Interpretation

"criminal injury" means an injury which appears in Part A or B of the tariff in Annex E.'

19.72 Reference will therefore need to be made to the Annex but by way of example includes burns, scaring, brain damage, paralysis, mental illness, fatality, physical abuse, sexual offences, loss of foetus, pregnancy or infection directly attributable to a sexual offence.

19.73 Mental illness will not qualify if it is limited to temporary mental anxiety. The Scheme requires that the mental illness is disabling in the sense of having a substantial adverse effect on a person's ability to carry out normal day-to-day activities.

19.74 Physical abuse of a child where it falls within a pattern of domestic abuse will normally be compensated by reference to the patterns rather than as instances of individual injury with a similar approach being adopted for sexual abuse.

19.75 A victim will not qualify if:

- They were injured before 1 August 1964.[32]

- The injury was sustained before 1 October 1979 and, at the time of the incident giving rise to the injury, the applicant and assailant responsible for the injury were living together as members of the same family.[33]

- The injury was sustained on or after the 1 October 1979and, at the time of the incident giving rise to that injury, the applicant and assailants were adults living together as members of the same family, unless the applicant and the assailant no longer live together and are unlikely to do so again.[34]

- They have previously applied for compensation for the same criminal injury, under the 2012 Scheme or under any earlier Scheme irrespective of whether or how that application was finally disposed of.[35]

---

[31] See para 9 in the 2008 Scheme for the previous wording.
[32] Paragraph 17 of the 2012 Scheme.
[33] Paragraph 19 of the 2012 Scheme.
[34] Paragraph 20 of the 2012 Scheme.
[35] Paragraph 18 of the 2012 Scheme.

- The assailant may benefit from the award.[36]

- The matter was not reported to the police as soon as reasonably practicable.[37]

- The injury and act of violence took place outside England, Scotland or Wales.[38]

Meaning of 'crime of violence'

19.76   Until the 2012 Scheme there was no definition within the scheme itself of the term 'crime of violence' so it was necessary to turn to the Scheme Guide and case law to gain an understanding as to what will be accepted or rejected by reference to this qualifying phrase. The 2012 Scheme now however includes an explanation of this term in Annex B.

19.77   Previously the 2008 Guide at paragraph 5 stated that 'we usually expect to have involved a physical attack although this is not always the case'. It continued then by listing examples which may give rise to an award including:

- assault (physical or sexual);

- wounding;

- injury direct result of a crime of arson;

- where there was a deliberate attempt to poison the victim;

- deliberate setting of an animal on the victim;

- where someone deliberately runs the victim down with a vehicle.[39]

19.78   Prior to the 2012 Scheme when considering the effect of the body of case law the best place to start was probably the principles stated by the Court of Appeal in *R v CICAP, ex p August; R v CICAP, ex p Brown*[40] and could be set out thus:

(a)   The concept of a crime of violence is not a term of art.

(b)   The issue of whether a crime of violence has taken place is a jury question for the authority or panel to decide. It depends on a 'reasonable and

---

36   Paragraph 21 of the 2012 Scheme.
37   Paragraph 22 of the 2012 Scheme.
38   Paragraph 8 and Annex C.
39   The requirement for this act to be 'deliberate' is contained in para 11 of the 2008 Scheme.
40   [2001] QB 774. Buxton LJ specifically considered 'the extent of current authority on the proper approach in law to the construction of the expression "crime of violence"' at paras 19–22.

literate man's understanding of the circumstances in which he could under the scheme be paid compensation for personal injury caused by a crime of violence'.

(c)   That question is not technical or complicated. The panel 'will recognise a crime of violence when they hear about it even though as a matter of semantics it may be difficult to produce a definition which is too narrow or so wide as to produce absurd consequence …'.

(d)   The correct approach was not to classify particular offences as crimes of violence but the task of the panel is to decide whether the events that actually occurred were:

   (i)   a crime; and
   (ii)   a crime of violence.

(e)   In performing that task, it was necessary to look at the nature and not at the results of the unlawful conduct.

19.79   Note that the proposition argued for 'that a test (or possible test) for the existence of a crime is whether there has been the infliction or threat of force or the doing of a hostile act' was not accepted as a principle. Earlier authority had approached this issue in the following manner:

> 'Most crimes of violence will involve the infliction or threat of force but some may not. I do not think it prudent to attempt a definition of words of ordinary usage in English which [the panel], as a fact finding body, have to apply to the case before them.'[41]

and applying the more dogmatic proposition as a universal rule was rejected in the *Brown* appeal as being inconsistent with the emphasis on the issue being a jury question that turns on all the circumstances.

2012 Scheme Annex B: definition of crime of violence

19.80   A 'crime of violence' is defined as a crime that involves:[42]

(a)   a physical attack;

(b)   any other act or omission of a violent nature which causes physical injury to a person;

(c)   a threat against a person, causing fear of immediate violence in circumstances which would cause a person of reasonable firmness to be put in such fear;

---

[41]   Taken from Lawton LJ in *R v CICB, Ex p Webb* [1987] QB 74.
[42]   Para 2(1) Annex B of the 2012 Scheme.

(d)   a sexual assault to which a person did not in fact consent; or

(e)   arson or fire-rising

In order to fall within the above definition it will need to be an act or omission which is done either intentionally or recklessly.[43]

19.81 Not surprisingly most instances therefore of common assault, actual bodily harm, grievous bodily harm,[44] as well as attempted murder, will be likely to be considered crimes of violence. The definition includes threats causing fear of immediate violence therefore making it clear that actual physical violence is not itself necessary.

19.82 However to qualify the act must still be accompanied by some degree of intent. This could be the intention to cause personal injury or death or recklessness as to whether personal injury or death might result. Purely accidental acts would not be included. Assaults only require basic intent' therefore self-induced intoxication or drug taking would not negate the offence. Self-defence however is a complete defence.

19.83 The 2012 Guide specifically excludes injuries sustained in utero as a result of harmful substances willingly ingested by the mother during pregnancy with intent to cause, or being reckless as to, injury to the foetus. No award will be made to a surviving child in these circumstances.

19.84 Injury from the use of a vehicle will only qualify if the vehicle was used with intent to cause injury to another person.

19.85 It will be for the applicant to establish the necessary intent and where necessary to rebut the defence of self-defence where it is raised on the evidence.

Meanings of 'loved one' and 'immediate aftermath'

19.86 For the purposes of para 6 eligibility[45] a 'loved one' is defined as a person with whom the applicant for the award:

(a)   at the time of the incident had a close relationship of love and affection;

(b)   if the loved one is alive at the date of the application, continues to have such a relationship.

19.87 The 2012 Guide gives the following explanation as to the meaning of 'immediate aftermath'. This must relate to the incident causing injury itself, not the events that follow the incident (such as dealing with the police and medical

---

[43]   Para 2(2) Annex B of the 2012 Scheme.
[44]   See for example the Offences Against the Persons Act 1861, ss 47, 20 and 18.
[45]   In para 6(a) and (b) of the 2012 Scheme.

authorities). The example given is that it would involve the arrival at the scene of the incident before the victim is moved to another location.

19.88 The Guide also indicates that in order to claim under this category a psychiatric diagnosis of a resulting mental injury will be required.[46]

19.89 Despite the reference to 'crime of violence' it is not necessary for the assailant to have been convicted in the UK or elsewhere.[47]

19.90 It is clear therefore by the terms of the Scheme that it is not necessary for an alleged offender to have been convicted of the offence that gave rise to the application for compensation in order for the claim to be successful. If however there has been a conviction then evidence of such conviction will usually be accepted by the Authority as proof of the occurrence of the events constituting the offence. If the conviction is for a lesser offence than the one alleged by the applicant, the onus will fall on the applicant to establish that the more serious offence occurred. Regard should be paid, however, to the circumstances in which an award may be withheld or reduced due to a delay in informing the police or a failure to co-operate with the police.[48]

Compensation in respect of sexual offences

19.91 This was a matter of some complexity in the old 2008 Scheme due to the presence of the requirement set out in para 9(c) of the 2008 Scheme that the applicant was the 'non-consenting victim of a sexual assault'.

19.92 This requirement no longer appears in the Scheme wording under the 2012 Scheme. It is worrying to note however that the 2012 Guide still makes reference to the issues of consent in this way. The explanation in section 2, para 4 of the Guide of the various eligibility criteria states that someone may be eligible for a payment if the criminal injury they sustained resulted from a sexual assault to which a person did not in fact consent.

19.93 Past case law on this aspect produced some surprising results. The past case authority interpretation of para 9(c) of the 2008 Scheme (and its predecessors) had been known, certainly in the eyes of family lawyers and workers involved with abused children, to throw up some surprising and unpalatable results.

19.94 *R v CICAP ex p JE*[49] was an appeal from a decision to dismiss an application for judicial review of the Criminal Injuries Appeal Panel decision to refuse *JE* compensation on the basis that he had consented to the sexual activities on which the application was based, even though it was agreed that

---

[46]   Section 2, paras 16–18 of the 2012 Guide.
[47]   Paragraph 9 of the 2012 Scheme.
[48]   See below at **9.113** et seq and paras 22–24 of the 2012 Scheme.
[49]   [2003] EWCA Civ 234.

JE was a 'defective' meaning his consent would not be a defence to a charge of indecent assault. The Court of Appeal elaborated on the meaning of consent stating at para 28:

> 'In our judgment, properly understood, the Court in *August* recognised that a crime could be a crime of violence as long as there was not 'real consent'. Real consent may exclude a crime from eligibility under the scheme. Consent that is not real will not do so. Nor will submission, which is not the same thing as consent. It is always important to assess, whether the applicant can still properly be regarded as a victim.'

The Court went on to indicate that whilst the fact that *JE* had consented was part, even an important part, of the issue to be determined, its resolution was not the end of the story. It was also necessary to ask whether, despite the consent, that consent was so real so as to prevent him from being a victim. Factors to consider in this exercise included the imbalance in the relationship between the people involved in the sexual acts and the relative degrees of responsibility for what happened.

19.95 Subsequent decisions of the panel have included rejection of the application of a girl (just shy of her 13th birthday at the time of the incident) based on rape by a 21-year-old man who pleaded guilty to unlawful sexual intercourse. The reasoning of the panel was said to include the fact that she had gone willingly with the man, that he had not used threats or violence, that she had previously stated that she had enjoyed the intercourse and that she had previous experience of sexual activity. Her consent was therefore regarded as a real consent excluding her from the scheme. The panel however were found, in a case involving the sexual assault of a 14-year-old by the son of her foster parents over a 3-year period, to have paid insufficient regard to the vulnerability of being in the care system with its associated lack of available support from her mother, her potential inability to make a complaint, the weakness of her position vis-a-vis the foster carer's son and to the possible consequences of her own previous sexual abuse.[50]

19.96 It remains to be seen just how this issue will be approached under the 2012 Scheme.

The assailant should not benefit

19.97 The 2012 Scheme, para 21 provides:

> 'An award will not be made if an assailant may benefit from the award.'

19.98 The 2012 Guide, section, para 37 simply states:

---

[50]   *R (CD) v CICAP and R (JM) v CICAP* [2004] EWHC 1674 (Admin).

'You cannot get a payment if the person who injured you could benefit from your award because there is a continuing close link between you (the victim) and the assailant.'

19.99   Where a child has been injured by a parent there is a real risk that a culpable parent may benefit, for example if the child pre-deceases the parent (a particular risk if the injury has been so severe as to have an impact on the child's life expectancy). Careful wording for trusts may need to be employed so that this risk is avoided and to enable an award to be made. Specific provision is made in para 106 of the 2012 scheme for the claims officer to make arrangements, directions, conditions, settlement or trusts and for the repayment of awards as he or she considers appropriate.[51]

19.100   This can include provision for the balance of any trust fund to revert to the Authority. These arrangements can be made not only to reflect the interests of the applicant but also to reflect public policy.

19.101   The Guide specifically explains that trusts can be set up where the Authority thinks that this will prevent an assailant from benefiting from the award. A trust can also be established if the authority thinks that it is not in the applicant's best interests to receive a lump sum.

Payments to victims under the age of 18 years

19.102   The 2012 Guide, section 6, paras 21–26 contain specific provision on the mechanics of payments to applicants under the age of 18 at the time of payment. These include that the authority would normally pay the award for a person under the age of 18 years directly into an interest earning bank account. The money would not be paid out until the applicant reaches the age of 18.[52]

19.103   Advances may be allowed on the award if they are needed for the sole benefit, education or welfare of the child or young person. If an advance payment is made the authority will normally require evidence in the form of a receipt that this is how the money has been used; absence of such evidence may prevent further advances being made. A young person aged 16 or 17 years and living independently may receive payment of the full award.[53]

---

[51]   The 2012 Guide, section 6, para 13 explains a trust as being a fund which is managed by a person or group of people (trustees) on the victim's behalf. If the CICA directs the setting up of a trust fund where the maximum level of payment has not been reached they may be able to pay the setting up costs in addition to the award. They will not cover any costs where the recipient decides to set up a trust where the setting up of the trust is not as a result of a direction from the CICA.

[52]   See requirements in FRP 2010, PD12D, para 6.2 for the payment into court of any CICA award made in favour of a ward of court. The Practice Direction appears in Part 4 (resources section) of this book.

[53]   2012 Guide, section 6, para 23.

Previous provisions relating to applicants under 18 years of age at time of determination

19.104 It is a relief that the old provisions set out below regarding applicants under the age of 18 at the time of determination have not been repeated in the 2012 Scheme.

19.105 In the 2008 Scheme, at para 16(b):

'A claims officer will make an award only where he or she is satisfied:

(a) where the applicant is under 18 years of age when the application is determined, that it would not be against his or her interest for an award to be made.'

19.106 The 1996 Guide contained the following explanation for the equivalent provision in the 1996 Scheme of the need to be satisfied that it would not be against the child's interests to make an award:

'An example might be that a child who was very young at the time of a very minor assault, who could reasonably be expected to make a full recovery and forget that it had happened. That might be a better outcome than if we made an award, invested it on the child's behalf and released it to him or her at age 18 which might well re-open the incident in the young persons mind and cause considerable distress.'

19.107 The 2001 guidance TS10 indicated that where a child was in care and the local authority had assumed responsibility the authority would normally expect that local authority to be responsible for investment and administration. The 2012 Guide makes no reference to children in care.

Previous provisions regarding withholding an award where victim and assailant living in same household

19.108 Under the old 2008 scheme there were additional provisions regarding the withholding of an award where the victim and assailant lived in the same household even where the victim managed to pass the eligibility criteria.

19.109 These are set out for reference below but it should be noted that these have not been repeated in the 2012 Scheme. It is therefore not likely to be the case that a child remaining in the care of a previously abusive parent will now fall foul of this approach (providing it cannot be brought within the scenario of allowing the assailant to benefit already discussed above). The exclusion from eligibility in para 20 of the new scheme only relates to adults who were living together at the time of the injury who are likely to do so again.

Old 2008 Scheme, para 17

19.110 This applied even where the injury is sustained after 1 October 1979:

'Where a case is not ruled out under paragraph 7(b) ... but at the time when the injury was sustained, the victim and any assailant (whether or not that assailant actually inflicted the injury) were living in the same household as members of the same family, an award will be withheld unless:

(a) the assailant has been prosecuted in connection with the offence, or a claims officer considers that there are practical, technical or other good reasons why a prosecution has not been brought; and

(b) [relates to case of violence between adults in the family]'.

19.111 The 2001 Guide TS10 based on identical wording in the 2001 Scheme spelt out that 'in cases of child abuse within the family where there has been no prosecution we will always require a full explanation on the child's behalf'. The 2008 Guide offers no further assistance as to what might be regarded as good reasons why a prosecution has not been brought.

19.112 Cases decided under earlier schemes informed the interpretation of 'living in the same household as members of the same family'. Earlier wording included the phrase living together at the same time as members of the same family and was held to apply to a child non-accidentally injured by his foster carers.[54] A child living with one parent and their cohabitee who was injured at the hands of the cohabitee was likely to be treated living as a member of the assailant's family under the old 2008 Scheme.

SECTION 8 – OTHER GROUNDS FOR WITHHOLDING OR REDUCING AN AWARD

19.113 Paragraph 22 of the 2012 Scheme provides:

'Failure to Report to the Police

An award under this Scheme will be withheld unless the incident giving rise to the criminal injury has been reported to the police as soon as reasonably practicable. In deciding whether this requirement is met, particular account will be taken of

(a) the age and capacity of the applicant at the date of the incident

(b) whether the effect of the incident on the applicant was such that it could not reasonably have been reported earlier.'

19.114 The 2012 Guide in fact offers very little further assistance on this issue. It stresses the expectation of immediate reporting to the police in order to give them the best chance of bringing the perpetrator to justice.

19.115 It stresses the likelihood of a refusal of an award if the matter is not reported to the police as soon as reasonably practicable. In deciding whether it was reasonably practicable the Authority will take into account whether:

---

[54]   *R (M) v CICAP* [2005] EWCA Civ 566.

- the applicant was too young to report the incident themselves;

- the applicant lacked the mental capacity to report the incident;

- the effect of the injuries meant that a full report could not be made to the police immediately.

19.116   Further grounds for withholding an award under the 2012 Scheme are:

'Paragraph 23

An award will be withheld unless the applicant has co-operated as far as reasonably practicable in bringing the assailant to justice.

Paragraph 24

An award may be withheld or reduced where the conduct of the applicant before during or after the incident giving rise to the criminal injury makes it inappropriate to make an award or a full award. For this purpose, conduct does not include intoxication through alcohol or drugs to the extent that such intoxication made the applicant more vulnerable to becoming a victim of a crime of violence.'

19.117   The Guide makes it clear that the scheme is intended to compensate blameless victims of crime.

Failure to co-operate/report

19.118   Under the 2008 Guide the position adopted was that whilst accepting that a claimant abused as a child may take some time before they felt able to report the abuse and that reporting may not in fact happen until they had become an adult, no matter how long ago the abuse took place it should be reported to the police before a claim is made to the CICA. If no reporting had taken place and there was no good reason for not reporting the incident than it is likely that the application will be rejected. The 2012 Guide makes it clear that if it has not been reported to the police the claim will be refused. There is no time limit put on the actual reporting to the police although delay clearly may hamper the ability to prove the essential elements of the claim.

19.119   Under the 2008 Scheme the expectation was that the report of the incident would be made to the police, although there was a discretion to accept reporting to another authority where it is reasonable for that to have taken place. The examples cited in the Guide include military police, prison wardens and chief officers in an institution for people with mental illnesses. It did not specifically mention a social worker or teacher, who are more likely to be the first authority figures that a child will report abuse to. This is not repeated in the 2012 Guide.

19.120   It is difficult to conceive that if any of these authority figures were told by a child, and they subsequently reported the matter to the police, that this would justify any adverse consequence for the claimant. It does however highlight the need for good practice in cases where a child makes allegations for the joint working of investigations by police and social services. If welfare reasons are adopted by the police for a decision not to prosecute a member of the child's household for the abuse it is also helpful if there is a record of this being the explanation for no further action on behalf of the police. The 2012 Guide specifically allows for the report to the police to be made by the victim or someone else.[55]

19.121   The 2001 TS10 guide included this as an illustration of the approach that would be taken:

> 'A more sympathetic view will be taken in the case of children who may be too young or too frightened to appreciate the right course of action. However we have to be satisfied on the balance of probabilities that the events alleged actually occurred and this will be much easier if the police have been informed on the child's behalf and been given the opportunity to investigate and prosecute.'

19.122   No doubt, even after prompt reporting, matters such as failing to cooperate for example by failing to provide a statement, failing to attend court to give evidence or the withdrawal of a statement could have an adverse impact on the award even if the lack of co-operation is only transient in nature. Where a child applicant is concerned no doubt the child's age would be taken into consideration when considering the impact of such lack of co-operation.

19.123   Failing to assist the CICA will also be taken into account. It is therefore essential that requests for further information are promptly acted upon and assistance given regarding access to medical or other records.

19.124   Once again it is assumed that where a child applicant is concerned there would be a sympathetic approach in cases of sexual abuse to any refusal by the child to undergo an intimate/invasive medical examination. However, failure to attend a medical examination to verify injuries is one of the bases upon which lack of co-operation with the Authority may result in reduction or refusal of the claim.

Conduct

19.125   Paragraph 25 of the 2012 Scheme provides:

> 'An award may be withheld or reduced where the conduct of the applicant before during or after the incident giving rise to the criminal injury makes it inappropriate to make an award or a full award. For this purpose conduct does

---

[55]   Section 5, para 2.

not include intoxication through alcohol or drugs to the extent that such intoxication made the applicant more vulnerable to becoming a victim of a crime of violence.'

19.126 The 2012 Guide specifically states that the payment of an award will not be withheld or reduced solely because consumption of alcohol or drug use made the victim more vulnerable to be attacked and clarifies that applicants who were sexually assaulted under the influence of alcohol or drugs will still be eligible to make an application.

Unspent convictions and character of applicant

19.127 Paragraphs 26 and 27 of the 2012 Scheme provide:

'Annex D sets out the circumstances in which an award under the scheme will be withheld or reduced because the applicant to whom an award would otherwise be made has unspent convictions.

An award may be withheld or reduced because of the Applicant's character, other than in relation to an unspent conviction referred to in paragraph 3 or 4 of Annex D, makes it inappropriate to make an award or a full award.'

19.128 Unspent convictions which result in a term of imprisonment (including youth custody, corrective training detention in YOI etc), service detention, or removal from her Majesty's Service will prevent an award being made under the Scheme. Even the imposition of community orders and youth rehabilitation orders will operate as a bar to an award.

19.129 Annex D to the 2012 Scheme and Appendix 2 to the 2012 Guide make it clear that the Authority must take account of unspent criminal convictions at the date of the application and before the making of a final decision. This is the case even where the applicant was blameless in the incident leading to the claim.

19.130 Unspent convictions attracting lesser sentences will also lead to the withholding or reduction of an award unless there are exceptional reasons not to withhold or reduce the award. This will not however apply to offences attracting only endorsements, penalty points and fines under Sch 2 of the Road Traffic Offenders Act 1988. For these lesser offences a penalty point system is set out in Appendix 2 to the Guide; it is said to enable the officers to operate the system consistently.

19.131 The more recent the conviction and the more serious the penalty the higher the number of penalty points attributed to the conviction. Tables set out the level of reduction according to the number of points (10 points will lead to a 100% reduction) and the number of points a sentence, when combined with the time elapsing before date of sentence and receipt of the compensation claim by the CICA, will attract.

19.132   The penalty point system will be the starting point for consideration   ·
but is not a fixed rule as the Authority must consider each case will exercise
their discretion.

19.133   There may therefore be room to argue in cases of longstanding abuse
there are exceptional reasons in that the existence of convictions are the direct
result of the abuse and should not be used to justify a refusal of the award.[56]

SECTION 9 – COMPENSATION IN FATAL CASES: DEATH OF A PARENT

19.134   An applicant will be a 'qualifying claimant' if at the time of the
deceased's death they were a child of the deceased.[57]

19.135   The 2012 Guide appears to clarify the meaning of 'child' for these
purposes as follows:[58]

- a child of the victim; or

- a person who the deceased accepted as their child and who was dependent
  on the deceased for parental services;

- the definition of child is not limited to someone who is under the age of
  18.

19.136   Further the definition of child as explained in the Guide is not limited
to someone who is under the age of 18.[59] It will include:

- adult children; and

- an unborn child of the deceased, conceived before they died and born
  alive after they died.

19.137   One caveat appears which may affect the ability of a child to claim this
award. The payment to a qualifying relative cannot be made if the qualifying
relative was estranged from the victim at the time of their death. It would be
harsh indeed if in the case of a minor child, removed from their parents into
care, with limited contact were to be taken as being estranged.

19.138   As a qualifying claimant the child may claim a bereavement award.
Under the 2012 Scheme this would be £11,000.00 if there is only one qualifying

---

[56]   For an example of such arguments see *R (M) v CICAP* [2001] EWHC 720 (Admin) where an
        application for judicial review succeeded in part as insufficient reasoning had been given to
        justify the reduction of two-thirds based on criminal convictions.
[57]   Paragraph 59(f) of the 2012 Scheme.
[58]   Section 2, para 19 of the 2012 Guide.
[59]   Section 2, para 20 of the 2012 Guide.

person or £5,500.00 if there is more than one qualifying person (other relevant people would include a partner living with the deceased at the date of death, a spouse, civil partner or parent of the deceased).[60]

19.139 Additional compensation may be payable if the claims officer is satisfied that the qualifying claimant was financially or physically dependent on the deceased (unless the deceased's only normal income was from social security benefits).[61]

19.140 If under 18 years at the date of the death and dependent on the deceased for parental services additional compensation may also be paid for loss of parental services and such other payments as the claims officer considers reasonable to meet other resultant losses.[62] The payment for loss of parental services is currently an annual rate of £2,000.00. This payment is known as a Child's Payment and will end on the day before the child's 18th birthday.

19.141 The child's payments are meant to provide some small recognition of what a child loses as a result of the death of parent such as:

- love and affection;

- care and supervision;

- being taken to and from clubs and activities; and

- treats.

---

[60] Paragraph 61 of the 2012 Scheme.
[61] Paragraphs 67–74 of the 2012 Scheme.
[62] Paragraphs 63–66 of the 2012 Scheme.

Part 4
RESOURCES

Contents

PRACTICE DIRECTION 12D –
INHERENT JURISDICTION (INCLUDING WARDSHIP)
PROCEEDINGS

This Practice Direction supplements FPR Part 12, Chapter 5

The nature of inherent jurisdiction proceedings

1.1 It is the duty of the court under its inherent jurisdiction to ensure that a child who is the subject of proceedings is protected and properly taken care of. The court may in exercising its inherent jurisdiction make any order or determine any issue in respect of a child unless limited by case law or statute. Such proceedings should not be commenced unless it is clear that the issues concerning the child cannot be resolved under the Children Act 1989.

1.2 The court may under its inherent jurisdiction, in addition to all of the orders which can be made in family proceedings, make a wide range of injunctions for the child's protection of which the following are the most common –

(a)   orders to restrain publicity;
(b)   orders to prevent an undesirable association;
(c)   orders relating to medical treatment;
(d)   orders to protect abducted children, or children where the case has another substantial foreign element; and
(e)   orders for the return of children to and from another state.

1.3 The court's wardship jurisdiction is part of and not separate from the court's inherent jurisdiction. The distinguishing characteristics of wardship are that –

(a)   custody of a child who is a ward is vested in the court; and
(b)   although day to day care and control of the ward is given to an individual or to a local authority, no important step can be taken in the child's life without the court's consent.

Transfer of proceedings to county court

2.1 Whilst county courts do not have jurisdiction to deal with applications that a child be made or cease to be a ward of court, consideration should be given to transferring the case in whole or in part to a county court where a direction has been given confirming the wardship and directing that the child remain a ward of court during his minority or until further order.

2.2 The county court must transfer the case back to the High Court if a decision is required as to whether the child should remain a ward of court.

2.3 The following proceedings in relation to a ward of court will be dealt with in the High Court unless the nature of the issues of fact or law makes them more suitable for hearing in the county court –

(a) those in which an officer of the Cafcass High Court Team or the Official Solicitor is or becomes the litigation friend or children's guardian of the ward or a party to the proceedings;
(b) those in which a local authority is or becomes a party;
(c) those in which an application for paternity testing is made;
(d) those in which there is a dispute about medical treatment;
(e) those in which an application is opposed on the grounds of lack of jurisdiction;
(f) those in which there is a substantial foreign element;
(g) those in which there is an opposed application for leave to take the child permanently out of the jurisdiction or where there is an application for temporary removal of a child from the jurisdiction and it is opposed on the ground that the child may not be duly returned.

Parties

3.1 Where the child has formed or is seeking to form an association, considered to be undesirable, with another person, that other person should not be made a party to the application. Such a person should be made a respondent only to an application within the proceedings for an injunction or committal. Such a person should not be added to the title of the proceedings nor allowed to see any documents other than those relating directly to the proceedings for the injunction or committal. He or she should be allowed time to obtain representation and any injunction should in the first instance extend over a few days only.

Removal from jurisdiction

4.1 A child who is a ward of court may not be removed from England and Wales without the court's permission. Practice Direction 12F (International Child Abduction) deals in detail with locating and protecting children at risk of unlawful removal.

Criminal Proceedings

5.1 Where a child has been interviewed by the police in connection with contemplated criminal proceedings and the child subsequently becomes a ward of court, the permission of the court deciding the wardship proceedings ("the wardship court") is not required for the child to be called as a witness in the criminal proceedings.

5.2 Where the police need to interview a child who is already a ward of court, an application must be made for permission for the police to do so. Where permission is given the order should, unless there is some special reason to the contrary, give permission for any number of interviews which may be required by the prosecution or the police. If a need arises to conduct any interview beyond the permission contained in the order, a further application must be made.

5.3 The above applications must be made with notice to all parties.

5.4 Where a person may become the subject of a criminal investigation and it is considered necessary for the child who is a ward of court to be interviewed without that person knowing that the police are making inquiries, the application for permission to interview the child may be made without notice to that party. Notice should, however, where practicable be given to the children's guardian.

5.5 There will be other occasions where the police need to deal with complaints, or alleged offences, concerning children who are wards of court where it is appropriate, if not essential, for action to be taken straight away without the prior permission of the wardship court, for example –

(a) serious offences against the child such as rape, where a medical examination and the collection of forensic evidence ought to be carried out promptly;

(b) where the child is suspected by the police of having committed a criminal act and the police wish to interview the child in respect of that matter;

(c) where the police wish to interview the child as a potential witness.

5.6 In such instances, the police should notify the parent or foster parent with whom the child is living or another 'appropriate adult' (within the Police and Criminal Evidence Act 1984 – Code of Practice C for the Detention, Treatment and Questioning of Persons by Police Officers) so that that adult has the opportunity of being present when the police interview the child. Additionally, if practicable the child's guardian (if one has been appointed) should be notified and invited to attend the police interview or to nominate a third party to attend on the guardian's behalf. A record of the interview or a copy of any statement made by the child should be supplied to the children's guardian. Where the child has been interviewed without the guardian's knowledge, the guardian should be informed at the earliest opportunity of this fact and (if it be the case) that the police wish to conduct further interviews. The wardship court should be informed of the situation at the earliest possible opportunity thereafter by the children's guardian, parent, foster parent (through the local authority) or other responsible adult.

Applications to the Criminal Injuries Compensation Authority

6.1 Where a child who is a ward of court has a right to make a claim for compensation to the Criminal Injuries Compensation Authority ("CICA"), an application must be made by the child's guardian, or, if no guardian has been appointed, the person with care and control of the child, for permission to apply to CICA and disclose such documents on the wardship proceedings file as are considered necessary to establish whether or not the child is eligible for an award plus, as appropriate, the amount of the award.

6.2 Any order giving permission should state that any award made by CICA should normally be paid into court immediately upon receipt and, once that payment has been made, application should made to the court as to its management and administration. If it is proposed to invest the award in any other way, the court's prior approval must be sought.

The role of the tipstaff

7.1 The tipstaff is the enforcement officer for all orders made in the High Court. The tipstaff's jurisdiction extends throughout England and Wales. Every applicable order made in the High Court is addressed to the tipstaff in children and family matters (eg "The Court hereby directs the Tipstaff of the High Court of Justice, whether acting by himself or his assistants or a police officer as follows ...").

7.2 The tipstaff may effect an arrest and then inform the police. Sometimes the local bailiff or police will detain a person in custody until the tipstaff arrives to collect that person or give further directions as to the disposal of the matter. The tipstaff may also make a forced entry although there will generally be a uniformed police officer standing by to make sure there is no breach of the peace.

7.3 There is only one tipstaff (with two assistants) but the tipstaff can also call on any constable or bailiff to assist in carrying out the tipstaff's duties.

7.4 The majority of the tipstaff's work involves locating children and taking them into protective custody, including cases of child abduction abroad.

****

PRACTICE DIRECTION 29A – HUMAN RIGHTS, JOINING THE CROWN

This Practice Direction supplements FPR Part 29, rule 29.5 (The Human Rights Act 1998)

Section 4 of the Human Rights Act 1998

1.1 Where a party has informed the court about –

(a) a claim for a declaration of incompatibility in accordance with section 4 of the Human Rights Act 1998; or

(b) an issue for the court to decide which may lead to the court considering making a declaration,

then the court may at any time consider whether notice should be given to the Crown as required by that Act and give directions for the content and service of the notice. The rule allows a period of 21 days before the court will make the declaration but the court may vary this period of time.

1.2 The court will normally consider the issues and give the directions referred to in paragraph 1.1 at a directions hearing.

1.3 The notice must be served on the person named in the list published under section 17 of the Crown Proceedings Act 1947.

1.4 The notice will be in the form directed by the court and will normally include the directions given by the court. The notice will also be served on all the parties.

1.5 The court may require the parties to assist in the preparation of the notice.

1.6 Unless the court orders otherwise, the Minister or other person permitted by the Human Rights Act 1998 to be joined as a party must, if he or she wishes to be joined, give notice of his or her intention to be joined as a party to the court and every other party. Where the Minister has nominated a person to be joined as a party the notice must be accompanied by the written nomination.

> (Section 5(2)(a) of the Human Rights Act 1998 permits a person nominated by a Minister of the Crown to be joined as a party. The nomination may be signed on behalf of the Minister.)

Section 9 of the Human Rights Act 1998

2.1 The procedure in paragraphs 1.1 to 1.6 also applies where a claim is made under sections 7(1)(a) and 9(3) of the Human Rights Act 1998 for damages in respect of a judicial act.

2.2 Notice must be given to the Lord Chancellor and should be served on the Treasury Solicitor on his behalf.

2.3 The notice will also give details of the judicial act, which is the subject of the claim for damages, and of the court that made it.

> (Section 9(4) of the Human Rights Act 1998 provides that no award of damages may be made against the Crown as provided for in section 9(3) unless the appropriate person is joined in the proceedings. The appropriate person is the Minister responsible for the court concerned or a person or department nominated by him or her (section 9(5) of the Act).

PRACTICE DIRECTION 29B – HUMAN RIGHTS ACT 1998

This Practice Direction supplements FPR Part 29

1 It is directed that the following practice shall apply as from 2 October 2000 in all family proceedings:

Citation of authorities

2 When an authority referred to in s 2 of the Human Rights Act 1998 ("the Act") is to be cited at a hearing:

(a) the authority to be cited shall be an authoritative and complete report;
(b) the court must be provided with a list of authorities it is intended to cite and copies of the reports:
  (i) in cases to which *Practice Direction (Family Proceedings: Court Bundles)* (10 March 2000) [2000] 1 FLR 536 applies, as part of the bundle;
  (ii) otherwise, not less than 2 clear days before the hearing; and
(c) copies of the complete original texts issued by the European Court and Commission, either paper based or from the Court's judgment database (HUDOC) which is available on the internet, may be used.

Allocation to judges

3

    (1)   The hearing and determination of the following will be confined to a High Court judge:

        (a)   a claim for a declaration of incompatibility under s 4 of the Act; or

        (b)   an issue which may lead to the court considering making such a declaration.

    (2)   The hearing and determination of a claim made under the Act in respect of a judicial act shall be confined in the High Court to a High Court judge and in county courts to a circuit judge.

Forms

Form N161

Appellant's notice

(All appeals except small claims track appeals)

For Court use only	
Appeal Court Ref. No.	
Date filed	

Notes for guidance are available which will help you complete this form. Please read them carefully before you complete each section.

SEAL

Section 1	Details of the claim or case you are appealing against

Claim or Case no.

Name(s) of the ☐ Claimant(s) ☐ Applicant(s) ☐ Petitioner(s)

Name(s) of the ☐ Defendant(s) ☐ Respondent(s)

Details of the party appealing ('The Appellant')

Name

Address (including postcode)

Tel No.	
Fax	
E-mail	

Details of the Respondent to the appeal

Name

Address (including postcode)

Tel No.	
Fax	
E-mail	

Details of additional parties (if any) are attached ☐ Yes ☐ No

Section 2   Details of the appeal

From which court is the appeal being brought?

☐   The County Court at

☐   High Court

☐   Queen's Bench Division

☐   Chancery Division

☐   Family Division

☐   Other (please specify)

What is the name of the Judge whose decision you want to appeal?

What is the status of the Judge whose decision you want to appeal?

☐ District Judge or Deputy   ☐ Circuit Judge or Recorder   ☐ Tribunal Judge

☐ Master or Deputy   ☐ High Court Judge or Deputy

What is the date of the decision you wish to appeal against?

To which track, if any, was the claim or case allocated?

☐   Fast track

☐   Multi track

☐   Not allocated to a track

Nature of the decision you wish to appeal

☐ Case management decision   ☐ Grant or refusal of interim relief

☐ Final decision   ☐ A previous appeal decision

Section 3   Legal representation

Are you legally represented?

☐ Yes ☐ No

If 'Yes', please give details of your solicitor below

Name of the firm of solicitors representing you

The address (including postcode) of the firm of solicitors representing you

	Tel No.	
	Fax	
	E-mail	
	DX	
	Ref.	

Are you, the Appellant, in receipt of a Legal Aid Certificate or a Community Legal Service Fund (CLSF) certificate?

☐ Yes ☐ No

Is the respondent legally represented?

☐ Yes ☐ No

If 'Yes', please give details of the respondent's solicitor below

Name and address (including postcode) of the firm of solicitors representing the respondent

	Tel No.	
	Fax	
	E-mail	
	DX	
	Ref.	

Section 4   Permission to appeal

Do you need permission to appeal?

☐ Yes ☐ No

Has permission to appeal been granted?

☐ **Yes** (Complete Box A)   ☐ **No** (Complete Box B)

Box A

Date of order granting permission

Name of Judge granting permission

Box B

I

the Appellant('s solicitor) seek permission to appeal.

If permission to appeal has been granted **in part** by the lower court, do you seek permission to appeal in respect of the grounds refused by the lower court?

☐ Yes ☐ No

Section 5	Other information required for the appeal

Please set out the order (or part of the order) you wish to appeal against

Have you lodged this notice with the court in time?
(There are different types of appeal -
see Guidance Notes N161A)

☐ Yes   ☐ No
If **'No'** you must complete
Part B of Section 9

Section 6	Grounds of appeal

Please state, in numbered paragraphs, **on a separate sheet** attached to this notice and entitled 'Grounds of Appeal' (also in the top right hand corner add your claim or case number and full name), why you are saying that the Judge who made the order you are appealing was wrong.

☐ I confirm that the grounds of appeal are attached to this notice.

Section 7	Arguments in support of grounds for appeal

☐ I confirm that the arguments (known as a 'Skeleton Argument') in support of the 'Grounds of Appeal' are set out **on a separate sheet** and attached to this notice.

OR

☐ I confirm that the arguments (known as a 'Skeleton Argument') in support of the 'Grounds of Appeal' will follow within 14 days of filing this Appellant's Notice

Section 8   What are you asking the Appeal Court to do?

I am asking the appeal court to:-
(please tick the appropriate box)

☐ set aside the order which I am appealing

☐ vary the order which I am appealing and substitute the following order. Set out in the following space the order you are asking for:-

☐ order a new trial

Section 9   Other applications

Complete this section **only** if you are making any additional applications.

Part A

☐ I apply for a stay of execution. (You must set out in Section 10 your reasons for seeking a stay of execution and evidence in support of your application.)

Part B

☐ I apply for an extension of time for filing my appeal notice. (You must set out in Section 10 the reasons for the delay and what steps you have taken since the decision you are appealing.)

Part C

☐ I apply for an order that:

(You must set out in Section 10 your reasons and your evidence in support of your application.)

Section 10	Evidence in support

In support of my application(s) in Section 9, I wish to rely upon the following reasons and evidence:

Statement of Truth – This must be completed in support of the evidence in Section 10

I believe (The appellant believes) that the facts stated in this section are true.

Full name

Name of appellant's solicitor's firm

signed   position or office held

Appellant ('s solicitor)   (if signing on behalf of firm or company)

Section 11 Supporting documents

To support your appeal you should file with this notice all relevant documents listed below. To show which documents you are filing, please tick the appropriate boxes.

If you do not have a document that you intend to use to support your appeal complete the box over the page.

- [ ] two additional copies of your appellant's notice for the appeal court;
- [ ] one copy of your appellant's notice for each of the respondents;
- [ ] one copy of your grounds for appeal for each of the respondents;
- [ ] one copy of your skeleton argument for each copy of the appellant's notice that is filed;
- [ ] a sealed *(stamped by the court)* copy of the order being appealed;
- [ ] a copy of any order giving or refusing permission to appeal, together with a copy of the judge's reasons for allowing or refusing permission to appeal;
- [ ] any witness statements or affidavits in support of any application included in the appellant's notice;
- [ ] a copy of the order allocating the case to a track *(if any)*; and
- [ ] a copy of the legal aid or CLSF certificate *(if legally represented)*.

A bundle of documents for the appeal hearing containing copies of all the papers listed below:-

- [ ] a sealed copy *(stamped by the court)* of your appellant's notice;
- [ ] a sealed copy *(stamped by the court)* of the order being appealed;
- [ ] a copy of any order giving or refusing permission to appeal, together with a copy of the judge's reasons for allowing or refusing permission to appeal;
- [ ] any affidavit or witness statement filed in support of any application included in the appellant's notice;
- [ ] a copy of the grounds for appeal;
- [ ] a copy of the skeleton argument;
- [ ] a transcript or note of judgment, and in cases where permission to appeal was given by the lower court or is not required those parts of any transcript of evidence which are directly relevant to any question at issue on the appeal;
- [ ] the claim form and statements of case (where relevant to the subject of the appeal);
- [ ] any application notice (or case management documentation) relevant to the subject of the appeal;
- [ ] in cases where the decision appealed was itself made on appeal (eg from district judge to circuit judge), the first order, the reasons given and the appellant's notice used to appeal from that order;
- [ ] in the case of judicial review or a statutory appeal, the original decision which was the subject of the application to the lower court;
- [ ] in cases where the appeal is from a Tribunal, a copy of the Tribunal's reasons for the decision, a copy of the decision reviewed by the Tribunal and the reasons for the original decision and any document filed with the Tribunal setting out the grounds of appeal from that decision;
- [ ] any other documents which are necessary to enable the appeal court to reach a decision; and
- [ ] such other documents as the court may direct.

Reasons why you have not supplied a document and date when you expect it to be available:-

Title of document and reason not supplied	Date when it will be supplied

Section 12 The notice of appeal must be signed here

Signed | Appellant('s Solicitor)

Guidance notes on completing form N161 – Appellant's notice (all appeals except small claims track appeals)

Please note form N161 is to be used for fast track and multi-track cases and statutory appeals from tribunals and other outside bodies only. Appeals in small claims track cases should use form **N164 – Appellant's notice (small claims track only)**.

A free leaflet **'EX340 – I want to appeal'** giving information about making an appeal in or to the High Court or a county court is available from:

- any county court,
- hmctsformfinder.justice.gov.uk; or
- the Clerk of the lists General Office/ Appeals Office at the Royal Courts of Justice, Strand, London WC2A 2LL.

The leaflet will also explain the meaning of some of the terms and expressions used in this guidance.

Information is available about making an appeal to the Court of Appeal, from the Civil Appeals Office Registry, Room E307, Royal Courts of Justice, Strand, London WC2A 2LL.

- Court staff can help you complete the appellant's notice and tell you about procedure, they cannot give legal advice - for example, whether you should appeal or whether your appeal will be successful.
- If you need legal advice about bringing your appeal, you should contact a solicitor or a Citizens Advice Bureau immediately.
- If you are legally represented, your solicitor should complete this form on your behalf.

N161A - Guidance notes on completing the appellant's notice (10.12)   © Crown copyright 2012

Important - time limits for issuing (filing) your appeal.

You have only a limited time in which to file your appellant's notice at the appeal court, so you must act quickly.

The leaflet **'EX340 – I want to appeal'** will tell you which is the appropriate appeal court in your case.

You must file your appellant's notice:-

- within the time limit set by the judge whose order you are appealing against; or
- where that judge set no time limit, within **21 days** after the date of the decision you wish to appeal against was made.

Time limits which apply in the Court of Appeal in specific types of appeal

If you are appealing a decision of the Administrative Court made at an oral hearing refusing permission to apply for judicial review, within **7 days** after the date the decision was made.

If you are appealing a decision of the Upper Tribunal Administrative Appeals Chamber, within **21 days** of the date on which the Upper Tribunal decision on permission to appeal to the Court of Appeal was given.

If you are appealing a decision of any other chamber of the Upper Tribunal Chamber, within **28 days** of the date on which the Upper Tribunal decision on permission to appeal to the Court of Appeal was given.

General notes on completing the notice

Set out below are notes to help you fill in the form. You should read the notes to each section carefully before you begin to complete that particular section.

Use a separate sheet if you need more space for your answers, marking clearly which section the information refers to. Write the claim or case number on it and attach it securely to the notice.

If you do not have all the documents or information you need for your appeal, you must **not** allow this to delay sending or taking the form to the appeal court within the correct time. Complete the form as fully as possible and provide what documents you have. The notes to Section 10 will explain more about what you have to do in these circumstances.

Section 1: Details of the claim or case you are appealing against

Give the claim or case number you wish to appeal against. You are required to provide the full name of all parties and to indicate whether they were the claimant, applicant or petitioner, defendant or respondent by ticking the appropriate box. You can find this and other information in the order or decision you are appealing against.

Give your (appellant's) full name, and the address to which you would like all documents relating to the appeal to be sent. Include contact information e.g telephone and any other contact information.

You will also need to include the above details for the respondent to enable the court to send correspondence and other details to the respondent. If there is more than one respondent, list their names, addresses and contact details on a separate sheet of

3

paper and tick the 'details of additional parties' box to indicate that you have done so. Write the claim number on it and attach it securely to your notice.

Section 2: Details of the appeal

Most of the information you will need to complete this section will be found on the order or decision you are appealing against.

Give the name of the court or tribunal whose order you are appealing against.

Give the name of the Judge, whose decision you wish to appeal and indicate, by ticking the relevant box, the status of the judge.

If the order being appealed was made in the High Court or a county court, and did not relate to a family matter, it will usually have been allocated to the fast track or multi-track for the purpose of preparation of evidence and trial. If it was allocated to a track, you should tick the appropriate box to show which. (The notice of allocation or other order should give this information.)

You should also tick the appropriate box if the order you are appealing against was a case management decision to indicate the nature of the decision you wish to appeal. Case management decisions include orders relating to:

- the timetable for trial;
- the filing and exchange of information (of witnesses and experts);
- disclosure of documents (papers the court said you must make available to the other parties); or
- adding a party to a claim.

4

A grant or refusal of interim relief might include an injunction, freezing order, an order for the detention or custody or preservation of relevant property, or a financial order. You should tick the previous appeal decision box if this is a second appeal and you wish to appeal against the outcome of the first appeal hearing.

Section 3: Legal representation

Confirm whether you are legally represented and if so, give your solicitor's name and contact details.

Indicate whether or not your case is being funded.

Confirm whether the respondent is legally represented and, if so, provide the name and contact details of their solicitor.

Section 4: Permission to appeal

You will usually need permission to appeal the decision of a judge of the High Court or a county court. If you are appealing the decision of a tribunal, you should check with that tribunal whether you need permission to appeal and, if so, whether you need to ask for that permission from the tribunal, or from the appeal court.

If you wish to make a **second appeal** against the same order, you can only do so if the Court of Appeal in London gives you permission. You must make your application for permission to that court permission for a second appeal will only be given exceptionally.

You should note that permission will only be given where the court considers that your appeal has a real prospect of success. Where your appeal is against a case management decision, the court will also consider:

- whether the issue is significant enough to justify the costs of an appeal;

- the overall effect on the case management timetable, e.g. whether the loss of the trial date is more significant than the procedural point you wish to appeal; and

- whether it would be more convenient to deal with your point at the trial.

You **do not** need permission if the order you are appealing against is one of the following:

- a committal order;

- an order refusing the grant of habeas corpus;

- a secure accommodation order under Section 25 of the Children Act 1989.

You need only request permission in this notice if:

- you did not ask for permission to appeal at the hearing at which the decision you are appealing against was made; or

- you asked for permission, but it was refused, and you wish the appeal court to reconsider your request.

> The court when giving permission to appeal may, **exceptionally,** direct that your appeal be referred to the Court of Appeal if it considers that it raises an important point of principle or practice or there is some other important reason for the Court of Appeal to hear it. Where the court gives this direction, it will be shown on form **N460 Reasons for allowing or refusing permission to appeal (including referral to the Court of Appeal)** which the court will send you.

6

If you need more time than is allowed for filing your appellant's notice, you must make an application in the notice itself. (See the notes to Section 9).

Section 5: Other information required for the appeal

You are required to state the order you wish to appeal. If you are appealing only part of an order or tribunal decision, you must write out that part (or parts) of the order in the box provided.

Sections 6 and 7: Grounds of appeal and arguments in support

An appeal must be based on relevant grounds (reasons for appealing). An appeal court will only allow an appeal against a decision that was either:

- wrong; or
- unjust because of a serious procedural or other irregularity in the lower court proceedings.

The appeal court will be unlikely to overturn a decision where no real difference would be made to the outcome of the case; or the appeal would involve re-examining the factual investigation undertaken by the lower court.

Set out briefly and **on a separate sheet** your reasons why you think the judge's decision was wrong or unjust. If possible, list your reasons in short separately numbered paragraphs and indicate you have done this by ticking the relevant box.

Remember that you **must not** include any grounds for appealing which rely on new evidence, that is evidence that has become available since the order was made. You may not produce new evidence in your appeal without first obtaining the permission of the appeal court. (See the notes to Section 4)

7

Please indicate by ticking the relevant box whether you are attaching your arguments (referred to as a skeleton argument) to this notice or whether you intend to send them separately within 14 days of filing this appellant's notice with the court.

The separate skeleton argument should be filed and served on the respondent either with your completed notice or, if you are unable to complete your skeleton argument in time, no later then 14 days after filing your notice.

Skeleton arguments should contain a numbered list of points that you intend to argue at the hearing. Each point should be stated in no more than a few sentences. Refer at each point to any documents you are filing with your appellant's notice which supports that argument (see Section 11 on documents).

Other useful information
Try to consider what other information the appeal court might find useful. For example, the court may find it helpful to have a list of people who feature in the case, an explanation of technical terms used in the papers, or a list of events in date order
(a chronology). If you are providing any of these, they should be on a separate piece of paper attached to your notice marked with the case or claim number and names of the parties.

Section 8: What you are asking the appeal court to do?

Indicate by ticking the relevant box whether you are asking the appeal court to set aside or vary the order you are appealing or whether you would like it to order a new trial.

8

Section 9: Other applications

You only need to complete this section if you are asking for orders in addition to those requested in Section 8.

Any application for an extension of time for appealing must be made in the appeal notice itself. You should state the reason for the delay and the steps taken up to the time of filing the notice. See page 2 for information on time limits.

You may wish to make additional applications to the appeal court in connection with your appeal. Any other applications may be made either in the notice, or in a separate application notice (Form N244 – Application notice). This form can be obtained from the court or our website. You may have to pay additional fees if it is filed at a later date than your appellant's notice.

Section 10: Evidence in support

Include here any information you have to support your application under Section 9.

State whether you are producing new evidence in your appeal or asking for permission to produce oral evidence at the appeal hearing. You will need to give reasons why the new evidence was not before the original court and, where oral evidence is requested, the reasons why you think it is necessary. You should sign the statement of truth at the bottom of this section to support any evidence you provide.

Section 11: Supporting documents

Do not delay filing your appellant's notice at the appeal court. If you have not been able to obtain any of the documents listed below within the time allowed, complete the notice as best you can and ensure the notice is filed on time. Tick the appropriate boxes to show the documents you are filing with the appeal notice. List any documents that you intend to use but which you do not have available in the box over the page. Set out the reasons why you have been unable to obtain any of the information or documents and give the date when you expect them to be available.

Whenever possible, the following documents should be filed with your appellant's notice:-

- two additional copies of your appellant's notice for the appeal court;

- one copy of your appellant's notice for each of the respondents;

- one copy of your skeleton argument for each copy of the appellant's notice that is filed;

- a sealed (stamped by the court) copy of the order being appealed;

- a copy of any order giving or refusing permission to appeal, together with a copy of the judge's reasons for allowing or refusing permission to appeal;

- any witness statements or affidavits in support of any application included in the appellant's notice;

- a copy of the order allocating the case to a track (if any); and

- a copy of the legal aid or CLSF certificate (if legally represented).

Your bundle of documents in support which should include copies of:

- a sealed copy (stamped by the court) of your appellant's notice;

- a sealed copy (stamped by the court) of the order being appealed;

- a copy of any order giving or refusing permission to appeal, together with a copy of the judge's reasons for allowing or refusing permission to appeal;

- any affidavit or witness statement filed in support of any application included in the appellant's notice;

- a copy of the skeleton argument;

- a transcript or note of judgment, and in cases where permission to appeal was given by the lower court or is not required those parts of any transcript of evidence which are directly relevant to any question at issue on the appeal;

- the claim form and statements of case (where relevant to the subject of the appeal);

- any application notice (or case management documentation) relevant to the subject of the appeal;

- in cases where the decision appealed was itself made on appeal (eg. from district judge to circuit judge), the first order, the reasons given and the appellant's notice used to appeal from that order;

- in the case of judicial review or a statutory appeal, the original decision which was the subject of the application to the lower court;

- in cases where the appeal is from a Tribunal, a copy of the Tribunal's reasons for the decision, a copy of the decision reviewed by the Tribunal and the reasons for the original decision and any document filed with the Tribunal setting out the grounds of appeal from that decision;

- any other documents which are necessary to enable the appeal court to reach a decision; and

- such other documents as the court may direct.

A transcript or note of judgment may be either an approved transcript of the judgment where the hearing was recorded or a copy of the written judgment (endorsed with the judge's signature) or a note of the judgment. If you were not legally represented in the lower court but the respondent was, the respondent's advocate should make their note of the judgment available to you free of charge.

You should remember that if you file any of the documents at a later date, you must check whether or not the information contained in the later documents alters any of the details already given in your appellant's notice. If it does, you will need to apply to the court for permission to amend the notice. The court can tell you how to do this.

What happens next?

Filing your completed notice and documents

Send or take the notice and copies of all the other documents to the appeal court office with the appropriate fee. The court can tell you how much this is. The court will seal the notice (stamp the notice with the court seal).

The court will serve your appellant's notice, your skeleton argument and any other documents on the respondent, unless you tell the court that you wish to serve them yourself.

Please note that the above paragraph does not apply to the Court of Appeal and the Civil Appeals Office will not serve documents where service is required by the Civil Procedure Rules (See CPR PD 52C para 7.1). For further guidance see the Civil Appeals website www.justice.gov.uk/guidance/ courts-and-tribunals/courts/court-of-appeal/civil-division/ index.htm

The respondent must be served with -

- **a sealed copy of your appellant's notice** as soon as practicable but no later than 7 days after it is filed at the court;

- **any separate skeleton argument** at the same time as the notice. If you have been unable to complete your skeleton argument in time, it must be served no later than 14 days after filing your notice at the court;

- **your bundle of documents**

- if you have already obtained permission to appeal or do not need permission, the bundle must be served at the same time as your notice; **or**

- if you have asked for permission to appeal in your notice and permission has been granted without a hearing, the bundle must be served within 7 days of receiving notice that permission has been given; **or**
- if you have asked for permission to appeal in your notice which is to be considered at a hearing, the bundle must be served within 7 days of receiving notice of that hearing.

Provisions as to service of bundles on respondent's in the Court of Appeal differ from the requirements above and are set out in PD52C para 21. Further guidance as to service of bundles in the Court of Appeal will be provided to you by way of letter from Civil Appeals Office after the issue of your appellant's notice.

Form N162

Respondent's Notice

In the	
Appeal Court Reference No.	

Notes for guidance are available which will help you complete this form. Please read them carefully before you complete each section.

For Court use only	
Date filed	

Seal

Section 1	Details of the claim or case

Name of court [   ]   Case or claim number [   ]

Name or title of case or claim [   ]

In the case or claim, were you the
(tick appropriate box)

☐ claimant   ☐ applicant   ☐ petitioner

☐ defendant   ☐ respondent   ☐ other *(please specify)* _____

Section 2	Your (respondent's) name and address

Your (respondent's) name _____

Your solicitor's name _____ *(if you are legally represented)*

Your (your solicitor's) address

	Your reference or contact name	
	Your contact telephone number	
	DX number	

Details of other respondents are attached ☐ Yes   ☐ No

Section 3	Time estimate for appeal hearing

Do not complete if appealing to the Court of Appeal

	Days	Hours	Minutes
How long do you estimate it will take to put your case to the appeal court at the hearing?			

Who will represent you at the appeal hearing?   ☐ Yourself   ☐ Solicitor   ☐ Counsel

N162 Respondent's Notice (04.07)   © Crown copyright 2007

Section 4	Details of the order(s) or part(s) of order(s) you want to appeal

Name of Judge

Date of order(s)

If only part of an order is appealed, write out that part (or those parts)

Section 5	Permission to file a respondent's notice

Has permission to appeal been granted?

☐ Yes   complete box **A**   ☐ No   complete box **B**
*if you are asking for permission
or it is not required*

A

Date of order granting permission _____

Name of judge_____

Name of court _____

B

☐ I do not need permission

☐ I _____
respondent('s solicitor) seek permission to appeal
the order(s) at **section 4** above.

Are you making any other applications?
If Yes, complete section 9   ☐ Yes   ☐ No

Is the respondent in receipt of legal aid certificate or a community
legal service fund (CLSF) certificate?   ☐ Yes   ☐ No

Does your appeal include any issues arising from the Human Rights Act 1998?   ☐ Yes   ☐ No

Section 6	Grounds for appeal or for upholding the order

I (the respondent)

☐ appeal(s) the order   ☐ wish(es) the appeal court to uphold the order on
                                different or additional grounds

because:-

3

Section 7	Arguments in support of grounds

My skeleton argument is:-

☐ set out below   ☐ attached   ☐ will follow within 14 days of receiving the appellant's skeleton arguments

I (the respondent) will rely on the following arguments at the hearing of the appeal:-

4

| Section 8 | What decision are you asking the appeal court to make? |

I (the respondent) am (is) asking that:-

(tick appropriate box)

☐   the order(s) at **section 4** be set aside

☐   the order(s) at **section 4** be varied and the following order(s) substituted :-

```



```

☐   a new trial be ordered

☐   the appeal court makes the following additional orders :-

```



```

☐   the appeal court upholds the order but for the following different or additional reasons

```



```

Section 9	Other applications

I wish to make an application for additional orders   ☐ in this section

☐ in the Part 23 application
form (N244) attached

Part A
I apply (the respondent applies) for an order (a draft of which is attached) that :-

because :-

Part B
I (the respondent) wish(es) to rely on :

☐   evidence in Part C

☐   witness statement (affidavit)

Part C
I (the respondent) wish(es) to rely on the following evidence in support of this application:-

---

Statement of Truth

I believe (the respondent believes) that the facts stated in Section 9 are true.

Full name _____

Name of respondent's solicitor's firm _____

Signed _____   position or office held _____

Respondent ('s solicitor)   (if signing on behalf of firm or company)

Section 10	Supporting documents

Please tick the papers you are filing in your bundle:-

☐ your respondent's notice and any skeleton arguments (if separate);

☐ any witness statements or affidavits in support of any application included in section 5 or 9 of your notice or in a separate Part 23 application notice;

☐ any other affidavit or witness statement filed in support of your arguments;

☐ a copy of the legal aid or CLSF certificate (if legally represented); and

☐ any other documents directed by the court to be filed in your appeal *(give details)*.

Reasons why you have not supplied a document and date when you expect it to be available:-

Signed_____   Respondent/'s Solicitor

Timetables for Appeals to the Court of Appeal[1]

Timetable Part 1 – Listing window notification to lodging bundle

Period within which step is to be taken	Action	Cross reference to relevant provisions in this Practice Direction
Within 14 days of service of: the appellant's notice if permission has been given by the lower court or is not needed; notification that permission has been granted by the Court of Appeal; or notification that the permission application will be listed with the appeal to follow	**Respondent's notice** (if any) must be filed and served	Paragraph 8 (respondent's notice)
Within 14 days of filing a respondent's notice	**If respondent has filed a respondent's notice**, respondent must lodge and serve a skeleton argument on every other party	Paragraph 9 (skeleton argument to be lodged with the respondent's notice or within 14 days of filing respondent's notice)
7 days after date of listing window notification	Appellant must serve **proposed bundle index** on every respondent	Paragraph 27 (bundle of documents)
14 days after date of listing window notification	**Appeal questionnaire** must be filed and served on every respondent	Paragraph 1 (listing window notification defined) Paragraph 23 (Appeal questionnaire)
7 days after service of Appellant's Appeal Questionnaire	**If a respondent disagrees with appellant's time estimate**, that respondent must file and serve on every other party its own time estimate	Paragraph 24 (time estimate)
21 days after listing window notification	**Appeal skeleton**: appellant must serve on every respondent an appeal skeleton (without bundle cross references)	Paragraph 31 (skeleton argument)

---

[1] Taken from CPR 1998, PD52C Appeals to the Court of Appeal, Part V, para 21.

Period within which step is to be taken	Action	Cross reference to relevant provisions in this Practice Direction
21 days after date of the listing window notification	**Agree bundle**: the respondent must either agree the contents of the appeal bundle or notify the appellant of the documents that the respondent considers should be included in, or removed from, the appeal bundle by sending a revised index. If there is no agreement in relation to inclusion of a particular document, it must be placed in a supplemental bundle prepared by the party who has proposed its inclusion.	Paragraph 27 (bundle of documents) Paragraph 28 (bundle: Appeals from Upper Tribunal Immigration and Asylum Chamber)
42 days after date of listing window notification	**Where Respondent has not filed a respondent's notice,** respondent must lodge skeleton argument and serve on every other party	Paragraph 13 (respondent's skeleton argument (where no Respondent's Notice filed)) Paragraph 31 (skeleton argument)

Timetable Part 2 – Steps to be taken once hearing date fixed: lodging bundles, supplemental skeletons and bundles of authorities

Time before hearing date when step is to be taken	Action	Cross reference to relevant provisions in this Practice Direction
No later than 42 days before the appeal hearing or as	Lodge, as directed by the court, the appropriate number of appeal bundles and serve a copy on all other parties to the appeal	Paragraph 27 (bundle of documents) Paragraph 28 (bundle: Appeals from Upper Tribunal Immigration and Asylum Chamber)
No later than 14 days before date of appeal hearing	Appellant must lodge and serve replacement skeleton argument	Paragraph 1 (replacement skeleton argument defined) Paragraph 31 (skeleton argument content, length and format) Paragraph 32 (supplementary skeleton argument)
No later than 7 days before the date of the hearing	Respondent must lodge and serve replacement skeleton argument	Paragraph 1 (replacement skeleton argument defined) Paragraph 32 (supplementary skeleton argument)
No later than 7 days before date of appeal hearing	Bundles of authorities must be lodged	Paragraph 29 (bundle of authorities)

Time before hearing date when step is to be taken	**Action**	**Cross reference to relevant provisions in this Practice Direction**
No later than 7 days before the date of the hearing	Every document needed for the appeal hearing (if not already lodged or filed) must be lodged or filed	

Form N235

Certificate of suitability of litigation friend

Name of court	
Claim No.	
Claimant (including ref.)	
Defendant (including ref.)	

If you are acting
- **for a child**, you must serve a copy of the completed form on a parent or guardian of the child, or if there is no parent or guardian, the carer or the person with whom the child lives
- **for a protected party**, you must serve a copy of the completed form on one of the following persons with authority in relation to the protected party as: (1) the attorney under a registered enduring power of attorney (2) the donee of the lasting power of attorney; (3) the deputy appointed by the Court of Protection; or if there is no such person, an adult with whom the protected party resides or in whose care the protected party is. You must also complete a certificate of service (obtainable from the court office)

You should send the completed form to the court with the claim form (if acting for the claimant) or when you take the first step on the defendant's behalf in the claim together with the certificate of service (if applicable).

You do not need to complete this form if you are a deputy appointed by the Court of Protection with power to conduct proceedings on behalf of the protected party.

I consent to act as litigation friend for _____
(claimant)(defendant)

I believe that the above named person is a

☐ child   ☐ protected party *(give your reasons overleaf and attach a copy of any medical evidence in support)*

I am able to conduct proceedings on behalf of the above named person competently and fairly and I have no interests adverse to those of the above named person.

delete if you are acting for the defendant *I undertake to pay any costs which the above named claimant may be ordered to pay in these proceedings subject to any right I may have to be repaid from the assets of the claimant.

Please write your name in capital letters

☐ Mr   ☐ Mrs   ☐ Miss   Surname _____

☐ Ms   ☐ Other _____   Forenames _____

Address to which documents in this case are to be sent.

I certify that the information given in this form is correct

Signed _____

Date _____

The court office at

is open between 10 am and 4 pm Monday to Friday. When corresponding with the court, please address forms or letters to the Court Manager and quote the claim number.
N235 Certificate of suitability of litigation friend (10.07)   ©Crown copyright 2007

Claim No.	

My reasons for believing that the (claimant)(defendant) is a protected party are:-

Letter before Claim (Judicial Review)

Section 1. information required in a letter before claim

Proposed claim for judicial review

1
To

(Insert the name and address of the proposed defendant – see details in section 2)

2
The claimant

(Insert the title, first and last name and the address of the claimant)

3
Reference details

(When dealing with large organisations it is important to understand that the information relating to any particular individual's previous dealings with it may not be immediately available, therefore it is important to set out the relevant reference numbers for the matter in dispute and/or the identity of those within the public body who have been handling the particular matter in dispute – see details in section 3)

4
The details of the matter being challenged

(Set out clearly the matter being challenged, particularly if there has been more than one decision)

5
The issue

(Set out the date and details of the decision, or act or omission being challenged, a brief summary of the facts and why it is contented to be wrong)

6
The details of the action that the defendant is expected to take

(Set out the details of the remedy sought, including whether a review or any interim remedy are being requested)

7
The details of the legal advisers, if any, dealing with this claim

(*Set out the name, address and reference details of any legal advisers dealing with the claim*)

8
The details of any interested parties

(*Set out the details of any interested parties and confirm that they have been sent a copy of this letter*)

9
The details of any information sought

(*Set out the details of any information that is sought. This may include a request for a fuller explanation of the reasons for the decision that is being challenged*)

10
The details of any documents that are considered relevant and necessary

(*Set out the details of any documentation or policy in respect of which the disclosure is sought and explain why these are relevant. If you rely on a statutory duty to disclose, this should be specified*)

11
The address for reply and service of court documents

(*Insert the address for the reply*)

12
Proposed reply date

(*The precise time will depend upon the circumstances of the individual case. However, although a shorter or longer time may be appropriate in a particular case, 14 days is a reasonable time to allow in most circumstances*)

Section 2. address for sending the letter before claim

Public bodies have requested that, for certain types of cases, in order to ensure a prompt response, letters before claim chould be sent to specific addresses.

- **Where the claim concerns a decision in an Immigration, Asylum or Nationality case:**

  - The claim may be sent electronically to the following UK Border Agency email address: UKBAPAP@UKBA.gsi.gov.uk
  - Alternatively the claim may be sent by post to the following UK Border Agency postal address:
    Judicial Review Unit
    UK Border Agency
    Lunar House
    40 Wellesley Rd
    Croydon CR9 2BY

- **Where the claim concerns a decision by the Legal Services Commission:**

  - The address on the decision letter/notification; and
    Legal Director
    Corporate Legal Team
    Legal Services Commission
    4 Abbey Orchard Street
    London SW1P 2BS

- Where the claim concerns a decision by a local authority:

  - The address on the decision letter/notification; and
  - Their legal department

- **Where the claim concerns a decision by a department or body for whom Treasury Solicitor acts *and Treasury Solicitor has already been involved in the case* a copy should also be sent, quoting the Treasury Solicitor's reference, to:**
  The Treasury Solicitor,
  One Kemble Street,
  London WC2B 4TS

In all other circumstances, the letter should be sent to the address on the letter notifying the decision.

Section 3. specific reference details required

Public bodies have requested that the following information should be provided in order to ensure prompt response.

- Where the claim concerns an Immigration, Asylum or Nationality case, dependent upon the nature of the case:

  - The Home Office reference number
  - The Port reference number

- – The Asylum and Immigration Tribunal reference number
- – The National Asylum Support Service reference number
  Or, if these are unavailable:

- – The full name, nationality and date of birth of the claimant.

- Where the claim concerns a decision by the Legal Services Commission:

  – The certificate reference number.

Letter in Response to the Letter before Claim (Judicial Review)

Information required in a response to a letter before claim

Proposed claim for judicial review

1
The claimant

(*Insert the title, first and last names and the address to which any reply should be sent*)

2
From

(*Insert the name and address of the defendant*)

3
Reference details

(*Set out the relevant reference numbers for the matter in dispute and the identity of those within the public body who have been handling the issue*)

4
The details of the matter being challenged

(*Set out details of the matter being challenged, providing a fuller explanation of the decision, where this is considered appropriate*)

5
Response to the proposed claim

(*Set out whether the issue in question is conceded in part, or in full, or will be contested. Where it is not proposed to disclose any information that has been requested, explain the reason for this. Where an interim reply is being sent and there is a realistic prospect of settlement, details should be included*)

6
Details of any other interested parties

(*Identify any other parties who you consider have an interest who have not already been sent a letter by the claimant*)

7
Address for further correspondence and service of court documents

(Set out the address for any future correspondence on this matter)

Form N461

Judicial Review
Claim Form

In the High Court of Justice
Administrative Court

Notes for guidance are available which explain how to complete the judicial review claim form. Please read them carefully before you complete the form.

For Court use only	
Administrative Court Reference No.	
Date filed	

Seal

SECTION 1   Details of the claimant(s) and defendant(s)

Claimant(s) name and address(es)

┌name────────────────────┐
└────────────────────────┘

┌address─────────────────┐
│   │
│   │
└────────────────────────┘

┌Telephone no.───┐ ┌Fax no.───┐
└────────────────┘ └──────────┘
┌E-mail address──────────┐
└────────────────────────┘

Claimant's or claimant's solicitors' address to which documents should be sent.

┌name────────────────────┐
└────────────────────────┘

┌address─────────────────┐
│   │
│   │
└────────────────────────┘

┌Telephone no.───┐ ┌Fax no.───┐
└────────────────┘ └──────────┘
┌E-mail address──────────┐
└────────────────────────┘

Claimant's Counsel's details

┌name────────────────────┐
└────────────────────────┘

┌address─────────────────┐
│   │
│   │
└────────────────────────┘

┌Telephone no.───┐ ┌Fax no.───┐
└────────────────┘ └──────────┘
┌E-mail address──────────┐
└────────────────────────┘

1st Defendant

┌name────────────────────┐
└────────────────────────┘

Defendant's or (where known) Defendant's solicitors' address to which documents should be sent.

┌name────────────────────┐
└────────────────────────┘

┌address─────────────────┐
│   │
│   │
└────────────────────────┘

┌Telephone no.───┐ ┌Fax no.───┐
└────────────────┘ └──────────┘
┌E-mail address──────────┐
└────────────────────────┘

2nd Defendant

┌name────────────────────┐
└────────────────────────┘

Defendant's or (where known) Defendant's solicitors' address to which documents should be sent.

┌name────────────────────┐
└────────────────────────┘

┌address─────────────────┐
│   │
│   │
└────────────────────────┘

┌Telephone no.───┐ ┌Fax no.───┐
└────────────────┘ └──────────┘
┌E-mail address──────────┐
└────────────────────────┘

SECTION 2 Details of other interested parties

Include name and address and, if appropriate, details of DX, telephone or fax numbers and e-mail

name

name

address

address

Telephone no.

Fax no.

Telephone no.

Fax no.

E-mail address

E-mail address

SECTION 3 Details of the decision to be judicially reviewed

Decision:

Date of decision:

Name and address of the court, tribunal, person or body who made the decision to be reviewed.

name

address

SECTION 4 Permission to proceed with a claim for judicial review

I am seeking permission to proceed with my claim for Judicial Review.

Is this application being made under the terms of Section 18 Practice Direction 54 (Challenging removal)? ☐ Yes ☐ No

Are you making any other applications? If Yes, complete Section 7. ☐ Yes ☐ No

Is the claimant in receipt of a Community Legal Service Fund (CLSF) certificate? ☐ Yes ☐ No

Are you claiming exceptional urgency, or do you need this application determined within a certain time scale? If Yes, complete Form N463 and file this with your application. ☐ Yes ☐ No

Have you complied with the pre-action protocol? If No, give reasons for non-compliance in the box below. ☐ Yes ☐ No

Have you issued this claim in the region with which you have the closest connection? (Give any additional reasons for wanting it to be dealt with in this region in the box below). If No, give reasons in the box below. ☐ Yes ☐ No

Does the claim include any issues arising from the Human Rights Act 1998?
If Yes, state the articles which you contend have been breached in the box below.   ☐ Yes   ☐ No

SECTION 5 Detailed statement of grounds

        ☐ set out below   ☐ attached

SECTION 6 Details of remedy (including any interim remedy) being sought

SECTION 7 Other applications

I wish to make an application for:-

SECTION 8 Statement of facts relied on

Statement of Truth

I believe (The claimant believes) that the facts stated in this claim form are true.

Full name_____

Name of claimant's solicitor's firm _____

Signed_____ Position or office held_____

      Claimant ('s solicitor)   (if signing on behalf of firm or company)

SECTION 9 Supporting documents

If you do not have a document that you intend to use to support your claim, identify it, give the date when you expect it to be available and give reasons why it is not currently available in the box below.

Please tick the papers you are filing with this claim form and any you will be filing later.

☐ Statement of grounds   ☐ included   ☐ attached

☐ Statement of the facts relied on   ☐ included   ☐ attached

☐ Application to extend the time limit for filing the claim form   ☐ included   ☐ attached

☐ Application for directions   ☐ included   ☐ attached

☐ Any written evidence in support of the claim or
  application to extend time

☐ Where the claim for judicial review relates to a decision of
  a court or tribunal, an approved copy of the reasons for
  reaching that decision

☐ Copies of any documents on which the claimant
  proposes to rely

☐ A copy of the legal aid or CSLF certificate *(if legally represented)*

☐ Copies of any relevant statutory material

☐ A list of essential documents for advance reading by
  the court *(with page references to the passages relied upon)*

If Section 18 Practice Direction 54 applies, please tick the relevant box(es) below to indicate which papers you are filing with this claim form:

☐ a copy of the removal directions and the decision to which   ☐ included   ☐ attached
  the application relates

☐ a copy of the documents served with the removal directions
  including any documents which contains the Immigration and   ☐ included   ☐ attached
  Nationality Directorate's factual summary of the case

☐ a detailed statement of the grounds   ☐ included   ☐ attached

Reasons why you have not supplied a document and date when you expect it to be available:-

Signed _____ Claimant ('s Solicitor)_____

Form N463

Judicial Review
Application for urgent consideration

This form must be completed by the Claimant or the Claimant's advocate if exceptional urgency is being claimed and the application needs to be determined within a certain time scale.

The claimant, or the claimant's solicitors must serve this form on the defendant(s) and any interested parties with the N461 Judicial review claim form.

To the Defendant(s) and Interested Party(ies)
Representations as to the urgency of the claim may be made by defendants or interested parties to the relevant Administrative Court Office by fax or email:-

For cases proceeding in

In the High Court of Justice Administrative Court	
Claim No.	
Claimant(s) *(including ref.)*	
Defendant(s)	
Interested Party(ies)	

London
Fax: 020 7947 6802   **email:** administrativecourtoffice.generaloffice@hmcts.x.gsi.gov.uk

Birmingham
Fax: 0121 250 6730   **email:** administrativecourtoffice.birmingham@hmcts.x.gsi.gov.uk

Cardiff
Fax: 02920 376461   **email:** administrativecourtoffice.cardiff@hmcts.x.gsi.gov.uk

Leeds
Fax: 0113 306 2581   **email:** administrativecourtoffice.leeds@hmcts.x.gsi.gov.uk

Manchester
Fax: 0161 240 5315   **email:** administrativecourtoffice.manchester@hmcts.x.gsi.gov.uk

SECTION 1 Reasons for urgency

SECTION 2 Proposed timetable *(tick the boxes and complete the following statements that apply)*

☐ a) The N461 application for permission should be considered within _____ hours/days

  If consideration is sought within 48 hours, you must complete Section 3 below

☐ b) Abridgement of time is sought for the lodging of acknowledgments of service

☐ c) If permission for judicial review is granted, a substantive hearing is sought by _____ (date)

SECTION 3 Justification for request for immediate consideration

Date and time when it was first appreciated that an immediate application might be necessary.

Date

Time

Please provide reasons for any delay in making the application.

What efforts have been made to put the defendant and any interested party on notice of the application?

SECTION 4 Interim relief *(state what interim relief is sought and why in the box below)*

A draft order must be attached.

SECTION 5 Service

A copy of this form of application was served on the defendant(s) and interested parties as follows:

Defendant

☐ by fax machine to   time sent

Fax no.   time

☐ by handing it to or leaving it with

name

☐ by e-mail to

e-mail address

Date served

Date

Interested party

☐ by fax machine to   time sent

Fax no.   time

☐ by handing it to or leaving it with

name

☐ by e-mail to

e-mail address

Date served

Date

I confirm that all relevant facts have been disclosed in this application

Name of claimant's advocate

name

Claimant (claimant's advocate)

Signed

Form N464

<table>
<tr>
<td colspan="2">Application for directions as to venue for administration and determination

Name and address of party making application

name

address

</td>
<td colspan="2">In the High Court of Justice
Administrative Court</td>
</tr>
</table>

<table>
<tr><td>Claim No.</td><td></td></tr>
<tr><td>Claimant(s)/
Appellant(s)</td><td></td></tr>
<tr><td>Defendant(s)/
Respondent(s)</td><td></td></tr>
<tr><td>Interested
Party(ies)</td><td></td></tr>
</table>

I/We apply to the court for a direction that this matter be administered and determined at the:

☐ Royal Courts of Justice in **London**

☐ District Registry of the High Court at **Birmingham**

☐ District Registry of the High Court at **Cardiff**

☐ District Registry of the High Court at **Leeds**

☐ District Registry of the High Court at **Manchester**

for the following reason(s): *(please refer to paragraph 5.2 of PD54D set out overleaf)*

(To be signed by you or by your solicitor or litigation friend)

Signed

Date

Name

(if signing on behalf of firm or company, court)

Position or office held

Please send your completed form to the Administrative Court Office which is currently administering this matter, within 21 days of service of the proceedings upon you. You must also serve copies of your completed application on all other parties.

N464 Application for directions as to venue for administration and determination (04.09)   © Crown copyright 2009

Practice Direction 54D 5.2

5.2 The general expectation is that proceedings will be administered and determined in the region with which the claimant/appellant has the closest connection, subject to the following considerations as applicable -

1) any reason expressed by any party for preferring a particular venue;

2) the region in which the defendant/respondent or any relevant office or department of the defendant/respondent is based;

3) the region in which the claimant's/appellant's legal representatives are based;

4) the ease and cost of travel to a hearing;

5) the availability and suitability of alternative means of attending a hearing (for example, by videolink);

6) the extent and nature of media interest in the proceedings in any particular locality;

7) the time within which it is appropriate for the proceedings to be determined;

8) whether it is desirable to administer or determine the claim in another region in the light of the volume of claims issued at, and the capacity, resources and workload of, the court at which it is issued;

9) whether the claim raises issues sufficiently similar to those in another outstanding claim to make it desirable that it should be determined together with, or immediately following, that other claim; and

10) whether the claim raises devolution issues and for that reason whether it should more appropriately be determined in London or Cardiff.

Form N462

Judicial Review
Acknowledgment of Service

	In the High Court of Justice
	Administrative Court

Name and address of person to be served

name	Claim No.	
	Claimant(s) *(including ref.)*	
address	**Defendant(s)**	
	Interested Parties	

SECTION A

Tick the appropriate box

1. I intend to contest all of the claim   ☐ ⎫
                                                        ⎬ complete sections B, C, D and E
2. I intend to contest part of the claim   ☐ ⎭

3. I do not intend to contest the claim   ☐   complete section E

4. The defendant (interested party) is a court or tribunal and **intends** to make a submission.   ☐   complete sections B, C and E

5. The defendant (interested party) is a court or tribunal and **does not intend** to make a submission.   ☐   complete sections B and E

Note: If the application seeks to judicially review the decision of a court or tribunal, the court or tribunal need only provide the Administrative Court with as much evidence as it can about the decision to help the Administrative Court perform its judicial function.

SECTION B

Insert the name and address of any person you consider should be added as an interested party.

name	name
address	address
Telephone no. Fax no.	Telephone no. Fax no.
E-mail address	E-mail address

SECTION C

Summary of grounds for contesting the claim. If you are contesting only part of the claim, set out which part before you give your grounds for contesting it. If you are a court or tribunal filing a submission, please indicate that this is the case.

SECTION D

Give details of any directions you will be asking the court to make, or tick the box to indicate that a separate application notice is attached.

If you are seeking a direction that this matter be heard at an Administrative Court venue other than that at which this claim was issued, you should complete, lodge and serve on all other parties Form N464 with this acknowledgment of service.

SECTION E

*delete as appropriate	*(I believe)(The defendant believes) that the facts stated in this form are true. *I am duly authorised by the defendant to sign this statement.	(if signing on behalf of firm or company, court or tribunal)	Position or office held
(To be signed by you or by your solicitor or litigation friend)	Signed		Date

Give an address to which notices about this case can be sent to you

name

address

Telephone no.

Fax no.

E-mail address

If you have instructed counsel, please give their name address and contact details below.

name

address

Telephone no.

Fax no.

E-mail address

Completed forms, together with a copy, should be lodged with the Administrative Court Office (court address, over the page), at which this claim was issued within 21 days of service of the claim upon you, and further copies should be served on the Claimant(s), any other Defendant(s) and any interested parties within 7 days of lodgement with the Court.

Administrative Court addresses

- Administrative Court in **London**

  Administrative Court Office, Room C315, Royal Courts of Justice, Strand, London, WC2A 2LL.

- Administrative Court in **Birmingham**

  Administrative Court Office, Birmingham Civil Justice Centre, Priory Courts, 33 Bull Street, Birmingham B4 6DS.

- Administrative Court in **Wales**

  Administrative Court Office, Cardiff Civil Justice Centre, 2 Park Street, Cardiff, CF10 1ET.

- Administrative Court in **Leeds**

  Administrative Court Office, Leeds Combined Court Centre, 1 Oxford Row, Leeds, LS1 3BG.

- Administrative Court in **Manchester**

  Administrative Court Office, Manchester Civil Justice Centre, 1 Bridge Street West, Manchester, M3 3FX.

Form N465

Response to application for directions as to venue for administration and determination	**In the High Court of Justice**	
	Administrative Court	
	Claim No.	
	Claimant(s)/ Appellant(s)	
	Defendant(s)/ Respondent(s)	
	Interested Party(ies)	

You must serve this form **within 7 days** of receiving form *N464 Application for directions as to venue for administration and determination.*

Name and address of party responding to application

name

address

I/We oppose the application for directions as to the venue for administration and determination, for the following reason(s):-

(To be signed by you or by your solicitor or litigation friend)	**Signed**
	Date
	Name
	(If signing on behalf of firm or company, court)
	Position or office held

Please send your completed form to the Administrative Court Office which is currently administering this matter, **within 7 days** of receiving form N464 Application for directions as to venue from administration and determination. You must also serve copies of your completed form on all other parties.

Form AC001

Request for an adjournment

Administrative Court Office
Room C324
Royal Courts of Justice
Strand
London WC2A 2LL

All requests must be made no later than 2 working days before the hearing.
A request for an adjournment can be considered only when the views of all parties have been received.
It is the responsibility of the party seeking the adjournment to ensure the views of all parties are included in this form before it is lodged with the court. All parties must sign this form before the court can deal with your request for an adjournment. Where there are more than 3 parties, please use additional forms. Please note that there is a fee payable for any application to adjourn made within 14 days of the hearing date, unless you are entitled to fee remission, in which case you must lodge an Application for a Remission of Fee (Form Ex160) with your application.

Case Title	
Case Ref No:	Date of hearing: / /

For completion by the party seeking the adjournment

Are you the ☐ Claimant ☐ Defendant ☐ Interested Party

Reasons for requesting adjournment:

Has a request for adjournment been made previously? ☐ Yes ☐ No

If Yes, please supply details:

Signed: Print name: Date: / /

For completion by other parties

Are you the ☐ Claimant ☐ Defendant ☐ Interested Party

Do you oppose the adjournment? ☐ Yes ☐ No

If Yes, please give reasons:

Signed: Print name: Date: / /

For completion by other parties

Are you the ☐ Claimant ☐ Defendant ☐ Interested Party

Do you oppose the adjournment? ☐ Yes ☐ No

If Yes, please give reasons:

Signed: Print name: Date: / /

Send your completed form and the appropriate fee or form Ex160 to the address above.

AC001 (09.08)   © Crown copyright 2008

Form N279

Notice of discontinuance

	In the
Note: Where another party must consent to the proceedings being discontinued, a copy of their consent must be attached to, and served with, this form.	
	Claim No.
	Claimant (including ref.)
	Defendant (including ref.)

To the court

The claimant (defendant)

(tick only one box)

☐   discontinues all of this (claim) (counterclaim)

☐   discontinues that part of this claim (counterclaim) relating to: *(specify which part)*

against the (defendant) (following defendants) (claimant) (following claimants)

(... *(enter name of Judge)* granted permission for the claimant to

discontinue (all) (part) of this (claim)(counterclaim) by order dated ....)

I certify that I have served a copy of this notice on every other party to the proceedings

Signed		**Position or office held**	
	(Claimant)(Defendant)('s solicitor)(Litigation friend)		(if signing on behalf of firm or company)
Date			

The court office at

is open between 10 am and 4 pm Monday to Friday. When corresponding with the court, please address forms or letters to the Court Manager and quote the claim number.

N279 - w3 Notice of discontinuance(6.99)   *Printed on behalf of The Court Service*

PF 244 – Administrative Court

Application Notice (Part 23)

IN THE HIGH COURT OF JUSTICE

QUEENS BENCH DIVISION

ADMINISTRATIVE COURT LIST

Claim No: ....

Claimant:

Defendant:

APPLICATION NOTICE

Part A – I/We[2]   the [Solicitor on behalf of the][3]

Apply for an order, a draft of which is attached, for[4]

I/We wish to have the application dealt with [at a hearing/without a hearing*] before a [Judge/Master] with a time estimate of   hour(s)   minutes agreed/not agreed.

*delete where applicable

This application will be heard before the Hon. Mr Justice / Master

on   day the   of   at   am/pm in Court/Room**

(**enter venue for hearing)

Part B – I/We wish to rely   [*]   the attached Witness Statement/Affidavit
on

                               [*]   my statement of case

                               [*]   the evidence in Part C on the reverse of this
                                        application

*tick as appropriate

Dated ....

Signed .... (name) ....

position or office held ....

---

[2]   State full name of Claimant or his/her Solicitor.
[3]   State title of party e.g. Claimant, Defendant etc.
[4]   State briefly the nature of the order sought and the reason it is sought including the material facts relied on and identifying any rule or statutory provision.

*(Claimant)(Litigation friend)(Claimant's Solicitor)(Signing on behalf of firm or company)

*delete as appropriate

PF 244 – Administrative Court (Continued)

Part C – Evidence

Statement of Truth (to be signed when part C is completed)

*(I believe)(The Claimant believes) that the facts stated in this application notice are true.

*I am duly authorised by the Claimant to sign this statement

Full name ....

Name of Claimant's Solicitor's firm ....

Signed .... position or office held ....

*(Claimant)(Litigation friend)(Claimant's Solicitor)(Signing on behalf of firm or company)

*delete as appropriate

To: Respondent/Respondent's Solicitor's address, DX or e-mail	To: Claimant/Claimant's Solicitor's address, DX or e-mail
Ref No.	Ref No.
Tel No.	Tel No.
Fax No.	Fax No.

Pre-action Protocol for Personal Injury Claims

1 Introduction

1.1

Lord Woolf in his final Access to Justice Report of July 1996 recommended the development of pre-action protocols:

To build on and increase the benefits of early but well informed settlement which genuinely satisfy both parties to dispute.

1.2

The aims of pre-action protocols are:

- more pre-action contact between the parties

- better and earlier exchange of information

- better pre-action investigation by both sides

- to put the parties in a position where they may be able to settle cases fairly and early without litigation

- to enable proceedings to run to the court's timetable and efficiently, if litigation does become necessary

- to promote the provision of medical or rehabilitation treatment (not just in high value cases) to address the needs of the claimant

1.3

The concept of protocols is relevant to a range of initiatives for good litigation and pre-litigation practice, especially:

- predictability in the time needed for steps pre-proceedings

- standardisation of relevant information, including documents to be disclosed.

1.4

The Courts will be able to treat the standards set in protocols as the normal reasonable approach to pre-action conduct. If proceedings are issued, it will be for the court to decide whether non-compliance with a protocol should merit adverse consequences. Guidance on the court's likely approach will be given from time to time in practice directions.

1.5

If the court has to consider the question of compliance after proceedings have begun, it will not be concerned with minor infringements, e.g. failure by a short period to provide relevant information. One minor breach will not exempt the 'innocent' party from following the protocol. The court will look at the effect of non-compliance on the other party when deciding whether to impose sanctions.

2 Notes of guidance

2.1

The protocol has been kept deliberately simple to promote ease of use and general acceptability. The notes of guidance which follows relate particularly to issues which arose during the piloting of the protocol.

Scope of the Protocol

2.2

This protocol is intended to apply to all claims which include a claim for personal injury (except those claims covered by the Clinical Disputes and Disease and Illness Protocols) and to the entirety of those claims: not only to the personal injury element of a claim which also includes, for instance, property damage.

2.3

This protocol is primarily designed for those road traffic, tripping and slipping and accident at work cases which include an element of personal injury with a value of less than the fast track limit and which are likely to be allocated to that track. This is because time will be of the essence, after proceedings are issued, especially for the defendant, if a case is to be ready for trial within 30 weeks of allocation. Also, proportionality of work and costs to the value of what is in dispute is particularly important in lower value claims. For some claims within the value 'scope' of the fast track some flexibility in the timescale of the protocol may be necessary, see also paragraph 3.8.

2.4

However, the 'cards on the table' approach advocated by the protocol is equally appropriate to higher value claims. The spirit, if not the letter of the protocol, should still be followed for multi-track type claims. In accordance with the sense of the civil justice reforms, the court will expect to see the spirit of reasonable pre-action behaviour applied in all cases, regardless of the existence of a specific protocol. In particular with regard to personal injury cases with a value of more than the fast track limit, to avoid the necessity of proceedings parties are expected to comply with the protocol as far as possible e.g. in respect of letters before action, exchanging information and documents and agreeing experts.

2.5

The timetable and the arrangements for disclosing documents and obtaining expert evidence may need to be varied to suit the circumstances of the case. Where one or both parties consider the detail of the protocol is not appropriate to the case, and proceedings are subsequently issued, the court will expect an explanation as to why the protocol has not been followed, or has been varied.

Early Notification

2.6

The claimant's legal representative may wish to notify the defendant and/or his insurer as soon as they know a claim is likely to be made, but before they are able to send a detailed letter of claim, particularly for instance, when the defendant has no or limited knowledge of the incident giving rise to the claim or where the claimant is incurring significant expenditure as a result of the accident which he hopes the defendant might pay for, in whole or in part. If the claimant's representative chooses to do this, it will not start the timetable for responding.

The Letter of Claim

2.7

The specimen letter of claim at Annex A will usually be sent to the individual defendant. In practice, he/she may have no personal financial interest in the financial outcome of the claim/dispute because he/she is insured. Court imposed sanctions for non-compliance with the protocol may be ineffective against an insured. This is why the protocol emphasises the importance of passing the letter of claim to the insurer and the possibility that the insurance cover might be affected. If an insurer receives the letter of claim only after some delay by the insured, it would not be unreasonable for the insurer to ask the claimant for additional time to respond.

2.8

In road traffic cases, the letter of claim should always contain the name and address of the hospital where the claimant was treated and, where available, the claimant's hospital reference number.

2.9

The priority at letter of claim stage is for the claimant to provide sufficient information for the defendant to assess liability. Sufficient information should also be provided to enable the defendant to estimate the likely size of the claim.

2.10

Once the claimant has sent the letter of claim no further investigation on liability should normally be carried out until a response is received from the defendant indicating whether liability is disputed.

2.10A

Where a claim no longer continues under the Pre-Action Protocol for Low Value Personal Injury Claims in Road Traffic Accidents the Claim Notification Form ('CNF') completed by the claimant under that Protocol can be used as the letter of claim under this Protocol unless the defendant has notified the claimant that there is inadequate information in the CNF.

Reasons for Early Issue

2.11

The protocol recommends that a defendant be given three months to investigate and respond to a claim before proceedings are issued. This may not always be possible, particularly where a claimant only consults a solicitor close to the end of any relevant limitation period. In these circumstances, the claimant's solicitor should give as much notice of the intention to issue proceedings as is practicable and the parties should consider whether the court might be invited to extend time for service of the claimant's supporting documents and for service of any defence, or alternatively, to stay the proceedings while the recommended steps in the protocol are followed.

Status of Letters of Claim and Response

2.12

Letters of claim and response are not intended to have the same status as a statement of case in proceedings. Matters may come to light as a result of investigation after the letter of claim has been sent, or after the defendant has responded, particularly if disclosure of documents takes place outside the recommended three-month period. These circumstances could mean that the 'pleaded' case of one or both parties is presented slightly differently than in the letter of claim and response. It would not be consistent with the spirit of the protocol for a party to 'take a point' on this in the proceedings, provided that there was no obvious intention by the party who changed their position to mislead the other party.

Disclosure of Documents

2.13

The aim of the early disclosure of documents by the defendant is not to encourage 'fishing expeditions' by the claimant, but to promote an early exchange of relevant information to help in clarifying or resolving issues in dispute. The claimant's solicitor can assist by identifying in the letter of claim or in a subsequent letter the particular categories of documents which they consider are relevant.

Experts

2.14

The protocol encourages joint selection of, and access to, experts. The report produced is not a joint report for the purposes of CPR Part 35. Most frequently this will apply to the medical expert, but on occasions also to liability experts, e.g. engineers. The protocol promotes the practice of the claimant obtaining a medical report, disclosing it to the defendant who then asks questions and/or agrees it and does not obtain his own report. The Protocol provides for nomination of the expert by the claimant in personal injury claims because of the early stage of the proceedings and the particular nature of such claims. If proceedings have to be issued, a medical report must be attached to these proceedings. However, if necessary after proceedings have commenced and with the permission of the court, the parties may obtain further expert reports. It would be for the court to decide whether the costs of more than one expert's report should be recoverable.

2.15

Some solicitors choose to obtain medical reports through medical agencies, rather than directly from a specific doctor or hospital. The defendant's prior consent to the action should be sought and, if the defendant so requests, the agency should be asked to provide in advance the names of the doctor(s) whom they are considering instructing.

Alternative Dispute Resolution

2.16

The parties should consider whether some form of alternative dispute resolution procedure would be more suitable than litigation, and if so, endeavour to agree which form to adopt. Both the Claimant and Defendant may be required by the Court to provide evidence that alternative means of resolving their dispute were considered. The Courts take the view that litigation should be a last resort, and that claims should not be issued prematurely when a settlement is still actively being explored. Parties are warned that if the protocol is not followed (including this paragraph) then the Court must have regard to such conduct when determining costs.

2.17

It is not practicable in this protocol to address in detail how the parties might decide which method to adopt to resolve their particular dispute. However, summarised below are some of the options for resolving disputes without litigation:

- Discussion and negotiation.

- Early neutral evaluation by an independent third party (for example, a lawyer experienced in the field of personal injury or an individual experienced in the subject matter of the claim).

- Mediation – a form of facilitated negotiation assisted by an independent neutral party.

2.18

The Legal Services Commission has published a booklet on 'Alternatives to Court', CLS Direct Information Leaflet 23 (www.clsdirect.org.uk/legalhelp/leaflet23.jsp), which lists a number of organisations that provide alternative dispute resolution services.

2.19

It is expressly recognised that no party can or should be forced to mediate or enter into any form of ADR.

Stocktake

2.20

Where a claim is not resolved when the protocol has been followed, the parties might wish to carry out a 'stocktake' of the issues in dispute, and the evidence that the court is likely to need to decide those issues, before proceedings are started. Where the defendant is insured and the pre-action steps have been conducted by the insurer, the insurer would normally be expected to nominate solicitors to act in the proceedings and the claimant's solicitor is recommended to invite the insurer to nominate solicitors to act in the proceedings and do so 7–14 days before the intended issue date.

3 The protocol

Letter of claim

3.1

Subject to paragraph 2.10A the claimant shall send to the proposed defendant two copies of a letter of claim, immediately sufficient information is available to substantiate a realistic claim and before issues of quantum are addressed in detail. One copy of the letter is for the defendant, the second for passing on to his insurers.

3.2

The letter shall contain **a clear summary of the facts** on which the claim is based together with an indication of the **nature of any injuries** suffered and of **any financial loss incurred**. In cases of road traffic accidents, the letter should provide the name and address of the hospital where treatment has been obtained and the claimant's hospital reference number. Where the case is funded by a conditional fee agreement (or collective conditional fee agreement), notification should be given of the existence of the agreement and where appropriate, that there is a success fee and/or insurance premium, although not the level of the success fee or premium.

3.3

Solicitors are recommended to use a **standard format** for such a letter – an example is at Annex A: this can be amended to suit the particular case.

3.4

The letter should ask for **details of the insurer** and that a copy should be sent by the proposed defendant to the insurer where appropriate. If the insurer is known, a copy shall be sent directly to the insurer. Details of the claimant's National Insurance number and date of birth should be supplied to the defendant's insurer once the defendant has responded to the letter of claim and confirmed the identity of the insurer. This information should not be supplied in the letter of claim.

3.5

Sufficient information should be given in order to enable the defendant's insurer/solicitor to commence investigations and at least put a broad valuation on the 'risk'.

3.6

The **defendant should reply within 21 calendar days** of the date of posting of the letter identifying the insurer (if any) and, if necessary, identifying specifically any significant omissions from the letter of claim. If there has been no reply by the defendant or insurer within 21 days, the claimant will be entitled to issue proceedings.

3.7

The **defendant**('s insurers) will have a **maximum of three months** from the date of acknowledgment of the claim **to investigate**. No later than the end of that period the defendant (insurer) shall reply, stating whether liability is denied and, if so, giving reasons for their denial of liability including any alternative version of events relied upon.

3.8

Where the accident occurred outside England and Wales and/or where the defendant is outside the jurisdiction, the time periods of 21 days and three months should normally be extended up to 42 days and six months.

3.9

Where the claimant's investigation indicates that the value of the claim has increased to more than the value of the fast track limit since the letter of claim, the claimant should notify the defendant as soon as possible.

Documents

3.10

If the **defendant denies liability**, he should enclose with the letter of reply, **documents** in his possession which are **material to the issues** between the parties, and which would be likely to be ordered to be disclosed by the court, either on an application for pre-action disclosure, or on disclosure during proceedings.

3.11

Attached at Annex B are **specimen**, but non-exhaustive, **lists** of documents likely to be material in different types of claim. Where the claimant's investigation of the case is well advanced, the letter of claim could indicate which classes of documents are considered relevant for early disclosure. Alternatively these could be identified at a later stage.

3.12

Where the defendant admits primary liability, but alleges contributory negligence by the claimant, the defendant should give reasons supporting those allegations and disclose those documents from Annex B which are relevant to the issues in dispute. The claimant should respond to the allegations of contributory negligence before proceedings are issued.

3.13

No charge will be made for providing copy documents under the Protocol.

Special damages

3.14

The claimant will send to the defendant as soon as practicable a Schedule of Special Damages with supporting documents, particularly where the defendant has admitted liability.

Experts

3.15

Before any party instructs an expert he should give the other party a list of the **name**(s) of **one or more experts** in the relevant speciality whom he considers are suitable to instruct.

3.16

Where a medical expert is to be instructed the claimant's solicitor will organise access to relevant medical records – see specimen letter of instruction at Annex C.

3.17

Within 14 days the other party may indicate **an objection** to one or more of the named experts. The first party should then instruct a mutually acceptable expert (which is not the same as a joint expert). It must be emphasised that if the Claimant nominates an expert in the original letter of claim, the defendant has 14 days to object to one or more of the named experts after expiration of the period of 21 days within which he has to reply to the letter of claim, as set out in paragraph 3.6.

3.18

If the second party objects to all the listed experts, the parties may then instruct **experts of their own choice**. It would be for the court to decide subsequently, if proceedings are issued, whether either party had acted unreasonably.

3.19

If the **second party does not object to an expert nominated**, he shall not be entitled to rely on his own expert evidence within that particular speciality unless:

(a)   the first party agrees,

(b)   the court so directs, or

(c)   the first party's expert report has been amended and the first party is not prepared to disclose the original report.

3.20

Either party may send to an agreed expert written questions on the report, relevant to the issues, via the first party's solicitors. The expert should send answers to the questions separately and directly to each party.

3.21

The cost of a report from an agreed expert will usually be paid by the instructing first party: the costs of the expert replying to questions will usually be borne by the party which asks the questions.

4 Rehabilitation

4.1

The claimant or the defendant or both shall consider as early as possible whether the claimant has reasonable needs that could be met by rehabilitation treatment or other measures.

4.2

The parties shall consider, in such cases, how those needs might be addressed. The Rehabilitation Code (which is attached at Annex D) may be helpful in considering how to identify the claimant's needs and how to address the cost of providing for those needs.

4.3

The time limit set out in paragraph 3.7 *of this Protocol* shall not be shortened, except by consent to allow these issues to be addressed.

4.4

The provision of any report obtained for the purposes of assessment of provision of a party's rehabilitation needs shall not be used in any litigation arising out of the accident, the subject of the claim, save by consent and shall in any event be exempt from the provisions of paragraphs 3.15 to 3.21 inclusive of this protocol.

5 Resolution of issues

5.1

Where the defendant admits liability in whole or in part, before proceedings are issued, any medical reports obtained under this protocol on which a party relies should be disclosed to the other party. The claimant should delay issuing proceedings for 21 days from disclosure of the report (unless such delay would cause his claim to become time-barred), to enable the parties to consider whether the claim is capable of settlement.

5.2

The Civil Procedure Rules Part 36 permit claimants and defendants to make offers to settle pre-proceedings. Parties should always consider before issuing if it is appropriate to make Part 36 Offer. If such an offer is made, the party making the offer must always supply sufficient evidence and/or information to enable the offer to be properly considered.

5.3

Where the defendant has admitted liability, the claimant should send to the defendant schedules of special damages and loss at least 21 days before proceedings are issued (unless that would cause the claimant's claim to become time-barred).

A Letter of Claim for Personal Injury Claims

To

Defendant

Dear Sirs

Re: Claimant's full name

Claimant's full address

Claimant's Clock or Works Number

Claimant's Employer (name and address)

We are instructed by the above named to claim damages in connection with an *accident at work/road traffic accident/tripping accident* on day of   *(year)* at *(place of accident which must be sufficiently detailed to establish location)*

Please confirm the identity of your insurers. Please note that the insurers will need to see this letter as soon as possible and it may affect your insurance cover and/or the conduct of any subsequent legal proceedings if you do not send this letter to them.

The circumstances of the accident are:-

(brief outline)

The reason why we are alleging fault is:

(simple explanation e.g. defective machine, broken ground)

A description of our clients' injuries is as follows:-

(brief outline)

(In cases of road traffic accidents)

Our client (state hospital reference number) received treatment for the injuries at name and address of hospital).

Our client is still suffering from the effects of his/her injury. We invite you to participate with us in addressing his/her immediate needs by use of rehabilitation.

He is employed as *(occupation)* and has had the following time off work *(dates of absence)*. His approximate weekly income is (insert if known).

If you are our client's employers, please provide us with the usual earnings details which will enable us to calculate his financial loss.

We are obtaining a police report and will let you have a copy of the same upon your undertaking to meet half the fee.

We have also sent a letter of claim to *(name and address)* and a copy of that letter is attached. We understand their insurers are *(name, address and claims number if known)*.

At this stage of our enquiries we would expect the documents contained in parts *(insert appropriate parts of standard disclosure list)* to be relevant to this action.

Please note that we have entered into a conditional fee agreement with our client dated in relation to this claim which provides for a success fee within the meaning of section 58(2) of the Courts and Legal Services Act 1990. Our client has taken out an insurance policy with [name of insurance company] of [address of insurance company] to which section 29 of the Access Justice Act 1999 applies. The policy number is and the policy is dated . Where the funding arrangement is an insurance policy, the party must state the name and address of the insurer, the policy number and the date of the policy, and must identify the claim or claims to which it relates (including Part 20 claims if any).

A copy of this letter is attached for you to send to your insurers. Finally we expect an acknowledgment of this letter within 21 days by yourselves or your insurers.

Yours faithfully

INDEX

References are to paragraph numbers.